Achieving Excellence

Educating the Gifted and Talented

Frances A. Karnes
The University of Southern Mississippi
Kristen R. Stephens
Duke University

Upper Saddle River, New Jersey
Columbus, Ohio

Library of Congress Cataloging in Publication Data

Achieving excellence: educating the gifted and talented / [edited by] Frances A. Karnes, Kristen R. Stephens.
p. cm.
Includes bibliographical references and index.
ISBN 0-13-175562-5 (pbk.)
1. Gifted children—Education—United States. 2. Gifted children—United States—Identification. I. Karnes, Frances A. II. Stephens, Kristen R.
LC3993.9.A655 2008
371. 95—dc22

2007017462

Vice President and Executive Publisher: Jeffery W. Johnston
Executive Editor: Ann Castel Davis
Editorial Assistant: Penny Burleson
Production Editor: Sheryl Glicker Langner
Production Coordination: Christian Holdener, S4Carlisle Publishing Services
Design Coordinator: Diane C. Lorenzo
Cover Design: Jason Moore
Cover Image: Fotosearch
Production Manager: Laura Messerly
Director of Marketing: David Gesell
Marketing Manager: Autumn Purdy
Marketing Coordinator: Brian Mounts

This book was set in Garamond by S4Carlisle Publishing Services. It was printed and bound by Bind Rite Graphics. The cover was printed by Phoenix Color Corp.

Pearson Education Ltd.
Pearson Education Singapore Pte. Ltd.
Pearson Education Canada, Ltd.
Pearson Education—Japan
Pearson Education Australia Pty. Limited
Pearson Education North Asia Ltd.
Pearson Educación de Mexico, S.A. de C.V.
Pearson Education Malaysia Pte. Ltd.

10 9 8 7 6 5 4 3 2
ISBN-13: 978-0-13-175562-8
ISBN-10: 0-13-175562-5

DEDICATION

We dedicate this book to all gifted children and youth and to our families.

Ray, John, Leighanne, Mary Ryan, Mo, Emma, Brooks and Betsy, Rich, Karen, David, and Jack for their love and support and to Christopher Karnes and Karen and David Stephens for their special love and guidance.

PREFACE

This text provides foundational information relating to the field of gifted education and details characteristics of gifted students from various populations, describes how such students are identified and assessed, and presents up-to-date, research-based pedagogy relating to curriculum design and instruction.

An outstanding feature of this text is the combination of the three critical issues (characteristics, methods and materials, and curriculum development) relating to the education of gifted students into one single volume. By combining the most critical aspects of these three issues, this text becomes a comprehensive volume in the field that can be used as a primary text and as a supplemental text in both graduate and undergraduate college course work related to gifted education. Possible courses for which this proposed text could be utilized include but are not limited to the following:

- Introduction to gifted education
- Nature and needs of gifted students
- Methods and materials in gifted education
- Curriculum development in gifted education
- Identification, current trends, and issues in gifted education

Each chapter draws on experts in the field. Selected authors are nationally renowned for their work in the chapter topics. Chapter authors have incorporated the most recent, cutting-edge research in support of the content presented. Subject matter is also presented in a practical way so that it is applicable to both preservice and practicing teachers. Practical strategies and tools are offered that make this text not only useful for teachers in their course work but also a valuable reference and resource throughout their professional careers.

Chapter summaries and questions for thought and reflection are included at the end of each chapter to help guide classroom discussion. In addition, each chapter provides a listing of useful resources (i.e., books, articles, websites, and organizations) that will enable the reader to extend their learning on a particular topic or issue.

This text will be a valuable resource to those seeking comprehensive knowledge in the field of gifted education; knowledge that will surely inform best practice.

ACKNOWLEDGMENTS

To the many people who have made valuable contributions to this book, we extend our deepest appreciation. We are deeply indebted to the chapter contributors who have offered their expertise across the many dimensions of gifted education. A special word of thanks is given to the staff at the Frances A. Karnes Center for Gifted Studies at The University of Southern Mississippi and to the staff at the Duke University Talent Identification Program. To our administrators and colleagues at the University of Southern Mississippi and Duke University, we thank you for your support of this book and our other professional publications and endeavors.

We would also like to extend our thanks to the individuals who reviewed this text and provided insightful comments and feedback: Mary Banbury, University of Nevada, Las Vegas; Gillian Eriksson, Central Florida University; Joyce E. Juntune, Texas A & M University; Bruce Mitchell, Eastern Washington University; Michael Saylor, University of North Texas; and Vicky L. Vaughn, Purdue University.

BRIEF CONTENTS

CONTENTS

CHAPTER 5
Characteristics of Gifted and Talented Learners: Similarities and Differences Across Domains 62

Sally M. Reis, Ph.D.

Angela M. Housand, M.A.

CHAPTER 6
Personal and Social Development 82

Sidney Moon, Ph.D.

CHAPTER 7
Culturally, Linguistically, and Economically Diverse Gifted Students 99

Michael S. Matthews, Ph.D.

Elizabeth Shaunessy, Ph.D.

CHAPTER 8
Special Populations 116

Sandra Manning, Ph.D.

Kevin D. Besnoy, Ph.D.

CHAPTER 9

Identifying Gifted and Talented Learners 135

Susan K. Johnsen, Ph.D.

CHAPTER 10

Instructional Strategies and Programming Models for Gifted Learners 154

Carol A. Tomlinson, Ed.D.

Jessica A. Hockett

CHAPTER 11

Teaching Models for Gifted Learners 170

Joan Franklin Smutny, Director

Note: Every effort has been made to provide accurate and current Internet information in this book. However, the Internet and information posted on it are constantly changing, so it is inevitable that some of the Internet addresses listed in this textbook will change.

ABOUT THE AUTHORS

Kevin D. Besnoy, Ph.D., is an assistant professor of elementary education at Northern Kentucky University. He earned his degree at The University of Southern Mississippi. He has taught gifted children in grades 7 to 8. He has authored several articles on gifted education and a book on twice-exceptional children. His research interests include integrating technology into the gifted education curriculum and serving at-risk gifted youth.

Jeffrey Calderon was born in San Jose, Costa Rica, in 1975. He graduated with a specialization in educational psychology from the Universidad Automoma Monterrey. Presently, he is studying in Munich, Germany, at the Ludwig-Maximilans-University, where he is concluding his graduate program with a focus on gifted education. He is in the process of working on his master's thesis regarding giftedness development and creativity. His future plans include a Ph.D. in the field of giftedness and the initiation of a center for gifted students in Costa Rica that will be dedicated to developing the skills of Latin American gifted and talented children in the field of arts.

Carolyn M. Callahan, Ph.D., Commonwealth Professor of Education at the University of Virginia, has been a principal investigator on projects of the National Research Center on the Gifted and Talented over the course of the past 16 years. She has published than 175 refereed articles and 35 book chapters across a broad range of topics, including the areas of identification of gifted students, program evaluation, the development of performance assessments, and curricular and programming options for highly able students. She has received recognition as Outstanding Faculty Member in the Commonwealth of Virginia, Outstanding Professor of the Curry School of Education, and Distinguished Higher Education Alumnae of the University of Connecticut and was awarded the Distinguished Scholar Award and the Distinguished Service Award from the National Association for Gifted Children. She is a past president of the Association for the Gifted and the National Association for Gifted Children.

Amber Esping is a Ph.D. student in educational psychology at Indiana University. Her specialization area is human learning and cognition. She also holds an associate credential from the Viktor Frankl Institute of Logotherapy in Abilene, Texas. Prior to graduate school, she completed the music therapy program at California State University, Northridge, and earned a bachelor of music in clarinet performance. Her current intellectual interests are focused in two areas: the relationship between domain expertise and teaching skill and existential aspects of the academic environment.

Jessica Hockett, M.A.T., M.A., is a doctoral student in educational psychology (gifted education emphasis) at the University of Virginia. As a research assistant at the National Research Center on the Gifted and Talented, Jessica conducted qualitative data analysis for a 5-year study of talent identification and development in underserved primary grade students. She has an M.A.T. in secondary education from National-Louis University and an M.A. in Gifted and Talented Education from the University of Connecticut. A former middle school teacher in the Chicago area, Jessica taught English, social studies, and math for academically gifted students. She won the 2005 National Association for Gifted Children Curriculum Studies Division award for her unit *In the Muck: A Study and Practice of Investigative Journalism* and is the coeditor of the division's newsletter, *SCOPE*. In addition, she works as a consultant on differentiated instruction to schools across the country.

Angela M. Housand, M.A., is a former teacher and holds master's degree in educational psychology. She is currently working toward a doctorate at the University of Connecticut with an emphasis on gifted and talented education. She has conducted workshops and professional development on creativity, curriculum differentiation, theories of cognitive development, and meeting the needs of talented readers.

Susan K. Johnsen, Ph.D., is a professor in the Department of Educational Psychology at Baylor University. She directs the Ph.D. program and programs related to gifted and talented education at both the graduate and the undergraduate level. She teaches assessment courses at the graduate level and courses in exceptionalities at both the undergraduate and the graduate level. She has written over 150 publications, including nine books, 12 chapters, and teacher curriculum materials. She is a frequent presenter at international, national, and state conferences. She is editor of *Gifted Child*

Today and serves on the editorial review boards of *Gifted Child Quarterly, Journal for the Education of Gifted and Talented, Journal for Secondary Gifted Education,* and *Roeper Review.* She is past president of the Texas Association for Gifted and Talented and currently serves on the board of The Association for the Gifted, International Council for Exceptional Children (TAG). She is the cochair of the graduate program standards task force of the National Association for Gifted Children and serves on the board of examiners of the National Council for Accreditation of Teacher Education.

Seon-Young Lee, Ph.D., is a research assistant professor of the Center for Talent Development, School of Education and Social Policy, Northwestern University, where she was a postdoctoral fellow for 2 years. After her bachelor's degree in psychology from Yonsei University and master's degree in educational psychology from Seoul National University, South Korea, she came to the United States to pursue her doctorate at the University of Georgia with a focus on gifted and creative education. While working on her doctorate, she was a consultant for statistical data analysis and also worked as a research assistant at the Torrance Center for Creative Studies. Her research interests encompass academic giftedness, talent development, educational programs for academically talented students, psychosocial development of gifted students, and family/parental roles in talent development.

Frances A. Karnes, Ph.D., received an undergraduate degree in elementary education from Quincy University in 1960 and was awarded an honorary doctorate by that institution in 1990. The University of Illinois at Champaign–Urbana granted her an M. S. degree in 1962 and a Ph.D. in 1973. At the University of Southern Mississippi, she directs the master's, specialist, and doctoral programs in special education with an emphasis in gifted education. In addition to her responsibilities as professor of curriculum, instruction, and special education and director of the Frances A. Karnes Center for Gifted Studies at the University of Southern Mississippi, she has coauthored over 250 professional articles and 38 books.

Sandra Manning, Ph.D., NBCT, is an assistant professor in the Department of Curriculum, Instruction, and Special Education at The University of Southern Mississippi. She earned her degree at The University of Southern Mississippi. She has taught gifted children in K–8 settings. In addition to teaching courses in gifted education at the University of Southern Mississippi, her research interests include curriculum programming for gifted children, young gifted children, and gifted adolescents. She has authored several articles on issues pertaining to gifted education and directed a grant funded by the U.S. Department of Education focusing on appropriate practices for screening, identifying, and serving young gifted children.

Michael S. Matthews, Ph.D., is an assistant professor in the Gifted Education Program of the Department of Special Education at the University of South Florida. He received his B.A. in chemistry, with a minor in anthropology, magna cum laude, from the University of Tennessee at Chattanooga, where he was a William E. Brock Scholar and member of the University Honors Program. His M.A. in anthropology (archaeology) is from the University of Wisconsin, Madison. After studying for a teaching certificate in secondary science, he taught science at a public high school in northern Georgia. In 2002, he received his Ph.D. in educational psychology with a concentration in gifted and creative education from the University of Georgia.

Erica R. McHard, J.D., is an attorney engaged in the private practice of law with Bryan Nelson P.A. in Hattiesburg, Mississippi. She received her bachelor's degree cum laude from Augustana College (Rock Island, Illinois) in business, political science, and public administration and her juris doctorate from the University of Iowa College of Law. She is admitted to practice in Illinois, Iowa, and Mississippi. In addition to practicing law, she is an advocate for children through her involvement with pro bono adoptions in conjunction with the Mississippi College School of Law Child Advocacy Program, chair of the Nursery Committee and member of the Christian Education Committee at her church, and a member of the Junior Auxiliary of Hattiesburg.

Sidney M. Moon, Ph.D., is director of the Gifted Education Resource Institute and associate dean for learning and engagement in the College of Education at Purdue University. She has been involved in the field of gifted education for almost 25 years. In that time, she has contributed more than 75 books, articles, and chapters to the field. She is active in the National Association for Gifted Children, where she has served as chair of the Research and Evaluation Division and a member of the board of directors. Her research interests include talent development in the STEM disciplines (science, technology, engineering, and mathematics), underserved populations of gifted students, and personal talent development.

Paula Olszewski-Kubilius, Ph.D., directs the Center for Talent Development at Northwestern University and is a professor in the School of Education and Social Policy. She earned her bachelor's degree in elementary education from St. Xavier University and her master's and doctoral degrees from Northwestern University in educational psychology. She has worked at the center for over 20 years, during which time she has designed and conducted educational programs for learners of all ages, including summer programs, weekend programs, distance-learning programs, programs for underrepresented gifted students, and workshops for parents and teachers. She has conducted research and published over 80 articles or book chapters on issues of talent development. She currently serves as the editor of *Gifted Child Quarterly* and formerly was a coeditor of the *Journal of Secondary Gifted Education.*

Jonathan A. Plucker, Ph.D., is professor of educational psychology and cognitive science at Indiana University, where he also directs the Center for Evaluation and Education Policy. Before returning to higher education, he taught science and gifted education at the elementary level. He is the author of over 80 publications on giftedness, creativity, intelligence, problem-based learning, and education policy, and he speaks widely to teacher, parent, and community groups on these and other topics. He is past president of the Research and Evaluation Division of the National Association of Gifted Children, and he has served as an officer and executive committee member of the Society for the Psychology of Aesthetics, Creativity, and the Arts (American Psychological Association Division 10). He is the creator and director of the website History of Intelligence Theory (*www.indiana.edu/~intell*).

Sally M. Reis, Ph.D., is a Board of Trustees Distinguished Professor of Educational Psychology at the Neag School of Education at the University of Connecticut. She has been involved in teaching and conducting research about gifted and talented students for over three decades and has written over 200 articles, technical reports, chapters, and books in the areas of gifted readers, curriculum differentiation, special populations, and the Schoolwide Enrichment Model. She is a past president of the National Association for Gifted Children and is the recipient of numerous national and state awards, including the Distinguished Scholar Award.

Sylvia Rimm, Ph.D., is a psychologist; directs the Family Achievement Clinic in Cleveland, Ohio; and is a clinical professor at the Case School of Medicine. She has authored many articles and books. Her book *See Jane Win®* was a *New York Times* best-seller and was featured on the *Oprah Winfrey* and *Today* shows and in *People* magazine. She also writes a parenting column syndicated nationally through Creators Syndicate. She speaks frequently to parents, teachers, and children on topics related to families and giftedness.

Julia Link Roberts, Ed.D., is the Mahurin Professor in Gifted Studies and the director of the Center for Gifted Studies at Western Kentucky University. She has spent 5 weeks for more than 20 summers directing residential programming for middle and high school young people who are gifted and talented. She is a member of the board of the National Association for Gifted Children, *Gifted Child Today*, the Kentucky Association for Gifted Education, and the Kentucky Advisory Board for Gifted and Talented Education, and she has served on the board of the Association for the Gifted, an affiliate of the Council for Exceptional Children. She has been recognized as a Distinguished Professor at Western Kentucky University, the first recipient of the National Association for Gifted Children David W. Belin Advocacy Award, and one of the 55 individuals in *Profiles of Influence in Gifted Education: Historical Perspectives and Future Directions* (2004). She is a graduate of the University of Missouri with a B.A. and Oklahoma State University with an Ed.D.

Elizabeth Shaunessy, Ph.D., NBPTS, is an assistant professor in the Department of Special Education and serves as the coordinator of the Gifted Education Program at the University of South Florida. She received her B. A. in English from the University of Miami, her M.A. in English from Florida State University, and her Ph.D. in special education with an emphasis in gifted education from The University of Southern Mississippi. At South Florida, she teaches in the online gifted program, which offers courses leading to the graduate certificate and master's degree in gifted education. Her research interests include culturally diverse gifted learners, the use of technology in gifted education, and public policy in gifted education.

Dorothy Sisk, Ph.D., specializes in the field of gifted education focusing on creative behavior and leadership development. She holds an endowed chair and is currently a professor in education at Lamar University, where she directs the C. W. and Dorothy Ann Conn Chair for Gifted Education and the Center for Creativity, Innovation and Leadership. She also coordinates teacher training in gifted education. She has also authored and coauthored numerous chapters, articles, and papers. She served as the director of the U.S. Office of the Gifted and Talented, playing an instrumental role in increasing the cadre of professionally trained consultants for the gifted, thereby expanding opportunities for students.

Joan Franklin Smutny is founder of the Center for Gifted at National-Louis University, where she directs yearly programs for thousands of gifted learners, age 4 through grade 10. In addition to teaching and consulting, she has authored, coauthored, and edited a number of books on gifted education for teachers and parents. In 1996, she won the National Association for

Gifted Children Distinguished Service Award for outstanding contribution to the field of gifted education.

Kristen R. Stephens, Ph.D., is an assistant professor for the Program in Education at Duke University. She also co-directs the Academically/Intellectually Gifted Licensure program for teachers at Duke University. She received her bachelor's degree in elementary education at the University of North Carolina at Chapel Hill; her master of arts in teaching at Webster University in St. Louis, Missouri; and her Ph.D. in special education with an emphasis in gifted education at The University of Southern Mississippi. She has presented at local, state, national, and international conferences; published numerous journal articles pertaining to gifted child education; and is the co-author of several books and book chapters.

Rena F. Subotnik, Ph.D., is director of the Center for Gifted Education Policy at the American Psychological Association. The center's mission is to generate public awareness, advocacy, clinical applications, and cutting-edge research ideas that will enhance the achievement and performance of children and adolescents with special gifts and talents in all domains, including the academic disciplines, the performing arts, sports, and the professions. She has coedited and coauthored several books pertaining to giftedness and talent development and was the 2002 recipient of the National Association for Gifted Children Distinguished Scholar award.

Carol Ann Tomlinson, Ed.D., is currently a professor of educational leadership, foundations and policy at the University of Virginia's Curry School of Education. She is codirector of the University of Virginia's Summer Institute on Academic Diversity and Best Practices Institute. She was named Outstanding Professor at Curry School of Education in 2004. She is a reviewer for eight journals and a section editor for one. She is author of over 150 articles, book chapters, books, and other professional development materials. She has served as consultant for and appeared in 12 videos for The Association for Supervision and Curriculum Development (ASCD). Her ASCD books have been translated into eight languages. She works with teachers across the United States and abroad on developing classrooms that are responsive to students with varied learning needs.

Joyce VanTassel-Baska, Ph.D., is the Jody and Layton Smith Professor of Education and executive director of the Center for Gifted Education at The College of William & Mary, where she has developed a graduate program and a research and development center in gifted education. She has published widely, including 20 books and over 375 refereed journal articles, book chapters, and scholarly reports. She has received numerous awards for her work, including the National Association for Gifted Children Early Leader Award in 1986, the State Council of Higher Education in Virginia Outstanding Faculty Award in 1993, the Phi Beta Kappa faculty award in 1995, the National Association for Gifted Children Distinguished Scholar Award in 1997, and the President's Award, World Council on Gifted and Talented Education, in 2005. Her major research interests are on the talent development process and effective curricular interventions with the gifted.

Susannah Wood, Ph.D., completed her doctoral degree in counselor education with a cognate in gifted education at The College of William & Mary, focusing on gifted adolescents' experiences in school counseling. Her background includes working as a middle school counselor in Newport News, Virginia, while spending summers providing residential counseling for programs such as the Johns Hopkins Center for Talented Youth and the Virginia Governor's School for the Visual and Performing Arts and Humanities. She has presented at a variety of national and state-level organizational conferences. She has won the Margaret, The Lady Thatcher Medallion for scholarship, character, and service within the School of Education and The College of William & Mary community in 2006. She will begin a tenure-track position as an assistant professor at the University of Iowa in the Department of Counseling, Rehabilitation and Student Development, helping prepare professional school counselors to work with gifted students in partnership with the Connie Belin and Jacquline N. Blank International Center for Gifted and Talented Education.

CHAPTER 1

HISTORICAL PERSPECTIVES IN GIFTED EDUCATION

Dorothy Sisk, Ph.D.
LAMAR UNIVERSITY

INTRODUCTION

Tracing the role of the federal government in gifted and talented education over the past 50 years or so, it is clear that its role has been cyclical. In some cases, it has represented responses to perceived national threat or to the image of America's students falling behind in comparison to students from other countries. When the Soviet Union launched *Sputnik,* there was an outcry for greater student preparation in science and mathematics resulting in the passing of the National Defense Education Act in 1958. This federal legislation represents the first major effort to support education. Under Title V of this act, states were provided funding for testing programs to identify able students and for counseling and guidance to encourage students to develop their aptitude and to attend colleges and universities, particularly to study mathematics and science. This point of view is quite similar to what President George W. Bush proposed in 2006 in an effort to encourage greater student and teacher involvement in mathematics and science and to upgrade secondary school programs. When the U.S. space program became more successful and the threat of the Soviet Union diminished, the support for gifted students also diminished. This chapter examines the early work of the 1968 White House Task Force on the Education of Gifted Persons, the *Marland Report,* the Jacob K. Javits Gifted and Talented Program, the *State of the States Report,* the Policy Workshop of the National Association for Gifted Children (NAGC), and the *Nation Deceived Report* to trace the federal history of gifted education, followed by a summary and implications for future directions.

TALENT DEVELOPMENT: AN INVESTMENT IN THE FUTURE OF THE NATION

In 1968, the White House Task Force on the Education of Gifted Persons made a report to President Lyndon Baines Johnson. The report stated,

> The blame for suppressing an inestimable amount of human talent rests not with our educational system alone, but with all of us who—by intention, ignorance, apathy, or myopia—condone the inequities of our social environment. (p. ii)

The task force was chaired by F. C. Ward and 12 members, including Jacob Getzels, a pioneer in creativity research, and John Goodlad, the former dean of the University of California, Los Angeles. The task force concluded that a national program of both action and research was needed and reported recognition and development of gifted individuals was "intermittent, unevenly distributed, and inadequate in amount" (p. 1).

The task force recommended that the president direct the secretary of the Department of Health, Education, and Welfare (HEW) to establish a Center for the Development of Exceptionally Talented Persons with responsibility to do the following:

1. Proclaim and expound the case for more effective development of a broad range of exceptional talents as a matter of national interest and individual fulfillment
2. Encourage and, where appropriate, provide support for local and state efforts to develop gifted persons over a wide range of ages and types of talents
3. Promote and support immediate long-term actions at local and state levels to provide for the development of high ability in urban ghettos, in disadvantaged rural areas, and among women
4. Sponsor, conduct, and/or coordinate at federal, state, and local levels basic and developmental research into the identification and nurture of gifted persons
5. Encourage and/or support projects or programs at state and local levels to increase the capacity of teachers to recognize and nurture gifted persons
6. Make regular reports to the hereinafter recommended Council and to provide the educational community and other concerned publics and agencies with information relevant to policies, plans, and programs for the development of exceptionally talented persons (pp. 1–2)

The task force further recommended that a National Advisory Council for the Development of Exceptionally Talented Persons be established with members from different spheres of attainment, including men and women from the public and private sectors. This council would review the operation of the center and all other federal programs that were relevant to the development of exceptionally talented persons and advise the president on policy matters concerning such programs and on needed federal legislation.

A final recommendation was to encourage the cooperation of the private sector in talent development efforts. To expedite their recommendations, the task force suggested that a meeting of leaders be convened with representatives from elementary, secondary, and higher education, including specialized institutions such as musical conservatories and schools of art to (a) review education practices that inhibit the effective development of gifted persons, (b) explore strategies for accommodating the development of a wide range of talents at all levels of education, and (c) recommend specific action to be taken by schools and colleges to foster achievement among the very able.

The task force stressed that states, communities, and individual institutions, both public and private, continue to maintain and have primary responsibility for initiating and implementing programs for the gifted, with the federal government taking an active role in encouraging, supporting, and coordinating national efforts to develop the exceptional talents of gifted persons.

The task force also emphasized the need for states and local educational agencies to develop sensitivity to giftedness in all education personnel and to recruit and provide special training for teachers of the gifted, including preservice and in-service, particularly in the areas of art, music, and the humanities. They suggested that school districts employ artisans, writers, musicians, composers, and artists in the field of education to provide real-life experiences.

Institutional rigidities and the fear of elitism were addressed:

> We will first have to overcome the idea that special treatment of the gifted student somehow contradicts democratic ideas. The basic democratic ideal—respect for human dignity—makes every individual "elite"; the basic educational problem is fashioning institutions which can instruct millions, but still instruct them one by one. (p. 9)

The task force made a strong case for educators to determine how a democratic society can devise *equal educational opportunity* to develop *unequal* talents. Four broad categories of attainment—scholarly inquiry, artistic creativity, professional service, and spiritual leadership—were identified. They underscored the danger of relying on the IQ as the sole or even the predominant criterion as to who is gifted and that outstanding achievement in academic pursuits, which is often the index for identification of giftedness in school, cannot be permitted to be the only criterion, nor should poor school work be considered a definite indication that a student lacks talent.

Three courses of action for identifying gifted students were suggested: (a) a long-term research program, (b) a teacher training program, and (c) an annual talent discovery program.

In terms of long-term research, the task force recommended that five cohorts of persons be randomly selected from age-groups 4 years apart beginning at 2 years of age and continuing through age 18. It was further suggested that each member be observed in detail every 2 years with attention given to his or her personal attributes, specific accomplishments, and the environmental conditions that facilitated or inhibited such accomplishments.

Teacher training programs were addressed by the task force, and they advised that programs include (a) preparation of materials to gain support and understanding of the importance of exceptional talent in society, (b) development of training materials to instruct school personnel and others on the nature and identification of talent, (c) establishment and support of various types of in-service and preservice teacher training programs, and (d) provision for systematic retraining in new techniques and theories.

The task force also recommended the promotion of an annual talent discovery exercise. The exercise would provide disadvantaged students from ages 8 to 17 the opportunity to engage in self-discovery and help motivate them.

Many of the recommendations of the 1968 task force have considerable relevancy for today. Several of the recommendations have been realized through the research of educators and psychologists, notably the work of E. Paul Torrance in planning and implementing annual creative problem-solving competitions to address the talent discovery need and his long-term research, over a 44-year period, of students identified at age 9 as creative children.

Other examples of how the task force recommendations for talent discovery have been realized include the Talent Search Model developed by Julian Stanley (1996). Four regional talent searches exist in the United States and are based on Stanley's work: the Center for Talented Youth at Johns Hopkins University, Duke University's Talent Identification Program, the Center for Talent Development at Northwestern University, and the Rocky Mountain Talent Search at the University of Denver. These programs address the need to assist gifted students in self-discovery and in increasing and maintaining their motivation to achieve.

EMPHASIS ON EQUITY

In the 1960s and 1970s, there was a priority to educate all children, with a special emphasis on serving the economically disadvantaged under the Title I federal legislation. In addition, there was a strong emphasis on ensuring that exceptional children receive the quality education that all children in public schools were provided. Gifted and talented children were included under the umbrella term of exceptional children by the Council for Exceptional Children (CEC), which represents the largest professional organization of teachers, administrators, parents, and others concerned with the education of exceptional children.

In 1969, there was a request by Congress, initiated by Senator John Erlenborn from Illinois, to study the status of gifted and talented education. Senator Erlenborn had been favorably impressed by the effort of the Illinois Department of Public Instruction to provide a comprehensive identification program for the gifted, by the variety of programs offered, and by the quality of in-service education for teachers through the state network of resource centers. The amendment he introduced included a congressional intent that gifted and talented children should benefit from federal legislation, particularly from Titles III and V of the Elementary and Secondary Education Act, as well as from the teacher education provisions of the Higher Education Act of 1965. However, most significant in Erlenborn's amendment was to direct the U.S. commissioner of education to launch a study to accomplish the following:

> a) Determine the extent to which special education assistance programs are necessary or useful to meet the needs of gifted and talented children; b) show which existing federal educational assistance programs are being used to meet the needs of gifted and talented children; c) evaluate how existing federal educational assistance programs can be more effectively used to meet these needs; and d) recommend which new programs, if any, are needed to meet these needs. (Jackson, 1979, p. 49)

The *Marland Report*

The congressional mandate was fulfilled on October 6, 1971, when the commissioner of education, Sydney Marland, submitted the document to Congress that became known among educators as the *Marland Report.* The report emphasized that services for the gifted and talented were almost nonexistent and stated,

> There was an enormous individual and social cost when talent among the Nation's children and youth goes undiscovered and undeveloped. These students cannot ordinarily excel without assistance.
>
> Identification of the gifted is hampered not only by costs of approved testing—when these methods are known and adopted—but also by apathy among teachers, administrators, guidance counselors, and psychologists.
>
> Gifted and talented children are, in fact, deprived and can suffer psychological damage and permanent impairment of their abilities to function well, which is equal to or greater than the similar deprivation suffered by any other population with special needs served by the Office of Education. (Marland, 1972, p. 3)

The *Marland Report* offered the first national definition of gifted students and listed six categories of giftedness:

> Gifted and talented children are those identified by professionally qualified persons who by virtue of outstanding abilities are capable of high performance. These are children who require differentiated educational programs and services beyond those normally provided by the regular school program in order to realize their contributions to self and society. Children capable of high performance include those with demonstrated achievement and/or potential ability in any of the following areas, singly or in combination:
> 1. General intellectual ability
> 2. Specific academic aptitude
> 3. Creative or productive thinking
> 4. Leadership ability
> 5. Visual and performing arts
> 6. Psychomotor ability. (pp. 13–14)

The second volume of the *Marland Report* contained seven appendices, including basic data for the findings and information for the recommendations. Ruth Martinson, a pioneer in gifted education and instrumental in crafting legislation for gifted education for the state of California, reviewed the research on the gifted and talented, and her review is included as an appendix to the report. She identified implications of this research and pointed out that the United States had been inconsistent in locating and identifying gifted and talented students, particularly in finding them early in their lives and individualizing their education. Martinson emphasized,

> Special programs have produced ample evidence of their merits. Widely varying arrangements have been found successful, and indicate clearly that excellence for the gifted can become a universal practice with less expenditure than in programs for other children with special learning needs. (p. 110)

The *Marland Report* offered recommendations for 11 actions to be carried out under existing legislative authority (Public Law [P.L.] 91-230, Sec. 806). The recommendations called for the following:

1. A planning report on implementing a federal role in educating the gifted and talented
2. The establishment of a staff within the Office of Education for gifted education
3. A national survey of programs to find costs, evaluation procedures, and model programs and to develop a clearinghouse on gifted and talented education
4. The utilization of Title V of the Elementary and Secondary Education Act to strengthen capabilities for gifted and talented education
5. Two national summer leadership training institutes to upgrade supervisory personnel in state education agencies
6. Program and research support for institutes interested in gifted children in minority groups
7. Program activities specific to career education for the gifted and talented
8. Special attention to one experimental school to project the relation between gifted and talented education and comprehensive school reform
9. Cooperation with Title III programs
10. One staff member from each of the 10 regional offices of education to be assigned to gifted and talented education
11. The study of Office of Education programs relating to higher education to optimize their potential for the gifted and talented

In response to the *Marland Report*, an Office of Gifted and Talented was established in HEW in 1974 and provided funding of $2.5 million to support grants to state and local agencies, to fund model projects, and to support universities in teacher training in gifted education. The director of the Office of Gifted and Talented, Harold C. Lyon, and program specialist Jane Case Williams were administratively housed in the Division of Exceptional Children under the bureau chief, Edwin Martin. The CEC conducted the national survey called for in the *Marland Report* under a grant from the Office of Gifted and Talented, and the findings included the following:

> 1. Differential educational provisions for the gifted and talented had an extremely low priority in the competition for the federal, state, and local educational dollar. Programmatic concern was found to be miniscule.
> 2. Minority and culturally different gifted and talented children were scarcely being reached.
> 3. While 21 states made some legislative or regulatory provisions for these children, more often than not such provisions represented mere intent. Only 10 states had full-time personnel in their state education agencies concerned with gifted child education. There was a gap between what should be and what actually was.
> 4. Gifted and talented children, contrary to myth, were not succeeding on their own. In fact, the reverse was true. Research had convincingly demonstrated that they required specialized educational programs to live up to their potential.
> 5. Identification of the gifted and talented suffered woefully from lack of adequate testing procedures and inadequate funds and in some cases from apathy and downright hostility to their education needs on the part of teachers and administrators.
> 6. When differentiated programs for the gifted and talented were implemented, the effects were measurable.
> 7. The federal role in the delivery of services to these children was for all practical purposes nonexistent. (Jackson, 1979, pp. 48–49)

In 1972, shortly after the *Marland Report* was submitted to Congress, the National/State Leadership Training Institute of Gifted and Talented (LTI) was formed. The LTI was funded primarily through a grant released under the authority of the Education Professions Development Act administered under the fiscal authority of Ventura

County in California. The LTI's codirectors, Dave Jackson and Irving Sato, held three national and nine regional conferences from 1973 to 1976. Five-member teams were recruited and invited to training sessions. Teams were comprised of one representative from each: the decision-making level, the operating level of the state agency, and the local education agency (LEA). Two or more representatives of the team were to include either teachers of the gifted and talented, parents, members of the academic community, local school board members, or an individual from the private sector. One noneducator was also to be represented on each team. The teams wrote long-range plans for the development of strategy and programming for gifted and talented children.

In each state, state-level goals, objectives, and strategies were delineated, and responsibilities were assigned with time frames. On returning to their states, the teams set about implementing their state plans and worked toward securing legislation and categorical funds. The collaborative work of the LTI and the states increased the national level of public awareness of gifted and talented education and increased opportunities for in-service training in gifted education.

In October 1975, the commissioner of education, Ernest Boyer, issued a policy statement declaring that the U.S. Office of Education recognized the education of the gifted and talented being an integral part of the educational system and supported the endeavors of all those who were involved in providing increased educational opportunities of these students. He pledged the resources of the Office of Education to provide technical and supportive services to state and local institutions and to persons in developing special programs.

Commissioner Boyer examined all 144 education programs in HEW and selected seven to focus on for collaboration and cooperation. Gifted education was selected among the seven. Dorothy Sisk, the director of the Office of Gifted and Talented at the time, and the other six program directors met monthly with Commissioner Boyer to report on their program efforts. During this time, funds for gifted were expended through career education and through Title III for model projects for gifted education. A national conference was held in Washington, D.C., that focused on minority and economically disadvantaged gifted students. Representative Shirley Chisholm was a major speaker, along with Assistant Secretary of Education Mary Berry and E. Paul Torrance. The purpose of the conference was to stimulate the states and the LEA's to submit projects in the next funding cycle for gifted education and to target economically disadvantaged students. When the projects were submitted, a very small number addressed the needs of minority and economically disadvantaged students. However, one model project was funded that focused on the creative arts and economically disadvantaged students in Connecticut.

Each state was provided a $50,000 grant to support leadership training at the state and local levels. The LTI and a teacher-training institute at Teachers College were funded to address the need for professional development. The Office of Gifted and Talented continued until 1981. When the Omnibus Budget Reconciliation Act was passed, the funds for gifted and talented were consolidated, along with 19 other programs, into a block grant where funds were allocated to the states for use at their discretion.

REFORM AND RESEARCH TO CULTIVATE EXCELLENCE

In 1983, *A Nation at Risk: The Imperative for Educational Reform* was published, and the Jacob K. Javits Program for Gifted and Talented was established as part of the reform in the Office of Educational Research and Improvement. Senator Javits, the father of a highly gifted daughter, had been most supportive of gifted education. He was convinced of the importance of identifying and developing the potential of gifted and talented children and youth.

The Jacob K. Javits Gifted and Talented Program

Congress reestablished a federal program for gifted and talented students under P.L. 100-297 in 1988. This funding provided for national demonstration grants, a national research and development center that was established at the University of Connecticut under the direction of Joe Renzulli, and national leadership activities. A program priority was specified with emphasis on economically disadvantaged students, limited-English-proficient students, and gifted and talented students with disabilities.

This program priority of the Javits Act has resulted in programs that address the identification of underserved students and the development of curriculum and unique services to meet their educational needs. The National Research Center, a collaborative of three universities—the University of Connecticut, the University of Virginia, and Yale University—works with 54 state and territorial departments of education and more than 280 public and private schools. In addition, there are over 135 content area consultants and stakeholders who work with the center on behalf of the needs of gifted and talented students and their families (Renzulli & Gubbins, 1997).

Over the years, the funds for the Javits program have ebbed and flowed with the support of Congress. In 2000, the funds available were $6.5 million; in 2001, $7.5 million; from 2002 to 2005, $11 million; and in 2006, $9.5 million.

National Education Goals

In 1989, President George H. W. Bush and the nation's governors met and developed a set of national goals providing a unified set of expectations for American education. The goals stated there should be higher standards for all children and that the American educational system should be the best in the world. Goal 3 of the national education goals stated,

> By the year 2000, all students will leave grades 4, 8, and 12 having demonstrated competency over challenging subject matter including English, mathematics, science, foreign languages, civics and government, economics, arts, history, and geography, and every school in America will ensure that all students learn to use their mind well, so that they may be prepared for responsible citizenship, further learning, and productive employment in our Nation's modern economy.
>
> (A) The objectives for this goal are that:
>
> i. The academic performance of all students at the elementary and secondary levels will increase significantly in every quartile, and the distribution of minority students in each quartile will more closely reflect the student population as a whole.
>
> ii. The percentage of all students who demonstrate the ability to reason, solve problems, apply knowledge, and write and communicate effectively will increase substantially. (U.S. Department of Education, 1995, p. 70)

This goal clearly stated that all students at all levels of accomplishment, including the gifted and talented, need to be performing at higher levels.

National Excellence Report

To more clearly establish a position for gifted and talented education in the overall effort in educational reform, a national report, *National Excellence: A Case for Developing American Talent,* was published by the U.S. Department of Education in 1993. The secretary of education, Richard Riley, in the preface to the report described the "quiet crisis" that continues in how we educate top students (p. iii). The report further stated,

> The United States is squandering one of its most precious resources—the gifts, talents, and high interests of many of its students. In a broad range of intellectual and artistic endeavors, these youngsters are not challenged to do their best work. This problem is especially severe among economically disadvantaged and minority students, who have access to fewer advanced educational opportunities and whose talents often go unnoticed. (p. 1)

The *National Excellence Report* found there were effective programs for gifted and talented students in the United States, but they were limited in scope and substance, and most gifted and talented students were spending most of their time in the regular classroom, where few provisions were offered. The report made several recommendations:

- set challenging curriculum standards,
- provide more challenging opportunities to learn,
- increase access to early childhood education,
- increase learning opportunities for disadvantaged and minority students,
- broaden the definition of gifted,
- emphasize teacher development, and
- match world performance. (pp. 10–11)

With educational reform focused on making education more substantial and rigorous, the *National Excellence Report* was consistent with this point of view. The need for meeting the needs of gifted and talented students not only was in the best interests of the nation but also would assist these students in developing their talents to their full potential. The following new definition of gifted and talented was provided in the *National Excellence Report*:

> Children and youth with outstanding talent perform or show the potential for performing at remarkably high levels of accomplishment when compared with others of their age, experience, or environment.
>
> These children and youth exhibit high performance capability in intellectual, creative, and/or artistic areas, possess an unusual leadership capacity, or excel in specific academic fields. They require services or activities not ordinarily provided by the schools.
>
> Outstanding talents are present in children and youth from all cultural groups, across all economic strata, and in all areas of human endeavor. (p. 3)

In 1994, Congress passed two pieces of legislation that substantially impacted gifted education. The Goals 2000: Educate American Act (U.S. Department of Education, 1994) provided funds to states to develop standards, frameworks, and assessments for what students should know and be able to do that were more demanding. In addition, the Elementary and Secondary Education Act (ESEA) was reauthorized with a focus on incorporating the idea that all children K–12 can achieve higher academic standards. The Improving American's Schools Act, as ESEA was renamed, called for acceleration and enrichment as strategies to improve the educational achievement of all students. At-risk students were expected to meet the same performance standards as other students and be assessed on the basis of the same standards. Through this legislation, it was suggested that all students need conceptually complex curriculum, problem-solving skills, instruction in the arts, and enrichment and acceleration. All these recommendations for conceptually complex curriculum have been the primary focus of gifted education over the past two or three decades.

No Child Left Behind

In 2001, Congress passed the educational plan of President George W. Bush called the No Child Left Behind Act of 2001 (NCLB), which reauthorized the ESEA and covered most of the federal programs for K–12 education. No Child Left Behind emphasized high standards and challenging opportunities for at-risk students; called for accountability and results; provided more choice for parents and students, particularly those in low-performing schools; offered more flexibility for states and LEAs in the use of federal funds; and emphasized reading for young children.

No Child Left Behind continued the Javits program to support research and development in gifted and talented education and placed a priority on serving poor and minority students. Patricia O'Connell-Ross (2003), director of the Javits program, summarized the potential impact of NCLB on students performing at high levels:

> One important result will be that there is better information on student achievement in reading and mathematics in grades 3–8. Parents and teachers will be able to make better, more objective judgments on students' progress in these two core subjects. In addition, low-income students who are performing at advanced levels can be identified. Further, states are provided with significant autonomy in the deployment of the increased funding that has been provided, so states with a commitment to services for advanced learners can build this into their plans in some federally funded programs. (p. 607)

O'Connell-Ross (2003) listed the most significant features of NCLB:

> *Accountability:* States are required to implement statewide accountability systems covering all public schools and students. These systems must be based on challenging state standards in reading and mathematics, annual testing of students in grades 3–8, and annual statewide progress objectives ensuring that all groups of students reach proficiency within 12 years. Results will be broken out by poverty, race, ethnicity, disability, and limited English proficiency. School districts and schools that fail to make adequate yearly progress toward statewide proficiency goals will, over time, be subject to improvement, corrective action, and restructuring measures.
>
> *Choice:* For students in persistently failing schools, LEAs must permit low-income students to use Title I funds to obtain supplemental educational services from public or private sector providers selected by parents and students.
>
> *Greater flexibility:* Authority is provided to states and LEAs to transfer up to 50% of the funding they receive in four major state grant programs to any one of the programs, or to Title I. The covered programs include Teacher Quality State Grants, Educational Technology, Innovative Programs, and Safe and Drug-Free Schools.
>
> *Reading:* A substantial increase in funding will support scientifically-based reading programs in the early grades. (p. 607)

The Center on Education Policy's fourth annual report on NCLB, *From the Capital to the Classroom: Year 4 of the No Child Left Behind Act* (2006), explores the legislation's effects. The report indicates that teaching and learning are changing as schools try to align curriculum and instruction with state academic standards and that assessment scores are rising on state achievement tests, with the greatest effect on urban school districts.

If nothing else, NCLB has launched an unprecedented focus on reading and math, and through disaggregated scores of achievement of poor and minority students, English-language learners, and students with disabilities, the progress of these student groups can be examined. It would be most helpful if gifted students could be included in this disaggregation to indicate their growth in achievement. Scherer (2006) says that the greatest shame of a failed NCLB would be that students will suffer from the withholding of a rich curriculum in favor of a test-heavy education. Gifted students certainly suffer from this test-heavy education since teachers are encouraged to design learning around test taking, thus sacrificing the rich curriculum that goes beyond the tested subjects.

In addition, NCLB has influenced teacher qualifications by requiring teachers to obtain a degree in their subject and complete additional course work to become highly qualified. Since so many gifted students are in the regular classroom, these highly qualified teachers would be more able to provide the advanced content gifted students need in a balanced curriculum.

Addressing the issue from an international perspective, Rotberg (2006) says that most countries use testing for tracking and selecting students for admission into academic secondary schools or universities but generally not for holding educators accountable. He points out that if a country ranks high on a given international comparison, people assume their schools must be good and that, if the country ranks low, the schools must be bad. The problem according to Rotberg is that international test score comparisons are the most difficult to interpret because of the enormous differences among nations in poverty rates, societal values, and objectives, and because of sampling problems.

The United States plays a major role in the international arena of gifted education through the World Council for Gifted and Talented Children (WCGTC), and many countries emulate the United States in policy-making and program development for gifted students. The WCGT provides a valuable source for interaction with over 55 member countries for sharing research, curriculum development, and administrative arrangements.

STATE AND LOCAL PROGRESS

Since the states and LEAs bear the majority of educational costs, it is to the states and local levels that we must look to for advances on program development for gifted students. One source of useful information on program development and on how well the states are making advances in gifted education is the biannual *State of the States Report*.

State of the States Report

The *State of the States Report* provides a biannual view of state regulations and support of programs and services for gifted and talented students. The report represents a joint effort of the NAGC and the Council of State Directors of Programs for the Gifted (2005). All 50 states were invited to participate in the study, and 47 states or territories responded to the survey for the 2004–2005 edition of the report. Thirty-seven responded online and 10 by fax or mail. Six state and territorial representatives failed to respond, indicating a shortage of staff or that no single individual was responsible for gifted education. The six were Nevada, New Hampshire, Vermont, Wisconsin, the District of Columbia, and Puerto Rico.

The findings from the 2004–2005 study were grouped under a number of issues, including lack of coordination and uniformity, limited service options, insufficient teacher training, inconsistent reporting and accountability measures, and lack of funds.

Lack of Coordination and Uniformity. The report indicated that many states do not provide direction regarding the education of gifted and talented students and that those states that do have little specificity and clarity in their policies and laws to guide LEAs in establishing identification procedures.

Findings of the 2004–2005 *State of the States Report* follow:

- Although 29 states mandated the identification of gifted students and 28 states mandated the provision of services, only 11 states provided funds to all LEAs by mandate; another 15 fund LEAs as part of general funding.
- 28 states did not require LEAs to follow the same identification guidelines or uniform identification procedures.
- In 17 states, gifted and talented education in the state education agency is a part-time responsibility, and there was no correlation between the size of a state and the staff allocation for gifted education.
- Only 15 states required LEAs to have a district coordinator for gifted and talented education. Of those that required coordinators, only four required the administrator to have gifted education training.
- 21 states had a standing state advisory committee, eight of which have produced a written report within the past 3 years that are available for public review. (p. v)

Limited Service Options. Services to gifted and talented students were found to be limited by district funding, geographic isolation, or other inhibiting factors. In spite of these limiting factors, 30 states fund the support of summer programs and/or special statewide schools (Figure 1–1).

Insufficient Teacher Training. The state requirements for credentialing/endorsement ranged from 6 credit hours (South Carolina) to 24 credit hours (Colorado). Only one state (Washington) required special training in gifted education for regular classroom teachers, even though most LEAs relied on the regular classroom teacher to meet the needs of gifted students (Figure 1–2).

Inconsistent Reporting and Accountability Measures. There was considerable variability in monitoring and reporting by the states:

- Only 13 states required all LEAs to report on the effectiveness of gifted and talented education through state accountability procedures or guidelines.

FIGURE 1–1 Service Options

- 14 states had a statewide school for math and science.
- 7 states had a statewide school for the fine and performing arts.
- 2 states had a statewide school for the humanities.
- 11 states had virtual high schools.
- 16 states offered summer programs, often called governor's schools.

Source: Adapted from National Association for Gifted Children (2005).

FIGURE 1–2 Teacher Training

- 23 states required classroom teachers working in specialized programs for gifted students to have a certificate or endorsement in gifted education.
- 20 states met full or partial criteria for requiring a minimum of 12 hours of university-based course work in gifted education.
- Only 7 states reported that they included gifted education program leadership in policy for personnel preparation.
- 7 states met full criteria and 1 met partial criteria for linking course work in gifted to NCATE standards.
- Only 6 states required gifted and talented training in initial teacher preparatory programs.
- Only 3 states (Oklahoma, Pennsylvania, and South Carolina) reported that they required annual staff development hours in gifted education for regular classroom teachers.

Source: Adapted from National Association for Gifted Children (2005).

FIGURE 1–3 Availability of State Funds

- 14 states spend less than $500,000 of state funds on gifted and talented education.
- 5 states with mandates provide no funds to LEAs to meet the mandate.
- 8 states report spending between $25 million and $50 million.
- 5 states report spending between $5 million and $10 million.
- 7 states report spending between $1 million and $4.99 million. dollars.
- 2 states report spending $67 million (Texas) and $155 million (Georgia).

Source: Adapted from National Association for Gifted Children (2005).

- 11 states published an annual report on gifted and talented education services in the state; another five states provided information as part of a larger report.
- 16 states included gifted and talented indicators on district report cards. (p. v)

Lack of State Funds. The availability of state funds for gifted varied among states from more than $155 million (Georgia) to eight states reporting no funds (Alabama, Connecticut, Illinois, Minnesota, New Jersey, Oregon, Rhode Island, and South Dakota; Figure 1–3).

The *State of the States Report* indicated a need for improvement in statewide identification procedures, teacher preparation and continuing education, funding, and service options. To secure the latest information on state funds expended for gifted education, all the states were contacted by e-mail and by phone. Figure 1–4 indicates this information.

The data from a national state policy workshop sponsored by NAGC further expand on the state of gifted education in the United States.

NAGC State Policy Workshop

In November 2004, all 50 state directors were invited to participate in a policy workshop at the NAGC. Twenty-seven states were represented, and they were provided a review of the literature and presentations on best practices in policy development and enactment for gifted learners. The participants worked in statewide teams to complete a standardized self-assessment (State Policy Assessment Form) with six sections:

1. Identification
2. Program, Curriculum, and Service Provisions
3. Personnel Preparation
4. Program Management
5. Supplemental Policies
6. Overall State Gifted Education Policy Assessment

FIGURE 1–4 Current State Funding for Gifted and Talented

$0 to $90,000	$182,000 to $500,000	$3 million to $19 million
Alabama Connecticut Florida Illinois New Hampshire Oregon Rhode Island Vermont	Massachusetts Michigan Montana North Dakota Wisconsin	Arkansas Colorado Hawaii Idaho Indiana Minnesota Pennsylvania Washington West Virginia
$25 million to $47 million	**$50 million to $69 million**	**$170 million**
Mississippi Missouri New Mexico Ohio South Carolina Virginia	California Texas	Georgia

Source: Adapted from National Association for Gifted Children (2005).

The teams were asked to rate each area as (a) meets criteria, (b) meets partial criteria, or (c) not included.

Identification. The criteria for the identification portion of the assessment included the following:

1. The existence of an operational definition
2. Use of multiple criteria in the identification process
3. Utilization of instruments sensitive to low socioeconomic status
4. Equal stringency for all categories of giftedness
5. Identification in any or all categories of giftedness
6. Consideration of the arts or other domains
7. Identification linked to service provisions
8. Equitable decision making
9. An appeals process

All 27 states indicated they met full or partial criteria for the existence of an operational definition of giftedness, and most states reported meeting full or partial criteria for using multiple criteria for identification in each category of giftedness, ensuring the use of instruments sensitive to underrepresented groups, and providing a process for equitable decision making. However, more than 50% of the participating states indicated their state policy did not include language that required equal effort in identification for all categories of giftedness, nor did they include an appeals process. One third of the 27 states indicated they did not specify the arts or other specific domain areas, nor did they link the process of identification to corresponding service provisions.

Programs and Services. The programs and services portion of the assessment collected information regarding the following:

1. Grouping arrangements
2. The match between grouping arrangements and programs
3. Contact time
4. Curriculum differentiation
5. Whether differentiation was aligned with state standards
6. The emphasis on higher-level skills
7. Assessment strategies
8. The modifications available for at-risk and highly gifted students
9. Social-emotional support
10. Guidance and career counseling
11. Requirements of a local advisory committee

Most of the 27 states reported having policies calling for the use of grouping arrangements matched to the nature of the service provision, a minimum of 150 minutes of contact aligned with state curriculum standards, assessment strategies matched to curriculum objectives, academic guidance and career counseling, and requirements for a local advisory committee. Approximately two thirds of the participating states indicated meeting full or partial criteria for citing necessary grouping arrangements. Only 16 of the 27 states indicated meeting full or partial criteria for having a policy describing curriculum differentiation options. Fourteen of the participating states met full or partial criteria for modifying the program for at-risk or highly gifted students, and 17 states included social-emotional support to some extent in program delivery. Responses for emphasizing higher-level skills through problem solving, critical thinking, and creative thinking were evenly divided among participating states with nine states meeting full criteria, nine states meeting partial criteria, and nine states indicating that it was not included.

Personnel Preparation. States were assessed on their personnel preparation efforts by collecting data regarding the following:

1. The minimum coursework in gifted required for all teachers
2. Whether the program goals were linked to the Standards of the National Council for Accreditation of Teacher Education (NCATE) and the CEC
3. Course work for supervisory personnel to provide program leadership

Twenty of the 27 states met full or partial criteria and required a minimum of 12 hours of university-based courses in gifted education. However, only seven of the states met full criteria for linking course work to NCATE standards for gifted education, and nine of the states reported partial credit on this issue. Seven of the states participating in the assessment indicated that they included gifted education program leadership in policies for personnel preparation in gifted education.

Program Management. The state policy assessment form also collected information regarding the following:

1. Annual review of LEA plans
2. State plan components
3. Monitoring plan for LEA compliance
4. Annual evaluation of LEA plans

Only seven of the participating states reported meeting the full criteria for an annual state-level review of LEA plans, and 11 of the states indicated no policy for an annual review. One state indicated meeting the full criteria for state plan components, and 21 of the 27 states indicated that they met partial criteria for plan components. Sixteen of the states completing the assessment reported requiring annual on-site visits and the monitoring of local district plans, and 15 of the states indicated that they did not require evaluation plans that included annual documentation of program assessment tied to state funding.

Supplemental Policies. Data regarding supplemental policies was also collected using the assessment. This includes information regarding the following:

1. Alignment of curriculum with content standards
2. Availability of the option for students to test out of the state standards
3. Analysis of state test proficiency data
4. Secondary options policies
5. Acceleration options

One state reported alignment of curriculum with content standards and acknowledgment of the accelerated learning needs of gifted students. Nineteen of the states did not address this policy. Nine of the states met full or partial criteria for allowing students to test out of state standards early, and 15 states did not meet this criterion. Thirteen of the states indicated that they monitored state proficiency data for achievement of gifted students. Eighteen of the states reported meeting full or partial criteria for policy regarding secondary options related to advanced placement, the International Baccalaureate program, and/or dual enrollment. Fourteen of the participating states met partial criteria for acceleration policies and acceleration options, while seven of the states indicated that they had no acceleration policies.

Supplemental policies including alignment with content standards, policies for testing out of state standards, and the analysis of state proficiency data were weak, with somewhat stronger reports in policies for secondary options and acceleration.

Policy. The 27 participating states were also asked to rate their state policies in regard to the following:

1. Clarity
2. Comprehensiveness
3. Connectedness
4. Feasibility for implementation
5. Being research based

Twenty-one of the states reported that their policies could be implemented with the current fiscal resources, 20 states indicated that their policies were grounded in research-based best practices, 20 states rated their policies as clear and unambiguous, and 18 states described their policies as logical and connected. Only six states rated their policies as comprehensive; and nine states indicated that their policies were not comprehensive.

Summary. Stambaugh, Worley, VanTassel-Baska, and Brown (2005) summarized the findings from the NAGC policy workshop. On the basis of the self-reported policy results, they determined that the majority of the states reporting operate gifted programs as loosely coupled systems without comprehensive alignment to best practices and connectivity to the major school reform agendas.

One of the strongest areas of policy development was the identification of gifted learners. Yet states were weak in linking service provisions to the categories of giftedness identified, and stringency was not equal across all categories of giftedness. The majority of the states required minimum courses for teachers in gifted education, but there was no unanimity on incorporation of policies for personnel preparation linked to NCATE standards, and few states required program leadership course work for supervisory personnel in gifted education. Programs and service policies were the weakest categories reported, particularly in assessment strategies, the incorporation of a policy for contact time, differentiation matched with state standards, and policies for guidance and career counseling.

Implications. Stambaugh et al. (2005) suggested the following steps in creating a model state policy agenda:

- Connect policies for gifted education to the larger standards and assessment reform agenda. This includes incorporating policies that require differentiated standards for gifted learners, testing out options for those students who know the grade-level standards, and reporting of standardized data for gifted learners.
- Increase the accountability of local districts to the state department of education to consistently monitor, assess, and report the quality of service provided to gifted learners, including growth gains within specific identified domains as matched to the identification area.
- Require a minimum number of contact hours for gifted learners to ensure direct services being delivered.
- Incorporate policies for guidance and career counseling of gifted learners to ensure the presence of this program component in local plans.
- Develop policies on service delivery options including acceleration, grouping, and curriculum differentiation to ensure inclusion of research-based approaches.
- Ensure the personnel preparation for teaching and coordination is at least 12 hours of course work calibrated to the current gifted education NCATE standards. (p. 10)

A NATION DECEIVED

The last major report to be examined in an effort to trace the federal history of gifted education is *A Nation Deceived: How Schools Hold Back America's Brightest Students,* which has had considerable impact on raising national awareness of gifted education programs.

A Nation Deceived, funded by the Templeton Foundation, evolved from a summit on acceleration held at the University of Iowa in 2003 (Colangelo, Assouline, & Gross, 2004). Distinguished scholars and educators from around the country were asked to help formulate a national report on acceleration. The participants deliberated about what schools need to know in order to make the best decisions about educating highly capable students, and these discussions led to a two-volume report. The first volume stressed the need for providing accelerative experiences for the brightest students in the nation.

Olenchak and VanTassel-Baska (2004) stated in the report that research continuously demonstrates the positive impact of the various forms of acceleration, yet the educational establishment, especially at the elementary and middle school levels, remains skeptical based on the implications of haphazard scope and sequence charts and ungrounded fears of hampering healthy social-emotional adjustment.

A Nation Deceived lists a number of reasons why schools hold back America's brightest students:

- limited familiarity with the research on acceleration,
- philosophy that children must be kept with their age group,
- belief that acceleration hurries children out of childhood,
- fear that acceleration hurts children socially,
- political concerns about equity, and
- worry that other students will be offended if one child is accelerated. (p. 53)

The report stresses that these widely held reasons are not supported by research, and it calls for a public awareness campaign to provide teachers and parents the knowledge, support, and confidence to consider acceleration. In order to make the report available to as many people as possible, it can be downloaded free of charge at *www.nationdeceived.org*.

The report reiterated that in times of war or crisis, high school students have been accelerated in programs because the nation needed more skilled workers and teachers. Colangelo et al. (2004) stressed the fallacy of being responsive to gifted students only in times of crisis:

> As a nation, we need to understand education is about our children. We can't wait for national emergencies to realize that matching people with appropriate opportunities is the best way to create a path to excellence. We must find options for students who are able to blaze through a standard high school curriculum, and we must publicize these options.
>
> Excellence is education's core—not its response to crisis. (p. 29)

A Nation Deceived listed 18 types of acceleration:

- Early admission to kindergarten
- Early admission to first grade
- Grade skipping
- Continuous progress
- Self-paced instruction
- Subject-matter acceleration/partial acceleration
- Combined classes
- Curriculum compacting
- Telescoping curriculum
- Mentoring
- Extracurricular programs
- Correspondence courses
- Early graduation
- Concurrent/dual enrollment
- Advanced placement
- Credit by examination
- Acceleration in college
- Early entrance into middle school, high school, or college

These 18 types of acceleration available to bright students fall into two broad categories: (a) grade-based acceleration, which shortens the number of years a student spends in the K–12 system, and (b) subject-based acceleration, which allows for advanced content earlier than customary. The key question addressed in *A Nation Deceived* is not whether to accelerate a gifted learner but rather how to do so. The report emphasizes that to encourage a major change in America's perceptions of educational acceleration, we will need to use all the engines of change: legislation, the courts, administrative rules, and professional initiatives.

PUBLIC OPINION AND POLICY

James Gallagher (2004), the former deputy assistant secretary of education in the Department of Education and professor emeritus at the University of North Carolina at Chapel Hill, suggested three ideas on ways to change public policy in *A Nation Deceived*:

1. Publicize interviews with adults who have been accelerated
2. Develop model legislation for early entrance to school
3. Form alliances with lawmakers to protect interests of gifted children

Importance of Public Policy

In examining the role of society in educating gifted students and the role of public policy, Gallagher (2006) identified cool and hot problems. Hot problems were violence in the schools, children with diabetes, national defense, cancer, heart disease, and terrorism. Cool problems were air and water pollution, mass transit, children with gifts and talents, universal health care, and global warning. Cool problems are typically put on the back burner, and by the time allocations are made for the hot problems, few resources are left for the cool problems. Consequently, policy development for gifted education is very important for continued support and maintenance of programs for gifted students. Policy statements emerge from administrative rules, state legislation, court decisions, and professional initiatives.

Administrative Rules

Local school districts and state education departments craft administrative rules and decisions, and many of these key rules spell out procedures and criteria for identifying gifted students and service options. A strong support system for gifted students needs to be activated through state and local gifted education organizations to influence this rule making. Parents are essential partners in these organizations, and they need to be diligent in protecting existing programs for gifted students and in advocating for future development. The addition or deletion of just one word in a rule can have an enormous effect on gifted education.

State Legislation

To secure state legislation to support gifted education, there must be public support for gifted students, and adequate support is not available at this time since the equity–excellence pendulum swings and influences both educators and the general public (Gallagher, 2006). However, most educators and legislators respond to success stories of talent denied and to case studies of students who are able to realize their potential and overcome considerable odds. This phenomenon is reflected in the emphasis on underrepresented students in the Javits program.

Almost every state has some legislative language concerning gifted students (Karnes, Troxclair, & Marquardt, 1997), and 22 states include gifted students under the broad category of exceptional children (Baker & Friedman-Nimz, 2001). In states that include gifted with exceptional children, the legislative budgets are much more generous, with the largest gifted education budgets reported in Florida, Georgia, and North Carolina. These states have strong exceptional child programs for students with unique needs that require appropriate differentiation, and gifted children are considered children with unique needs. The downside of gifted students being included under the umbrella of exceptional children is the necessity of meeting the "spirit of the law" for exceptional children, which includes developing individualized education plans (IEPs) and inclusion. Many educators of the gifted make the case that the least restrictive environment for gifted students is outside the regular classroom, and they report that the paperwork involved in designing large numbers of IEPs for gifted students can be problematic.

Court Decisions

Another source of policy statements and decisions concerning gifted education are court decisions. Most court decisions have been made at the state level, and consequently there has been little national attention (Karnes & Marquardt, 2000). However, there are three issues being addressed: (a) early admission to programs for gifted students; (b) the racial balance in gifted programs, including reverse discrimination in gifted programs through the use of different criteria for underserved students; and (c) the responsibility of the local school districts to provide services for the gifted (Karnes & Marquardt, 2003).

Professional Initiatives

The NAGC and The Association for the Gifted, a division of the CEC, have developed a set of standards (*Initial Knowledge and Skill Standards for Gifted and Talented Education*) that can impact policy development for gifted education at the local and state level. These standards address the following:

- Foundations
- Development and characteristics of learners
- Individual learning differences
- Instructional strategies
- Learning environments and social interactions
- Language and communication
- Instructional planning
- Assessment
- Professional and ethical practice
- Collaboration

With the strong influence of two major associations in gifted education and the major exceptional child education organization, these standards have great potential to shape and influence policymakers at the local, state, and national levels.

SUMMARY AND CONCLUSIONS

The federal government continues to be an important and expanding contributor to state and local policy in education. Clearly the federal role in the education of gifted and talented children and youth has been one of support and encouragement, yet the role has been cyclical in nature. The states are responsible for education of all students; therefore, a strong state role in education of gifted students is crucial in establishing policy, in long-range planning, and in seeking categorical funding and mandates for teacher preparation. The early work of the LTI was instrumental in assisting all the states in initiating long-range plans and in collaboratively planning and learning from one another. This effort has been continued by the National Association for Gifted and Talented Children and the Council of State Directors of Programs for the Gifted in conducting research efforts on the state of gifted education.

No Child Left Behind has had a positive effect on increasing student achievement in urban schools and ensuring that more teachers become highly qualified. The disaggregation of student achievement data has been very useful to districts to note the achievement of different student groups. It would be most helpful if gifted students could be added to this list to indicate their growth in achievement.

One issue that needs to be addressed is the lack of alignment of gifted program efforts with educational reform; consequently, it is essential that state and LEA efforts on behalf of gifted students seek to become viable partners in the larger reform efforts in education. Gifted education and educators of the gifted over the past three decades have identified and championed many innovative practices that are now being introduced in the regular classroom. Therefore, the challenge for educators of the gifted is to continue to innovate and design new program efforts that can be shared.

Another challenge for the field of gifted education is to develop strong advocacy at the state education and legislative levels to ensure federal and state awareness, support, and involvement. An example of political advocacy yielding positive results was the support of Senator De La Parte and Representative Richard Hodes, who was accelerated from junior high to high school, in introducing legislation for gifted students in Florida. These legislators were instrumental in securing legislation to include gifted students under the umbrella of exceptional student education. They were aware of the gifted program efforts in Tampa, Florida, as a result of parents, teachers, and university educators working collaboratively through the Hillsborough County Association for Gifted Education and the Florida Association for the Gifted. Tampa's advocacy efforts secured a comprehensive program of funding for gifted students, including a mandate for teacher preparation and a mandate for program services for gifted students. Representative Hodes and Senator De La Parte assured the advocates in Florida that the narrow definition of intellectual giftedness as identified primarily by an IQ score would be temporary; however, unfortunately, it still stands today. There are countless stories of advocacy in other states and in LEAs that can be validated and shared to stimulate future advocacy building.

It is essential that educators recognize the power and influence of parents of gifted children as potential advocates. Their advocacy stories can serve as a needed stimulus for developing educational experiences that will contribute to the full development of giftedness and talent in our children and youth.

A significant finding of the *Marland Report* was that a commitment to gifted and talented education by professionals at the state level was a determining factor in the development of strong programming (Jackson, 1979). Many states were recognized leaders in the field of gifted education prior to federal interest and funding, notably California, Connecticut, Florida, Georgia, Illinois, and North Carolina. This was due primarily to the strong leadership of state consultants in the early 1960s and 1970s, including Paul Plowman, Bill Vassar, Joyce Runyon, William Roggee, and Cornelia Tongue.

Future directions will need to reemphasize the state role and look to the state and local levels for support. During the early years of the Office of Gifted and Talented, fully half the total federal allocation went to the state education agencies for professional staff development, and this effort will need to be strengthened and renewed in the future. In some cases, the state allocation was used to fund the salary of the state contact person for gifted education.

Another area that will need to be readdressed is the "ripple effect" achieved by model projects at the LEA and community levels. One model project funded in the 1970s, New York City's Arts Connection, is still actively functioning, providing visibility for the targeted program area of visual and performing arts. One of their program efforts, the Community Encounter, serves the city's most disenfranchised population, children living in temporary housing facilities. In this program, the arts and artistic productions are introduced, as they build understanding and respect for cultural diversity (*http://artsconnection.org/whoweare.html*). Successful programs for the gifted and talented with high visibility can help stabilize the educational focus on gifted and talented students and help ensure that their needs will be met on a continuing basis, rather than on perceptions of threats and crises.

The ongoing struggle between equity and excellence in the United States may be resolved in the future as the nation recognizes that being competitive in a global market and the world will require intensive efforts to develop the mathematical and scientific knowledge of gifted students and to develop their leadership in technology.

The challenge is to convince policymakers that the goal for gifted education is to provide gifted students a world-class education to enable them to attain careers and professions that will allow the United States to remain globally competitive. To do this, educators in gifted education will need to design and implement highly challenging curricula in math and science, which can lead to meaningful partnerships with business and industry. Educators in gifted education will need to step forward and work collaboratively with regular educators with expertise in math and science to develop accelerated and challenging programs that impact the quality of education for all students.

The need for quality teachers of the gifted with strong professional development will be essential if we are to address the development of high-quality curricula. Teacher education represents one of the more serious weaknesses in the Javits program, with no specific funding being available for teachers to seek higher education at universities. Many universities have dropped teacher training programs in gifted education when their student enrollment wasn't substantial enough to merit additional funding. Finally, gifted educators will need to continue to reach out to other professional organizations, such as the CEC, the International Reading Association, and the Association for Supervision and Curriculum Development, to plan and develop collaborative efforts. These efforts can help move the issues of gifted education from the category of a cool issue to that of a hot issue.

QUESTIONS FOR THOUGHT AND REFLECTION

1. What are some of the reasons the federal government historically has taken a minimal role in gifted education?
2. Drawing on what you know about the field of gifted education, what would you suggest to raise the consciousness of educators and the public concerning the need for gifted education?
3. If you were to write a letter to a senator or representative, what would you urge him or her to work toward in gifted education legislation?
4. Where do you think gifted education "fits in" within the realm of education reform?
5. The federal government has responded to gifted education in crises such as the Cold War and the launching of *Sputnik*. What do you think are the major forces behind the current support efforts in gifted education?

RESOURCES

Websites

American Association for Gifted Children
www.aagc.org
The nation's oldest advocacy organization for gifted children. The site highlights working papers, articles, and other information resources.

Center for Development and Learning
www.cdl.org
Organization that specializes in the development and dissemination of research, knowledge, and best practices from multiple disciplines that impact teaching and learning.

Council for Exceptional Children, The Association for the Gifted
www.cectag.org
Organization that promotes the welfare of children and youth with high abilities.

Harvard Family Research Project
www.gse.harvard.edu/hfrp
Assists philanthropies, policymakers, and practitioners in developing strategies that promote the educational and social success and well-being of children, families, and their communities.

National Association for Gifted Children
www.nagc.org
A national organization of parents, teachers, educators, other professionals, and community leaders who unite to support the needs of gifted and talented children.

World Council for Gifted and Talented Children
www.worldgifted.ca
Organization formed to focus world attention on gifted and talented children so that they may realize their potential.

READINGS

Gallagher, J. J. (2002). *Society's role in educating gifted students: The role of public policy.* Storrs, CT: National Research Center on the Gifted and Talented.

Gallagher, J. J. (2004). *Public policy in gifted education.* Thousand Oaks, CA: Corwin.

Haskins, R., & Gallagher, J. J. (1981). *Models for analysis of social policy: An introduction.* Norwood, NJ: Ablex.

Kober, N. (2001). *It takes more than testing: Closing the achievement gap.* Washington, DC: Center for Education Policy.

Pipho, C. (2000). Governing the American dream of universal public education. In R. S. Brandt (Ed.), *Education in a new era* (pp. 5–19). Alexandria, VA: Association for Supervision and Curriculum Development.

Renzulli, J. (2005, May 25). A quiet crisis is clouding the future of R&D. *Education Week, 24,* 32–33, 40.

Sapon-Shevin, M. (1996). Beyond gifted education: Building a shared agenda for school reform. *Journal for the Education of the Gifted, 19,* 194–214.

Watson, J. (2002). *Education report.* Washington, DC: National Education Association.

REFERENCES

Baker, B., & Friedman-Nimz, R. (2001, Spring). *State policies and equal opportunity: The example of gifted education.* Paper presented at the annual meeting of the American Education Finance Association, Cincinnati, OH.

Center on Educational Policy. (2006). *From the capital to the classroom: Year 4 of the No Child Left Behind.* Retrieved January 29, 2007, from *http://www.cep-dc.org/nclb/year4/ Press*

Colangelo, N., Assouline, S., & Gross, M. (Eds.). (2004). *A nation deceived: How schools hold back America's brightest students* (Vols. 1 and 2). Retrieved May 11, 2006, from *http://nationdeceived.org*

Gallagher, J. (2004). Public policy and acceleration of gifted students. In N. Colangelo, S. Assouline, & M. Gross (Eds.), *A nation deceived: How schools hold back America's brightest students* (Vol. 2, pp. 39–45). Retrieved May 11, 2006, from *http://nationdeceived.org*

Gallagher, J. (2006). *Driving change in special education.* Baltimore: Paul H. Brookes.

Improving America's Schools Act of 1994, Pub. L. No. 103-882, 108 Stat. 3707 (1994).

Jackson, D. M. (1979). The emerging national and state concern. In A. H. Passow (Ed.), *The gifted and talented: Their education and development* (pp. 45–62). Chicago: University of Chicago Press.

Jacob K. Javits Gifted and Talented Students Education Act of 1988, Pub. L. No. 100-297, Title IV, Part B, § 4101 *et seq.* (1988).

Karnes, F., & Marquardt, R. (2000). *Gifted children and legal issues: An update.* Scottsdale, AZ: Gifted Psychology.

Karnes, F., & Marquardt, R. (2003). Gifted education and legal issues and recent decisions. In N. Colangelo & G. Davis (Eds.), *Handbook of gifted education* (3rd ed., pp. 590–603). Boston: Allyn & Bacon.

Karnes, F., Troxclair, D., & Marquardt, R. (1997). The Office of Civil Rights and the gifted: An update. *Roeper Review, 19,* 162–163.

Marland, S. P. (1972). *Education of the gifted and talented* (Report to Congress by the U.S. Commissioner of Education). Washington, DC: U.S. Government Printing Office.

National Association for Gifted Children & Council of State Directors of Programs for the Gifted. (2005). *State of the states.* Washington, DC: National Association for Gifted Children.

No Child Left Behind Act of 2001, 20 U.S.C. 70 § 6301 *et seq.* (2001).

O'Connell-Ross, P. (2003). Federal involvement in gifted and talented education. In N. Colangelo & G. Davis (Eds.), *Handbook of gifted education* (3rd ed., pp. 604–608). Boston: Allyn & Bacon.

Olenchak, F., & VanTassel-Baska, J. (2004). Guest foreword. In N. Colangelo, S. Assouline, & M. Gross (Eds.),

A nation deceived: How schools hold back America's brightest students (Vol. 1, p. ix). Retrieved May 11, 2006, from *http://nationdeceived.org*

Renzulli, J., & Gubbins, J. (1997). The national research center on the gifted and talented: Lessons learned and promises to keep. In J.A. Leroux (Ed.), *Connecting the gifted community worldwide: Selected proceedings from the 12th world conference of the World Council for Gifted* and *Talented Children,* July 29–August 2. Seattle, WA.

Rotberg, I. (2006, November). Assessment around the world. *Educational Leadership, 64,* 58–63.

Scherer, M. (2006, November). The NCLB issue. *Educational Leadership, 64,* 7.

Stambaugh, T., Worley, B., VanTassel-Baska, J., & Brown, E. (2005). *Analysis of state gifted education policy: Self-assessment forms.* Williamsburg, VA: College of William & Mary.

Stanley, J. (1996). In the beginning: The study of mathematically precocious youth. In C. Benbow, D. Lubinski, & J. Stanley (Eds.), *Intellectual talent: Psychometric and social issues* (pp. 223–230). Baltimore: Johns Hopkins University Press.

U.S. Department of Education. (1993). *National excellence: A case for developing America's talent.* Washington, DC: Author.

U.S. Department of Education. (1994). *Goals 2000: A world class education for every child.* Washington, DC: Author.

U.S. Department of Education. (1995). *Teachers and Goals 2000: Leading a journey toward high standards for all students.* Washington, DC: Author.

White House Task Force for the Education of the Gifted. (1968). *Talent development: An investment in the nation's future* (Report to the president). Copies available through the Lyndon Baines Johnson Library.

CHAPTER 2

LEGAL ISSUES IN GIFTED EDUCATION

Frances A. Karnes, Ph.D.
THE UNIVERSITY OF SOUTHERN MISSISSIPPI

Kristen R. Stephens, Ph.D.
DUKE UNIVERSITY

Erica R. McHard, J.D.
BRYAN NELSON P.A.

INTRODUCTION

Students with disabilities are protected by a federal mandate under the Individuals with Disabilities Education Act (IDEA). In 2004, this significant legislation was reauthorized and renamed the Individuals with Disabilities Education Improvement Act. However, gifted children and youth are not protected under this legislation. Each state has the authority to develop state law, rules and regulations, and state board of education policies and procedures that address how gifted students will be identified and served. As of 2005, approximately 27 states had laws requiring identification and services for the gifted (National Association for Gifted Children [NAGC], 2005). The remaining states have permissive legislation that does not require school districts to serve these students, but school systems may still do so if they choose.

Without a federal mandate, it becomes difficult to determine the legal developments in the education of the gifted. There is no systematic procedure to determine the current status of legal conflicts regarding gifted students and how such disputes are resolved.

METHODS FOR RESOLVING LEGAL ISSUES

Legal issues can be resolved in a variety of ways. Negotiation, mediation, due process, and the courts are the usual methods. With each step, time and costs escalate.

Negotiation

As disputes arise pertaining to gifted education, the first step in resolving an issue is negotiation (Karnes & Marquardt, 1991, 1997, 2000). Beginning at the heart of the conflict, this informal procedure follows administrative channels.

To be prepared for negotiation, each person must know what is and is not possible for gifted students. State law, state and local board policies, local district guidelines, and state rules and regulations must be located and analyzed. If court cases exist on the topic, those should also be assembled and evaluated. Resolution should start with the source of the issue, which is typically the teacher, then should proceed up the administrative channels as necessary: to the principal, superintendent, and school board. Both parties involved should keep accurate notes of all meetings, including time, place, parties present, and the essential details of the conversations and correspondence, until the issue is resolved. If the dispute can't be settled through negotiation, then the next step should be mediation.

Mediation

Mediation is a voluntary, nonadversarial process that allows disputing parties to meet with an impartial, third-party facilitator in order to reach an agreement. Although states have been utilizing mediation for a number of years, it wasn't until the reauthorization of IDEA in 1997 that states were mandated to offer mediation whenever a due process hearing was requested. In states where mediation was being used, litigation was reduced; therefore, Congress thought it reasonable to strengthen the availability of mediation through the 1997 IDEA amendments for the disabled.

Mediation Provisions. Provisions regarding mediation cited in the 1997 amendments to IDEA include the following:

1. Mediation must be voluntary and not delay or deny a parent's request for a due process hearing.
2. A qualified, impartial mediator who is trained in effective mediation techniques must conduct the mediation.
3. The state must maintain a list of qualified mediators who are knowledgeable in the laws and regulations regarding the provision of special education and related services.
4. The mediator must be selected at random from a list or the parties may agree on the selection of a qualified mediator.
5. The mediation sessions must be scheduled in a timely manner and held at a location convenient to both parties.
6. Discussions that take place during the mediation process must be confidential and may not be used as evidence in any subsequent due process hearings or civil proceedings.
7. The mediated agreement must be put in writing.
8. All costs related to the mediation process are the responsibility of the state. (IDEA, 1997)

Most state mediation systems are managed through the state department of education (usually within the exceptional children division), though some may manage their mediation systems jointly with another state agency (e.g., a university law school or office of conflict resolution).

Advantages of Mediation. There are a number of advantages in using mediation to resolve conflicts:

1. Reduced Cost—While mediation costs vary from state to state, they rarely exceed $1,500.
2. Expeditious Process—The mediation process is usually completed within 20 to 30 days.
3. Improved Relationships—Mediation helps reconcile differences between disputing parties and assists in enhancing communication.
4. Collaborative Resolution—In due process, decisions are made by a third party, and one or both parties may be unhappy with the outcome. In mediation, collaborative resolutions are developed by the participants themselves.
5. Confidential—Issues discussed in mediation remain confidential and cannot be admissible in any future legal proceedings.
6. Empowered Participants—Both parties determine who the participants are, who the mediator will be, and where and when the mediation sessions will occur and contribute to the creation of the final agreement.
7. Allowance for Flexibility—Because mediation sessions are not limited by issues of law, parties can develop new, creative options that benefit the child. (Bar-Lev, Neustadt, & Marshall, 2002)

Status Across States. According to the 2004–2005 *State of the States Report* (NAGC, 2005), mediation is available for issues involving gifted education in 10 states. Four states (Florida, Kansas, New Mexico, and Utah) afford gifted students the same rights to mediation as those students who qualify for services under IDEA. Others (Hawaii, Kentucky, Louisiana, Nebraska, North Carolina, and Pennsylvania) require mediation for gifted students under state law separate from IDEA.

Some states allow attorneys to be present at mediation sessions, while others prohibit the attendance of an attorney. In those that allow attorneys, some require that both parties must first agree on their presence.

Qualifications and Training of Mediators. Since the IDEA requirements regarding mediator qualifications are somewhat vague, requirements vary among states, with some having mediators that are highly qualified and others having mediators with minimal training and limited knowledge (Feinberg, Beyer, & Moses, 2002). A survey of state directors for special education (National Association of State Directors of Special Education [NASDSE], 1998) revealed that the majority of states have established qualifications for individuals serving as mediators, with the most common requirement being the completion of a specified number of training hours. All states surveyed provide mediators initial training and ongoing support.

Due Process

If an agreement can't be reached through mediation, then the next step, if available, is due process. Due process is a procedure by which an aggrieved party has an opportunity to be heard by an impartial hearing officer. For example, when parents and schools cannot settle a dispute at the local school board level, some states by law or regulation offer the parties the right to due process. Both parties may or may not have legal representation at a due process hearing. Although children with disabilities have had the right to due process since 1975, only in recent years has due process become an appropriate method of resolving conflicts in gifted education after all other channels have been exhausted (Karnes, Troxclair, & Marquardt, 1998).

The due process hearing officer, trained and appointed by the state department of education, listens to all witnesses and reads all documents pertaining to the issue. He or she usually has 45 days to write the decision and disseminate it to the parties involved. If the decision of the hearing officer is not agreeable to one or both of the parties involved, an appeal can be made.

Opuda (1999), in a study of due process in Maine, found that families who initiated hearings tended to have a higher income and higher level of paternal education than those who just initiated complaints. Such findings raise questions regarding the accessibility of due process hearings to all families. In addition, Opuda found that 71% of parents who initiated a hearing received assistance from an attorney or an advocate.

Requirements of Due Process. While states may differ in the initial hearing level, jurisdiction, hearing officer's selection and training, and appeals routes, due process hearings do have several common requirements across states. These include the following:

1. Timely notice to all parties involved that a hearing has been scheduled
2. Opportunity to present evidence, witnesses, and oral arguments to an impartial hearing officer
3. Opportunity to have counsel present
4. An oral or written record of the proceedings
5. A written decision from the hearing officer based on the arguments presented at the hearing

The NASDSE reported that although due process hearings are structured similarly across the states, there is one major distinction: about two thirds of states use a one-tier system in which a hearing is held only at the state level, while one third of states utilize a two-tiered system whereby a hearing occurs at the local level (school or district) with the right of appeal to a state-level hearing officer or panel (U.S. Government Accountability Office [GAO], 2003). The trend in recent years has been to move toward a one-tier system to avoid delays in the dispute process. Table 2–1 details the state due process structures as they existed in 2001.

Hearing Officer Decisions. Locating hearing officer decisions on gifted students is not an easy process. There is no federal mandate for the collection of such data (Ahearn, 2002). In addition, according to Ahearn, some two-tiered states do not collect data at the local level concerning the hearings held so obtaining information regarding such hearings can be tedious if not impossible. Most states retain confidentiality of due process discussions by deleting the names of the children, parents, and hearing officers. In some situations, the designation of the school district is also withheld, and some states even destroy documentation of due process hearings after a certain number of years. Furthermore, requests for due process hearings are typically withdrawn or the parties eventually resolve their issues through other avenues; thus, most requests may not even lead to formal hearings (GAO, 2003).

Status Across States. As previously mentioned, the provisions for due process pertaining to gifted children vary from state to state. The *2004–2005 State of the States Report* (NAGC, 2005) indicates that seven states (Colorado, Hawaii, Kansas, New Mexico, Tennessee, Utah, and West Virginia) offer the right to due process to the gifted under the same provision as afforded to students with disabilities (IDEA). Nine states (Arkansas, Florida, Georgia, Kentucky, Louisiana, Nebraska, Ohio, Pennsylvania, and Texas) cite the right to due process for gifted students by state law different from IDEA. Fourteen states (Alabama, Alaska, Arizona, Delaware, Maryland, Massachusetts, Michigan, Mississippi, Montana, New Jersey, North Carolina, Oregon, Rhode Island, and Virginia) indicate that they do not require due process for the gifted. The remaining states (California, Connecticut, District of Columbia, Idaho, Illinois, Indiana, Iowa, Maine, Minnesota, Missouri, Nevada, New Hampshire, New York, North Dakota, Oklahoma, South Carolina, South Dakota, Vermont, Washington, Wisconsin, and Wyoming) did not respond to the question regarding due process on the questionnaire.

In those states where gifted and talented programs are housed under "exceptional children," the statutory

TABLE 2–1 State Due Process Structures in 2001

One-Tier			Two-Tier
AK	ME	VT	AZ
AL	MO	WA	CO
AR	MS	WV	IN
CA	MT	WI	KS
CT	NE	WY	KY
DC	NH		LA
DE	NJ		MI
FL	ND		MN
GA	OR		NV
HI	RI		NM
ID	SD		NY
IL	TN		NC
IA	TX		OH
MD	UT		PA
MA	VA		SC

Note: This table represents states that afford students with disabilities due process under IDEA. Gifted students may not have the same right to due process in some states.

Source: Adapted from Ahearn (2002), retrieved May 15, 2006, from *http://www.projectforum.org/docs/due_process_hearings_2001.pdf.*

TABLE 2–2 States with Due Process Provisions Specifically Cited Within the State Regulations/Rules for Gifted and Talented

Alabama
Connecticut
Florida
Louisiana
New Mexico[a]
North Carolina
Pennsylvania
West Virginia

[a] Gifted children fall under the umbrella of exceptional children. All the applicable rules for children with disabilities apply to gifted children with the exception of child find in private schools, home-schooled children, those enrolled in state-supported schools, or children in detention and correctional facilities and the provisions afforded children with disabilities regarding disciplinary changes of placement.

mandates of Public Law 94-142 regarding due process hearings are typically followed unless otherwise specified. In addition to federal requirements, some states have adopted their own regulations or developed guidelines and policies regarding due process procedures for students with disabilities (Ahearn, 2002). A few states (Table 2–2) specifically cite provisions for due process hearings within their state rules, regulations, or legislation regarding the education of gifted and talented students. State-level data from a recent inquiry to state departments of education and extensive Internet research regarding due process hearings for the gifted are detailed in Table 2–3.

Disputed issues presented in due process hearings typically fall into the following categories: programming/placement and compensatory education, program eligibility and/or identification, tuition reimbursement, and miscellaneous matters.

Programming/Placement and Compensatory Education. The largest number of due process hearings pertain to issues surrounding appropriate placement/programming and compensatory education, with Pennsylvania reporting the largest number of such hearings. Following are a few selected summaries of due process hearings regarding this issue by state.

Illinois (2003). Parents requested a hearing alleging that their child had reached the goals and objectives within the individualized education plan (IEP) and should be transitioned to a less restrictive placement that could meet the needs of a gifted student. While the parties agreed that the student was ready to transition, they disagreed as to the location of the regional gifted center where the student should be placed. The hearing officer held that by law and by consideration of the facts specific to this student, the district's choice of regional gifted center was correct.

Iowa: Sioux City Community School District (2002). Parents sought the reversal of the local school board's decision to deny a request that their gifted son transfer intradistrict from one high school to another. The parents wanted the transfer because the high school in which their son was placed was low performing, offered fewer advanced placement courses, had fewer students taking postsecondary education option courses, and had fewer students identified as gifted and talented. The administrative law judge affirmed the district's decision to deny the intradistrict transfer application.

Kansas (2004). Parents of a gifted third grader requested a due process hearing after parties could not agree on whether the student should be skipped to the fifth grade. The hearing offer concluded that the IEP provided the student with a meaningful education and was reasonably calculated to confer benefit. It was further ordered that the student would remain in the third grade with enrichment services provided in the general education and enrichment class rooms.

Pennsylvania: Charleroi Area School District (2005). A parent of a twelfth grader asserted that the student's gifted individualized education plan (GIEP) was not appropriate or implemented properly, specifically in regard to aspects pertaining to the student's French program. The parent's complaint was that the French teacher failed to individualize the French program to fit the student's specially designed instruction per the GIEP. The hearing officer found that the GIEP was appropriately written in regard

TABLE 2–3 Due Process Hearings for Gifted Students

State	Hearing Status
Alabama	From 1990 to 2006, Alabama reported having nine due process requests. Only two, both occurring prior to 1998, progressed to a due process hearing.
Alaska	No response.
Arizona	Reported no due process hearing involving gifted students from 1990 to 2005.
Arkansas	Reported no due process hearing involving gifted students from 1990 to 2005.
California	No hearings reported. California districts are not required to provide services to gifted students unless they submit an application for funding that is approved by the state.
Colorado	Reported no due process hearing involving gifted students from 1998 to 2005.
Connecticut	Reported four requests for due process hearings that involved issues related to gifted and talented education. None of these cases resulted in a fully adjudicated decision, as they were either withdrawn or dismissed.
Delaware	Reported no due process hearing involving gifted students from 1990 to 2005.
Florida	Reported seven due process hearings between 1992 and the present. Two of these cases were dismissed. Three involved identification issues, one pertained to tuition reimbursement, and one dealt with issues regarding an interpreter for a gifted, hearing-impaired child.
Georgia	No response.
Hawaii	No response.
Idaho	Reported no due process cases involving gifted students from 1995 to 2005.
Illinois	A search of due process summaries from 2000 to 2004 available online at *http://www.isbe.net/spec-ed/html/due_process.htm* revealed one hearing involving placement in 2003.
Indiana	Gifted education in Indiana is not mandated. Therefore, there is no legislation for due process in gifted education. Only children who are found in need of special education and related services under IDEA or Article 7 of the state special education regulations have the right to due process.
Iowa	Summaries of due process hearings can be found online at *http://www.edinfo.state.ia.us/web/appeals.asp?aptype=se.* Three cases involving gifted students were located between 1995 and 2005. Two of these cases involved appropriate placement, and the third dealt with tuition reimbursement.
Kansas	Reported one due process hearing from 1995 to 2005 regarding a gifted student. In 2004, a parent challenged a student's IEP because the IEP team refused to permit the student to skip the fourth grade.
Kentucky	No due process hearings were reported involving gifted students from 1995 to 2005.
Louisiana	One due process hearing was reported from 1995 to 2005. In 2005, a parent tried to apply IDEA discipline protections to a gifted child. The claim was dismissed.
Maine	No due process for gifted and talented. The 2005–2006 school year marked the first year in this state that schools had to have gifted and talented programs in place.
Maryland	Reported that they do not track due process hearings by area of exceptionality. Furthermore, all due process hearing transcripts are destroyed after 3 years.
Massachusetts	There have been no due process hearings involving gifted students since there is no legislative mandate to serve gifted students in this state.
Michigan	Due process decisions are posted at *http://web1mdcs.state.mi.us/NXT/gateway.dll?f=templates&fn=default.htm&vid=mdoeal:public.* However, special education decisions are not complete, and those issued prior to 1996 and after 2004 are not yet posted on the site. A review of decisions that are posted yielded no cases involving gifted children.
Minnesota	None reported. Minnesota has no mandates for gifted education.
Mississippi	There is no due process afforded to gifted students.
Missouri	Due process decision summaries from 1998 to 2006 can be found at *http://www.dese.mo.gov/divspeced/Complaint_System/index.htm.* A review of all the decisions posted yielded no cases involving gifted students.

(continued)

TABLE 2–3 *(continued)*

State	Hearing Status
Montana	No due process cases involving gifted students were reported.
Nebraska	No response.
Nevada	Reported no due process decisions regarding gifted students.
New Hampshire	No response.
New Jersey	Three relevant cases from 1996 to 2003 were located that involved gifted students.
New York	Decisions from 1990 to 2004 are posted at *http://www.sro.nysed.gov.* A search yielded two cases involving gifted students. Both had to do with provision of services and were with students classified with dual exceptionalities (gifted/learning disabled).
North Carolina	No due process cases involving gifted students were reported.
North Dakota	No due process cases involving gifted students were reported. Gifted education is not mandated within the state.
Ohio	Case summaries from 2003 to the present are available online at *http://webapp2.ode.state.oh.us/exceptional_children/default.asp.* A search yielded no cases involving gifted students. All school districts are required to have appeals policies, but districts are not required to report to the state whether appeals have been filed or the outcomes of those appeals. Because Ohio mandates that districts provide at least two opportunities a year for screening for gifted identification and because there is no state mandate for gifted services, appeals at the state level for identification and placement are rare.
Oklahoma	No due process cases were reported from 1995 to 2005.
Oregon	No due process cases were reported from 1995 to 2005.
Pennsylvania	Over 30 due processes cases involving gifted students were found from 1995 to 2005.
Rhode Island	Six due process hearings were reported from 1997 to 2004. Most pertained to appropriate placement.
South Carolina	No response.
South Dakota	No response.
Tennessee	No due process hearings involving gifted students were reported.
Texas	Four hearings were located through an online search.
Utah	No due process hearings involving gifted students were reported.
Vermont	No due process hearings involving gifted students were reported.
Virginia	No response.
West Virginia	Data regarding due process by area of exceptionality are not collected. Since 2000, there has been one hearing filed regarding a gifted student, and this was withdrawn before it went to a hearing.
Wisconsin	A review of the online database, located at *http://dpi.wi.gov/sped/dueproc.html,* yielded no due process hearings involving gifted students from 1997 to 2005.
Wyoming	Reported no awareness of due process hearings involving gifted student, as such hearings would more than likely be conducted at the district rather than the state level.

to the French program but deficient in implementation. As a remedy, the hearing officer ordered that the student be supplied with supplementary French software and consultation with the French teacher. The parent filed exceptions, objecting to the hearing officer's award, specifically objecting to the software, which was considered repetitive and inappropriate. The parent requested compensatory education for 42 minutes each school day. The appeals panel found no failure in the wording of the GIEP in regard to French instruction and further found no failure in implementation.

Program Eligibility/Identification. More often than not, hearing officers have sided with the district's decision regarding program eligibility and identification. Once again, Pennsylvania reported the most hearings regarding this issue. Several of the Florida hearings revolve around the Plan B initiative, which allows flexibility in identifying gifted students from underrepresented populations. "Race" was subsequently eliminated as a criterion under Plan B in light of numerous lawsuits.

Florida: Leon County School Board (1998). The issue of whether the IEP concerning a student would provide a free and appropriate public education (FAPE) and specifically whether the student was entitled to be enrolled in the district's gifted program on the basis of being a member of an underrepresented racial or ethnic group or of limited English proficiency (Plan B) was presented. The student was Asian of Sri Lankan origin, and she was bilingual. The administrative law judge found Asian/Pacific Islanders as a category well represented proportionally in the gifted program and that it had not been demonstrated by a preponderance of evidence that the student was of limited English proficiency. Thus, the student could not be recommended to the gifted program on the basis of Plan B.

Florida: Miami-Dade County School Board (2002). Parents alleged that the school district improperly denied their fifth-grade autistic child a place in the gifted program, for which, they asserted, he is eligible under the Plan B criteria. The district explained to the parents that as of December 12, 2001, they had stopped using the race and ethnicity factors for evaluating students under Plan B but that it was still considering limited English proficiency and low socioeconomic status. Since the student was neither, he was not eligible for the gifted program under Plan B. Furthermore, he was not eligible under Plan A because his IQ was below the score prescribed by the state. Thus, the administrative law judge found that the student was ineligible for the district's gifted education program.

New Jersey: Lower Camden County Regional School District Number One (1999). Parents of a gifted 13-year-old with a subtle learning disability challenged the decision of the local school board to deny the student participation in the school district's academically gifted and talented enrichment class. Students with disabilities must meet the same cutoff score for entry into the gifted and talented program as their nondisabled peers. The parents contended that the student was gifted with a potential higher than was demonstrated due to the subtle learning disability in speech and language and motor coordination. The district contended that the student would be easily frustrated by the extensive writing, rapid pace, and keyboarding skills of the gifted program and felt that the student would not function well in the class. Since the student was performing well academically, he did not qualify for Section 504 accommodations. The administrative law judge affirmed the decision of the board of education, thus dismissing the parents' appeal.

Pennsylvania: Wilson School District (2005). Parents of a 9-year-old sought an evaluation to determine eligibility for the gifted program. Evaluation revealed that the student was high functioning but not gifted. The hearing officer found that the preponderance of the evidence overwhelmingly supported this conclusion since the parents put forth only subjective assessment to challenge the decision.

Pennsylvania: Haverford Township School District (2005). A student was identified as gifted, and the parents filed a request for a due process hearing seeking compensatory education for previous years when the student had not qualified for the gifted program. A hearing officer determined the parents were not entitled to compensatory education, reimbursement for independent evaluations, or any other relief. The parents filed exceptions to the hearing officer's decision. The appeals panel unanimously affirmed the hearing officer's orders.

Rhode Island: Warwick School Committee (2005). A boy's parents raised the issue of a student's eligibility to remain in the Chemistry I honors class, from which he was unilaterally transferred. The district informed the parents that their son was ineligible for the class because of his withdrawal from the Biology I honors class the previous school year. The parents contended that the policy referenced by the school officials couldn't be applied to their son because it is not contained in the written regulations that govern operation of the honors program at the school. The district argued that while there wasn't any written policy, it was a consistent practice. The commissioner concluded that the school district was legally required to operate the honors program through written regulations and that the student should be assigned to the Chemistry I honors course.

Rhode Island: Warwick School (2004). On appeal, a parent challenged school authorities' denial to permit a student enrolled in a private school to seek enrollment in the district's Accelerated Learning Activities Program, a public school program for gifted children that meets 90 minutes per week. The commissioner concluded that (a) there is no constitutional obligation for public schools to admit non–public school students into public school programs, (b) there is no Rhode Island statute that requires public schools to admit non–public school students into public school programs, and (c) the Rhode Island Board of Regents has encouraged (not required) public schools to allow non–public school students to enroll in public school programs on a space-available basis.

Tuition Reimbursement. Although tuition reimbursement has been a right afforded to students under IDEA, hearing officers have not granted it to gifted and talented students.

Iowa: Cardinal Community School District (1996). A parent sought reversal of a decision by the board of directors of a district denying her request for payment of two classes her twelfth-grade gifted son was taking at a community college. The school board had declined payment under the Postsecondary Enrollment Options Act because they felt that comparable courses were already offered at the high school. The hearing panel found that the board acted reasonably in denying the request for tuition reimbursement since the parent did not seek permission from the district before enrolling her son in the courses and since the high school offered comparable courses.

Pennsylvania: Mechanicsburg School District (2004). A gifted twelfth grader requested freeing up two blocks of time at the beginning of each school day in order to enroll in a local college with tuition subsidy. The high school principal denied the tuition subsidy, as the college courses the student wanted were similar to courses already offered at the high school. The hearing officer found that an appropriate GIEP was offered by the district, leaving space in the schedule for a college course of the student's choosing. Although the scheduling choices may have not been the most convenient, they were appropriate given the student's level of academic functioning and interests. The parents appealed, and the decision was affirmed in December 2004. The appeals panel found that the district never made college-level classes a part of the student's GIEP and were therefore under no mandate to provide such courses.

Miscellaneous Issues. Additional issues regarding dual exceptionalities, sign language interpreters, calculation of grade-point averages, district fees, course waivers, and more have resulted in due process hearings.

Pennsylvania: West York Area School District (2002). Parents of a 14-year-old gifted student requested a due process hearing following a dispute over district fees (i.e., field trips and supplies) that the parents believed were educational services that are required as part of the student's gifted education. The hearing officer ordered that the district was to make no revisions to the student's GIEP. The parents filed exceptions to the hearing officer's decision. The appeals panel affirmed the hearing officer's decision, citing that a gifted student's entitlement to an appropriate education arises from the state regulations and not IDEA.

Pennsylvania: Bucks School District (2003). A district voluntarily provided a 9-year-old gifted student with specialized instruction in a gifted program while he was dually enrolled in second grade at a parochial school. In 2003, the district notified the parents that they would be ceasing the practice of providing the student with specialized instruction as an eligible gifted student unless he enrolled as a full-time student in the district's elementary school. The parents requested, in a letter from their attorney, that the district reverse its decision and permit the student to continue to participate in the gifted program while attending third grade at the local parochial school.

On the district's denial of the request, the parents filed for a due process hearing requesting that the district be ordered to allow the student to continue participating in the gifted program on district grounds while enrolled at the parochial school. The hearing officer granted the district's motion to dismiss, which challenged the hearing officer's jurisdiction to determine whether the district was required to allow a student to dually enroll. The parents filed exceptions.

The appeals panel reversed the hearing officer's decision to dismiss and ordered that the district continue to provide the student with appropriate gifted education services in the public school pursuant to the parties' agreed-on GIEP.

Pennsylvania: Stroudsburg Area School District (2004). Parents of a gifted 17-year-old requested that the course Health and Career Planning be waived. The district opposed the request because the course is a requirement for graduation. The hearing officer ruled that hearing officers lack jurisdiction to address graduation requirements. The hearing officer was not persuaded that requiring the course in question would deny the student a FAPE.

Rhode Island: Pawtucket School Committee (2004). A fourth-grade student was dropped from the gifted and talented program for failing to submit an assignment on time, resulting in his class average being below a B. District policy requires students in the gifted and talented program to maintain a B average. The commissioner found that the grade being contested was not arbitrary, incorrectly computed, or made in bad faith and therefore that it must stand. Although the district's policy excludes him from the gifted program temporarily, the policy also provides that once the student's grades again meet requirements, he can once again participate in the program.

Discussion. Because of various procedures across states, it is difficult to find due process hearings regarding gifted and talented students. The NASDSE (Ahearn, 2002) reported that in 1999 and 2000, the total number of special education hearings *heard* declined, even though the total number of hearings *requested* increased. The 1997 amendments to IDEA required that states establish mediation procedures at state cost for the settlement of disputes. As a result, it is reasonable to expect that the number of due process hearings may continue to decline with the availability of other dispute resolution strategies (Ahearn, 2002).

Nevertheless, parents report the need for increased information and support with regard to hearing and complaint procedures (Opuda, 1999), particularly parents of gifted students who may not realize the availability of such dispute resolution options. Finally, parents need assurances that the due process system will not harm their long-term relationships with schools, as many may fear retaliation against their children by the school because of their use of the due process system (Opuda, 1999).

Courts

When due process isn't available for the gifted or when it doesn't resolve the issue, parents, teachers, administrators, and others may decide to go to court. State laws and regulations provide the framework for educational issues, although some may fall under federal law (i.e., the Civil Rights Act).

Before going to court, there are several concepts to keep in mind. Court cases are costly in terms of time and money and can be emotionally and psychologically draining for both parties. However, it may be the only recourse left to a party seeking relief. If the decision is to go to court, one should seek an attorney knowledgeable in education law.

Case Summaries. Admissions, early entrance, expense reimbursement/transportation, compensatory education, grades, appropriate programming, twice-exceptional students, and personnel issues are but some of the matters that create conflicts among school districts, teachers, and parents. Following are summaries of some of the court cases that have involved gifted students.

Federal Cases. The federal courts become involved when disputed issues involve constitutional or statutory law challenges. Matters typically involve discrimination under the Fourteenth Amendment equal protection clause or procedural due process. Interestingly, the *Lisa H., Student Doe,* and *Student Roe* cases detailed next all involved the same family.

In *Lisa H. v. Board of Education* (1982), two students who were evaluated but not selected to participate in the gifted program claimed that the Pennsylvania Code that defines gifted and talented students was unconstitutional under both the U.S. and the Pennsylvania constitution because the program infringes on their fundamental property right to a free public education appropriate to their needs.

The plaintiffs argued that the program excluded them from available educational instruction without just cause, provided them with an education inferior to that afforded to students in the program, and resulted in the expenditure of fever tax dollars on their education than on the education of students categorized as gifted. As relief, the plaintiffs sought a declaration that the Pennsylvania Code pertaining to the gifted and talented be unconstitutional and that they be awarded $60,000 in damages.

The court found that education is not among one of the rights, either implicitly or explicitly, that is guaranteed under the U.S. Constitution. In addition, the court held that the state constitution does not confer an individual the right to a particular level or quality of education; it only imposes on the legislature the duty of providing a thorough and efficient system of schools throughout the state. The court also held that the plaintiffs did not utilize their right to due process prior to seeking litigation; therefore, the objections of the defendants were sustained, and the case was dismissed.

In *Student Doe v. Commonwealth of Pennsylvania* (1984), a plaintiff claimed that the use of an IQ test to exclude her from the gifted program violated the equal protection and due process clauses of the U.S. Constitution. The court dismissed the complaint and concluded "that use of a minimum cut-off score might not be the best procedure available but that the court could not conclude that such a method cannot be reasonably used" (Pennsylvania Department of Education, 2004, p. 58).

In *Student Roe v. Commonwealth of Pennsylvania* (1987), parents raised various statutory and constitutional challenges after their child, who scored 121 on an IQ test, was denied entrance into the gifted program. The court found that Pennsylvania's minimum cutoff score for eligibility into gifted programs did not violate the equal protection or due process clauses of the Fourteenth Amendment (Pennsylvania Department of Education, 2004).

In *Rosenfeld v. Montgomery County Public Schools* (1999), parents of two students challenged various procedures and policies that they alleged were used by the school system in selecting students for participation in the gifted and talent program. The parents claimed the policies and procedures discriminated against students who are not members of "preferred" minority racial groups by creating different, less stringent selection criteria for minority students for entry into gifted programs, thereby disadvantaging White and Asian students in the competition for a limited number of spaces. The parents sought injunctive relief under the equal protection clause of the Fourteenth Amendment and under Title VI of the Civil Rights Act.

The district court sided with the school system, indicating that both students lacked standing to challenge the admissions policy. One student lacked standing because her prospective injury was not imminent enough to meet the constitutional requirement of injury, and the other student's claim for injunctive relief was barred, as he had already been accepted in the International Baccalaureate program at his high school, which was considered the "gifted program." The Rosenfelds appealed the district court's order. The circuit court affirmed the district court's decision regarding injunctive relief.

State Supreme Court Decisions. Two seminal cases have reached state high courts. Although these cases have differing outcomes, subsequent courts have relied on the decisions from these cases in making their rulings.

The Supreme Court of Connecticut in *Broadley v. Board of Education* (1994) held that a gifted student's right to a free public education did not include the right to a special education, including an IEP, and that the failure of the state to provide special education programs did not violate any of the student's rights.

In *Centennial School Dist. v. Commonwealth Department of Education* (1988), the court held that gifted children were entitled to specialized programs but did not require individual tutors or programs that were beyond the district's current offerings.

Admissions. How students are admitted into programs for the gifted has been the basis for litigation. Lottery systems and discriminatory practices have been under dispute.

In *Bennett v. City School Dist. of New Rochelle* (1985), the New York Supreme Court Appellate Division reviewed a school district's use of a lottery system to select participants in a full-time talented and gifted program from a pool of eligible students.

On the basis of the laws and guidelines of the state and with the use of government funds and school surplus funds, the school district had designed a variety of programs for gifted students. However, the school district had only a limited number of slots available in the full-time gifted program.

The court held that the school district was not statutorily required to place a child into an educational program of choice and that the court system was not the proper forum to challenge such educational placement issues, which should instead be filtered through the administrative processes provided for by statute. The court further held that the use of a lottery system was not a violation of the equal protection clause but was instead an impartial and fair manner of selecting participants.

The court analyzed its prior jurisdictional grant regarding school desegregation in *Keyes v. Congress of Hispanic Educators* (1995). The court held that as long as the school district showed awareness and sensitivity to differences in participation levels in educational programs, including the gifted programs, by improving its identification and placement methods, it was not committing any racially based violations of rights.

Early Entrance. Parents have had limited success in litigating for early entrance for their gifted children. For the most part, courts have left entrance requirements to the discretion of the local school boards.

In *Wright v. Ector County Independent School District* (1993), the plaintiff sought admission of her 5-year, 10-month-old child into the first grade despite the Texas Education Code requirement that a child be at least 6 years of age. The court held that the Texas Education Code intended to grant school boards discretion regarding the admission of underage and overage children and that the board's policy in the case at issue to totally exclude admission of children to the first grade prior to their achieving age 6 was wholly within the board's discretion. Furthermore, the court held that the plaintiff was not entitled to an evidentiary hearing because the school had a total exclusion policy in place.

In Wisconsin, the state's highest court rejected the assertions of parents who sought early admission to kindergarten for their gifted child (*Zweifel v. Joint District No. 1, Belleville* [1977]). The court found the matter to be at the discretion of the school board and that the district's policy requiring students to be 5 years old "was not an abuse of this discretion" (Zirkel, 2005, p. 7).

Expense Reimbursement/Transportation. Cases involving reimbursement for tuition, transportation, or course materials have typically favored school systems. Courts have limited the educational options for gifted students to those already existing in the district's curriculum.

In *Ellis v. Chester Upland School District* (1994), the court held that gifted students were not eligible for reimbursement of expenses resulting from tuition or transportation at private schools. The *Ellis* court indicated that the curriculum available to a gifted student need not maximize the student's ability to benefit from an IEP but is required only to provide an appropriate program for the student.

Likewise, in *New Brighton Area School Dist. v. Matthew Z.* (1997), the court held that a school district couldn't be compelled to pay for transportation or college courses beyond the district's current curriculum because it would be more than a FAPE. The state's regulations required each public school district to create an IEP but did not require the school district to act beyond the scope of the district's existing curriculum for gifted children. In making its decision, the *New Brighton* court relied on rulings in *Centennial* (1988) and in *Ellis* (1994). On the basis of these previous rulings, the *New Brighton* court extended its holdings to encompass the inability of a gifted student to recover expenses related to tuition or transportation for college courses, unless the school district specifically agrees to reimburse such expenses.

The court held in *Huldah v. Easton Area School District* (1992) that it was not bound by IDEA because it did not provide coverage to gifted children. Therefore, a gifted student could not use IDEA as a basis to claim reimbursement for an independent evaluation or for the purchase of educational materials.

In *Woodland Hills School District v. Commonwealth Department of Education* (1986), a Pennsylvania court held that a school district had an obligation to furnish free midday transportation to non-public elementary school students who were participating in the district's gifted education program. When the district initially developed its gifted program, it gave non-public students the opportunity for dual enrollment. When the district reorganized its gifted program, transportation for the non-public school students was eliminated. The court relied on the *Centennial* decision to determine that the gifted, non–public school students had the right to be identified and provided with an education program to meet their needs.

Compensatory Education. Compensatory education is a legal term used to describe future educational services that courts provide students as a result of their being denied a FAPE. Although compensatory education has been a right of exceptional students covered under IDEA, such awards have been limited for gifted students.

In *Brownsville Area School Dist. v. Student X* (1999), the court discussed in detail the remedy of compensation education. Compensatory education was found to be an appropriate remedy for gifted children whose district failed to provide them with an adequate program that would ensure they were provided with a FAPE but was limited to the education that was available within the school district's curriculum. The court found the limitation was essential to respect each school district's autonomy while simultaneously requiring each school district to provide a FAPE to all of its students. On the basis of these discussions, the court held that an appeals panel could not require, as compensatory education, college-level instruction, private tutoring, or any education beyond that currently offered by the school district.

Building on the court's ruling in *Brownsville*, the court in *Saucon Valley School District. v. Robert O.* (2001) held that a reviewing panel could order certain remedies, which included compensatory education, but that the panel could not impose any requirements on the school district that were outside the scope of existing regulations, including requiring the school district to hire a special education expert or classifying a student as a member of another grade level.

In *Carlynton School District v. D.S.* (2003), a school district filed a petition for review of a special education appeals review panel decision that the district design a compensatory education plan that was to include weekend and/or summer enrichment classes in study and organizational skills and that they provide the student in question with a review course in algebra. The district argued that the review panel had erred in determining that no statute of limitation applied to the request of compensatory education and that the compensatory education awarded by the panel extended beyond the school's current curriculum. The court vacated the panel's determination that no statute of limitations applied to the claims and to the compensatory education award and remanded the matter back to the appeals review panel.

Grades. Conflicts over grades and the computation of grade point averages have also been the source of disputes. As competition for college entrance increases, it is likely that litigation regarding this matter will continue.

In *Luping Qu v. North Carolina School of Science and Mathematics* (2005), a father sued the North Carolina Schools of Science and Mathematics, a residential high school for gifted students, for capricious grading and false presentation. He asked that the judge overrule a teacher who gave a bad grade to his daughter for failure to turn in a homework assignment, which resulted in the student not receiving credit for the course.

The father did not deny that his daughter had failed to do the homework, but he claimed that the missing homework was assigned in the third grading quarter but was calculated in the fourth-quarter grading period. The school argued that as a state agency, the school, teachers, and administrators were immune from liability for discretionary actions and that even if no such immunity existed, Mr. Qu's claim should be barred because he failed to follow the school's administrative procedures for contesting grades. Supporting the authority of schools in grading matters, the court dismissed Mr. Qu's complaint.

In *Gateway School District v. Commonwealth of Pennsylvania, Department of Education* (1989), a school system appealed the secretary of education's adoption of the recommendation by a hearing officer that they develop an IEP for a student that included college-level courses he had taken during the 1987–1988 school year for grade-point calculation. The court, because of the district's failure to respond within a 30-day allotted period, quashed the appeal. The district claimed that a recent decision (*Centennial*) was not available at the time the original exceptions were filed, and the *Centennial* case offered new case law regarding a school district's obligation to gifted students. The court found the district's argument insufficient to overcome the waiver rule.

Appropriate Programming. A large number of cases have involved issues regarding the availability of appropriate programming for gifted students. Disputes typically arise regarding a school's obligation to provide services beyond what they currently offer and how such programs will be funded. Court decisions have varied regarding this matter.

In one such case, a school district, having lost its case at the due process hearing level, appealed to the Commonwealth Court of Pennsylvania (*Central York School District v. Commonwealth of Pennsylvania, Department of Education* [1979]). The district argued that its duty to provide programs to gifted students was contingent on reimbursement from the state for the cost of such programs. The court rejected this argument, citing that the provision of programs for the gifted "was a condition to its right of reimbursement rather than vice versa" (Zirkel, 2005, p. 9).

Parents of a gifted high school student challenged the district's IEP for their son on the grounds that it did not provide an advanced math course (*Scott S. v. Commonwealth Department of Education* [1986]). The district argued that the student had already exhausted all the school's math courses and that the student's acceleration had been detrimental to performance in other courses. The parents requested that the district offer a classroom course in math beyond Calculus B.C. or reimburse them for the cost of a college calculus course. Citing the *Centennial* (1988) case, the court sided with the district stating that "a school district is not required to devise an educational program which makes the best use of each student's abilities, but only to identify exceptional children and develop educational programs appropriate to their particular needs."

In *York Suburban School District v. S.P.* (2005), the court ruled that the school district was required to provide an education sufficient to confer an educational benefit on the student and it must be tailored to the child's unique needs by means of the IEP. The school district was further required to provide each gifted child with an adequate individualized program. The student at issue had previously been provided with an IEP that incorporated partial grade skipping, and the court held that the school district could not remove future partial grade-skipping provisions from the IEP without explanation. The court held that the school district's failure to attempt to tailor the student's course work to her needs amounted to a failure to provide an adequate IEP and entitled the student to an award of compensatory education.

Twice-Exceptional Children. Zirkel (2005) suggests that two distinct categories should be considered when reviewing case law regarding the gifted: (a) "gifted alone," those students eligible for gifted education without any other special legal protection, and (b) "gifted plus," those students who are gifted but are also eligible for other federal, legal protections (e.g., students with disabilities under IDEA and minority gifted students under Title IV of the Civil Rights Act). The cases detailed here involve "gifted plus" students, those who are both gifted and disabled.

In *Fowler v. Unified School District No. 259* (1997), the Kansas court held that a school district was responsible for paying for a hearing-impaired interpreter for a gifted child with a hearing disability enrolled in a private school but only up to and not to exceed the average cost to the school district to provide the same services to a student with a similar disability in a public school.

In *Ford v. Long Beach Unified School District* (2002), the parents of a student challenged a district's determination that their daughter was not disabled despite the fact that their daughter scored high on IQ tests but was doing very poorly in school. The parents believed that their daughter was entitled to services under IDEA because of a central auditory processing disorder. They relied on a California regulation that makes students eligible for services if they have a severe discrepancy between intellectual ability and achievement. The parents challenged the assessments given by the district and their right to reimbursement for an independent evaluation. The court found that the district's assessments were adequate and that the parents were responsible for the cost of any independent evaluations.

A mother wanted her son to attend a magnet school for the gifted so that he would be competitive for scholarships at Ivy League schools. In seeking admission to the magnet program, she asked her son's middle school principal to write a letter on his behalf, indicating that his attention deficit disorder (ADD) had adversely affected his grades. The magnet school agreed to admit the student on the condition he maintain a B average.

During his first 2 years, the student neglected to take his ADD medication regularly, skipped classes, and failed to do homework assignments. As a result, his grades fluctuated, and he failed his French class. Administrators of the school informed the student that if his grades did not improve, he would be reassigned to his home school. Eventually, the student was reassigned.

Pursuant to IDEA, a due process hearing was held before a special education hearing officer. The hearing officer found that the student was eligible for special education services as a child who is other health impaired and emotionally disturbed, that the school system had failed to provide him with a FAPE, and that his mother was entitled to reimbursement of $3,032.47 for over a year of high school courses.

The school system filed a motion for summary judgment (*Austin Independent School District v. Robert M.* [2001]). The court granted the school system's motion for summary judgment, vacated the order of the hearing officer, and closed the case, making any pending motions moot.

In its decision, the court disagreed with the hearing officer's decision that the student qualified for other health impaired and emotionally disturbed and stated that this case "nicely illustrates many of the problems with twenty-first century America—parents push their children in ill-considered directions; blame for failures is placed in the most convenient, rather than the most deserving spot; the best interests of the child are ignored while the 'adults' in the situation resort to legal action." The court went on to say, "Schools are not required to force or motivate students to take advantage of the education they offer—this is the parent's role. Schools are also not required to spoon-feed students to maximize their potential." In summary, the court determined that failing classes is not by itself sufficient evidence that an educational benefit is not being conferred on the student.

In *Conrad Weiser Area School District v. Department of Education* (1992), a school district appealed a special education hearing panel's decision that a student had a specific learning disability in the area of written expression and needed special education to address his disability. The district claimed that the hearing panel erred in failing to recognize that the student's success in the regular education program precluded classification of him as an exceptional student with a specific learning disability. The district conceded that discrepancies between the student's intellectual level and level of achievement existed but argued that the student was not entitled to special education because the student did not "need" special education provisions. The court agreed with the panel in that, despite his classification as gifted, the student was also a child with a learning disability whose performance level was not sufficient to guarantee success in the regular classroom without supplementary aids and services to address his disability.

Personnel Issues. Several cases involve personnel issues related to gifted and talented programs. Two of the cases discussed here involve the unethical actions of school district personnel. The other two deal with teacher qualification issues that arose in West Virginia.

In *Howze-Campbell v. Mound Bayou School District* (2005), the contract of the superintendent of Mound Bayou School District was terminated because of deficiencies in the elementary school's gifted program and alleged violations of federal law regarding the school system's confidential records pertaining to the gifted program. Campbell appealed the school system's decision, indicating that (a) there was no substantial evidence presented to support her termination, (b) a board member of the school system should have recused herself from the proceedings because of prejudice against Campbell, and (c) the board had an illegal public meeting prior to the hearing. The state consultant for gifted education in Mississippi testified that the district reported that 23 students in grades 2 through 6 were participating in the district's program and that no other documentation regarding the existence of a program was produced; therefore, it was recommended that funding be withdrawn.

A site visit by a state department of education representative found no evidence or documentation to prove that a gifted program existed. The representative asked to view samples of student work and meet with students in the program, but no samples could be produced, and no students were available. The principal of the elementary school testified that she was unaware of a gifted program in her school and that the gifted teacher (who happened to be Campbell's sister) was not teaching a class during the 2001–2002 school year. The court found all of Campbell's arguments to be without merit and supported the school board's decision to terminate her employment.

A teacher's changing of answers on a child's Iowa Test of Basic Skills (ITBS) test from correct to incorrect was the issue in *Professional Standards Commission v. Denham* (2001). A paraprofessional reported the incident to the principal, and the teacher admitted her actions. The school board issued a written reprimand and barred the teacher from administering the ITBS test.

The Professional Standards Commission in the state of Georgia referred the matter to the Office of State Administrative Hearings with a recommendation that the teacher's teaching certificate be suspended for 6 months. The administrative law judge adopted the commission's recommendations. On appeal, the superior court concluded that the commission had "acted in an arbitrary and capricious manner" by failing to consider the impact of their decision on the school system and its students. However, on appeal by the Professional Standards Commission, the Court of Appeals of Georgia decided that since the commission had determined that the state interest in ensuring the integrity of standardized test results outweighed other considerations (e.g., the impact on the school system), the decision by the commission to suspend the teacher's teaching certification did have a rational basis and that the superior court exceeded its authority by overturning it.

In a West Virginia case, Robert Johnson petitioned the circuit court for a writ of prohibition to stop the school board from placing an unqualified teacher in a vacant position for the gifted and talented program for which he was qualified (*Johnson v. Cassell* [1989]). Johnson held a master's degree in special education and was certified by the state to teach in gifted education programs. He had 11 years of teaching experience in the specialized area of gifted education. Charles Streisel, the individual hired for the position, was certified to teach in the areas of general science and mathematics only. At the time he was selected for the position, he did not have a master's degree, was not certified in gifted education, and had no experience teaching in a gifted program.

West Virginia Code indicates that boards of education shall make decisions regarding the filling of any classroom teacher's position on the basis of qualifications. Johnson's qualifications were undeniably superior to those of Streisel. Therefore, the court found that the board of education abused its hiring discretion by failing to place the most qualified applicant in the open position and ordered that Johnson be placed in the position of gifted education teacher with salary and other applicable benefits retroactively applied.

In a similar case (*Egan v. Board of Education of Taylor County* [1991]), Sarah Egan applied for a position as a teacher for the gifted (grades 5 to 8) and as a teacher for the learning disabled (grade 6). The district selected another candidate, and Egan filed a petition with the circuit court arguing that she was better qualified than the teacher hired. The teacher selected for the position had a bachelor's degree and was certified to teach grades 1 through 6. She had been employed as a substitute teacher with the district for the past 2 years and had experience with teaching the learning disabled and gifted. The appellant had 14 years of teaching experience, held a master's degree, and was certified to teach grades K through 8. At the time of the decision, neither teacher held certification to teach gifted children, though the appellant was in the process of obtaining such certification.

The circuit court determined that the board of education did not act inappropriately or abuse its discretion in determining that the teacher selected for the position was the most qualified applicant. On appeal, the Supreme Court of Appeals of West Virginia found that the appellant was clearly the individual most qualified to fill the position and held that the board of education acted arbitrarily and capriciously by failing to place the most qualified candidate in the position. The court ordered that the appellant be hired and awarded back pay and other work-related benefits and her attorney fees.

Discussion. Clearly, there is a lack of legal precedence for "gifted only" students. This, combined with the absence of a federal mandate and permissive state legislation regarding the educational rights of gifted students, has hindered parents in successfully resolving disputes with schools.

While federal and state legislation has served to guide policy development regarding the education of gifted students, court cases and administrative hearings are another viable source of policy development (Gallagher, 2002). As such, supporters of gifted programs need to pay attention to those cases involving gifted students that proceed through legal channels, as they may hold precedence for future decisions impacting the gifted.

THE OFFICE FOR CIVIL RIGHTS AND GIFTED STUDENTS

In the U.S. Department of Education, the Office for Civil Rights (OCR) is designated to enforce five federal civil rights laws prohibiting discrimination on the basis of race, color, national origin, sex, disability, and age in programs and activities receiving federal assistance. The overall mission of OCR is to ensure equal access to education and to promote educational excellence across the United States.

Karnes and Marquardt (1994) identified the major responsibilities of OCR, which include investigating complaints filed by an individual or representative who believes he or she has been discriminated against. In addition, OCR may initiate compliance reviews and monitor the progress of institutions and agencies in eliminating discriminatory practices. It also provides technical assistance to help institutions achieve voluntary compliance with OCR.

Karnes and Marquardt (1994) and Karnes, Troxclair, and Marquardt (1997) have reported on the investigations conducted by OCR involving gifted students and their education. In each study, the Freedom of Information Act (1966) was employed, and letters of findings were requested. The OCR agreed to the request for information and eliminated all personally identifiable information from the reports shared. From 1985 to 1991, there were 48 letters of OCR findings (Karnes & Marquardt, 1994) regarding gifted students. The second study of OCR findings from 1992 to 1995 revealed 38 incidents involving gifted students (Karnes et al., 1997). Of the 86 letters of findings analyzed over a 10-year period, districts were found to be in compliance in 52 instances. Fifty-four of the letters of findings pertained to African Americans. Hispanics, the disabled, persons with limited English proficiency, Native Americans, East Indians, and a White followed in descending order. The major issues were admission to gifted programs and the identification of gifted students. Others focused on staff assignments, IEPs, and the location of a fine arts program. It should be noted that most of the activity occurred in the southern states of Arkansas (10), Texas (9), South Carolina (6), Oklahoma (6), Virginia (5), and Georgia (5). California also had nine letters of findings.

In 2006, the letters of findings were requested from OCR from 2000 to the present. Over the 6 years, there were 56 letters of findings from 25 states. Florida had the highest number at seven. Twenty-seven of the letters of findings pertained to race, 17 to disabilities, 8 to national origin, 2 to sex, and 2 to age. The major issues were admission to gifted programs and the identification of gifted students.

It must be emphasized that there are no quotas or percentages of protected classes of students in gifted education set forth by OCR. Rather, school districts must prove that their policies do not discriminate. Some guidelines to take into consideration to help ensure OCR compliance follow:

- Appoint a biracial committee to establish guidelines for screening and identification procedures that do not discriminate on the basis of race, color, disability, gender, and age.
- Determine the eligibility criteria, including multiple criteria for eligibility and multiple assessment measures, and inform all parents, students, and the community about the screening and identification procedures and program(s).
- Provide staff development on an annual basis for all certified school personnel about the characteristics, nature, and needs of all gifted and talented students.
- Utilize nondiscriminatory screening criteria and procedures that are directly related to the purpose of the gifted program.
- Ensure that all approved assessment instruments/measures are validated with respect to the population for whom they are being used, that the instruments/measures accurately assess the abilities/skills intended to be measured, and that the abilities/skills are consistent with the definition of the gifted used at the local and state levels.
- Monitor by race, disability, gender, and age the number of students nominated and identified in each individual school in the district to determine that discrimination does not occur.

- Initiate change, if and when needed.
- Appoint a biracial appeals committee for the district.

Karnes and Marquardt (1994) emphasize that complainants can delineate the issues, provide information, and discuss proposed solutions without worrying about technical court procedures. The underserved gifted must continue to be represented and protected, and this federal agency works to accomplish that goal.

SUMMARY AND CONCLUSIONS

Negotiation, mediation, and due process are the most expeditious ways to resolve a dispute in gifted education. Parents, teachers, administrators, and others should use the formal and quasi-formal means before proceeding to a more expensive, often anxiety-ridden, cumbersome world of courts and attorneys. The costs of going to court are not only court and attorney's fees but also the time lost from work and the emotional stress. When an issue pertains to race, national origin, sex, disability, and age, the Office for Civil Rights should be contacted. Local and state educational agencies and boards as well as private and public schools, must take caution in describing all dimensions of their gifted education programs. Every aspect must be in print and widely disseminated to all interested parties.

It is extremely important that everyone concerned know the state laws and regulation. States should examine the policies on early admission, screening and identification, programming options, teacher certification, and other important topics to avoid legal action. Decisions made at the state court level impact only the specific state. It should be remembered that the Jacob Javits Gifted and Talented Education Act gives no legal protection to the gifted of our nation.

QUESTIONS FOR THOUGHT AND REFLECTION

1. What are some reasons that litigation should be the final route for parents wishing to resolve disputes?
2. Locate your state or school system's policies regarding dispute resolution. What are their strengths regarding gifted students? Weaknesses?
3. Write a job description for a mediator. What qualifications should they possess?
4. Develop a brochure or pamphlet that informs parents of their rights regarding dispute resolution. How can this information be disseminated?
5. In *Brownsville Area School Dist. v. Student X,* the courts found that a free and appropriate education should be limited to the education that was available with the school district's curriculum. Do you agree or disagree with this ruling? Why or why not? How does this decision impact gifted learners?

RESOURCES

Websites

Consortium for Appropriate Dispute Resolution in Special Education (CADRE)
www.directionservice.org/cadre
Provides technical assistance to state departments of education on implementation of the mediation requirements under IDEA'97. CADRE also supports parents, educators, and administrators in dispute resolution.

Genius Denied
www.geniusdenied.com/StatePolicy.aspx
Provides information about respective state policies in gifted education.

National Association of State Directors of Special Education
www.nasdse.org/index.cfm
Organization that helps state agencies promote and support specially designed instruction and related services for children and youth with disabilities.

U.S. Department of Education's Office for Civil Rights
www.ed.gov/ocr
Ensures equal access to education and promotes educational excellence throughout the nation through enforcement of civil rights.

State of the States Report
www.nagc.org/index.aspx?id=10
Offers a biannual snapshot of how states regulate and support programs and services for gifted students.

BOOKS

Karnes, F. A., & Marquardt, R. G. (1991). *Gifted children and legal issues in education: Parents' stories of hope.* Scottsdale, AZ: Great Potential.

Karnes, F. A., & Marquardt, R. G. (1991). *Gifted children and the law: Mediation, due process, and court cases.* Scottsdale, AZ: Great Potential.

Karnes, F. A., & Marquardt, R. G. (2000). *Gifted children and legal issues: An update.* Scottsdale, AZ: Great Potential.

REFERENCES

Ahearn, E. (2002, April). *Due process hearings: 2001 update.* Retrieved on May 15, 2006, from *http://www.projectforum.org/docs/due_process_hearings_2001.pdf*

Bar-Lev, N. B., Neustadt, S., & Marshall, P. (2002). *Considering mediation for special education disputes: A school administrator's perspective* [Brochure]. Eugene, OR: Consortium for Appropriate Dispute Resolution in Special Education. (ERIC Reproduction Document Service No. ED471809)

Feinberg, E., Beyer, J., & Moses, P. (2002). *Beyond mediation: Strategies of appropriate early dispute resolution in special education* [Briefing Paper]. Eugene, OR: Consortium for Appropriate Dispute Resolution in Special Education. (ERIC Reproduction Document Service No. ED476294)

Freedom of Information Act, 5 U.S.C. § 552 (1966).

Gallagher, J. J. (2002). *Society's role in educating gifted students: The role of public policy* [Monograph]. Storrs, CT: National Research Center on the Gifted and Talented. (ERIC Document Reproduction Service No. ED476370)

Individuals with Disabilities Education Act, 20 U.S.C. § 1401 *et seq.* (1990).

Individuals with Disabilities Education Act Amendments of 1997, 20 U.S.C. § 1400 *et seq.* (1997).

Individuals with Disabilities Education Improvement Act of 2004, 20 U.S.C. § 1400 *et seq.* (2004).

Karnes, F. A., & Marquardt, R. G. (1991). *Gifted children and the law: Mediation, due process, and court cases.* Scottsdale, AZ: Great Potential.

Karnes, F. A., & Marquardt, R. G. (1994). Gifted education and discrimination: The role of the Office for Civil Rights. *Journal for the Education of the Gifted, 18,* 87–94.

Karnes, F. A., & Marquardt, R. G. (1997). *Know your legal rights in gifted education.* Reston, VA: Council for Exceptional Children. (Eric Reproduction Document Service No. ED415590)

Karnes, F. A., & Marquardt, R. G. (2000). *Gifted children and legal issues: An update.* Scottsdale, AZ: Great Potential.

Karnes, F. A., Troxclair, D. A., & Marquardt, R. G. (1997). The Office of Civil Rights and the gifted: An update. *Roeper Review, 19,* 162–165.

Karnes, F. A., Troxclair, D. A., & Marquardt, R. G. (1998). Due process in gifted education. *Roeper Review, 20,* 297–301.

National Association for Gifted Children. (2005). *The state of the states report.* Washington, DC: Author.

National Association of State Directors of Special Education. (1998). *State mediation systems: A NASDSE report.* Retrieved July 18, 2006, from *http://www.directionservice.org/cadre/qta-1a.cfm#*

Opuda, M. J. (1999). A comparison of parents who initiated due process hearings and complaints in Maine. *Dissertation Abstracts International, 60,* 1081.

Pennsylvania Department of Education. (2004). *Gifted guidelines.* Harrisburg, PA: Author. Retrieved August 3, 2006, from *http://www.pagiftededucation.info/pdf/GiftedGuidelines.pdf*

U.S. Government Accountability Office. (2003, September). *Special education: Numbers of formal disputes are generally low and states are using mediation and other strategies to resolve conflicts.* Retrieved on May 15, 2006, from *http://www.gao.gov/cgi-bin/getprt?gao-03-897*

Zirkel, P. A. (2005). *The law on gifted education* (Rev. ed.) [Research Monograph 05178R]. Storrs, CT: National Research Center on the Gifted and Talented.

ADMINISTRATIVE HEARINGS

Bucks School District, Special Education Opinion No. 1438 (Pa. 2003).

Charleroi School District, 43 IDELR ¶ 262 (Pa. SEA 2005).

C. J. D. v. Miami-Dade County School Board, Case No. 02-2286E, Division of Administrative Hearings (Fla. 2002).

D. B. and J. B. on behalf of minor child A. B. v. Board of Education of Lower Camden County Regional School District No. 1, OAL Dkt. No. EDU391-99 (N.J. 1999).

Haverford Township School District, Special Education Opinion #1664 (Pa. 2005).

Illinois State Board of Education Due Process Summaries, Case No. 003349 (Ill. 2003).

Kansas, Special Education Due Process Hearing (Kan. March 1, 2004).

Mechanicsburg Area School District, Special Education Opinion No. 1542 (Pa. 2004).

N. K. v. Leon County School Board, Case No. 98-000026E, Division of Administrative Hearings (Fla. 1998).

Pat Davis v. Cardinal Community School District, 14 D.o.E. App. Dec. 199 (Iowa SBE, 1996).

Stroudsburg Area School District, Special Education Opinion No. 1669 (Pa. 2005).

Student Doe v. Warwick School Community, Commissioner of Education (R.I. October 7, 2004).

Student K. S. Doe v. Pawtucket School Committee, Commissioner of Education (R.I. July 9, 2004).

Student M. P. v. Warwick, Commissioner of Education (R.I. January 30, 2004).

West York Area School District, Special Education Opinion No. 1256 (Pa. 2002).

William and Janette Deck v. Sioux City Community School District, 21 D.o.E. App. Dec. 242 (Iowa SBE 2001).

Wilson School District, ODR #4732 (Pa. 2005).

COURT CASES

Austin Independent School District v. Robert M., 168 F. Supp.2d 635 (W. D. Tex. 2001).

Bennett v. City School Dist. of New Rochelle, 497 N.Y. S.2d 72 (App. Div. 1985).

Broadley v. Board of Education, 639 A.2d 502 (Conn. 1994).

Brownsville Area School Dist. v. Student X, 729 A.2d 198 (Pa. Commw. 1999).

Carlynton School District v. D. S., 815 A.2d 666 (Pa. Commw. Ct. 2003).

Centennial School District v. Commonwealth of Pennsylvania, Department of Education, 539 A.2d 785 (Pa. 1988).

Central York School District v. Commonwealth Department of Education, 41 Pa. Commw. 383; 399 A.2d 167 (Pa. Commw. Ct. 1979).

Conrad Weiser Area School District v. Department of Education, 603 A.2d 701 (Pa. Commw. Ct. 1992)

Egan v. Board of Education of Taylor County, 406 S.E.2d 733 (W. Va. 1991).

Ellis v. Chester Upland School Dist., 651 A.2d 616, 618 (Pa. Commw. Ct. 1994).

Ford v. Long Beach Unified School District, 291 F.3d 1086 (9th Cir. 2002).

Fowler v. Unified School Dist. No. 259, 128 F.3d 1431 (10th Cir. 1997).

Gateway School District v. Commonwealth of Pennsylvania, Department of Education, 559 A.2d 118 (Pa. Commw. Ct. 1989).

Howze-Campbell v. Mound Bayou School District, 914 So.2d 1284 (Miss. App. 2005).

Huldah A. v. Easton Area School District, 601 A.2d 860 (Pa. Commw. Ct. 1992).

Johnson v. Cassell, 387 S.E.2d 553 (W. Va. 1989).

Keyes v. Congress of Hispanic Educators, 902 F. Supp. 1274 (D. Colo. 1995).

Lisa H. v. State Board of Education, 447 A.2d 669 (Pa. Commw. Ct. 1982).

Luping Qu v. North Carolina School of Science and Mathematics, No. 04 CV 06351 (N.C. Super. Ct. 2005).

New Brighton Area School Dist. v. Matthew Z., 697 A.2d 1056, 1058 (Pa. Commw. 1997).

Professional Standards Commission v. Denham, 252 Ga. App. 785 (Ga. App. 2001).

Rosenfeld v. Montgomery County Public Schools, 41 F. Supp. 2d (D. Md. 1999).

Saucon Valley School Dist. v. Robert O., 785 A.2d 1069, 1075 (Pa. Commw. 2001).

School Dist. of the City of York v. Lincoln-Edison Charter School, 772 A.2d 1045, 1050 (Pa. Commw. 2001).

Scott S. v. Commonwealth Department of Education, 512 A.2d 790 (Pa. Commw. Ct. 1986).

Student Doe v. Commonwealth of Pennsylvania, 593 F. Supp. 54 (E.D. Pa. 1984).

Student Roe v. Commonwealth of Pennsylvania, 638 F. Supp. 929 (E.D. Pa. 1987).

Woodland Hills School District v. Commonwealth Department of Education, 516 A.2d 875 (Pa. Commw. Ct. 1986).

Wright v. Ector County Independent School Dist., 867 S.W.2d 863 (Tx. App. Ct. 1993).

York Suburban School Dist. v. S.P., 872 A.2d 1285, 1287 (Pa. Commw. 2005).

Zweifel v. Joint District No. 1, Belleville, 251 N.W.2d 822 (Wis. 1977).

CHAPTER 3

THEORIES OF INTELLIGENCE

Amber Esping
Indiana University

Jonathan A. Plucker, Ph.D.
Indiana University

INTRODUCTION

Take a moment to think about the most intelligent person you know. This person can be someone you know personally or someone you have heard or read about. Once you have decided on an individual, write a list of the characteristics that make this person "intelligent." When you have completed your list, use it to create your personal definition of intelligence. Start it this way: "Intelligence is ___________."

What items were on your list and definition? It is likely that if you compared your responses with those of others, you would find many of the same items. Sternberg, Conway, Ketron, and Bernstein (1981) found that Americans tend to define intelligence in terms of verbal ability, social competence, and practical problem-solving ability, so items in these categories would probably be popular responses. However, it is very rare that any two people will create exactly the same definition. Think about these questions: Does an intelligent person need to think and respond quickly? Can a person be intelligent but not be creative? What about "street smarts" or common sense? Are these things necessary to call someone "intelligent"? What about the case of an autistic savant who cannot function well enough to live independently but can instantaneously calculate the weekday on which you were born. Is this person intelligent?

There are several competing theories about what intelligence is, and psychologists have proposed many different approaches to testing it. One reason for this diversity of opinion is that intelligence is a psychological construct, not a "thing" that can be seen. Psychological constructs are hypothetical entities or processes that cannot be observed directly. They are driven by theory, and their existence can only be inferred from relationships among observable behaviors.

Of course, there is a certain mystery surrounding the construct of intelligence. This is due to several factors. First, most cultures hold intelligent individuals in high regard, which often leads to stereotyping about what a "genius" is. Second, in order to preserve the integrity of the instruments used to measure it, the exact contents of intelligence tests are carefully guarded secrets, known only to the licensed psychologists who write and administer the tests. Access to intelligence test materials is denied even to other professional psychologists, and the penalties for any violation of this ethics code can be severe (American Psychological Association, 2002). This secrecy is vitally important. If the contents of these tests were well known, students could skew results by practicing for the tests. It does lead to misconceptions about the concept of intelligence and the type of information that intelligence tests provide. For example, many college students do not know that there is little relationship between the so-called intelligence tests published in popular books and on Web sites and the carefully controlled psychometric instruments used by licensed psychologists working in the schools or in private practice. Even professional educators sometimes misinterpret their students' IQ scores, implicitly assuming that they provide more information or different kinds of information than they actually do.

These misconceptions are troubling because research suggests that what people believe about the nature of intelligence can have a measurable impact on their behavior in terms of the choices they make in their own lives (Dweck & Leggett, 1988) and how they relate to their students (Rosenthal, 1995; Rosenthal & Jacobson, 1968). For example, teachers appear to treat students differently on the basis of teacher estimations of students' levels of intelligence. Educators of the gifted often have access to students' intelligence test scores and may be in a position to make instructional decisions on the basis of those scores. Therefore, there is a certain ethical imperative in learning about the theories of intelligence that form the basis for this kind of testing. What one knows or doesn't know about intelligence has the potential either to help or to hinder students.

This chapter will help one understand what intelligence testing looks like and will also attempt to demystify the intelligence theories that support these practices. A historical perspective is taken by looking at how philosophers and psychologists have explored human intellectual abilities from the time of Plato and Aristotle to the present day. For example, psychologists do not yet know with certainty how much intelligence depends on nature or nurture, although we do have some compelling evidence. Nor is it known if intelligence is the result of a single, metaphorical "pool" of mental energy in the brain or if different intellectual abilities (e.g., linguistic, mathematical, and musical aptitudes) arise from different pools. Indeed, for all our sophisticated theoretical and statistical machinery, even the experts cannot agree on precisely how to *define* intelligence.

A BRIEF HISTORY OF INTELLIGENCE THEORY

How have philosophers and psychologists dealt with the problem of defining and conceptualizing human mental abilities? Even though 21st-century psychologists have access to very sophisticated tools for studying human intelligence, some of the same questions are still being asked today that Plato and Aristotle posed before the turn of the first millennium. The historical eras used to organize this chapter are somewhat arbitrary. Other researchers would probably organize the material differently (Gardner, 2003; Gardner, Kornhaber, & Wake, 1996; Sternberg, 1990). The proposed time periods presented here conform closely with the material at the History of Intelligence Theory Web site (*www.indiana.edu/~intell*).

Historical Foundations

Although space limitations prevent a detailed discussion of the historical influences on modern intelligence theory, these influences are numerous and long standing. Human beings have always been fascinated with our own mental lives, and the origins of modern intelligence theories can be traced as far back in Western philosophy as Plato (427–347 B.C.E.) and Aristotle (384–322 B.C.E.). In the *Meno,* Plato addressed the nature/nurture question when he asked, "Can you tell me, Socrates, whether excellence can be taught? Or can it not be taught, but acquired through practice? Or can it neither be acquired through practice nor learned, but is something which men possess by nature or in some other way?" (Plato, 1985, p. 35). Another salient question in contemporary intelligence theory involves the debate over multiple intelligences. Does intelligence arise from a single metaphorical pool of mental energy, or are there many different pools in the human mind? Some researchers believe that Plato's pupil Aristotle prefigured this question by distinguishing intellectual excellence from moral excellence and by separating mental activities into three ontological kinds: understanding, action, and production (Tigner & Tigner, 2000). Given that the field of psychology is an offshoot of the field of philosophy, the role of philosophy in shaping modern thought about intelligence is not surprising. Other philosophers whose work has influenced contemporary intelligence theory include Thomasius, Hobbes, and Kant, among others.

Modern Foundations

During the 1800s, significant theoretical and empirical advances were made in the study of intelligence. Building on the strong philosophical foundation of Hume, Kant, Adam Smith, and others, philosophers and psychologists made significant advances in theories about intelligence and methods for studying and applying these theories. Two major figures from this time are the psychologist Francis Galton, building on the work of his cousin Charles Darwin, and the philosopher John Stuart Mill, who held very different views of intelligence and its development.

Galton's Work on Heredity and Intelligence. One of the most significant events in the development of intelligence theory was the publication of Charles Darwin's *The Origin of Species by Means of Natural Selection* in 1859.

According to Darwin's theory, animals that are best suited to their environments have a natural survival advantage and are therefore more likely to live long enough to pass on their hereditary contribution to offspring. In this way, advantageous characteristics become increasingly common in local populations, and species gradually evolve. Simple explanations of evolution often emphasize changes in physical characteristics, but Darwin believed that natural selection applies to mental traits as well because of inherited changes in brain structure (Darwin, 1896). Animals that learn more efficiently will have the best chance of reproducing, and in this way the overall intelligence of each species should gradually increase.

The British psychologist Sir Francis Galton (1822–1911) was one of the first to systematically investigate how this phenomenon might manifest in human beings. He combed through biographical dictionaries to identify individuals who had made culturally significant contributions and then carefully examined their family trees. The culmination of this work, *Hereditary Genius: An Inquiry into Its Laws and Consequences* (1962), reported several findings. First, it was clear to Galton that eminence ran in families. Approximately 10% of the eminent individuals in his sample had at least one close relative who was also eminent. This may seem like a small number, but it is much larger than mere chance would predict. Moreover, sons and fathers were more likely to appear together in a biographical dictionary than more distant relatives like cousins or an uncle and a nephew. Finally, Galton discovered that close relatives usually shared the particular field of eminence; if a father was an eminent scientist, it was probable that his eminent son was also a scientist. Since this pattern mirrored the already established hereditary pattern for certain physical traits, Galton concluded that intellectual characteristics must also have a hereditary origin (Fancher, 1985).

To further investigate this hypothesis, Galton initiated the very first adoption and twin studies. Unfortunately, this work was hampered by sloppy research methodology and the inability to scientifically differentiate between monozygotic and dizygotic twins; he simply assumed that the twins who behaved more alike were monozygotic, which of course provided support for his argument that nature invariably trumps nurture (Fancher, 1985).

This research led Galton to conclude that the human race could be improved through selective breeding. He called this idea *eugenics*. He believed that society could evolve in a positive direction if eminent individuals could be encouraged to intermarry and produce large numbers of children. Conversely, typical individuals and those with mental defects would need to be discouraged from procreating. A practical problem had to be solved before this plan could be put into action: intellectually talented individuals would have to be identified before they were old enough to choose mates. Eminence could not be used as a criterion because it does not usually manifest until later in life. This lead to discussions about how one might go about testing innate intellectual ability; in essence, Galton was proposing the need for an intelligence test. His preliminary work measuring physiological variables like reaction time and sensory acuity failed to generate useful results, but this approach caught on and was further developed by later researchers in the next historical period (Fancher, 1985).

Mill's Blank Slate. Despite Darwin's formidable presence, not all researchers during this time period adopted a strong hereditarian position. John Stuart Mill (1773–1836) exemplified the other side of the nature–nurture debate. Mill was attracted to John Locke's idea that the infant mind is a *tabula rasa,* or blank slate. Mill did not unequivocally reject the possibility that some mental abilities might be innate; since lower animals are born with instincts, it made sense to him that human animals are also born with something analogous. However, Mill believed that many seemingly innate characteristics could be acquired through experience. For example, he argued that differences between the so-called scientific and artistic temperaments could be explained by closely examining the mental associations these individuals made in childhood. Thus, intelligent individuals were made, not born (Fancher, 1985).

Unlike Galton, Mill did not develop a systematic method for exploring this hypothesis, but he did propose one. He hoped that in the future psychologists would receive training in a new field he called *ethology*. Ethologists would be specialists in the field of individual differences. In time they would discover which mental characteristics are innate, and they would also be able to explain precisely how all other mental abilities arise through experience (Fancher, 1985). Although the term *ethology* is no longer used in psychology, the general idea is preserved in the field of behavior genetics. This is where Galton's scientific methodology and Mill's philosophy intersect. In the 21st century, behavior geneticists study twins and adopted individuals in order to estimate the heritability of intelligence. This research, combined with studies of early intervention programs like Head Start, is helping psychologists understand how and which environmental influences impact intellectual functioning.

The Great Schools

The late 1800s saw the growth of psychology as a distinct, scientific field, with much of this activity focused on the great schools or laboratories of psychologists in Europe, primarily in Germany. The most notable development of this time period is the refinement of the work of Galton and other earlier researchers, particularly by James McKeen Cattell in Germany, England, and later the United States.

Cattell's Extension of Galton's Work. Psychologists working during this historical period made important contributions to the scientific study of intellectual functioning. As discussed previously, Francis Galton had been the first to articulate the need for a test of innate mental ability. Since mental ability is a construct that cannot be seen or measured directly, he had to focus his research on things that can be seen and measured. One area of interest was *anthropometric testing,* which involved the measurement of physiological variables like reaction time and sensory acuity. This approach made intuitive sense and provides evidence of how early psychologists conceptualized intelligence. Reaction time and sensory acuity were likely indicators of neural efficiency and, by logical extension, innate mental ability. Galton did not have access to the statistical tools necessary to make systematic analyses of his results, but future psychologists who extended his research would benefit from the field's more sophisticated understanding of quantitative psychology (Fancher, 1985).

One such researcher was the American psychologist James McKeen Cattell (1860–1944). After studying anthropometric testing in Wilhelm Wundt's experimental psychology laboratory in Germany, Cattell returned to the United States and began his own series of anthropometric experiments. He developed a set of 50 tests measuring such variables as reaction time to auditory stimuli, pain thresholds, ability to detect differences in the weight of two seemingly identical objects, memory for a random stream of letters, and the speed with which an individual could name colors presented on strips of paper. In 1890, Cattell published a paper describing some of these experiments, and in it he introduced the term "mental test" (Cattell, 1890; Fancher, 1985).

Cattell's systematic approach to mental testing helped move the psychology of individual differences away from philosophy and toward science, and this was an important step in the development of intelligence testing. However valuable Cattell's approach, the tests themselves contributed very little to our understanding of intellectual ability. Advances in statistical techniques made it possible for one of Cattell's graduate students to show empirically that there were no systematic relationships between the mental tests and other indicators of intellectual ability, such as college grades. In fact, computation of correlation coefficients demonstrated that there were no meaningful relationships between any single mental test and the other tests. This meant that the constellation of variables Cattell was measuring failed as a construct of mental ability. However, Cattell's objective and quantitative approach to mental testing was a success inasmuch as it set a new standard for the scientific measurement of intelligence (Mackintosh, 1998).

The Great Schools' Influence

As psychology matured as a discipline, the students from the great schools in Europe began to spread throughout Western cultures. As psychologists such as Cattell and others created labs and psychology programs in other countries, the impact of this work was magnified. It is within this context that a great deal of seminal work on intelligence was conducted, including the work of Binet, Terman, Spearman, Goddard, and the U.S. Army testing team during World War I.

Binet and Intelligence Testing. In 1904, the French psychologist Alfred Binet (1857–1911) became a member of a committee appointed by the French government to diagnose low-achieving children who might be in need of special education services. In the past this had been a rather slipshod and subjective process, and the committee recognized the need for a more objective measure as France moved to a system of universal public education. Binet enlisted the aid of his student, the French physician Theodore Simon (1873–1961), and began work on what would eventually become the world's first true intelligence test.

Binet and Simon approached their task differently than psychologists from the earlier time periods. Binet had long been dissatisfied with the anthropometric approach of Galton and Cattell on the grounds that physiological variables, while relatively easy to measure, were not necessarily appropriate indicators of intellectual functioning and did not provide enough variability in performance to discriminate adequately among individuals. He proposed instead that mental tests should focus on higher and more psychometrically elusive psychological processes like judgment, memory, and attention. Although Binet is often criticized for not having a theoretical basis to his work, he was actually quite specific about his conceptualization of intelligence, noting, "In intelligence there is a fundamental faculty. . . . This faculty is judgment, . . . practical sense, initiative, the faculty of adapting one's self to circumstances. To judge well, to comprehend well, to reason well, these are the essential activities of intelligence" (Binet & Simon, 1973, p. 43). Binet and Simon began by piloting several experimental tests on children who had previously been identified as being normal or mentally deficient, and it soon became clear that the main difference between these two groups of children was not which tests they could pass but rather the age at which they could pass them. Normal children were able to pass the tests at an earlier age than the mentally deficient ones (Fancher, 1985). This discovery led to the creation of the Binet-Simon Intelligence Scales, which they published in 1905, with revisions in 1908 and 1911.

The 1905 Binet-Simon Intelligence Scale was designed for use with children between the ages of 3 and 13, and it was hampered by a ceiling effect that limited its usefulness for diagnosing high-ability individuals. The 2003 version of the test, called the Stanford-Binet V, can be used with individuals ages 2 to 90 and is capable of discriminating across the full range of intelligence from very low to very high (Roid, 2003), although there is some controversy about whether a ceiling effect still exists.

Terman, Testing, and Giftedness. Lewis Terman's intelligence research is of special interest to the field of gifted education. In 1921, he initiated the Stanford Studies of Genius, the first comprehensive longitudinal study of intellectually talented individuals. The 1,528 children who were selected for the study achieved an IQ score of at least 135 or 140 on the Stanford-Binet scales and as such represented about the top 1% of the U.S. population. The researchers collected empirical data on their subjects from the time they entered the study (usually at age 12 or 13) throughout their adult lives and into old age (Feldhusen, 1994). The information they obtained included data on their physical growth, motivation, psychosocial functioning, family life, and career accomplishments (Fetterman, 1994).

Terman's study accomplished many things. First, it helped the general public become more aware of the singular abilities of gifted children. It also provided data that could be used by Terman in his advocacy on their behalf. Terman believed that gifted children were a "national resource" and as such that they deserved special attention. He was one of the first to popularize the need for grade acceleration, special educational programs, and specially trained teachers. Finally, the psychosocial data collected as part of the study helped to challenge some of the negative stereotypes about gifted individuals (Feldhusen, 1994).

Spearman and *g*. One of the most enduring technical contributions to the field of intelligence theory during this period grew out of the work of the British psychologist Charles Spearman (1863–1945). Spearman offered robust statistical evidence to support his ideas, and therefore he has been called the "first systematic psychometrician" and is considered to be the father of classical test theory (Jensen, 1994). In a famous article, "'General Intelligence' Objectively Determined and Measured," Spearman (1904) proposed the idea that intelligent behavior is generated by a single, unitary entity within the human mind or brain. Spearman derived this theoretical entity, called the *general factor,* or simply *g,* through a new statistical technique that analyzed the correlations among a set of variables. This technique, called factor analysis, remains one of the most important tools in 21st-century intelligence theory.

Like his predecessors Cattell and Galton, Spearman had been a student in William Wundt's experimental psychology laboratory, and he also found the idea of a single, biologically based source of human intelligence appealing. However, as mentioned earlier, there were no statistically meaningful relationships between each one of Cattell's mental tests and any of his other tests. Since the tests did not correlate with one another, it appeared to contemporary researchers that they could not be measuring the same thing. Spearman saw it differently and pursued the idea mathematically. He was able to demonstrate that uncorrected correlation coefficients will always underestimate the true degree of the relationships among any set of variables and that this underestimate is particularly severe when the scores on the tests have a restricted range of values, as was the case with Cattell's tests. Spearman derived a statistical formula to correct for this underestimation. When he applied his corrective procedure to Cattell's data, he found substantial positive correlations among all the variables measured by the mental tests and also between the mental tests and other variables that could be considered measures of mental ability. Through an extended formula, he was able to demonstrate that a common source of variance accounted for the correlations among all the mental tests, and he called this the general factor, or *g*. This finding reinvigorated the idea that intelligent behavior arises from a single metaphorical entity, and it forms the foundation for many present-day theories of human intelligence (Jensen, 1994).

Goddard and the Kallikaks. Darwin's evolutionary theory continued to exert significant influence during this time period, and this is illustrated by the life and work of the American psychologist Henry Herbert Goddard (1866–1957). Like Francis Galton, Goddard was a strong hereditarian and a proponent of eugenics. His most famous publication, *The Kallikak Family: A Study in the Heredity of Feeble-Mindedness* (1912), purported to prove the heritability of intelligence by tracing the family lineage of a "feebleminded" student named Deborah Kallikak. The name Kallikak is actually a pseudonym created from the Greek words *kallos* (beauty) and *kakos* (bad). The Kallikak family was divided into two branches—one "good" and one "bad"—both of which originated from Deborah's great-great-great grandfather, Martin Kallikak. When Kallikak was a young soldier, he had a liaison with an "unnamed, feebleminded tavern girl" that resulted in the birth of an illegitimate son, Martin Kallikak Jr., from whom the bad branch of the family descended. Later in his life, Martin Kallikak Sr. married a Quaker woman from a good family. The good branch descended from this marriage. Goddard's genealogical research revealed that the union with the feebleminded girl resulted in generations of feeblemindedness, illegitimacy, prostitution, alcoholism, and lechery. The marriage of Martin Kallikak Sr. to the Quaker woman yielded generations of normal, accomplished offspring. Goddard failed to take environmental factors into account and asserted that the remarkable differences separating the two branches of the family were due entirely to the different hereditary influences from the two women involved with the senior Kallikak (Plucker & Esping, 2003).

Goddard's influence on the development of intelligence theory during this time period extended beyond the scientific community into the political and popular sphere. In 1910, Goddard was invited to help create a screening program that could be used to enforce an 1882 law prohibiting the entry of mental defectives into the United States. His "moron detection" program at Ellis Island involved visually screening immigrants as they passed the checkpoint, at which time those suspected of being mentally defective were pulled aside and administered a revised version of the Binet-Simon scales. Although this controversial program resulted in many unfortunate consequences, it did help advance the idea of intelligence testing in the United States by demonstrating that it had large-scale practical applications. Goddard also helped to popularize intelligence testing in other ways. In the years between 1908 and 1918, he supervised the English translation of the Binet-Simon scales, distributed 22,000 copies of the test throughout the United States, and advocated for its use in the public schools (Fancher, 1985; Zenderland, 1998).

Yerkes and the Army Testing Teams. This time period also saw the advent of the first group intelligence tests. In 1917, a committee headed by Robert Mearns Yerkes (1876–1956) and organized by the American Psychological Association was charged with the task of developing an intelligence test that could be used to classify the large numbers of recruits entering the army for service in World War I. The research team created two tests, the *army alpha* and the *army beta*. Both tests could be administered to large groups under the supervision of an army psychologist. Most recruits took the alpha test, which required them to solve a variety of verbal, mathematical, and logical tasks in less than 50 minutes. Recruits who were illiterate in English were given the beta test, which presumably assessed the same underlying abilities using symbols and pictures instead of words and numbers. By the end of the war, the army's alpha and beta tests had been administered to approximately 2 million men (McGuire, 1994).

The alpha and beta tests are considered to be a pivotal moment in the history of American psychology and intelligence testing. The eventual availability of a civilian version of alpha test built on the contributions of Binet, Terman, and Stern helped create the psychological testing industry as it exists in the United States today (McGuire, 1994).

Modern Explorations

The period between the end of World War I and the late 1960s is best known for the development of intelligence testing and advanced statistical techniques to study intelligence, but several important theoretical advances were also made by Thurstone, Wechsler, Guilford, and Horn and Cattell, among others, each of whom advanced very different conceptions of intelligence. However, a defining characteristic of these four research programs is the reliance on psychometrics and statistical methodology for studying intelligence. This stands in contrast to later efforts, which are more diverse in their theoretical and methodological approaches.

Thurstone and Multiple Intelligences. The American psychologist L. L. Thurstone was active from just after World War I until his death in 1955. Thurstone, reacting to a perceived overemphasis on stimulus–response behaviors in experimental psychology in the first half of the 20th century, proposed an alternative focus on studying how people achieved their goals and solved problems. In this work, he became interested in the nature of human intelligence (Thurstone, 1924; Thurstone & Thurstone, 1941). His major contribution to intelligence theory was his model of primary mental abilities (Thurstone, 1938), which was a direct reaction to Spearman's work with *g*. Rather than posit a unitary factor of intelligence, which Thurstone believed was a useless average of multiple, specific intelligences, he proposed a seven-factor model of the following intelligences: verbal comprehension, word fluency, number facility, spatial visualization, associative memory, perceptual speed, and reasoning.

Wechsler's Assessment Approach. David Wechsler, a contemporary of Thurstone and a veteran of the U.S. Army testing teams during World War I, is best known for developing several popular intelligence tests, including the *Wechsler Intelligence Scale for Children* and the *Wechsler Adult Intelligence Scale* (Wechsler, 1939, 1949). Wechsler, who studied briefly with Spearman, believed that his mentor's conceptualization of intelligence as being dominated by a general factor with additional specific intelligences was too narrow and restrictive, which lead to people seeing intelligence as the cause of human behavior rather than an effect of various influences, which contrasted to his personal views. Although Wechsler's contributions to the study of intelligence are usually limited to testing, it is easy to see how the widespread use of these assessments, which continues today, has influenced perceptions of intelligence. Mirroring the army's alpha and beta tests, Wechsler's tests generally had two sets of tasks, one performance based and one dealing with verbal activities. Wechsler further defined intelligence as "the global capacity to act purposefully, to think rationally, and to deal effectively with his environment" (Wechsler, quoted in Bartholomew, 2004, p.4).

Guilford and the SOI Model. J. P. Guilford, working as a psychologist in California, believed that both *g* and Thurstone's seven-factor model oversimplified intelligence. Guilford, who is also given credit for encouraging the psychological study of creativity (see Guilford, 1950), proposed the structure of the intellect (SOI) model of intelligence (Guilford, 1967). He conceptualized the model as a cube with three dimensions—operations, content, and products—with each dimension consisting of four to six subdimensions. For example, *operations* includes evaluation, cognition, memory, and both divergent and convergent production. Over time, Guilford added subdimensions that grew the model from its original 120 components to 150 or more. Although the SOI model has not had the popularity of subsequent theories, it was among the first to be applied on a large scale to both general and gifted education (see Meeker, 1969).

Cattell-Horn Theory. The two-factor theory of intelligence proposed by Raymond B. Cattell and John Horn (Cattell, 1941; Horn & Cattell, 1966) separates intelligence broadly into two statistically derived, second-order group factors that load just below *g*. Fluid abilities drive the individual's ability to think and act quickly, solve novel problems, and encode short-term memories. They have been described as the source of intelligence that an individual uses when he or she doesn't already know what to do. The other factor, crystallized intelligence, represents intentional learning; thus, it is reflected in tests of vocabulary, general information, or previously acquired skills (Jensen, 2002). These two types of intelligence can also be thought of in terms of hardware and software. Fluid abilities are the individual's biologically determined hardware, whereas crystallized intelligence is the software that the individual obtains through life experience. Research has consistently shown that fluid and crystallized abilities change in opposite directions as people age. Fluid intelligence tends to peak around age 30 and then steadily declines. Older people tend to think and respond more slowly than younger ones. This may be because fluid abilities rely heavily on optimal functioning of the central nervous system. Crystallized abilities, on the other hand, remain stable or continue to increase into old age (Belsky, 1997).

Indeed, one large-scale study found that verbal ability peaked at a mean age of 67 years (Hertzog & Schaie, 1986). Psychologist Paul Baltes integrated this idea into his "selective optimization with compensation" theory of human development. As people age, they can learn to optimize their crystallized abilities or use them to compensate for age-related losses in fluid intelligence. For example, an aging chess master may find that he is no longer at the top of his game in speed chess. He could choose to compensate by playing speed chess only with other senior citizens or to selectively optimize by focusing instead on traditional chess. The chess master's expertise in this domain (crystallized abilities) will continue to be an advantage when he competes against less experienced players (Baltes & Carstensen, 1996).

The late 1960s and early 1970s serve as the end of this period because of the controversies surrounding intelligence that peaked around this time. The primary debate involved the roles of environment and genetics in the development of intelligence (Eysenck & Kamin, 1981; Kamin, 1974), with a heated debate about whether racial differences in intelligence are environmental or genetic (Jensen, 1969). Space limitations prevent a detailed discussion of these debates, but the negative fallout from the topic of race and intelligence may account for a "cooling off" in the development of intelligence theories for the next several years.

Current Efforts

Over the past 25 years, several important contributions have been made in the development of intelligence theory. Much of the 1980s was marked by analysis of Gardner's and Sternberg's work with multiple intelligences, and over the past 10 to 15 years, a diverse set of theoretical approaches has been proposed, studied, and refined, including PASS theory and emotional intelligence. A flurry of controversy in the mid-1990s provided evidence that the death of *g* has been greatly exaggerated.

Theory of Multiple Intelligences. One theory of human intelligence that has been embraced by many educators is Howard Gardner's (2003) theory of multiple intelligences. This theory proposes that intelligent behavior does not arise from a single unitary quality of the mind, as *g*-based theories suggest, but rather that different kinds of intelligence are generated from separate metaphorical pools of mental energy. Each of these pools enables the individual "to solve problems, or to create products, that are valued within one or more cultural settings" (Gardner, 2003, p. x).

The initial seven intelligences proposed by Gardner are linguistic, logical-mathematical, spatial, bodily-kinesthetic, musical, interpersonal, and intrapersonal. Linguistic intelligence enables individuals to read, write, and speak well. Logical-mathematical intelligence encompasses logical thinking (e.g., as might be used in chess or deductive reasoning) as well as mathematical and scientific problem solving. Spatial intelligence makes its appearance when an individual navigates an unfamiliar set of streets or when an architect visualizes his or her plans for a building. Musical intelligence generates the set of skills that allow musicians to play a tune by ear or to execute a phrase with sensitivity and grace. Bodily-kinesthetic intelligence is necessary for problem solving that requires the individual to use his or her physical body, as would be necessary for performing a complex surgical procedure, executing a series of dance steps, or catching a fly ball. Interpersonal intelligence drives social skills and things like empathy and intuition about what motivates other people—a type of understanding that is necessary for salespersons, teachers, and clergy, for example. Intrapersonal intelligence involves a similar set of abilities, but these are turned toward the self; individuals who have high intrapersonal intelligence have an accurate self-understanding and can use this to their advantage in problem solving. Gardner asserts that logical-mathematical and linguistic intelligences are overemphasized in traditional models of human intelligence but that this is a cultural artifact; in different life circumstances, different intelligences would gain higher priority (Gardner, 1993).

Since his initial proposal of the seven intelligences, Gardner has added two more candidates: naturalist and existential (Gardner, 1999). Individuals with high naturalist intelligence have the ability to identify and classify patterns in nature and often show unusual interest in the natural world early in life. People who possess high existential intelligence are better able than most to make sense out of the "ultimate" concerns of human beings, such as the meaning of life and death or the puzzle of the existence of single individuals in a vast and empty universe. Although Gardner proffers this final intelligence very cautiously, the limited evidence that has been gleaned suggests that it meets the same empirical criteria as the original seven.

Gardner derived his conceptualization of intelligence in part from his experiences working with members of extreme populations, in which certain cognitive abilities are preserved, often to a remarkable degree, even in the absence of other, very basic abilities. For example, some autistic savants display extraordinary musical or mathematical abilities despite severely impaired language development and social awareness. Likewise, individuals with localized brain damage often demonstrate severe deficits that are circumscribed to a single cognitive domain. Each of these domains is a candidate intelligence. There are six other prerequisites. First, an intelligence must have an identifiable core operation or set of operations; that is, a basic information-processing mechanism must exist in the brain that is designed to deal specifically with that type of information. Neural scientists have yet to discover unequivocal evidence of these neural substrates. Second, the intelligence must have a distinctive developmental history and a definable set of "end-state" performances. This means that it must be appropriate to think of "experts" and "novices" in the domain. Third, the intelligence must suggest evolutionary plausibility; its precursors should be evident in lower life forms, as in the cases of birdsong (musical intelligence) or social organization in primates. Fourth, support for the existence of the intelligence must be evident from experimental tasks; many tests have been developed that can provide evidence that a given set of abilities arises from a single intelligence or more than one intelligence. Fifth, psychometric findings should support the existence of the intelligence as something separate from other intelligences. This criterion has generated the most criticism for Gardner's multiple intelligences theory. Proponents of traditional intelligence testing point out that since a general factor is always present to some degree in all tests of cognitive ability, Gardner's intelligences should be more appropriately conceptualized as talents or abilities (Jensen, 2002). Finally, the intelligence must be susceptible to encoding in a symbol system, as in the case with writing, musical notation, or football plays.

Triarchic Theory. Another contemporary approach to redefining human intelligence can be found in the triarchic theory of successful intelligence proposed by the American psychologist Robert Sternberg (1988, 1996, 1999b). His triarchic theory contends that intelligent behavior arises from a balance between analytical, creative, and practical abilities and that these abilities function collectively to allow individuals to achieve success within particular sociocultural contexts. Analytical abilities enable the individual to evaluate, analyze, compare, and contrast information. Creative abilities generate invention, discovery, and other creative endeavors. Practical abilities tie everything together by allowing individuals to apply what they have learned in the appropriate setting.

An important feature of the triarchic theory of successful intelligence is that analytical, creative, and practical abilities operate within sociocultural contexts. To be successful in life, the individual must make the best use of his or her analytical, creative, and practical strengths while at the same time compensating for weaknesses in any of these areas. This might involve working on improving weak areas to become better adapted to the needs of a particular environment or choosing to work in an environment that values the individual's particular strengths. For example, a person with highly developed analytical and practical abilities but with less well-developed creative abilities might choose to work in a field that values technical expertise but does not require a great deal of imaginative thinking. Conversely, if the chosen career does value creative abilities, the individual can use his or her analytical strengths to come up with strategies for improving this weakness. Thus, a central feature of the triarchic theory of successful intelligence is adaptability, both within the individual and within the individual's sociocultural context (Cianciolo & Sternberg, 2004).

The triarchic theory of successful intelligence comprises three subtheories. The componential subtheory addresses intelligence as it relates to the information-processing capabilities of the individual. Three information-processing mechanisms are specified. The first involves the ability to learn to do things. The second involves both planning what to do as well as how to do it. The third mechanism involves carrying out the specified action. The two-facet subtheory emphasizes the role of both novelty and automaticization as they relate to the individual's use of his or her intelligence. The contextual subtheory focuses on intelligence in regard to the individual's ability to shape, adapt, and select his or her environment. These three subtheories provide a contextual perspective on the nature of intelligence and suggest alternative approaches to the design of intelligence tests.

According to Sternberg, traditional intelligence tests are limited by their overemphasis on facets of the componential subtheory and largely neglect the other two (Sternberg, 1984). Sternberg and his colleagues have extensively studied applications of his work to educational contexts, with positive results (Sternberg, 2003).

PASS Theory. Psychologists J. P. Das and Jack Naglieri have proposed an alternative to *g*-based theories of cognitive ability. Their planning, attention-arousal, simultaneous, and successive (PASS) model of processing (Das, Kirby, & Jarman, 1975; Das, Naglieri, & Kirby, 1994) challenges *g* theory on the grounds that neuropsychological research has consistently demonstrated that the brain is made up of interdependent but separate functional systems. Neuroimaging studies and clinical studies of individuals with brain lesions make it clear that the brain is modularized; for example, damage to a very specific area of the left temporal lobe will impair the production but not the comprehension of spoken and written language. Damage to an adjacent area will have the opposite impact, preserving the individual's ability to produce but not understand speech and text. Therefore, proponents of PASS theory argue that it is not appropriate to view human intelligence as arising from a single, unitary quality (Das, 2002).

The PASS theory divides intelligence into four interrelated cognitive processes: planning, attention-arousal, simultaneous processing, and successive processing. Planning is the ability to make decisions about how to solve problems and perform actions. It involves setting goals, anticipating consequences, and using feedback. Planning also involves the attention-arousal, simultaneous, and successive processing functions and is associated with the frontal lobes of the brain. Attention-arousal involves the ability to selectively attend to stimuli while ignoring other distractions. Individuals with attention deficit disorder have impairments in this area. The arousal functions are generally associated with the brain stem and thalamus, whereas the higher attentional processes are thought to be related to the planning functions of the frontal lobe.

Simultaneous processing involves the ability to integrate separate stimuli into a cohesive, interrelated whole. Simultaneous processing is necessary for language comprehension, as in "Bill is taller than Sue, but Mary is taller than Bill; who is the tallest?" (Das et al., 1994, p. 72). The occipital and parietal lobes are thought to be important for these functions. Finally, successive processing involves the ability to integrate stimuli into a sequential order. An example of this process is the sequencing of letters and words in reading and writing. This type of processing is believed to be related to frontal-temporal lobe functioning (Das, 2002).

According to the PASS theory, information first arrives at the senses from external and internal sources, at which point the four cognitive processes activate to analyze its meaning within the context of the individual's knowledge base (e.g., semantic and episodic knowledge, implicit and procedural memories, and so on). Thus, the same information can be processed multiple ways (Das, 2002).

Emotional Intelligence. The construct of emotional intelligence (EI) has received a great deal of attention over the past decade. Although other recent theories included noncognitive facets (e.g., Gardner and Sternberg), EI theories specifically focus on the role of emotion and emotional competencies (Mayer & Salovey, 1997). Perhaps the most serious line of research in this area has been conducted by Peter Salovey, Jack Mayer, and their colleagues (Mayer, Perkins, Caruso, & Salovey, 2001; Salovey & Mayer, 1990). They propose a four-factor EI model that is largely self-explanatory: perceiving emotions, using emotions to facilitate thought, understanding emotions, and managing emotions. These factors are seen as abilities, and the entire framework provides a lens through which to examine the complex interactions of emotion and reason (Salovey & Pizarro, 2003).

The Resurgence of *g*. Although all these recent theories mark a clear move away from unitary theories such as *g*, the publication of Herrnstein and Murray's (1994) *The Bell Curve,* with its defense and application of *g*, provoked a great deal of debate (Jacoby & Glauberman, 1995). Those scholars who traditionally have criticized unitary theories or psychometric approaches in general heavily criticized the book, yet many researchers supported the book's *g*-centric focus and conclusions about human ability (but not the book's eugenics-flavored social implications). If nothing else, the furious debate provided evidence that many psychologists and educators remain supportive of unitary theories and models of intelligence.

Criticisms of Contemporary Approaches. Much has been made of the lack of empirical support for contemporary conceptualizations of intelligence (e.g., see Waterhouse's [2006] analysis of multiple intelligence [MI] and EI theories). These criticisms often go so far as to question whether these "theories" are merely wishful thinking by scholars who are unhappy with classic, psychometric approaches such as *g* but are unable to create a suitable alternative.

We find these criticisms to be selective (e.g., Waterhouse overlooks some research on MI theory), impatient (e.g., researchers have had a century to gather support for *g*), or historically amusing (e.g., MI theory and EI are often seen as telling people what they want to hear—a criticism lobbed at Galton 130 years earlier). At the same time, strong empirical support for some of the contemporary theories is not accumulating at the pace one would expect. The breadth of contemporary theory should be seen as a positive development. Historically, researchers unsatisfied with psychometric conceptualizations had few alternatives; contemporary theories have their weaknesses, but their methodological breadth is refreshing.

RELATIONSHIP BETWEEN CREATIVITY AND INTELLIGENCE

A final topic to discuss is the relationship between intelligence and creativity. Researchers who concentrate on this relationship have argued that it "is theoretically important, and its answer probably affects the lives of countless children and adults" (Sternberg & O'Hara, 1999, p. 269). For example, Wallach and Kogan (1965) suggested that students with high creativity but low intelligence are more disadvantaged in the traditional classroom setting than students with low creativity and low intelligence.

Although the acknowledgement of these potential benefits has led to the creation of a substantial body of research, the issue remains controversial. For example, the threshold theory suggests that intelligence is a necessary but not a sufficient condition of creativity (Barron, 1969), and an interference hypothesis suggests that very high levels of intelligence may interfere with creativity (Simonton, 1994; Sternberg, 1996).

Sternberg (1999a) has suggested five possible intelligence–creativity relationships, each of which enjoys some empirical support (Sternberg & O'Hara, 1999). Creativity may be a subset of intelligence, such as in Guilford's or Gardner's work; intelligence may be a subset of creativity, as exemplified in Sternberg and Lubart's investment theory of creativity; creativity and intelligence may be overlapping sets, as implied in Renzulli's three-ring conception of giftedness and PASS theory (Naglieri & Kaufman, 2001); creativity and intelligence may be coincident sets (i.e., both are the result of problem solving), as reflected in the research of Weisberg (1988); or creativity and intelligence may be disjoint sets, as exemplified by Ericsson's (Ericsson & Charness, 1994) work on expertise. Plucker and Lim (in press) have recently suggested that, when studying implicit theories of intelligence and creativity, more than one relationship may be pertinent in a given context.

The complexity of possible intelligence–creativity relationships is not surprising. Whenever one compares two constructs, the way in which each construct is conceptualized and assessed will have a significant impact on any empirical results. In general, researchers and theorists clearly believe that intelligence and creativity are related. How they are related is still very much in question.

SUMMARY AND CONCLUSIONS

A case could be made that intelligence theory has never been more diverse, complex, and potentially confusing. Emerging from the primarily statistical and psychometric approaches in the early and mid-20th century, psychologists and educators are approaching intelligence from different fields and with diverse backgrounds and influences. And, as never before, these theories are being applied enthusiastically to education and children. Although *g*-based theories continue to find support among psychologists and psychometricians, alternative explanations of intelligent human behavior are gaining ground. Gardner's work is a popular guide for curriculum development, Sternberg and his colleagues are using his work to address difficult educational problems, and the use of PASS theory is becoming increasingly widespread in special education and school psychology. There can be no doubt that intelligence theory can provide rich opportunities for psychologists and educators interested in exploring this fascinating and somewhat elusive topic.

QUESTIONS FOR THOUGHT AND REFLECTION

1. Define these terms: construct, general intelligence (*g*), ethology, eugenics, and anthropometric testing.
2. Take a look at the list and definition of intelligence that you made at the beginning of this chapter. Which of the theories covered in your reading does it most closely resemble? What changes would you make on the basis of your newly acquired understanding about intelligence theories? Which theory of human intelligence most appeals to you? Why?
3. Take a few minutes to review the contemporary intelligence theories explored in the last section of this chapter. What are their implications for classroom practice? How would your approach to teaching gifted children change if you accepted Gardner's theory as true? How would your pedagogical approach be different if your personal theory was more in line with Sternberg's triarchic theory or Naglieri and Das's PASS theory?

RESOURCES

Websites

History of Intelligence Theory

www.indiana.edu/~intell

A resource offering profiles of historical figures and prominent contemporary intelligence theorists. The site offers photographs, interviews, and interactive video clips that cannot be found elsewhere. A first stop for anyone interested in this topic.

Reflections on Stephen Jay Gould's *The Mismeasure of Man (1981)*
www.psych.utoronto.ca/~reingold/courses/intelligence/cache/carroll-gould.html
Gould's scathing critique of intelligence theorists and psychometricians is often required reading in college courses. However, many of his facts and assertions have been challenged. Among the best critiques is Carroll's review.

Classics in the History of Psychology
http://psychclassics.yorku.ca/author.htm
Full text of many classic works in psychology.

BOOKS

Deary, I. J. (2001). *Intelligence: A very short introduction.* Oxford: Oxford University Press.

A clear and concise overview of intelligence testing with emphasis on contemporary theories and issues. This book will give the reader a deeper understanding of present-day psychometric testing.

Fancher, R. E. (1985). *The intelligence men: Makers of the IQ controversy.* New York: Norton.

This book provides vivid portraits of the pioneers of intelligence testing, with emphasis on the interactions between the researcher's personal lives and their views on human intelligence.

Gould, S. J. (1981). *The mismeasure of man.* New York: Norton.

Gould's scathing critique of intelligence theorists and psychometricians is often required reading in college courses. However, many of his facts and assertions have been challenged.

REFERENCES

American Psychological Association. (2002). *Ethical principles of psychologists and code of conduct.* Retrieved March 24, 2006, from *http://www.apa.org/ethics/code2002.html*

Baltes, P. B., & Carstensen, L. L. (1996). The process of successful aging. *Ageing and Society, 16,* 397–422.

Barron, F. (1969). *Creative person and creative process.* New York: Holt, Rinehart and Winston.

Bartholomew, D.J. (2004). *Measuring intelligence: Facts and fallacies.* New York: Cambridge University Press.

Binet, A., & Simon, T. (1973). New methods for the diagnosis of the intellectual level of subnormals. In *The development of intelligence in children* (E. S. Kite, Trans.). New York: Arno Press. (Original work published 1916)

Belsky, J. (1997). *The adult experience.* St. Paul, MN: West.

Cattell, J. M. (1890). Mental tests and measurements. *Mind, 15,* 373–381.

Cattell, R. B. (1941). Some theoretical issues in adult intelligence testing. *Psychological Bulletin, 38,* 592.

Cianciolo, A. T., & Sternberg, R. J. (2004). *Intelligence: A brief history.* Malden, MA: Blackwell.

Darwin, C. (1896). *The descent of man and selection in relation to sex.* New York: D. Appleton and Company. (Original work published 1871)

Das, J. P. (2002). A better look at intelligence. *Current Directions in Psychological Science, 11* (1), 28–33.

Das, J. P., Kirby, J. R., & Jarman, R. F. (1975). Simultaneous and successive syntheses: An alternative model for cognitive abilities. *Psychological Bulletin, 82,* 87–103.

Das, J. P., Naglieri, J. A., & Kirby, J. R. (1994). *Assessment of cognitive processes: The PASS theory of intelligence.* Boston: Allyn & Bacon.

Dweck, C. S., & Leggett, E. L. (1988). A social-cognitive approach to motivation and personality. *Psychological Review, 95,* 256–273.

Ericsson, K. A., & Charness, N. (1994). Expert performance: Its structure and acquisition. *American Psychologist, 49,* 725–747.

Eysenck, H. J., & Kamin, L. J. (1981). *The intelligence controversy: H. J. Eysenck versus Leon Kamin.* New York: Wiley.

Fancher, R. E. (1985). *The intelligence men: Makers of the IQ controversy.* New York: Norton.

Feldhusen, J. F. (1994). Terman, Lewis M. In R. J. Sternberg (Ed.), *Encyclopedia of intelligence* (Vol. 1, pp. 1059–1063). New York: Macmillan.

Fetterman, D. A. (1994). Terman's giftedness study. In R. J. Sternberg (Ed.), *Encyclopedia of intelligence* (Vol. 1, pp. 1063–1068). New York: Macmillan.

Galton, F. (1962). *Hereditary genius: An inquiry into its laws and consequences.* London: Collins. (Original work published 1869)

Gardner, H. (1993). *Multiple intelligences: The theory in practice.* New York: Basic Books.

Gardner, H. (1999). *Intelligence reframed: Multiple intelligences for the 21st century.* New York: Basic Books.

Gardner, H. (2003). *Frames of mind. The theory of multiple intelligences.* New York: Basic.

Gardner, H. (2003). Three distinct meanings of intelligence. In R. J. Sternberg, J. Lautrey, & T. I. Lubart (Eds.), *Models of intelligence: International perspectives* (pp. 43–54). Washington, DC: American Psychological Association.

Gardner, H., Kornhaber, M. L., & Wake, W. K. (1996). *Intelligence: Multiple perspectives.* Fort Worth, TX: Harcourt Brace.

Goddard, H. (1912). *The Kallikak family: A study in the heredity of feeble-mindedness.* New York: Macmillan.

Guilford, J. P. (1950). Creativity. *American Psychologist, 5,* 444–454.

Guilford, J. P. (1967). *The nature of human intelligence.* New York: McGraw-Hill.

Herrnstein, R. J., & Murray, C. (1994). *The bell curve.* New York: Free Press.

Hertzog, C., & Schaie, K. W. (1986). Stability and change in adult intelligence: I. Analysis of longitudinal covariance structures. *Psychology and Aging, 1,* 159–171.

Horn, J. L., & Cattell, R. B. (1966). Refinement and test of the theory of fluid and crystallized general intelligences. *Journal of Educational Psychology, 57,* 253–270.

Jacoby, R., & Glauberman, N. (Eds.). (1995). *The bell curve debate.* New York: Times Books.

Jensen, A. (2002). Psychometric g: Definition and substantiation. In R. J. Sternberg & E. L. Grigorenko (Eds.), *The general factor of intelligence: How general is it?* (pp. 39–53). Mahwah, NJ: Lawrence Erlbaum Associates.

Jensen, A. R. (1969). How much can we boost IQ and scholastic achievement? *Harvard Educational Review, 39,* 1–123.

Jensen, A. R. (1994). Spearman, Charles Edward. In R. J. Sternberg (Ed.), *Encyclopedia of intelligence* (Vol. 1, pp. 1007–1014). New York: Macmillan.

Kamin, L. J. (1974). *The science and politics of IQ.* New York: Wiley.

Mackintosh, N. J. (1998). *IQ and human intelligence.* New York: Oxford University Press.

Mayer, J. D., Perkins, D. M., Caruso, D. R., & Salovey, P. (2001). Emotional intelligence and giftedness. *Roeper Review, 23,* 131–137.

Mayer, J. D., & Salovey, P. (1997). What is emotional intelligence? In P. Salovey & D. Sluyter (Eds.), *Emotional development and emotional intelligence: Educational implications* (pp. 3–31). New York: Basic Books.

McGuire, F. (1994). Army alpha and beta tests of intelligence. In R. J. Sternberg (Ed.), *Encyclopedia of intelligence* (Vol. 1, pp. 125–129). New York: Macmillan.

Meeker, M. (1969). *The Structure of Intellect: Its Interpretation and Uses.* Columbus, OH: Charles Merrill.

Naglieri, J. A., & Kaufman, J. C. (2001). Understanding intelligence, giftedness and creativity using PASS theory [Special Issue]. *Roeper Review, 23* (3), 151–156.

Plato. (1985). *Meno* (R. W. Sharples, Trans.). Chicago: Bolchazy-Carducci. (Original work published ca.390 B.C.E.)

Plucker, J. A., & Esping, A. (2003). Henry Goddard and the Kallikak family. In J. Guthrie (Ed.), *Encyclopedia of education* (2nd ed.). New York: Macmillan.

Plucker, J. A., & Lim, W. (in press). Viewing through one prism or two? Discriminant validity of Koreans' implicit theories of creativity and intelligence. *Creativity Research Journal.*

Roid, G. (2003). *Stanford-Binet Intelligence Scales* (5th ed.). Itasca, IL: Riverside.

Rosenthal, R. (1995). Critiquing Pygmalion: A 25 year perspective. *Current Directions in Psychological Science, 4* (6), 171–172.

Rosenthal, R., & Jacobson, L. (1968). *Pygmalion in the classroom: Teacher expectation and pupils' intellectual development.* New York: Holt, Rinehart and Winston.

Salovey, P., & Mayer, J. D. (1990). Emotional intelligence. *Imagination, Cognition, and Personality, 9,* 185–211.

Salovey, P., & Pizarro, D. A. (2003). Emotional intelligence. In R. J. Sternberg, J. Lautrey, & T. I. Lubart (Eds.), *Models of intelligence: International perspectives* (pp. 263–278). Washington, DC: American Psychological Association.

Simonton, D. K. (1994). *Greatness: Who makes history and why.* New York: Guilford.

Spearman, C. E. (1904). "General intelligence" objectively determined and measured. *American Journal of Psychology, 15,* 201–293.

Sternberg, R. J. (1984). What should intelligence tests test? Implications of a triarchic theory of intelligence for intelligence testing. *Educational Researcher, 13,* 5–15.

Sternberg, R. J. (1988). *The triarchic mind: A new theory of human intelligence.* New York: Viking.

Sternberg, R. J. (1990). *Metaphors of mind: Conceptions of the nature of intelligence.* New York: Cambridge University Press.

Sternberg, R. J. (1996). *Successful intelligence: How practical and creative intelligence determine success in life.* New York: Simon & Schuster.

Sternberg, R. J. (1999a). Intelligence. In M. A. Runco & S. R. Pritzker (Eds.), *Encyclopedia of creativity* (Vol. 2, pp. 81–88). San Diego, CA: Academic Press.

Sternberg, R. J. (1999b). The theory of successful intelligence. *Review of General Psychology, 3,* 292–316.

Sternberg, R. J. (2003). Construct validity of the theory of successful intelligence. In R. J. Sternberg, J. Lautrey, & T. I. Lubart (Eds.), *Models of intelligence: International perspectives* (pp. 55–77). Washington, DC: American Psychological Association.

Sternberg, R. J., Conway, B. E., Ketron, J. L., & Bernstein, M. (1981). People's conceptions of intelligence. *Journal of Personality and Social Psychology, 41*(1), 37–55.

Sternberg, R. J., & O'Hara, L. A. (1999). Creativity and intelligence. In R. J. Sternberg (Ed.), *Handbook of creativity* (pp. 251–272). New York: Cambridge University Press.

Thurstone, L. L. (1924). *The nature of intelligence.* New York: Harcourt Brace.

Thurstone, L. L. (1938). *Primary mental abilities.* Chicago: University of Chicago Press.

Thurstone, L. L., & Thurstone, T. G. (1941). *Factorial studies of intelligence.* Chicago: University of Chicago Press.

Tigner, R. B., & Tigner, S. S. (2000). Triarchic theories of intelligence: Aristotle and Sternberg. *History of Psychology 3*(2), 168–176.

Wallach, M., & Kogan, N. (1965). *Modes of thinking in young children.* New York: Holt, Rinehart and Winston.

Waterhouse, L. (2006). Multiple intelligences, the Mozart effect, and emotional intelligence: A critical review. *Educational Psychologist, 41,* 207–225.

Wechsler, D. (1939). *The measurement of adult intelligence.* Baltimore: Williams & Wilkins.

Wechsler, D. (1949). *Wechsler Intelligence Scale for Children Manual.* New York: Psychological Corporation.

Weisberg, R. W. (1988). Problem solving and creativity. In R. J. Sternberg (Ed.), *The nature of creativity: Contemporary psychological perspectives* (pp. 148–176). New York: Cambridge University Press.

Zenderland, L. (1998). *Measuring minds: Henry Herbert Goddard and the origins of American intelligence testing.* New York: Cambridge University Press.

CHAPTER 4

DEVELOPING GIFTEDNESS AND TALENT

Rena F. Subotnik, Ph.D.
American Psychological Association

Jeffrey Calderon
University of Munich

INTRODUCTION

Terman's (1916) longitudinal study of high IQ children beginning at the turn of the 20th century spawned America's scientific examination of the phenomenon of giftedness. Terman assumed that if children were born with appropriately high IQs, then they would become gifted adults. His high IQ adults were, for the most part, extremely productive, but perhaps the most important lesson learned from the Terman and Oden (1959) study is that other factors, including educational opportunity, pursuit of a passion, and other psychological and sociological (psychosocial) components, are likely to determine whether a gifted child fulfills his or her potential and experiences life satisfaction.

This chapter is designed to display what has been learned in the past 30 years about the interaction of human abilities and development. It must be remembered that the concept of talent development is not that old in psychological theory. For centuries, societies have believed that talents develop spontaneously and effortlessly, and this myth has only recently been examined rigorously by psychological research.

Today, hardly anyone in the field would argue against the notion of giftedness needing to be developed. Whether researchers stress genetic or psychosocial variables, it seems clear that talents do not remain constant over time. In sum, talents valued by society (Ziegler, 2005) show a certain state of transformation. Therefore, further efforts should be taken to find the key developmental practices that lead to attaining outstanding performance or innovative ideas.

At present, talent development constitutes a major area of interest for researchers. It is through a well-designed model of development that gifted individuals may be assisted throughout their life span, knowing which factors become more or less important during the development of their core abilities.

MODELS DESCRIBING THE TRANSFORMATION OF POTENTIAL INTO FULFILLMENT OF TALENT

A number of scholars in the field have undertaken efforts to explain and describe the process of transforming high-level abilities into expressions of "Big C Creativity" (Csikszentmihalyi, 1996). That is to say, the desired outcomes of talent development programs should be outstanding performance and innovative ideas in a domain. This view is in contrast with education and counseling models, which focus on optimizing the general creativity employed day to day by all individuals ("small c creativity"). Without exception, the talent development models reviewed here portray the active pursuit of excellence in a domain on the part of gifted individuals.

The review of the talent development literature is structured into three broad categories:

- Models that identify key components of talent development
- Models that place key components into a trajectory of development
- Models that place key components into a trajectory in the form of developmental stages

Each category of models is then organized according to the following descriptors:

- The *developmental range* addressed by the model. Most models are designed to be comprehensive from childhood to adulthood. Some, however, go up to but not beyond professional life or address the talent development process only of women.
- Whether any *core abilities* are identified in the model to serve as starting points of the talent development process.
- The inclusion of *psychosocial variables* in the model. Most models, although not all, stress the importance of psychosocial variables, such as motivation, drive, or intrinsic motivation.
- The *unique aspects* of the model.
- The *desired outcomes* of the talent development process as viewed by the model's author.

Category 1: Models That Identify Key Components

This first category includes models that propose a list of elements or components essential to the process of talent development, the building blocks that transform abilities into creative productivity or outstanding performance. These models do not focus explicitly on how this process takes place or at what points over time the existence of each component enhances high performance. Table 4–1 summarizes these models and their main characteristics.

WICS (Wisdom, Intelligence, Creativity) Model of Giftedness. Sternberg (2005) conceives of intelligence as the ability to adapt to the environment and to learn from experience. For Sternberg, a synthesis of three attributes—intelligence, creativity, and wisdom—is necessary for an individual to achieve his or her highest potential. Intelligence serves as the basis for creativity, and wisdom incorporates both intelligence and creativity yet goes beyond both. Although Sternberg suggests a type of developmental path from intelligence to creativity to wisdom, the transitions are not explicitly described.

Psychosocial Model. Tannenbaum (1986) addresses the importance of matching the gifted person's particular talent with society's readiness to appreciate that talent. Thus, Tannenbaum emphasizes how internal qualities of the individual need to interact with appropriate external conditions in order to produce outstanding ideas and performances. According to his model, there are five psychological and social variables that must interact to transform potential into fulfillment: (a) general ability, (b) special aptitudes, (c) nonintellective facilitators, (d) environmental influences, and (e) chance.

Personal Talent Model. Moon (2003) proposes the concept of *personal talent* as a form of developing expertise in the interpersonal and intrapersonal domains. According to Moon, personal talent can be developed through systematic training and individual effort. The components required to attain personal talent include knowledge of one's own history, weaknesses and strengths, and sociocultural influences. This knowledge can then be applied to personal decision-making skills and self-regulation.

Csikszentmihalyi's Systems Approach Model. Finally, Csikszentmihalyi (1996) conceives of "Big C Creativity" as the interaction of three elements: domain, field, and the individual. Csikszentmihalyi has found that highly creative individuals present a "complex personality"; they are found along the whole spectrum of behaviors and emotions. His research reports that individuals who perform at the highest levels show a great amount of energy, responding to the environment in innovative and enthusiastic ways. Csikszentmihalyi stresses how important it is for talented individuals to internalize the rules and language of their field of interest. Concurrently, changes in social and cultural events open new possibilities to express creative work in different domains.

Synthesis. The models in this first category all address the range of ages. Csikszentmihalyi and Tannenbaum (but not Moon or Sternberg) presuppose that core abilities must be in place to ensure that sufficient potential exists to be developed. All four models recognize the important contribution of psychosocial variables, with Moon focusing the greatest importance on this dimension

TABLE 4–1 Models That Identify Key Components of the Talent Development Process

Model	**WICS**	**Psychosocial Model**	**Personal Talent**	**Systems Approach**
Author	Sternberg (2005)	Tannenbaum (1986)	Moon (2003)	Csikszentmihalyi (1996)
Developmental range	Comprehensive.	Comprehensive.	Expertise in personal domain. It has special resonance for subpopulations of gifted females or gifted children with attention-deficit/hyperactivity disorder (ADHD).	Comprehensive.
Core abilities	None.	General ability, special aptitudes.	None.	Ability to internalize the language of the domain and field.
Supporting psychosocial variables	• Intrinsic motivation, tolerance, courage. • With the proper environment, anyone may be motivated to achieve.	Internal qualities of the individual need to interact in a special way with appropriate external conditions in order to produce giftedness.	Self-knowledge, personal talent skills such as personal decision skills and self-regulation.	Personal talent, interest, curiosity, drive.
Unique aspects	• Broad definition of intelligence as adapting to or shaping, modifying, or selecting one's environment or condition. • This model suggests capitalizing on strengths and shoring up weaknesses.	First to introduce the role of chance in the fulfillment of potential.	• Personal talent skills can be learned through systematic instruction. • Research of the frontal lobes of the brain may explain executive abilities such as personal decision skills. • This theory may explain underachievement and the case of ADHD gifted children.	• Creative products result from the interaction of a domain, a field, and the individual. • Importance of historical, economic, political, social, and cultural contexts in influencing high levels of creativity.
Desired outcomes of the talent development process	Application of intelligence and creativity toward the achievement of a common good by balancing among intrapersonal, interpersonal, and extrapersonal interests.	• Producing important new ideas or material inventions. • Performing brilliantly before appreciative audiences.	• Domain-specific achievements. • Proposes predictive validity for high success. • Personal Talent theory may also predict whether a gifted child would exhibit resilience or vulnerability.	Big "C" Creativity.

of talent development. While three of the four models—those of Csikszentmihalyi, Moon, and Tannenbaum—see the end point of talent development as outstanding creative performance or ideas, Sternberg argues that these ideas and performances must also serve the common good.

Category 2: Models That Place Key Components into a Trajectory of Development

This category contains a group of models that not only identify key components of talent development but also imply a trajectory toward a desired outcome. Although these models assert transformation of potential into fulfillment, the components are not presented in the form of developmental stages or phases, leading one to assume that each component is constant in importance during the whole developmental process. Table 4–2 presents an overview of these models.

Female Talent Development Model. Noble, Subotnik, and Arnold (1996) address female talent development. In this model, the authors stress the importance of the context of a woman's life, demographic and psychosocial factors, and filters leading to individual women choosing to pursue self-actualization, leadership, and eminence. The distance a gifted female may travel in her talent development often depends on how far from the mainstream her journey began.

The Three-Ring Conception of Giftedness. Renzulli (2005) proposes a view of giftedness as the interaction of above-average ability, task commitment, and creativity. The Renzulli model provides three types of enrichment opportunities that can assist children in their pursuit of creative-productive giftedness, that is, ideas that change our culture in some important respect.

The Differentiated Model of Giftedness and Talent (DMGT). Proposed by Gagné (2005), DMGT discusses the long-term process of talent development, proposing dynamic interactions among the following components: (a) gifts, (b) talents, (c) learning and practice processes, (d) environmental catalysts, (e) intrapersonal catalysts, and (f) chance. The first trio describes the core of the talent development process, while the last three components are what Gagné calls *catalysts*, factors that facilitate or inhibit the talent development process. Gagné suggests a hierarchy of these components in terms of influence: chance and genetic endowment play the most important roles in the development of gifts, followed by cognitive and physical abilities, intrapersonal catalysts, and finally environmental catalysts.

Feldman's Coincidence Model. In his developmental model, Feldman (1986) addresses the phenomenon of prodigies. According to Feldman, an individual who performs well must master a sequence of major mental reorganizations of the subject matter or field in question. Feldman argues that prodigies master a domain more rapidly and deeply than others their age. The model focuses on five "coincidental" factors: (a) the child's special proclivity for a field or study or domain; (b) personality, including a drive to exercise one's talents; (c) a receptive culture or time in history; (d) access to mentors or other resources; and (e) complementary family traditions and values.

Emergenic and Epigenetic Model. Simonton (2005) examines the development of giftedness and talent from two interrelated perspectives: an emergenic and an epigenetic approach. According to Simonton, most forms of giftedness require the simultaneous inheritance of certain traits or components; these include all physical, physiological, cognitive, and dispositional traits that facilitate the manifestation of superior achievement according to inherited trajectories. Talent development in certain domains may be initiated with the presence of only one component, yet several domains of giftedness can set off only when all components have emerged developmentally. In other words, according to Simonton, components such as exceptional visual acuity or memory may be sufficient to succeed in a certain field (although such a field is not identified by Simonton), while others, such as opera composition or choreography, are talent domains that require several components to start the developmental trajectory.

Piirto's Pyramid of Talent Development. Piirto (2004) proposes a contextual framework for her model that considers person, process, product, and environmental factors in the fulfillment of potential talent. At the base of the model are genetic components, on which rest personality attributes an individual needs to succeed. Next is the cognitive dimension of the model (necessary and helpful IQ minimums), and at the top is well-defined talent domains. The whole process is influenced by the home environment, the community and culture, the school, gender, and chance.

Actiotope Model of Giftedness. Ziegler (2005) presents a model that focuses on the development of specific actions within complex systems rather than by way of personal attributes. In his approach, Zeigler stresses the capacity of individuals to perform actions in every valued field of human activity through a sequence of partial actions. For example, playing the piano requires several actions, such as moving the fingers and monitoring the notes being played. It also requires self-regulation in the form of effort and intensity and examining the output for desired effects.

Synthesis. The models in this second category have roots in childhood just as the models in the first category do. Unlike most of the models in the first category, however,

TABLE 4–2 Models That Place Key Components into a Trajectory of Development

Model	Female Talent Development	Enrichment Triad Model	DMGT	Coincidence	Emergenic and Epigenetic Model	Pyramid of Talent Development	Actiotope Model
Author	Arnold et al. (1996)	Renzulli (2005)	Gagné (2005)	Feldman (1986)	Simonton (2005)	Piirto (2004)	Ziegler (2005)
Developmental range	Females, children ⇒ adults	Early identification (children/youth).	Comprehensive.	Childhood.	In complex domains, development can be retarded.	Comprehensive.	Depends on the specific domain.
Core abilities	Personality traits, psychological resilience.	Above-average ability, creativity, and task commitment.	Natural abilities (intellectual, creative, socioaffective, and sensorimotor).	Biological proclivity toward domain.	Emergenic inheritance and epigenetic development.	Genes, personality and cognitive skills.	Demonstrated actions an individual is able to execute; goal-setting skills.
Supporting psychosocial variables	Filters: • Opportunities • Degree of social marginalization • chosen sphere of influence	Consider context of cultural and situational factors.	Catalysts (IC, EC, LP, C) facilitate or inhibit talent development.	Master teacher, family recognition and support; deep passion for a specific domain of interest.		Family, school, community, and culture influence the development of an individual's abilities.	An individual's goals and action repertoire must interact with the systems of the field to produce excellence.
Unique aspects	Remarkable attainment varies with the degree of women's initial marginalization and chosen sphere of influence.	Provides three types of enrichment aspiring to advanced levels of achievement. Talent pool of the top 15% or 20%.	• Clear differentiation between gifts and talents. • Detailed description of prevalence estimates.	• Importance of the status of the domain in current context. • Domain has to be in physical and conceptual reach of children (they can grasp its meaning).	• Giftedness does not develop until the last component kicks into gear. • Environmental factors enter into the developmental process in relation to genetic factors.	Personality attributes outweigh measured intelligence in determining the attainment of high or creative achievement.	Gifts and talents are not personal attributes since there are no entities within the human psyche that correspond to these terms; they are assumptions extracted from social norms.
Desired outcomes of the talent development process	(a) Self-actualization, (b) leadership, and (c) creative contributions that transform a profession or field.	• Creative-productive giftedness. • Type III products.	Outstanding mastery in at least one field that places an individual at least among the top 10% of age peers who are or have been active in that field or fields.	Prodigious achievement—performance at an extremely high level within a specific field at a very early age.	High level of performance, eminence.	Respectable mastery and recognition by peers in the field for making something momentarily new.	Excellence in a specific domain or field.

these models identify core abilities that are essential as starting points of the talent development process. All but Simonton's model explicitly highlight the role of psychosocial variables in transforming potential into fulfillment. In addition, all the models aspire to the achievement of "Big C Creativity," although Renzulli and Feldman focus most of their expected outcomes on school-age children or prodigies, respectively.

Category 3: Models That Place Key Components into a Trajectory in the Form of Developmental Stages

This third set of models incorporates the components of talent development promoted by the models in categories 1 and 2 and builds on the trajectories of the category 2 models by proposing stages that parallel the developmental process. Table 4–3 shows these models and their principal features according to the different stages of talent development, from fostering core abilities to aspiring for and reaching eminence.

Bloom's Talent Development Model. Bloom (1985) recognized that no one reaches the limits of learning in a talent field on his or her own. In describing the positive and optimal conditions for the development of talent, he underscores the role played by talented individuals, their parents, teachers, and others at each stage of the talent development process.

According to Bloom, during the early years of development, parents of talented individuals can be described as child oriented, willing to devote their time, resources, and energy to provide the best conditions for their children. In most of the cases studied by Bloom, parents placed great stress on achievement, success, and doing one's best at all times. During the middle years, Bloom states that parents' major role consists of settling schedules and plans for practice, while setting expectations and demands was assumed by teachers or mentors. Teachers and mentors also emphasized technical proficiency, identifying flaws or difficulties to overcome, and monitoring the talented individual's progress. Finally, the later years were marked by an emphasis on helping talented and well-prepared individuals find ways to express their unique talents. According to Bloom, the role of parents changes over time, as do the qualities and the qualifications of the teachers, and these modifications set the stage for exceptional learning.

Munich Model of Giftedness. As shown in Table 4–3, Heller, Perleth, and Lim (2005) present a multidimensional model of giftedness (MMG) stressing the fit between individual cognitive and noncognitive factors, learning processes, and environmental influences. Talent factors, noncognitive personality characteristics, environmental conditions, and performance areas form the building blocks of this model. In terms of gifted development, a differentiated curriculum is needed to address and nurture gifted characteristics; such a program of study should provide opportunities to focus on a wide variety of issues, themes, ideas, and making connections within and across systems of knowledge.

An extension of the MMG developed by Heller et al. (2005) distinguishes three stages of achievement or expertise development that are related to the main phases of school and vocational training. Using Plomin's (1994) classification, these stages can be distinguished as *passive* (early school age), *reactive* (middle school age), and *active* (adolescence and older). During the early school years, general domain-related competencies are formed. These abilities or talents are depicted in the MMG as giftedness factors (intellectual abilities, creative abilities, social competencies, and so on). During the middle school years, the formation of knowledge is acquired by way of active, goal-specific learning processes. The third stage, which also takes place during adolescence and early adulthood, focuses on increased specialization and development of expertise in a respective domain up to the beginning of professional life.

Scholarly Productivity or Artistry (SP/A) Model. For Subotnik and Jarvin (2005), abilities are forms of developing expertise (Sternberg, 1998). An individual may then surpass the acquisition of expertise by achieving scholarly productivity or artistry or SP/A (Subotnik, 2000, 2004). The transition from abilities to SP/A is mediated by psychosocial components developed through instruction in analytical, creative, and practical skills.

During the first stage of the SP/A model, core abilities are transformed into competencies by way of exposure to content knowledge and guided skill practice. The success of this effort is mediated by the talented individual's ability to learn fast and be able to apply knowledge and skills proficiently. Although students need intrinsic motivation in order to fulfill the promise of their abilities, they also respond to extrinsic rewards, especially in the form of recognition for the success of their efforts, helping them persist through good and bad times.

Parents may both pressure and support their child, although neither strategy is uniquely successful with every child. Using their expertise, the best teachers for this stage of talent development assess their students' strengths and weaknesses, seeking students who are responsive to learning, and do not hold rigid views of the world and the way it works.

The second stage in the Subotnik and Jarvin SP/A model describes the transition from demonstrating competency to demonstrating expertise. The focus of this stage is moving beyond mastery of skills and knowledge to creative problem solving and finding. At this stage, the talented individual is expected to demonstrate proficiency in creative problem solving and finding. They may need emotional or financial support from their parents but certainly not pressure. Teachers appropriate to this

TABLE 4–3 Models That Place Key Components into a Trajectory in the Form of Developmental Stages

Model	Talent Development Model	SP/A	Munich Model of Giftedness
Author	Bloom (1985)	Subotnik and Jarvin (2005)	Heller, Perleth, and Lim (2005)
Developmental range	Comprehensive.	Comprehensive.	Life span up to, but not including, professional life.
Core abilities	High level of demonstrated abilities (physical conditioning, motor coordination, hand–eye coordination, academic aptitude).	Domain-specific acuities, such as verbal or mathematical acuity or musicality, intrinsic motivation, charisma.	Talent factors (intelligence, creativity, social competence, psychomotor skills, etc.)
Supportive psychosocial variables	Family, teachers, and mentors play an important role in the development of gifts.	Parental support or pressure, "teachability," quality of the student–teacher experience, external rewards, social skills, persistence, knowing your strengths and weaknesses, self-promotion, learning how to play the game, self-confidence, and risk taking.	Personality characteristics and interests, deliberate practice, and support systems.
Unique aspects	Provides clear differentiation of the role of teachers and parents at different stages in the talent development process.	• Abilities are combination of nature and nurture. • Psychosocial variables assist in the transition from one stage to another. • Several variables become less important or more important over time. • Recognizes the role of extrinsic rewards.	• Individual characteristics such as attention, memory, and so on are seen as innate prerequisites or "cognitive equipment" (core abilities). • Personality characteristics are viewed as traits and remain stable. • Some attention to factors that change in importance over time.
Desired outcomes or end points of the talent development process	Top performers in academics, sports, and artistic fields.	• Artistry or scholarly productivity. • Elite performance	• Preparation for professional achievement or expertise.
Early years	Romance period: • Recreational involvement. • Informal, playful learning. • Reinforcement by family and teachers. • Rapid progress.	Abilities to competencies with a focus on exposure to content knowledge and guided skill practice: • Learns fast. • Proficient with application of skills and knowledge. • Parental support or pressure. • Teachability. • Teacher assesses student strengths and weaknesses. • External rewards such as recognition. • Persistence.	Passive: • Forming general domain-related competencies. • Formation of knowledge in different areas.

Middle years	Technique period: • Acquisition of technique, content knowledge, and rules. • Expert teachers. • Decrease of parental roles. • Increase of teacher's role. • Socialization in the values of the domain. • Detail oriented.	Competencies to expertise with a focus on moving beyond mastery of skills and knowledge to creative problem solving and finding: • Proficiency in creative problem solving and finding. • Parental support. • Teachability—but start to break from teacher. • External rewards. • Persistence. • Knowing your strengths and weaknesses. • Promoting oneself. • Learning how to "play the game." • Social skills. • Restoring self-confidence.	Reactive: • This knowledge has to be acquired in active, goal-specific learning process. • Deliberate practice. Active: • Increase of specialization. • Development of expertise in a respective domain.
Adulthood	Mastery period: • From technical precision to personal expression. • Tremendous amount of time and attention expended. • Search for feeling, meaning, and expression. • Master teacher finds flaws and helps overcome particular difficulties. • Details are less important than the larger conception. • Students become more responsible for their own motivation. • Full commitment to the field.	Expertise to scholarly productivity or Artistry: SP/A with a focus on socialization into a field and networking. • Capitalizing on strengths. • External rewards, such as financial independence. • Persistence. • Someone else promotes you. • Mastering "the game." • Social skills, including soliciting patrons. • Exuding self-confidence. • Risk taking.	

stage of talent development expect that students will be receptive to new knowledge but also hold their own opinions about how to interpret this knowledge and what gaps in the knowledge exist. Talented individuals still need recognition and will encounter good and bad times. They can assess their own strengths and weaknesses and can strategize how to work with both.

During the second stage, psychosocial variables play a greater role with regard to success in a talent domain. It is important to be able to promote one's work, learn the system, use one's social skills effectively by being a dependable colleague, and restore self-confidence lost in the process of encountering more challenging work and competition.

Finally, SP/A relies on the opportunity for mentors, teachers, agents, and other gatekeepers to impart their tacit knowledge and networks unto their protégés. Rather than focus on both strengths and weaknesses, the talented individual capitalizes on his or her strengths. Talented individuals need to remain persistent through good and bad times, and recognition and financial independence (along with intrinsic motivation) help keep them going. Having achieved some success and recognition, the talented individual is free to take more risks, exude self-confidence, and solicit patrons and promoters.

During the third stage, the role played by parents and teachers diminishes and changes over time. Psychosocial variables increase in importance, as do the role of others, such as mentors and agents, who can help promote the ideas and innovations developed by the scholar or artist.

Synthesis. Table 4–3 displays some general patterns of agreement among the three developmental stage models: (a) Bloom, (b) Subotnik and Jarvin, and (c) Heller, Perleth, and Lim. The three models share many common attributes, although the Munich model ends at the preprofessional level, while the other two models describe the talent development process through professional life. All three models identify domain-specific core abilities that serve as the base of the talent development trajectory. Further, each model recognizes the importance of psychosocial components to success in the domains as well as support from families, teachers, and peers. Most important, these models recognize that, developmentally, certain variables and supporters play more important roles at certain stages than at others.

GENERALIZATIONS ACROSS STAGES OF DEVELOPMENT

In this section, the developmental ranges addressed by each of the three models in category 3 are discussed. It is important to note that each model promotes the idea that the ideal end point of the talent development process is outstanding performance or creative ideas in a specific domain, whether science, music, poetry, or architecture. Further, each domain has a trajectory that begins at earlier or later times than others. For example, in music, talent development in violin and other string instruments begins earlier than talent development in wind instruments or voice. Similarly, talent in mathematics tends to emerge earlier than talent in social sciences or the humanities. Specific ages to the talent development process have not been deduced; instead, the stages are defined as early, middle, or adulthood. Finally, because schools have limited resources and opportunities to individualize instruction, a significant proportion of talent development takes place after school, on weekends, and in the summer.

Early Years

This is a great period for field trips, exposure to different careers, and enrichment in the arts and sciences. Once a young person discovers a special affinity for a particular topic or subject, the early years are characterized by playful exploration in a domain, learning the basic skills, and getting lots of attention for effort and success in learning content and skills quickly.

Teachers need to assess each student's strengths and weaknesses and provide a program of study and practice that capitalizes on the child's enthusiasm. Parents who are deeply involved in a domain for which the child exhibits strengths may play a double role of teacher and parent, offering both support and pressure to stay focused and personalized instruction.

Middle Years

Children can lose interest in playful exploration without (a) others to engage with at their level and (b) sufficient instruction in the rules and techniques associated with their area of passion. If parents need to pressure a child constantly at this point, it is not a good sign that the talented individual will persist. Yet parents need to remain involved as supporters, whether driving to events or lessons, purchasing equipment, or cheering from the stands.

Teachers guide their students into becoming experts, learning the values of the field or subject (including a commitment to studying or practicing), and engaging opportunities for young people with similar interests to meet and support as well as compete with one another as a stimulus for extrinsic motivation. Good teachers will expect their students on occasion to "bite back," or defend a position, opinion, or stand that might differ from that of the teacher.

Most important, the teachers need to encourage psychosocial strength in their pupils. Increased competition and advanced work often leads to reduced self-confidence. This is a normal course of events, but it may not feel that way to the developing adolescent. Talented young people need to pay attention to being a good teammate and a dependable colleague, to thank people who help them, to encourage friends when they do not succeed at a difficult task, and to accept accolades graciously. All of these are teachable skills that can be conveyed by mentors or teachers.

Adulthood

During the transition to adult manifestations of talent, the individual must commit extraordinary time and psychic resources to a field or domain. After mastering techniques, content, and skills, the most important task for gifted adults is to channel their personal expression and passions into creative work. Gifted adults must operate in a competitive environment at the highest levels. The biggest challenge they will encounter is to take the risks needed to develop breakthroughs while seeking recognition within their field or profession. This may require supreme confidence and charisma, which are difficult attributes to develop.

SUMMARY AND CONCLUSIONS

Core abilities of gifted individuals follow a developmental path throughout the life span. In this chapter, the principal theoretical explanations of this phenomenon have been discussed and the different models categorized into three different groups: (a) models that identify key components of talent development, (b) models that place key components into a trajectory of development, and (c) models that place key components into a trajectory in the form of developmental stages.

Research has shown that although most theories of giftedness indirectly refer to the topic of development, only a few of them have tried to organize this process into specific stages. The overwhelming conundrum for those struggling with this challenge is how to address the particular and singular requirements and traditions of each domain. Every domain demands instruction beginning at different ages, and each stage of the process is unique even within the domain (e.g., string and piano earliest, wind next, and voice last).

Even with these difficulties, some general principles can be delineated: (a) a basic stage during which one is exposed to the romance and rudimentary rules of the field, (b) a middle stage in which individuals perfect their skills and master the rules, and (c) a final stage when talented individuals work to move the field forward through creative efforts. All the stages have some role for parents, teachers, and mentors that diminish over time, and all involve psychosocial dimensions that become increasingly significant.

QUESTIONS FOR THOUGHT AND REFLECTION

The following questions are designed to elicit discussion. Answer these questions from both an individual and a policy perspective. With regard to individual children, the response should consider contextual factors, such as individual interest, maturity, or family values. When it comes to policy, however, decisions are made with the notion of greatest good for the greatest number of people or for society in general.

1. What might be the unintended consequences of early specialization in a talent domain?
2. What might be the unintended consequences of rejecting early specialization in a talent domain?
3. How can direct measures of core abilities be employed instead of abstract tests when those abilities are not standardized, subject to bias, and not even agreed on?
4. How can we ensure access to the needed content, skill, and psychosocial components of talent development for any young person who exhibits deep interests and core abilities in a domain?
5. Are some talent domains more worthy of investment by society than others?

BOOKS

Horowitz, F., & O'Brien, M. (Eds.). (1985). *The gifted and talented: Developmental perspectives.* Washington, DC: American Psychological Association.

This classic is on the bookshelves of most researchers of "a certain age." Many of the chapters are outstanding and often cited. The 15 chapters are divided into sections on the nature of giftedness, aspects of giftedness, and reflections on the study of giftedness. The editors of this volume took the innovative step of commissioning articles by developmental psychologists to consider how giftedness might be addressed in theories of development.

van Lieshout, C., & Heymans, P. (Eds.). (2000). *Developing talent across the lifespan*. Philadelphia: Taylor & Francis.

This volume includes 14 chapters of work by European, Asian, and American researchers covering a range of topics from the derivation of talent to the role of intelligence, morality, personality, context, and subject matter in talent development.

JOURNAL ARTICLES

Kay, S. I. (2001). A talent profile for facilitating talent development in schools. *Gifted Child Quarterly, 45,* 45–53.

As a scholar practitioner, Kay has created a brilliant mechanism for organizing files for students that can be used for planning of extracurricular activities, for résumés, and for curriculum development. Each student has a record with his or her activities noted in various domains. Each domain includes benchmarks for judging the competitive level of the student's contribution to promote aspiration to the next level of achievement.

Kogan, N., & Kangas, B. (2006). Careers in the dramatic arts: Comparing genetic and interactional perspectives. *Empirical Studies of the Arts, 24,* 43–54.

Kogan's model parallels the work by Heller, Subotnik and Jarvin, and Bloom from category 3 described in this chapter. In this article, Kogan compares his model to that of Simonton's, described in category 2. Kogan and Kangas analyze responses from 122 students attending the prestigious Actors Studio Drama School with regard to the age they began to consider a career in theater, their undergraduate majors, and earlier experiences in the arts.

Forthcoming Projects

High Ability Studies Issue

Two new projects are underway that may enhance our knowledge about the development of giftedness and talent. One project will appear in an upcoming issue of *High Ability Studies* edited by Marion Porath. The issue includes four articles designed to explore neo-Piagetian principles and stage development with implications for teachers and psychologists.

The Development of Giftedness and Talent Across the Life Span

This second project will be published in 2007 by the American Psychological Association and is titled *The Development of Giftedness and Talent Across the Life Span*. This volume is a 12-year follow-up to *The Gifted and Talented: Developmental Perspectives,* cited previously. This volume, coedited by Frances Horowitz, Rena Subotnik, and Dona Matthews, argues that advances in developmental psychology provide information and insights with potential application to research, practice, and policy in gifted education and talent development. Concurrently, investigations of giftedness may also inform developmental psychologists' understandings of optimal human development. Subthemes of the volume include the following:

- Prediction: What are we trying to predict when we identify giftedness? How valid and stable over time are the available and prevalent measures (e.g., IQ tests)?
- Diversity: What roles do race, ethnicity, gender, and culture play in giftedness and talent?
- Psychosocial factors: What role do psychosocial variables play in the development of giftedness and talent?
- Domain specificity: What do we know about how giftedness develops over time in different domains? What is needed at different developmental stages to support gifted development?

REFERENCES

Arnold, K.D., Noble K.D., & Subotnik, R.F. (Eds.) (1996). *Remarkable Women: Perspectives on female talent development.* Cresskill, NJ: Hampton Press.

Bloom, B. S. (Ed.). (1985). *Developing talent in young people*. New York: Ballantine.

Csikszentmihalyi, M. (1996). *Creativity: Flow and the psychology of discovery and invention*. New York: HarperCollins.

Feldman, D. H. (1986). *Nature's gambit: Child prodigies and the development of human potential*. New York: Basic Books.

Gagné, F. (2005). From gifts to talents: The DMGT as a developmental model. In R. J. Sternberg & J. E. Davidson (Eds.), *Conceptions of giftedness* (2nd ed., pp. 98–119). New York: Cambridge University Press.

Heller, K. A., Perleth, C., & Lim, T. K. (2005). The Munich model of giftedness designed to identify and promote gifted students. In R. J. Sternberg & J. E. Davidson (Eds.), *Conceptions of giftedness* (2nd ed., pp. 147–170). New York: Cambridge University Press.

Moon, S. M. (2003). Personal talent. *High Ability Studies, 14,* 5–21.

Noble, K. D., Subotnik, R. F., & Arnold, K. D. (1996). A new model for adult female talent development: A synthesis of perspectives from remarkable women. In K. Arnold, K. D. Noble, & R. F. Subotnik (Eds.), *Remarkable women: Perspectives on female talent development* (pp. 427–439). Cresskill, NJ: Hampton.

Piirto, J. (2004). *Understanding creativity.* Scottsdale, AZ: Great Potential.

Plomin, R. (1994). *Genetics and experience: The interplay between nature and nurture.* Thousand Oaks, CA: Sage.

Renzulli, J. S. (2005). The three-ring conception of giftedness: A developmental model for promoting creative productivity. In R. J. Sternberg & J. E. Davidson (Eds.), *Conceptions of giftedness* (2nd ed., pp. 246–279). New York: Cambridge University Press.

Simonton, D. K. (2005). Genetics of giftedness: The implications of an emergenic-epigenetic model. In R. J. Sternberg & J. E. Davidson (Eds.), *Conceptions of giftedness* (2nd ed., pp. 312–326). New York: Cambridge University Press.

Sternberg, R. J. (1998). Abilities are forms of developing expertise. *Educational Researcher, 27,* 11–20.

Sternberg, R. J. (2005). The WICS model of giftedness. In R. J. Sternberg & J. E. Davidson (Eds.), *Conceptions of giftedness* (2nd ed., pp. 327–342). New York: Cambridge University Press.

Subotnik, R. F. (2000). Developing young adolescent performers at Juilliard: An educational prototype for elite level talent development in the arts and sciences.

In C. F. Van Lieshout & P. G. Heymans (Eds.), *Developing talent across the lifespan* (pp. 249–276). Philadelphia: Taylor & Francis.

Subotnik, R. F. (2004). Transforming elite musicians into professional artists: A view of the talent development process at the Juilliard School. In L. V. Shavinina & M. Ferrari (Eds.), *Beyond knowledge: Extra cognitive aspects of developing high ability*. Mahwah, NJ: Lawrence Erlbaum Associates.

Subotnik, R. F., & Jarvin, L. (2005). Beyond expertise: Conceptions of giftedness as great performance. In R. J. Sternberg & J. E. Davidson (Eds.), *Conceptions of giftedness* (2nd ed., pp. 343–357). New York: Cambridge University Press.

Tannenbaum, A. J. (1986). Giftedness: A psychosocial approach. In R. J. Sternberg & J. E. Davidson (Eds.), *Conceptions of giftedness* (pp. 21–52). New York: Cambridge University Press.

Terman, L. M. (1916). *The measurement of intelligence.* Boston: Houghton Mifflin.

Terman, L. M., & Oden, M. (1959). *Genetic Studies of Genius,* Volume 5: The gifted group in mid-life: Thirty years' follow up of the superior child. In University Press.

Ziegler, A. (2005) *The actiotope model of giftedness.* In R. J. Sternberg & J. E. Davidson (Eds.), *Conceptions of giftedness* (2nd ed., pp. 411–436). New York: Cambridge University Press.

CHAPTER 5

CHARACTERISTICS OF GIFTED AND TALENTED LEARNERS: SIMILARITIES AND DIFFERENCES ACROSS DOMAINS

Sally M. Reis, Ph.D.
UNIVERSITY OF CONNECTICUT

Angela M. Housand, M.A.
UNIVERSITY OF CONNECTICUT

INTRODUCTION

A century ago, Lewis Terman used IQ tests to identify 1,000 gifted students for participation in a longitudinal study using scores on the *Stanford-Binet Intelligence Scale* (Davis & Rimm, 1998) that ostensibly provided a clearly defined line between students who were gifted and those who were not. Terman's belief that an IQ score of 135 or higher was synonymous with giftedness set a precedent in the identification of gifted students and started a movement that continues to affect students' placement in gifted programs decades later. Current researchers continue to debate which measures to use but often need clear and quantifiable methods to define individuals as gifted. In a review of published articles of research in gifted journals for a period of one year, Tannenbaum (2000) found that in one well-respected journal, all reports listed IQ, using similar or alternate tests that correlate highly with IQ, as the selected measure for identifying gifted individuals. It is understandable in research on gifted students that a clear method for identification must exist, but when considering ways to identify students as gifted and to identify the characteristics of these students, the line is not always so clear. This chapter discusses how conceptions of giftedness interact with characteristics of giftedness and introduces the federal definition of gifted individuals, which is used as a basis for the discussion of the characteristics of gifted and talented students.

CONCEPTIONS AND CHARACTERISTICS

Multiple conceptions of giftedness have been suggested by many researchers that range from general, broad, overarching characterizations to more specific definitions of giftedness identified by *specific* actions, products, or abilities within certain domains (Sternberg & Davidson, 2005). Some of the more general conceptions that incorporate a broad variety of characteristics and traits into their conceptions of giftedness are Renzulli's (1986, 2005) Three-ring Conception of Giftedness and Sternberg's (1997) Triarchic Theory of Intelligence. Renzulli (1986) defines giftedness as an interaction among three attributes: task commitment, above-average achievement, and creativity applied to an area of interest and talent. Sternberg's theory of intelligence combines dynamic skills that blend and change as intelligence is developed. These conceptions encompass a wide range of domains and include a variety of abilities and skills that result in creative and/or culturally valuable products. Neither of these conceptions of intelligence suggests that the traits, characteristics, or attributes exhibited by individuals are innate or finite. Renzulli's (1986, 2005) conception refers to "gifted behaviors" that are manifested in varying degrees, applied to various areas at varying times, while Sternberg's conception refers to various combinations of skills and traits that can combine and transform over time. Both of these perspectives suggest that the traits and characteristics of giftedness, especially in young people, are dynamic and malleable and that they comprise a potential rather than a more static and reliable set of traits that defines giftedness in any absolute sense.

Renzulli (1986) believes that existing research about giftedness can be divided into two broad categories, which he appropriately refers to as either schoolhouse/high-achieving giftedness or creative/productive giftedness. Schoolhouse giftedness refers to high performance in test taking, high-achievement learning, or academic giftedness. Individuals who excel in this category score well on more traditional intellectual or cognitive assessments and perform well in school and on traditional analytic skills. Creative/productive giftedness, on the other hand, is reflected in individuals who tend to be producers (rather than consumers) of original knowledge, materials, or products and who employ thought processes that tend to be inductive, integrated, and problem oriented. Longitudinal research supports Renzulli's distinction between schoolhouse giftedness and creative/productive giftedness. Perleth, Sierwald, and Heller (1993), in their Munich Longitudinal Study of Giftedness (1985–1989), found clear differences between students who demonstrated creative/productive as opposed to schoolhouse giftedness. Renzulli believes that both types of giftedness should be developed and that an interaction exists between them (Renzulli & Reis, 1997).

Other perspectives define giftedness as talents manifested in specific domains. Gottfried and Gottfried's (2004) & Gottfried, Cook, Gottfried & Morris's (2005) construct of *gifted motivation*, for example, suggests that individuals who have advanced determination for an enterprise are, by nature of extreme motivation, gifted. Other examples of specific forms of giftedness are the exceptional ability in selecting and attaining life goals suggested by Moon's (2003) theory of personal talent and Gardner's (1983, 1993) notion of specific talents in his theory on multiple intelligences with eight distinct intelligences: musical, linguistic, logical-mathematical, interpersonal, intrapersonal, bodily-kinesthetic, naturalistic, and spatial.

Gardner defines an intelligence as the ability to solve problems or create products that are valued within one or more cultural settings. Giftedness in his conception might be characterized by advanced performance or abilities in a specific domain, but Gardner believes that these intelligences do not work in isolation but rather "are continuous with one another" (1983, p. 70). He also believes that educators are much more comfortable using the term *talents*, that *intelligence* is generally reserved to describe linguistic or logical "smartness," and that some human abilities should not arbitrarily qualify as *intelligence* over others (e.g., language as an intelligence vs. dance as a talent; Gardner, 1993), leading to a wide variety of characteristics of giftedness that may be represented by this conception of intelligence.

The Federal Definition

The U.S. government also subscribed to a multifaceted approach to giftedness as early as 1972 when Sidney Marland, the commissioner of education, submitted a report that was later passed as Public Law (P.L.) 91-230, Section 806. The Marland, or U.S. Department of Education, definition has dominated most states' definitions of giftedness and talent (Passow & Rudnitski, 1993; Stephens & Karnes, 2000), and it defined giftedness in specific domains:

> Gifted and talented children are those identified by professionally qualified persons who by virtue of outstanding abilities are capable of high performance. These are children who require differentiated educational programs and services beyond those normally provided by the regular school program in order to realize their contribution to self and society.
>
> Children capable of high performance include those with demonstrated achievement and/or potential in any of the following areas:
>
> 1. General intellectual ability
> 2. Specific academic aptitude
> 3. Creative or productive thinking
> 4. Leadership ability
> 5. Visual and performing arts
> 6. Psychomotor ability (Marland, 1972, pp. 13–14)

Marland's report was the basis for the development of a federal definition that evolved through multiple iterations. The current version of the federal definition of gifted and talented, part of the reauthorization of the Jacob K. Javits Gifted and Talented Students Education Act of 1988 (U.S. Congress, 1988), expands the domain specific definition of the previous report:

> The term "gifted and talented students" means children and youth who give evidence of high performance capability in areas such as intellectual, creative, artistic, or leadership capacity, or in specific academic fields, and who require services or activities not ordinarily provided by the school in order to fully develop such capabilities. (P.L. 103-382, Title XIV, p. 388)

While the two definitions are similar, noticeable changes exist in the most recent federal definition. Psychomotor ability was removed as one domain of ability, as some districts used funds to promote athletic talent, which is often well financed outside of gifted and talented programs. Another noticeable change from the original report to the current definition was the exclusion of the phrase "in order to realize their contribution to self and society" (Davis & Rimm, 1998, p. 18), leading to questions about the purposes for identifying talent. Further, questions were raised about whether this was a cohesive definition of giftedness when, as Renzulli (1978, 1986) points out, it is nonparallel, as specific academic aptitude and visual and performing arts are fields of *accomplished performance,* whereas the other three areas of the definition (i.e., general intellectual ability, creative or productive thinking, and leadership ability) are cognitive processes that may or may not lead to eminence or superior achievement in a field.

Does an overlap exist in the traits or characteristics exhibited by eminent individuals as adults and those that can be used to identify gifted children and adolescents? If so, would any of these characteristics fall into the categories of the federal definition of giftedness? Some studies of eminent individuals suggest that there are common, identified traits that are shared. These include the following:

- Resilience
- Perseverance to overcome seemingly insurmountable obstacles
- Superior capacity for communication
- A sense of destiny about work
- The ability to focus for long periods of time (Reis, 1995, 1998, 2005; Renzulli, 1978, 1986; Sternberg & Lubart, 1993; VanTassel-Baska, 1989; Walberg & Paik, 2005).

These shared traits are somewhat similar to characteristics that distinguish talented adolescents from their average counterparts, such as the following:

- Strong interest and emotional commitment to a particular field
- Persistence
- Perseverance despite difficulties
- Need to display and receive recognition for work
- Desire to reach high levels of attainment in particular domains
- Belief in self
- Willingness to invest considerable amounts of time in a field of endeavor and interest (Bloom, 1985; Csikszentmihalyi, Rathunde, & Whalen, 1993; Hébert & Reis, 1999; Reis & Díaz, 1999; Walberg & Paik, 2005).

Similar cognitive traits are also suggested in research about high levels of intellectual giftedness. These include the following:

- Rapid learning in some areas (as well as some asynchronous development in other areas)
- Ability to grasp complex and abstract concepts
- Advanced verbal ability
- Well-developed thinking skills (Clark, 1988, 2002; Feldhusen, 1986; Renzulli, 1978, 1996).

With multiple perspectives on giftedness and individual variability, it is impossible to delineate between those children and young adults who have the potential for high levels of accomplishment and those who do not, perhaps because of the absence of motivation or ability to achieve at high levels. Some traits are commonly acknowledged among gifted students that may differentiate them from their average achieving age peers, including cognitive abilities, personality traits, past experiences, and affective characteristics (Clark, 2002; Renzulli, 1978, 1996; Treffinger, Young, Selby, & Shepardson, 2002). It must be noted that the use of these traits is not suggested to identify or classify students as gifted, particularly when the opportunities have not been available that would enable some of these traits and behaviors to emerge (Renzulli & Reis, 1985, 1997). Further, no one individual has all of these characteristics or displays them all of the time. Sometimes the characteristics involve the integration of opposites or the ability to accommodate conflicting traits in their self-concept (e.g., selfish/unselfish, receptive to new ideas/sarcastic; Renzulli, 1986, 2005; Sternberg, 1997; Treffinger et al., 2002).

Finally, these characteristics vary among individuals; across gender, cultures, and socioeconomic status; and across disciplines and time (Bloom, 1985; Frasier & Passow, 1994; Reis, 2005; Treffinger et al., 2002). Therefore, caution must be taken to avoid use of a checklist of characteristics based on one group of gifted individuals to try to identify another group or to use characteristics for one period of time as an indication of a child's abilities forever. Any list of characteristics in a group of mainly White gifted students, for example, should not be used to identify giftedness in a group of Hispanic high-potential students, and an understanding must exist that even though a child does not demonstrate gifted abilities at one point in time, he or she may still exhibit characteristics of giftedness at another point.

As previously mentioned, the current federal definition (U.S. Congress, 1988) has been used as the basis for many state definitions of gifted students, and it is this definition that is used to guide this chapter's discussion of specific characteristics and traits. The five areas of focus in the federal definition are intellectual ability, specific academic aptitude, creative or productive thinking, leadership ability, and the visual and performing arts. This parsimonious view of giftedness is useful when considering the ways in which talent manifestation can vary from one domain to another, but it must be viewed with caution. Bloom (1985), in his research on gifted individuals in multiple talent domains, found that specific qualities necessary for talent development in one domain generally are not the same qualities necessary for talent development in another domain. For example, the qualities necessary for talent manifestation in mathematics and neurology may be quite different from each other and may be completely unlike those qualities necessary for leadership and music.

In an exploration of characteristics in each of the areas defined in the current federal definition, differences also emerge between domains. Despite these differences, some traits and characteristics also overlap, making it impossible to characterize giftedness quickly or narrowly. While a parsimonious perspective would be easier, it is not supported by current research, explaining why a consensus in the field of gifted education that *only one* absolute attribute of giftedness exists is impossible (Frasier & Passow, 1994; Renzulli, 1978). Positive and negative characteristics of giftedness across domains also recur in research (Table 5–1A), but these characteristics also vary in gifted students from multicultural and diverse backgrounds. Frasier and Passow (1994) identified the traits, aptitudes, and behaviors consistently identified by researchers as common to all gifted students (Table 5–1B), noting that these basic elements of giftedness are similar across cultures (though each is not displayed by every student). Use of these traits, aptitudes, and behaviors should be monitored as well, for each of these common characteristics may be manifested in various ways in different students, and educators should be especially careful in attempting to identify these characteristics in students from diverse backgrounds (i.e., disadvantaged, ethnically or racially diverse, and so on), as specific behavioral manifestations of the characteristics may vary with context in much the same way that cultural values may influence manifestations in behavior associated with certain characteristic traits (Frasier & Passow, 1994). With these cautions in mind, the following sections describe some of the characteristics of giftedness and advanced potential that may be associated with the federal definition.

Outstanding Intellectual Ability

By definition, outstanding intellectual ability is regarded as a high level of intelligence or having the ability to reason or understand. Outstanding intellectual ability is exhibited when individuals' mental abilities exceed their same-aged peers and their own physical development (Davis & Rimm, 2004). This *asynchronous* develop-ment may be accompanied by heightened sensitivity that some researchers and scholars in the field believe can create internal experiences for the gifted individual that can be qualitatively different from the norm (Silverman, 1994). Intellectual ability is measured by IQ tests that assess one's ability to manipulate abstract symbols and ideas, early language development, (including advanced reading comprehension), ability to think logically, and capacity to retrieve and use previous knowledge (Clark, 2002; Frasier & Passow, 1994; Reis, 2005; Renzulli, 1978; Renzulli, et al., 1976, 2002; Sternberg, 1986; VanTassel-Baska, 1989). Some researchers argue that the variety of attributes and traits that characterize individuals with advanced intellectual ability have less to do with what is measured on an IQ test and more to do with affective personality characteristics, such as originality and creative productivity (Renzulli, 1978), humor (Frasier & Passow, 1994), reasoning, independence, motivation (Renzulli, 1978), insightfulness (Simonton, 2003) and emotional intensity (Reis, 2005).

When and how are the traits of intellectual ability manifested, and do children with this advanced aptitude translate this into adult productivity? One might expect children with high levels of advanced ability to gain eminence in adulthood, but a conflict exists in this reasoning. As Simonton (2003) noted, more children in Terman's research should have become eminent adults. The Terman participants became doctors, scientists, professors, accountants, as well as stay-at-home parents, but few became eminent individuals, such as well-known artists or Nobel Prize winners. Some were even "misfits and failures" (Simonton, 2003, p. 358). Cox (1926), a colleague of Terman's, conducted a retrospective study of eminent adults and found that many of the individuals in her study would not have met the criteria for inclusion in Terman's study. Cox found that personality characteristics such as motivation and determination could compensate for very high IQ scores and that to attain eminence, an individual must have personality characteristics in addition to advanced intellectual ability (Simonton, 2003). While a certain level of intellectual ability seems to be necessary for eminence in adulthood, some researchers have found that IQ levels beyond a certain threshold do not result in proportional increases in distinction (Barron & Harrington, 1981; Renzulli, 1986, 2005; Simonton, 2003). It is clear that IQ tests may measure advanced intellectual ability as it relates to precocious development of language, abstract reasoning,

TABLE 5–1A Recurrent Characteristics of Students Who Are Gifted

Positive Characteristics	Negative Characteristics
Intellectual/Academic	
Unusual alertness in infancy and later	Uneven mental development
Early and rapid learning	Interpersonal difficulties, due often to intellectual differences
Rapid language development as a child	Underachievement, especially in uninteresting areas
Superior language ability—verbally fluent, large vocabulary, complex grammar	
Enjoyment of learning	
Academic superiority, large knowledge base, sought out as a resource	
Superior analytic ability	
Keen observation	
Efficient, high-capacity memory	
Superior reasoning, problem solving	
Thinking that is abstract, complex, logical, insightful	
Insightful, sees "big picture," recognizes patterns, connects topics	
Manipulates symbol systems	
Uses high-level thinking skills, efficient strategies	
Extrapolates knowledge to new situations, goes beyond what is sought	
High concentration, long attention span	
Greater metacognition (understanding own thinking)	
Advanced interests	
Needs for logic and accuracy	
Wide interests, interested in new topics	
High curiosity, explores how and why	
Multiple capabilities (multipotentiality)	
Affective and Emotional	
High career ambitions	Nonconformity, sometimes in disturbing directions
Expanded awareness, greater self-awareness	Perfectionism, which can be extreme
Overexcitability	Excessive self-criticism
Emotional intensity and sensitivity	Self-doubt, poor self-image
High alertness and attention	Variable frustration and anger
High intellectual and physical activity level	Depression
High motivation, concentrates, perseveres, persists, task oriented	
Active—shares information, directs, leads, offers help, eager to be involved	
Strong empathy, moral thinking, sense of justice, honesty, intellectual honesty	
Aware of social issues	
Reflectiveness	
Good self-concept—usually	
Strong internal control	
Independent, self-directed, works alone	
Inquisitive, asks questions	
Excellent sense of humor	
Creative	
Imaginative, creative, solves problems	
Preference for novelty	

Source: From *Education of the Gifted and Talented*, 5th Ed. (p. 33), by G. A. Davis and S. B. Rimm, 2004, Boston: Allyn and Bacon. Copyright © 2004 by Pearson Education. Reprinted by permission of the publisher.

and logical thinking, but it also remains clear that intellectual ability is only one attribute of giftedness.

What, then, are the characteristics of outstanding intellectual abilities in children? Which characteristics should teachers consider when nominating diverse children for gifted and talented programs? A review of selected literature (Davis & Rimm, 2004; Feldhusen, 1986; Renzulli et al., 2002; Rogers, 1991; Sternberg & Davidson, 1985, 2005; Tannenbaum, 1986) suggests the list of characteristics in Table 5–2 that may help guide

TABLE 5–1B Common Attributes of Giftedness

• Motivation	• Advanced interests
• Communication skills	• Problem-solving ability
• Well-developed memory	• Inquiry
• Insight	• Reasoning
• Imagination/creativity	• Sense of humor
• Advanced ability to deal with symbol systems	

Source: From *Toward a New Paradigm for Identifying Talent Potential* (pp. 49–51), by M. M. Frasier and A. H. Passow, 1994, Storrs, CT: National Research Center on the Gifted and Talented, University of Connecticut. Copyright © 1994 by NRC/GT. Reprinted with permission.

TABLE 5–2 General Characteristics of Intellectual Abilities

• Strong communication skills (including advanced and extensive vocabulary)
• Good problem-solving, reasoning, and questioning skills
• Well-developed and extensive memory
• Insight about connections
• Rapid capacity to learn
• Ability to think using abstract ideas
• Possesses or has the potential to gain broad background knowledge
• Demonstrates curiosity and the desire to learn
• Ability to focus for long periods of time in areas of interest

Source: Adapted from Davis and Rimm (2004), Feldhusen (1986), Renzulli et al. (2002), Rogers (1991), Sternberg and Davidson (1985, 2005), and Tannenbaum (1986).

teacher judgment in the identification of general intellectual abilities.

Specific Academic Aptitude

How does specific academic aptitude, also a category of the federal definition, differ from general intellectual ability? First, academic aptitude is generally tied to performance in academic or educational settings and is most often exhibited through superior performance in reading, mathematics, science, history, and the humanities. Specific academic aptitude is usually measured by achievement tests that test content knowledge as well as rapid and accurate retrieval of information, verbal and numerical reasoning, and reading fluency. Some of these tests are standardized nationally, while others may reflect specific standards of the state government, districts, and national organizations (such as the National Council of Teachers of Mathematics). Renzulli (1986) suggests that academic aptitude exists in varying degrees but is most often characterized by a student's ability to learn curricular material at advanced rates and levels of understanding. It is apparent from current research that both general and specific content area characteristics exist for gifted and talented and high-potential youth (Renzulli, 1972, 1986; Tannenbaum, 1986). General characteristics include the following:

- Intense interests in an area
- Rapidity of learning in an area of interest when compared with chronological peers
- Hobbies or pastimes in the area
- Motivation or task commitment in an area
- Curiosity and questioning skills in the area of interest

Comprehensive research on the *Scales for Rating the Behavioral Characteristics of Superior Students* (*SRBCSS*) have been conducted by Renzulli and his colleagues (1976, 2002), and recent additions include three scales with high validity and reliability that measure academic aptitude in mathematics, reading, and science. Originally developed in 1976 and subsequently translated into several languages, the first three scales in the series on learning, motivation, and creativity have been widely used to guide identification of high-potential students based on the theory related to the three-ring conception of giftedness (Renzulli, 1978). Comprehensive studies have examined the *SRBCSS,* and revisions have occurred over time (Renzulli et al., 2002). Reviews (Argulewicz, 1985; Rust, 1985) of the *SRBCSS* suggest that the 10 factors used in this scale correlate favorably with other

TABLE 5–3 Characteristics of Academic Aptitude in Mathematics, Reading, and Science

Mathematic Characteristics
• Is eager to solve challenging math problems.
• Organizes data and information to discover mathematical patterns.
• Enjoys challenging math puzzles, games, and logic problems.
• Understands new math concepts and processes more easily than other students.
• Has creative (unusual and divergent) ways of solving math problems.
• Displays a strong number sense (e.g., makes sense of large and small numbers, estimates easily and appropriately).
• Frequently solves math problems abstractly, without the need for manipulatives or concrete materials.
• Has an interest in analyzing the mathematical structure of a problem.
• When solving a math problem, can switch strategies easily, if appropriate or necessary.
• Regularly uses a variety of representations to explain math concepts (written explanations, pictorial, graphic, equations, etc.).
Reading Characteristics
• Eagerly engages in reading related activities.
• Applies previously learned literary concepts to new reading experiences.
• Focuses on reading for an extended period of time.
• Demonstrates tenacity when posed with challenging reading.
• Shows interest in reading other types of interest-based reading materials.
Science Characteristics
• Demonstrates curiosity about scientific processes.
• Demonstrates creative thinking about scientific debates or issues.
• Demonstrates enthusiasm in discussion of scientific topics.
• Is curious about why things are as they are.
• Reads about science-related topics in his/her free time.
• Expresses interest in science project or research.
• Clearly articulates data interpretation.

Source: From *Scales for Rating the Behavioral Characteristics of Superior Students* (online at *www.creativelearningpress.com*) by J. S. Renzulli, L. H. Smith, A. J. White, C. M. Callahan, R. K. Hartman, and K. L. Westberg, M. K. Gavin, S. M. Reis, D. Siegle, and R. E. Sytsma, 2002, Mansfield, CT: Creative Learning Press. Copyright © 2002 by Creative Learning Press. Reprinted with permission.

instruments measuring similar constructs, and the instrument has strong reliability and validity. The most recent scales describe the characteristics and behaviors of superior students in specific academic areas, including math, reading, technology, and science, and include research-based characteristics based on extent literature. Reading characteristics include items examining accelerated reading, enjoyment of reading, advanced reading processing, and advanced language (Renzulli et al., 2002). As specified in Table 5–3, mathematics characteristics include students' interests and approaches to solving mathematical problems and their ease in understanding mathematical concepts (Renzulli et al., 2002), while science items focus on students' interests and approaches to solving problems in science and their ease in understanding scientific concepts (Renzulli et al., 2002).

What is the rationale for the distinction between outstanding intellectual abilities, academic aptitude, and creativity in the federal definition? Tannenbaum (1986) differentiated between academically talented and intellectually gifted individuals by suggesting that academically talented individuals are organized and hard working, traits that enable high potential to translate into high achievement. He also believes that the performance of these individuals can lack innovation or creativity, leading perhaps to the reason that creativity exists as a separate component of the federal definition. Gottfried and Gottfried's (2004) conceptualization of giftedness supports Tannenbaum's delineation between academic and intellectual giftedness. Gottfried, et al. (2005) extend the ideas of *academic intrinsic motivation* or *gifted motivation,* finding that students with exceptionally high academic motivation have superior academic achievement and eventually progress further in their education during postsecondary years, while others with lower motivation have lower academic achievement. Gottfried et al. (2005) defined academic intrinsic motivation as "the enjoyment of school learning characterized by an orientation toward mastery, curiosity, persistence, task-endogeny, and the learning of challenging, difficult, and novel tasks" (p. 173). They concluded that while gifted motivation and general intellectual ability were not mutually exclusive, they were separate constructs and that "academic intrinsic motivation was significant above and beyond IQ in predicting cumulative high school GPA" (p. 184). Gottfried et al. also identified several attributes that characterized the motivationally gifted, such as better self-concepts, superior academic achievement, and the ability to work harder and be able to learn relatively more when compared with their cohort group. These students are well organized and hardworking, but their products and performance seem to lack innovation. It would appear, then, that motivation could be considered an intrinsic part of the characteristics of giftedness by some researchers, a theory posited by Renzulli (1978) almost 30 years ago. It also seems that creativity, according to some researchers, should be an essential characteristic of giftedness (Renzulli, 1978; Tannenbaum, 1986).

Creativity and Creative Productivity

Is there a relationship between outstanding academic ability and creativity? Children with high potential for creativity often demonstrate fluency, flexibility, originality, and elaboration as well as the ability to think in creative or divergent ways (Guilford, 1950; Torrance, 1976). Creativity is an area of interest for many scholars, and multiple lists of characteristics and attributes of the highly creative have been offered. Treffinger et al. (2002) conducted a comprehensive appraisal of literature on creativity in which they reviewed 120 definitions of creativity discussed in more than 100 books and journal articles. There is no universally accepted definition of creativity (Treffinger et al., 2002). Many researchers and theorists use the term *creativity,* but each may have a different interpretation of the concept, and characteristics of creativity vary within and among people and across disciplines. These researchers clustered the characteristics that are "commonly accepted by the education research community" (Treffinger et al., 2002, p. 6), into four broad categories: generating ideas, digging deeper into ideas, openness and courage to explore ideas, and listening to one's "inner voice." According to these researchers, these characteristics are represented in three general areas of personal characteristics that differentiate highly creative individuals from their less creative peers:

- *Cognitive characteristics,* which refer to how people think
- *Personality traits,* which include individual values, temperament, and motivations
- *biographical events,* or experiences that lead to creative achievement (Treffinger et al. 2002a).

As noted, academic giftedness and creative giftedness may be distinct concepts, as Sternberg and Lubart's (1993) assertion that the "academically successful children of today are not necessarily the creatively gifted adults of tomorrow" (p. 12). Individuals with high intelligence may or may not have high creative ability as well (Davis & Rimm, 1998; Renzulli & Reis, 1997). There is evidence, however, to suggest that a relationship exists between these two constructs, as the "threshold concept" discussed by MacKinnon in 1978 includes a base level of intelligence, an IQ of about 120, as essential for creative productivity. Beyond that threshold, no relationship between creativity and intelligence appears to be measured by IQ tests (Davis & Rimm, 1998; Sternberg & Lubart, 1993). Getzels and Jackson's (1960, 1961, 1962) work supports the idea that there is no relationship between IQ and creativity after a certain threshold (IQ = 120) is passed. In a study of adolescents in one private secondary school, Getzels and Jackson found multiple discrepancies between a group of high-IQ-students and a group of highly creative students. For example, when rated by teachers in the school, the high-IQ-students were found to be a more desired group of students than average students, but the highly creative students were not. Additionally, a much higher percentage of students in the creative group had "unconventional" career aspirations than the high-IQ-group, and the creative students valued a sense of humor more often than high-IQ-students and produced more playfulness, humor, and unexpected conclusions when writing stories than did their high-IQ-counterparts (Getzels & Jackson, 1960, 1961, 1962).

What are the traits and characteristics that define an individual with high creative ability or potential? Gardner's (1983, 1993) conception of a creative individual is one who *"regularly* solves problems or fashions products in a *domain,* and whose work is considered both novel and acceptable by knowledgeable members of a field" (p. xvii). Creativity should not be regarded as a construct in the mind or personality of an individual; rather, it is something that emerges from the interactions of intelligence (personal profile of competences), domain (disciplines or crafts within a culture), and field (people and institutions that judge quality within a domain) (Gardner, 1983, 1993).

Sternberg and Lubart (1993) view creativity as a separate type of giftedness rather than as one dimension of intelligence, proposing that a person's *resources* for creativity enable the process of creative production to occur. They believe that six separate resources combine to interactively yield creativity and find creative giftedness a rare occurrence because so many components must interact at once.

Sternberg and Lubart's (1993) six resources succinctly describe many of the traits of creative individuals, including their use of *intellectual processes* for problem definition, using insight (selective encoding, selective comparison, and selective combination) to solve problems, and using divergent thought as a problem-solving strategy. They also use their *knowledge of the domain* to identify areas where new and novel work is needed. Creatively gifted people understand their *intellectual* (cognitive) *styles* and prefer a legislative style (creating, formulating, and planning) and a global mode of processing information (thinking abstractly, generalizing, and extrapolating). They also appear to have key *personality attributes,* such as tolerance for ambiguity, moderate risk taking, willingness to surmount obstacles and persevere, willingness to grow, and belief in self and ideas. They have a *task-focused orientation* (drive or goal that leads a person to work on a task) as opposed to a goal-focused orientation (extrinsic motivators, rewards, or recognition that lead people to see a task as a means to an end). Last, they exist in an *environmental context* that interacts with the development of creativity as well. Implications for educators include providing surroundings that promote creativity, a reward system for creative ideas, and an evaluation of creative products by appropriate audiences.

Renzulli and Reis (1997) identify the characteristics of creativity in children as fluency, flexibility and originality of thought, being open to new experiences and ideas, curiosity, willingness to take risks, and sensitivity to aesthetic characteristics. What, then, are the "resources" and environments for creativity that children might need in school that will enable their creative characteristics to be nurtured and developed? According to Sternberg and Lubart's (1993) theory, it would involve creating an environment that nurtures problem definition, using insight to solve problems, and using divergent thought as a problem-solving strategy. Classrooms or schools would enable students to gain knowledge of the domain to identify areas where new and novel work is needed. It would enable creatively gifted children to create, formulate, and plan ideas and projects while also processing information through abstract thinking and generalizing. Teachers and parents would help to nurture personality attributes such as tolerance of ambiguity, moderate risk taking, willingness to surmount obstacles and persevere, willingness to grow, and belief in self and ideas. A task-focused orientation that would enable children to work on creative tasks would also be encouraged, as would an environment in which creativity is rewarded and creative ideas are celebrated. The work of Renzulli and Reis (1985, 1997) focuses on gifted education and enrichment programs that encourage the development of characteristics that promote the identification of interests, learning and product styles, and enrichment opportunities. These opportunities are also considered to be positive forces in the development of creative potential in children.

The generally positive attributes of creativity summarized briefly in this chapter do not represent a comprehensive list of traits. Davis (1999, 2003) identified a broad array of positive characteristics, including the following:

- Awareness of one's own creativeness
- Originality
- Independence
- Willingness to take risks
- Energy
- Curiosity
- Keen sense of humor
- Attraction to complexity and novelty
- Artistic tendencies
- Open-mindedness
- Need for privacy and alone time
- Perceptiveness

Davis (1999, 2003) also identified negative traits that characterize the creatively gifted individual and may include actions that appear to be the following:

- Impulsive
- Egotistical
- Argumentative
- Rebellious
- Uncooperative
- Stubborn
- Childish
- Absentminded
- Neurotic
- Temperamental
- Indifferent to conventions or courtesies
- Capricious
- Careless
- Disorganized
- Demanding

It is important to remember, however, that any overgeneralization of these traits would be imprudent and that to suggest that a creatively gifted individual will exhibit all of these traits all of the time or even some of these traits all of the time is erroneous.

Characteristics of Talented Leaders

Leadership has generally been characterized by specific personal qualities and traits, particularly one's ability to influence others. The qualities that are valuable in one leadership situation may vary from those in another leadership role, depending on the circumstances. For example, emergency situations necessitate the immediate emergence of a leader who can rapidly restructure the group, appropriately assign tasks to effectively utilize the skills of the members of the group, make decisions, take action, and act outside of normal parameters (Torrance, 1988). One who manages the daily operations of a research enterprise, however, may be more conducive to a facilitative leadership role—supporting, encouraging, and directing members of a group. Their colleagues, however, may not consider individuals who maintain facilitative leadership roles to be gifted leaders. How, then, do we identify the characteristics for leadership? One way is to focus on the qualities of emergent leaders, or those individuals who are nominated by their peers or superiors on the basis of demonstrated ability and who emerge as leaders from a leaderless group or participate in leadership activities (Judge, Colbert, & Ilies, 2004).

What are the important qualities necessary for one to be considered a leader? In a meta-analysis examining the relationship between intelligence and leadership, Judge, et al. (2004) suggested that certain characteristics or traits combine multiplicatively in their effects on leadership:

> It is possible that leaders must possess the intelligence to make effective decisions, the dominance to convince others, the achievement motivation to persist, and multiple other traits if they are to emerge as a leader or be seen as an effective leader. (pp. 548–549)

According to Guastello (2002), the emergent leader becomes a role model, inspires or motivates the group to forge ahead when ideas are stalled, provides intellectual stimulation, and sees matches between group member traits and the tasks to be accomplished and thereby delegates work accordingly. Guastello (1995) also found that emerging leaders were able to keep a group focused, suggest compromises that were acceptable to members in a group, and were respected by group members and that the group frequently agreed with them (Jolly & Kettler, 2004). These traits are similar to those identified in the *SRBCSS* (Renzulli et al., 2002). The leadership qualities identified in these scales include the following:

- Responsible behavior
- Follow-through on projects
- Respect and willing compliance of others
- Self-confidence
- Ability to organize
- Ability to cooperate
- Tendency to direct activities when involved with others

The characteristics of young leaders suggest that these individuals have a predisposition to facilitate and direct actions necessary to correct problems (Davis & Rimm, 2004). If young leaders with these qualities can have a positive influence on our communities, an altruistic component must be embedded within their potential for leadership. Tannenbaum (2000) defined social leadership as the ability to enable a group to reach its goal and, in the process, improve human relationships. Renzulli (2002) also discussed the need for high-potential students to develop leadership capabilities coupled with a concern for less fortunate individuals. He used the term "social capital" to identify a set of intangible assets that address the collective needs and problems of other individuals and communities at large. The co-cognitive characteristics identified by Renzulli (2002, 2003) as the backdrop of his three-ring conception of giftedness include the following:

- *Optimism*—cognitive, emotional, and motivational components that reflect the belief that the future holds good outcomes
- *Courage*—the ability to face difficulty or danger while overcoming physical, psychological, or moral fears
- *Romance with a topic or discipline*—passion about a topic or discipline
- *Sensitivity to human concerns*—sensitively communicating understanding through action
- *Altruism and empathy*—the unselfish concern for others and the capacity to identify with others' feelings
- *Physical/mental energy*—individual is willing and able to invest effort and energy in the achievement of a goal
- *Vision/sense of destiny*—interrelated concepts, such as internal locus of control, motivation, volition, and self-efficacy that lead to making a difference in the world

Renzulli believes that when leaders have a vision or sense of destiny about future activities, events, and involvements, vision serves to stimulate planning and direct behavior. Renzulli's theory is supported by research on personality and leadership by Judge, Bono, Ilies, and Gerhardt (2002), who found that, among other qualities, conscientiousness had a statistically significant relationship to leadership. Because gifted leaders have the potential to positively influence society, it helps educators to know that some research suggests that leadership skills can be developed (Smith, Smith, & Barnette, 1991).

Karnes and colleagues (Karnes & Bean, 1995; Karnes & Chauvin, 1986, 2000; Karnes & D'Ilio, 1989) define leadership in gifted students as demonstrating a desire to be challenged, to solve problems creatively, to reason critically, to see new relationships, to be flexible in thought and action, to tolerate ambiguity, and to motivate others. They suggest several strategies for developing leadership characteristics in young people, including leadership education activities that enable individuals to problem solve, plan, and critically develop leadership training in science or social studies or other content area projects (Karnes & Bean, 1990, 1996). Children can also benefit from reading or hearing biographies about past leaders and discussing what made these leaders successful (VanTassel-Baska, 1994).

Characteristics of Talents in the Visual and Performing Arts

Both general and specific characteristics appear to be associated with artistic, musical, and dramatic talent (Clark & Zimmerman, 1984; Renzulli et al., 1976, 2002). Within the various characteristics for each artistic domain described in the *SRBCSS* (Renzulli et al., 1976), several that seem to be consistent across the visual, musical, and performing arts are elaboration; creating varied, unique, and unconventional products; setting high standards of quality; being self-critical; and having a heightened sensitivity to the environment.

Winner and Martino (2003), in a study of artistically gifted children, suggest that these students actually see the world in a qualitatively different way. For example, they encode visual information in terms of what they see, in forms and shapes, rather than what they know about an object. Artistically gifted students have superior memory capacity for visual attributes, and the process of drawing enables them to see when something they are drawing does not look right. The result is that artistically gifted children will demonstrate the ability to draw recognizable shapes a full year or more before this skill emerges in their same-aged peers. In addition to skills emerging in advance of expectation, very young children who are gifted in drawing use lines to represent the edges of objects, whereas typical children of the same age use lines to represent things.

Winner and Martino (2003) also contend that at an age when a child would be creating schematic, two-dimensional objects, artistically gifted children create complex images and begin to represent the third dimension and elaborate details in their visual products. It seems clear that the advanced abilities of the artistically talented child are asynchronous with their chronological age and physical development, but does this influence affective characteristics? Sternberg and Davidson (1985) suggest that it does, for in their conception of creative giftedness, artists have been found to be concerned with aesthetic values. Artists, they believe, also exhibit a lower concern for economic values when compared to their same-age peers, and they exhibit tendencies toward introspection, imaginativeness, radical thought and action, and self-sufficiency that are not typical of individuals of their chronological age. Gifted artists also tend to be highly sensitive to form, line, color, and texture in a way that is advanced for their age (Bloom, 1985), supporting Renzulli et al.'s (2002) research on arts characteristics that suggests that the artistically gifted student "is particularly sensitive to the environment; is a keen observer [and] sees . . . what may be overlooked by others" (p. 34).

Creativity continues to be discussed as a goal for both average and gifted students in art, but research indicates that tests of creativity and abilities in the arts are only minimally related (Clark & Zimmerman, 1984; Hurwitz, 1983); thus, caution must be used in relying on creativity assessment in the identification of artistically talented students. Caution, too, should be used in differentiating between general artistic characteristics and specific characteristics within each art form (Clark & Zimmerman, 1984; Renzulli et al., 1976, 2002). General characteristics may include interest in and possession of general artistic talents, love and passion for art, interest in improving artistic skills, ability to focus on the selected art form, intrinsic standards, and sensitivity to aesthetics (Clark & Zimmerman, 1984; Renzulli et al., 1976, 2002; Winner & Martino, 2003). The best-researched scale for artistic talent is the *SRBCSS* (Renzulli et al., 1976), and the use of the individual scales is one way to enable teachers to become aware of the manifestations of artistic talent in young people (Table 5–4).

MANIFESTATION OF CHARACTERISTICS ACROSS POPULATIONS AND CULTURES

Several populations of gifted students are underidentified and underserved in gifted programs. Underserved populations include students who are not provided with appropriate time and level of opportunities for their talents to be nurtured, stimulated, or guided so that the individual may reach his or her full potential (Whitmore, 1986). Linguistically, culturally, and economically diverse individuals, gifted underachievers, and gifted students with disabilities are representative of populations that are underserved and often overlooked for provisions afforded by gifted programs. This underrepresentation in programs may be due to the absence of appropriate assessment procedures (Frasier, García, & Passow, 1995; Frasier & Passow, 1994). Discrepancies between teachers' perceptions of diverse students' abilities and their actual ability or between their performance and their ability may also contribute to underrepresentation. Frasier and Passow (1994) found that the way a Navajo child from an isolated reservation or an African American child from an urban setting exhibits high degrees of motivation will differ from the way a middle-class, White child from the suburbs will show evidence of this characteristic. Educators

TABLE 5–4 Artistic, Musical, and Dramatics Characteristics

Artistic Characteristics
• Likes to participate in art activities; is eager to visually express ideas.
• Incorporates a large number of elements into art work; varies the subject and content of art work.
• Arrives at unique, unconventional solutions to artistic problems as opposed to traditional, conventional ones.
• Concentrates for long periods of time on art projects.
• Willingly tries out different media; experiments with a variety of materials and techniques.
• Tends to select art media for free activity or classroom projects.
• Is particularly sensitive to the environment; is a keen observer—sees the unusual, what may be overlooked by others.
• Produces balance and order in art work.
• Is critical of his or her own work; sets high standards of quality; often reworks creation in order to refine it.
• Shows an interest in other students' work—spends time studying and discussing their work.
• Elaborates on ideas from other people—uses them as a "jumping-off point" as opposed to copying them.
Musical Characteristics
• Shows a sustained interest in music—seeks out opportunities to hear and create music.
• Perceives fine differences in musical tone (pitch, loudness, timbre, duration).
• Easily remembers melodies and can produce them accurately.
• Eagerly participates in musical activities.
• Plays a musical instrument (or indicates a strong desire to).
• Is sensitive to the rhythm of music; responds to changes in the tempo of music through body movements.
• Is aware of and can identify a variety of sounds heard at a given moment—is sensitive to "background" noises, to chords that accompany a melody, to the different sounds of singers or instrumentalists in a performance.
Dramatics Characteristics
• Volunteers to participate in classroom plays or skits.
• Easily tells a story or gives an account of some experience.
• Effectively uses gestures and facial expressions to communicate feelings.
• Is adept at role-playing, improvising, acting out situations "on the spot."
• Can readily identify himself or herself with the moods and motivations of characters.
• Handles body with ease and poise for his or her particular age.
• Creates original plays or makes up plays from stories.
• Commands and holds the attention of a group when speaking.
• Is able to evoke emotional responses from listeners—can get people to laugh, frown, feel tense, etc.
• Can imitate others—is able to mimic the way people speak, walk, gesture.

Source: From *Scales for Rating the Behavioral Characteristics of Superior Students* (pp. 34–36), by J. S. Renzulli, L. H. Smith, A. J. White, C. M.Callahan, R. K. Hartman, K. L. Westberg, M. K. Gavin, S. M. Reis, D. Siegle, and R. E. Sytsma, 2002, Mansfield, CT: Creative Learning Press. Copyright © 2002 by Creative Learning Press. Reprinted with permission.

TABLE 5–5 Characteristics of Giftedness and Cultural Values of Minorities and Possible Behavioral Manifestations of Giftedness Resulting from Their Interaction

Absolute Aspects of Giftedness	Characteristic Cultural Values
Hispanics	
Leadership	Collaborative, rather than competitive dynamic
Emotional depth and intensity	"Abrazo," a physical or spiritual index of personal support
Native American Indians	
Unusual sensitivity to expectations and feelings of others	Collective self—the tribe
Creativity in endeavors	Traditions, heritage, beliefs
Asian Americans	
High expectations of self	Confucianist ethic—people can be improved by proper effort and instruction
Perfectionism	Conformity, correctness, respect for and obedience to authority
Low Socioeconomic Status	
Persistent, goal-directed behavior	Survival in circumstances
Accelerated pace of thought processes	Physical punishment, blunt orders rather than discussion

Source: From *Critical Issues in Gifted Education: Defensible Programs for Cultural and Ethnic Minorities* (Vol. 2, pp. 4, 78, 152, 211), by C. J. Maker and S. W. Schiever, 1989, Austin, TX: PRO-ED. Copyright © 1989 by PRO-ED. Adapted with permission.

must understand that opportunities to display certain characteristics are dependent on the provisions of the environment and cultural perspectives. Maker and Schiever (1989) identify how cultural differences may influence how gifted behaviors are manifested within different cultural groups (Table 5–5). For example, the expression of creativity may be influenced by the traditions, heritage, or beliefs of an individual's cultural group.

Gifted students with disabilities represent another population that may be underrepresented in gifted programs. These students vary, depending on the type of disability and the way their disabilities interact with their gifts and talents (Reis, Neu, & McGuire, 1995). Students with both gifts and learning disabilities often have unrealistic expectations of themselves, and they may exhibit frustration with difficult tasks. This frustration can contribute to disruptive or withdrawn behavior or a lack of motivation. These students may experience learned helplessness or feelings of low self-esteem (Baum & Owen, 1988; Baum, Owen, & Dixon, 1991; Reis et al., 1995). Reis et al. (1995) compiled a list that describes the characteristics of gifted and learning-disabled individuals that may lead to their underrepresentation in gifted programs (Table 5–6). Often, the aptitude–achievement discrepancy is the emphasis when identifying or describing this group, and, unfortunately, this classification gives the impression that they are underachievers (Boodoo, Bradley, Frontera, Pitts, & Wright, 1989), causing them to be associated with another group that can be underidentified for gifted programs.

Gifted underachievers also demonstrate discrepancies between performance and ability, falling short of their potential and representing a major challenge for educators in meeting their needs. Sometimes these students underachieve because of unidentified disabilities, but it is just as likely that they are bored in school and are being forced to regularly engage in repetitive, understimulating, or unchallenging tasks (Reis & McCoach, 2000). The reasons for underachievement vary from boredom to poor self-regulation skills or poor self-esteem. Reis and McCoach (2000) identified a wide variety of characteristics associated with underachievement that are summarized in Table 5–7 Regardless of the personality traits and factors that contribute to underachievement, a student who is not performing at a level matching his or her ability presents a frustrating challenge for both teachers and parents (Reis & McCoach, 2000).

TABLE 5–6 Characteristics of Gifted Students with Learning Disabilities

Characteristics that Hamper Identification as Gifted
• Frustration with inability to master certain academic skills
• Learned helplessness
• General lack of motivation
• Disruptive classroom behavior
• Perfectionism
• Supersensitivity
• Failure to complete assignments
• Lack of organizational skills
• Demonstration of poor listening and concentration skills
• Deficiency in tasks emphasizing memory and perceptual abilities
• Low self-esteem
• Unrealistic self-expectations
• Absence of social skills with some peers
Characteristic Strengths
• Advanced vocabulary use
• Exceptional analytic abilities
• High levels of creativity
• Advanced problem-solving skills
• Ability to think of divergent ideas and solutions
• Specific aptitude (artistic, musical, or mechanical)
• Wide variety of interests
• Good memory
• Task commitment
• Spatial abilities
Social and Emotional Characteristics of Gifted/Learning-Disabled Students
• Exhibit feelings of inferiority
• Show an inability to persevere in the accomplishment of goals
• Demonstrate a general lack of self-confidence
• Exhibit confusion as they struggle to understand why they can know an answer but are not able to say it or write it correctly
• Have their abilities mask their disabilities
• Have their disabilities mask their giftedness
• Demonstrate a strong, personal need for excellence in performance and in outcomes that nears and often embodies unhealthy perfectionism
• Exhibit an intensity of emotions
• Have unrealistic expectations of self
• Also have a tendency to experience intense frustration with difficult tasks that often produces a general lack of motivation
• Experience feelings of learned helplessness
• Exhibit low self-esteem

Source: From *Talent in Two Places: Case Studies of High Ability Students with Learning Disabilities Who Have Achieved* (pp. 16–17), by S. M. Reis, T. W. Neu, and J. M. McGuire, 1995, Storrs, CT: National Research Center on the Gifted and Talented, University of Connecticut. Copyright © 1995 by NRC/GT. Adapted with permission.

TABLE 5–7 Characteristics of Gifted Underachievers

Personality Characteristics
• Low self-esteem, low self-concept, low self-efficacy
• Feelings of pessimism, distrust
• Anxious, impulsive, inattentive
• Aggressive, hostile
• Depressed
• Dependent
• Socially immature
Internal Mediators
• Fear of failure
• Fear of success
• Negative attitude toward school
• Antisocial, rebellious
• Self-critical or perfectionistic
Maladaptive Strategies
• Lack goal-directed behavior
• Poor coping skills
• Poor self-regulation strategies
• Use defense mechanisms
Positive Attributes
• Creative
• Intense outside interests
• Demonstrate honesty and integrity when rejecting inappropriate schoolwork

Source: From "The Underachievement of Gifted Students: What Do We Know and Where Do We Go?," by S. M. Reis and D. B. McCoach, 2000, *Gifted Child Quarterly,* 44, pp. 152–170. Copyright © 2000 by NAGC. Adapted with permission.

SUMMARY AND CONCLUSIONS

> Giftedness is being reconceptualized and redefined to encompass a broad range of cognitive and affective traits and qualities that are dynamically displayed as potential to be nurtured and developed. New constructs of giftedness reflect multifaceted, multicultural, multidimensional perspectives and are defined by traits, aptitudes, and behaviors to be nurtured. (Frasier & Passow, 1994, p. 63)

In the past, the general approach to the study of gifted persons could easily lead the casual reader to believe that giftedness is an absolute condition that is magically bestowed on a person in much the same way that nature endows us with blue eyes, red hair, or a dark complexion (Renzulli, 1980). This position is not supported by the current research cited in this chapter, for multiple lists of traits and characteristics exist, and some apply to students in the majority culture and others to students of diverse cultural backgrounds. Educators cannot identify gifted children in an absolute and unequivocal manner, and this belief has further led to the mistaken assumption that the right combination of traits will identify gifted children.

Most of the confusion and controversy surrounding characteristics of giftedness can be placed into proper perspective if a few key questions are examined. Do we use specific characteristics of one group of people to identify another group? Are the characteristics of giftedness reflected in high-ability Puerto Rican students in the Northeast the same characteristics of giftedness as those demonstrated by above-average Mexican students in Texas? Are some characteristics common to each group? If so, how are they exhibited? What happens to a child who consistently manifests gifted characteristics in the primary grades but who learns to underachieve in school because of a lack of intellectual stimulation or an unchallenging curriculum? What about a gifted child with a learning disability that masks his or her talents? Are characteristics of giftedness static (i.e., you have or you don't have them), or are they dynamic (i.e., they vary within persons and among learning/performance situations)?

These questions suggest that a fundamental change in the ways the characteristics and traits of giftedness should take place in the future. That is, characteristics of advanced learners must be identified within various population groups, and educators should attempt to identify the characteristics of talented students within educational contexts and populations. The use of characteristics and checklists are but one type of information that can be used to identify gifted students and should never be considered an absolute method. Rather, information from characteristics should be used to help teachers provide differentiated levels of service or a continuum of services (Renzulli & Reis, 1997) to help nurture students' characteristics and, ultimately, develop their gifts and talents. This shift might appear insignificant, but it has implications for the ways that schools should structure identification and programming endeavors. This change may also provide the flexibility in both identification and programming that will encourage the inclusion of more culturally and linguistically diverse students in gifted and talented programs.

Defining our populations (e.g., artistic talent, scientific talent, or outstanding intellectual ability) and then using characteristics to identify students and deciding which services are offered to students and what is qualitatively appropriate will help develop programs that are internally consistent. Educators must understand that children from different cultures will express gifts and talents in different ways, and we must develop identification tools and program services and practices that will take into account the diverse characteristics displayed by all students in our changing society.

QUESTIONS FOR THOUGHT AND DISCUSSION

1. Should a list of characteristics be included in identification processes? How might a list of characteristics influence an identification process?
2. How might one incorporate the characteristics of gifted individuals into a conception of giftedness? What might that conception entail?
3. What changes could be made to the federal definition to make it more inclusive? What changes would make it more exclusive? If you had to advocate for changes in the federal definition, what would you advocate for and why?
4. How do differences in gender, culture, achievement, or socioeconomic status influence the manifestation of gifted characteristics? How might these differences influence diverse representation in gifted programs? What might you, as an educator, do to influence the representation of a diverse population in gifted programs?
5. Which category of giftedness (schoolhouse/creative productive) might be most often provided for in gifted programs? Which form of giftedness is most likely to lead to eminence? Support your answers with examples.

RESOURCES

Websites

National Research Center on the Gifted and Talented

www.gifted.uconn.edu/nrcgt.html

A research site from the University of Connecticut on talent development; the National Research Center conducts research on the education and identification of the gifted and talented.

Neag Center for Gifted Education and Talent Development

www.gifted.uconn.edu

This website provides numerous resources for the education of the gifted and talented as well as links to advanced training opportunities for teachers who want to learn more about the education of gifted and talented students.

Jacob K. Javits Gifted and Talented Students Education Program

www.ed.gov/programs/javits/index.html

The purpose of the Javits program is to support and enhance the ability of elementary and secondary schools to meet the special educational needs of gifted and talented students. The major emphasis of the program is on serving students traditionally underrepresented in gifted and talented programs, particularly economically disadvantaged, limited-English-proficient, and disabled students.

BOOKS

Colangelo, N., & Davis, G. A. (Eds.). (2003). *Handbook of gifted education* (3rd ed.). Boston: Allyn & Bacon.

Davis, G. A., & Rimm, S. B. (2004). *Education of the gifted and talented* (5th ed.). Boston: Pearson.

Karnes, F. A., & Bean, S. M. (Eds.). (2005). *Methods and materials for teaching the gifted* (2nd ed.). Waco, TX: Prufrock.

Neihart, M., Reis, S. M., Robinson, N. M., & Moon, S. M. (Eds.). (2002). *The social and emotional development of gifted children: What do we know?* Waco, TX: Prufrock.

Reis, S. M. (Series Ed.). (2004). *Essential readings in gifted education.* Thousand Oaks, CA: Corwin.

Renzulli, J. S., Smith, L. H., White, A. J., Callahan, C. M., Hartman, R. K., Westberg, K. L., et al. (2002). *Scales for Rating the Behavioral Characteristics of Superior Students* (Rev. ed.). Mansfield Center, CT: Creative Learning Press.

Sternberg, R. J., & Davidson, J. E. (Eds.). (2005). *Conceptions of giftedness* (2nd ed.). New York: Cambridge University Press.

REFERENCES

Argulewicz, E. N. (1985). Review of the Scale for Rating the Behavior Characteristics of Superior Students. In J. V. Mitchell (Ed.), *Ninth mental measurements yearbook* (Vol. 2, pp. 1311–1312). Lincoln, NE: Buros.

Barron, F., & Harrington, D. M. (1981). Creativity, intelligence, and personality. *Annual Review of Psychology, 32,* 439–476.

Baum, S., & Owen, S. V. (1988). High ability/learning disabled students: How are they different? *Gifted Child Quarterly, 32,* 321–326.

Baum, S., Owen, S. V., & Dixon, J. (1991). *To be gifted and learning disabled: From identification to practical intervention strategies.* Mansfield Center, CT: Creative Learning Press.

Bloom, B. S. (Ed.). (1985). *Developing talent in young people.* New York: Ballantine.

Boodoo, G. M., Bradley, C. L., Frontera, R. L., Pitts, J. R., & Wright, L. P. (1989). A survey of procedures used for identifying gifted learning disabled children. *Gifted Child Quarterly,* 33, 110–114.

Clark, B. (1988). *Optimizing learning. A leadership accessing monograph: Education of gifted and talented youth.* West Lafayette, IN: Gifted Education Resource Institute, Purdue University. (ERIC Document Reproduction Service No. ED315947)

Clark, B. (2002). *Growing up gifted* (6th ed.). Upper Saddle River, NJ: Merrill/Prentice Hall.

Clark, G., & Zimmerman, E. (1984). Toward a new conception of talent in the visual arts. *Roeper Review, 6,* 214–216.

Cox, C. M. (1926). *The early mental traits of three hundred geniuses.* Stanford, CA: Stanford University Press.

Csikszentmihalyi, M., Rathunde, K., & Whalen, S. (1993). *Talented teenagers: The roots of success and failure.* New York: Cambridge University Press.

Davis, G. A. (1999). *Creativity is forever* (4th ed.). Dubuque, IA: Kendall/Hunt.

Davis, G. A. (2003). Identifying creative students, teaching for creative growth. In N. Colangelo & G. A. Davis (Eds.), *The handbook of gifted education* (3rd ed., pp. 311–324). Boston: Allyn & Bacon.

Davis, G. A., & Rimm, S. B. (1998). *Education of the gifted and talented* (4th ed.). Boston: Allyn & Bacon.

Davis, G. A., & Rimm, S. B. (2004). *Education of the gifted and talented* (5th ed.). Boston: Allyn & Bacon.

Feldhusen, J. F. (1986). A conception of giftedness. In R. J. Sternberg & J. E. Davidson (Eds.), *Conceptions of giftedness* (pp. 112–127). New York: Cambridge University Press.

Frasier, M. M., García, J. H., & Passow, A. H. (1995). *A review of assessment issues in gifted education and their implications for identifying gifted minority students.* Storrs: National Research Center on the Gifted and Talented, University of Connecticut.

Frasier, M. M., & Passow, A. H. (1994). *Toward a new paradigm for identifying talent potential.* Storrs: National Research Center on the Gifted and Talented, University of Connecticut.

Gardner, H. (1983). *Frames of mind: The theory of multiple intelligences.* New York: Basic Books.

Gardner, H. (1993). *Frames of mind: The theory of multiple intelligences* (10th anniversary ed.). New York: Basic Books.

Getzels, J. W., & Jackson, P. W. (1960). Occupational choice and cognitive functioning: Career aspirations of highly intelligent and of highly creative adolescents. *Journal of Abnormal and Social Psychology, 61,* 119–123.

Getzels, J. W., & Jackson, P. W. (1961). Family environment and cognitive style: A study of the sources of highly intelligent and of highly creative adolescents. *American Sociological Review, 26,* 351–359.

Getzels, J. W., & Jackson, P. W. (1962). *Creativity and intelligence: Explorations with gifted students.* New York: Wiley.

Gottfried, A. W., Cook, C. R., Gottfried, A. E., & Morris, P. E. (2005). Educational characteristics of adolescents with gifted academic intrinsic motivation: A longitudinal investigation from school entry through early adulthood. *Gifted Child Quarterly,* 49, 172–186.

Gottfried, A. E., & Gottfried, A. W. (2004). Toward the development of a conceptualization of gifted motivation. *Gifted Child Quarterly, 48,* 121–132.

Guastello, S. J. (1995). Facilitating style, individual innovation, and emergent leadership in problem solving groups. *Journal of Creative Behavior, 29,* 225–239.

Guastello, S. J. (2002). *Managing emergent phenomena: Nonlinear dynamics in work organizations.* Mahwah, NJ: Lawrence Erlbaum Associates.

Guilford, J. P. (1950). Creativity. *American Psychologist, 5,* 444–454

Hébert, T. H., & Reis, S. M. (1999). Culturally diverse high-achieving students in an urban high school. *Urban Education, 34,* 428–457.

Hurwitz, A. (1983). *The gifted and talented in art: A guide to program planning.* Worcester, MA: Davis Publications.

Jolly, J., & Kettler, T. (2004, Winter). Authentic assessment of leadership in problem-solving groups. *Gifted Child Today, 27,* 32–39.

Judge, T. A., Bono, J. E., Ilies, R., & Gerhardt, M. W. (2002). Personality and leadership: A qualitative and quantitative review. *Journal of Applied Psychology,* 87, 765–780.

Judge, T. A., Colbert, A. E., & Ilies, R. (2004). Intelligence and leadership: A quantitative review and test of theoretical propositions. *Journal of Applied Psychology, 89,* 542–552.

Karnes, F. A., & Bean, S. M. (1990). *Developing leadership in gifted youth.* Reston, VA: Council for Exceptional Children. (ERIC Document Reproduction Service No. ED321490)

Karnes, F. A. & Bean, S. M. (1995). *Leadership for Students: A practical guide.* Waco, TX: Prufrock.

Karnes, F. A., & Bean, S. M. (1996). Leadership and the gifted. *Focus on Exceptional Children, 29,* 1–12.

Karnes, F. A., & Chauvin, J. C. (1986, May/June). The leadership skills: Fostering the forgotten dimension of giftedness. *Gifted Child Today, 9,* 22–23.

Karnes, F. A., & Chauvin, J. C. (2000). *Leadership development program.* Scottsdale, AZ: Gifted Psychology.

Karnes, F. A., & D'Ilio, V. R. (1989). Personality characteristics of student leaders. *Psychological Reports, 64,* 1125–1126.

MacKinnon, O. (1978). *In Search of human effectiveness.* Buffalo, NY: Bearly.

Maker, C. J., & Schiever, S. W. (1989). *Critical issues in gifted education: Defensible programs for cultural and ethnic minorities* (Vol. 2). Austin, TX: PRO-ED.

Marland, S. P. (1972). *Education of the gifted and talented* (Vol. 1) (Report to the Congress of the United States by the U.S. Commissioner of Education). Washington, DC: U.S. Government Printing Office.

Moon, S. M. (2003). Personal talent. *High Ability Studies,* 14, 5–21.

Passow, A. H., & Rudnitski, R. A. (1993). *State policies regarding education of the gifted as reflected in legislation and regulation.* Storrs: National Research Center on the Gifted and Talented, University of Connecticut.

Perleth, C., Sierwald, W., & Heller, K. A. (1993). Selected results of the Munich longitudinal study of giftedness: The multidimensional/typological giftedness model. *Roeper Review, 15,* 149–155.

Reis, S. M. (1995). Older women's reflections on eminence: Obstacles and opportunities. *Roeper Review, 18,* 66–73.

Reis, S. M. (1998). *Work left undone: Choices and compromises of talented females.* Mansfield Center, CT: Creative Learning Press.

Reis, S. M. (2005). Feminist perspectives on talent development: A research-based conception of giftedness in women. In R. J. Sternberg & J. E. Davidson (Eds.), *Conceptions of giftedness* (2nd ed., pp. 217–245). New York: Cambridge University Press.

Reis, S. M., & Díaz, E. I. (1999). Economically disadvantaged urban female students who achieve in school. *The Urban Review, 31,* 31–54.

Reis, S. M., & McCoach, D. B. (2000). The underachievement of gifted students: What do we know and where do we go? *Gifted Child Quarterly, 44,* 152–170.

Reis, S. M., Neu, T. W., & McGuire, J. M. (1995). *Talent in two places: Case studies of high ability students with learning disabilities who have achieved.* Storrs: National Research Center on the Gifted and Talented, University of Connecticut.

Renzulli, J. S. (1972). *An evaluation of Project Gifted 1971–1972.* Washington, DC: Bureau of Elementary and Secondary Education. (ERIC Document Reproduction Service No. ED093135)

Renzulli, J. S. (1978). What makes giftedness? Reexamining a definition. *Phi Delta Kappan, 60,* 180–184, 261.

Renzulli, J. S. (1980). Will the gifted child movement be alive and well in 1990? *Gifted Child Quarterly, 24,* 3–9.

Renzulli, J. S. (1986). The three-ring conception of giftedness: A developmental model for creative productivity. In R. J. Sternberg & J. E. Davidson (Eds.), *Conceptions of giftedness* (pp. 53–92). New York: Cambridge University Press.

Renzulli, J. S. (1996). Schools for talent development: A practical plan for total school improvement. *School Administrator, 53,* 20–22.

Renzulli, J. S. (2002). Expanding the conception of giftedness to include co-cognitive traits and to promote social capital. *Phi Delta Kappan, 84,* 33–40, 57–58.

Renzulli, J. S. (2003). Conception of giftedness and its relationship to the development of social capital. In N. Colangelo & G. A. Davis (Eds.), *The handbook of gifted education* (3rd ed., pp. 75–87). Boston: Allyn & Bacon.

Renzulli, J. S. (2005). The three-ring conception of giftedness: A developmental model for promoting creative productivity. In R. J. Sternberg & J. E. Davidson (Eds.), *Conceptions of giftedness* (2nd ed., pp. 246–279). New York: Cambridge University Press.

Renzulli, J. S., & Reis, S. M. (1985). *The schoolwide enrichment model: A comprehensive plan for educational excellence.* Mansfield Center, CT: Creative Learning Press.

Renzulli, J. S., & Reis, S. M. (1997). *The schoolwide enrichment model: A how-to guide for educational excellence* (2nd ed.). Mansfield Center, CT: Creative Learning Press.

Renzulli, J. S., Smith, L. H., White, A. J., Callahan, C. M., Hartman, R. K., & Westberg, K. L. (1976). *Scales for Rating the Behavioral Characteristics of Superior Students.* Mansfield Center, CT: Creative Learning Press.

Renzulli, J. S., Smith, L. H., White, A. J., Callahan, C. M., Hartman, R. K., Westberg, K. L., et al. (2002). *Scales for Rating the Behavioral Characteristics of Superior Students* (Rev. ed.). Mansfield Center, CT: Creative Learning Press.

Rogers, K. B. (1991). *A best-evidence synthesis of the research on accelerative options for gifted students.* Unpublished doctoral dissertation. Minneapolis, MN: University of Minnesota.

Rust, J. O. (1985). Review of the scale for rating the behavior characteristics of superior students. In J. V. Mitchell (Ed.), *Ninth mental measurements yearbook* (Vol. 2, pp. 1312–1313). Lincoln, NE: Buros.

Silverman, L. K. (1994). The moral sensitivity of gifted children and the evolution of society. *Roeper Review, 17,* 110–116.

Simonton, D. K. (2003). When does giftedness become genius? And when not? In N. Colangelo & G. A. Davis (Eds.), *The handbook of gifted education* (3rd ed., pp. 358–372). Boston: Allyn & Bacon.

Smith, D. L., Smith, L., & Barnette, J. (1991). Exploring the development of leadership giftedness. *Roeper Review, 14,* 7–12.

Stephens, K. R., & Karnes, F. A. (2000). State definitions for the gifted and talented revisited. *Exceptional Children, 66,* 219–238.

Sternberg, R. J. (1986). A triarchic theory of intellectual giftedness. In R. J. Sternberg & J. E. Davidson (Eds.), *Conceptions of giftedness* (pp. 223–243). New York: Cambridge University Press.

Sternberg, R. J. (1997). A triarchic view of giftedness: Theory and practice. In N. Colangelo & G. A. Davis (Eds.), *Handbook of gifted education* (pp. 43–53). Boston: Allyn & Bacon.

Sternberg, R. J., & Davidson, J. E. (1985). Cognitive development in the gifted and talented. In F. D. Horowitz & M. O'Brien (Eds.), *The gifted and talented: Developmental perspectives* (pp. 37–74). Washington, DC: American Psychological Association.

Sternberg, R. J., & Davidson, J. E. (Eds.). (2005). *Conceptions of giftedness* (2nd ed.). New York: Cambridge University Press.

Sternberg, R. J., & Lubart, T. I. (1993). Creative giftedness: A multivariate investment approach. *Gifted Child Quarterly, 37,* 7–15.

Tannenbaum, A. J. (1986). Giftedness: A psychosocial approach. In R. J. Sternberg & J. E. Davidson (Eds.), *Conceptions of giftedness* (pp. 21–52). New York: Cambridge University Press.

Tannenbaum, A. J. (2000). A history of giftedness in school and society. In K. A. Heller, F. J. Mönks, R. J. Sternberg, & R. F. Subotnik (Eds.), *International handbook of giftedness and talent* (2nd ed., pp. 23–53). New York: Elsevier.

Torrance, E. P. (1976). *Guiding creative talent.* Huntington, NY: Krieger.

Torrance, E. P. (1988). The nature of creativity as manifest in its testing. In R. J. Sternberg (Ed.), *The nature of creativity: Contemporary psychological perspectives* (pp. 43–75). New York: Cambridge University Press.

Treffinger, D. J., Young, G. C., Selby, E. C., & Shepardson, C. (2002). *Assessing creativity: A guide for educators* (Research Monograph No. 02170). Storrs, CT: National Research Center on the Gifted and Talented.

U.S. Congress. (1988). *Jacob K. Javits Gifted and Talented Students Education Act of 1988.* Washington, DC: U.S. Government Printing Office.

VanTassal-Baska, J. (1989). Characteristics of the developmental path of eminent and gifted adults. In J. L. VanTassel-Baska & P. Olszewski-Kubilius (Eds.), *Patterns of influence on gifted learners: The home, the self, the school* (pp. 146–162). New York: Teachers College Press.

VanTassel-Baska, J. (1994). *Comprehensive curriculum for gifted learners* (2nd ed.). Boston: Allyn & Bacon.

Walberg, H. J., & Paik, S. J. (2005). Making giftedness productive. In R. J. Sternberg & J. E. Davidson (Eds.), *Conceptions of giftedness* (2nd ed., pp. 395–410). New York: Cambridge University Press.

Whitmore, J. (1986). Conceptualizing the issue of underserved populations of gifted students. *Journal for the Education of the Gifted, 10,* 141–153.

Winner, E., & Martino, G. (2003). Artistic giftedness. In N. Colangelo & G. A. Davis (Eds.), *The handbook of gifted education* (3rd ed., pp. 335–349). Boston: Allyn & Bacon.

PERSONAL AND SOCIAL DEVELOPMENT

Sidney Moon, Ph.D.
PURDUE UNIVERSITY

INTRODUCTION

Much of the research and writing in the field of gifted education focuses on issues like how to differentiate curriculum and instruction so that these students will be appropriately challenged. These are important issues. Teachers need to understand the learning characteristics of academically talented youth and have the skills needed to provide an appropriate level and pace of instruction for them. Teachers also need to understand the social and emotional issues of gifted youth at different stages of development and build skills that promote positive social and emotional development among gifted youth. In this chapter, strategies promoting the *holistic development* of talented learners will be discussed. Holistic development means the development of the whole person with balanced attention to cognitive (learning), personal (emotional and motivational), and social issues (Moon & Dixon, 2006).

The focus of this chapter is on academically talented students who score well on traditional tests of intelligence and achievement and/or students who demonstrate talent in one or more academic subject areas through outstanding performances. The first two sections of this chapter are designed to help the reader understand common themes in the social, emotional, and motivational development of gifted students. In the final section, ideas for promoting holistic development in gifted and talented students are discussed.

PERSONAL AND SOCIAL DEVELOPMENT

Developmental Tasks

Personal and social tasks for gifted youth are depicted in Table 6–1 for each of the typical divisions of K–12 schooling: elementary, middle, and high school. Like all children, gifted children who are on a positive developmental trajectory will develop self-confidence, build friendships easily, and become increasingly autonomous and self-directed as they grow. By high school, they will have developed positive identities that incorporate all aspects of themselves, including their ability and personality profiles, as well as their age, gender, culture, ethnicity, and sexual orientation.

At the same time, there are some aspects of personal and social developmental tasks for gifted youth that differ from those of typically developing students. For example, some developmental tasks for gifted students are *accelerated* in comparison to typically developing children. This is true of friendship development. Research has shown that gifted students move more quickly than most children through the stages of friendship development (Gross, 2000, 2004). They have more advanced friendship preferences than their chronological peers and are ready for more sophisticated types of friendship earlier. Gifted youth also need to begin career development work earlier than most typical adolescents both because they are ready for such development earlier and because the choices they make in middle school can influence their college and career options (Hébert & Kelly, 2006).

TABLE 6–1 Personal and Social Developmental Tasks for K–12 Gifted Youth

Elementary School (ages 5–10)
Developing self-regulation abilities
Developing a strong work ethic
Building friendships and prosocial skills
Developing self-confidence
Developing resilience when encountering obstacles or failure
Managing long-term projects
Expressing and labeling feelings
Resisting the "just get by" attitude
Coping effectively with teasing and/or bullying
Middle School (ages 11–14)
Negotiating affiliation and achievement conflicts
Building a positive identity around giftedness
Managing more complex and volatile emotions
Increasing time management skills
Building friendships with a wider variety of people
Exploring career fields
Beginning long-term educational and career planning
Resisting anti-achievement and/or antisocial peer pressures
Resisting cultural stereotypes
High School (ages 14–18)
Differentiating from family while remaining close to family members
Making autonomous decisions
Completing college and career planning
Choosing challenging course work
Maintaining motivation in more demanding academic classes
Balancing extracurricular activities with school work
Developing a sexual identity
Making good relationship and sexual choices
Resisting cultural stereotypes

Other developmental tasks are the same as those of typically developing children but may be more difficult for gifted students to accomplish. For example, it may be harder for a gifted elementary student to develop a strong work ethic if he or she is placed in a regular classroom with little academic challenge. When schoolwork is always easy, it is easy to develop a maladaptive "just do enough to get by" attitude and very difficult to develop resilience.

Finally, there are differences because giftedness can create greater developmental challenges. This is true in the areas of emotional development, achievement–affiliation conflicts, and time management. Gifted children may feel their emotions more intensely than other children and so have greater challenges in learning to manage those emotions during the elementary school years (Mendaglio, 2003; Piechowski, 1997; Piechowski & Cunningham, 1985). In middle school, achievement–affiliation conflicts may be particularly acute for gifted youth because they have such high achievement potential (Clasen & Clasen, 1995). Gifted high school students may have greater time management challenges than their average-ability peers because they are taking more demanding classes and involved in more extracurricular activities (Moon, 2003b). While all high school students need to develop time management skills, the skills academically gifted youth need will be more difficult to master.

Table 6–1 gives teachers a picture of what a gifted student who is developing well will be able to do by the time he or she leaves each stage of development. Gifted students who have mastered the tasks of the elementary level are ready for the challenges of middle school; gifted students who have mastered the tasks of middle school are ready for high school. Students who have not mastered the tasks of one of the levels will benefit from interventions to help them get back on track. Table 6–1 provides a picture of positive holistic development in gifted students. All gifted students are capable of accomplishing these typical developmental tasks, though some may need special assistance to do so.

Personal and Social Talent

Some gifted students may be especially talented in the personal and/or social domains. Teachers need to know how to recognize the behavioral characteristics of students with exceptional talent in the personal

TABLE 6–2 Characteristics of Students with Personal and Social Talent

Personal Talent	Social Talent
Abilities	Abilities
Intrapersonal intelligence	Interpersonal intelligence
Skills	Skills
Self-awareness	Empathy
Awareness of contexts	Friendship creation and maintenance
Adaptability	Conflict management
Goal setting	Leadership
Decision making	Communication
Planning	Listening
Goal attainment	Assertiveness
Self-regulation	
Time management	
Personal problem solving	
Dispositions	Dispositions
Optimism	Openness
Hardiness	Tolerance
Self-confidence	Appreciation for human diversity
Integrity	Commitment to social justice
Achievement motivation	High ethical standards

and social domains and how to nurture and guide students with these talents. The characteristics of students with personal and/or social talents are summarized in Table 6–2.

Students with *personal* talent who are motivated to do well in school are fairly easy for teachers to identify. These are the students most teachers would describe as "motivated." They know how to succeed in academic environments; they make good decisions, work hard, and manage time well. To nurture these students, teachers can provide learning environments that balance challenge and support, allow students as much choice as possible, emphasize instructional strategies the build personal talent such as problem-based learning and independent study, and scaffold the development of skills in decision making and self-regulation (Moon & Ray, 2006).

Students with personal talent whose interests lie outside of school are much more difficult for teachers to recognize and nurture. For example, a high school student with personal talent who is aware that she has talent in theater and wants to be an actress may make a conscious choice to invest limited energy in her academic classes. As a result, she puts in only enough effort to get passing grades in order to free up time for both school and community drama productions. This decision may represent an excellent choice and reflect a high degree of personal talent, enabling the student to chart her own path through high school rather than conforming blindly. However, it may not appear to be a good choice to the teachers of her academic classes. To those teachers, this student will appear to be an underachiever. The teachers who coach drama productions will be in a better position to nurture personal talent in this student than the teachers of her academic subjects.

In general, social talents will be more obvious in elementary classrooms than secondary classrooms because elementary teachers generally have students in their room for most of the school day and supervise students in informal settings such as recess. Their experience of their students is holistic. In secondary classrooms, social talents will be most visible when teachers engage students in experiential, informal, or group learning projects. Secondary teachers may also be able to observe social talent in students when they advise extracurricular clubs or teams. Extracurricular activities allow leadership talents to emerge and provide numerous opportunities for peer interactions. Social talent can be invisible to teachers who use traditional styles of instruction because students in traditional classrooms have few opportunities to interact with their peers or demonstrate leadership. It follows from these observations that teachers who wish to recognize and nurture social talents need to provide opportunities for students to interact with their peers and demonstrate leadership.

SOCIAL AND EMOTIONAL ISSUES

All gifted children should be able to master the basic personal and social developmental tasks shown in Table 6–1, but some are not able to do so. It might seem that smart students should have an easy time with social and emotional development, yet that is not always the case. The reasons gifted students can have difficulties with social and emotional adjustment fall into three categories: *endogenous* (internal or individual), *exogenous* (external or environmental), and *interactive* (both internal and external).

Endogenous Issues

Endogenous issues are internal characteristics of the individual like personality traits or low self-esteem. Gifted children are similar to each other with respect to cognitive abilities and different from each other with respect to social, emotional, and personal development. By definition, gifted students all have advanced cognitive development in at least one area that is relevant for academic work in school. However, they are not at all the same with respect to personal and social development. Some cognitively gifted students are quite advanced or even talented in the personal and social domains, while others are average or below average. In addition, certain subgroups of gifted students may face special challenges with social, emotional, and personal development. Three examples of endogenous characteristics that can create social and emotional difficulties for some gifted students in classroom settings follow.

Self-Concept. For various reasons, some gifted children and adolescents have low self-concepts. As a group, gifted children generally have higher-than-normal academic self-concepts and average self-concepts in other areas, such as social and physical (Hoge & Renzulli, 1993; Schneider, 1987). Discrepancies between academic (high) and social (average to low) self-concepts can create adjustment difficulties for gifted children. Self-concept discrepancies may arise because a gifted child perceives him- or herself to have high cognitive abilities and only relatively average social abilities. Making internal comparisons with respect to their strengths and weaknesses, gifted children conclude that their average abilities are low abilities because they feel low to them in comparison with their cognitive abilities. As a result, children can develop a low social self-concept and may become withdrawn and isolated. A low social self-concept is especially troublesome in adolescence, where it can lead to depression or to immersion in academics at the expense of social relationships. Hence, one of the endogenous issues that teachers should be alert to with gifted children is the overall profile of their self-concept across different areas. There are also interactive self-concept issues that can affect gifted children. For example, their self-concepts can dip when they are first placed in a more challenging educational situation, such as a self-contained classroom (Coleman & Fults, 1982, 1985).

Multiple Exceptionalities. *Twice-exceptional* students are students who have co-occurring giftedness and disabilities. For example, a student who is verbally gifted and also has a learning disability in math is twice exceptional. Similarly, a student who is intellectually gifted and has an attention-deficit/hyperactivity disorder (ADHD) is also twice exceptional. Twice-exceptional students are at risk for difficulties with social-emotional adjustment (Moon, 2002; Moon & Hall, 1998; Moon, Zentall, Grskovic, Hall, & Stormont, 2001; Olenchak & Reis, 2002). Gifted students with learning disabilities have been found to demonstrate the following maladaptive affective characteristics: a tendency toward intense frustration with difficult tasks, disruptive or withdrawn behavior, and feelings of learned helplessness (Olenchak & Reis, 2002). For example, academically gifted second-grade boys with co-occurring ADHD who were placed in a self-contained classroom for gifted students were found to be at risk for social maladjustment because their gifted peers could not understand or tolerate the immature, annoying, and irresponsible behaviors typical of their disorder (Moon et al., 2001). As a result, the students experienced social rejection. "They were described as being friendless loners in school who were tolerated by their gifted peers, but seldom picked as work or play partners" (Moon et al., 2001, p. 225). Twice-exceptional students are at risk for emotional disorders and may struggle with peer relationships.

Perfectionism. For many years, perfectionism was thought to be a trait that was associated with giftedness (Adderholdt-Elliot, 1987). However, studies comparing gifted students to general students have found little difference between the groups, suggesting that the incidence of perfectionism is about as frequent among gifted students as among other students (Parker & Adkins, 1995; Parker & Mills, 1996). What appears to be important for social and emotional adjustment is not whether a student is a perfectionist but the type of perfectionism the student exhibits. Some kinds of perfectionism are positive, and others are negative (Dixon, Lapsley, & Hanchon, 2004; Neumeister, 2004a, 2004b; Parker & Adkins, 1995). Adaptive perfectionism promotes personal growth and achievement; maladaptive perfectionism does just the opposite. Adaptive perfectionists set high standards for themselves and are confident they can meet those standards; if they fail or make a mistake, they don't overreact or criticize themselves excessively. They tend to have parents and teachers who have high expectations while being very supportive. Maladaptive perfectionists, on the other hand, are full of doubts and very concerned about making mistakes. Because they are so worried about making mistakes, they are afraid to take risks, set low goals, and choose easy classes. They tend to have parents or teachers who set high standards and are very critical of them if they can't meet those standards. It is not the high standards that create the problem; it is the constant criticism. In summary, the research on perfectionism suggests that it is important to combine warmth and support with high standards when working with gifted youth.

Exogenous Issues

In addition to these individual issues, external forces can make the optimal social and emotional development described in Table 6–1 challenging for gifted students. Exogenous issues are environmental factors such as family and school environments. Some of these are specific to certain individuals; others affect most gifted students. Three exogenous influences on the social and emotional development of gifted students are explored here: schools, peers, and families.

School Placements. Neihart, Reis, Robinson, and Moon (2002) conducted an extensive review of the empirical literature on the social and emotional development of gifted students. They concluded that most of the social and emotional difficulties that exist in this population "reflect the interaction of an ill-fitting environment with an individual's personal characteristics" (Neihart et al., 2002, p. 268). By far the most common ill-fitting environment experienced by these students is a school placement with chronological peers instead of cognitive peers. For gifted children, the typical elementary school classroom is an ill-fitting environment. Because they are so cognitively advanced, gifted children who are placed in a heterogeneous classroom on the basis of their chronological age often experience boredom, frustration, and peer rejection. They are too young to understand why they must spend hours each day relearning material they have already mastered, so they may act out or withdraw into daydreaming. In either case, they fail to develop a strong work ethic, one of the developmental tasks of the elementary school years.

In addition, because they think differently, talk differently, and have more advanced conceptions of friendships, gifted children may have great difficulty building friendships with their classmates in a regular elementary school classroom. This is especially true for verbally gifted students and for highly gifted students because their differences from typically developing students are quite pronounced at the elementary level. Such students may experience rejection, loneliness, or bullying (Kaiser & Berndt, 1985; Kennedy, 1995; Peterson & Ray, 2006). Placement in a self-contained class for gifted students (Moon, Swift, & Shallenberger, 2002) or radical acceleration (Gross, 1993) can improve social and emotional adjustment in highly gifted students who have been experiencing boredom or social rejection in a regular classroom.

One reason younger gifted children can have difficulty forming friendships and building prosocial skills when they are placed in heterogeneous classrooms is that they have more advanced conceptions of friendship (Gross, 2000). In a series of studies comparing average, moderately gifted, highly gifted, and exceptionally gifted students in grades 3 to 8, Gross found that all the gifted students had more advanced conceptions of friendship than their average-ability peers in grades 3 to 4. The five developmental stages of friendship in this study ranged from play partnerships at the lowest level to relationships characterized by fidelity, authenticity, and emotional security at the highest level. Gifted students progressed through these stages faster than their average-ability peers, especially before 10 years of age. Even moderately gifted children generally had conceptions of friendship that were 2 to 3 years in advance of their average-ability peers. Exceptionally gifted children, with IQs higher than 160, begin searching for friendships based on unconditional acceptance 4 or 5 years earlier than their peers (Gross, 2002). This means that highly gifted children aged 6 or 7 have conceptions of friendship not typically seen until age 11 or 12, which makes it very difficult for them to form friendships with average-ability children their own age. These differences in conceptions of friendship are greatest when children are younger. They begin to moderate in the middle school years and may disappear entirely in high school when the circle of potential friends is wider.

Peer Relationships. Peer relationships are a potential stressor for gifted students regardless of school placement, during the adolescent years (Rimm, 2002). In the United States, there is a pervasive anti-intellectual peer culture in adolescence. This anti-intellectualism pervades all aspects of U.S. adolescent culture but is particularly pronounced among African Americans and Latinos (Schneider, 1987). As a result, many gifted adolescents believe they must make a choice between being intelligent and being popular (Clasen & Clasen, 1995; Cross, Coleman, & Terhaar-Yonkers, 1991). They face achievement–affiliation conflicts that can prevent them from accomplishing the social and emotional tasks of the middle school years.

Highly gifted adolescents have more difficulties with peer acceptance than more moderately gifted children (Dauber & Benbow, 1990; Gross, 2002). As noted previously, they have great difficulties relating to average-ability children when placed in a regular classroom setting (Gross, 2004; Kennedy, 1995), and they have such advanced friendship conceptions that it is almost impossible for them to form deep friendships with chronological peers who are at a lower stage of friendship development (Gross, 2000). Highly gifted adolescents are also more likely to manage the stigma of giftedness by denying their gifts in order to fit in with their peers, which results in failure to achieve their intellectual and academic potential (Cross et al., 1991; Swiatek, 1995).

Bullying is another aspect of peer relationships that can cause social and emotional difficulties for a some gifted students (Peterson & Ray, 2006). A national study of the incidence of bullying among gifted students in grades K to 8 found that 27% to 46% had experienced at least one bullying incident and that 2% to 11% had been the victim of repeated bullying (more than 10 times). Bullying peaked in the middle school years. For example, 46% of gifted sixth graders had experienced bullying (54% of males and 38% of females), and 11% of these had experienced repeated bullying. The types of bullying these students experienced included name-calling, teasing about their intelligence, and physical violence. Teasing about intelligence and grades peaked during seventh and eighth grade. When asked how much they were affected by bullying, 8% to 13% of students in grades 5 to 8 said "a lot" (Peterson & Ray, 2006). Thus, a sizable minority of gifted students across several geographic locations, types of communities, and racial and ethnic groups experience an exogenous threat to social and emotional well-being in the form of peer bullying, and this bullying is often related to their giftedness.

Family Life. Families are very influential in the development of gifted students (Moon, Jurich, & Feldhusen, 1998; VanTassel-Baska & Olszewski-Kubilius, 1989). Families influence academic talent development (Csikszentmihalyi, Rathunde, & Whalen, 1993) as well as social and emotional development (Moon & Hall, 1998; Sowa & May, 1997). Complex families appear to be most effective in promoting the holistic development of gifted students (Csikszentmihalyi et al., 1993). Complex families balance *integration* and *differentiation*. Integration is developed through strong bonds of connection with one another, efficient organization, and consistent rules. Differentiation involves encouraging each family member to develop his or her individuality by seeking out new challenges and opportunities. Complex families provide an appropriate balance of integration and differentiation. They are supportive and organized without being stifling, and they encourage individual interests and personal growth.

Dysfunctional families, on the other hand, have a negative impact on the development of gifted children, as they do for all children (Frey & Wendorf, 1985; Sowa & May, 1997). Problem families come in many types and affect all children negatively. Parents can be too permissive or too strict. Parents can neglect their children because they are struggling with their own issues, such as alcoholism, mental illness, or extreme poverty. Family conflict may be pervasive because parents or siblings do not have the skills to resolve their differences amicably. Any of these situations are likely to have a negative impact on the social and emotional development of gifted children.

Families with gifted children are vulnerable to a negative family dynamic called *parentification*. Gifted children who are parentified are given too much family responsibility too early because they seem so adult in their language and behavior. Another negative family dynamic unique to families with gifted children can occur when the advanced development of a gifted child pushes the family into the adolescent life cycle transition before the family is ready (Moon, Nelson, & Piercy, 1993). Both of these dynamics are most likely to occur with firstborn or only children.

In summary, exogenous or environmental forces are critical influences on the social and emotional development of gifted students. The most important exogenous influences are schools, peers, and families. When all three of these environmental influences are supporting a particular gifted child, that child is likely to develop well. When one or more of these environmental influences is a poor fit or dysfunctional, the gifted child is likely to develop related social-emotional adjustment problems. "Fit" is a relative term. A family that is a good fit for a young child because it provides appropriate amounts of support and structure may be a poor fit when that child reaches adolescence because it fails to encourage the development of an independent identity. Similarly, a classroom environment that works well for gifted second graders may be inappropriate for eleventh graders taking advanced placement physics. The important question is whether a particular environmental influence is growth promoting, for a particular gifted student, at a particular time.

Interactive Issues

Many of the challenges to the social-emotional development of gifted students arise from interactions between endogenous characteristics like gender and exogenous forces like sociocultural conditioning. Teachers need to be especially sensitive to these issues so they can counteract the often insidious effects of social inequities and biases on talented youth. In the next section, three interactive issues are examined: gender, ethnicity, and underachievement.

Gender. Reis (2002) reviewed the literature on gifted females and found that they face both endogenous and exogenous barriers to achievement: "Gifted females," she wrote, "find themselves in a world of limiting stereotypes and barriers to achievement presented by parents, school, and the larger society" (pp. 126–127). Teachers can have a more difficult time identifying gifted girls because many gifted girls are quite adept at hiding their intelligence in order to fit in with their peers (Kramer, 1985; Sadker & Sadker, 1994). In addition, many of the standardized instruments that are used to identify giftedness have sex biases against girls (Reis, 2006). Both male and female teachers tend to hold gender-stereotypical views of talent distribution, believing that smart boys are more competent in thinking and problem-solving skills while smart girls are superior in creative writing (Cooley, Chauvin, & Karnes, 1984). Teachers also reinforce gender-stereotypical attributions for success and failure, believing that the success of male students is due to ability while the success of female students is due to effort (Fennema, Peterson, Carpenter, & Lubinski, 1990). This attributional pattern is beneficial for males and detrimental to females, contributing to lowered self-efficacy and performance for gifted females. In addition, gifted females tend to be more socially oriented than males and so may experience intense achievement–affiliation conflicts, especially during the middle school years. Concerns about balancing family and career can lead to reduced career aspirations for gifted girls (Arnold, 1995; Reis, Callahan, & Goldsmith, 1996). In summary, gifted females face internal, external, and interactive barriers to career achievement that are not as salient for gifted males. In order to succeed in life, they need supportive parents and teachers and high levels of personal talent (Moon, 2003b; Rimm, 2003a).

Gifted males have not been studied as much as gifted females. The small amount of research that exists on gifted males suggests that it is very important for high-achieving males to believe in themselves, especially when they are immersed in a culture that provides little support for achievement, such as an impoverished, urban community (Hébert, 2002b). Cultural stereotypes affect gifted males as well as gifted females, but the stereotypes and their effects are different for each gender. Gifted males can struggle with how to develop and express emotional intelligence because males in Western society are socialized not to share or show their emotions. It can be harder for gifted males than females to develop *androgyny,* or the ability to be both dominant and submissive as well as independent and nurturing, yet androgyny is an important characteristic of creative adults (Csikszentmihalyi, 1996). Many creative fields are more associated with females than males such as creative writing, theater, and ballet. Males who have talents in these areas face the same kinds of sociocultural barriers that females face in fields like physics and engineering. Gifted males who enter traditionally female fields like elementary education need to be comfortable displaying empathic, caring behaviors (Hébert, 2000b).

In summary, gifted males who follow traditional career paths toward professions such as law, medicine, or engineering face far fewer sociocultural barriers to achievement than gifted females. However, there are several types of gifted males who experience intense barriers to their goals. These include (a) sensitive, emotionally talented males who grow up in urban or rural cultures that do not value education and achievement (Hébert, 2001, 2002a; Hébert & Beardsley, 2001); (b) gifted males who pursue traditionally female career paths (Hébert, 2000b); and (c) gifted males who devote themselves to homemaking and child rearing rather than career pursuits. These gifted males face strong sociocultural barriers to their aspirations and so need a strong belief in themselves, high levels of personal talent, and psychological resilience to persist in their chosen lifestyles.

Ethnicity. Gifted students come from every racial, ethnic, and cultural background (Ross, 1993). In the United States, however, gifted students of color experience barriers to cognitive, social, and emotional development that are not experienced by White students (Ford & Moore, 2006). These barriers create difficulties with recruiting and retaining students of color in gifted programming. Students of color are underrepresented in gifted education (Ford, 2003; Grantham, 2003). Percentages of underrepresentation from 1978 to 1992 ranged from 33% to 57% for African Americans, 25% to 53% for Hispanic Americans, and 40% to 62% for American Indians. Asian Americans, on the other hand, were overrepresented in gifted programs by 43% to 59% during the same time period. Little progress has been made in recent years in improving this situation. Ford (2003) believes that the primary reason for the underrepresentation of diverse students in gifted programs is "the pervasive deficit orientation that prevails in society and our schools" (p. 507), which has an extremely negative impact on the social and emotional development of students of color. Other reasons that have been proposed for the underrepresentation include cultural value conflicts (Ogbu & Simmons, 1998); internal, psychological factors, such as stereotype threat (Steele, 1997; Steele & Aronson, 1995); inability to believe that academic effort will lead to positive long-term outcomes (Ogbu, 2003); and anti-achievement peer pressures (Steinberg, 1996).

Value conflicts and anti-achievement peer pressures are particularly salient in adolescence when the values of the peer culture of students of color often deviate sharply from the values of teachers and the larger society (Steinberg, 1996). Steinberg's research suggests that the African American and Hispanic peer cultures in large urban high schools value affiliation over achievement, while the Asian American peer culture values achievement over affiliation. As a result, strong pressure is exerted on gifted African American and Latino students to underachieve in order to remain part of the peer and ethnic culture. Students of color who resist this anti-achievement peer pressure to develop their talents by doing well in school generally have a strong belief in themselves; peer mentors, or supportive families, teachers, and counselors (Hébert, 2000a; Ogbu, 2003; Reis, Hébert, Díaz, Maxfield, & Ratley, 1995). Peer mentoring programs may be a particularly effective way to help those of color resolve achievement–affiliation conflicts because they enable the students to simultaneously satisfy achievement and affiliation needs (Ogbu, 2003).

Underachievement. Underachievement in gifted students almost always arises as a result of interactions between characteristics of students and their environments (Moon & Hall, 1998). Sometimes the causes are more internal, as with the underachievement of twice-exceptional students; in other cases the causes are more external, as with the underachievement of highly gifted students placed in regular classrooms. Usually, however, some type of interaction between internal, individual characteristics and a students' environment contributes to underachievement in gifted students. In an exhaustive review of the literature on underachievement, Reis and McCoach (2000) identified several internal factors that have been associated with underachievement, including low self-concept, depression, social immaturity, fears of failure or success, maladaptive attributional patterns, maladaptive perfectionism, and poor self-regulation strategies. In addition, inappropriate school and family environments have been associated with underachievement (Rimm, 2003b). For unknown reasons, more gifted males than females underachieve in high school (Peterson & Colangelo, 1996). For the reasons explored in the previous section on ethnicity, underachievement is also prevalent among students of color (Ford, 1996).

Regardless of the etiology of underachievement, gifted students who underachieve are at risk for difficulties with social and emotional adjustment. It is important to try to reverse the underachievement before irreparable damage is done to the student and his or her future. Factors that can reverse underachievement include careful assessment to diagnose possible hidden disabilities (Moon & Hall, 1998; Rimm, 2003b); strength-based educational programs and curricula (Baum, 1995; Whitmore, 1980); psychological interventions designed to improve self-efficacy, goal setting, and self-regulation skills (Siegle & McCoach, 2002); parental coaching and role modeling (Rimm, 2003b); and counseling (Moon & Hall, 1998; Zuccone & Amerikaner, 1986).

NURTURING PERSONAL AND SOCIAL DEVELOPMENT

There are many ways to nurture the personal and social development of gifted students. Teachers can have a dramatic impact on the well-being of gifted students through the ways they manage their classrooms and through the instructional strategies employed. With sufficient training, teachers can also provide direct instruction in social and emotional skills. Counselors also have a role in promoting social and emotional development. School counselors can work with groups of gifted students at critical transition points or with individuals who face overwhelming challenges to their development. In this section, three types of strategies that are effective in promoting the holistic development of gifted students are discussed: indirect instructional strategies, affective curriculum, and counseling.

Indirect Instructional Strategies

Teachers influence the development of gifted students both indirectly and directly. Indirect instructional strategies that promote holistic development include (a) modeling adaptive behaviors, (b) creating adaptive classrooms, and (c) using instructional strategies that promote personal and social talent development.

Modeling Affective Behavior. Social learning theory suggests that modeling is a powerful way to teach new behaviors (Bandura, 1986; Schunk, 1981). Whether teachers are aware of it or not, they are constantly modeling behavior patterns. Teachers who model adaptive behaviors like self-confidence, empathy, organization, creativity, fairness, persistence, and resilience influence students to develop those same adaptive behaviors.

In addition, teachers can select curricular materials that model positive behaviors without gender or culture bias. This is an important principle behind multicultural curricula (Ford, Grantham, & Harris, 1996; Ford & Trotman, 2001). Curricular materials that celebrate the accomplishments of diverse individuals and show individuals from all races and cultures contributing to society influence students of color to believe that education is a route to success and happiness in adult life. Because modeling is so powerful, teachers need to review all their curricular materials for possible cultural, ethnic, or gender biases. If such biases are detected, teachers can either use different materials or counteract the biases through direct instruction or supplementary materials that present less stereotypical viewpoints. In addition, teachers need to monitor their classroom behavior to ensure that their interactions with students are free of bias and stereotyping.

Creating Adaptive Classrooms. Classrooms that provide a balance of support and challenge tend to be adaptive for all students (Midgley & Edelin, 1998). The same is true for gifted students. Challenging and supportive learning environments promote holistic development (Robinson, Reis, Neihart, & Moon, 2002). Support without challenge inhibits the development of persistence and can create boredom and depression. Challenge without support inhibits the development of self-confidence and can lead to anxiety and maladaptive perfectionism.

Gentry, Gable, and Springer (2000) have identified four empirically distinct components of adaptive learning environments for elementary and middle school students: interest, challenge, choice, and enjoyment. Unfortunately, in a study of 787 middle school students, 114 of whom were gifted, none of the students perceived any of these dimensions to be high in their classrooms. Gifted students felt their choices were particularly limited. This suggests that most middle school classrooms are not adaptive learning environments for gifted students and that middle school teachers need to find ways to provide gifted students with more choices, especially if they want to foster the development of personal talent (Moon, 2003a). Gentry, Rizza, and Gable (2001) have also found that gifted elementary students in rural schools perceive their classrooms to be less interesting and challenging but more enjoyable than their urban and suburban peers. This suggests that teachers in rural schools need to work effectively to be sure their classrooms are sufficiently challenging for gifted students, while teachers in urban and suburban environments need to be sure they are providing sufficient support and fun to balance the greater challenge they are providing. Teachers in all contexts need to provide students with more choices.

Creating an adaptive classroom for gifted students requires teachers to differentiate curriculum and adjust for individual differences (Tomlinson et al., 2002; VanTassel-Baska, 1992, 1994; VanTassel-Baska & Little, 2003). In other words, teachers must do something different than they would ordinarily do to appropriately challenge and support gifted students. Challenging gifted students requires teachers to be able to deliver advanced content in a less structured, more complex learning environment (VanTassel-Baska, 1994). In general, gifted learners thrive in low-structure learning environments that emphasize instructional strategies such as inquiry and problem-based learning, while low-ability learners do best in teacher-controlled, high-structure, mastery-oriented learning environments (Snow, 1993). Hence, teachers who have both types of learners in their classroom can have a difficult time creating a learning environment that meets the needs of both their low- and their high-ability students. As noted previously, when teachers fail to create an appropriate learning environment for the gifted students in their classrooms, the social and emotional development of those students may suffer.

Grouping gifted students together for instruction can make it easier for teachers to provide an appropriately challenging learning environment, especially if some within class differentiation is provided to address different learning styles, interests, ability profiles, and levels of motivation (Feldhusen & Moon, 1992; Kulik, 2003). However, homogeneous grouping sometimes has the negative effect of lowering self-concept, at least temporarily (Marsh, Chessor, Craven, & Roche, 1995; Vaughn, Feldhusen, & Asher, 1991). In a study examining middle and high school student perceptions of homogeneous and heterogeneous grouping, the gifted students in the study perceived each grouping method to have different strengths and weaknesses with respect to social and emotional adjustment (Adams-Byers, Whitsell, & Moon, 2004). Homogeneous grouping had the advantage of decreasing teasing and increasing peer understanding; it also had few disadvantages for most students. Students were split in their opinions about the social and emotional impact of heterogeneous grouping. Some saw no advantages to this grouping strategy. Others perceived prosocial advantages like being able to help others or having a greater diversity of friends. The primary disadvantage of heterogeneous grouping for these students was peer teasing and abuse. The findings of this study suggest that the social and emotional effects of different grouping arrangements are complex and individualized.

Teachers need to be aware that the same classroom may have a positive impact on one student's social and emotional growth and a negative impact on another student. For example, a study of a self-contained fifth-grade classroom for gifted students found that the class had a very positive effect on the social and emotional development of one highly gifted student who had exhibited behavior problems in his previous, undifferentiated, regular classroom environment; a moderately positive effect on most of the students in the class; and a negative impact on one student who entered the classroom with a hidden disability (Moon et al., 2002). The latter student functioned well in the classroom the following year, after her disability was identified and appropriate accommodations were made. Hence, teachers must constantly monitor the social and emotional impact of their classroom environments with respect to each individual student in the class and take steps to ameliorate any negative effects they notice.

Instructional Strategies That Promote Personal and Social Talent. In addition to creating classrooms that have appropriate amounts of choice, challenge, interest, and enjoyment for all students, teachers can use instructional strategies that provide indirect support for the personal and social development of gifted students. In general, instructional strategies that are learner centered, where the teacher acts as a facilitator of learning, are most effective in building personal and social talent. Examples of such strategies include problem-based learning in a social studies class (Gallagher, 1997), a model eliciting activity in a math class (Chamberlin & Moon, 2005; Lesh & Doerr, 2003; Lesh, Hoover, Kelly, & Post, 2000), or an inquiry-based unit in a science class (Reger, 2006). Students who are involved in these types of instructional activities have opportunities to make choices, collaborate with their peers, and self-regulate their behavior (Moon & Ray, 2006).

Another instructional strategy that can be an effective, indirect stimulus to personal growth is independent study (Moon, 2003a). Many of the recommended programming models in gifted education encourage involving gifted students in substantial, long-term, independent projects (Betts & Kercher, 1999; Feldhusen & Kolloff, 1978; Kolloff & Feldhusen, 1981; Moon, 1993; Reis & Renzulli, 1989; Renzulli & Reis, 1997). Independent study helps build self-awareness because students must select projects based on their abilities and interests. Independent work builds self-regulation because students must develop an action plan for their project, implement their plan, monitor their progress, share their results, and self-evaluate their work. Independent study is one of the best instructional vehicles available for building skills in self-regulation. If students work in teams on their independent projects, as is common in the sciences and engineering, independent projects can also build social skills, such as teamwork, conflict management, and communication skills. Some direct instruction may be needed when students are working on independent projects to scaffold independent learning skills. For example, high school students being prepared to design and carry out a scientific investigation may need direct instruction on how to conduct a review of the scientific literature related to their research question, use specific laboratory equipment safely, or develop a poster presentation of their findings (Whitman & Moon, 1993).

Other experiential learning activities that can promote social and emotional development in gifted students include service learning (Terry, 2003) and simulations (Sisk, 2005). All these types of activities require the teacher to function as a facilitator of learning rather than as an expert dispensing knowledge of a subject. Some of them require relatively large amounts of instructional time. All engage students in active learning experiences that can enhance the learning of more traditional subject-matter content while building personal and social competencies.

Direct Instructional Strategies

Experiential learning activities develop personal and social competence by activating student emotions, encouraging social interactions, and facilitating self-direction. They represent an implicit approach to social and emotional skill development. Direct instructional strategies, on the other hand, provide explicit instruction in specific personal, social, or emotional skills. Since most teachers do not have extensive training in the teaching of these skills, developed curricula can provide helpful guidance. The best of such curricula teach skills in the context of a specific theory of social and emotional development. Three examples of such curricula are discussed here.

The Curriculum of Identity. The Parallel Curriculum Model is a theoretically based model for designing curricula to develop high potential and challenge high-ability learners (Tomlinson et al., 2002). The model includes four parallel approaches to curriculum development. Three of these are academic in nature and so won't be discussed here. The fourth, the curriculum of identity, is affective. This strand of the Parallel Curriculum Model suggests that all curricula for gifted and talented students should integrate activities that help students build skills such as introspection, a personal compass for decision making, self-affirmation, courage, and wisdom. The strand is "responsive to learner variance" (Tomlinson et al., 2002; p. 233) on two levels. First, it expects that different learners will have different needs and learning profiles with respect to each discipline of study and that teachers will explicitly address these differences. Second, it encourages learners to monitor changes in learning goals and interests over time. The curriculum of identity is particularly helpful in developing the self-awareness component of personal talent and in assisting learners to determine their degree of fit with the disciplines that organize human knowledge.

Teaching for Successful Intelligence. Another example of direct instruction in personal skills comes from the work of Sternberg and his colleagues on developing successful intelligence (Sternberg, 1996; Sternberg & Grigorenko, 2000, 2003). *Successful intelligence* is the ability to be successful in a particular sociocultural context. Successful intelligence includes the following components: (a) recognition of personal strengths and the ability to make the most of them, (b) recognition of personal weaknesses and the ability to compensate for them, and (c) the ability to adapt to, shape, and select environments to accomplish specific goals, which involves analytic, creative, and practical thinking. Sternberg and Grigorenko (2000) developed a series of lessons based on this theory. The lessons are divided into three types: teaching for analytic thinking, teaching for creative thinking, and teaching for practical thinking. The first two are more cognitive and are similar to the types of indirect, experiential activities discussed previously. The practical thinking section of this curriculum is more affective. It focuses on development of the skills needed to accomplish personal goals, such as impulse control, perseverance, planning, priority setting, and development of self-confidence. Each lesson focuses on one target skill and includes brief ideas for ways that skill might be developed in eight subject areas. For example, the lesson on setting priorities focuses on the target skill of keeping the goal in view rather than getting bogged down in small details. To build this skill, social studies teachers can remind students that understanding past events can help them understand current ones, and science teachers help students understand that a good grasp of physics will help them design a fast race car when they enter an engineering competition.

Emotional Intelligence Curriculum. Mayer and Salovey and their colleagues have developed a theoretically sound and empirically validated theory of emotional intelligence (Mayer, Perkins, Caruso, & Salovey, 2001; Mayer & Salovey, 1997; Salovey & Mayer, 1990; Salovey, Mayer, & Caruso, 2002). In their theoretical framework, emotional intelligence involves four, hierarchical levels of skills. VanTassel-Baska (2006) has developed sample lessons for secondary students at each skill level. Each lesson teaches secondary gifted students about emotions and assists them in developing emotional skills. For example, students who are currently functioning on the lowest level of the emotional intelligence hierarchy learn how to perceive, appraise, and express emotions through activities such as analyzing their feelings as they respond to art, music, poetry, or video clips of human interactions and expressing their feelings through a variety of media. Lessons for the second and third levels of the emotional intelligence hierarchy involve students in activities such as explaining how emotions can affect perceptions of problems like terrorism or analyzing and evaluating the emotional content of fiction. At the highest level of the emotional intelligence hierarchy, individuals develop expertise in regulating emotions in themselves and others (Mayer & Salovey, 1997). To develop this skill in gifted students, VanTassel-Baska (2006) suggests discussing moral dilemmas or role-playing conflict mediation scenarios with a focus on monitoring, analyzing, and regulating the emotions that arise.

Such a curriculum would be particularly helpful to gifted students who have high levels of emotional sensitivity and intensity (Ackerman, 1997; Kuhl & Kraska, 1989; Mendaglio, 2003; Piechowski, 1997; Piechowski & Cunningham, 1985; Piechowski, Silverman, & Falk, 1985). A curriculum designed to develop emotional skills could help them turn a potential weakness (overreactions to situations) into a strength (expertise in understanding, communicating, regulating, and utilizing emotions to solve human or artistic problems). Although this curriculum is called an emotional intelligence curriculum, it builds social skills as well as emotional ones.

Counseling Interventions

Direct and indirect instructional strategies are helpful in preventing social and emotional adjustment difficulties, facilitating holistic development, and developing personal and social talents in gifted students. Counseling strategies are helpful in addressing the social and emotional issues that can arise for gifted students because of endogenous, exogenous, or interactive forces. School counselors can provide many useful services to gifted students and their families. For example, group counseling with gifted students at the middle school level can help students resolve achievement–affiliation conflicts in positive ways that allow them to be fully themselves while building supportive peer relationships (Colangelo & Peterson, 1993; Peterson, 1993, 1995). School counselors are also trained to assist students with transitions, such as the transition into a more challenging educational environment (Peterson, 2006). Psychoeducational parent support groups led by school counselors can assist the holistic development of young gifted children (Webb & DeVries, 1993). Group or individual career counseling at the upper elementary or middle school levels can help gifted students develop strong identities, make sound course selections in high school, and develop an appropriate postsecondary education plan (Greene, 2002; Hébert & Kelly, 2006).

Bibliotherapy (reading and discussion of novels) and videotherapy (viewing and discussion of films) are useful additions to all types of group counseling with gifted students and their parents. These techniques have been recommended for assisting gifted students with typical affective issues facing gifted students (Milne & Reis, 2000) and for addressing more specific problems, such as math anxiety (Hébert & Furner, 1997). Both strategies involve gifted students in guided discussions of books or movies that deal with themes that are salient in their lives. For example, Hébert provided suggestions for books that can help gifted males address the following common issues: image management/search for self-identity, self-inflicted pressure, being labeled different, male bonding, feeling alone within one's culture, and gender role conflicts. Milne and Reis provided suggestions for films that could be used to address the issues of subpopulations of gifted students such as those with disabilities, African Americans, females, and students with talents in the performing arts. Counselors are trained to lead emotionally charged discussions so that they are in an ideal position to implement bibliotherapy or videotherapy with groups of gifted students. However, teachers who are skilled in creating a safe environment for many of the issues discussed here can use bibliotherapy or videotherapy in their classrooms, especially the curriculum of identity. Both bibliotherapy and videotherapy encourage gifted students to identify intensely with story characters; this identification, coupled with skilled guided discussions, can lead them to new insights about themselves and their classmates. Bibliotherapy is likely to be especially effective with verbally talented students who love literature. Videotherapy is useful with learning-disabled students who have difficulty reading. Both techniques require careful prescreening of materials to be sure that the content, presentation, and language are suitable for the age and experience of the students who will be reading and discussing the materials.

Gifted students with affective disorders such as depression or a conduct disorder can benefit from one-on-one counseling with school counselors or community counselors. Similarly, underachieving and twice-exceptional gifted students may benefit from individual sessions with a school counselor, support groups, and family therapy designed to help the family understand and support the twice-exceptional child (Moon & Hall, 1998). Such counseling will be more effective if the counselors involved have training in working with gifted students and their families. Many school counselors do not have training in the unique developmental concerns and counseling issues related to high-ability youth. According to an unpublished 2005 study of university-based school counseling programs conducted at Purdue University, preparatory curricula for school counselors provides very little emphasis on working with gifted and talented students (Peterson, 2006). In fact, only 65% of the programs surveyed gave any attention to giftedness at all, with most of those devoting 3 or fewer contact hours. The Counseling and Guidance Division of the National Association for Gifted Children is currently working with the Council for the Accreditation of Counseling and Related Educational Programs to improve this situation by including affective concerns of gifted youth in accreditation standards for school counseling programs (J. S. Peterson, personal communication, June 22, 2006).

SUMMARY AND CONCLUSIONS

In the first section of this chapter, optimal personal and social development was explored by looking at the developmental tasks gifted youth must accomplish across the years from kindergarten through twelfth grade and by describing the characteristics of gifted youth with high levels of personal and social talent. The purpose of this section was to convey a clear picture of what optimal personal and social development looks like in gifted youth.

In the second section, ways in which giftedness can create special challenges for K–12 students were discussed. Some of the challenges were internal, or *endogenous*. For example, maladaptive perfectionism creates internal challenges to personal development in gifted students. Other challenges can stem from the environment. These challenges were called *exogenous*. Examples of exogenous challenges included bullying by peers and inappropriate school placements. Finally, three interactive issues were discussed: gender, ethnicity, and underachievement. Interactive issues are ones where internal characteristics of individual students interact with the characteristics of their environments to create special developmental challenges. The purpose of this section was to build understanding of the special social and emotional challenges gifted students can experience and provide ideas for how teachers can assist students who are facing particular challenges.

The final section of the chapter focused on nurturing social and emotional development in gifted students through indirect instructional strategies, affective curriculum, and counseling. Indirect instructional strategies are learner-centered, experiential learning strategies that can be integrated into any content area. Examples include problem-based learning, independent study, service learning, and simulations. Affective curriculum provides more direct instruction in specific affective skills, such as regulating emotions, mediating conflicts, or setting priorities. Counseling strategies include group counseling, support groups, individual counseling, and family counseling. Preventive counseling strategies, such as support groups, can be helpful in promoting optimal social and emotional development in all gifted students. Counseling intervention is highly recommended for gifted youth with more serious adjustment difficulties.

QUESTIONS FOR THOUGHT AND REFLECTION

1. What are the developmental tasks that gifted students need to accomplish by the end of high school? What factors assist and impede them in accomplishing these tasks?
2. How do individual differences such as gender, ethnicity, and disabilities affect social and emotional development of gifted youth?
3. Describe three strategies you plan to use to promote optimal *personal* development in the gifted students you teach. Describe three strategies you plan to use to promote optimal *social* development. Compare the strategies with each other.
4. Pretend you are the superintendent of a rural school district. You have the opportunity to apply for a grant to implement a counseling program for the gifted students in your district. What kind of program would you design? What type of counseling would you provide? What grade levels and students would you serve? Give reasons for your choices.

RESOURCES

Websites

The Collaborative for Academic, Social, and Emotional Learning (CASEL)

www.casel.org

Devoted to promoting social and emotional learning for all students. Although this site does not specifically address gifted issues, it does have classroom materials designed to develop social and emotional skills.

The National Association for Gifted Children (NAGC)

www.nagc.org

The primary national organization devoted to gifted and talented children. The organization's Web site has social and emotional resources for parents and educators.

Supporting the Emotional Needs of the Gifted (SENG)

www.sengifted.org

A national organization devoted to the social and emotional development of gifted students. Provides information about publications and the organization's annual conference.

BOOKS

Cross, T. L. (2004). *On the social and emotional lives of gifted children: Issues and factors in their psychological development* (2nd ed.). Waco, TX: Prufrock.
This book is a compilation of columns originally written for *Gifted Child Today* magazine on social and

emotional issues. It provides helpful guidance for parents and teachers.

Ford, D. Y. (1996). *Reversing underachievement among gifted black students: Promising programs and practices.* New York: Teachers College Press. An excellent resource for teachers in diverse communities, this volume discusses social, cultural, and psychological factors that are related to underachievement in black youth.

Moon, S. M. (Ed.). (2004). *Social/emotional issues, underachievement, and counseling of gifted and talented students.* Thousand Oaks, CA: Corwin. A useful supplementary textbook for courses on social and emotional development, this book compiles in one volume the most influential research on giftedness published in *Gifted Child Quarterly.*

Neihart, M., Reis, S. M., Robinson, N. M., & Moon, S. M. (2002). *The social and emotional development of gifted children: What do we know?* Waco, TX: Prufrock. A standard textbook for graduate classes on the social and emotional development of gifted students, this book provides an easy-to-read summary of research on the social and emotional development of gifted children.

Rimm, S. (2003). *See Jane win for girls: A smart girl's guide to success.* Minneapolis: Free Spirit. A self-help book for gifted girls based on Dr. Rimm's study of 1,000 successful women.

REFERENCES

Ackerman, C. M. (1997). Identifying gifted adolescents using personality characteristics: Dabrowski's overexcitabilities. *Roeper Review, 19,* 229–236.

Adams-Byers, J., Whitsell, S. S., & Moon, S. M. (2004). Gifted students' perceptions of the academic and social/emotional effects of homogeneous and heterogeneous grouping. *Gifted Child Quarterly, 48,* 7–20.

Adderholdt-Elliot, M. (1987). *Perfectionism: What's bad about being too good?* Minneapolis: Free Spirit.

Arnold, K. D. (1995). *Lives of promise: What becomes of high school valedictorians? A 14-year study of achievement and life choices.* San Francisco: Jossey-Bass.

Bandura, A. (1986). *Social foundations of thought and action: A social cognitive theory.* Englewood Cliffs, NJ: Prentice Hall.

Baum, S. M. (1995). Reversing underachievement: Creative productivity as a systematic intervention. *Gifted Child Quarterly, 39,* 224–235.

Betts, G., & Kercher, J. (1999). *Autonomous learner model: Optimizing ability.* Greeley, CO: ALPS.

Chamberlin, S. A., & Moon, S. M. (2005). Model-eliciting activities as a tool to develop and identify creatively gifted mathematicians. *Journal for Secondary Gifted Education, 17,* 37–47.

Clasen, D. R., & Clasen, R. E. (1995). Underachievement of highly able students and the peer society. *Gifted and Talented International, 10,* 67–76.

Colangelo, N., & Peterson, J. S. (1993). Group counseling with gifted students. In L. K. Silverman (Ed.), *Counseling the gifted and talented* (pp. 111–129). Denver: Love.

Coleman, J. M., & Fults, B. (1982). Self-concept and the gifted classroom: The role of social comparisons. *Gifted Child Quarterly, 26,* 116–119.

Coleman, J. M., & Fults, B. A. (1985). Special-class placement, level of intelligence, and the self-concepts of gifted children: A social comparison perspective. *Remedial and Special Education, 6,* 7–11.

Cooley, D., Chauvin, J., & Karnes, F. (1984). Gifted females: A comparison of attitudes by male and female teachers. *Roeper Review, 6,* 164–167.

Cross, T. L., Coleman, L. J., & Terhaar-Yonkers, M. (1991). The social cognition of gifted adolescents in schools: Managing the stigma of giftedness. *Journal for the Education of the Gifted, 15,* 44–55.

Csikszentmihalyi, M. (1996). *Creativity: Flow and the psychology of discovery and invention.* New York: HarperCollins.

Csikszentmihalyi, M., Rathunde, K., & Whalen, S. (1993). *Talented teenagers.* New York: Cambridge University Press.

Dauber, S. L., & Benbow, C. P. (1990). Aspects of personality and peer relations of extremely talented adolescents. *Gifted Child Quarterly, 34,* 10–15.

Dixon, F. A., Lapsley, D. K., & Hanchon, T. A. (2004). An empirical typology of perfectionism in gifted adolescents. *Gifted Child Quarterly, 48,* 95–106.

Feldhusen, J. F., & Kolloff, M. B. (1978, September/October). A three-stage model for gifted education. *Gifted Child Today, 1,* 39–50.

Feldhusen, J. F., & Moon, S. M. (1992). Grouping gifted students: Issues and concerns. *Gifted Child Quarterly, 36,* 63–67.

Fennema, E., Peterson, P. L., Carpenter, T. P., & Lubinski, C. A. (1990). Teachers' attributions and beliefs about girls, boys, and mathematics. *Educational Studies in Mathematics, 21,* 55–69.

Ford, D. Y. (1996). *Reversing underachievement among gifted black students: Promising practices and programs.* New York: Teachers College Press.

Ford, D. Y. (2003). Equity and excellence: Culturally diverse students in gifted education. In N. Colangelo & G. A. Davis (Eds.), *Handbook of gifted education* (pp. 506–520). Boston: Allyn & Bacon.

Ford, D. Y., Grantham, T. C., & Harris, J. J. (1996). Multicultural gifted education: A wake up call to the profession. *Roeper Review, 19,* 72–78.

Ford, D. Y., & Moore, J. L. (2006). Being gifted and adolescent: Issues and needs of students of color. In F. A. Dixon & S. M. Moon (Eds.), *The handbook of secondary gifted education* (pp. 113–136). Waco, TX: Prufrock.

Ford, D. Y., & Trotman, M. F. (2001). Teachers of gifted students: Suggested multicultural characteristics and competencies. *Roeper Review, 23,* 235–239.

Frey, J., & Wendorf, D. J. (1985). Families of gifted children. In L. L'Abate (Ed.), *Handbook of family psychology and therapy* (Vol. 2, pp. 781–809). Homewood, IL: Dorsey.

Gallagher, S. A. (1997). Problem-based learning: Where did it come from, what does it do, and where is it going. *Journal for the Education of the Gifted, 20,* 332–362.

Gentry, M., Gable, R. K., & Springer, P. (2000). Gifted and nongifted middle school students: Are their attitudes toward school different as measured by the new affective instrument, My Class Activities . . . *Journal for the Education of the Gifted, 24,* 74–95.

Gentry, M., Rizza, M. G., & Gable, R. K. (2001). Gifted students' perceptions of their class activities: Differences among rural, urban, and suburban student attitudes. *Gifted Child Quarterly, 45,* 115–129.

Grantham, T. C. (2003). Increasing black student enrollment in gifted programs: An exploration of the Pulaski Country Special School District's advocacy efforts. *Gifted Child Quarterly, 47,* 44–65.

Greene, M. J. (2002). Career counseling for gifted and talented students. In M. Neihart, S. M. Reis, N. M. Robinson, & S. M. Moon (Eds.), *The social and emotional development of gifted children: What do we know?* (pp. 223–236). Waco, TX: Prufrock.

Gross, M. (1993). *Exceptionally gifted children.* London: Routledge.

Gross, M. (2000, May). *From "play partner" to "sure shelter": How do conceptions of friendship differ between average-ability, moderately gifted, and highly gifted children?* Paper presented at the fifth biennial Henry B. and Jocelyn National Wallace Research Symposium on Talent Development, Iowa City, IA.

Gross, M. (2002). Social and emotional issues for exceptionally intellectually gifted students. In M. Neihart, S. M. Reis, N. M. Robinson, & S. M. Moon (Eds.), *The social and emotional development of gifted children: What do we know?* (pp. 19–29). Waco, TX: Prufrock.

Gross, M. (2004). *Exceptionally gifted children* (2nd ed.). London: Routledge Falmer.

Hébert, T. P. (2000a). Defining belief in self: Intelligent young men in an urban high school. *Gifted Child Quarterly, 44,* 91–114.

Hébert, T. P. (2000b). Gifted males pursuing careers in elementary education: Factors that influence a belief in self. *Journal for the Education of the Gifted, 24,* 7–45.

Hébert, T. P. (2001). "If I had a new notebook, I know things would change": Bright underachieving young men in urban classrooms. *Gifted Child Quarterly, 45,* 174–194.

Hébert, T. P. (2002a). Educating gifted children from low socioeconomic backgrounds: Creating visions of a hopeful future. *Exceptionality, 10,* 127–138.

Hébert, T. P. (2002b). Gifted males. In M. Neihart, S. M. Reis, N. M. Robinson, & S. M. Moon (Eds.), *The social and emotional development of gifted children: What do we know?* (pp. 137–144). Waco, TX: Prufrock.

Hébert, T. P., & Beardsley, T. M. (2001). Jermaine: A critical case study of a gifted black child living in rural poverty. *Gifted Child Quarterly, 45,* 85–103.

Hébert, T. P., & Furner, J. M. (1997). Helping high ability students overcome math anxiety through bibliotherapy. *Journal of Secondary Gifted Education, 8,* 164–178.

Hébert, T. P., & Kelly, K. R. (2006). Identity and career development in gifted students. In F. A. Dixon & S. M. Moon (Eds.), *The handbook of secondary gifted education* (pp. 35–64). Waco, TX: Prufrock.

Hoge, R. D., & Renzulli, J. S. (1993). Exploring the link between giftedness and self-concept. *Review of Educational Research, 63,* 449–465.

Kaiser, C. F., & Berndt, D. J. (1985). Predictors of loneliness in the gifted adolescent. *Gifted Child Quarterly, 29,* 74–77.

Kennedy, D. M. (1995). Glimpses of a highly gifted child in a heterogeneous classroom. *Roeper Review, 17,* 164–168.

Kolloff, M. B., & Feldhusen, J. F. (1981, May/June). PACE (Program for Academic and Creative Enrichment): An application of the Purdue Three-Stage Model. *Gifted Child Today, 5,* 47–50.

Kramer, L. R. (1985, April). *Social interaction and perceptions of ability: A study of gifted, adolescent females.* Paper presented at the annual meeting of the American Educational Research Association, Chicago.

Kuhl, J., & Kraska, K. (1989). Self-regulation and metamotivation: Computational mechanisms, development, and assessment. In R. Kanfer, P. L. Ackerman, & R. Cudeck (Eds.), *Abilities, motivation, and methodology: The Minnesota Symposium on individual differences* (pp. 343–374). Hillsdale, NJ: Lawrence Erlbaum Associates.

Kulik, J. A. (2003). Grouping and tracking. In N. Colangelo & G. A. Davis (Eds.), *Handbook of gifted education* (pp. 268–281). Boston: Allyn & Bacon.

Lesh, R., & Doerr, H. (2003). *Beyond constructivism: Models and modeling perspective on mathematics problem solving, learning, and teaching.* Mahwah, NJ: Lawrence Erlbaum Associates.

Lesh, R., Hoover, M., Kelly, A., & Post, T. (2000). Principles for developing thought-revealing activities for students and teachers. In A. Kelly & R. Lesh (Eds.), *The handbook of research design in mathematics and science education* (pp. 591–646). Mahwah, NJ: Lawrence Erlbaum Associates.

Marsh, H. W., Chessor, D., Craven, R., & Roche, L. (1995). The effects of gifted and talented programs on academic self-concept: The big fish strikes again. *American Educational Research Journal, 32,* 285–319.

Mayer, J. D., Perkins, D. M., Caruso, D. R., & Salovey, P. (2001). Emotional intelligence and giftedness. *Roeper Review, 23,* 131–137.

Mayer, J. D., & Salovey, P. (1997). What is emotional intelligence? In P. Salovey & D. Sluyter (Eds.), *Emotional development and emotional intelligence: Educational implications* (pp. 3–31). New York: Basic Books.

Mendaglio, S. (2003). Heightened multifaceted sensitivity of gifted students: Implications for counseling. *Journal for Secondary Gifted Education, 14,* 72–82.

Midgley, C., & Edelin, K. C. (1998). Middle school reform and early adolescent well-being: The good news and the bad. *Educational Psychologist, 33,* 195–206.

Milne, H. J., & Reis, S. M. (2000). Using videotherapy to address the social and emotional needs of gifted children. *Gifted Child Today, 23,* 24–29.

Moon, S. M. (1993, Winter). Using the Purdue Three-Stage Model: Developing talent at the secondary level. *Journal of Secondary Gifted Education, 5,* 31–35.

Moon, S. M. (2002). Gifted children with attention-deficit/hyperactivity disorder. In M. Neihart, S. M. Reis, N. M. Robinson, & S. M. Moon (Eds.), *The social and emotional development of gifted children: What do we know?* (pp. 193–201). Waco, TX: Prufrock.

Moon, S. M. (2003a). Developing personal talent. In F. J. Mönks & H. Wagner (Eds.), *Development of human potential: Investment into our future. Proceedings of the 8th conference of the European Council for High Ability (ECHA)* (pp. 11–21). Bad Honnef, Germany: Bock.

Moon, S. M. (2003b). Personal talent. *High Ability Studies, 14,* 5–21.

Moon, S. M., & Dixon, F. A. (2006). Conceptions of giftedness in adolescence. In F. A. Dixon & S. M. Moon (Eds.), *The handbook of secondary gifted education* (pp. 7–33). Waco, TX: Prufrock.

Moon, S. M., & Hall, A. S. (1998). Family therapy with intellectually and creatively gifted children. *Journal of Marital and Family Therapy, 24,* 59–80.

Moon, S. M., Jurich, J. A., & Feldhusen, J. F. (1998). Families of gifted children: Cradles of development. In R. C. Friedman & K. B. Rogers (Eds.), *Talent in context: Historical and social perspectives on giftedness* (pp. 81–99). Washington, DC: American Psychological Association.

Moon, S. M., Nelson, T. S., & Piercy, F. P. (1993). Family therapy with a highly gifted adolescent. *Journal of Family Psychotherapy, 4*(3), 1–16.

Moon, S. M., & Ray, K. (2006). Personal and social talent development. In F. A. Dixon & S. M. Moon (Eds.), *The handbook of secondary gifted education* (pp. 249–280). Waco, TX: Prufrock.

Moon, S. M., Swift, S., & Shallenberger, A. (2002). Perceptions of a self-contained class of fourth- and fifth-grade students with high to extreme levels of intellectual giftedness. *Gifted Child Quarterly, 46,* 64–79.

Moon, S. M., Zentall, S. S., Grskovic, J. A., Hall, A., & Stormont, M. (2001). Emotional and social characteristics of boys with AD/HD and giftedness: A comparative case study. *Journal for the Education of the Gifted, 24,* 207–247.

Neihart, M., Reis, S., Robinson, N., & Moon, S. M. (Eds.). (2002). *The social and emotional development of gifted children: What do we know?* Waco, TX: Prufrock.

Neumeister, K. L. S. (2004a). Factors influencing the development of perfectionism in gifted college students. *Gifted Child Quarterly, 48,* 259–274.

Neumeister, K. L. S. (2004b). Understanding the relationship between perfectionism and achievement motivation in gifted college students. *Gifted Child Quarterly, 48,* 219–231.

Ogbu, J. U. (2003). *Black American students in an affluent suburb: A study of academic disengagement.* Mahwah, NJ: Lawrence Erlbaum Associates.

Ogbu, J. U., & Simmons, H. D. (1998). Voluntary and involuntary minorities: A cultural-ecological theory of school performance with some implications for education. *Anthropology and Education Quarterly, 29,* 155–188.

Olenchak, F. R., & Reis, S. M. (2002). Gifted students with learning disabilities. In M. Neihart, S. M. Reis, N. M. Robinson, & S. M. Moon (Eds.), *The social and emotional development of gifted children* (pp. 267–289). Waco, TX: Prufrock.

Parker, W. D., & Adkins, K. K. (1995). The incidence of perfectionism in honors and regular college students. *Journal of Secondary Gifted Education, 7,* 303–309.

Parker, W. D., & Mills, C. J. (1996). The incidence of perfectionism in gifted students. *Gifted Child Quarterly, 40,* 194–199.

Peterson, J. S. (1993). *Talk with teens about self and stress: 50 guided discussions for school and counseling groups.* Minneapolis: Free Spirit.

Peterson, J. S. (1995). *Talk with teens about feelings, family, relationships, and the future: 50 guided discussions for school and counseling groups.* Minneapolis: Free Spirit.

Peterson, J. S. (2006). Superintendents, principals, and counselors. In F. A. Dixon & S. M. Moon (Eds.), *The handbook of secondary gifted education* (pp. 649–671). Waco, TX: Prufrock.

Peterson, J. S., & Colangelo, N. (1996). Gifted achievers and underachievers: A comparison of patterns found in school files. *Journal of Counseling and Development, 74,* 399–407.

Peterson, J. S., & Ray, K. E. (2006). Bullying and the gifted: Victims, perpetrators, prevalence, and effects. *Gifted Child Quarterly, 50,* 148–168.

Piechowski, M. M. (1997). Emotional giftedness: The measure of intrapersonal intelligence. In N. Colangelo & G. A. Davis (Eds.), *Handbook of gifted education* (pp. 366–381). Boston: Allyn & Bacon.

Piechowski, M. M., & Cunningham, K. (1985). Patterns of overexcitability in a group of artists. *Journal of Creative Behavior, 19*(3), 153–174.

Piechowski, M. M., Silverman, L. K., & Falk, R. F. (1985). Comparison of intellectually and artistically gifted on five dimensions of mental functioning. *Perceptual and Motor Skills, 60,* 539–545.

Reger, B. (2006). *How does participation in inquiry-based activities influence gifted students' higher order thinking?* West Lafayette, IN: Purdue University Press.

Reis, S. M. (2002). Gifted females in elementary and secondary school. In M. Neihart, S. M. Reis, N. M. Robinson, & S. M. Moon (Eds.), *The social and emotional development of gifted children: What do we know?* (pp. 125–135). Waco, TX: Prufrock.

Reis, S. M. (2006). Gender, adolescence, and giftedness. In F. A. Dixon & S. M. Moon (Eds.), *The handbook of secondary gifted education* (pp. 87–111). Waco, TX: Prufrock.

Reis, S. M., Callahan, C. M., & Goldsmith, D. (1996). Attitudes of adolescent gifted girls and boys toward education, achievement, and the future. In K. D. Arnold, K. D. Noble, & R. F. Subotnik (Eds.), *Remarkable women: Perspectives on female talent development* (pp. 209–224). Cresskill, NJ: Hampton.

Reis, S. M., Hébert, T. P., Díaz, E. I., Maxfield, L. R., & Ratley, M. E. (1995). *Case studies of talented students who achieve and underachieve in an urban high school.* Storrs, CT: National Research Center on the Gifted and Talented, University of Connecticut.

Reis, S. M., & McCoach, D. B. (2000). The underachievement of gifted students: What do we know and where do we go? *Gifted Child Quarterly, 44,* 152–170.

Reis, S. M., & Renzulli, J. S. (1989). The secondary triad model. *Journal for the Education of the Gifted, 13,* 55–77.

Renzulli, J. S., & Reis, S. M. (1997). *The schoolwide enrichment model: A how-to guide to educational excellence.* Mansfield Center, CT: Creative Learning.

Rimm, S. B. (2002). Peer pressures and social acceptance of gifted students. In M. Neihart, S. M. Reis, N. M. Robinson, & S. M. Moon (Eds.), *The social and emotional development of gifted children: What do we know* (pp. 13–18). Waco, TX: Prufrock.

Rimm, S. B. (2003a). *See Jane win for girls: A smart girl's guide to success.* Minneapolis: Free Spirit.

Rimm, S. B. (2003b). Underachievement: A national epidemic. In N. Colangelo & G. A. Davis (Eds.), *Handbook of gifted education* (pp. 424–443). Boston: Allyn & Bacon.

Robinson, N. M., Reis, S. M., Neihart, M., & Moon, S. M. (Eds.). (2002). *Social and emotional issues: What have we learned and what should we do now?* Waco, TX: Prufrock.

Ross, P. O. (1993). *National excellence: A case for developing America's talent.* Washington, DC: U.S. Department of Education.

Sadker, M., & Sadker, D. (1994). *Failing at fairness: How America's schools cheat girls.* New York: Charles Scribner's Sons.

Salovey, P., & Mayer, J. D. (1990). Emotional intelligence. *Imagination, Cognition, and Personality, 9,* 185–281.

Salovey, P., Mayer, J. D., & Caruso, D. R. (2002). The positive psychology of emotional intelligence. In C. R. Snyder & S. J. Lopez (Eds.), *Handbook of positive psychology* (pp. 159–171). New York: Oxford University Press.

Schneider, B. H. (1987). *The gifted child in peer group perspective.* New York: Springer-Verlag.

Schunk, D. H. (1981). Modeling and attributional effects on children's achievement: A self-efficacy analysis. *Journal of Educational Psychology, 73,* 93–105.

Siegle, D., & McCoach, D. B. (2002). Promoting positive achievement attitude with gifted and talented students. In M. Neihart, S. M. Reis, N. M. Robinson, & S. M. Moon (Eds.), *The social and emotional development of gifted children: What do we know?* (pp. 237–249). Waco, TX: Prufrock.

Sisk, D. (2005). Teaching the gifted through simulations. In F. A. Karnes & S. M. Bean (Eds.), *Methods and materials for teaching the gifted* (pp. 543–574). Waco, TX: Prufrock.

Snow, R. E. (1993). Aptitude development and talent achievement. In N. Colangelo, S. G. Assouline, & D. L. Ambroson (Eds.), *Talent development: Proceedings from the 1993 Henry B. and Jocelyn Wallace National Research Symposium on Talent Development* (pp. 101–120). Dayton, OH: Ohio Psychology.

Sowa, C. J., & May, K. M. (1997). Expanding Lazarus and Folkman's paradigm to the social and emotional adjustment of gifted children. *Gifted Child Quarterly, 41,* 36–43.

Steele, C. M. (1997). A threat in the air: How stereotypes shape the intellectual identities and performance of women and African Americans. *American Psychologist, 52,* 613–629.

Steele, C. M., & Aronson, J. (1995). Stereotype threat and the intellectual test performance of African-Americans. *Journal of Personality and Social Psychology, 69,* 797–811.

Steinberg, L. (1996). *Beyond the classroom.* New York: Simon & Schuster.

Sternberg, R. J. (1996). *Successful intelligence.* New York: Simon & Schuster.

Sternberg, R. J., & Grigorenko, E. (2000). *Teaching for successful intelligence.* Arlington Heights, IL: Skylight Professional Development.

Sternberg, R. J., & Grigorenko, E. L. (2003). Teaching for successful intelligence: Principles, procedures, and practices. *Journal for the Education of the Gifted, 27,* 207–228.

Swiatek, M. A. (1995). An empirical investigation of the social coping strategies used by gifted adolescents. *Gifted Child Quarterly, 39,* 154–161.

Terry, A. W. (2003). Effects of service learning on young, gifted adolescents and their communities. *Gifted Child Quarterly, 45,* 295–308.

Tomlinson, C. A., Kaplan, S. N., Renzulli, J. S., Purcell, J., Leppien, J., & Burns, D. E. (2002). *The parallel curriculum: A design to develop high potential and challenge high ability learners.* Thousand Oaks, CA: Corwin.

VanTassel-Baska, J. (1992). *Planning effective curriculum for gifted learners.* Denver: Love.

VanTassel-Baska, J. (1994). *Comprehensive curriculum for gifted learners* (2nd ed.). Boston: Allyn & Bacon.

VanTassel-Baska, J. (2006). Secondary affective curriculum and instruction for gifted learners. In D. N. Dixon & S. M. Moon (Eds.), *The handbook of secondary gifted education* (pp. 481–503). Waco, TX: Prufrock.

VanTassel-Baska, J., & Little, C. A. (Eds.). (2003). *Content-based curriculum for high-ability learners.* Waco, TX: Prufrock.

VanTassel-Baska, J., & Olszewski-Kubilius, P. (Eds.). (1989). *Patterns of influence on gifted learners.* New York: Teachers College Press.

Vaughn, V. L., Feldhusen, J. F., & Asher, W. J. (1991). Meta-analysis and review of research on pull-out programs in gifted education. *Gifted Child Quarterly, 35,* 92–98.

Webb, J. T., & DeVries, A. R. (1993). *Training manual for facilitators of SENG model guided discussion groups.* Dayton, OH: Ohio Psychology.

Whitman, M. W., & Moon, S. M. (1993, September/October). Bridge building: Conducting scientific research redefines the roles of teacher and student. *Gifted Child Today, 16,* 47–50.

Whitmore, J. R. (1980). *Giftedness, conflict, and underachievement.* Boston: Allyn & Bacon.

Zuccone, C. F., & Amerikaner, M. (1986). Counseling gifted underachievers: A family systems approach. *Journal of Counseling and Development, 64,* 590–592.

CHAPTER 7

CULTURALLY, LINGUISTICALLY, AND ECONOMICALLY DIVERSE GIFTED STUDENTS

Michael S. Matthews, Ph.D.
University of South Florida

Elizabeth Shaunessy, Ph.D.
University of South Florida

INTRODUCTION

From the point of view of a teacher or administrator working with potentially gifted students, addressing issues of diversity is essential. Gifted education exists for the purpose of providing appropriate enrichment and acceleration that will allow able learners to realize their full potential.

Unfortunately, discussions of diverse students often implicitly feature a deficit thinking perspective that focuses primarily on remediation of presumed weaknesses rather than on fostering the development of areas of strength. Fully examining the origins of these common beliefs would extend well beyond the scope of this chapter, encompassing multiculturalism (e.g., Gay, 2003), historical intergroup relations, and complex value judgments. As such, it is important to present some fundamental ideals on which the present chapter is based.

The following are critical in understanding gifted learners from culturally, linguistically, and economically diverse (CLED) populations:

1. There are multiple dimensions of diversity, including ethnicity, linguistics, gender, sexual orientation, and ability, though this is not an exhaustive list. This chapter provides information about recent projects and research about CLED populations as discussed in a report issued by the National Research Council (2002). Ethnic and racial groups addressed here follow the terminology utilized in this national report (i.e., Black, White, Hispanic, and Asian). These terms have been subject to criticism; efforts to provide more specific information about these populations as discussed in representative works are provided when possible in this chapter. The complexities inherent in ethnic terms are discussed in this chapter in the section titled "Conceptualizing Diversity."
2. Although there are various special populations of gifted learners, many of who have been considered in the research, each is a unique group even within the population. No two gifted learners are alike, even if they represent similar cultural, ethnic, linguistic, or socioeconomic backgrounds.
3. Giftedness is not culturally bound. It is a broad construct that may be manifested in various ways but is not defined by characteristics unique to a single culture.
4. Understanding the complexity of giftedness is an ongoing goal for the field of gifted education as well as for teachers who work with gifted learners.
5. Competent understanding of appropriate services for gifted students must include the experiences and voices of diverse groups of gifted.
6. Culturally competent educators of the gifted must strive to understand and serve these groups of learners beyond categorical group definitions.
7. Teacher preparation in gifted education should include a broad conceptualization of culture, language, ethnicity, and socioeconomic status as well as how these constructs relate to educating all students, including those who have been identified for gifted programs.
8. Policy at the national, state, and local levels should promote a broad, inclusive understanding of giftedness and encourage openness and transparency in screening and identification, including the use of multiple criteria for eligibility during the referral, screening, and individual assessment phases. While single instruments such as IQ tests can in some settings be effective for the purpose of *including* students in gifted programs, performance on a single measure should never be used to exclude a child from these opportunities.

BENEFITS OF GIFTED PROGRAM PARTICIPATION

There have been surprisingly few empirical studies in gifted education that hold up to emerging standards of evidence for best practice (Bass & Ries, 2006; see also Callahan & Plucker, 2007). Furthermore, few studies have examined gifted program effectiveness. Gifted education services vary widely with regard to important features such as level of funding, program structure, content area emphasis, and personnel preparation. Most studies have examined one particular program model or curriculum (Feng, VanTassel-Baska, Quek, Bai, & O'Neill 2005) rather than seeking to address program effectiveness questions at a regional or state level.

Additional research is needed to document the effectiveness of gifted programming, globally construed. Considering those investigations that also have made comparisons across diverse groups of gifted learners, little difference in performance has been found across cultural, linguistic, or economic minority groups in comparison with mainstream students participating in the same curricula (Borland, Schnur, & Wright, 2000; Duran and Weffer, 1992; Ford, 1998; Smith, LeRose, & Clasen, 1991).

A related body of literature has considered the affective needs of diverse students in gifted education programs (Grantham & Ford, 2003; Reis, Colbert, & Hébert, 2005). Although diverse students face unique pressures in the gifted program setting, findings also have shown that diverse gifted learners receive social and emotional benefits from participating in gifted programs. It appears that in some respects, diverse students may gain proportionally greater benefit from gifted programs than mainstream gifted students.

Benefits at the Public School Level

In an important early study, Smith and colleagues (1991) examined outcome measures among high-ability minority students randomly assigned to a gifted program or to no specialized program treatment. The authors found that long-term gifted program participation sharply reduced the dropout rate and increased the rate of college attendance for these students. Much attention in the gifted literature continues to be devoted to identification issues, but this study and others (Borland et al., 2000; Ford, 1998) suggest that retention in gifted programs is also a vital component in promoting successful outcomes for diverse gifted students.

Research with gifted students from CLED households has demonstrated that a talent development approach can increase the likelihood of these students meeting formal criteria for participation in programs for academically gifted students (Baldwin, 1994; Borland et al., 2000; Matthews, 2002; Olszewski-Kubilius Lee, Ngoi, & Ngoi, 2004). Such programs may be located within schools or offered as an extracurricular option. For example, Olszewski-Kubilius and colleagues (2004) studied students enrolled in the EXCITE enrichment program and found a 300% increase in minority children qualifying for an advanced math class after 2 years of involvement in the program.

Extracurricular educational programs also produce other tangible benefits for diverse gifted students. Duran and Weffer (1992) studied 88 academically talented Mexican American high school students participating in an extracurricular math and science enrichment program. Participation led to significantly higher ACT exam scores in those areas in comparison to college-bound seniors who did not participate in the program.

In sum, the limited evidence available does appear to show that long-term participation in gifted programs can have substantial benefits for learners from diverse populations. These positive outcomes appear to be more likely due to affective components of these programs than to academic ones (Gabelko & Sosniak, 2002; Reis et al., 2005; Swanson, 2006; Valenzuela, 1999), although the importance of appropriate academic content should not be overlooked.

Beyond Public School: Benefits in College

Recent demographic and social trends have led to an increasing demand at the university level for highly qualified minority high school graduates. Although highly able minority university students likely face many of the same roadblocks that such students face in high school (Gándara, 2005), it is also true that top universities compete fiercely to attract qualified diverse learners, chiefly by offering substantial financial aid, transitional programming, and other forms of support (e.g., Emerson, 2006). Because of such competition, if public schools can help traditionally underrepresented students to prosper, attain high achievement in appropriately advanced course work (Borman, Stringfield, & Rachuba, 2000), and receive informed college counseling, such students should be able to attract sufficient financial support to complete a university education at the school of their choice (Emerson, 2006).

CONCEPTUALIZING DIVERSITY

For the purposes of this chapter, focus is given primarily to three broad dimensions of diversity. These dimensions incorporate cultural, linguistic, and economic components. Although these certainly are not the only forms diversity may take, together these three elements subsume a majority of the variation that is conspicuously absent from most K–12 gifted educational settings.

Much of the research on diversity issues in education has been limited to the categories used by the U.S.

Census Bureau (2000) and other government sources (e.g., Florida Department of Education, 2004; Georgia Department of Education, 2004, 2006). However, as the alert reader may recognize, these traditional categories are extremely broad. Although available categories were greatly expanded at the time of the 2000 census (Office of Management and Budget, 1997), published studies typically still categorize students as simply Black, White, Asian, Hispanic, American Indian, or multiracial. In such a scheme, it can be impossible to disaggregate important individual differences (Artiles, Rueda, Salazar, & Higareda, 2005). For example, the designation "Black" or "African American" might include a Haitian immigrant with few financial resources and a student whose parents are doctors from Kenya in addition to the child whose ancestors have lived in the United States for seven generations. Each of these students may be gifted, and each might bring to school vastly different background experiences, worldviews, and educational needs. In large-scale educational studies, however, all these students might be grouped together into a single category.

Culture in a general sense is the term used to describe shared systems of learned behaviors that are passed along from one generation to the next. Because it is such a broad term, the term carries many nuanced meanings. For example, one may hear of "school culture" in the context of administrative leadership, of student behaviors in a particular instructional setting, or of teacher attitudes. Each of these uses would have a somewhat different meaning and may also carry different implications depending on the speaker and the context.

Research Findings About Culture and Giftedness

Underrepresentation. Research in gifted education in recent years has examined the underrepresentation of culturally and linguistically diverse groups in programs for the gifted (Shaunessy, Matthews, & Smith, 2006; Tomlinson, Ford, Reis, Briggs, & Strickland, 2004). Despite national, state, and local efforts to increase the representation of culturally and linguistically diverse youth in K–12 gifted education, Asians and White students still make up the majority of learners in these programs (Ford & Harris, 1999; National Research Council, 2002).

According to the most recent data available about the representation of diverse populations of gifted learners, African Americans made up 17% of the K–12 public school population, but only 6.6% were identified as gifted (National Research Council, 2002; U.S. Department of Education, 2001). Latino/a students were also underrepresented, as they accounted for 15% of the total school enrollment, but only 8.64% were served in gifted education. White students represented 64% of the total U.S. K–12 public school population, though they accounted for 77% of the gifted population. Like White students, Asian students are overrepresented in gifted programs in the United States; though they comprise 3% of the total school population, 6.6% were identified for gifted education. It is important to emphasize that research efforts to understand underrepresentation at the national level are affected by both the lack of a federal mandate for gifted identification and the variation in education practices and data management strategies across states (National Association for Gifted Children, 2005; National Research Council, 2002).

Figures 7–1 to 7–4 illustrate underrepresentation of gifted learners from CLED populations within one selected U.S. state. These figures include state-level data from four school districts (including two of the largest 10 school districts in the nation), serving a combined total of over 1 million K–12 learners.

Efforts to address the underrepresentation of CLED gifted learners have resulted in modifications in identification practices and increases in services for CLED children and youth (Shaunessy, Karnes, & Cobb, 2004). Despite these strides, the overall demographics of the K–12 gifted student population in the United States has remained generally the same, with White and Asian learners overrepresented and African American, Hispanic, Native American, and Pacific Islander underrepresented in these programs (National Association for Gifted

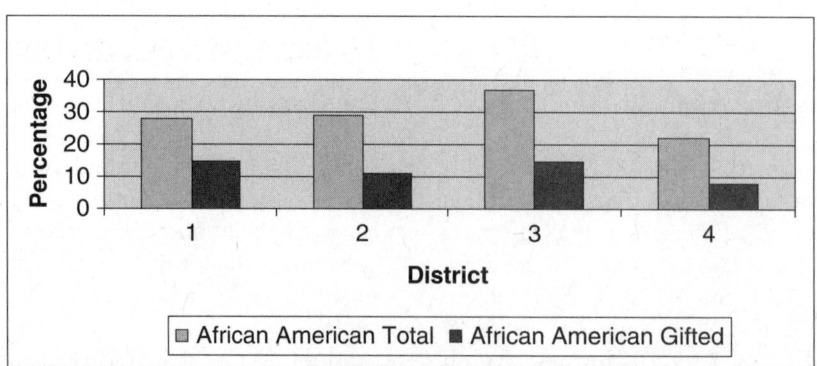

FIGURE 7–1 Percentage of K–12 African American Learners Enrolled in the Four Largest Districts in a Southeastern State

Children, 2005; National Research Council, 2002). Although less frequently considered as a unique group, students from low-income households are also underrepresented in programs for the gifted (Borland et al., 2000; Slocumb & Payne, 2000), as are learners enrolled in programs for students who are learning English (Matthews, 2006; Shaunessy et al., 2006).

Without a federal mandate to identify and serve gifted students, including those from CLED populations, the identification of these learners falls under state-level policies, which vary greatly. For example, Georgia and Florida, two states with diverse K–12 student populations, address criteria for identification in very different ways (Florida Department of Education, 2004; Georgia Department of Education, 2004, 2006). As shown in Table 7–1, Georgia's identification procedures are the same for all learners, including those from CLED populations, allowing gifted learners to be identified either through ability or achievement or by demonstrating three of four facets of giftedness. Florida's policies, however, focus on specific criteria all learners must meet in order to qualify for gifted identification under "Plan A" but also allow limited-English-proficient or low-socioeconomic status (SES) learners to qualify for services through alternate criteria known as "Plan B." At the time of this writing, Florida has drafted a proposed rule revision that

TABLE 7–1 Two States' Criteria for Identifying Mainstream and Diverse Gifted Learners

	Georgia	Florida
What is measured?	Four areas: mental ability, achievement, creativity, and motivation	Three areas: intelligence quotient (IQ), characteristics of gifted students, and need for program
How do most students qualify for gifted program services?	Psychometric approach: mental ability and achievement results only; no student may qualify on the basis of a mental ability test score alone	"Plan A" requires "an intelligence quotient of two standard deviations or more above the mean on an individually administered standardized test of intelligence"
Additional criteria designed to increase the number of diverse students who qualify for gifted program services?	Multiple-criteria approach: a student also may qualify by meeting the standards in any three of the four data categories, at least one of which must be on a nationally normed standardized test	"Plan B" currently applies only to students who are limited English proficient or who are from a low-socioeconomic-status family. Identification plans are developed by the districts and must be approved by the state department of education. Identification criteria do not require the same IQ cutoff as under Plan A, and districts may also base identification on demonstrated ability or potential in specific areas of leadership, motivation, academic performance, and creativity

Note: Georgia information adapted from *Classroom Instruction: Gifted Education* (retrieved April 30, 2006, from *http://www.doe.k12.ga.us/curriculum/instruction/gifted.asp*). Florida information adapted from *State Board of Education, Administrative Rules, Chapter 6A–6—Continued* (retrieved April 30, 2006, from *http://www.firn.edu/doe/rules/6a–63.htm*). Georgia and Florida are two of the four U.S. states having the strongest gifted education policies, as described on the website *Gifted Education Policies* (retrieved April 30, 2006, from *http://www.gt-cybersource.org/StatePolicy.aspx?NavID=4_o*).

SIDEBAR 7–1

Research Perspectives Used to Investigate Underrepresentation of Diverse Youth in Programs for the Gifted

(a) Identification (Callahan, Hunsaker, Adams, Moore, & Bland, 1995; Fernández, Gay, Lucky, & Gavilán, 1998; Frasier & Passow, 1994; Frasier et al., 1995b; Maker & Schiever, 1989; Masten, Plata, Wenglar, & Thedford, 1999; McBee, 2006; Shaunessy, Matthews, & Smith, 2006).
(b) Assessment (Ford & Harris, 1999; Ford & Trotman, 2001; Frasier et al., 1995a).
(c) Teachers' perceptions (National Research Council, 2002; Elhoweris et al., 2005; Peterson, 1999; Peterson & Margolin, 1997; Swanson, 2006).
(d) Teacher preparation (Ford & Harris, 1999; Frasier et al., 1995a; Tomlinson et al., 2004).
(e) Educational supports, including curricular modifications (Baldwin, 1994; Grantham & Ford, 2003; Hébert, 2002; Kaplan, 1999; Kitano & Espinosa, 1995; Moon & Callahan, 2001; Stormont, Stebbins, & Holliday, 2001).

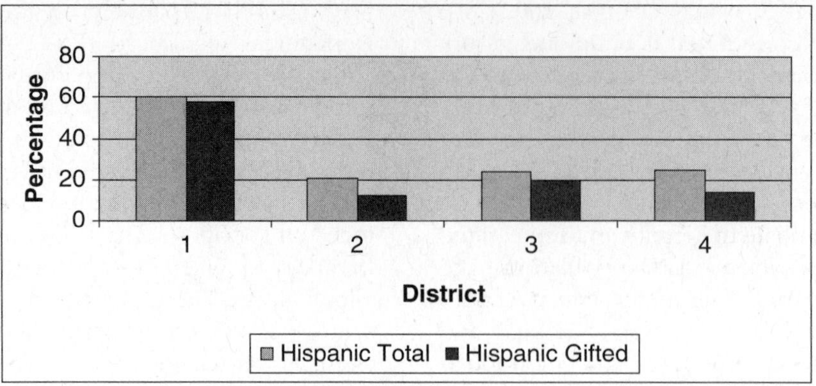

FIGURE 7–2 Percentage of K–12 Hispanic Learners Enrolled in the Four Largest Districts in a Southeastern State

would enact uniform identification criteria for all learners based in intelligence and achievement test scores. The outcome of this proposal is as yet unknown.

Groups of Diverse Learners

Investigations of specific underrepresented diverse populations of gifted and high achieving students have been undertaken and have provided much-needed information about gifted learners who are African American (Ford, 1996, 1998; Hébert, 1998), Hispanic (Bernal, 1979; Gándara, 2005; Plata, Masten, & Trusty, 1999), linguistically diverse (Fernández, Gay, Lucky, & Gavilán, 1998; Valdés, 2003), and economically diverse (Hébert, 2002; Moon & Callahan, 2001; Stormont, Stebbins, & Holliday, 2001).

African American Learners. Investigations focusing on African American students have been reported extensively in the literature in comparison to what has been written about other diverse groups of gifted learners. Figure 7–1 provides a graphic of the percentage of African American students in both the total school population and the gifted education program as reported by four large school districts from the southeastern United States.

Ford's work (1992, 1993, 1996, 1998) provides insights about underrepresentation and social and emotional needs of African American gifted learners. Grantham and Ford (2003) articulate specific strategies for educators working with gifted African American students, including multicultural counseling to foster confidence and motivation and to promote school achievement.

Hébert (1998, 2002) underscores the need for schools to provide gifted programs tailored to the unique cognitive and affective needs of individual African American learners. Recommended considerations include providing during- and after-school gifted program experiences, linking learners with communities, and supporting students' academic goal setting.

Milner (2002) also emphasizes the importance of affective considerations in working with high-achieving and gifted African American students, many of whom face social repercussions if they succeed in school. Milner echoes the recommendations of Ford (1993, 1996) and Hébert (1998, 2002), suggesting that school personnel carefully consider the pressures African American students may experience at home, in school, and in their community, presenting challenges that may lead to social exclusion for the learner if high achievement is pursued. Thus, teachers are encouraged to understand (a) how African American students may manifest their abilities and (b) the importance of providing opportunities for creative learning experiences so that gifts and talents can be identified and nurtured.

Additionally, teachers should cultivate partnerships with parents of African American gifted students, recognizing that learners may come from a variety of homes where parenting, socioeconomic characteristics, and valuing of school may vary (Milner, 2002). Teachers are encouraged to listen to the interests of their students and connect with the world in which the students live—listen to the music they like, watch the television shows they enjoy, or visit the stores in which they frequent—to better understand and relate to students' experiences and realities.

Hispanic Learners. It is important to note that the term *Hispanic* is used mostly in government documents and applies to those individuals whose heritage is based in a Spanish-speaking country; however, many of these individuals prefer either the terms *Latino/Latina* or descriptors specific to a particular heritage, such as *Mexican American.* For consistency with the majority of sources, the term *Hispanic* is used throughout this chapter.

Research about Hispanic learners in gifted education dates back to the contributions of Bernal (1979; Bernal & Reyna, 1974), a pioneer in the education of and advocacy for gifted Latino/a students. Bernal's work underscores the lack of Hispanic students identified and served in gifted education. The representation of Hispanic students from four large school districts is provided in Figure 7–2. The total district population of Hispanic learners as well as the percentage of Hispanic learners identified is illustrated.

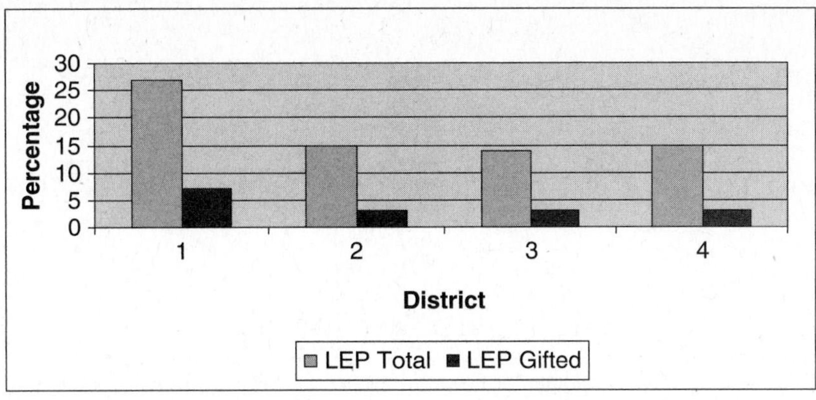

FIGURE 7–3 Percentage of K–12 Learners Eligible for LEP Services in the Four Largest Districts in a Southeastern State

Although some research has considered Hispanics together with other diverse populations, research specific to these students is gaining interest nationally (Castellano, 2004; Castellano & Díaz, 2002), especially in recent years with the rapid growth in the number of Hispanic students attending schools in the United States (U.S. Census Bureau, 2000). Teacher nominations of Hispanic students for gifted programs have been identified as a central consideration in the referral-to-identification process (Cunningham, Callahan, Plucker, Roberson, & Rapkin, 1998). Plata and colleagues (1999) investigated general education teachers' nominations of Anglo and Hispanic students for gifted programming using an early version of the *Scales for Rating the Behavior Characteristics of Superior Students* (*SRBCSS*) (Renzulli, Hartman, & Callahan, 1971). These researchers found that teachers consistently (a) rated Hispanic students lower than Anglo peers, (b) rated acculturated Hispanic learners higher than their less acculturated peers, and (c) considered Hispanic learners nominated for gifted programming to have "less potential" than their gifted-nominated Anglo peers (p. 119). In this study, the Leadership subscale score of the *SRBCSS* was found to be the strongest predictor of giftedness for both Anglo and Hispanic students when leadership was identified for the participants as a central characteristic of giftedness. These findings suggest teacher bias plays a significant role in the nomination and gifted education experience for Hispanic learners.

Peterson and Margolin (1997) also investigated teachers' perceptions of giftedness and found culture to be a critical component in teachers' nominations for gifted eligibility. Their study, set in a midwestern middle school made up of 13% Hispanic students, examined teachers' discussions about giftedness and nominations of students for gifted services. Findings indicated that in the absence of guidelines for defining giftedness, teachers were absolute in their definitions of this construct. Teachers' beliefs were found to be congruent with those beliefs held by the dominant culture. Teachers thought that giftedness was evident in assertive students who openly shared opinions with peers and teachers during class discussions. These educators also connected proficiency in English and verbal acumen with exceptional ability.

Irby and Lara-Alecio (1996) investigated perceived attributes of gifted Hispanic learners (and their Hispanic peers who came close to meeting district identification criteria) as rated by certified bilingual educators in their schools. The 61 teacher raters reported that several characteristics were observed "often," including some traits common to gifted characteristics checklists such as the *SRBCSS* (Renzulli, Smith, White, Callahan, & Hartman, 1976; Renzulli et al., 1971). These traits included (a) motivation for learning, (b) speaking multiple social and academic languages, (c) being culturally sensitive, (d) having strong familial bonds, (e) collaborating frequently, (f) using imagery in conversation, (g) achieving in school, (h) performing in creative ways, and (i) being a problem solver.

Linguistically Diverse Learners. Research about linguistically diverse children, often referred to as *limited English proficient* (LEP) or by the less deficit-oriented term *English-language learners* (ELLs), has addressed biases in the screening, referral (Fernández et al., 1998; Masten, Plata, Wenglar, & Thedford, 1999; Peterson & Margolin, 1997), and identification processes for gifted education (U.S. Department of Education, 1998). Figure 7–3 provides a graphic representation of linguistically diverse learners in four school districts. The percentage of LEP students in the total district population and in the gifted population is depicted for each district.

Research indicates that academically oriented LEP students may not have the same opportunities as their native-English-speaking peers to pursue academically rigorous options such as advanced placement program courses (U.S. Department of Education, 1998). According to the federal government, schools rarely provide LEP students with opportunities to develop higher-level thinking skills; such students often are relegated to low-level instruction. Thus, LEP students may not be afforded classroom experiences in which they might display

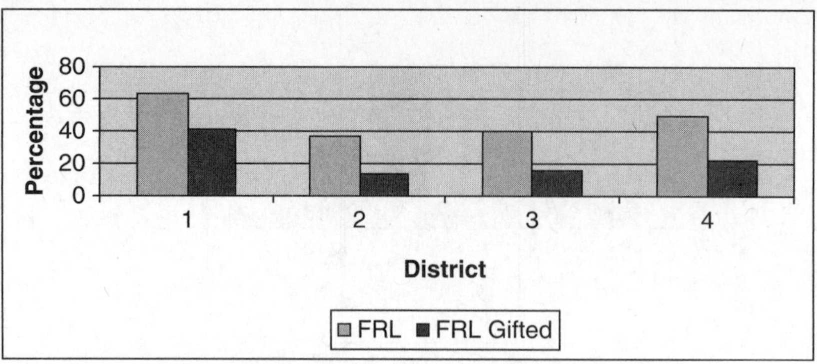

FIGURE 7–4 Percentage of K–12 Learners Eligible for Free or Reduced Lunch (FRL) Program in the Four Largest Districts in a Southeastern State

characteristics associated with giftedness, particularly if they are presented with tasks offering minimal interest, teachers with little to no training in gifted education, and schools with few resources (Losey, 1995).

Fernández et al. (1998) caution teachers and examiners to be aware of possible language-related biases during the identification process. They also note that differences in language skills may be evident between (a) Anglo gifted and general education students and (b) Latino/a LEP students who are gifted. Using a modified version of a measure of characteristics unique to gifted learners, together with items specific to Hispanic and LEP populations (adapted from Márquez, Bermúdez, & Rakow, 1992), researchers surveyed two groups of K–12 teachers who ultimately deemed curiosity to be the most important characteristic of giftedness (Fernández et al., 1998).

These researchers also found variations in participant group perceptions of characteristics of Hispanic LEP gifted. Differences based on the ethnicity of the respondent were noted; both Hispanic and African American teachers ranked two characteristics (doing well in school and preference for studying) as more important indicators of giftedness than did their White colleagues (Fernández et al., 1998). No differences in rankings of characteristics were found between native and foreign-born Hispanic teachers. This study underscored the belief that perceptions of giftedness may vary across cultures.

Economically Diverse Gifted Learners. Representation of economically diverse populations has been a concern in the field of gifted education in recent years. A review of educational practices and policies (National Association for Gifted Children, 2005) indicates that few states have specifically addressed identification of low-SES groups (often defined in practice as students enrolled in programs for free or reduced lunch) in their definitions of giftedness or in their gifted program eligibility criteria. Florida is one state that currently does provide special provisions in its definition of gifted learners and acknowledges the underrepresentation of low-SES children in gifted programs. Efforts to address this concern are evident in the additional identification criteria public school districts may use to increase the identification of low-SES learners in this state (see Table 7–1). Figure 7–4 provides a snapshot of four school districts in the same state, each district's percentage of students enrolled in a free or reduced lunch program, and the respective district's percentage of gifted learners who receive free or reduced priced lunches.

Hunsaker, Finley, and Frank (1997) examined the use of two teacher nomination instruments: the *Traits, Attitudes, and Behaviors Summary Form* (Frasier et al., 1995a) and the *SRBCSS* (Renzulli et al., 1976). Findings indicate that trained educators can successfully identify a variety of behavioral characteristics that are correlated with student success in gifted education programs. Furthermore, these nomination instruments were found to be helpful in identifying "low income and/or culturally diverse populations" (Hunsaker et al., 1997, p. 19).

Identification of gifted learners from low-income households also requires special consideration (Frasier et al., 1995b). Schools have been urged to consider the use of alternative assessments, including nonverbal measures and dynamic assessments where learners are provided learning opportunities and are evaluated for mastery of these educational tasks (Kirschenbaum, 1998; Matthews, 2002). These efforts parallel in some respects the "response to instruction" approach that is increasingly being applied within special education settings. Additionally, as with other exceptional student populations, the role of the classroom teacher in recognizing individual attributes of the learner is a key step in the eligibility determination process (Elhoweris, Mutua, Alsheikh, & Holloway, 2005). Teachers who work with gifted learners should provide opportunities for students to engage in a variety of tasks so as to showcase their talents; educators should look for unique advanced skills in a variety of domains, including performing arts, problem solving, and leadership (VanTassel-Baska, 1998).

Underachievement among gifted learners from low-income households is a specific concern noted in the literature (Stormont et al., 2001), as these children may not have access to resources afforded to children from higher socioeconomic backgrounds (VanTassel-Baska, 1998). Low-SES gifted learners may require specific forms of support from educators to compensate for this resource disparity, particularly during the critical developmental period of elementary school.

To minimize the likelihood of underachievement and to promote positive schooling experiences, Hébert (2002) recommends that educators "maintain high expectations" (p. 135), offer enrichment experiences tailored to the needs of each learner, provide opportunities for engaging extracurricular activities, and make mentors available to guide and provide support to gifted learners from low-income backgrounds. Additionally, VanTassel-Baska (1998) suggests that these learners be provided leadership development, involvement in community activities, social-emotional support, and a strengths-focused curriculum in order to develop their gifts and talents.

EXTENDING TRADITIONAL REPRESENTATIONS OF DIVERSITY

In this section, the additional dimensions of diversity that teachers should consider are examined. These include home language, country of origin, generation in the United States, immigration status, and SES. Aspects of each area that might influence academic performance are considered.

Home Language and Country of Origin

Students' home language and country of origin can provide the astute teacher with an additional source of information about a child's educational and affective needs. The degree of similarity between the home language and English may offer some indication of how rapidly the child will be able to learn English, and the teacher who is familiar with the general structure of the child's home language may be able to anticipate particular areas of grammar or usage where the child will benefit from additional explanation or scaffolding in learning English. Although rapid acquisition of English has long been considered a hallmark of the linguistically diverse gifted child (Bernal & Reyna, 1974), the evidence supporting this proposed relationship is largely anecdotal. Nevertheless, the teacher should keep this possible trait in mind in working with linguistically diverse students, as rapid acquisition of English may present an early indicator of high verbal ability.

Immigrant Status and Generation in the United States

The immigration status of a student and his or her family can have a strong influence on academic achievement (Valdés, 2003). Because children who are born in the United States automatically become U.S. citizens, it is possible for one sibling to be a legal resident even if the remainder of his or her family is not in the United States legally. Such a situation can lead to vast differences in students' potential for success, as some states have imposed punitive restrictions on higher-education access for illegal immigrants even for those students who have lived in the United States virtually their entire lives. It is not uncommon for families with limited financial resources to focus on sending some of their children to college, while other children (often the girls, although this is not always the case) may be encouraged to leave school to pursue work in support of the rest of the family.

Generation in the United States also has a demonstrated influence on academic achievement. Despite possible languages-learning issues, students who are first-generation immigrants tend to have higher academic achievement than those in subsequent generations, for reasons that are still not clearly understood (Valenzuela, 1999). Some or all of these factors may be salient when considering the experiences of culturally and linguistically diverse gifted learners.

Socioeconomic Status

Socioeconomic status is the term used to refer to "a multidimensional construct that is used to denote one's relative position and power within the social and economic hierarchy of our society" (Murdock, 2000, p. 114). Understanding SES is vital to educators; SES is a strong predictor of academic achievement, one that may imply greater cultural commonalities than other, more obvious attributes, such as gender or ethnicity (Murdock, 2000). Unfortunately, researchers in education as a whole are only beginning to consider SES as a routine concern, and although it has long been considered of importance in gifted education (e.g., Frasier, 1991; Matthews, 2002; Slocumb & Payne, 2000), the SES of research participants is rarely described in a fully satisfactory manner.

Several important components constitute SES, although often only one or two of these may be provided in published descriptions of research. Major components of SES include *parental occupation*, *household income*, and *parental education*. Household income is often represented by the child's free or reduced lunch status, as this tends to be the easiest aspect of family income to measure in the public education setting. Additional indicators of relative SES may include *family size*, *household structure*, and *residential mobility*. For students whose families are migrant farmworkers, for example, these last three characteristics may be particularly important in understanding the student's school experience.

Few states' gifted identification procedures explicitly recognize the challenges associated with finding and serving low-SES gifted learners. Complicating matters, low SES often occurs together with limited English proficiency and minority status, requiring additional specific interventions and teacher competencies to promote student success (Castellano, 2004). Table 7–1 compares identification procedures from two states that have implemented processes designed to increase the participation of gifted students from minority and low-SES backgrounds. The reader should be aware that Florida's gifted education mandate, which as of 2006 is characterized by parallel tracks having different entrance criteria for mainstream versus low-SES and English-language learners, has been the subject of repeated legal challenges that have shaped its present structure (Matthews, 2001).

BEHAVIORS OF INTEREST: RESILIENCY, ACCULTURATION, AND CODE SWITCHING

Resiliency

Resiliency describes how individuals respond to challenges, or how they maintain a positive sense of self (Rutter, 1981; Werner, 1984). Bland, Sowa, and Callahan (1994) examined giftedness and resiliency and suggested that not all gifted learners will respond positively to adversity. Reis and Díaz (1999) investigated nine high-achieving female students from an urban high school and found several protective factors that contributed to academic achievement among this population, including strong belief in self; ability to overcome situational challenges presented by the learning environment; a support network of friends, teachers, and family; enrollment in advanced course work; and participation in extracurricular experiences. Other authors outside the field of gifted education have identified similar factors among high-achieving diverse students (e.g., Valenzuela, 1999).

Acculturation and Assimilation

Acculturation is a term used to describe the transition from one's home cultural perspective to that embraced by the dominant culture. An understanding of this process is an important component in understanding the experiences of CLED children. Acculturation is recognized as an interactive process between multiple cultures or ethnic groups wherein the characteristics of both groups evolve to take on traits of the other (Banks, 2002). A more radical transition is typified in *assimilation*, where one's original ethnic or cultural characteristics are surrendered as those of another group are adopted (Gordon, 1964).

Because cultural and ethnic beliefs affect student achievement, school performance, and identification for gifted programs, teachers should be aware that their practices may be greatly influenced by their own beliefs and experiences in this area as well as by the acculturation or assimilation of students, other teachers, parents, community members, and other school personnel.

Students of color may come from homes where Standard English is not spoken or where it is not the parents' native language; these students may encounter different cultural and linguistic perspectives in the home, school, and community. Learning to adjust to the varied beliefs and expectations in each setting can be challenging for students who seek to function in multiple environments. Variation between parent and child values and perspectives can affect how learners perceive and interact with classmates, teachers, administrators, and community members. Therefore, educators are encouraged to consider these multiple perspectives and how each may affect a child. Students' adjustment to the varied expectations of the home, school, and community is a dynamic process, not simply a static trait. Teachers need to be aware of the ways in which varied degrees of adjustment with regard to culture, socioeconomics, and language may affect students' classroom performance as well as their interactions with others. The messages that teachers convey to students about the students' status in society can have a powerful influence on how learners understand their own use of language and their interactions in school and other settings (Alvarez-McHatton, Shaunessy, Hughes, Brice, & Ratliff, in press).

The role of acculturation has been considered in the identification of CLED learners for gifted programs. Peterson and Margolin (1997) examined general education teachers' understanding of giftedness and found the teachers believed English-language skills in writing and speaking to be indicators of giftedness. Among the few Latino/a students recommended for gifted education by the general education teachers, none had ever been served in programs for LEP students.

Likewise, Hispanic students in a middle school gifted education program were also described as more acculturated than their Hispanic peers not identified for gifted programs (Shaunessy, Hughes, McHatton, Brice, & Ratliff, 2005). According to Fernández et al. (1998), teachers' perceptions of acculturation may be a critical component in educators' recognition of giftedness; traditional conceptions of giftedness continue to influence the under identification of Hispanic and LEP students, and understanding of variations in how giftedness may be manifested among different CLED groups is not fully understood by teachers.

Attitudes of peers, teachers, and administrators toward CLED youth can greatly affect the success of these learners (U.S. Department of Education, 1998). As such, the eligibility process for gifted education is also greatly affected by beliefs about language, ethnicity, and culture held and communicated by teachers, administrators, and school psychologists (Fernández et al., 1998).

Teachers are encouraged to recognize the price learners may pay in becoming acculturated or assimilated. Stanton-Salazar (2004) notes that individuals may become marginalized from both family and community. As these students struggle to establish a balance between acculturation and assimilation, they may also encounter great stress and increased conflicts with parents, many of who hold different cultural and linguistic values and may not experience acculturation or assimilation to the same degree as their children.

Code Switching and Bilingualism

During the 1900s in the United States, the education system embraced a subtractive view of bilingualism; schools advocated the increase of English and a reduction of other languages spoken (Williams, Alvarez, & Hauck, 2002). The debate about how to best serve LEP or ELL students has not decreased in intensity over the years despite the increasing exposure to diversity that one may observe in K–12 schools and their surrounding communities.

Research about bilingualism has established that a second language is most successfully acquired when the learner has a "strong foundation in the mother tongue" (Spener, 1995, p. 76). Additionally, bilingualism may offer students a small cognitive advantage over monolingual learners. One study found that California students who were bilingual had a slightly higher grade-point average than their monolingual English classmates (Tse, 2001). Stanton-Salazar's (2004) work emphasizes the positive associations between bilingualism, academic achievement, and cognitive growth. Furthermore, lower dropout rates (Rumbaut, 1995) and greater social connections with adults in schools and communities (Stanton-Salazar & Dornbusch, 1995) have been reported for highly bilingual students (i.e., those with advanced proficiency in at least two languages).

Despite these findings, most schools continue to promote a deficit approach with regard to English skills rather than attempting to provide language enhancement in both the native tongue and English (Matthews & Matthews, 2004). Heritage language classes would provide enrichment and acceleration in language for gifted and high-ability students while honoring their cultural and linguistic inheritance.

RECOMMENDATIONS FOR SCREENING AND IDENTIFICATION

Although those screening and identification practices in use continue to focus primarily on grades and individual intelligence test scores, both of which favor verbal abilities, a more inclusive approach to screening and identification is essential if the goal of identifying and serving CLED children and youth is to be achieved (Frasier & Passow, 1994; Frasier et al., 1995b; Torrance, 1977). However, such new approaches must be balanced with the requirement that identification methods correspond in some fashion to the programs or services that will be provided for those who are identified.

For Teachers

As teacher nominations are a common component of the screening and identification process (McBee, 2006), educational practitioners should reflect on the implications of this process and should avail themselves of findings and recommendations from the research in this area.

Formal and ongoing professional training in the development of cultural competence is highly recommended for teachers as well as for parents, administrators, and community members. These stakeholders in the screening, identification, and service delivery process should attend to their personal and professional growth in understanding biases toward those not like themselves. Through a self-reflective and information-sharing process, individuals can allow themselves the opportunity to become more aware of various views of the world, including those of CLED children and youth (Banks, 2002; Ford & Harris, 1999).

For Schools and Districts

Procedural considerations are also critical to the screening, identification, and instruction of gifted learners from CLED populations. Although the teacher has traditionally held the keys to the gate through which students must pass to become eligible for gifted education services, schools and districts should monitor and evaluate trends in their referral and identification process to pinpoint possible areas for improvement. Parents should also be invited to share knowledge of their child's giftedness and talent as expressed in varied areas of giftedness that may include academic and intellectual ability, achievement, creativity, leadership, and performing arts. If available, the use of instruments designed specifically for these purposes is encouraged, especially when the measures' psychometric integrity has been established across multiple populations. When developing local gifted identification procedures, educators should also keep in mind the type of programs their setting will be able to offer for the learners they identify. Effective identification practices must be in alignment with program curricula, a requirement that is all too often ignored in practice.

Another strategy for screening is the use of group assessments, which often can be administered and scored by trained classroom teachers. Group screenings should be used for the identification of diverse learners, and individual learners' strengths as assessed on these group measures should be used to select appropriate individual assessments—whether nonverbal or verbal—as well as to design subsequent educational opportunities (Shaunessy & Karnes, 2004).

Individual intelligence testing seems likely to continue to be a key component of the gifted identification process; as such, psychologists are encouraged to match the strengths of the learner with the selected instrument. Psychologists and gifted program coordinators should also be aware of the ethical use of translation and of professionally translated versions of tests with students who are English-language learners. Although the *Wechsler Intelligence Scale* (Wechsler, 2003) is mentioned as one of the most commonly used identification instruments for gifted eligibility, providing both verbal and performance scores, some authorities suggest that CLED learners may be more appropriately assessed with an instrument measuring nonverbal skills exclusively, such as the *Universal Nonverbal Intelligence Test* (Bracken & McCallum, 1998). The reader should be aware that the use of nonverbal tests has been the subject of ongoing debate in the literature (e.g., Lohman, 2005), and these arguments should be examined closely before attempting to select any particular measure for use with diverse individual learners.

PROMISING PROGRAMS

Some promising programs for gifted learners from CLED populations have been identified in the literature (Tomlinson et al., 2004), as have programs that are successful in meeting the needs of general education students from specific populations (Miramontes, Nadeau, & Commins, 1997). Such programs share common features that include novel approaches to identification, collaborative efforts that focus on parent involvement, and provision of innovative curricula that are tailored to students' unique experiences and perspectives. Several such programs report positive outcomes for CLED gifted learners, at levels from pre-K to grade 12 and in varied geographic locales in the United States (Parker, 1998; Tomlinson et al., 1994). Philosophically, individualization of the curriculum and the development of student potential are central features of these promising approaches. We encourage the reader to seek further guidance from this literature and to draw on descriptions of successful gifted programs that share specific features with your location and school population.

SUMMARY AND CONCLUSIONS

Diversity may be conceptualized with regard to varied sources of observable differences that include social, cultural, linguistic, and economic factors. For the classroom teacher, competency with respect to other cultures as well as awareness of one's own culture are vital components in working successfully with diverse learners.

Gifted program participation may be even more beneficial for diverse students than it is for those from culturally and linguistically mainstream backgrounds. As when working with gifted children from mainstream backgrounds, educators should seek to individualize instruction to develop the strengths of diverse gifted learners rather than focusing exclusively on perceived areas of weakness.

The needs of gifted learners from CLED backgrounds include being understood by educators and professionals, receiving appropriate screening and identification during the process of determining eligibility for gifted services, and engaging in educational opportunities that address these students' unique cognitive and affective needs. Teachers serve a central function in each of these considerations, as they are often charged with making nominations for gifted programs, providing educational opportunities, and collaborating with other school personnel to advocate for appropriate services for these learners. The informed teacher seeks to become aware of the needs of a multitude of gifted learners, including those from CLED populations. The successful teacher of CLED youth will understand the unique strengths of each child and will advocate accordingly for each child to receive an appropriate educational experience.

QUESTIONS FOR THOUGHT AND REFLECTION

1. Who are culturally and linguistically diverse gifted learners?
2. How are CLED learners currently represented in programs for the gifted in your school, district, and state?
3. What policies in your district and state affect the identification and retention of gifted learners from CLED populations? How might these policies be improved?
4. What is the difference between assimilation and acculturation? How do you feel these should be balanced, and how has your personal experience informed your perspective?
5. How does your classroom promote multiple perspectives, even of learners and viewpoints not represented in your classroom?
6. How can your school better serve CLED youth? What specific steps would be necessary to implement this plan of action?

RESOURCES

Websites

Expanding Appropriate Assessment and Differentiated Instruction for Culturally Diverse Gifted Students

www.usm.edu/gifted/gifted_culturally_diverse.pdf

Information guide about screening, identification, and instruction of gifted learners from culturally and linguistically diverse populations, compiled by the Frances A. Karnes Center for Gifted Studies.

Hot Topics: Fostering Diversity in Gifted Education
www.nagc.org/index.aspx?id=1217
The National Association for Gifted Children offers links to related articles addressing giftedness, diversity, parenting, socioeconomics, and culture.

Linking Academic Scholars to Educational Resources
www.coedu.usf.edu/LASER
A U.S. Department of Education–supported program that provides a forum for discussions as well as multicultural resources for educators and funding for urban youth programs.

Multicultural Pavilion
www.edchange.org/multicultural
Website developed by EdChange and P. Gorski for sharing resources about multicultural education, including lesson plans, action research ideas, materials, professional development, and research.

Pew Hispanic Center
http://pewhispanic.org
Contains research about Hispanics, including education, demographics, and a searchable database with connections to research briefs and full reports.

Smithsonian
www.smithsonianeducation.org/educators/index.html
Searchable lesson plan database by grade level and selected subjects of interest, including African American, Hispanic, multicultural perspectives, and worldviews.

BOOKS

Baldwin, A., & Reis, S. A. (Eds.). (2004). *Culturally diverse and underserved populations of gifted students.* Thousand Oaks, CA: Corwin.

Castellano, J. (Ed.). (2003). *Special populations in gifted education: Working with diverse learners.* Boston: Allyn & Bacon.

Castellano, J., & Díaz, E. (2001). *Reaching new horizons: Gifted and talented education for culturally and linguistically diverse students.* Boston: Allyn & Bacon.

Ford, D. Y., & Harris, J. J. (1999). *Multicultural gifted education.* New York: Teachers College Press.

Ford, D. Y., & Milner, H. R. (2005). Teaching culturally diverse gifted students. In F. A. Karnes & K. R. Stephens (Eds.), *The practical strategies series in gifted education.* Waco, TX: Prufrock.

Matthews, M. S. (2006). *Working with gifted English language learners.* Waco, TX: Prufrock.

Nieto, S. (2004). *Affirming diversity: The sociopolitical context of multicultural education.* Boston: Allyn & Bacon.

JOURNAL ARTICLES

Baker, B. D. (2001). Living on the edges of state school-funding policies: The plight of at-risk, limited-English-proficient, and gifted children. *Educational Policy, 15,* 699–723.

Ford, D. Y., & Moore, J. L. (2004, Fall). Creating culturally responsive gifted education classrooms: Understanding "culture" is the first step. *Gifted Child Today, 27,* 34–43.

Ford, D. Y., & Trotman, M. F. (2001). Teachers of gifted students: Suggested multicultural characteristics and competencies. *Roeper Review, 23,* 235–239.

Hébert, T. P. (2002). Educating gifted children from low socioeconomic backgrounds: Creating visions of a hopeful future. *Exceptionality, 10,* 127–138.

Irby, B. J., & Lara-Alecio, R. (1996). Attributes of Hispanic gifted bilingual students as perceived by bilingual educators in Texas. *SABE Journal, 11,* 120–142.

Matthews, P. H., & Matthews, M. M. (2004). Heritage language instruction and giftedness in language minority students: Pathways toward success. *Journal of Secondary Gifted Education, 15,* 50–55.

Moon, T. R., & Callahan, C. M. (2001). Curricular modifications, family outreach, and a mentoring program: Impacts on achievement and gifted identification in high-risk primary students. *Journal for the Education of the Gifted, 24,* 305–321.

Olszewski-Kubilius, P., & Laubscher, L. (1996). The impact of a college counseling program on economically disadvantaged gifted students and their subsequent college adjustment. *Roeper Review, 18,* 202–208.

Passow, A. H., & Frasier, M. M., (1996). Toward improving identification of talent potential among minority and disadvantaged students. *Roeper Review, 18,* 198–202.

Reis, S. M., & Díaz, E. (1999). Economically disadvantaged urban female students who achieve in schools. *Urban Review, 31*(1), 31–54.

Swanson, J. D. (2006). Breaking through assumptions about low-income, minority gifted students. *Gifted Child Quarterly, 50,* 11–25.

U.S. Department of Education. (1998). *Talent and diversity: The emerging world of limited English proficient students in gifted education* (Report No. ORAD-98-1100). Washington, DC: Office of Educational Research and Improvements. (ERIC Document Reproduction Service No. ED419426)

Wright, L., & Borland, J. H. (1993). Using early childhood developmental portfolios in the identification and education of young, economically disadvantaged, potentially gifted students. *Roeper Review, 15,* 205–210.

ORGANIZATIONS

National Association for Multicultural Education
www.nameorg.org
Provides resources for teachers and resources interested in multicultural education.

National Council of La Raza
www.nclr.org/content/policy/detail/998
Addresses achievement, policy, and issues about Latino/a learners.

United Nations Educational, Scientific, and Cultural Organization
http://portal.unesco.org
Provides information on gatherings regarding gifted education.

Fight Hate and Promote Tolerance
www.tolerance.org/teach/web/power_of_words/index.jsp
A Web project of the Southern Poverty Law Center. Addresses how language is used in society; information for teachers provided.

REFERENCES

Alvarez-McHatton, P. A., Shaunessy, E., Hughes, C., Brice, A., & Ratliff, M. A. (in press). You gotta represent! Ethnic identity development among Hispanic adolescents. *Multicultural Perspectives.*

Artiles, A. J., Rueda, R., Salazar, J. J., & Higareda, I. (2005). Within-group diversity in minority disproportionate representation: English language learners in urban school districts. *Exceptional Children, 71,* 283–300.

Baldwin, A. Y. (1994). The *seven* plus story: Developing hidden talent among students in socioeconomically disadvantaged environments. *Gifted Child Quarterly, 38,* 80–84.

Banks, J. A. (2002). *An introduction to multicultural education* (3rd ed.). Boston: Allyn & Bacon.

Bass, G., & Ries, R. (2006, April 10). *What works: Clearinghouse criteria for gifted education.* Paper presented at the annual meeting of the American Educational Research Association, San Francisco.

Bernal, E. M. (1979). The education of culturally different gifted. In A. H. Passow (Ed.), *The gifted and the talented: Their education and development* (pp. 395–400). Chicago: National Society for the Study of Education.

Bernal, E. M., & Reyna, J. (1974). *Analysis of giftedness in Mexican American children and design of a prototype identification instrument.* Austin, TX: Southwest Educational Development Laboratory.

Bland, L. C., Sowa, C. J., & Callahan, C. M. (1994). An overview of resilience in gifted children. *Roeper Review, 17,* 77–80.

Borland, J. H., Schnur, R., & Wright, L. (2000). Economically disadvantaged students in a school for the academically gifted: A postpositivist inquiry into individual and family adjustment. *Gifted Child Quarterly, 44,* 13–32.

Borman, G. D., Stringfield, S., & Rachuba, L. (2000). Advancing minority high achievement: National trends and promising programs and practices [Electronic version]. New York: The College Board. Retrieved June 8, 2006, from *http://www.collegeboard.com/repository/minorityhig_3948.pdf*

Bracken, B. A., & McCallum, R. S. (1998). *Universal Nonverbal Intelligence Test.* Itasca, IL: Riverside.

Callahan, C. M., Hunsaker, S. L., Adams, C. M., Moore, S. D., & Bland, L. C. (1995). *Instruments used in the identification of gifted and talented students* (Research Monograph 95139). Storrs: National Research Center on the Gifted and Talented, University of Connecticut.

Callahan, C. M., & Plucker, J. A. (Eds.) (2007). *What the research says about . . . An encyclopedia on research in gifted education.* Waco, TX: Prufrock.

Castellano, J. A. (2004). Empowering and serving Hispanic students in gifted education. In D. Boothe & J. C. Stanley (Eds.), *In the eyes of the beholder: Critical issues for diversity in gifted education* (pp. 1–13). Waco, TX: Prufrock.

Castellano, J. A., & Díaz, E. I. (Eds.). (2002). *Reaching new horizons: Gifted and talented education for culturally and linguistically diverse students.* Boston: Allyn & Bacon.

Cunningham, C. M., Callahan, C. M., Plucker, J. A., Roberson, S. C., & Rapkin, A. (1998). Identifying Hispanic students of outstanding talent: Psychometric integrity of a peer nomination form. *Exceptional Children, 64,* 197–209.

Duran, B. J., & Weffer, R. E. (1992). Immigrants' aspirations, high school process, and academic outcomes. *American Educational Research Journal, 29,* 163–181.

Elhoweris, H., Mutua, K., Alsheikh, N., & Holloway, P. (2005). Effect of children's ethnicity on teachers' referral and recommendation decisions in gifted and talented programs. *Remedial and Special Education, 26,* 25–31.

Emerson, A. (2006, April 30). Universities' priority: Winning Cesar. *Tampa Tribune.* Retrieved May 1, 2006, from *http://www.tampatrib.com//MGB13HSRMME.html*

Feng, A. X., VanTassel-Baska, J., Quek, C., Bai, W., & O'Neill, B. (2005). A longitudinal assessment of gifted students' learning using the Integrated Curriculum Model (ICM): Impacts and perceptions of the William and Mary language arts and science curriculum. *Roeper Review, 27,* 78–83.

Fernández, A. T., Gay, L. R., Lucky, L. F., & Gavilán, M. R. (1998). Teacher perceptions of gifted Hispanic limited English proficient students. *Journal for the Education of the Gifted, 21,* 335–351.

Florida Department of Education. (2004). *Florida education and community data profiles (Series 2005-05).* Retrieved May 1, 2006, from *http://www.firn.edu/doe/eias/eiaspubs/pdf/fecdp2004.pdf*

Ford, D. Y. (1992). Determinants of underachievement as perceived by gifted, above-average, and average Black students. *Roeper Review, 14,* 130–136.

Ford, D. Y. (1993). Support for the achievement ideology and determinants of underachievement as perceived by gifted, above-average, and average Black students. *Journal for the Education of the Gifted, 16,* 280–298.

Ford, D. Y. (1996). *Reversing underachievement among gifted black students: Promising practices and programs.* New York: Teachers College Press.

Ford, D. Y. (1998). The underrepresentation of minority students in gifted education: Problems and promises in recruitment and retention. *Journal of Special Education, 32,* 4–14.

Ford, D. Y., & Harris, J. J. (1999). *Multicultural gifted education.* New York: Teachers College Press.

Ford, D. Y., & Trotman, M. F. (2001). Teachers of gifted students: Suggested multicultural characteristics and competencies. *Roeper Review, 23*, 235–239.

Frasier, M. M. (1991). Response to Kitano: The sharing of giftedness between culturally diverse and non-diverse gifted students. *Journal for the Education of the Gifted, 15*, 20–30.

Frasier, M. M., Hunsaker, S. L., Lee, J., Finley, V. S., Garcia, J. H., Martin, D., et al. (1995a). *An exploratory study of the effectiveness of the Staff Development Model and the Research-Based Assessment Plan in improving the identification of gifted economically disadvantaged students.* Storrs: National Research Center on the Gifted and Talented, University of Connecticut.

Frasier, M. M., Hunsaker, S. L., Lee, J., Mitchell, S., Cramond, B., Krisel, S., et al. (1995b). *Core attributes of giftedness: A foundation for recognizing the gifted potential of economically disadvantaged students* (RM95210). Storrs: National Research Center on the Gifted and Talented, University of Connecticut.

Frasier, M. M., & Passow, A. H. (1994). *Toward a new paradigm for identifying talent potential* (Research Monograph 9412). Storrs: National Research Center on the Gifted and Talented, University of Connecticut.

Gabelko, N. H., & Sosniak, L. A. (2002). "Someone just like me": When academic engagement trumps race, class, and gender. *Phi Delta Kappan, 83*, 400–405.

Gándara, P. (2005). *Fragile futures: Risk and vulnerability among Latino high achievers.* Princeton, NJ: Educational Testing Service.

Gay, G. (Ed.). (2003). *Becoming multicultural educators: Personal journey toward professional agency.* San Francisco: Jossey-Bass.

Georgia Department of Education. (2004). *Eligibility standards for free and reduced price meals.* Retrieved June 9, 2006, from *http://www.gadoe.org/_documents/schools/nutrition/nutrition_frp_eligibility_standards.pdf*

Georgia Department of Education. (2006). *School year enrollment 2005–2006, enrollment by gender, race/ethnicity and grade (PK–12).* Retrieved June 9, 2006, from *http://app.doe.k12.ga.us/ows-bin/owa/fte_pack_ethnicsex. display_proc*

Gordon, M. M. (1964). *Assimilation in American life: The role of race, religion, and national origins.* New York: Oxford University Press.

Grantham, T. G., & Ford, D. Y. (2003). Beyond self-concept and self-esteem: Racial identity and gifted African American students. *High School Journal, 87*, 18–29.

Hébert, T. P. (1998). Gifted Black males in an urban high school: Factors that influence achievement and underachievement. *Journal for the Education of the Gifted 21*, 385–414.

Hébert, T. P. (2002). Educating gifted children from low socioeconomic backgrounds: Creating visions of a hopeful future. *Exceptionality, 10*, 127–137.

Hunsaker, S. L., Finley, V. L. S., & Frank, E. L. (1997). An analysis of teacher nominations and student performance in gifted programs. *Gifted Child Quarterly, 41*, 19–24.

Irby, B. J., & Lara-Alecio, R. (1996). Attributes of Hispanic gifted bilingual students as perceived by bilingual educators in Texas. *SABE Journal, 11*, 120–142.

Kaplan, S. N. (1999). Teaching up to the needs of the gifted English language learner. *Tempo, 14*, 20.

Kirschenbaum, R. J. (1998). Dynamic assessment and its use with underserved gifted and talented populations. *Gifted Child Quarterly, 42*, 140–147.

Kitano, M. K., & Espinosa, R. (1995). Language diversity and giftedness: Working with gifted English language learners. *Journal for the Education of the Gifted, 18*, 234–254.

Lohman, D. F. (2005). Review of Naglieri and Ford (2003): Does the Naglieri Nonverbal Ability Test identify equal proportions of high-scoring White, Black, and Hispanic students? *Gifted Child Quarterly, 49*, 19–28.

Losey, K. M. (1995). Mexican American students and classroom interaction: An overview and critique. *Review of Educational Research, 65*, 283–318.

Maker, C. J., & Schiever, S. W. (1989). *Critical issues in gifted education: Defensible programs for cultural and ethnic minorities.* Austin, TX: PRO-ED.

Márquez, J. A., Bermúdez, A. B., & Rakow, S. J. (1992). Incorporating community perceptions in the identification of gifted and talented Hispanic students. *Journal of Educational Issues of Language Minority Students, 10*, 117–130.

Masten, W. G., Plata, M., Wenglar, K., & Thedford, J. (1999). Acculturation and teacher ratings of Hispanic and Anglo-American students. *Roeper Review, 22*, 64–65.

Matthews, M. S. (2001). *Southeastern public education responds to change in Hispanic population, 1985–2000.* Paper presented at the 82nd annual meeting of the American Educational Research Association, Seattle, WA. (ERIC Document Reproduction Service No. ED 453 305)

Matthews, M. S. (2002). Dynamic assessment of academic ability of bilingual immigrant Latino children (Doctoral dissertation, University of Georgia, 2002). *Dissertation Abstracts International, 63*, 498.

Matthews, M. S. (2006). *Working with gifted English language learners.* Waco, TX: Prufrock.

Matthews, P. H., & Matthews, M. S. (2004). Heritage language instruction and giftedness in language minority students: Pathways toward success. *Journal of Secondary Gifted Education, 15*, 50–55.

McBee, M. T. (2006). A descriptive analysis of referral sources for gifted identification screening by race and socioeconomic status. *Journal of Secondary Gifted Education, 17*, 103–111.

Milner, H. R. (2002). Affective and social issues among high achieving African American students: Recommendations for teachers and teacher education. *Action in Teacher Education, 24*, 81–89.

Miramontes, O. B., Nadeau, A., & Commins, N. L. (1997). *Restructuring schools for linguistic diversity: Linking decision making to effective programs.* New York: Teachers College Press.

Moon, T. R., & Callahan, C. M. (2001). Curricular modifications, family outreach, and a mentoring program: Impacts on achievement and gifted identification in high-risk primary students. *Journal for the Education of the Gifted, 24*, 305–321.

Murdock, T. B. (2000). Incorporating economic context into educational psychology: Methodological and conceptual challenges. *Educational Psychologist, 35,* 113–124.
National Association for Gifted Children. (2005). *State of the states 2004–2005.* Washington, DC: Author.
National Research Council. (2002). *Minority students in special and gifted education.* (M. S. Donovan & C. T. Cross, Eds.). Committee on Minority Representation in Special Education, Division of Behavioral and Social Sciences and Education. Washington, DC: National Academy Press.
Office of Management and Budget. (1997). *Revisions to the standards for the classification of federal data on race and ethnicity* (Federal Register Notice, October 30, 1997). Retrieved December 15, 2006, from *http://www.whitehouse.gov/omb/fedreg/1997standards.html*
Olszewski-Kubilius, P., Lee, S.-Y., Ngoi, M., & Ngoi, D. (2004). Addressing the achievement gap between minority and nonminority children by increasing access to gifted programs. *Journal for the Education of the Gifted, 28,* 127–158.
Parker, J. P. (1998). The Torrance Creative Scholars Program. *Roeper Review, 21,* 32–36.
Peterson, J. S. (1999). Gifted through whose cultural lens? An application of the postpositivistic mode of inquiry. *Journal for the Education of the Gifted, 22,* 354–383.
Peterson, J. S., & Margolin, L. (1997). Naming gifted children: An example of unintended "reproduction." *Journal for the Education of the Gifted, 21,* 82–100.
Plata, M., Masten, W. G., & Trusty, J. (1999). Teachers' perception and nomination of fifth-grade Hispanic and Anglo students. *Journal of Research and Development in Education, 32,* 113–123.
Reis, S. M., Colbert, R. D., & Hébert, T. P. (2005). Understanding resilience in diverse, talented students in an urban high school. *Roeper Review, 27,* 110–120.
Reis, S. M., & Díaz, E. (1999). Economically disadvantaged urban female students who achieve in schools. *Urban Review, 31,* 31–54.
Renzulli, J. S., Hartman, R. K., & Callahan, C. A. (1971). Teacher identification of superior students. *Exceptional Children, 38,* 211–214, 243–248.
Renzulli, J. S., Smith, L. H., White, A. J., Callahan, C. M., & Hartman, R. K. (1976). *Scales for rating the behavioral characteristics of superior students.* Mansfield Center, CT: Creative Learning Press.
Rumbaut, R. G. (1995). The new Californians: Comparative research findings on the educational progress of immigrant children. In R. G. Rumbaut & W. A. Cornelius (Eds.), *California's immigrant children: Theory, research and implications for educational policy* (pp. 17–69). San Diego: Center for U.S.-Mexican Studies, University of California.
Rutter, M. (1981). Stress, coping, and development: Some issues and some questions. *Journal of Child Psychology and Psychiatry and Allied Disciplines, 24,* 323–356.
Shaunessy, E., Hughes, C., McHatton, P. A., Brice, A., & Ratliff, M. A. (2005, November). *You gotta represent! Understanding bilingual Hispanic adolescents in gifted and general education.* Session presented at the annual conference of the National Association for Gifted Children, Louisville, KY.
Shaunessy, E., & Karnes, F. A. (2004, Summer). Assessing culturally diverse potentially gifted students with nonverbal measures of intelligence. *The School Psychologist,* pp. 99–102.
Shaunessy, E., Karnes, F. A., & Cobb, Y. (2004). Assessing potentially gifted students from lower socioeconomic status with nonverbal measures of intelligence. *Perceptual and Motor Skills, 98,* 1129–1138.
Shaunessy, E., Matthews, M. S., & Smith, D. (2006, November). *District practices in the identification of underrepresented populations in gifted education.* Paser presented at the 53rd annual convention of the National Association for Gifted Children, Charlotte, NC.
Slocumb, P. D., & Payne, R. K. (2000). *Removing the mask: Giftedness in poverty.* Highlands, TX: RFT.
Smith, J., LeRose, B., & Clasen, R. E. (1991). Underrepresentation of minority students in gifted programs: Yes! It matters! *Roeper Review, 35,* 81–83.
Spener, D. (1995). Transitional bilingual education and the socialization of immigrants. In P. Leistyna, W. A. Sherblom, & S. A. Sherblom (Eds.), *Breaking free: The transformative power of critical pedagogy.* (pp. 59–82) Cambridge, MA: Harvard Educational Review.
Stanton-Salazar, R. D. (2004). The integration of Latino students. In P. Strum & A. Selec (Eds.), *The Hispanic Challenge? What we know about Latino Immigration.* (pp. 23–25). Washington, DC: Woodrow Wilson International Center for Scholars.
Stanton-Salazar, R. D., & Dornbusch, S. M. (1995). Social capital and the reproduction of inequality: Information networks among Mexican-origin high school students. *Sociology of Education, 68,* 116–135.
Stormont, M., Stebbins, M. S., & Holliday, G. (2001). Characteristics and educational support needs of underrepresented gifted adolescents. *Psychology in the Schools, 38,* 413–431.
Swanson, J. D. (2006). Breaking through assumptions about low-income, minority gifted students. *Gifted Child Quarterly, 50,* 11–25.
Tomlinson, C. A., Ford, D. Y., Reis, S. M., Briggs, C. J., & Strickland, C. A. (2004). *In search of the dream: Designing schools and classrooms that work for high potential students from diverse cultural backgrounds.* Washington, DC: National Association for Gifted Children.
Torrance, E. P. (1977). *Discovery and nurturance of giftedness in the culturally different.* Reston, VA: Council for Exceptional Children.
Tse, L. (2001). *"Why don't they learn English?": Separating fact from fallacy in the U.S. language debate.* New York: Teachers College Press.
U.S. Census Bureau. (2000). *State profiles: 2000 census.* Washington, DC: U.S. Department of Commerce, Economics, and Statistics Division.
U.S. Department of Education. (1998). *Talent and diversity: The emerging world of limited English proficient students in gifted education.* (Office of Educational Research and Improvement Report No. ORAD 98-1100). Retrieved May 10, 2005, from *http://www.ed.gov/PDFDocs/talentdiversity.pdf*

U.S. Department of Education. (2001). *Digest of education statistics, 2000* (NCES 2001-034). Washington, DC: Author.

Valdés, G. (2003). *Expanding definitions of giftedness: The case of young interpreters from immigrant communities.* Mahwah, NJ: Lawrence Erlbaum Associates.

Valenzuela, A. (1999). *Subtractive schooling: U.S.-Mexican youth and the politics of caring.* Albany: State University of New York Press.

VanTassel-Baska, J. (Ed.). (1998). *Excellence in educating gifted and talented learners* (3rd ed.). Denver: Love.

Wechsler, D. (2003). *Manual for the Wechsler Intelligence Scale for Children—Fourth Edition.* San Antonio, TX: Psychological Corporation.

Werner, E. E. (1984). Research in review: Resilient children. *Young Children 40*, 68–72.

Williams, L. S., Alvarez, S. D., & Hauck, K. S. A. (2002). My name is not María: Young Latinas seeking home in the heartland. *Social Problems, 49*, 563–584.

CHAPTER 8

SPECIAL POPULATIONS

Sandra Manning, Ph.D.
THE UNIVERSITY OF SOUTHERN MISSISSIPPI

Kevin D. Besnoy, Ph.D.
NORTHERN KENTUCKY UNIVERSITY

INTRODUCTION

Attempting to define traits and needs of all gifted students is difficult because of each child's individuality. However, grouping the gifted population into a few categories makes it easier to discuss the characteristics, special issues, and curriculum/programming considerations for the entire population. This chapter provides foundational information related to highly gifted, twice-exceptional students, young gifted, rural gifted, gifted adolescents, and gifted females. The overlapping and interrelatedness of these special populations (e.g., gifted females as adolescents, characteristics of the highly gifted as young children, and so on) is also communicated. The reader is encouraged to consider how giftedness interacts with the conditions unique to each special population.

HIGHLY GIFTED

Because of the relatively small size of this group of exceptional students and the paucity of research currently available, defining the highly gifted population can be difficult. Researchers (Gagné, 1998; Gross, 2000; Jackson & Peterson, 2003; Kline & Meckstroth, 1985; Lovecky, 1994; Silverman, 1989; Tolan, 1992), the field of gifted education have labeled students with tremendous cognitive ability using terms such as *highly, exceptionally,* and *profoundly gifted.* Some agreement has been reached on the psychometric baseline of highly gifted as three or more standard deviations above the mean on an individually administered standardized intelligence test. Being an extremely diverse group, students with high cognitive ability vary significantly. As such, instructional practices employed with these students are often inadequate to meet their unique needs.

Definitions

Early studies of gifted individuals lead to the recognition of distinct differences in intellectual functioning among the gifted population. Lewis Terman, a pioneer in gifted education and coauthor of the longitudinal study *Genetic Studies of Genius* (Terman & Oden, 1925), originally selected individuals for participation in his study who obtained an intelligence quotient (IQ) of 140 or above on the Stanford-Binet Intelligence Test. Qualifying this score, he stated, "The standard set was purely arbitrary and was intended to insure that the subjects included for the study should be in the highest 1 percent of the school population in general intelligence as measured by the test used" (Terman & Oden, 1959, p. 3). Leta Hollingworth, a Terman contemporary and early leader in the field of gifted education, was among the first to research children with exceptional IQs. She posited an IQ of 180 as the benchmark for labeling extremely gifted students (Hollingworth, 1942). Similar to Terman, she qualified her choice by stating that the score "is obviously arbitrary and is adopted merely for the purpose of defining a point at and above which there are very few children who score" (p. 23). While there is a difference of 40 IQ points between the subjects in Hollingworth's and Terman's studies, the value of their efforts to identify gifted individuals did much to draw attention to the differences in children within the gifted range of cognitive ability.

Prior to their work, such scholars as Sir Francis Galton were able to base their ideas of intellectual eminence only on the earned accomplishments of individuals (Hollingworth, 1942). With the advent of psychometric testing, it became possible for researchers to identify the potential for success during childhood. This advance has resulted in the study of these children and the ways educational opportunities can build on heritable potential to train and enhance gifted student development.

TABLE 8–1 Levels of Giftedness

Level of Giftedness	Range of IQ Scores	Prevalence in the Population
Mildly	115–129	1 in 6 to 1 in 44
Moderately	130–144	1 in 44 to 1 in 1,000
Highly	145–159	1 in 1,000 to 1 in 10,000
Exceptionally	160–179	1 in 1,000 to 1 in 1,000,000
Profoundly	180+	Fewer than 1 in 1 million

Source: Adapted from Gross (2000).

More recently, researchers appear to have reached a consensus on what constitutes extreme potential. Currently, the defining concept of three standard deviations above the mean on a standardized measure of intelligence serves as the threshold for the label "highly gifted" (Gagné, 1998; Gross, 2000; Jackson & Peterson, 2003; Kline & Meckstroth, 1985; Lovecky, 1994; Tolan, 1992). Silverman (1989) described the highly gifted as individuals "whose advancement is significantly beyond the norm of the gifted" (p. 71). Gross defined the exceptionally gifted as different as "chalk and cheese" (cited in Lovecky, 1994, p. 117) from the moderately gifted and presents levels of giftedness to support her point (Table 8–1). However, theorists continue to redefine these levels of differentiation. Gagné (1998) postulated his most recent leveled scale of giftedness based on the metric system. Despite a few differences, the group classified as highly gifted remains at an IQ equivalent score of 145 or three standard deviations above the mean of 100.

Characteristics

One major concern for educators is a lack of knowledge as to the specific characteristics of highly gifted students (Gross, 2000). Table 8–2 gives an overview of the common characteristics of this student population. Another consideration is that while highly gifted students may exhibit many of the same baseline characteristics as mildly or moderately gifted students, they often possess these in extreme proportions or what Dabrowski termed "overexcitiablities" or heightened sensitivity (for further discussion, see Bouchard, 2004; Dabrowski, 1967; Jackson and Peterson, 2003; Lovecky, 1994; Tucker & Hafenstein, 1997).

Individual case studies from Terman and Oden (1925) to Hollingworth (1942) and most recently the research of Gross (1999, 2000), Lovecky (1994), and Silverman (1989, 2002) reveal differences in these extremely gifted children from birth. They often excel in locomotion with many learning to walk as early as

TABLE 8–2 Observed Characteristics of the Highly Gifted

• Early mastery of gross motor skills
• Superb memory
• Intense interest areas
• Keen attention span
• Early mastery of verbal and written language
• Advanced logical thinking skills
• Extreme sensitivity to the feeling of others
• Vivid imagination

Source: Adapted from Clark (2002), Kearney (2000), and Silverman (2002).

8 months. As a result, these children will begin to explore the world around them at an earlier age.

Additionally, early language skill is common among this group with many speaking their first words as early as 5 months of age. Within this early verbal ability, observations have been made of very young children being fascinated with words and proficient in the use of metaphor. Take, for example, the case of the 27-month-old highly gifted child who, on seeing the ocean for the first time, remarked, "The ocean is waving at me" (Lovecky, 1994, p. 118). Hand in hand with precocious verbal ability, highly gifted youngsters often learn to read at an exceptionally early age. Hollingworth (1942) reported in a review of her study of extremely bright children that reading commenced between the ages of $3\frac{1}{2}$ and 4 years of age. Others have observed the same propensity for early reading with many highly gifted children reading before the age of 4 (Gross, 1999; VanTassel-Baska, 1983).

Lovecky (1994), in her work with children with IQs above 170, made distinct comparisons between moderately and exceptionally gifted children. Their great need for precision, coupled with their ability to make the simple complex, reveals the extreme range of their cognitive abilities. For example, Lovecky recounted the story of Zachary, who, at age 7 and with an IQ of 200, had trouble answering what might be considered a simple question, "What is a doctor?" The problem for this child lay in his extensive knowledge about the various kinds of physicians. In an effort to give a precise answer, he ultimately turned an easy question into one he had difficulty answering. Lovecky (1994) indicated that the moderately gifted children in her study were able to answer the question quickly, intelligently, and with relative ease because they were not burdened by the need for precision or extensive, in-depth knowledge about a variety of medical specialties.

The social and emotional issues associated with high intellectual ability have also been addressed in the literature. Hollingworth (1942), Gross (1994), Jackson and Peterson (2003), and Rodell (1984) found that many of these children and youth display deficits in social development, often preferring to work alone and lacking the ability to form meaningful peer relationships, thus making them susceptible to such emotional maladies as depression and perfectionism. One reason given for this is the scarcity of same age peers functioning at similar cognitive levels (Gross, 2000). Other researchers, however, have found the opposite to be true; that is, highly gifted students appear to be more socially and emotionally well adjusted than average-ability or moderately gifted students (Garland & Zigler, 1999; Norman, Ramsay, Martray, & Roberts, 1999). It should be noted, however, that the later studies were conducted with students attending summer programs for academically talented youth. The presence of intellectual peers in such a setting may account for the report of higher levels of social and emotional stability.

Educational Considerations

Despite the fact that research shows a distinction among gifted individuals, the highly gifted may be one of the most underserved populations of gifted students (Gross, 2000). Popular program options for the gifted, such as pullout resource rooms and curriculum differentiation in the general education classroom, have not proven to be as beneficial to the highly gifted as to their mildly and moderately gifted counterparts (Kennedy, 2002). Often, highly gifted students possess a learning preference for total immersion (Lovecky, 1994) in an area of interest to satisfy their extreme curiosity. Consequently, few educational programs are equipped to offer these students consistent rigor and challenge, which provide the depth and breadth of learning they crave.

Many highly gifted students find nonconventional educational settings such as home schooling or acceleration programs more appropriate to their unique educational needs. Programs such as the Talent Search originated at Johns Hopkins University offer highly able students the opportunity for recognition and participation in radically accelerated academic programs (Lubinski & Benbow, 1994). In addition, many highly gifted individuals have found mentorships to be valuable educational experiences when the offerings at both public and private schools are lacking (Gross & van Vliet, 2005). With the recent release of the national acceleration report *A Nation Deceived* (Colangelo, Assouline, & Gross, 2004), drawing attention to the low-cost effectiveness of early school admission, grade skipping, and advanced placement programs for the gifted, progress may soon be made in the area of offering appropriate educational options to the highly gifted.

For educators seeking to study the highly gifted, lack of information can be a stumbling block to serious exploration. Because of the small proportion of students being considered (as few as 1 in every 1,000 students; Gross, 2000), it is not uncommon to find experts grouping the highly, exceptionally, and profoundly gifted into one category in order to explore the characteristics and educational needs of these students. Add to that the idea that highly gifted individuals may also possess specific talents in areas such as art, music, and athletics (Morelock & Feldman, 2003), and one can understand why the dearth of research regarding this student population is problematic.

These concerns can result in an illusive understanding of the highly gifted, especially when one considers the potential differences between a child with an IQ score of 145 (highly gifted) and another with a score higher than 180 (profoundly gifted). Imagine this 35-point difference in IQ at the other end of the intelligence spectrum. One would hardly expect to find in the educational literature grouping and discussion of students with IQ scores of between 65 and 100 as common practice.

Problems are also encountered in the screening and identification of highly gifted students. Locating an intelligence test with a ceiling high enough to accurately measure their intelligence has prompted some in the field to advocate for the use of an older version of the Stanford-Binet, Form L-M (Lovecky, 1994; Silverman, 1989). As Silverman and Kearney (1992) indicate, newer tests discriminate against gifted students "because when an item can be solved 'only' by children in a gifted class, it is removed from the test" (p. 34).

Summary of Highly Gifted Students

Although initiated decades ago, the study of the highly gifted has grown slowly, perhaps in part because of the small number of students this group represents. Individual observations and case studies of students with remarkable ability reveal their existence as distinct among the gifted and talented population. While educational options for the highly gifted may be limited, the implementation of radical acceleration practices may prove to be the most effective means of differentiating the curriculum for these students. Research in this area is growing, but much more is needed to bring this special population of gifted learners to the attention of policymakers in hopes of providing these students with opportunities for rigor and challenge in our nation's educational system.

TWICE-EXCEPTIONAL STUDENTS

To many educators, it is inconceivable that a child can be both gifted and have a learning disability. Unfortunately, this misconception prevents gifted students with learning disabilities (i.e., twice-exceptional students) from receiving appropriate educational services. The solution to this dilemma is to raise awareness among educators as to the general characteristics of and appropriate programming for twice-exceptional students.

Definitions

Classifying twice-exceptional students into one of three categories permits educators to concretely discuss this population. Baum (1990) groups twice-exceptional students into one of the following three categories: (a) identified gifted students whose learning disability is undiagnosed, (b) identified learning disabled students whose giftedness is unrecognized, and (c) students whose giftedness and disabilities are both unidentified. No matter how you categorize them, many educators are unfamiliar with these students' characteristics. As such, school programs are unable to provide the necessary educational services to allow any of these three categories of twice-exceptional students to maximize their potential (Baum, 1990).

There is a fourth category of twice-exceptional students that Baum does not describe. This is the student whose giftedness and disability have both been recognized. Students who fall into this category are fortunate because schools can provide services that address the giftedness and learning disability.

Identified Gifted. Students with identified giftedness but unrecognized learning disabilities often tend to be underachievers. As these students progress through school, the gap between their potential and displayed performance widens. Meanwhile, this group of twice-exceptional students begins to experience greater levels of frustration. Baum (1990) suggests that their self-concept and motivation suffer.

Vaidya (1993) states that gifted students with unidentified learning disabilities find learning a difficult and painful process. More specifically, they generally have poor handwriting and spelling skills (Fetzer, 2000), have high verbal abilities (Little, 2001), and are forgetful, sloppy, and disorganized (Baum, 1990). Many times teachers and parents, knowing the potential of these students, become extremely frustrated with the students' underachievement. According to Baum, concerned adults believe that these students only need to try harder in order to meet their potential. However, without appropriate intervention programs, greater effort is not enough.

Researchers (Brody & Mills, 1997; Coleman, 2005) cite many examples of gifted students' whose learning disabilities were not identified until late in their educational careers. Unfortunately, this lapse was a real issue for these students because they did not learn the appropriate coping strategies that would have enabled them to successfully compensate for their disability.

Identified Learning Disabled. Students with an identified learning disability but unidentified giftedness typically receive only specialized educational services that address their disability. The lack of concentration of gifted programming and services makes it more difficult for these types of twice-exceptional children to maximize their potential (Fetzer, 2000).

Without appropriate curriculum services, a student's disability can depress his or her academic performance (Fetzer, 2000), and as a result they are rarely referred for gifted services (Brody & Mills, 1997; Lidz, 2002; Winebrenner, 2003). Baum (1990) declares that teachers and other adults become focused on the problem because they do not recognize the gifts.

Not only are these students at risk for not maximizing their potential, but the learning disability label places them at risk for either dropping out of high school or completing school without the necessary skills and mind-set to succeed in adult life. Researchers (Baum, 1990; Little, 2001; Mather, 2003) state that these children often have high-level interests at home, so educators may have little knowledge of or exposure to these strengths in the school setting.

Unidentified Gifted or Learning Disabled. Students whose gifts and disabilities are both unidentified are perhaps the largest group of twice-exceptional students (Fetzer, 2000; Hua & Coleman, 2002; Olenchak & Reis, 2002). In essence, their giftedness and disability mask one another. Thus, it is not uncommon for these twice-exceptional students to have one or two academic areas where they excel and a couple where they struggle. Many will perform at grade level on achievement tests and in course work. They are often perceived as "average" students who are just "getting by." Such factors make it difficult to identify this population as twice exceptional. Although the masked talents and disabilities might surface in specific content areas or be brought out by a teacher's unique teaching methods, neither the disability nor the gift is typically discovered, if at all, until college or adulthood. On discovering their skills and disabilities, these students are able to successfully navigate adulthood (Besnoy, 2006; Olenchak & Reis, 2002).

Gifted ADHD/ADD. Giftedness can also be found among those children diagnosed with attention-deficit/hyperactivity disorder (ADHD) and/or attention deficit disorder (ADD). Distinguishing behaviors of ADHD/ADD include constant inattentiveness and/or impulsive/hyperactive conduct atypical of a similarly developing child (American Psychiatric Association, 2000) without a definitive medical rationale of cause. ADHD/ADD and gifted children share many of the same attributes. Such attributes include (a) intense focus, (b) eagerness, (c) hyperactivity (Willard-Holt, 2002), (d) restlessness, (e) minimal need of sleep, (f) sensitivity, and (g) strong-mindedness since early childhood (Mendaglio, 1995). Mendaglio asserted that a considerable number of parents have described their gifted child as having an extraordinary amount of energy as compared to a typically developing child. Thus, according to Mendaglio, distinguishing between giftedness and ADHD/ADD can be difficult.

When a child is identified as both gifted and ADHD/ADD, the outcome may adversely affect the child's outlook on academic success. According to Mendaglio (1995), gifted children with ADHD/ADD may feel they now have an excuse not to do their best. In addition, a child who is gifted ADHD/ADD will exhibit assertive and argumentative behavior toward instructors and parents. Children who are gifted and ADHD/ADD are more likely to express themselves through intense outbursts directed toward teachers and family.

Characteristics

There are many students who are twice exceptional (Baum, 1990; Little, 2001). Little (2001) estimates that there are between 120,000 and 180,000 students in the United States with learning disabilities and above-average IQs. In addition, it is estimated that the number of unidentified twice exceptional is quite large.

Describing the characteristics of twice-exceptional students is difficult because there are numerous definitions of giftedness and various types of learning disabilities. Still, researchers (Beckley, 1998; Besnoy, 2006; Lidz, 2002; Winebrenner, 2003) have attempted to provide practitioners with a list of characteristics. Accordingly, twice-exceptional students possess advanced abstract reasoning skills and the ability to make astute generalizations. Furthermore, these students quickly understand new concepts and enjoy deciphering complex tasks independently. Additional characteristics include but are not limited to (a) intelligence, (b) impulsivity, (c) advanced abstract reasoning skills (d) failure to complete assignments, (e) poor study skills, and (f) high motivation in areas of interest.

Educational Considerations

An appropriate curriculum for twice-exceptional students has two fundamental components: flexibility and empowerment. It should be flexible enough to allow twice-exceptional children the freedom to develop their talents through varied programming. At the same time, the curriculum must empower twice-exceptional students with the capacity to utilize their abilities as a tool to overcome any learning disability. Curricula with these two components will help develop self-efficacy while providing necessary rigor. In order to meet this goal, educators must understand this population's unique characteristics. Besnoy (2006) describes several practical approaches to serving twice-exceptional students. Each of these methods is designed to provide flexible classroom instruction that enables the teacher to empower the student with the confidence and skills necessary to successfully compensate for the learning disability. These strategic approaches range from teaching to the student's learning style and interests to teaching organizational skills and good study habits that help teachers create such an environment.

Self-Efficacy. One hindrance to the academic success of twice-exceptional children is the frustration they feel with not always being successful (Winebrenner, 2003). As such, educators must create learning environments that enable these students to be successful and deliberately build their self-efficacy (Little, 2001). Bandura (1986) defines self-efficacy as the belief in ones' capabilities to organize and execute the sources of action required to manage prospective situations. Even though twice-exceptional students possess the abilities to excel, their diminished confidence prevents them from always maximizing their potential.

One method for helping twice-exceptional students to enhance their self-efficacy is to create a problem-based curriculum. According to Hmelo-Silver (2004), a problem-based curriculum is one where classroom learning is centered on solving a complex problem. While students are required to work together to find a solution, individuals assume specific responsibilities in the process. Benefits of this type of curriculum include development of problem-solving skills, collaboration skills, and intrinsic motivation (Hmelo-Silver, 2004). Because of the diversity of possible solutions, it permits the twice-exceptional learner greater control of his or her learning. The problem-based curriculum also allows teachers to create learning environments that provide support for the disability while maintaining an appropriate amount of academic and intellectual rigor (Coleman, 2005).

Learning Styles. Each student has his or her own unique learning style. As such, it is important for teachers of twice-exceptional students to identify and teach to the student's learning style (Coleman, 2005; Winebrenner, 2003). Many times, teachers only teach to their own learning style. While this might be easier for the teacher, it limits the opportunities for twice-exceptional students to utilize their gifts to compensate for their learning disability.

One of the greatest struggles that twice-exceptional students face is trying to adapt their metacognitive approach to classroom situations. This "extra" effort often becomes an obstacle to academic success. Learning according to one's learning style makes it easier for the student to make strong metacognitive associations to prior knowledge and to produce work that accurately demonstrates learning.

Designing activities centered on the student's preferred learning style allows children to utilize their giftedness. Not only will the children feel greater confidence in their abilities, but they will also gain the ability to develop coping strategies. The increased learning that will occur will build self-confidence and result in a more academically skilled child.

Student Interest. Identifying and teaching to a twice-exceptional student's interests is another successful strategy (Besnoy, 2006; Coleman, 2005; Winebrenner, 2003) that requires the teacher to create activities that are flexible enough for the student to meet objectives while learning information that is of interest. By employing this simple strategy, students will engage in the activity with more enthusiasm and a greater willingness to overcome their learning disability.

Fortunately, identifying a student's interests can be accomplished at the beginning of the year through a student interest inventory. While every lesson does not have to center around a student's interests, teachers of twice-exceptional children must be cognizant of subjects that spark enthusiasm among students. Not only will it permit the teacher to design more meaningful lessons, but it will also provide greater insight into the child's special talents (Besnoy, 2006; Dole, 2000). Finally, determining students' interests allows teachers to know what topics act as motivators.

Organizational Skills. The idea of teaching organizational skills goes beyond instilling an ability to organize a notebook and a day planner. Many times, twice-exceptional students unsuccessfully complete assignments because they either lose the assignment or do not know when it is due. However, many twice-exceptional students also struggle with mental organizational skills (Cline & Schwartz, 1999; Swanson, 2001; Winebrenner, 2002). Consequently, teachers need to teach students how to organize their physical and metacognitive space.

Students must be taught how to organize a notebook, desk, book bag, and locker (Winebrenner, 2003). Learning organizational skills will help improve the frequency and accuracy of completed assignments. In addition, teachers should instruct twice-exceptional students on the benefits of advanced organizers such as KWLs charts (what you Know, Want to know, and have Learned), Venn diagrams, and concept mapping (Swanson, 2001). These tools are designed to integrate students' prior knowledge with current content.

Summary of Twice-Exceptional Students

While all twice-exceptional students have the potential to succeed, without knowledgeable educators, many of these students might never fully maximize their potential. As such, school officials must understand that a child can potentially be gifted and have a learning disability. Furthermore, to meet their various needs, educators and parents must work together to improve intervention strategies (Baum, 1990; Brody & Mills, 1997; Winebrenner, 2003). Gifted students with learning disabilities must receive instruction that attends to both their gifts and their disability.

YOUNG GIFTED CHILDREN

Some educators are hesitant to identify young children as gifted because of the expectations often associated with this label. Additionally, researchers state that it is difficult to make accurate IQ determinations at an early age. However, by identifying the abilities and potential of young children, educators can design appropriate educational opportunities for this population that promote intellectual and social and emotional growth.

Definitions

The young gifted child has been defined as a child between the ages of 3 and 6 years old who displays advanced cognitive abilities well beyond his or her agemates (Harrison, 2004; Jackson & Peterson, 2003; Parke & Ness, 1988). As simple as this statement sounds, identifying and educating these children can be a difficult task. Giftedness is a multidimensional construct. The discovery of advanced cognitive performance in concert with the underlying promise of potential can be a daunting revelation to parents and early childhood educators. Combine this with the asynchronous developmental patterns of young gifted children, and it is easy to understand the challenges offered by this special population of gifted students (Barbour & Shaklee, 1998; Cline & Schwartz, 1999; Parke & Ness, 1988; Rodell, 1990).

The term *asynchronous* refers to the manner in which young children develop advanced skills in one area while displaying average abilities in another (Silverman, 1997). This pattern of development makes it difficult for young children to be identified as gifted using traditional measures such as IQ testing (Hall, 1993). For young children who have been identified as gifted, patterns of asynchronous development can confuse parents and educators as to the best methods for serving the child's educational needs. Since social, emotional, and psychomotor development in young children rarely keep pace with cognitive growth, early school placement may not meet the needs of these children (Gross, 1999; Rodell, 1990), leaving parents and educators unsure of how to best support young gifted children.

Characteristics

Young gifted children display many observable characteristics. These may serve as a starting point for parents and educators in the identification process. Table 8–3 gives an overview of the most noticeable characteristics in this special population of gifted children. The young gifted child's early and easy grasp of the abstract results in an advanced ability to draw conclusions, make inferences, and transfer learning from one situation to another. Additionally, their intense curiosity, combined with early verbal skills, often leads to numerous questions on a variety of topics (Harrison, 2004).

TABLE 8–3 Cognitive and Affective Characteristics of the Young Gifted Child

Cognitive Characteristics	Affective Characteristics
Curiosity	Emotional Intensity
Long-term memory	Emotional Sensitivity
Advanced vocabulary	Depth of feeling
Learns easily	High expectations of self and others
Sustained interest in one area	Early empathy development
Generates original ideas	Independence
Thinks abstractly	Overexcitability
Transfers knowledge	Concern for truth/fair play
Creative/imaginative	Cares for others

Source: Adapted from Clark (2002), Cline and Schwartz (1999), Hafenstein and Tucker (1995), and Jackson and Peterson (2003).

Researchers suggest that multiple steps be taken to identify giftedness in young children (Gross, 1999; Hall, 1993; Tucker & Hafenstein, 1997). Contrary to popular belief, parents are often very adept at recognizing potential giftedness in their children (Gross, 1999). For this reason, parent surveys and interviews are an important part of the identification process. Teacher checklists and child interviews should also be included (Sandel, McCallister, & Nash, 1993). Multiple assessments, using both verbal and nonverbal measures of intelligence, must be considered when identifying young gifted children to get an accurate overall picture of the child's abilities (Cline & Schwartz, 1999).

Assessors should also keep in mind the fatigue aspect for young children inherent in a testing situation and provide ample time for the session (Gross, 1999). Most important, parents and early childhood providers must realize that assessment of cognitive ability is a process. The administration of one instrument provides a snapshot of the child's performance on that one instrument at a given point in time. A true understanding of giftedness in young children can be gained only by building a portfolio, or many snapshots, of the child's abilities. This may include not only test scores but also work samples and anecdotal records of the child's conversations and behaviors (Karnes, Manning, Besnoy, Cukierkorn, & Houston, 2004).

Educational Considerations

The importance of providing appropriate programs to young gifted children is evident when one considers the problems associated with its absence. Cline and Schwartz (1999) assert that underachievement in later years can be a result of not beginning gifted programs early. Inherent to underachievement are the problems of loss of interest and motivation, boredom, rebellious behavior, and social and emotional concerns. In addition, Rodell (1990) points out that uneven development can cause extreme frustration in young gifted children. Early intervention in addressing the needs of young gifted children can help to alleviate these problems and provide a firm foundation for helping these children understand their giftedness.

Parke and Ness (1988) list four basic tenets for designing curricula for this special population of gifted students. Their ideas are based on the goals of developmentally appropriate practice posited by the National Association for the Education of Young Children (Bredekamp & Copple, 1997). Such goals reflect research findings of the best practices for teaching young children.

The first tenet advocated by Parke and Ness (1988) is quite obvious—address the special learning needs of the young gifted child. The young gifted child's ability to learn more quickly and deeply and his or her varied interests should be taken into consideration when planning. Referring to an intense internal motivation to communicate, Halliday (1975) pointed out the urgency in young children to construct meaning. This common attribute of early language development, coupled with the young gifted child's extreme desire to learn, makes developing meaningful curricula for young gifted learners imperative.

Second, the curriculum should be based on the interests of children rather than the pressures of parents for early schooling (Parke & Ness, 1988). An integrated and balanced curriculum implemented during the critical early learning period can motivate and set the stage for continued growth and development (Hall, 1993). By basing the curriculum on children's interests rather than parent or educator interests, they are given the opportunity to engage in creative expression and motivating content.

The third tenet purposed by Parke and Ness (1988) states that the curriculum must emphasize play and exploration. Based on the idea of developmentally appropriate practice, research has found that young children learn best through play (Bredekamp & Copple, 1997). Even though young gifted children think in abstract terms earlier than their age peers, they still need the opportunity to explore and manipulate concrete materials. The opportunities for problem solving and creativity afforded by dramatic play helps children develop many of the higher-order thinking skills beneficial to their growth.

The last tenet purposed by Parke and Ness (1988) advises that young gifted children be included in making curricular decisions. This helps them develop self-confidence, motivates them to mastery, and prepares them to become lifelong learners. Because of their high interest levels, young gifted children often know which kinds of activities they need for growth.

An example of curriculum based on student input is the Reggio Emilia approach developed in Italy by Louis Malaguzzi (Barbour & Shaklee, 1998). This program is referred to as an "emergent curriculum" (p. 233) because teachers observe their students to find out what their precise needs and interests are to plan future activities. Based on the tenets of special programming for young gifted children presented by Parke and Ness (1988), the Reggio Emilia approach addresses student needs and interests, provides the opportunity for developmentally appropriate and meaningful play, and gives the young gifted child an opportunity to be actively involved in curricular decision making. Barbour and Shaklee (1998) present it as a viable alternative to present programs for young gifted children.

The Reggio Emilia approach is based on six principles:

1. Careful preparation of the learning environment to meet learner needs
2. Focus on the importance of the relationships between parents, teachers, and children
3. Education as an active process
4. Teacher behaviors that define, reflect, and redefine their teaching philosophies as an ongoing process
5. Child centered and focused on children's rights
6. Belief in the inherent value of developing curriculum based on the observed interests and activities of young gifted children that emerge through social and environmental interactions (Barbour & Shaklee, 1998)

Summary of Young Gifted

This brief exploration of the characteristics and education of young gifted children should serve as a springboard for the gifted educator interested in the growth and development of this special population of gifted students. The need for early childhood education initiatives throughout America's public school system is gaining attention (Barnett, Hustedt, Robin, & Schulman, 2005). Continued research and training for both parents and early childhood educators must be pursued to develop the cognitive promise of young gifted children.

RURAL GIFTED

Students with gifts and talents being educated in rural school districts are faced with many roadblocks in their educational journeys. Several characteristics of rural schools combine to make it difficult for gifted students in these educational settings to receive the services and programs they need to reach their potential. Among these are small populations of gifted students, limited availability of resources, and a teaching staff that may not be qualified to teach advanced subject areas. These difficulties must be addressed if the rural gifted are to be educated according to their needs.

Definition

Depending on the formula used to define rural (for further discussion, see Colangelo, Assouline, & New, 1999; Snyder, 2006), estimates range from 42% to 50% of the nation's public schools are located in rural areas. Given that, one would expect more attention to be directed at solving the problems of rural school districts. However, with the plethora of complexities faced by urban and inner-city schools, rural education initiatives have not taken the national spotlight until recently. In 2004, the National Research Center on Rural Education Support (NRCRES) was created by the U.S. Department of Education and is housed at the University of North Carolina at Chapel Hill. Its mission is to act as a catalyst for academic improvements in educational opportunities provided for children and youth in rural schools. The specific aims of the center include retention of quality teachers, improved student achievement through advanced placement courses, the reduction of dropout rates, and staff development models to increase teacher quality (NRCRES, n.d.). Currently, three research projects are underway, including rural literacy, adolescent learning, and distance education; however, gifted students in rural schools have yet to be addressed.

Individual states have put forth initiatives to address the needs of gifted students in their rural settings. One such program is the Rural Gifted Task Force established in Louisiana to identify and remedy some of the problems faced by these students (Picard, 2002). The major goals of this endeavor include identification of gifted students, providing differentiated curriculum, allocating resources to the rural gifted programs, implementing staff development for teachers of the gifted, and developing a criteria for certification of gifted education teachers (Picard, 2002).

A recent report issued by researchers at the Belin Blank International Center for Gifted Education and Talent Development housed at the University of Iowa (Colangelo, Assouline, Baldus, Ihrig, & New, 2006) highlighted initiatives for serving gifted ethnically diverse students in rural Alabama, Iowa, Washington, and Hawaii. These programs focus on identifying underrepresented student populations for gifted programming, providing challenging academic course work, and increasing community and family involvement.

Characteristics

High-ability students often represent such a small portion of the total student population within a district that they are frequently overlooked (Colangelo, Assouline, & New, 2001). Other issues take precedence, such as federally mandated special education programs for students with disabilities. With little attention being given to developing educational programs and services to meet the unique educational needs of gifted students, many do not receive appropriate opportunities for rigor and challenge. Gifted rural students often lack the opportunity to work and learn in settings with their intellectual peers, which can be vital in building self-esteem and avoiding the pitfalls of underachievement that frequently plague gifted youth deprived of suitable peer group interaction (Montgomery, 2004).

The teacher and administrative workforce in rural schools is often younger with fewer advanced degrees and less experience than faculty in other school types (Luhman & Fundis, 1989). With many staff members at the beginning of their careers, remuneration may be lower. Although inadvertent, this scenario may have a negative psychological effect, resulting in a lack of professionalism or a "waiting to move on attitude." Additionally, rural school district faculty are often called on to teach courses outside their areas of expertise because of teacher shortages. With the advent of the No Child Left Behind Act (NCLB) of 2002 and its requirements for highly qualified teachers, this may change; however, with teacher shortages in rural areas, the highly qualified stipulations of NCLB may prevent rural districts from offering advanced courses entirely. Further, many rural districts experience a high staff turnover. For all students in rural schools—but especially the gifted and talented who thrive on rigor and challenge—this can be problematic.

Another characteristic of rural schools often detrimental to the education of gifted students is the limited availability of resources (Colangelo et al., 2001; Picard, 2002). Students have fewer opportunities for enriching cultural experiences such as excursions to art museums, theatrical productions, and the like. Teaching materials and technological resources are often limited as well. A strong emphasis may be placed on athletic activities. While this is not entirely negative, the practice of rewarding students for athletic ability over and above academic ability may create a climate for gifted adolescents that devalues their intellectual and academic gifts and talents and leads to resentment (Davalos & Griffin, 1999).

Educational Considerations

Despite small size and limited resources, rural schools possess some strengths that can be utilized to meet the needs of gifted students. Strengths of schools in rural communities include smaller teacher–pupil ratios and community support (Montgomery, 2004). It should be noted, however, that a higher percentage of individuals in rural communities view gifted and talented programs as elitist and often resist their implementation (Colangelo et al., 2001). The most common service option for gifted students is pullout enrichment programs (Howley, 2002). This may not be a viable option for rural school districts because of budgeting concerns and low numbers of identified gifted students. More economical alternatives must be considered. Curriculum differentiation and acceleration may be the easiest and most cost-effective strategies for improving the educational opportunities for gifted youth in rural settings (Colangelo, et al., 2004). Smaller class sizes in rural districts may make these suggestions easier to implement. However, the primary drawback here lies in delivering the staff development necessary to train general education teachers in these strategies (Picard, 2002).

The most frequently suggested and perhaps easiest curriculum differentiation strategy for teachers to implement is open-ended and higher-level questioning techniques (Johnsen & Ryser, 1996; Manning 2005; Shaunessy, 2005). One study by Friedman and Lee (1996) involved fourth-and fifth-grade teachers from ethnically diverse schools in Kansas. Although the teachers had no prior training in gifted education, the study showed that training in higher-level questioning strategies can be a successful way to help general classroom teachers differentiate curriculum for their gifted students. Findings indicated that classroom teachers should not only plan their lesson content and activities but also implement effective questioning strategies that will tap into students' higher cognitive abilities. Further, consistent teacher attention to planning and implementing higher-level questioning with their students may naturally increase teacher skill to the point where asking high-level questions occurs as often or more so than use of lower-level inquiries.

Another common method used to differentiate curriculum for gifted learners is curriculum compacting. This term refers to procedures employed "to streamline the regular curriculum for students who are capable of mastering it at a faster pace" (Reis, Burns, & Renzulli, 1992, p. 5). Curriculum compacting allows students to pretest out of curriculum materials they have already learned and use instructional time to explore related information in depth, often based on individual interest. This may be a viable option for educators in rural districts because of overall smaller class size. However, effective use of the strategy to meet gifted learner needs can occur only through exposure and repeated implementation.

Davalos and Griffin (1999) assert that the needs of gifted students can be met in the regular classroom if certain teacher attitudes are present. These include a belief in the value of individualized instruction, high motivation to meet the needs of gifted students, a shift to a more responsive and student-centered learning environment, and attention to the social and emotional needs of gifted students. Of course, these requirements cannot be met without effective staff development programs in gifted education, which, unfortunately, are frequently lacking (Manning, 2005). The implementation of strategies to differentiate the curriculum in the general education classroom is especially salient for teachers in rural school districts. With limited staff and funding to provide for the needs of gifted students, rural districts would do well to devote a portion of their required staff development sessions to curriculum differentiation.

Acceleration and distance learning are two other options often recommended for meeting the needs of gifted students in rural settings. Colangelo et al. (2004) reported on 18 different types of acceleration that could easily and economically be implemented for high-ability students in all types of school settings. Among those most suited to rural school situations are early school admittance, grade skipping, early high school graduation, and dual enrollment, or taking college courses while still enrolled in high school. With the advent of the World Wide Web and other technological advances, distance learning, telementoring (mentoring via e-mail and other technology), and online courses should be considered as possible solutions to the problems faced by gifted students in rural settings (Adams & Cross, 1999/2000; Belcastro, 2002). However, limited availability of the equipment needed for these activities could be problematic.

Summary of Rural Gifted

Given the unique realities of rural school settings, much research into effective programming for gifted students is needed. Time, effort, and attention to providing substantive staff development for rural educators must be provided along with evaluative assessments to gauge the effectiveness of the training provided. A strong collaborative commitment by parents, educators, administrators, and those responsible for funding programs in rural schools is essential if rural gifted students are to be educationally empowered to reach their potential.

GIFTED ADOLESCENTS

The importance of addressing the social and emotional concerns of gifted adolescents is paramount. Peer relations, career planning, and the development of leadership skills play critical roles in the development of these students. There are several variables that influence the lives of gifted adolescents, such as peer relationships, parental expectations, educational environment, and personal goals. Striking a positive balance among these influences requires an understanding of how impactful each one can be.

Definition

In many respects, gifted teens are no different than their nongifted peers. In addition to developing their own identity, most adolescents are searching for peer acceptance while masking their personal vulnerabilities and trying to form lifelong aspirations (Lee, 2002; Stormont, Stebbins, & Holliday, 2001; Tieso, 1999). However, gifted adolescents have characteristics that distinguish them from their nongifted peers.

Characteristics

According to researchers (Plucker & Stocking, 2001; Schilling, Sparfeldt, & Rost, 2006), trying to fulfill their precocious abilities can cause some gifted adolescents stress not usually experienced by their nongifted peers. A few examples of these unique stressors include (a) meeting high self-imposed expectations, (b) satisfying lofty expectations of others, (c) administering asynchronously developing talents, and (d) controlling hypersensitivity (Plucker & Stocking, 2001; Richards, Encel, & Shute, 2003; Tieso, 1999).

In addition to these stressors, much of the literature on gifted adolescents describes multipotentiality as a common characteristic that may be catalyst for indecision, pressure, and stress. Multipotentiality is defined as a diversity of precocious talents (Achter, Lubinski, & Benbow, 1996; Tieso, 1999). This multiplicity makes it difficult for some gifted adolescents to select and pursue a single interest. In essence, these students have such a variety of talents and interests that it becomes difficult to decide on one or two to pursue. However, with appropriate guidance, curriculum planning, and career counseling, many gifted adolescents can learn how to focus their interests and select a course of action that enables them to achieve success in their postsecondary life (Sajjadi, Rejskind, & Shore, 2001).

Despite these stressors, many gifted adolescents recognize their unique aptitudes and believe they will be successful in life. In general, Plucker and Stocking (2001) report that gifted adolescents have a positive self-concept of their intellectual abilities. They recognize their precocious intellectual skills and generally feel they can use these assets to their advantage.

Still, while many gifted adolescents are aware of their potential and recognize their ability, they do not always have a strong academic self-concept (Plucker & Stocking, 2001). Plucker and Stocking theorize that this incongruity is most evident in those students who succeed in one academic discipline yet struggle in another.

A common characteristic of gifted students is asynchronous development, meaning their intellectual development is uneven and beyond the norm of their age peers (Silverman, 1998). As such, many gifted adolescents wrestle with both internal and external expectations. Internally, the student expects to excel in all disciplines and endeavors. Externally, society (e.g., peers, parents, and teachers) expects the adolescent to master all academic subjects. Failure to meet these high expectations can negatively affect the student's total academic self-concept and overall self-efficacy.

The discrepancy between perceived ability and actual performance can manifest itself into feelings of frustration and anxiety. Thus, meeting the needs of gifted adolescents requires a coordinated effort on the part of parents, teachers, school officials, and community leaders (Tieso, 1999).

Sexual orientation issues must also be considered when discussing the social and emotional needs of gifted adolescents. A Policy Statement by the National Association for Gifted Children (NAGC, 2001) addressed best practices for educating gifted gay, lesbian, bisexual, and transgendered (GLBT) students. Gifted GLBT students often experience emotional burdens related to both their giftedness and their sexual identities. They may be harassed and ridiculed by peers or have inner feelings of conflict associated with their journey toward sexual understanding (Cohn, 2003; Kerr & Nicpon, 2003).

It goes without saying that a psychologically safe school environment is important for every student. However, educators working with gifted GLBT students should take extra care to help create a safe haven of acceptance and appreciation for these students and their unique needs (NAGC, 2001).

Educational Considerations

Gifted adolescents have needs that require special considerations. Unfortunately, many educators feel that gifted students will be successful throughout their entire educational career. However, many gifted adolescents struggle with underachievement, peer relationships, leadership skill development, and career planning. Educators, parents, community leaders, and gifted/adolescents themselves must take into consideration pressures and expectations of an adolescent who has extraordinary potential.

Underachievement. There are many factors that cause gifted adolescents to underachieve, including inappropriate curricula, negative home environments, poor teaching practices, and inadequate interpersonal/intrapersonal coping skills (Hayes, Norris, & Flaitz, 1998; Rayneri, Gerber, & Wiley, 2003). While each of these factors can be a contributor to a student's underachievement, teachers cannot always control those that occur outside of school. However, while the gifted adolescent is in school, educators have a great deal of jurisdiction over what and how the student learns. Engaging gifted adolescents with a rigorous curriculum is an effective method for combating underachievement.

As gifted adolescents mature, they encounter many issues that may erode their academic performance and threaten their social and emotional stability. Accordingly, educators must create a challenging curriculum that fosters positive peer relations, provides opportunities for career exploration, and promotes leadership skills (Achter et al., 1996; Lee, 2002; Manning, 2005; Rayneri et al., 2003; Tieso, 1999). Providing a rigorous curriculum challenges gifted adolescents to utilize their intellectual capacities to their fullest, thus allowing them to demonstrate their maximum potential.

An essential benefit of a rigorous curriculum is that it permits gifted adolescents to learn at their instructional level. Kanevsky and Keighley (2003) report that many gifted adolescents who underachieve find school boring and unchallenging. In fact, these students articulated that learning was the opposite of school boredom (Kanevsky & Keighley, 2003). In other words, when gifted adolescents are engaged with learning activities that are designed to meet their precocious abilities, school becomes an intellectually stimulating place. In such an environment, gifted adolescents are more likely to be successful both academically and socially.

Peer Relations. Lee (2002) states that gifted adolescents often rely on their peer relations for social and emotional support. While parental influence is strong during adolescence, it is not as powerful as in previous developmental stages. As gifted adolescents begin to develop their interests, they find intellectual peers to satiate their social and emotional needs and rely less on parental input. As a result, the peer group in which these children are accepted is critically important.

Lee (2002) indicates that gifted adolescents are influenced by their peers in three ways. First, peers offer social and emotional support. Second, they act as a motivator to excel. Third, they serve as moral and career role models. For these reasons, parents and educators must create opportunities for gifted adolescents to interact with affirming and positive peers.

One way to provide such opportunities is to involve gifted adolescents in extracurricular activities. Research has demonstrated that participation not only increases self-concept and academic performance but also affords gifted adolescents a better chance to interact with peers who can make a positive contribution to society (Garzarelli & Everhart, 1993; Tieso, 1999). Moreover, it allows these students to develop strong and healthy friendships.

Leadership Skills. As gifted adolescents begin to take stock of the larger world around them, many begin to feel the need to make a positive contribution to society. The difficulty for them is not finding the desire to affect positive change; rather, it is turning that desire into activism. While research is mixed as to whether leadership ability is innate or cultivated, most agree that these skills can be enhanced (Manning, 2005). Through strategic programming, educators can develop gifted adolescents' leadership abilities.

According to Manning (2005), many characteristics of gifted adolescents, such as a penchant for solving complex tasks, keen language ability, and heightened empathy, make them excellent candidates to assume leadership positions.

Career Planning. As a gifted adolescent, trying to make a career decision that will affect one's entire life is daunting. Not only can their talents be exceptional and vast, but there are countless careers from which to choose as well. The pressure to make "the correct" decision is strong. Without formal career counseling, many gifted adolescents are unable to make a sound decision on how to pursue their postsecondary goals (Greene, 2002).

Greene (2002) asserts that gifted high school students often involve themselves in a multitude of extracurricular activities hoping to ensure their place in an elite college or university. This by-product of their multipotentiality provides these adolescents with numerous informal opportunities to explore areas of interest. Unfortunately, many schools do not offer formal career-counseling opportunities to help them decide which area of interest to pursue. As such, deciding on a postsecondary career path may become unnecessarily difficult.

Although multipotentiality might be a possible hindrance to fulfilling career aspirations, there are many proactive steps that gifted adolescents can take to help make the right career choice. Sajjadi et al. (2001) assert that gifted adolescents who actively participate in career planning courses or are mentored by a career counselor are more likely to successfully navigate through postsecondary settings.

Summary of Gifted Adolescents

When adults understand the unique characteristics and needs of gifted adolescents, they can provide programming that empowers these young people to make significant contributions for the betterment of society. The unique characteristics of this population require specialized programming that addresses their social and emotional, academic, and career needs. Those educators who are fortunate enough to work with these students should relish the opportunity to shape the future of society.

GIFTED FEMALES

While there is no empirical evidence that females are more or less likely to be gifted than their male peers, there are some unique characteristics and issues facing this special population. Understanding these characteristics is crucial in enabling young females to maximize their potential.

Definition

Research on women and young girls has shown that females experience a variety of culturally based concerns stemming from their gender (Rimm, Rimm-Kaufman, & Rimm, 1999). These include stereotyping (e.g., pretty girls are not bright), discouragement of competitiveness, and promotion of submissiveness. When the element of giftedness is interjected into the equation, females often find themselves juggling multiple issues in order to excel in academic, social, and career settings (Reis, 2005; Rimm, & Rimm-Kaufman, 2001).

Characteristics

Gifted females possess many of the same characteristics as other special populations of gifted children. These include but are not limited to precocious intellectual abilities, asynchronous development, underachievement, and multipotentiality. In addition, gifted females are constantly bombarded with the expectations of family members, peers, and society (Stormont et al., 2001). Unique to this special population is how these characteristics and expectations impact the lives of gifted females.

Gifted females face many pressures that can negatively impact their academic performance. As a result, some gifted females will mask their giftedness in an attempt to avoid the stress. Furthermore, many of these pressures can adversely affect these females' self-concept. In order to help gifted females overcome these obstacles, educators must be willing to provide an educational program that empowers these young women.

Masking Giftedness. As with many other young gifted people, gifted females have a strong desire for social acceptance (Stormont et al., 2001). However, in an attempt to fit into a particular peer group, gifted females often mask their giftedness (Klein & Zehms, 1996; Reis, 2002; Stormont et al., 2001). This particular characteristic is troublesome because it represents an intentional attempt on the part of the gifted female to sabotage academic performance and potential.

Another cause of masking and intentionally underachieving is the pressure to meet societal expectations. In fact, researchers cite this as a major case for underachievement among gifted females (Freeman, 2004; Schober, Reimann, & Wagner, 2004; Stormont et al., 2001; Wilgosh, 2001). According to Reis (2002), many young gifted girls are encouraged to pay greater attention to their looks, social status, and manners than they are to educational pursuits. As a result, these females view their giftedness as a source of embarrassment. While this might seem like an archaic view that is no longer in vogue, it still exists and is a major obstacle as to why many adolescent females hide their giftedness (Hébert, Long, & Neumeister, 2001; Reis, 2002).

Lowered Self-Concept. Stormont et al. (2001) report that on average classroom teachers overlook the mathematical and science talents of females. Reasons for this oversight range from gender stereotypes to the assertiveness of their male peers. The results of failing to recognize these talents negatively impacts gifted females' self-concept and can manifest into feelings of inferiority, unhappiness, and lowered career aspirations (Luscombe & Riley, 2001; Reis, 2002).

Gifted females' have a precocious ability to observe socialization patterns of their peers (Reis, 2002; Stormont et al., 2001). Kerr and Sodano (2003) state that this heightened sensitivity can negatively impact self-concept. Research has demonstrated that as these females enter middle school, they begin to seek social acceptance among their peers. Generally, one of two scenarios occurs. First, young females are unable to make socially prominent friends. Second, they are able to fit into desirable social groups but sacrifice academic performance to do so. These scenarios manifest themselves into feelings of lowered self-concept socially, academically, or both.

Educational Considerations

Researchers (Nugent, 2000; Reis, 2002; Stormont et al., 2001; Wilgosh, 2001) have identified several programming elements that contribute to the overall self-concept of young gifted females. Effective school programming ensures that gifted females are enrolling in intellectually challenging classes, mentorships, and extracurricular activities. The benefits of this is to empower girls to visualize themselves as achieving success and enabling them to realize their dreams.

Bibliotherapy. One effective method to help gifted females overcome societal and peer expectations is bibliotherapy. Nugent (2000) defines bibliotherapy as the process of meeting a student's affective needs through literature. Through this process, the reader forms a personal connection with the story or characters within and finds inspiration. Bibliotherapy exposes young gifted females to women of achievement and offers examples of other women with potential who overcame challenges in order to be successful.

According to Hébert et al. (2001), exposing young females to real-life examples of accomplished women serves two purposes. First, bibliotherapy introduces gifted females to role models who may not be present in their personal lives or local communities. Second, it serves as a source of inspiration to overcome environmental obstacles and to maximize their potential (Hébert et al., 2001).

Mentorships. The literature is complete with instances demonstrating the beneficial effects of mentorships with all special populations of gifted children, including gifted females (Casey, 2000; Siegle & McCoach, 2005; Wilgosh, 2001). Benefits of mentoring programs include increased self-esteem, heightened awareness of potential, and improved career aspirations. In addition to improving a young woman's self-concept, Casey (2000) reports that mentorships are an effective intervention for encouraging gifted females to pursue science- or math-focused degree and career paths.

Mentorships can greatly improve the services schools offer young gifted females. By placing them in real-world situations, gifted females are free to explore the endless possibilities of their talents. Furthermore, schools that sponsor mentorships benefit because it demonstrates their commitment to an individual's development (Milam, 2001).

Summary of Gifted Females

In order for gifted females to maximize their potential, they need to view their giftedness as a special oppotunity to pursue any career path. Educators must understand this population's inimitable talents and characteristics if they are going to provide gifted females with the necessary educational experience. Recognizing that many gifted females will grow to mask their talents enables school officials to help create mentorships and develop positive peer relationships for these young women.

SUMMARY AND CONCLUSIONS

While there are some common characteristics and programming options for all gifted children, the diversity of gifted children requires educators to individualize curricula planning. The special populations described in this chapter have unique needs that must be met in order for each individual to maximize his or her potential. To accomplish this, teachers and gifted program administrators must understand the challenges that each population faces and empower them to overcome any obstacle.

Curricular individualization is not an easy task; however, with training and a deep commitment to all children and youth, it is not a task beyond reach. When educational policymakers embrace the goal of providing every child educational opportunities fitted to maximize potential based on individual strengths, our public school system will have taken the critical first step toward meeting the needs of all children. Special populations of gifted students are a small group in the "big picture" of education; nonetheless, this group is made up of individuals who represent our future. It is imperative they be provided educational opportunities to prepare them for that role.

QUESTIONS FOR THOUGHT AND REFLECTION

1. Create a matrix identifying the various groups of gifted children discussed in this chapter. For each group, choose what you would consider the most pressing issue facing educators in the delivery of services to that particular student population. Engage in additional research to develop an action plan for meeting the needs of these students in your current or future educational setting.
2. Visit the websites listed in the resource section of this chapter related to distance-learning opportunities for students. Prepare an informative resource flyer or pamphlet for parents, students, and educators highlighting the strengths of each.
3. From a practical classroom management perspective and in light of standards-based curriculum, discuss the positive and negative aspects of the concept of "emergent curriculum" in meeting the needs of young gifted children.
4. Discuss the cognitive and affective characteristics of a selected special population of gifted children and how the characteristics of this population vary from that of typically developing children.
5. Choose one of the educational options for special populations of gifted students discussed in this chapter. List the positive and negative aspects of the option.

RESOURCES

Websites

Davidson Institute for Talent Development
www.ditd.org
Links to several articles that offer scholarly information about highly gifted individuals.

Hoagies Gifted
www.hoagiesgifted.org
Provides a wealth of information on "all things gifted." The search option can be used to find information about any of the topics presented in this chapter.

National Association for Gifted Children
www.nagc.org
Provides educators and parents with up-to-date information about legislation affecting gifted children. Additionally, the resource link page can direct interested individuals to a number of resources specific to special populations of gifted students.

National Association of Young Children
www.naeyc.org
Offers the latest information about the education of young children. Many of the publications and resources offered by this national group are "must reads" for individuals concerned with appropriate educational practices for young children.

Center for Rural Gifted Education
www.coe.iup.edu/gifted
Details support services to schools and communities in rural areas. The primary goal of the center is to provide guidance to high-ability students and their parents in locating educational opportunities.

Frances A. Karnes Center for Gifted Studies
www.usm.edu/gifted
Provides information and services about center programs for gifted children and youth and houses a number of research documents to educate teachers, administrators, and parents on special populations of gifted students.

BOOKS AND OTHER RESOURCES

Colangelo, N., Assouline, S. G., & Gross, M. U. M. (2004). *A nation deceived: How schools hold back America's brightest students.* Iowa City: Connie Belin and Jacqueline N. Blank International Center for Gifted Education and Talent Development, University of Iowa.

Provides the reader with specific information about 18 different types of acceleration and may be a valuable resource for advocates of highly gifted children. The report can be downloaded for free at *www. nationdeceived. org.*

Davidson, J., Davidson, B., & Vanderkam, L. (2004). *Genius denied: How to stop wasting our brightest young minds.* New York: Simon & Schuster.

A wake-up call to the nation's educational policymakers, *Genius Denied* gives the reader an inside look at the growing concern over the dearth of educational opportunities available to our nation's brightest students.

Henderson, M. E. (2005). *Gifted and talented females speak out on parental influences and achievement!* Lanham, MD: Hamilton.

Provides firsthand information directly from high-ability females on the critical issues faced by this special population of gifted individuals.

NAGC's Frequently Asked Questions (FAQ) Brochures
This informative collection of easy-to-read brochures covers many pertinent topics related to special populations of gifted students. Available for nominal fee at *www.nagc.org/acb/stores/1/FAQ-Brochures-P182C32.aspx.*

REFERENCES

Achter, J. A., Lubinski, D., & Benbow, C. P. (1996). Multipotentiality among the intellectually gifted: "It was never there and already it's vanishing." *Journal of Counseling Psychology, 43,* 65–76.

Adams, C. M., & Cross, T. L. (1999/2000, Winter). Distance learning opportunities for academically gifted students. *Journal of Secondary Gifted Education, 11,* 88–97.

American Psychiatric Association. (2000). *Diagnostic and statistical manual of mental disorders* (4th ed.). Washington, DC: Author.

Bandura, A. (1986). *Social foundations of thought and action: A social cognitive theory.* Englewood Cliffs, NJ: Prentice Hall.

Barbour, N. E., & Shaklee, B. D. (1998). Gifted education meets Reggio Emilia: Visions for curriculum in gifted education for young children. *Gifted Child Quarterly, 42,* 228–237.

Barnett, W. S., Hustedt, J. T., Robin, K. B., & Schulman, K. L. (2005). *The state of preschool: 2005 state preschool yearbook.* New Brunswick, NJ: National Institute for Early Education Research, Rutgers University.

Baum, S. (1990). *Gifted but learning disabled: A puzzling paradox.* Retrieved April 5, 2006, from *http://ericec.org/digests/e479.html* (ERIC Document Reproduction Service No. ED321484)

Beckley, D. (1998, Spring). Gifted and learning disabled: Twice-exceptional students. *NRC/GT Newsletter.* Retrieved July 25, 2006, from *http://www.sp.uconn.edu/~nrcgt/news/spring98/sprng984.html*

Belcastro, F. P. (2002). Electronic technology and its use with rural gifted students. *Roeper Review, 25,* 14–17.

Besnoy, K. D. (2006). Successful strategies for twice-exceptional students. In F. A. Karnes & K. R. Stephens (Eds.), *Practical strategies series in gifted education.* Waco, TX: Prufrock.

Bouchard, L. L. (2004). An instrument for the measure of Dabrowskian overexcitabilities to identity gifted elementary students. *Gifted Child Quarterly, 48,* 339–350.

Bredekamp, S., & Copple, C. (Eds.). (1997). *Developmentally appropriate practice in early childhood programs.* Washington, DC: National Association for the Education of Young Children.

Brody, E. L., & Mills, J. C. (1997). Gifted children with learning disabilities: A review of the issues. *Journal of Learning Disabilities, 30,* 282–286.

Casey, K. M. A. (2000). Mentors' contributions to gifted adolescents' affective, social, and vocational development. *Roeper Review, 22,* 227–230.

Clark, B. (2002). *Growing up gifted* (6th ed.). Upper Saddle River, NJ: Merrill/Prentice Hall.

Cline, S., & Schwartz, D. (1999). *Diverse populations of gifted children.* Upper Saddle River, NJ: Merrill.

Cohn, S. (2003). The gay gifted learner: Facing the challenge of homophobia and anithomosexual bias in schools. In J. A. Castellano (Ed.), *Special populations in gifted education: Working with diverse gifted learners* (pp. 123–134). Boston: Allyn & Bacon.

Colangelo, N., Assouline, S. G., Baldus, C. M., Ihrig, D., & New, J. (2006). *Gifted in rural America: Faces of diversity.* Iowa City: Connie Belin and Jacqueline N. Blank International Center for Gifted Education and Talent Development, University or Iowa.

Colangelo, N., Assouline, S. G., & Gross, M. U. M (2004). *A nation deceived: How schools hold back America's brightest students.* Iowa City: Connie Belin and

Jacqueline N. Blank and International Center for Gifted Education and Talent Development, University of Iowa.

Colangelo, N., Assouline, S. G., & New, J. K. (1999). *Gifted education in rural schools: A national assessment.* Iowa City: Connie Belin and Jacqueline N. Blank International Center for Gifted Education and Talent Development, University of Iowa.

Colangelo, N., Assouline, S. G., & New, J. K. (2001). *Gifted voices from rural America.* Iowa City: Connie Belin and Jacqueline N. Blank International Center for Gifted Education and Talent Development, University of Iowa.

Coleman, M. R. (2005, September/October). Academic strategies that work for gifted students with learning disabilities. *Teaching Exceptional Children, 38,* 28–32.

Dabrowski, K. (1967). *Personality shaping through positive disintegration.* New York: Little, Brown.

Davalos, R. & Griffin, G. (1999). The impact of teachers' individualized practices on gifted students in rural, heterogeneous classrooms. *Roeper Review, 21,* 308–315.

Dole, S. (2000). The implications of the risk and resilience literature for gifted students with learning disabilities. *Roeper Review, 23,* 91–106.

Fetzer, E. A. (2000, July/August). The gifted/learning-disabled child. *Gifted Child Today, 23,* 44–51.

Freeman, J. (2004). Cultural influences on gifted gender achievement. *High Ability Studies, 15,* 7–23.

Friedman, R. C., & Lee, S. W. (1996). Differentiating instruction for high-achieving/gifted children in regular classrooms: A field test of three gifted-education models. *Journal for the Education of the Gifted, 19,* 405–436

Gagné, F. (1998). A proposal for subcategories within gifted and talented populations. *Gifted Child Quarterly, 42,* 87–95.

Garland, A. F., & Zigler, E. (1999). Emotional and behavioral problems among highly intellectually gifted youth. *Roeper Review, 22,* 41–44.

Garzarelli, P., & Everhart, B. (1993). Self-concept and academic performance in gifted and academically weak students. *Adolescence, 28* (109), 235–237.

Greene, M. J. (2002). Gifted adrift? Career counseling of the gifted and talented. *Roeper Review, 25,* 66–72.

Gross, M. U. M. (1994, Summer). Radical acceleration: Responding to the academic and social needs of extremely gifted adolescents. *Journal of Secondary Gifted Education, 5,* 27–34.

Gross, M. U. M. (1999). Small poppies: Highly gifted children in the early years. *Roeper Review, 21,* 207–214.

Gross, M. U. M. (2000, Winter). Exceptionally and profoundly gifted students: An underserved population. *Understanding Our Gifted, 15,* 8–12.

Gross, M. U. M., & van Vliet, H. E. (2005). Radical acceleration and early entry to college: A review of the research. *Roeper Review, 49,* 154–171.

Hafenstein, N. L., & Tucker, B. (1995). *Psychological intensities in young gifted children.* Paper presented at the Esther Katz Rosen Symposium on the Psychological Development of Gifted Children, Lawrence, KS. (ERIC Document Reproduction Service No. ED387975)

Hall, E. G. (1993, May/June). Educating preschool gifted children. *Gifted Child Today, 16,* 24–27.

Halliday, M. (1975). *Learning how to mean: Explorations in the development of language.* New York: Elsevier.

Harrison, C. (2004). Giftedness in early childhood: The search for complexity and connection. *Roeper Review, 26,* 78–84.

Hayes, P. A., Norris, J., & Flaitz, J. R. (1998). A comparison of the oral narrative abilities of underachieving and high-achieving gifted adolescents: A preliminary investigation. *Language, Speech, and Hearing Services in Schools, 29,* 158–171.

Hébert, T. P., Long, L., & Neumeister, K. (2001). Using biography to counsel gifted young women. *Journal of Secondary Gifted Education, 12,* 62–79.

Hmelo-Silver, C. E. (2004). Problem based learning: What and how do students learn? *Educational Psychology Review, 16,* 235–266.

Hollingworth, L. S. (1942). *Children above 180 IQ: Stanford-Binet origin and development.* Yonkers-on-Hudson, NY: World Book Company.

Howley, A. (2002). The progress of gifted students in rural district that emphasized acceleration strategies. *Roeper Review, 24,* 158–161.

Hua, C. B., & Coleman, M. R. (2002, Winter). Preparing twice-exceptional children for adult lives: A critical need. *Understanding Our Gifted, 14,* 17–19.

Jackson, P. S., & Peterson, J. (2003). Depressive disorder in highly gifted adolescents. *Journal of Secondary Education, 14,* 175–186.

Johnsen, S. K., & Ryser, G. R. (1996). An overview of effective practices with gifted students in general-education settings. *Journal for the Education of the Gifted, 19,* 379–404.

Kanevsky, L., & Keighley, T. (2003). To produce or not to produce? Understanding boredom and the honor in underachievement. *Roeper Review, 26,* 20–28.

Karnes, F. A., Manning S., Besnoy, K., Cukierkorn, C., & Houston, H. (2004). *Appropriate practices for screening, identifying, and serving potentially gifted preschoolers.* Hattiesburg: Frances A. Karnes Center for Gifted Studies, The University of Southern Mississippi.

Kearney, K. (2000). *Early signs of extreme intelligence.* Retrieved July 25, 2006, from *http://www.gt-cybersource.org/Record.aspx?NavID=2_0&rid=11487*

Kennedy, D. M. (2002). Glimpses of a highly gifted child in a heterogeneous classroom. *Roeper Review, 24,* 120–124.

Kerr, B. A., & Nicpon, M. F. (2003). Gender and giftedness. In N. Colangelo & G. A. Davis (Eds.), *Handbook of gifted education* (3rd ed., pp. 493–505). Boston: Allyn & Bacon.

Kerr, B., & Sodano, S. (2003). Career assessment with intellectually gifted studennts. *Journal of Career Assessment, 11,* 168–186.

Klein, A. G., & Zehms, D. (1996). Self-concept and gifted girls: A cross sectional study of intellectually gifted females. *Roeper Review, 19,* 30–34.

Kline, B., & Meckstroth, E. (1985). Understanding and encouraging the exceptionally gifted. *Roeper Review, 8,* 24–30.

Lee, S. Y. (2002). The effects of peers on the academic and creative talent development of a gifted adolescent male. *Journal of Secondary Gifted Education, 14,* 19–29.

Lidz, C. S. (2002). Mediated learning experience (MLE) as a basis for an alternative approach to assessment. *School Psychology International, 23,* 68–84.

Little, C. (2001, Summer). A closer look at gifted children with disabilities. *Gifted Child Today, 24,* 46–52.

Lovecky, D. V. (1994). Exceptionally gifted children: Different minds. *Roeper Review, 17,* 116–120.

Lubinski, D., & Benbow, C. T. (1994). The study of mathematically precocious youth: The first three decades of a planned 50-year study. In R. F. Subotnik & K. D. Arnold (Eds.), *Beyond Terman: Contemporary longitudinal studies of giftedness and talent* (pp. 255–281). Norwood, NJ: Ablex.

Luhman, A., & Fundis, R. (1989). *Building academically strong gifted programs in rural schools.* Retrieved May 1, 2006, from *http://www.ericdigests.org/pre-9211/gifted.htm* (ERIC Document Reproduction Service No. ED308060).

Luscombe, A., & Riley, T. L. (2001). An examination of self-concept in academically gifted adolescents: Do gender differences occur? *Roeper Review, 24,* 20–22.

Manning, S. (2005, Winter). Young leaders: Growing through mentoring. *Gifted Child Today, 28,* 14–20.

Mather, D. S. (2003). Dyslexia and dysgraphia: More than written language difficulties in common. *Journal of Learning Disabilities, 36,* 307–317.

Mendaglio, S. (1995, July/August). Children who are gifted/ADHD. *Gifted Child Today,* 18, 37–38, 40.

Milam, C. P. (2001). Extending learning through mentorships. In F. A. Karnes & S. M. Bean (Eds.), *Methods and materials for teaching the gifted* (pp. 523–558). Waco, TX: Prufrock.

Montgomery, D. (2004). Broadening perspectives to meet the needs of gifted learners in rural schools. *Rural Special Education Quarterly, 23,* 3–7.

Morelock, M. J., & Feldman, D. H. (2003). Extreme precocity: Prodigies, savants, and children of extraordinarily high IQ. In N. Colangelo & G. A. Davis (Eds.), *Handbook of gifted education* (3rd ed., pp. 455–469). Boston: Allyn & Bacon.

National Association for Gifted Children. (2001). *Position paper: Appropriate education for gifted GLBT students.* Retrieved January 1, 2007, from *http://www.nagc.org/uploadedFiles/PDF/Position_Statement_PDFs/pp_GLBT.pdf*

National Research Center on Rural Education and Support (n. d.). Retrieved May 1, 2006, from *http://www.nrcres.org*

Norman, A. D., Ramsay, S. G., Martray, C. R., & Roberts, J. L. (1999). Relationship between levels of giftedness and psychosocial adjustment. *Roeper Review, 22,* 5–9.

Nugent, S. A. (2000). Perfectionism: Its manifestations and classroom-based interventions. *Journal of Secondary Gifted Education, 11,* 215–221.

Olenchak, F. R., & Reis, S. M. (2002). Gifted students with learning disabilities. In M. Neihart, S. M. Reis, N. M. Robinson, & S. M. Moon (Eds.), *The social and emotional development of gifted children: What do we know?* (pp. 177–191). Waco, TX: Prufrock.

Parke, B. N., & Ness, P. S. (1988, Winter). Curricular decision-making for the education of young gifted children. *Gifted Child Quarterly, 32,* 196–199.

Picard, C. J. (2002). *Report from the rural gifted task force: Findings and recommendations.* Louisiana Department of Education. Retrieved April 25, 2006, from *http://www.doe.state.la.us/lde/uploads/962.pdf*

Plucker, J. A., & Stocking, V. B. (2001). Looking outside and inside: Self-concept development of gifted adolescents. *Exceptional Children, 67,* 534–548.

Rayneri, L. J., Gerber, B. L., & Wiley, L. P. (2003, Summer). Gifted achievers and gifted underachievers: The impact of learning style preference in the classroom. *Journal of Secondary Gifted Education, 14,* 197–204.

Reis, S. M. (2002, Winter). Internal barriers, personal issues, and decisions faced by gifted females. *Gifted Child Today, 25,* 14–28.

Reis, S. M. (2005). Feminist perspectives on talent development: A research-based conception of giftedness in women. In R. J. Sternberg & J. E. Davidson (Eds.), *Conceptions of giftedness* (2nd ed., pp. 217–245). New York: Cambridge University Press.

Reis, S. M., Burns, D. E., & Renzulli, J. S. (1992). *Curriculum compacting: The complete guide to modifying the regular curriculum for high ability students.* Mansfield Center, CT: Creative Learning.

Richards, J., Encel, J., & Shute, R. (2003). The emotional and behavioural adjustment of intellectually gifted adolescents: A multi-dimensional, multi-informant approach. *High Ability Studies, 14,* 153–164.

Rimm, S., & Rimm-Kaufman, S. (2001). *How Jane won.* New York: Crown.

Rimm, S., Rimm-Kaufman, S., & Rimm, I. (1999). *See Jane win.* New York: Crown.

Rodell, W. C. (1984). Vulnerabilities of highly gifted children. *Roeper Review, 6,* 127–130.

Rodell, W. C. (1990). *Nurturing giftedness in young children.* Washington, DC: Office of Educational Research and Improvement. (ERIC Document Reproduction Service No. ED321492)

Sajjadi, S. H., Rejskind, F. G., & Shore, B. M. (2001). Is multipotentiality a problem or not? A new look at the data. *High Ability Studies, 12,* 27–43.

Sandel, A., McCallister, C., & Nash, W. R. (1993). Child search and screening activities for preschool gifted children. *Roeper Review, 16,* 98–102.

Schilling, S. R., Sparfeldt, J. R., & Rost, D. H. (2006). Families with gifted adolescents. *Educational Psychology, 26,* 19–32.

Schober, B., Reimann, R., & Wagner, P. (2004). Is research on gender-specific underachievement in gifted girls an obsolete topic? New findings on an often discussed issue. *High Ability Studies, 15,* 43–62.

Shaunessy, E. (2005). Questioning strategies for teaching the gifted. In F. A. Karnes & K. Stephens (Eds.) Practical Strategies Series in Gifted Education. Waco, TX: Prufrock

Siegle, D., & McCoach, D. B. (2005). Making a difference: Motivating gifted students who are not achieving. *Teaching Exceptional Children, 38,* 22–27.

Silverman, L. K. (1989). The highly gifted. In J. F. Feldhusen, J. VanTassel-Baska, & K. Seeley (Eds.), *Excellence in educating the gifted.*(pp. 71-83). Denver: Love.

Silverman, L. K. (1997). The construct of asynchronous development. *Peabody Journal of Education, 72* (3/4), 36–59.

Silverman, L. K. (1998). Through the lens of giftedness. *Roeper Review, 20*, 204–210.

Silverman, L. K., (2002). What have we learned about gifted children. Retrieved May 1, 2006, from *http://www.hoagiesgifted.org/we_have_learned.htm*

Silverman, L. K., & Kearney, K. (1992). The case for the Stanford-Binet L-M as a supplemental test. *Roeper Review, 15*, 34–38.

Snyder, T. (2006). *Navigating resources for rural schools.* Retrieved May 1, 2006, from *http://nces.ed.gov/surveys/ruraled*

Stormont, M., Stebbins, M. S., & Holliday, G. (2001). Characteristics and educational support needs of underrepresented gifted adolescents. *Psychology in the Schools, 38*, 413–423.

Swanson, H. L. (2001). Research on interventions for adolescents with learning disabilities: A meta-analysis of outcomes related to higher-order processing. *Elementary School Journal, 101,* 331–348.

Terman, L. M., & Oden, M. H. (1925). *Genetic studies of genius: Mental and physical traits of a thousand gifted children* (Vol. 1). Stanford, CA: Stanford University Press.

Terman, L. M., & Oden, M. H. (1959). *Genetic studies of genius: The gifted group at mid-life,* (Vol. 2). Stanford, CA: Stanford University Press.

Tieso, C. (1999, May/June). Meeting the socio-emotional needs of talented teens. *Gifted Child Today, 22*, 38–43.

Tolan, S. S. (1992). Parents vs. theorists: Dealing with exceptionally gifted. *Roeper Review, 15*, 14–18.

Tucker, B, & Hafenstein, N. L. (1997). Psychological intensities in young gifted children. *Gifted Child Quarterly, 41*, 66–75.

Vaidya, S. R. (1993). Gifted children with learning disabilities: Theoretical implications and instructional challenge. *Education, 113,* 568–574.

VanTassel-Baska, J. (1983). Profiles of precocity: The 1982 Midwest Talent Search finalists. *Gifted Child Quarterly, 27*, 139–144.

Wilgosh, L. (2001). Enhancing gifts and talents of women and girls. *High Ability Studies, 12*, 45–59.

Winebrenner, S. (2002, Winter). Strategies for teaching twice-exceptional students. *Understanding Our Gifted, 13*, 3–6.

Winebrenner, S. (2003). Teaching strategies for twice-exceptional students. *Intervention in School and Clinic, 38*, 131–137.

CHAPTER 9

IDENTIFYING GIFTED AND TALENTED LEARNERS

Susan K. Johnsen, Ph.D.
Baylor University

INTRODUCTION

Assessment is a process for gathering information. The process may include the use of tests, procedures, and techniques that are effective for a specific purpose, such as (a) screening, (b) classification or selection, (c) curriculum planning, (d) program planning, and/or (e) progress evaluation. While identification information may sometimes be used in curriculum and program planning, this chapter focuses primarily on the purposes of screening and selection of students for gifted and talented programs. It discusses the issues and procedures related to identification, including selecting assessments, establishing procedures, and organizing data for making placement decisions.

ISSUES RELATED TO DEFINITIONS, MODELS, AND CHARACTERISTICS

Knowing the characteristics of gifted and talented students is an essential first step in their identification. Consider these students:

- Olivia had become interested in black holes, wormholes, and white holes when she was in the second grade. She had formed her own definitions about these astronomical constructs and had a theory about the shape of the universe's fabric. She is learning algebra in the fifth grade.
- His middle school teacher describes Sam as an average student. He makes Cs at school—just enough to pass from one grade level to the next. His peers have a different perspective of his ability because they have seen the working rockets that he builds from scraps he finds in neighborhood trash cans.
- Teachers and students at Sunny High might describe Jeff as a Renaissance man. He has so many interests, plays several instruments, reads voraciously, writes poetry, takes artistic photographs, and is quite popular among his peers. When he is interested, Jeff does exceptional schoolwork; otherwise, he does not complete assignments.
- Marlo, a high school sophomore, has been writing stories at home since she was able to hold a pencil. At first, they were pictures that were described to her mother; later, they were narrative short stories about dogs. Now she is engrossed in writing a novel that she plans to submit to a publisher within the next few years. She has never shared her writing with her teachers at school. While she completes the required schoolwork and makes As on her report cards, she prefers to pursue her passion at home.

Based on true stories about gifted students, these snapshots describe some of the diversity of the gifted and talented population. Gifted students may be talented in one or more domains, demonstrate their gifts at school and/or at home, make excellent or poor grades, and come from a variety of backgrounds. They are all learners who are curious to know more about everything, as in the case of Jeff, or about their passions, as in the cases of Olivia, Sam, and Marlo. This diversity is captured in the federal definition:

> The term "gifted and talented" when used in respect to students, children, or youth means students, children, or youth who give evidence of high performance capability in areas such as intellectual, creative, artistic, or leadership capacity, or in specific academic fields, and who require services or activities not ordinarily provided by the school in order to fully develop such capabilities. (Improving America's Schools Act, 1994, p. 388)

Of the 44 states that reported diversity in their definitions, 30 (68%) recognize intellectually gifted, 29 (66%) academically gifted, 20 (45%) performing/visual arts, 19 (43%) creatively gifted, and 13 (29.5%) leadership (National Association for Gifted Children and Council of State Directors of Programs for the Gifted, 2005). This diversity has also been acknowledged by researchers and incorporated into their conceptual models (Gagné, 1995, 1999; Tannenbaum, 2003).

Models

In their conceptual models of giftedness, researchers have described not only the diversity of gifts and talents but also the multiplicity of factors that influence their development. For example, Tannenbaum (2003) identifies general ability (e.g., "*g*" or general intelligence), special ability (e.g., aptitude in a specific area), nonintellective facilitators (e.g., metalearning, dedication to a chosen field, strong self-concept, willingness to sacrifice, and mental health), environmental influences (e.g., parents, classroom, peers, culture, and social class), and chance (e.g., accidental, general exploratory, sagacity, and personalized action) as influencing the emergence of excellence in a specific domain. These factors are static and dynamic—influencing the individual at a single point in time and also changing over time.

Gagné's (1995, 1999) *Differentiated Model of Giftedness and Talent* also describes a multiplicity of factors, that are placed in two categories: intrapersonal and environmental catalysts. Intrapersonal catalysts are influenced by genetic background and include physical (e.g., health and physical appearance) and psychological (e.g., motivation, personality, and volition) factors. Environmental catalysts are surroundings (e.g., geographic, demographic, and sociological), persons (e.g., parents, teachers, siblings, and peers), undertakings (e.g., programs for gifted and talented students), and events (e.g., death of a parent, major illness, and winning a prize). *Gifts*, which are natural abilities, are influenced by catalysts and develop into *talents*, which emerge through systematic learning, training, and practicing skills specific to a particular domain. In Gagné's model, programs need to focus on the development of the student's gift in a specific domain or field at the level of the student's giftedness or talent (e.g., performing in the top 10%, 5%, 2%, 1%, or less than 1%).

Characteristics

The virtually unlimited combinations of factors and talent domains produce a variety of characteristics that describe the gifted and talented student. Researchers have identified sets of characteristics that are categorized within each of the broad areas of the federal definition (Table 9–1; Clark, 1997; Clark & Zimmerman, 1984; Colangelo & Davis, 1991; Coleman & Cross, 2001; Davis & Rimm, 1994;

TABLE 9–1 Characteristics of Gifted and Talented Students

Intellectual (general ability—"g")	Creative (within knowledge area)	Artistic (within artistic field)	Leadership (within specific situations)	Academic (within field of interest)
• Has detailed memory • Uses advanced vocabulary • Asks intelligent questions • Identifies essential concept/attributes of problems • Solves difficult and unusual problems • Learns quickly • Uses logic • Has a large base of knowledge • Understands abstract ideas and complex concept • Uses analogical reasoning • Observes relationships • Understands principles, generalizations • Transfers knowledge to new situations • Is curious • Concentrates in area of interest • Uses various symbol systems • Reflects about learning	• Has in-depth knowledge • Prefers complexity and novelty • Contributes new ideas, products, performances • Has fluency of ideas • Is observant • Uses unique solutions in solving problems • Challenges existing ideas • Connects disparate ideas • Asks questions constantly • Criticizes constructively • Is a risk taker • Accepts disorder • Tolerates ambiguity • Is persistent • Is intellectually playful • Is emotionally sensitive • Is intuitive • Has a sense of humor	• Chooses artistic activity during free time • Practices without being told • Studies to improve skill • Demonstrates artistic talent over time • Concentrates for long periods of time • Picks up skills in the arts with little instruction • Possesses high sensory sensitivity • Observes and shows interest in others who are proficient • Uses artistic area to communicate • Experiments in artistic area • Sets high standards • Demonstrates confidence	• Is well organized • Can do backward planning • Is visionary • Is a problem finder • Able to see problems from multiple perspectives • Adaptable to new situations • Can manipulate systems • Is highly responsible • Maintains on-task focus • Is self-confident • Is a persuasive communicator • Works well in groups • Enjoys being around people • Recognized as leader by peers • Is respected by others • Recognizes verbal and nonverbal cues • Is emotionally stable	• Has intense interest that is sustained • Has hobbies related to field • Enjoys complex problems • Analyzes problems • Understands abstract ideas • Is self-motivated • Has broad base of knowledge • Reads widely • Learns quickly • Asks intelligent questions • Recalls details • Uses advanced vocabulary • Translates information into other forms • Sees connections and relationships • Transfers knowledge

Source: Adapted from Johnsen (2004a).

Feldhusen, Hoover, & Sayler, 1990; Gardner, 1993; Gilliam, Carpenter, & Christensen, 1996; Goertzel & Goertzel, 1962; Gruber, 1981; Guilford, 1950; Karnes, 1991; Khatena, 1992; Perkins, 1981; Piirto, 1999; Renzulli et al., 2002; Rogers, 2001; Ryser & McConnell, 2004; Sternberg, 1988; Sternberg & Davidson, 1986; Swassing, 1985; Tannenbaum, 1983; Torrance, 1974).

While some commonalities exist across these general areas of giftedness (e.g., keen observer, problem solver or problem finder, and question asker), diversity is present not only in the characteristics but also in their expression. For example, one student may be gifted in math, another in language arts. In the former case, the gifted student may appreciate parsimony, simplicity, and economy in solutions; in the latter case, the gifted student may enjoy elaborating ideas in writing or in speaking. Similarly, a creative student may accept disorder, tolerate ambiguity, and produce products that push the limits of the current system, whereas a future leader may be very organized, focused on a goal, and have the ability to develop a plan that is coherent and sequenced.

Issues

This diversity raises important issues when identifying gifted students.

Issue 1. Giftedness is exhibited not only within a specific area or category but also within a specific area of interest or expertise within that category. For example, when identifying students who have a talent in writing, that talent may be exhibited only when writing about a particular topic, such as science fiction. Similarly, leadership may emerge only within an area of expertise, such as building bridges, not in all situations. Within the identification process, professionals must seek ways to gather examples across a variety of domains and contexts.

Issue 2. The presence or absence of a gift is dynamic, not static. Educators who adhere to a strict cutoff score on intelligence or other aptitude tests frequently believe that the "gift" is innate or set (e.g., once gifted, always gifted). Students are tested at one point in time and must meet the criterion to be accepted into the gifted and talented program. On the other hand, those whose conception of giftedness is toward a more talent development model (e.g., Gagné, 1999) assume that specific conditions need to be created for the talent to emerge and to be developed. Limited experiences to display gifts is particularly true for children from poverty who may not have had learning resources at home or been involved in out-of-school enrichment activities (Johnsen, Robins, Witte, & Feuerbacher, 2003). Therefore, the identification process needs to occur over time with opportunities for the students to exhibit their gifts through products and performances.

Issue 3. Giftedness is exhibited across all racial, ethnic, income levels, and exceptionality groups. While most states have definitions, policies, or rules that address the identification of gifted students from special populations, underrepresentation still occurs (Coleman, Gallagher, & Foster, 1994; National Association for Gifted Children and Council of State Directors of Programs for the Gifted, 2005). Ford (1996) estimates that African American, Hispanic American, and Native American students are underrepresented by about 50% in programs for the gifted. Various explanations have been provided for this underrepresentation, such as (a) exclusive definitions, (b) attitudes, and (c) test fairness (Ryser, 2004).

Exclusive Definitions. Narrow definitions requiring superior performance on intelligence or achievement tests (e.g., 130 or 98th percentile) may limit the number of students who are gifted, particularly those who are English-language learners and those from lower income groups. Broader definitions that encompass a wider range of characteristics similar to the federal definition and use multiple assessments are more likely to identify students who exhibit their talents in a variety of ways (Passow & Frasier, 1996).

Attitudes. In light of high-stakes testing, teachers of children from economically disadvantaged backgrounds may view their job as one of remediation rather than talent development and not nominate students for gifted programs because they are looking only for students who are academic achievers (Johnsen & Ryser, 1994). Similarly, teachers who do not recognize that giftedness takes many forms may view language as important in identification and rate English-language learners lower than native-English-speaking students (Fernandez, Gay, Lucky, & Gavilán, 1998; Plata & Masten, 1998). Gifted children with disabilities also pose special problems because their disability may mask their ability or vice versa (Whitmore, 1981). Since special education services most often focus on the disability, the exceptional student's gift may go unrecognized. In all these cases, if the students' characteristics are too different from the macroculture or from a stereotyped view of model, gifted students, they are less likely to be identified. While parents from lower-income backgrounds may be helpful in identifying their children for gifted programs (Johnsen & Ryser, 1994), some minority parents may not request evaluations of their child for future placement in the gifted program (Scott, Perou, Urbano, Hogan, & Gold, 1992). Parents and teachers need to be educated about the range of characteristics within the gifted population so that more children from diverse backgrounds are nominated. Parent education may occur through orientations at the beginning of the school year, special meetings, brochures that are written in languages that parents will understand, and announcements through public media, such as local television channels or newspapers. Since only six states require gifted and talented training at the preservice level and only 23 states require professionals in specialized programs for gifted and talented to have a certificate or a license, school districts will want to establish their own professional development programs in gifted education, offering staff development hours. In all cases, special attention needs to be paid not only to the range of characteristics but also to attitudes toward underrepresented populations (National Association for Gifted Children and Council of State Directors of Programs for the Gifted, 2005).

Test Fairness. Fairness relates to the characteristics of the norming population, the linguistic demands of the instrument, and item bias (Ryser, 2004). First, test norms should reflect the population of individuals who live in the United States but may not reflect local norms. Given changing demographics, some school districts with a greater number of individuals from minority or ethnic groups may establish local norms for comparison purposes. In this case, the schools would accumulate norms on students who have been nominated for the gifted and talented program. Using these data, the school would then examine its own score distribution and identify standards that would be used during the identification process. For example, the mean or average score on a test might vary significantly for the local population compared to the national population. This variation would be considered when the committee reviews test data. Second, tests with high language demands may create barriers for culturally and linguistically diverse students and those from economically disadvantaged backgrounds (Bernal, 1981; Johnsen & Ryser, 1994; Reid, Udall, Romanoff, & Algozzine, 1999). To reduce these barriers, professionals have recommended the use of nonverbal or individually administered tests (Ryser, 2004). These types of tests not only limit linguistic requirements but also reduce the amount of previous information required in responding to the items. Finally, items may be biased against certain cultural and socioeconomic groups (e.g., knowledge is required that is unknown within a particular culture). Most test developers have professionals review the items for gender or cultural stereotyping and analyze each item statistically (e.g., differential item functioning) to ensure that every special group has the same probability of answering the item correctly.

In summary, more equal representation across groups is enhanced when (a) definitions are broader, (b) professional development for teachers and parents is provided, and (c) tests that are fair to all populations in the identification process are used.

Issue 4. Early identification improves the likelihood that gifts will be developed into talents. When minority students are identified early and attend schools and classes for gifted and talented students, they have higher achievement than those who are placed in general education classrooms (Borland, Schnur, & Wright, 2000; Cornell, Delcourt, Goldberg, & Bland, 1995). On the other hand, when no gifted education services are provided for children from lower-income backgrounds, their scores may decrease at twice the rate as those who are not identified as gifted (Johnsen & Ryser, 1994). With no services, these young children receive not differentiated instruction that nurtures early indications of potential but rather a skill-based curriculum that focuses on their weaknesses. The identification of talents needs to begin early, particularly for minority students and those students from low-income backgrounds.

Characteristics of gifted students and these issues influence the entire identification process and are essential considerations when selecting instruments.

SELECTING ASSESSMENTS

Assessments need to (a) be aligned with the characteristics of gifted and talented students within a specified domain or talent area, (b) gather information across a variety of contexts from different sources, and (c) be technically adequate.

Assessment Alignment

The diversity of the gifted and talented population requires a variety of assessments that are aligned with characteristics of gifted and talented students within a specific domain and talent area. For example, when identifying students who are gifted and talented in mathematics, assessments will need to show the student's ability to analyze, reason, organize data, creatively solve math problems, and acquire new math concepts more rapidly than other students. On the other hand, for a student who is gifted and talented in language arts, assessments will need to demonstrate the student's enjoyment of language or of conducting research in an area of interest and the student's ability to see details, organize ideas in speaking and writing, entertain alternative points of view, use original ideas in speaking or writing, and visualize and translate images into written or spoken forms.

Multiple Assessments

The variety of characteristics and performance contexts within each of the areas within the federal definition (intellectual, creative, artistic, leadership, and specific academic fields) require more than one assessment to identify a student who is gifted and talented. Using multiple assessments is important because they (a) sample a wider range of behaviors; (b) provide more sources of information, such as from peers, parents, teachers, and the student; and (c) add reliability and validity to the process (i.e., consistency in scores and multiple viewpoints; Coleman & Cross, 2001; Johnsen, 2005; Salvia & Ysseldyke, 2001). To ensure that the assessments accurately represent the student's performance in an area of talent and across contexts, qualitative and quantitative instruments are frequently used. Quantitative instruments are those that use numbers to describe the student's performance in relation to others (e.g., norm-referenced tests such as an intelligence test) or the degree that a student may possess a particular characteristic in relationship to a standard level of performance (e.g., criterion-referenced achievement tests). Qualitative instruments are those that use words to describe a student's strengths or weaknesses, such as interviews, observations, and portfolios of work.

Returning to our examples of students who may be gifted and talented in math and/or language arts, these assessments might be selected:

- **Achievement tests in math or language arts to determine what the students already have learned and if they are more advanced than their grade-level peers**—These assessments should not have a ceiling such as state proficiency tests so that students are able to show what they know. Schools may use out-of-grade-level tests or those that are specifically designed for gifted populations, such as the *Test of Mathematical Abilities for Gifted Students* (Ryser & Johnsen, 1998) or the *Screening Assessment for Gifted Elementary Students,* second edition (SAGES-2; Johnsen & Corn, 2001).
- **Peer, teacher, and/or parent checklists of characteristics related to math or language arts**—These observations may be made using a rating scale, checklist, or an anecdotal "jot down" procedure where teachers list names of students when they exhibit a particular characteristic during instruction (Texas Education Agency, n.d., a). In collecting anecdotal information, teachers plan instructional tasks that show how students organize ideas in speaking and writing for linguistically talented students or data in solving problems for mathematically talented students.

- **Portfolios of work that include the students' reflections of their products or performance that are collected over time (e.g., math problems or writing/oral speeches)**—These products are collected at home, at school, or both to demonstrate a specific set of characteristics (Johnsen & Ryser, 1997). Criteria that might be used for both math and language arts include details in the presentation of an idea, creative responses to tasks, work advanced beyond grade level, and in-depth understanding of an idea (Texas Education Agency, n.d., b). Other criteria might be developed that relate specifically to math or language arts.
- **Observations of improvements in student performance over time where the teacher assesses, teaches, and reassesses (e.g., dynamic assessment; Borland & Wright, 1994; Johnsen, 1997; Kirschenbaum, 1998)**—The teaching task needs to be problem based and require complex strategies so that potential may be discovered (Geary & Brown, 1991; Kurtz & Weinert, 1989; Scruggs & Mastropieri, 1985). When related to student interest and talent, this type of assessment is particularly helpful in identifying potentially gifted, economically disadvantaged students (Borland & Wright, 1994).
- **General reasoning assessments, such as intelligence tests that focus on flexibility in solving nonverbal or verbal problems**—Nonverbal or individually administered tests may be more effective for students from culturally and linguistically different or economically disadvantaged backgrounds (Ryser, 2004). Examples of nonverbal tests include the *Naglieri Nonverbal Ability Test* (Naglieri, 2003), the *SAGES-2* Reasoning subtest (Johnsen & Corn, 2001), the *Test of Nonverbal Intelligence,* third edition (Brown, Sherbenou, & Johnsen, 1997), and the *Universal Nonverbal Intelligence Test* (Bracken & McCallum, 1998).

Technical Adequacy

These questions may be helpful in determining the technical adequacy of qualitative and/or quantitative assessments (Jolly & Hall, 2004):

1. What is the age of the assessment? The age of the instrument is based on the date when the norms were collected and *not* the date of the latest edition. An assessment that uses norms that are more than 12 years old should not be used because of the changing demographics of schools in the United States.
2. What is the purpose for the assessment? The assessment should relate to the area of giftedness, to the identification of gifted and talented students, and to the program option. For example, a creativity test would not be an effective measure for identifying students with a potential talent in mathematics. Similarly, an achievement test would not be an effective measure for identifying students who are talented in the performing arts. In this case, an audition would be better than a paper-and-pencil task.
3. Is the assessment valid for the purpose? Validity is based on how well the assessment relates to the desired criterion and the domain.
   a. Questions about the desired criterion might include these: Does the assessment relate to the student's performance within the domain? Does it discriminate between students who are talented in the domain from those who are not? Does it relate to other assessments that are judged to be effective in identifying talent in the domain? Does it predict those who perform well in the domain? Is the student's performance similar to those who are considered expert within the domain?
   b. Questions about the domain might include these: Does the assessment sample a range of knowledge and skills within the domain? Are these knowledge and skills important within the domain? Do the knowledge and skills examine more complex behaviors, such as problem solving?
4. Is the assessment nonbiased? The technical manual should describe how the norms are representative of national norms, particularly racial and ethnic groups; how each item has been examined for bias; and, in the case of nonverbal assessment, the language requirements for the assessment. Even if the assessment is fair, bias may enter the identification procedure if those involved in the nomination process have negative attitudes or stereotypes toward certain groups of students (Frasier, 1997; Ryser, 2004). Training is essential to ensure that the instrument is used fairly and effectively.
5. Is the assessment reliable? Reliability studies address how consistently the assessment measures the domain (e.g., internal consistency), is consistent over time (e.g., test–retest reliability), and is consistent between raters or observers (e.g., interrater/scorer reliability). Without consistency, a student might receive different scores from one time to the next or different ratings from different individuals. For this reason, those who provide qualitative ratings on assessments, such as portfolios or checklists, need to be trained to ensure consistency across students, classrooms, and schools.
6. Do the norms match national census data and reflect the school district's population? For norm-referenced tests, the technical manual should provide a table that shows the percentage of students in each of the norming groups (e.g., ethnicity, race, gender, geographic area, family income, parent educational attainment, and urban

vs. suburban vs. rural) and how these percentages relate to national census data. If a particular school varies considerably from the national norms, the district may want to consider local norms for meaningful comparisons.

7. What types of scores does the instrument provide? Tests provide a variety of scores, including raw scores, percentile ranks, grade-equivalent scores, and standard scores. When using multiple assessments, standard scores are essential for comparison purposes.
8. How is the test administered? Clear instructions need to be provided for both qualitative and quantitative instruments. In this way, consistency will be ensured across individuals, settings, and schools. Group-administered tests are useful if a school is going to screen a large number of students. If students are referred for screening, similar to special education, then an individual administered format would be preferable. Another important aspect to consider when selecting instruments is the degree of training required for administration. For example, only school psychologists may administer some tests, such as the *Wechsler Intelligence Scale for Children.* Some qualitative assessments, such as portfolios, require more professional development. In any case, all who are involved in the administration of assessments should have training and be aware of the standards of the American Educational Research Association, American Psychological Association, and National Council on Measurement in Education (1999).
9. What is the cost of administering the assessment? Once strong assessments have been identified, administrators will want to consider costs in terms of both human and material resources. How much does the assessment cost? How much training is needed? How long does it take to administer the assessment?

A number of resources are available that review instruments. These include the *Buros Mental Measurements Yearbooks* (Buros Center for Testing, n.d.); *Test Critiques,* volumes 1 to 10 (Keyser & Sweetland, 2004); *Tests in Print,* volume 6 (Murphy, Plake, Impara, & Spies, 2002); *Tests: A Comprehensive Reference for Assessments in Psychology, Education, and Business,* fifth edition (Maddox, 2003); and Jolly and Hall's (2004) chapter on technical information regarding assessment that reviews assessments frequently used in gifted education.

ESTABLISHING PROCEDURES

Identification procedures generally include a systematic winnowing process to find students that need services beyond the general education program that is free of bias. Some questions that need to be addressed in the procedures include these:

1. How often will students be assessed for the gifted education program? Will it be once or twice a year or ongoing? When will transfer students be assessed?
2. Will students be reassessed when the program or their performance changes? How frequently will the reassessment occur?
3. How many phases will be included in the procedure? Will all students be administered all assessments?
4. How might the identification procedure ensure equal access for all students?
5. How will parents and guardians appeal a placement decision?
6. How will students be exited from the program?

The answers to these questions will be addressed in the three following sections: multilevel phases, bias, and due process.

Multilevel Phases

While the majority of states do not require local education agencies to follow the same identification process (National Association for Gifted Children and Council of State Directors of Programs for the Gifted, 2005), most school districts choose to establish a multilevel procedure. This procedure generally includes a nomination or identification phase, a screening or selection phase, and a placement phase.

Nomination Phase. During the nomination phase, a variety of sources, such as teachers, parents, peers, counselors, and the student him- or herself, may identify a student who may need services or activities not ordinarily provided by the general education program. The purpose of this phase is to cast a broad net in identifying as many students as possible who might need special services. Typical assessments used during this phase include checklists, observations, portfolios of work, group-administered intelligence and/or achievement tests, and information in students' cumulative records (e.g., grades, state tests, and teacher anecdotal information). Some schools even advertise in the local newspaper or post flyers in churches and grocery stores to ensure that everyone is aware of services for gifted and talented students.

In a few states, particularly those where gifted education is within special education, such as Kansas and Pennsylvania, a prereferral process is added to the nomination phase. During this phase, the teacher uses dynamic assessment (e.g., assesses, teaches, and reassesses) and observes the student's responses to a variety of interventions (Table 9–2). Those students who demonstrate behaviors that show talents or performances above grade level are referred to the next phase: screening.

TABLE 9–2 Prereferral Interventions

Intervention	Possible Observation Question
Contracting	In what ways is the student able to work independently when pursuing an area of interest?
Open ended	When given opportunities, how does the student show creativity or more complexity in the content or in an area of interest?
Independent study	What interests or passions does the student have?
Research skills	After learning research skills, in what ways is the student able to pursue a topic of interest over time?
Formative assessment/compacting	How much of the basic grade-level knowledge and skills has the student already learned?
Acceleration	How does the student learn above-grade-level content?
Mentorship	When guided by a mentor, how does the student perform in an area of interest?
Varied methods of presentations	In what ways does the student learn best?
Questioning	What types of questions are most stimulating to the student?
Differentiated assessment	How does the student respond to more complex levels of questions on assessments?
Long-term assignments	How does the student respond to activities that allow for more in-depth study, particularly in an area of interest?
Ability group	How does the student respond when grouped with other students of similar interest and/or ability?
New knowledge and skills	How quickly does the student learn new knowledge and skills in his or her talent area?

Screening Phase. During this phase, individually administered assessments or assessments that are specifically designed to identify gifted students are used. These assessments provide more in-depth information about the student's characteristics and include interviews, auditions, observations of learning new knowledge or skills, portfolios of specific talent areas, and individually administered intelligence, aptitude, and/or achievement tests.

Placement Phase. At this phase, all the data collected during the nomination and screening phases are compiled and reviewed by a committee of professionals who make a decision about the types of services that the student requires to fully develop his or her talent.

The information may be organized for the committee's consideration in a variety of ways, such as in case studies or profiles, as long as it provides access to all special groups and meets the following guidelines (Johnsen, 2004b).

Equal Weighting of Assessments. If qualitative and quantitative assessments are technically adequate, then the committee needs to consider each one equally in making placement decisions. Weighting may occur in a number of different ways. First, if the teacher provides information for several assessments, such as grades, classroom checklists, and portfolios, then the committee is weighting this one source more than other sources. Second, the committee might view quantitative assessments as more valid and/or reliable than qualitative assessments (e.g., intelligence tests are better indicators than product portfolios). Third, a specific cutoff score might be needed on one of the assessments before the rest of the data are considered. For example, a student might need to perform in the top 5% on an intelligence test to be considered for the gifted program. Finally, one assessment's subtests might be used as separate criteria in the process, which would weight heavily on the performance of a single instrument (e.g., math, reading, social studies, and science subtests on one achievement test each receive points toward the placement of a student).

Best Performance. The student's best performance is likely to be indicative of potential (Tolan, 1992a, 1992b). Students don't always perform similarly across assessments because they sample different behaviors in different domains. For this reason, scores on each assessment and each assessment's subtest should be separated so that the committee can view the student's relative strengths and weaknesses. Summing and averaging scores may lead to misinterpretation of the student's potential.

Description of the Student over Time. Given that talent is developed over time, information needs to be provided regarding the student's performance and/or products over time. This description might include clinical impressions from those who administered quantitative assessments, anecdotal information from classroom or home observations, students' reflections regarding their products, and/or students' responses to teaching tasks.

Comparable Scores. Quantitative assessments generate different types of scores: raw scores, percentile ranks, grade-equivalent scores, and standard scores. These scores need to be transformed for comparison purposes.

Raw scores are original numeric values before they are transformed to other scores. They do not have any inherent meaning because it is difficult to determine if the score indicates above- or below-average test performance. For example, a student who scored 78 points on a chemistry test might have made the "best score" or the "worst score" in comparison to the rest of her class. Similarly, a score of 95 in one teacher's class may be quite different than the same score in another class. Therefore, raw scores cannot meaningfully be compared with each other.

Percentiles are derived from raw scores. It is important not to confuse percentile ranks with percentages. Percentages are simply the number of items that a student passed divided by the total number of items and are therefore raw scores. Percentiles, on the other hand, are ordinal data that show the relative rank of how a student performed in relationship to other students who took the same test. For example, a student who obtained a percentile rank of 95 performed better than 95% of the students who took the test. While these scores are useful and easily understood, they cannot be averaged or otherwise operated on arithmetically since they are not interval data. They cluster heavily around the mean, or 50th percentile, and are more sparsely distributed at the top and bottom (e.g., the tails) of a normal curve distribution. A difference between a 50 and a 55 represents a much smaller difference than a difference between a 95 and a 99.

The mean raw score is obtained for children in each grade. Using interpolation, extrapolation, and smoothing, *grade-equivalent scores* are then generated for each raw score point achieved on a test. Psychometrists have criticized the use of these scores because the content of instruction varies from grade to grade, and they are open to serious misinterpretation (Anastasi & Urbina, 1997; Salvia & Ysseldyke, 2001). For example, a third-grade student who received a 7.5 grade-equivalent score on a math achievement test does not mean that she has mastered the math knowledge and skills at a seventh-grade level. It simply means that she is performing above grade level. A curriculum-based assessment is more likely to indicate the knowledge that she has learned. Grade equivalents should therefore not be used in making placement decisions.

Standard scores are derived from the raw scores and are transformed into a normalized score distribution (e.g., bell-shaped curve). These scores come in a variety of forms, such as *z* scores, *T* scores, normal curve equivalents, quotients, and stanines, all of which are expressed in standard deviation units to indicate the score's distance from the mean or average performance of the group. Because these scores are on an equal interval scale, they are much more versatile than the other types of scores because they can be compared to other standard scores with the same mean and standard deviation and can be added and subtracted. For example, a score of 130 on an intelligence test with a standard deviation of 15 is comparable to a score of 130 on an achievement test with a standard deviation of 15. Books about tests and measurement and test publishers provide conversion charts to compare various test scores with one another and to a normal distribution. Scores in the top 2.34% of the normal distribution are generally recognized as being in the very superior range, in the top 6.8% in the superior range, in the top 16.12% in the above-average range, and in the top 49.51% in the average range. Note that in Table 9–3, a performance of 125 is similar to a percentile rank of 95, a normalized curve equivalent score of 85, a *T* score of 67, a *z* score of 1.67, and a stanine of 8. This score at the 95th percentile (in the top 5%), therefore, indicates that the student is scoring well above average, in the superior range. Since these derived scores are on an equal interval scale, they should never be assigned a rank order number, such as in matrices, where a range of standard scores is assigned a rank, making them less versatile and open to misinterpretation.

All these scores represent the performance of a group of students who were administered the test (e.g., the norm-reference group). This norm-reference group may be comprised of a national, state, or local sample and should be considered when comparing scores. For example, a student whose performance is compared to the performance of only students nominated for the gifted program may score lower than when compared to *all* the students in the school district. Similarly, a student who is compared to a national *gifted* sample may not perform as well when compared to the entire national sample. In addition, young kindergarten children who have summer birthdays may appear to do less well when compared to children who have fall birthdays. At early grade levels, age may be a more useful comparison. In some cases, for more accurate comparisons, local norms may need to be developed for students who are from districts that have a dominant minority or income level group or whose

TABLE 9–3 Relationships Among Various Standard Scores and Percentile Ranks

Percentile Ranks	Quotients	Normalized Curve Equivalent Scores	*T* Scores	*Z* Scores	Stanines
99	150	99	83	+3.33	9
99	145	99	80	+3.00	9
99	140	99	77	+2.67	9
99	135	99	73	+2.33	9
98	130	92	70	+2.00	9
95	125	85	67	+1.67	8
91	120	78	63	+1.33	8
84	115	71	60	+1.00	7
75	110	67	57	+0.67	6
63	105	64	53	+0.33	6
50	100	50	50	0.00	5
37	95	43	47	−0.33	4
25	90	36	43	−0.67	4
16	85	29	40	−1.00	3

scores differ dramatically from the nationally normed scores offered for comparison purposes.

Test Error. Every assessment has error. With quantitative assessments, this error is based on the reliability and the standard deviation of the test. A single test score is therefore not absolute and is merely an estimate of test performance that can be affected by any number of variables that relate to the test itself, the situation, or the test taker. The standard error of measurement (*SEM*) is one way of calculating the upper and lower limits of the range in which the student's true score actually lies. This range is defined by adding and subtracting the *SEM* from a student's obtained score. For example, 68% of the time, a student's true score will likely fall within a range ±1 *SEM* from the obtained test score, 95% of the time between ±2 *SEM*, and 99% of the time between about ±2.5 *SEM*. For example, suppose that Krystal scored 115 on an intelligence test with an *SEM* of five points. One would expect that 68% of the time, her true score would be within the range of 110 to 120, 95% of the time within the range of 105 to 125, and 99% of the time within the range of 100 to 130. In interpreting Krystal's score, she might conceivably score within the average (e.g., 100) to superior (e.g., 130) range 99% of the time. Therefore, test error is important when interpreting scores and making placement decisions.

Once the committee organizes, interprets, and makes decisions regarding placement, they recommend possible services that match the student's characteristics and talent domain. Similar to special education, individual student services might include specialized materials or human support provided to the general education teacher, opportunities to work with other gifted and talented students with similar interests and abilities for part or all of the day (e.g., a resource room, self-contained classroom, or magnet school setting), working with a mentor who has expertise in the student's area of talent, acceleration (e.g., full grade, single subject, or concurrent enrollment in a college setting), or special contests or competitions, summer or year-round enrichment programs. These options may vary, depending on the school district's resources. Since the number of identified students may vary from year to year, the program options need to be flexible and matched to individual student characteristics.

Example Case Study. While many forms meeting these suggested guidelines might be used to display data for placement decisions, a sample case study form is provided in Figure 9–1. Case study approaches have been recommended as one of the best ways of identifying children from lower-income backgrounds (Borland & Wright, 1994) and are able to show growth in performance across a variety of settings.

This cover page from a folder of work based on a composite of identified students provides a summary of the evidence for "Tony Ramirez," a first-grade student at Daily Elementary in the Ely Public School District. The top part of the form provides student demographic information, including first language and date of birth, which is important in interpreting the data. In this case, the committee needs to consider two factors that might contribute to Tony's performance. His primary language is Spanish, so he is in the process of learning English, and he was born in July, which places him with the younger-age children in his classroom.

The data have been organized into types of assessments: observations, products/performances, aptitude tests, and achievement tests. The school has provided information from a variety of sources—teacher, parent, peer, and Tony (e.g., reflections in the portfolio and his performance on assessments). For qualitative data, the committee makes a recommendation on the basis of the presented evidence; for quantitative data, the committee considers the stanine scores and determines if they

Date Referred 11-6-06 **ELY PUBLIC SCHOOLS** ID# 807506
GIFTED EDUCATION

Student Name Tony Ramirez School/Grade Daily/1st DOB July 8, 2000
Parent Name E. D. Ramirez Phone (H) 712-5873 (W) 776-5339
Address 534 Speight City Moderno ZIP 76795

First Language Spanish Other Language English Ethnicity H
Nominated by Salinas Teacher Salinas **Male** /Female

	Assessment		Standard	Student's Actual Score or Summary			Comments
Observation	Teacher		Recommend	Learning math content two grade levels above grade. Uses creative math methods in solving problems; learns quickly. Enjoys logic problems.			**(Check One)** ✓1. Highly Recommend 2. Recommend 3. With reservation 4. Not recommend
	Parent		Recommend				
	Peer		Recommend				
	Teaching Task		Recommend				
Portfolio of Products or Performance	Portfolio samples may include writing, math, drawings, drafts, books read, unusual products, planned experiences, awards, and so on.		Recommend	Math work shows advanced problem solving at higher grade levels. Integrates math into independent study projects (see statistics in baseball study).			**(Check One)** ✓1. Highly Recommend 2. Recommend 3. With reservation 4. Not recommended
Aptitude Tests	Test	Date	Superior Range on total and/or one or more subtests	V	NV	T	Superior range on total scores on both instruments; superior range on CoGAT nonverbal.
	CoGAT	2005		7	9	8	
	TONI-3	2006				9	
Achievement Tests	Test ITBS	Date 2006	Superior Range on total and/or one or more subtests				Additional Testing: Achievement test shows strength in mathematics.
	LA	7		Above Average			
	Math	9		Very Superior			
	Total	8		Superior			

Recommendation for Placement:
Tony should be accelerated in the subject area of math and receive services from the GT teacher. In the general education program, Ms. Salinas should continue with curriculum compacting in math, which allows Tony to use statistics in a topic of interest. Tony appears to be doing well in learning English and should be reevaluated at the end of the year to determine other areas where he might need GT services.

Admission/Review/Exit (ARE) Committee signatures:
Administrator ____________________
Teacher ____________________
GT Specialist ____________________
Counselor ____________________
Other ____________________

FIGURE 9–1 Case Study Form
Source: Adapted from the Carrollton-Farmers Branch School District, Carrollton, TX, 2006.

are in the superior range. The school has chosen to use stanine scores because they are comparable and provide a range of performance that takes into account some of the error in the assessments.

Before the committee met, each of the members reviewed the evidence for Tony. After talking with Tony's parents, Ms. Salinas, his teacher, referred Tony for additional testing. She noticed that in kindergarten, he had performed well on the *Cognitive Abilities Test* (CoGAT; Lohman & Hagen, 2001). Using a variety of formative assessments and teaching tasks, she discovered that he already knew many math concepts and acquired new ones rapidly. Given that Tony was an English-language learner, the school decided to administer the *Test of Nonverbal Intelligence*, third edition (TONI-3; Brown et al., 1997), because it would not be linguistically demanding. In addition, they administered the *Iowa Test of Basic Skills* ITBS; (Hoover, Dunbar, & Frisbie, 2001/2003) to determine Tony's level of achievement in his area of strength, mathematics, and to determine any additional strengths or weaknesses.

At the time of the meeting, the committee shared their initial reviews and summarized their comments in the "student's actual score/summary" or "comments" columns, depending on the type of assessment. In reviewing the observation and product examples, the committee recognized the characteristics of a student who was talented in math and gave Tony a high recommendation. His quantitative assessments corroborated the evidence from the qualitative ones. He received a stanine score of 9 on the nonverbal portion of the CoGAT, the full-scale quotient of the TONI-3, and the math subtest of the ITBS, placing him in the top 4% of those who took each of these tests. Relative to his math performance, Tony did not perform as well on the verbal portion of the CoGAT or the ITBS (e.g., both were stanine scores of 7, top 12%), which may result from the fact that he is still becoming fluent in English. Given these data, the committee recommended that Tony be placed in an accelerated math class within the gifted and talented program and also receive services within the general education program. Recognizing that he is an English-language learner, they also want to reevaluate him again at the end of the year to see if he demonstrates talents in other areas.

This case study form meets the suggested guidelines and addresses the issues presented earlier in this chapter. First, both quantitative and qualitative data are considered equally and are used to provide a broad picture of the student across contexts. In addition, the qualitative data provide dynamic assessment and growth over time (e.g., the teaching tasks and the portfolio of work from the beginning of the school year). Second, the committee is also able to see the student's relative strengths and weaknesses on all the assessments since subtests are listed for the quantitative assessments and each piece of qualitative evidence is in Tony's folder. Third, in addition to the descriptions provided by teachers, parents, peers, and Tony, the committee has provided a brief summary in each assessment area. Finally, stanine or standard scores are used for comparison purposes across the quantitative instruments. These scores provide for error in the assessments.

Bias in the Procedure

Even with the design of technically adequate procedures, bias may occur at any phase in the identification process. A key to a fair assessment is professional development for administrators, teachers, parents, and other interested community members. Research suggests that teachers identify more children (Gear, 1978; Strange, 2005) and that parents are better than teachers at identifying very young children (Jacobs, 1971) when they are trained. Otherwise, teachers may consider only students who are similar to their preconceived conceptions of giftedness (e.g., teacher pleaser, verbal, assertive, positive vs. negative characteristics, and mainstream cultural values; Hany, 1993; Peterson & Margolin, 1997; Rohrer, 1995; Schack & Starko, 1990; Spindler & Spindler, 1990). Teachers who are trained also provide more classroom activities that are open ended and problem based and that require higher-level thinking so that students may demonstrate their talents (Strange, 2005). Finally, a *trained* committee of professionals is necessary to identify students who need services. This committee is generally comprised of a general education teacher, gifted teacher, principal, counselor or school psychologist, and/or director of the gifted programs who make placement decisions.

Another key to fair assessment is the use of *multiple sources of information* and multiple measures. Movement from one phase to the next phase should not be based on a single criterion or a single source of information, such as a teacher nomination or a specific score on a standardized test. At the final placement phase, the committee may want to identify students by number only to ensure objectivity with anecdotal information added later. In addition, all data from all phases (nomination and screening) should be considered and used in developing an individual program.

Flexibility among selected assessments is important and should be based on student characteristics so that students who are not fluent in English or who do not have linguistically enriched backgrounds (e.g., economically disadvantaged) may be administered nonverbal measures or assessments in their native language. Similarly, students with disabilities may need modifications such as extended time, different forms of directions (e.g., verbal vs. written), or aural versus written formats (e.g., for visually or auditorally impaired).

The Office for Civil Rights has created guidelines to assist school districts in providing equal access at all phases of the school district's gifted program (Table 9–4) (Trice & Shannon, 2002). Their guide includes a statistical

TABLE 9–4 Office for Civil Rights Guidelines

Statistical Analysis

_____Racial/ethnic composition of the district's student enrollment.
_____Racial/ethnic composition of student population receiving gifted services.
_____Determine if minority students are statistically underrepresented in gifted programs.
_____Number (%) of students by race/ethnicity referred for evaluation for gifted eligibility.
_____Number (%) of students by race/ethnicity determined eligible for gifted services.
_____Number (%) of students by race/ethnicity withdrawing from, or otherwise discontinuing participation in, gifted programs/services.

Notice

_____ Notice simply and clearly explains the purpose of the program, referral/screening procedures, and eligibility criteria and identifies the district's contact person.
_____ Notice is provided annually to students, parents, and guardians, in a manner designed to reach all segments of the school community.

Referral/Screening

_____Multiple alternative referral sources, e.g., teachers, parents, etc., are, in practice, accessible to and utilized by all segments of the school community.
_____Teachers and other district staff involved in the referral process have been trained and/or provided guidance regarding the characteristics of giftedness.
_____Referral/screening criteria are applied in a nondiscriminatory manner.
_____All referral/screening criteria/guidelines are directly related to the purpose of the gifted program.
_____Standardized tests *and* cutoff scores are appropriate (valid and reliable) for the purpose of screening students for gifted services.

Evaluation/Placement

_____ Eligibility criteria are applied in a nondiscriminatory manner.
_____ Eligibility criteria are consistent with the purpose and implementation of the gifted program: Eligibility is based on multiple criteria; criteria include multiple assessments; eligibility incorporates component test scores as appropriate.
_____ Assessment instruments/measures and cutoff scores are appropriate (valid and reliable) for the purpose of identifying students for gifted services.
_____ To the extent that subjective assessment criteria are utilized, those individuals conducting the assessments have been provided guidelines and training to ensure proper evaluations.
_____ Alternative assessment instruments are utilized in appropriate circumstances.
If private testing is permitted as the basis for an eligibility determination, it does not have a disparate impact on minority students or, if it does, the use of such testing is legitimately related to the successful implementation of the program and no less discriminatory alternative exists that would achieve the same objective.

Program Participation

_____ Continued eligibility standards/criteria are applied in a nondiscriminatory manner.
_____ Continued eligibility standards/criteria are consistent with the purpose and implementation of the gifted program.
_____ Implementation procedures and practices facilitate equal access for all students.

Source: Trice and Shannon (2002).

analysis of the representation of various racial and ethnic groups; notice of identification procedures that reach all segments of the community; nondiscriminatory referral, screening, evaluation, and placement procedures; and program participation of all qualified students.

Due Process and Appeals

The Fifth and Fourteenth Amendments require that school districts adopt due process procedures (Karnes & Marquardt, 1991). To ensure these rights, school districts need to develop a time frame for a sequence of steps that progress from a local appeal to a state or federal appeal. These steps might include (a) an initial parent meeting with the principal, (b) a meeting with the school district placement committee, (c) a parent meeting with the school district director of the gifted program, and (d) a presentation to the board of trustees and/or superintendent. If none of the meetings at the district level resolves the issues, then the district may want to involve an impartial, professional mediator. If the mediation is unsuccessful, then the parents or the school district may want to contact the state education agency and initiate a formal hearing. At the state level, both sides may have counsel and present expert witnesses. Finally, if none of these steps resolves the conflicts, then the parents and/or the school district may want to litigate in state or federal courts.

SUMMARY AND CONCLUSIONS

This chapter has focused on the screening and selection of students for gifted and talented programs. The starting point for determining the need for services beyond those offered in the general education program is the student. Since the gifted student's characteristics and the development of his or talent are influenced by a variety of factors, these issues have been raised to improve the identification process:

1. *Diversity of talent.* Assessment examples need to come from across a variety of domains and contexts since talent is often exhibited in a specific interest area.
2. *Dynamic concept of giftedness.* Since the emergence of giftedness is dynamic, the identification process needs to occur over time with opportunities for students to exhibit their gifts through products and performance.
3. *Underrepresentation.* Representation of special groups can be enhanced through broader definitions, professional development, and fair tests.
4. *Early identification.* Since gifts need to be nurtured, early identification can improve the development of talents, particularly for students from minority and low-income backgrounds.

Considering these issues, assessments need to be aligned with the students' characteristics, provide both qualitative and quantitative information across contexts and over time, and be technically adequate and free from bias.

Selected assessments are generally used in a multiphase winnowing process that includes nomination or identification, screening or selection, and placement. When organizing data from multiple assessments for placement decisions, the committee needs to consider weighting of specific sources or types of assessments, the best performance of the student, a description of the student's performance and products over time, scores that are comparable, and test error. Programs should be flexible and match each student's strengths and weaknesses and may vary from year to year. To ensure equal access to all students, professional development for administrators, teachers, parents, and other interested community members is critical so that nondiscriminatory procedures and program participation is available to all qualified students.

QUESTIONS FOR THOUGHT AND REFLECTION

1. Some states require schools to identify students who score at or above the 97th percentile on an intelligence test, based on national norms. How might this rule affect the students who are identified in those states?
2. If you were planning a workshop for teachers, counselors, administrators, parents, and other professional and community members in identifying gifted students, what topics would you include? Why would you include these topics?
3. If you were the director of advanced academics in a school district and discovered that there was an underrepresentation of students from lower socioeconomic groups in the gifted program, what would you do? Why?
4. What types of assessments might you select for the different areas of giftedness in the federal definition?
5. Do you think it is acceptable for school districts to establish different identification standards for different groups of students? Why or why not?

RESOURCES

Following is a list of publishers, their contact information, and the tests that are frequently used in gifted education.

American Guidance Services
4201 Woodland Road
Circle Pines, MN 55014
Phone: (800) 328-2560
www.agsnet.com

Developmental Indicators for the Assessment of Learning (Speed DIAL)

Kaufman Assessment Battery for Children, second edition (KABC-2)

Kaufman Brief Intelligence Test, second edition (KBIT-2)

Kaufman Survey of Early Academic and Language Skills (K-SEALS)

Kaufman Test of Educational Achievement, second edition (KTEA-II)

Peabody Individual Achievement Test—Revised—Normative Update (PIAT-R/NU)

Peabody Picture Vocabulary Test, third edition (PPVT-III)

Creative Learning Press
P.O. Box 320
Mansfield, CT 06250
Phone: (800) 518-8004
www.creativelearningpress.com

Scales for Rating the Behavioral Characteristics of Superior Students

CTB-Macmillan-McGraw-Hill
20 Ryan Ranch Road
Monterey, CA 93940
Phone: (800) 538-9547
www.ctb.com

California Achievement Tests, fifth edition (CAT/5)

Primary Test of Cognitive Skills (PTCS)

SUPERA

TerraNova, The Second Edition (CAT/6)

TerraNova Algebra Assessment System

TerraNova Performance Assessments

Test of Cognitive Skills (TCS/2)

Great Potential Press
P.O. Box 5057
Scottsdale, AZ 85261
Phone: (602) 954-4200
www.giftedbooks.com

Iowa Acceleration Scale, Second Edition: A Guide for Whole-Grade Acceleration K–8
Leadership Development Program

Harcourt Assessment, Inc.
19500 Bulverde Road
San Antonio, TX 78259
Phone: (800) 211-8378
www.harcourtassessment.com

Raven's Progressive Matrices and Vocabulary Scales

Wechsler Individual Achievement Test, second edition (WIAT-II)

Wechsler Intelligence Scale for Children, fourth edition (WISC-IV)

Wechsler Preschool and Primary Scale of Intelligence, third edition (WPPSI-III)

Hawthorne Educational Services
800 Gray Oak Drive
Columbia, MO 65201
Phone: (800) 542-1673
www.hes-inc.com/hes.cgi

Gifted Evaluation Scale, second edition (GES-2)

PRO-ED
8700 Shoal Creek Boulevard
Austin, TX 78757-6897
Phone: (800) 897-3202
www.proedinc.com

Comprehensive Test of Nonverbal Intelligence (CTONI)

Draw-A-Person Intellectual Ability Test for Children, Adolescents, and Adults (DAP:IQ)

Gifted and Talented Evaluation Scales (GATES)

Screening Assessment for Gifted Elementary and Middle School Students, second edition (SAGES-2)

Slosson Intelligence Test—Revised (SIT-R)

Test of Early Language Development, third edition (TELD-3)

Test of Early Mathematics Ability, third edition (TEMA-3)

Test of Early Reading Ability, third edition (TERA-3)

Test of Early Written Language, second edition (TEWL-2)

Test of Language Development—Intermediate, third edition (TOLD-I: 3)

Test of Language Development—Primary, third edition (TOLD-P: 3)

Test of Mathematical Abilities (TOMA-2)

Test of Mathematical Abilities for Gifted Students (TOMAGS)

Test of Nonverbal Intelligence, third edition (TONI-3)

Test of Written Language, third edition (TOWL-3)

Prufrock Press
P.O. Box 8813
Waco, TX 76714-8813
Phone: (800) 998-2208
www.prufrock.com

Gifted and Talented Evaluation Scales (GATES)

Scales for Identifying Gifted Students (SIGS)

Screening Assessment for Gifted Elementary and Middle School Students, second edition (SAGES-2)

Test of Nonverbal Intelligence, third edition (TONI-3)

Riverside Publishing Company
8420 Bryn Mawr Avenue
Chicago, IL 60631-3476
Phone: (800) 323-9540
www.riverpub.com

Cognitive Abilities Test, Form 6 (CogAT)

Iowa Algebra Aptitude Test, fifth edition (IAAT)

Iowa Tests of Basic Skills, Forms A and B (ITBS)

Stanford-Binet Intelligence Scales, fifth edition (SB5)

Universal Nonverbal Intelligence Test (UNIT)

Woodcock-Johnson III

Scholastic Testing Service
480 Meyer Road
Bensenville, IL 60106-1617
Phone: (800) 642-6787
www.ststesting.com

Khatena-Morse Multitalent Perception Inventory (KMMPI)

Thinking Creatively in Action and Movement (TCAM)

Torrance Test of Creative Thinking (TTCT)

Slosson Educational Publications
P.O. Box 280
East Aurora, NY 14052
Phone: (716) 652-0930
www. slosson. com

Slosson Intelligence Test—Primary (SIT-P)

Slosson Full Range Intelligence Test (S-FRIT)

Websites

American Psychological Association (APA)
www.apa.org/science/testing.html
The APA provides a wealth of information about assessments including these online reports:

1. Finding Information About Psychological Tests
2. The ABC's of School Testing
3. Code of Fair Testing Practices in Education
4. Rights and Responsibilities of Test Takers
5. Bibliography on Relevant Literature Addressing Testing and Assessment of Cultural, Ethnic, and Linguistically Diverse Populations
6. Reference on Testing of People of Color, Women, Language Minorities, and People with Disabilities

Buros Center for Testing
www.unl.edu/buros
The Buros Institute of Mental Measurements publishes review of tests each year in the *Mental Measurements Yearbook* series. The yearbook may be found in most university libraries. Critiques can also be accessed online for a fee per test title.

National Association for Gifted Children (NAGC)
www.nagc.org/index.aspx?id=404
The NAGC has published a position statement titled *Using Tests to Identify Gifted Students* and has other publications related to assessment that may be accessed online.

National Council on Measurement in Education (NCME)
www.ncme.org/pubs
The NCME publishes a newsletter and has a *Code of Professional Responsibilities in Educational Measurement* that may be accessed online and was prepared by the NCME Ad Hoc Committee on the Development of a Code of Ethics.

The National Research Center on the Gifted and Talented (NRC-GT)
www.gifted.uconn.edu/nrcgt.html
The NRC-GT lists 26 monographs related to assessment, evaluation, and identification. The abstracts and conclusions may be accessed online.

Office for Civil Rights (OCR)
www.ed.gov/about/offices/list/ocr/index.html
The OCR provides technical assistance to help institutions achieve voluntary compliance with the civil rights laws that OCR enforces. Topics from ability grouping to tracking are found on the "Topics from A to Z" page and focus on discrimination among different groups.

REFERENCES

American Educational Research Association, American Psychological Association, & National Council on Measurement in Education. (1999). *Standards for educational and psychological testing.* Washington, DC: Author.

Anastasi, A., & Urbina, S. (1997). *Psychological testing* (7th ed.). Upper Saddle River, NJ: Prentice Hall.

Bernal, E. (1981, February). *Special problems and procedures for identifying minority gifted students.* Paper presented at the annual meeting of the Council for Exceptional Children, New Orleans, LA. (ERIC Document Reproduction Service No. ED203652)

Borland, J. H., Schnur, R., & Wright, L. (2000). Economically disadvantaged students in a school for the academically gifted: A postpositivist inquiry into individual and family adjustment. *Gifted Child Quarterly, 44,* 13–32.

Borland, J. H., & Wright, L. (1994). Identifying young, potentially gifted, economically disadvantaged students. *Gifted Child Quarterly, 38,* 164–171.

Bracken, B. A., & McCallum, S. R. (1998). *Universal nonverbal intelligence test.* Itasca, IL: Riverside.

Brown, L., Sherbenou, R., & Johnsen, S. (1997). *Test of nonverbal intelligence* (3rd ed.). Austin, TX: PRO-ED.

Buros Center for Testing. (n.d.). *Buros mental measurement yearbooks.* Retrieved May 3, 2006, from *http://www.unl.edu/buros*

Clark, B. (1997). *Growing up gifted* (5th ed.). Upper Saddle River, NJ: Merrill.

Clark, G. A., & Zimmerman, E. (1984). *Educating artistically talented students.* Syracuse, NY: Syracuse University Press.

Colangelo, N., & Davis, G. A. (1991). *Handbook of gifted education.* Boston: Allyn & Bacon.

Coleman, L. J., & Cross, T. L. (2001). *Being gifted in school: An introduction to development, guidance, and teaching.* Waco, TX: Prufrock.

Coleman, M. R., Gallagher, J. J., & Foster, A. (1994). *Updated report on state policies related to the identification of gifted students.* Chapel Hill: University of North Carolina Press. (ERIC Document Reproduction Service No. ED372591)

Cornell, D. G., Delcourt, M. A. B., Goldberg, M. D., & Bland, L. C. (1995). Achievement and self-concept of minority students in elementary school gifted programs. *Journal for the Education of the Gifted, 18,* 189–209.

Davis, G. A., & Rimm, S. B. (1994). *Education of the gifted and talented* (3rd ed.). Boston: Allyn & Bacon.

Feldhusen, J. F., Hoover, S. M., & Sayler, M. (1990). *Identifying and educating gifted students at the secondary level.* Monroe, NY: Trillium.

Fernández, A. T., Gay, L. R., Lucky, L. F., & Gavilán, M. R. (1998). Teacher perceptions of gifted Hispanic limited English proficient students. *Journal for the Education of the Gifted, 21,* 335–351.

Ford, D. Y. (1996). *Reversing underachievement among gifted Black students: Promising practices and programs.* New York: Teachers College Press.

Frasier, M. M. (1997). Multiple criteria: The mandate and the challenge. *Roeper Review, 20,* 2–4.

Gagné, F. (1995). From giftedness to talent: A developmental model and its impact on the language of the field. *Roeper Review, 18,* 103–111.

Gagné, F. (1999). Is there any light at the end of the tunnel? *Journal for the Education of the Gifted, 22,* 191–234.

Gardner, H. (1993). *Creating minds.* New York: Basic Books.

Gear, G. (1978). Effects of training on teachers' accuracy in identifying gifted children. *Gifted Child Quarterly, 22,* 90–97.

Geary, D. C., & Brown, S. C. (1991). Cognitive addition: Strategy choice and speed-of-processing differences in gifted, normal, and mathematically disabled children. *Developmental Psychology, 27,* 398–406.

Gilliam, J. E., Carpenter, B. O., & Christensen, J. R. (1996). *Gifted and Talented Evaluation Scales.* Austin, TX: PRO-ED.

Goertzel, V., & Goertzel, M. G. (1962). *Cradles of eminence.* Boston: Little, Brown.

Gruber, H. E. (1981). *Darwin on man: A psychological study of scientific creativity* (2nd ed.). Chicago: University of Chicago Press.

Guilford, J. P. (1950). Creativity. *American Psychologist, 5,* 444–454.

Hany, E. A. (1993). Methodological problems and issues concerning identification. In K. A. Heller, F. J. Mönks, & A. H. Passow (Eds.), *International handbook of research and development of giftedness and talent* (pp. 209–232). New York: Pergamon.

Hoover, H. D., Dunbar, S. B., & Frisbie, D. A. (2001/2003). *Iowa Test of Basic Skills* (Forms A and B). Chicago: Riverside.

Improving America's Schools Act of 1994, Pub. L. No. 103–382, Tit. XIV General Provisions.

Jacobs, J. (1971). Effectiveness of teacher and parent identification as a function of school level. *Psychology in the Schools, 9,* 140–142.

Johnsen, S. K. (1997). Assessment beyond definitions. *Peabody Journal of Education, 72,* 136–152.

Johnsen, S. K. (2004a). Definitions, models, and characteristics. In S. K. Johnsen (Ed.), *Identifying gifted students: A practical guide* (pp. 1–22). Waco, TX: Prufrock.

Johnsen, S. K. (2004b). Making decisions about placement. In S. K. Johnsen (Ed.), *Identifying gifted students: A practical guide* (pp. 107–131). Waco, TX: Prufrock.

Johnsen, S. K. (2005). Identifying gifted students: A step-by-step guide. In F. A. Karnes & K. R. Stephens (Eds.), *Practical strategies series in gifted education.* Waco, TX: Prufrock.

Johnsen, S. K., & Corn, A. L. (2001). *SAGES-2: Screening Assessment for Gifted Elementary Students* (2nd ed.). Austin, TX: PRO-ED.

Johnsen, S. K., Robins, J., Witte, M., & Feuerbacher, S. (2003, April). *Developing social and academic characteristics among gifted students labeled at-risk.* Paper Presented at the annual conference of the International Council for Exceptional Children, Seattle, WA.

Johnsen, S., & Ryser, G. (1994). Identification of young gifted children from lower income families. *Gifted and Talented International, 9,* 62–68.

Johnsen, S. K., & Ryser, G. R. (1997). The validity of portfolios in predicting performance in a gifted program. *Journal for the Education of the Gifted, 20,* 253–267.

Jolly, J. L., & Hall, J. R. (2004). Technical information regarding assessment. In S. K. Johnsen (Ed.), *Identifying gifted students: A practical guide* (pp. 51–105). Waco, TX: Prufrock.

Karnes, F. A. (1991). Leadership and gifted adolescents. In M. Bireley & J. Genshaft (Eds.), *Understanding the gifted adolescent* (pp. 122–138). New York: Teachers College Press.

Karnes, F. A., & Marquardt, R. G. (1991). *Gifted children and the law: Mediation, due process and court cases.* Scottsdale, AZ: Great Potential.

Keyser, D., & Sweetland, R. (2004). *Test critique,* (Vols 1–10). Austin, TX: PRO-ED.

Khatena, J. (1992). *Gifted: Challenge and response for education.* Itasca, IL: Peacock.

Kirschenbaum, R. (1998). Dynamic assessment and its use with underserved gifted and talented populations. *Gifted Child Quarterly, 42,* 140–147.

Kurtz, B. E., & Weinert, F. E. (1989). Metacognition, memory performance, and causal attributions in gifted and average children. *Journal of Experimental Child Psychology, 48,* 45–61.

Lohman, D. F., & Hagen, E. P. (2001). *Cognitive Abilities Test* Form 6. Chicago: Riverside.

Maddox, T. (2003). *Tests: A comprehensive reference for assessments in psychology, education, and business* (5th ed.). Austin, TX: PRO-ED.

Murphy, L. L., Plake, B. S., Impara, J. C., & Spies, R. A. (Eds.). (2002). *Tests in print* (Vol. 6). Lincoln: University of Nebraska Press.

Naglieri, J. A. (2003). *Naglieri Nonverbal Ability Test.* San Antonio, TX: Psychological Corporation.

National Association for Gifted Children and Council of State Directors of Programs for the Gifted. (2005). *State of the states: A report by the National Association for Gifted Children and the Council of State Directors of Programs for the Gifted, 2004–2005.* Washington, DC: Author.

Passow, A. H., & Frasier, M. M. (1996). Toward improving identification of talent potential among minority and disadvantaged students. *Roeper Review, 18,* 198–202.

Perkins, D. N. (1981). *The mind's best work.* Cambridge, MA: Harvard University Press.

Peterson, J. S., & Margolin, L. (1997). Naming gifted children: An example of unintended reproduction. *Journal for the Education of the Gifted, 21,* 82–100.

Piirto, J. (1999). *Talented children and adults: Their development and education* (2nd ed.). Upper Saddle River, NJ: Merrill.

Plata, M., & Masten, W. (1998). Teacher ratings of Hispanic and Anglo students on a behavior rating scale. *Roeper Review, 21,* 139–144.

Reid, C., Udall, A., Romanoff, B., & Algozzine, B. (1999). Comparison of traditional and problem solving assessment criteria. *Gifted Child Quarterly, 43*, 252–264.

Renzulli, J. S., Smith, L. H., White, A. J., Callahan, C. M., Hartman, R. K., & Westberg, K. L. (2002). *Scales for Rating the Behavioral Characteristics of Superior Students*. Mansfield Center, CT: Creative Learning.

Rogers, K. B. (2001). *Re-forming gifted education: Matching the program to the child.* Scottsdale, AZ: Great Potential.

Rohrer, J. C. (1995). Primary teacher conceptions of giftedness: Image, evidence, and nonevidence. *Journal for the Education of the Gifted, 18*, 269–283.

Ryser, G. R. (2004). Culture-fair and nonbiased assessment. In S. K. Johnsen (Ed.), *Identifying gifted students: A practical guide* (pp. 41–49). Waco, TX: Prufrock.

Ryser, G. R., & Johnsen, S. K. (1998). *Test of Mathematical Abilities for Gifted Students*. Austin, TX: PRO-ED.

Ryser, G. R., & McConnell, K. (2004). *Scales for Identifying Gifted Students.* Waco, TX: Prufrock.

Salvia, J., & Ysseldyke, J. E. (2001). *Assessment* (8th ed.). Boston: Houghton-Mifflin.

Schack, G. D., & Starko, A. J. (1990). Identification of gifted students: An analysis of criteria preferred by preservice teachers, classroom teachers, and teachers of the gifted. *Journal for the Education of the Gifted, 13*, 346–363.

Scott, M. S., Perou, R., Urbano, R., Hogan, A., & Gold, S. (1992). The identification of giftedness: A comparison of white, Hispanic and black families. *Gifted Child Quarterly, 36*, 131–139.

Scruggs, T. E., & Mastropieri, M. A. (1985). Spontaneous verbal elaboration in gifted and nongifted youths. *Journal for the Education of the Gifted, 9*, 1–10.

Spindler, G., & Spindler, L. (1990). *The American cultural dialogue and its transmission.* New York: Falmer.

Sternberg, R. J. (Ed.). (1988). *The nature of creativity.* New York: Cambridge University Press.

Sternberg, R. J., & Davidson, J. E. (Eds.). (1986). *Conceptions of giftedness.* New York: Cambridge University Press.

Strange, C. J. (2005). *Perceptions and practices that influence the identification of gifted students from low socioeconomic backgrounds.* Unpublished doctoral dissertation, Baylor University, Waco, TX.

Swassing, R. H. (1985). *Teaching gifted children and adolescents.* Columbus: Merrill.

Tannenbaum, A. J. (1983). *Gifted children: Psychological and educational perspectives.* New York: Macmillan.

Tannenbaum, A. (2003). Nature and nurture of giftedness. In N. Colangelo & G. A. Davis (Eds.), *Handbook of gifted education* (3rd ed., pp. 45–59). Boston: Allyn & Bacon.

Texas Education Agency. (n.d., a). *Non-traditional assessment of gifted students.* Austin, TX: Advanced Academic Services (formerly Division of Gifted/Talented Education).

Texas Education Agency (n.d., b). *Texas student portfolio.* Austin, TX: Advanced Academic Services (formerly Division of Gifted/Talented Education).

Tolan, S. S. (1992a). Parents vs. theorists: Dealing with the exceptionally gifted. *Roeper Review, 15*, 14–18.

Tolan, S. S. (1992b). Special problems of highly gifted children. *Understanding Our Gifted, 4* (3), 3, 5.

Torrance, E. P. (1974). *Torrance Tests of Creative Thinking.* Bensenville, IL: Scholastic Testing Service.

Trice, B., & Shannon, B. (2002, April). *Office for Civil Rights: Ensuring equal access to gifted education.* Paper presented at the annual meeting of the Council for Exceptional Children, New York.

Whitmore, J. (1981). Gifted children with handicapping conditions: A new frontier. *Exceptional Children, 48*, 106–114.

CHAPTER 10

INSTRUCTIONAL STRATEGIES AND PROGRAMMING MODELS FOR GIFTED LEARNERS

Carol A. Tomlinson, Ed.D.
University of Virginia

Jessica A. Hockett
University of Virginia

INTRODUCTION

Two recurrent concerns in gifted education are *where* to teach gifted students and *how.* The reality, however, is that neither gifted students nor any other group of students are uniform, and no single setting or strategy is uniformly effective for all individuals in the group.

More helpful than a search for unitary answers about where and how to teach gifted learners is consideration of a range of options available for serving high-performing and high-potential students. Integrating the profiles of four highly able students, this chapter examines how teachers and schools can use varied instructional strategies, program types, and administrative arrangements to effectively accommodate the variety of needs in the diverse population of high-ability learners.

FOUR STUDENTS

Adam

Adam is the highest-performing student in his first-grade class. He skipped kindergarten and, despite being younger than his classmates, is popular among his peers. Adam's parents have been able to provide their son with extensive and unique out-of-school educational experiences, including foreign travel and chess lessons.

Inquisitive, motivated, and gregarious, Adam enjoys writing his own stories about dinosaurs or space aliens after finishing a required assignment quickly. On several occasions, he has been allowed to read these compositions aloud to the class. Adam's verbal abilities are so strong that his teacher wonders if he should send him to a second- or third-grade class for language arts instruction.

Bettina

Since kindergarten, Bettina has shown aptitude and affinity for math. She learns new concepts quickly and consistently earns perfect scores on end-of-unit assessments. Standardized test data reveal that Bettina performs in the 99th percentile in math. Recently, as a fifth grader, she took the SAT-M and scored above 600. Her language skills, however, test as average.

The gifted and talented program at Bettina's school is focused on reading and writing. Although Bettina performs well in these areas, she does not qualify for services based on district criteria. Her classroom teachers have typically accommodated her abilities by assigning independent work and placing her in the most advanced math group for instruction.

Catie

Catie is a bright, hardworking eighth grader who has a learning disability. While teachers recognize her high potential, the special education services Catie receives are offered at the same time services for gifted and talented students are scheduled. She maintains a solid B average—a testament to her diligence but not high enough to meet the A minimum required to enroll in honors-level courses. As they look toward high school, Catie's parents are worried about how their daughter's dual exceptionality will be viewed and accommodated in the classroom.

Diego

Now in eleventh grade, Diego has experienced limited success in school. When his family immigrated to the United States several years ago, Diego assumed responsibility for watching his two younger siblings until his parents returned from their late-night shifts. Between cooking dinner, keeping the apartment tidy, and helping his brother and sister with homework, Diego found little time for his own studies. In his sophomore year, increased family financial struggles motivated Diego to secure an after-school job.

Despite lackluster grades, many teachers have noted Diego's talents in science. Because his spoken language skills are not strong, however, Diego's counselor advised him against enrolling in advanced science courses. Once hopeful about going to college, Diego has begun to think he can do better for himself and his family by entering the workforce full time following graduation.

A VARIETY OF GIFTED LEARNERS

As these four student profiles illustrate, there is no "typical" or "all-around" gifted learner. Adam, Bettina, Catie, and Diego represent the spectrum of highly able learners in virtually every school, encompassing those whose abilities are readily apparent and those whose abilities are concealed by learning challenges, cultural differences, language barriers, physical disabilities, economic challenges, or other circumstances. Some high-ability students come to school very well prepared for academic success by virtue of economic advantages and family supports, while other students of equal potential arrive with significant barriers to learning. Even focusing on a seemingly narrow category such as academic giftedness may not be useful. A student identified as gifted is just as likely to prefer inductive reasoning as he or she is deductive reasoning. The same student who has easily memorized the periodic table might not be able to fill out a blank map of the United States. He or she may demonstrate remarkable computation speed but poor composition skills. The inevitable variance within highly able learners individually and across groups makes it impossible to subsume them under a single label—and certainly makes it inappropriate to think about serving all of them in the same way. In light of this variability, it is suggested that highly able learners be thought of in the classroom in at least two ways: as high performing and as high potential.

The category of *high-performing students* typically includes more "traditionally identified" gifted students, or students that classroom teachers can more readily recognize as having high abilities. High performance may manifest itself as advanced content knowledge, skill, or conceptual understanding but may also surface as the ability to move through previously unknown material more quickly, with greater interest, or greater insight than age-mates. Students might be consistently high performing across or within subject areas, like Adam, or they may perform at an advanced level with respect to specific subjects or units of study, as Bettina does. These students need opportunities and support to work at advanced levels in their areas of strength.

High-potential students are those whose talents are emerging but not consistently demonstrated or evident. In other words, while they have the capacity to perform academically at higher levels, their academic performance does not typically mirror that capacity. Thus, these students require a curriculum and instruction that provides opportunities and conditions to *develop* certain knowledge, skills, or conceptual understanding. Some high-potential students may need to acquire specific grade-level competencies while simultaneously accessing advanced content. This might include students from low-economic, culturally diverse, and twice-exceptional groups who would benefit from a quality curriculum and instruction that serves as a catalyst for both discovery and development of capacity. Catie and Diego exemplify these learners.

In order to enable all very bright students to develop their possibilities, it is important for teachers to both extend the talent of high-performing students like Adam and Bettina and to develop the talent of high-potential students like Catie and Diego. At the same time, teachers are cautioned against seeing students as either high performing *or* high potential. Because giftedness is domain specific—that is, a person is gifted *at* or *in* something—students will often evidence both high potential and high performance, depending on a particular subject, portion of a subject, or point in time. In addition, teachers should be steadfast in offering chances for *all* students to demonstrate behaviors characteristic of advanced knowledge, skill, or understanding.

Throughout this chapter, the terms *gifted, highly able*, and *advanced* are used interchangeably to suggest that both high-performing and high-potential students are included in our understanding of these terms.

MEETING GIFTED STUDENTS' NEEDS THROUGH INSTRUCTIONAL STRATEGIES

Purposes of Instructional Strategies

In general, instructional strategies have two main purposes: (a) to allow students to explore and master high-quality curriculum and (b) to address the specific learning needs of individual students. Using an instructional strategy for its own sake or to try out something learned at a conference without considering a specific set of lesson objectives will almost certainly be ineffective in the long term. Even when afforded opportunities to work with exemplary curriculum, highly able students still require flexibility for varied pacing needs, provisions for appropriate challenge, opportunities to develop specific strengths and passions, and support for bridging areas of weakness (Tomlinson, 2005). It makes sense, then, for teachers to select instructional strategies on the basis of curricular goals and to make adjustments on the basis of learner traits rather than selecting them on the basis of learner traits and force-fitting them to curricular aims.

Instructional Strategies and Gifted Learners

There are no instructional strategies *exclusively appropriate to* teaching gifted learners (Tomlinson, 1997). However, certain strategies have come to be *associated with* or *advocated for* teaching gifted learners. Simulations are one example (e.g., Sisk, 2005). Simulations approximate real-world conditions, events, experiences, or processes. They might be implemented in one class period, or they might encompass an entire unit of study or classroom environment. A 2-day simulation may take students through labor negotiations; a simulation extending several weeks might setup the classroom as a news bureau. While simulation can be an exciting and engaging strategy when properly planned and aligned with curricular goals, there is little reason to believe that they are necessarily more appropriate for gifted students than other groups of learners or that gifted students learn more from simulations per se than from other strategies.

Some strategies associated with high challenge were actually created for specific purposes that had little to do with bright learners. For example, *Synectics* was created in the business world to harness the mental connections that yield creative ideas (Gordon, 1961). Similarly, *brainstorming* was developed by an advertising executive to help employees generate new ideas (Osborn, 1948). *Shared Inquiry*, the basis for Socratic Seminars, was developed to facilitate book group discussions in dissecting literary works (Great Books Foundation, 1987). *Complex Instruction* was created to address inequities in cooperative learning for low-economic and second language learners (Cohen, Lotan, Scarloss, & Arellano, 1999). Although strategies *can* be developed with a certain group of learners in mind, most substantial instructional approaches have the potential to benefit many different kinds of learners, including those with high potential and high performance. What matters most is *how* the strategies are used as a means of responding to particular learner needs. To allow the flexibility needed for effective instruction of the diverse pool of high-ability learners, it is likely that some form of differentiated instruction is necessary.

Traits of Effective Differentiated Instruction

To address the diverse needs of all students—including high-potential and high-performing students—teachers must adapt instruction on the basis of the varying needs of learners. One way of thinking about adapting instruction in response to learner variance has been characterized as *differentiated instruction*. The term differentiation has been used in two key ways. One is in discussing curriculum and instruction for gifted learners specifically (Kaplan, 1974; Maker, 1982; Passow, 1982; Renzulli, 1977; Tannebaum, 1986; VanTassel-Baska, 1985; Ward, 1961). A second, more recent conception of differentiation is that of teaching a range of diverse learners—including but not limited to high-performing and high-potential learners—with emphasis on the general education setting (Tomlinson, 2004). In the latter context, differentiation is an instructional model for addressing learner variance in readiness, interest, and learning profile through proactive modification of curricula, instructional methods, resources, student products, and learning activities (Tomlinson, 1999, 2001).

There are no doubt hundreds of instructional strategies available to teachers for purposes of differentiation. Because strategies should be purposefully chosen and proficiently modified to be effective in addressing learners' varied needs and profiles, it is beneficial to consider the hallmarks of instruction that is differentiated to effectively address a range of student needs—including the needs of gifted and talented learners. Key indicators of quality differentiation (Tomlinson et al., 2003) with specific examples of their application using Adam, Bettina, Catie, and Diego as cases in point are listed here.

Differentiated Instruction is Learner Centered. Differentiated instruction that is learner centered positions students not in terms of general ability (e.g., "Diego is a good student.") but in terms of how ready they are for a particular set of learning goals at a particular time (e.g., "Diego has mastered three of the learning goals for this unit."). Toward this end, the teacher must use a combination of formative and summative assessments to gauge student readiness. These assessments can be as formal as pretests from textbooks or as informal as writing one or two questions on the chalkboard for students to answer on an index card before they leave class.

Learner-centered differentiated instruction also ensures that all students consistently (though not always uniformly) make choices about their learning throughout the year. Choice should not be the privilege only of Adam when he finishes classroom tasks quickly or of Bettina when she performs well on a test. Likewise, teachers should not use basic skills mastery as a barrier to pursuing areas of interest, broader or deeper content knowledge, or enrichment activities.

Bettina. In Bettina's class, students are grouped for math instruction according to their standardized test scores from the previous year. The teacher, Ms. Alvarez, has kept students in the same groups since September because she says that in her experience the test scores predict student performance well. She has been impressed by Bettina's math talents but is puzzled why her top student is currently struggling with a unit on exponents while some students in the group who are usually less proficient are grasping the concepts easily.

Because even the highest-performing students will not (and should not) avert struggle if they are well challenged, creating static instructional groups is likely to inhibit Bettina's growth—whether the content is not advanced enough for her or whether she needs additional support and practice with concepts and skills that are less clear to her. Ms. Alvarez can avoid pigeonholing Bettina and other students into fixed groups by preassessing their skills prior to beginning a new unit and using a variety of groupings that are based on specific strengths, weaknesses, interests, and learning preferences during a unit.

Differentiated Instruction is Planned Proactively Rather Than Reactively. A teacher is *proactive* in differentiating instruction when he or she plans for student differences prior to instruction based on formative or summative assessment data or on other information about students. In other words, the teacher plans assignments and lessons with student differences in mind. By contrast, the teacher is *reactive* when he or she waits for the student to demonstrate a need for an instructional intervention or curricular modification before making adjustments.

Diego. Ms. Shaker, Diego's chemistry teacher, assigns all students in her class the same lab. Soon, she observes that it is too easy for Diego but challenging for his partner. In the past, she has responded by grading Diego harder than his partner, expecting higher-quality work from him, or giving him additional questions to answer. These reactive adjustments have frustrated Diego, who is still confused about why his counselor would not let him enroll in the honors section of the course.

More proactively, Ms. Shaker can design two labs, one of which is a more advanced application of the principles in the lesson. Then she can assess how well the students understand the concepts necessary for each version. By pairing students on the basis of their readiness and assigning each pair the lab commensurate with their current readiness, students like Diego are not limited by the standard curriculum.

Differentiated Instruction Employs Flexible Teaching–Learning Groups. Because students learn at different rates, respond to instruction in different ways, and have a range of interests, effective differentiated instruction allows students to move fluidly between a variety of whole-group, small-group, and individual configurations. Within these groupings, teachers can employ many strategies, such as direct instruction, cooperative learning, discussion, investigations, problem solving, and so on.

It is tempting for teachers to fall into the habit of grouping according to students' academic performances. Specific to advanced learners, more tempting still may be to adopt one of two practices exclusively: either always grouping advanced learners together or always grouping them to teach other students. But classrooms in which teachers successfully accommodate advanced learners are also places where flexible grouping is a way of life (e.g., Westberg & Archambault, 1997). Depending on the task, groups may need to be homogeneous or heterogeneous. Determining the best-fit grouping should depend on the learner's relationship to the curricular goals, not on whether the student is generally high performing.

As a general guideline, teachers should group according to *readiness* when the primary goal is student *progress*, according to *learning profile* when the primary goal is task *efficiency*, and according to student interest when the primary goal is *motivation*. At the same time, flexible grouping must, over time, allow students to work with a variety of peers—both students like and students dissimilar from themselves (Tomlinson, 2001).

Catie. Language arts isn't Catie's strongest subject, but she frequently contributes fresh, thoughtful ideas to class discussions and pursues writing assignments with enthusiasm. When the class is doing small-group or partner tasks, the teacher, Mr. Jarvis, assigns Catie to work with other special education students. An upcoming journalism unit has given him a chance to think more flexibly about grouping.

Figure 10–1 illustrates an instructional segment from Mr. Jarvis's unit and how he will avoid grouping students according to the fuzzy, subjective criterion of "general ability." Note how the segment moves back and forth from whole-class arrangements to small and individual groupings. Clearly, there are opportunities for discussion and analyzing in which Catie might be paired with students who have similar verbal skills, complementary interests, and interdependent learning preferences.

Differentiated Instruction Varies the Materials Used by Individuals and Small Groups of Students in the Classroom. Materials and resources should be varied according to medium, learner need, and learning goals. A teacher cannot expect resources to be "self-differentiating." For example, the same reading material is not necessarily appropriate for all readiness levels simply because students will approach the text with different needs and capacities. The expert teacher acknowledges learner differences by providing reading materials at varying levels of complexity that address the same ideas or topic and ensure that all students have access to important ideas.

Adam. According to district curriculum benchmarks, all first-grade students will be able to use nonstandard units to measure length. Typically, this has meant using 1-inch wood blocks. On giving a preassessment, Mr. Clemons discovers that several students in his class are able to use a ruler to measure items by the inch. Adam is able to use a ruler to measure objects to the half inch. Mr. Clemons plans an activity in which all students are measuring items using the instruments and increments commensurate with their readiness. He uses small-group and individual instruction to teach some students how to use the ruler in a more advanced way than their current skill level dictates. Consequently, Adam is able to experiment with measuring length to the quarter inch.

Diego. Diego's chemistry course culminates in a project Ms. Shaker calls "Sludge." Throughout the year, students learn methods for identifying and separating different substances. Ms. Shaker assigns the same mixture to all students and gives each pair structured directions on how to approach the task as well as a list of possible substances and methods.

Making sure all students are using at least the skills and concepts required by the curriculum, Ms. Shaker creates mixtures of varying degrees of difficulty and assigns each pair the most challenging sludge for them. Additionally, she will give Diego and his partner open-ended directions and offer the list of substances and methods only if they need it.

Differentiated Instruction Uses Variable Pacing as a Means of Addressing Learner Needs. The pace of instruction should increase and decrease in response to students' interactions with the curriculum. This includes provisions for students when they grasp concepts and skills quickly. Variable pacing also builds in time for advanced learners to reinforce skills or probe a topic or concept with greater depth or breath. The teacher recognizes that early finishers and fast movers may need more complex tasks to begin with. In any case, giving high-performing students more work or letting them engage in activities not appropriate for school learning are not tenable ways to adjust pacing.

Adam and Bettina. Because they are high-performing, traditionally talented students, it is easy to see that Adam and Bettina would be able to move quickly through the grade-level curriculum in their strongest subjects. Not as obvious are their relative weaknesses within those talent areas.

For example, Mr. Clemons has noticed that when Adam reads his dinosaur stories aloud to the class, he adds details and sentences not written on his paper.

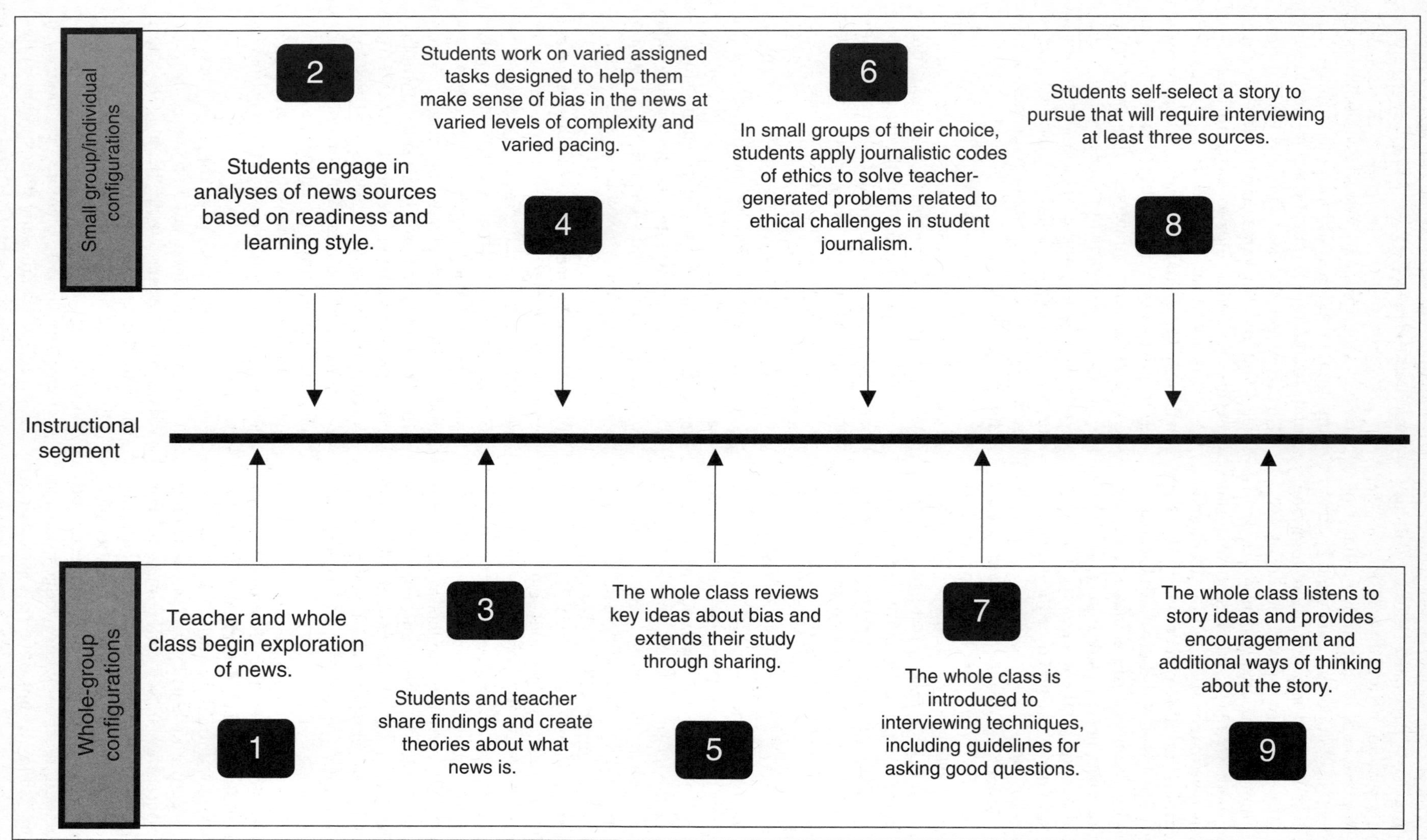

FIGURE 10–1 An Example of Flexible Grouping in Mr. Jarvis's Classroom

In essence, Adam is a stronger oral storyteller than he is a story writer. Instead of allowing Adam to write his usual two or three stories during the class's next Writer's Workshop, Mr. Clemons limits his student to one well-organized, elaborately detailed story. The teacher uses various strategies—including having Adam tape-record himself—to ensure that Adam is better able to express his creative ideas in writing.

Similarly, Bettina struggles with keeping the problems on her math homework neat and organized. In the past, teachers usually overlooked the messiness because Bettina's answers were correct. As she started to work with multistep equations this year, this weakness became a barrier not only to Bettina being able to evaluate her answers when they were incorrect but also to her receiving partial credit on tests for steps she had done correctly. To help her student, Ms. Alvarez showed her how to align the problems using graph paper and assigns her fewer problems for homework. Although Bettina is spending more time on each lesson, ultimately, her math talents will benefit from the slower pace and focus on organization.

Catie and Diego. Having been characterized academically according to their weaknesses, Catie's and Diego's teachers might be tempted to focus on what they can't do at the expense of what they can. While there may be times when the pace of instruction should account specifically for Catie's learning disability and Diego's language skills, their full range of traits calls for pacing that varies according to task. Two illustrations follow.

Eager to watch the morning news daily, Catie has been consistently completing her in-class current events assignments quickly and accurately. Rather than have Catie start reading the next chapter in the history textbook or sit quietly until the rest of the class has finished, Catie's teacher, Mrs. Williams, creates a more advanced version of the assignment for Catie that requires in-depth analysis and corroborating news sources. Mindful of her student's reading difficulties, Mrs. Williams requires Catie to use online audio and video sources.

On the first day of class, Diego noticed that organic compounds were the last topic on the chemistry course syllabus. Ms. Shaker said they might not have enough time for that unit, so in his spare time after tests and quizzes, Diego read the organic compounds chapter. Interest in the concepts prompted him to check out additional books on the topic from the school library. He asked Ms. Shaker repeatedly whether the class would have time for the unit. Knowing they would not have time but wanting to foster Diego's fascination, Ms. Shaker set up the unit as an independent study for Diego. He completed the work throughout the rest of the semester, both in spare class time and during selected class activities that Ms. Shaker had determined he had already mastered.

ACCELERATION AND ENRICHMENT: TWO TYPES OF PROGRAMS, STRATEGIES, AND ADMINISTRATIVE ARRANGEMENTS FOR MEETING THE NEEDS OF GIFTED STUDENTS

Acceleration and Enrichment: What's the Difference?

Acceleration and *enrichment* are two terms widely used in gifted education to describe certain program types, strategies for organizing curriculum, and administrative arrangements for grouping highly able learners. The nature of the relationship between enrichment and acceleration is challenging to articulate because both are usually conceived as relationships between the student and the grade-level curriculum and/or the teacher and the grade-level curriculum (Davis & Rimm, 2004; Kaplan, 1974; Rogers, 2002; Shore, Cornell, Robinson, & Ward, 1991; Southern & Jones, 1991). Enrichment is seen as extending, supplementing, or otherwise going beyond the regular curriculum in greater depth or breadth and acceleration as moving through grade-level or subject-matter curriculum faster or sooner than same-age peers. For example, a student is *accelerated* from first grade to second grade, or the math curriculum is *enriched*. Davis and Rimm (2004) made this distinction: "Any strategy that results in advanced placement or credit may be titled *acceleration*; strategies that supplement or go beyond standard grade-level work but do not result in advanced credit may be called *enrichment*" (p. 121).

Regardless of how the terms are defined, it is likely that to serve highly able learners well, both acceleration and enrichment must be a part of curriculum and instruction.

Acceleration

One national report defines acceleration as "an educational intervention that moves students through an educational program at a faster than usual rate or younger than typical age" (Colangelo, Assouline, & Gross, 2004, p. 5). As related to gifted education, acceleration is usually recommended for high-performing students whose academic needs are so advanced that they have not been or cannot be met in the regular classroom and whose overall development allows for curriculum and instruction to be delivered via acceleration.

Acceleration is frequently cited as the most researched instructional and administrative provision for gifted students (Colangelo, et al., 2004; Davis & Rimm, 2004; Rogers, 2002; Shore, et al., 1991; Southern & Jones, 1991). Indeed, studies in acceleration illustrate well the importance of curriculum and instruction that provides moderate, attainable challenge just above what the student is able to do without support (Gross, 2004; Kulik & Kulik, 1984; Rogers, 2004; Stanley, 1976).

Strategies and Administrative Arrangements that Support Acceleration. Drawing on the 18 types of acceleration identified by Southern and Jones (2004), we note here those most likely to be encountered and used by teachers in K–12 settings.

- *Early entrance or exit* occurs when the student enters or graduates from a level of schooling earlier than his or her same-age peers. Entering kindergarten prior to a district's cut off age or matriculating to college at 16 years old are examples.
- *Grade skipping* places a student in a grade-level higher than his or her same-age peers. In contrast to early entrance, grade skipping occurs during or at the end of the academic year.
- In *subject-matter acceleration*, students take a specific subject in a higher grade level without being grade skipped.
- *Telescoping* is a process of condensing the grade-level or subject-matter curriculum into an abbreviated course of study. Through telescoping, a school can allow a student to take a year long math course in one semester or finish high school in 3 years instead of 4.
- For students in schools that do not offer advanced or special-interest courses in certain disciplines, *distance-learning* is an accelerative option that allows students to take advanced courses for school credit. Increasingly, distance learning opportunities are delivered via the Internet as online courses.
- When students take courses at two levels of schooling simultaneously, it is called *concurrent* or *dual enrollment*. For example, an elementary school student might take a math course at the middle school, or a high school student may enroll in an advanced composition course at a local college.
- Advanced Placement (AP) and International Baccalaureate are two of the most well known examples of programs that offer *credit by examination*, but a school might allow a student to test out of a course or grade-level subject before advancing the student to the next grade or course using tests created at the district level.
- *Curriculum compacting* is a multistep strategy by which the teacher preassesses student readiness relative to lesson or unit learning goals and replaces the objectives the student has mastered with more challenging alternatives or interest-based activities (Renzulli & Reis, 1997). Studies in curriculum compacting have documented its effectiveness in helping teachers eliminate portions of the grade-level curriculum for some high-ability students (Reis & Westberg, 1994; Reis et al., 1993).
- *Continuous progress* is allowing a student to progress through grade-level or subject-matter curriculum as he or she masters it. When the student surpasses the performance of his or her classmates, the strategy has become accelerative. When a student makes his or her own decisions about the pace at which to progress, it is called *self-paced instruction*.

Implications. The variety of options described here highlight some of the many ways through which curriculum and instruction can be modified for high-performing and high-potential students. Depending on her middle school's offerings, Bettina's talents in math may warrant dual enrollment in a high school math course. Diego's chemistry teacher could use compacting in allowing him time to study advanced topics. Despite not being enrolled in an advanced chemistry course, through self-paced instruction, telescoping, or studying on his own, Diego might also take and pass the AP chemistry test. Any of the four students we've profiled may benefit from distance learning courses, especially if their current or future schools either do not offer those courses at an appropriate level of challenge or do not offer them at all.

Although acceleration can be an appropriate first step in meeting the academic needs of some students who show exceptionally advanced abilities beyond their same-age peers, moving a student to a different grade or giving a student a curriculum intended for older students does not necessarily ensure him or her an appropriate education. Consider Adam, who skipped kindergarten. Suppose his school is one where the general education curriculum does not exhibit markers of high quality. Given curricula at all grade levels that is unchallenging, disengaging, and based on attainment of rote facts and basic skills, early entrance to kindergarten or first grade may expose Adam to new content but not to the challenge and engagement he needs. Similarly, if the curriculum is defensible but the first-grade teacher is using a one-size-fits-all approach or relies solely on grade-level discussions and worksheets, the classroom is likely just as ill fitting as the kindergarten room—not only for Adam but likely for most students in the class as well.

Similarly, accelerated courses and programs are not necessarily differentiated. A teacher may assume that the students in an honors class can or should be taught the same content in the same ways. Research indicates that classroom teachers have difficulty with and often lack training in how to consistently provide appropriately challenging alternatives for advanced learners (Archambault et al., 1993; Moon, Callahan, Tomlinson, & Miller, 2002; Moon, Tomlinson, & Callahan, 1995; Reis & Purcell, 1993). This can be an obstacle to classroom-based acceleration strategies and administrative arrangements, which are dependent on the teacher knowing how to provide curriculum and instruction commensurate with the students' readiness. A teacher might not have the depth or breadth of content knowledge to know what the next step or level "looks like" or the strategies to manage students working on different things at the same time.

In addition, a teacher in a higher grade level or more advanced course is not necessarily more likely to differentiate instruction. Recall that Diego was denied access to advanced science courses. If he is in a general education science class where the teacher accommodates student differences and is committed to moving all students toward scientific expertise, he may do just as well, if not better, than in a course that is inflexible. In other words, a classroom where students' needs are efficiently addressed may be preferable to acceleration without differentiation.

Thinking further about Diego as well as Catie—both students we described as high potential—they may also require accelerative strategies that simultaneously equip them with skills and knowledge they lack or have been previously denied *and* that deliver high-level content. For this reason, schools and teachers must avoid thinking of acceleration only as a strategy or programming option for students who show exceptionally advanced performance. In addition to Diego, who entered the American school system later than his peers, or Catie, whose special education services have preempted other opportunities, consider the transient student or the student who has missed class time because of disciplinary action. There are highly capable learners among these populations as well. They need to simultaneously "catch up" and develop their talents. Delivery systems for realizing these goals might include compacted lessons or units, a telescoped grade-level curriculum, or enrollment in an honors class supplemented by a foundational-level online course in the same subject.

The Accelerated Schools Project, conceived by Henry Levin from Stanford University, is based on a similar way of thinking about acceleration. Founded on the premise that students from disadvantaged backgrounds benefit not from remediation but rather from the same kind of instruction and programs academically advanced students receive, accelerated schools use heterogeneous grouping, high-level courses, and an enrichment program called "powerful learning" to ensure that the skills of students in high-poverty situations are comparable with their more advantaged peers (Goldberg, 2001; Levin, 1987). For these schools, then, acceleration is a vehicle for educational equity.

Students do not learn in the same ways, at the same pace, or under the same conditions. Whether because of advanced performance, gaps in proficiency, missed time in school, economic disadvantages, or other factors, it is likely that many students—not only those identified as highly gifted—will need provisions for accelerated learning in some form.

Enrichment

Definitions of *enrichment* generally include descriptors like *richer*, *more varied, deeper*, and *greater breadth*. The broad, widespread use of the term makes it difficult to summarize research on enrichment (Schiever & Maker, 1997). The lack of clarity about what kind of enrichment is best suited for gifted learners may account for the gap between research-based support for acceleration and similar support for enrichment (Shore et al., 1991). If enrichment is conceived as any and all additions to the core curriculum, many provisions can be considered enrichment, from grouping arrangements to competitions to after-school programs.

Supports for Enrichment. There are numerous strategies, programs, and administrative arrangements that can support enrichment. Here are a few of these:

- **Curriculum compacting**—Although described in this chapter under strategies that support acceleration, when a student has been compacted out of a grade-level curriculum, the teacher may assign tasks or projects classified as enrichment.
- **The Enrichment Triad Model**—The Enrichment Triad Model was developed in part as a response to shallow enrichment programs for gifted students (Renzulli, 1977). Three of its components—Type I, Type II, and Type III activities—provide useful ways of thinking about enrichment. General exploratory activities make up Type I enrichment. Type II activities involve group training in methodological or "how-to" skills inspired by Type Is, and Type III activities are individual and small-group investigations aimed at developing real products or solutions to real problems and real audiences.
- **Enrichment clusters**—Enrichment clusters are nongraded groups of students who share a common interest and are directed toward creating a product or offering a service with an authentic purpose. Facilitated by teachers, parents, staff, or community members, the clusters meet at a designated time of month, week, or day (Renzulli & Reis, 1997).
- **Interest centers**—A designated place in the classroom where students can explore topics they are interested in. The topics may or may not be an extension of a current curricular focus, but in any case, the materials and tasks are directed toward important learning goals, promote individual student growth, and vary from simple to complex, concrete to abstract, and structured to open ended (Tomlinson, 1999).
- **Anchor activities**—Similar to interest centers, anchor activities are motivating tasks that students do when they have completed required work at a level of high quality (Tomlinson, 2001). As a vehicle for enrichment, the activities should allow

students to access the curriculum in greater breadth, depth, or complexity.
- **Independent projects**—Customized opportunities for students to develop talent and interest areas (Tomlinson, 1999). Independent projects are not ways of privileging advanced students or giving them "something to do" but rather chances for all students to work at some point during the year on a meaningful, authentic, research-based pursuit at their current level of readiness.
- **Orbital studies**—Three- to 6-week investigations that revolve, or orbit, around a particular aspect of the curriculum (Stevenson, 1992; Tomlinson, 1999). With teacher coaching, students develop expertise on self-selected topics and independent research skills.
- **WebQuests/Web inquiries**—Inquiry-oriented activities that use the Internet as a primary resource. WebQuests are structured to lead students through a predetermined inquiry and process. Web inquiries are designed to help teachers scaffold the inquiry process for and give more responsibility to students. The teacher follows a Web-based lesson plan organized into six sections: hook, questions, procedures, data investigation, analysis, and findings. All students start the inquiry by viewing the "hook" Web page. Then the teacher decides what level of inquiry—from more structured to more open ended—is most appropriate for individual students to progress successfully through the investigation (Molebash, Dodge, Bell, Mason, & Irving, n.d.).

Implications. Similar to instructional strategies, these examples of vehicles for enrichment are not themselves intrinsic guarantees of differentiated learning experiences for students. Without a thorough understanding of its purpose, an enrichment cluster could turn into a teacher-dominated club or an interest center into contrived busywork. Deprived a foundation in a high-quality curriculum, a WebQuest might become little more than a scavenger hunt. And if a teacher does not make adjustments for student readiness, interest, and learning profile, an independent or orbital study is likely to bore some students and frustrate others. Used expertly, however, these structures can cultivate students' talents and interests—both manifest and latent.

In practice, teachers may use the term *enrichment* to denote activities for students who have mastered or completed regular classroom work and/or activities they use with some or all students when there is left-over time in a curricular or instructional sequence. Enrichment might be viewed as anything *extra* or of interest to the teacher or student that the regular curriculum does not allow. But because a teacher provides activities or instruction that are not covered by the regular curriculum does not mean they should be called enrichment. For example, if Adam demonstrates readiness with respect to a particular set of learning goals or skills and his teacher provides enrichment in the form of fun word puzzles, however challenging, we contend that this kind of enrichment (a) does not constitute differentiation as we understand it and (b) might not constitute appropriate school curriculum for anyone.

Textbooks or other curricular materials may also designate certain sections or questions as enrichment. In the absence of clear ideas about how to differentiate for gifted learners, Diego's teacher might rely on these labels to guide decisions about adjustments for him and other students. While the enrichment activities in his science book might make better use of his time than another worksheet, they are not likely to help his teacher develop a coherent approach to enriching curriculum and instruction for her students' range of readiness, interests, and learning profiles.

By contrast, high-quality enrichment is marked by tasks and products that do the following:

- Are rooted in authentic, discipline-based content
- Enhance/extend students' understanding of, attitude toward, or application of a concept or topic
- Provide ample guidance to support students in working at a high level of quality
- Are aligned with important curricular goals
- Move students toward greater expertise in content, process, and product
- Increase students' capabilities to work independently

These qualities are vital for the students demonstrating advanced readiness and for students who are less ready. Like acceleration, access to enrichment should not be limited to students identified as gifted.

The Equalizer. Faced with providing enrichment for a range of student readiness levels, interests, and learning preferences, teachers may wonder how to modify enrichment activities for high-performing and high-potential learners. The Equalizer (see Figure 10–2) is one tool that teachers can use to think practically about how to differentiate instruction for all levels of readiness, including advanced readiness (Tomlinson, 2001). The buttons on The Equalizer represent continua across which a teacher can mentally adjust content, processes, or products.

At first glance, it may seem like the dimensions on the left side of the figure are those most appropriate for gifted students. However, given content and concepts that are significantly challenging, the highly able learner may need to work more slowly rather than faster. The procedure a bright student uses in an initial approach to a complex problem might be simple rather than complex. He or she might work with advanced ideas on a concrete level before moving toward abstraction. At various points in their development, most students will be at a range of points along the continua.

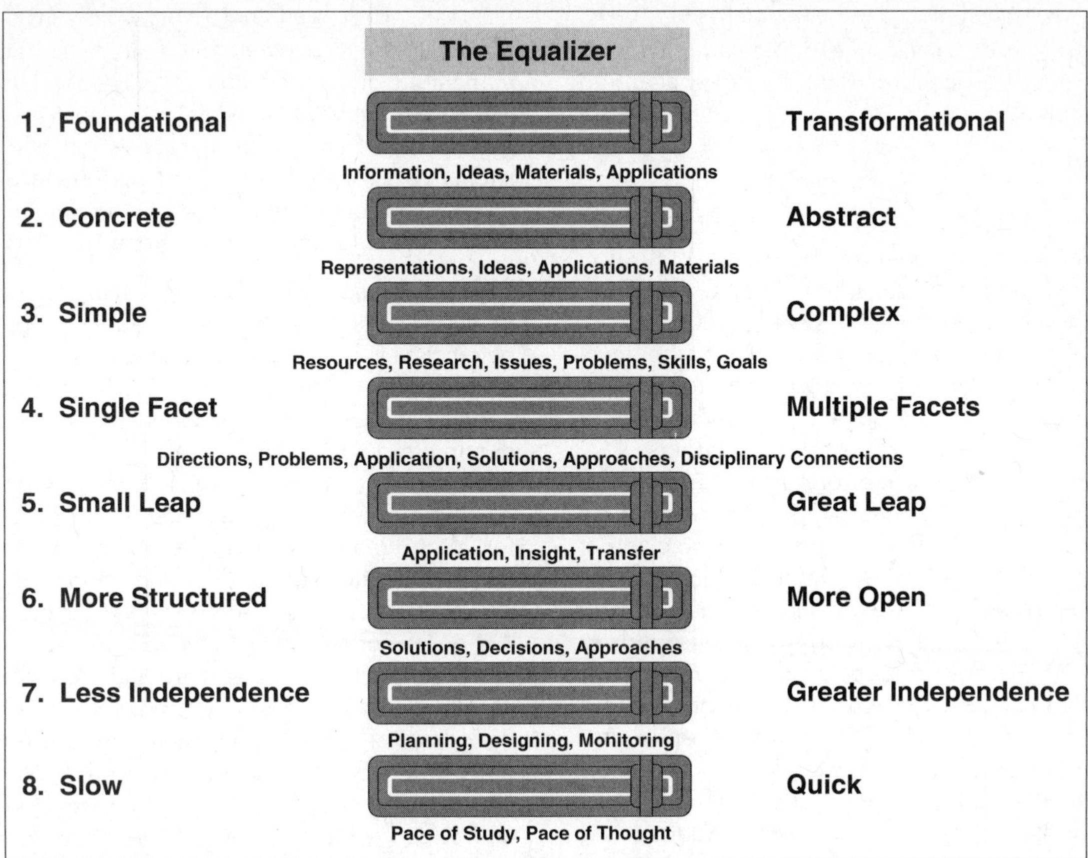

FIGURE 10–2 The Equalizer
Source: From The Differentiated Classroom: Responding to the Needs of All Learners, *by C. A. Tomlinson, 1999, Alexandria, VA: Association for Supervision and Curriculum Development. Copyright © 1999 by ASCD. Reprinted by Permission. The Association for Supervision and Curriculum Development is a worldwide community of educators advocating sound policies and sharing best practices to achieve the success of each learner. To learn more, visit ASCD at www.ascd.org.*

Using The Equalizer for Enrichment. As an extension of a recent math unit, Bettina's teacher wants all her students to gather and analyze data. She decides that the topic for the research will be summer vacation plans. From there, her students will have to refine their research questions for specificity. For a student working on a less complex level, the question might be, "What are the summer vacation plans of the students in Mr. Hopper's fourth grade class?" This question is authentic and purposeful and will require important math skills; however, the student will be working with a well-defined, easy-to-sample population. A more complex question for Bettina might be, "Is there a statistical difference between the summer vacation plans of girls and boys at our school?" This question requires a larger sample size, more complicated data collection, and inferential statistics. Because of the high level of her task, Bettina will likely need greater teacher support for structuring and carrying out her investigation. She may also be working more slowly than the other students, as the methods she will be using are more time consuming and unfamiliar.

GROUPING AS AN ADMINISTRATIVE ARRANGEMENT

Ways of grouping flexibly for classroom instruction that are vital for effectively differentiating instruction have been noted thus far in this chapter. In this section, grouping as an administrative arrangement or way of organizing students for instruction at the school level is addressed. These structures can be used to support acceleration, enrichment, or both. Relevant research, two potentially flexible administrative arrangements for gifted learners, the implications of these groupings, and how they might be applied for Adam, Bettina, Catie, and Diego are discussed.

Definitions of Grouping

Kaplan (1974) explained grouping as "provisions which facilitate the student's access to learning opportunities" (p. 46). This definition suggests that (a) grouping is a means to an end, not the end itself, and (b) grouping is a means for granting (and, conversely, denying) access to learning opportunities. In line with this view, teachers should use a *variety* of grouping arrangements on behalf of all learners, including high-potential and high-performing learners.

Research

Questions about and research on how to best group students for instruction abound in both gifted education (Gentry, 1999; Kulik & Kulik, 1992) and general education (Berliner & Biddle, 1995; Oakes, 2005; Slavin, 1991). Generally, grouping students at the school level requires administrators to consider how to provide challenging curriculum and engaging instruction for all students, not just specific populations of learners.

Although grouping in some form is an inherent part of how schools are structured, traditionally, schoolwide grouping has not been flexible. Academic tracking is one example. Oakes (2005) defined tracking as "the process whereby students are divided into categories so that they can be assigned in groups to various kinds of classes" (p. 3). Because students in higher tracks have tended to have access to higher-status content, more time to learn, better teachers, and more positive attitudes toward teachers, learning, and peers, tracking has contributed to inequities between students in various tracks (Gamoran, 1992; Oakes, 1986). Additionally, tracking is associated with "locking students in" to a prescribed educational pathway.

In a "best-evidence" synthesis of research specific to gifted learners, Rogers (1993) found several grouping arrangements beneficial to gifted students: full-time placement in an enrichment or acceleration gifted program, subject-specific regrouping, subject-specific cross-grade grouping, pullout grouping for enrichments, cluster grouping in an academically heterogeneous classroom, and within-class ability grouping. Depending on how they are practiced, these strategies may be flexible or inflexible.

Taken together, research on grouping—including grouping advanced students—reveals that independent of curricular and instruction modifications, grouping configurations and compositions themselves do not determine learning outcomes. In other words, the act of assembling a group of students according to some similar criteria or characteristics in the same room or within the same room does not by itself guarantee benefits for those learners (e.g., Schumm, Moody, & Vaughn, 2000). Rather, it is how curriculum and instruction are adjusted and used within the group that impacts student performance (Kulik, 1992; Rogers, 1991).

Cluster Grouping

Definition. A *cluster* is a group of students with a common trait (e.g., English-language learners) purposely placed in the same classroom for instructional purposes. Specific to gifted education, cluster grouping is an arrangement in which several students identified as high performing or gifted are placed with similar-ability peers in the classroom of a teacher who either has training in differentiating curriculum and instruction for high-ability learners or otherwise wants to do so (Gentry, 1999). Often, these groups are formed on the basis of subject-specific strengths or on general school performance. Between-class groupings—most common at the elementary level—allow teachers to group and regroup by subject.

Implications. Like many of the strategies and arrangements discussed in this chapter, cluster grouping can be beneficial for some highly able learners and pose obstacles for others. Further, clustering students without appropriate attention to differentiating the curriculum is not an effective practice.

Potentially, benefits of cluster grouping high-performing students can include increasing achievement for all students, assisting the teacher in meeting the needs of highly able students, and raising teacher expectations for learners (Gentry, 1999; Gentry & Owen, 1999). Having a concentrated, identified group of students in the classroom who are high performing and/or identified as gifted could prompt a teacher to accommodate those students. Adam might be in classroom with more students who share his strengths. Catie could be cluster grouped with other twice-exceptional learners and Diego with other second-language learners who exhibit talent in science. The fifth-grade teachers at Bettina's school could use between-class groupings to flexibly configure students for different units of study.

Still, cluster grouping is not without its potential pitfalls. If a school identifies students for cluster groups using less inclusive means, such as test scores or teacher recommendations, learners like Diego and Catie could be missed. Catie is already cluster grouped in her classes with other students who are learning disabled, and scheduling conflicts might prevent her from being grouped with a cluster of advanced students. Even Bettina, whose strengths are exceptional in one subject area, may not experience higher-quality differentiated instruction or curriculum by being cluster grouped than she would by being grouped with other high-readiness math students in her current classroom. Adam's teacher may attend to the needs of the cluster group as a whole but not make plans to maximize Adam's particular talents.

Ultimately, all teachers should assume they will have clusters of high-performing and high-potential students in their classrooms—whether or not they are purposely put there—and should plan accordingly.

Pullout and Push-In

Definitions. Pullout and push-in are two types of programs or services a school may use to facilitate acceleration or enrichment. As a model for gifted programming at the elementary level, *pullout* refers to the practice of identifying students for services that remove them from one or more regular classroom subjects and place them in alternative setting for services. Pullout can also describe any separate individual or small-group instruction in a specific subject area that takes place outside the general education classroom.

Push-in refers to a service option through which a specialist with training in gifted education or another area of exceptionality works in collaboration with the classroom teacher to meet the instructional needs of students identified by a particular trait, such as talent in one or more subject areas.

Implications. When pullout is limited to one subject, like the program for identified gifted students at Bettina's school, it may give the impression that only demonstrated advanced capabilities in the chosen program area call for extra classroom attention. A pullout program could disadvantage students like Catie, whose scheduling conflicts with her special education pullout and prevents her from participating in services for gifted learners at her school. Finally, in some schools, pullout programs may have a primarily process-based orientation. That is, their focus may be on thinking, research, and creativity skills taught and applied in isolation from meaningful, discipline-based content.

Two major obstacles to successfully implementing a push-in model are staffing and scheduling. Most districts employ few classroom-based specialists in general and even fewer gifted or differentiated instruction specialists. Even the school with its own one or two gifted resource instructors may find itself hardpressed to ensure the specialists are spending ample time in classrooms across grade levels and subjects. Regular, productive time for collaborative planning between the teacher and the specialist may also be challenging to schedule.

Both pullout and push-in services can provide students with curriculum and instruction targeted to their learning needs from a teacher specially trained to meet those needs. These systems are flexible and complementary when used in tandem as a means for all students to work with different teaching professionals who are collaborating to meet a range of learner needs. Research indicates not only that many general education classroom teachers and gifted specialists want to collaborate with one another to meet the needs of high-performing students (Purcell & Leppien, 1998) but also that they can experience success in doing so (Landrum, 2001).

Like the other arrangements described in this chapter, exclusive reliance on any single means of servicing gifted students—or any students—is likely to shortchange many learners.

SUMMARY AND CONCLUSIONS

In this chapter, ways for teachers to think about meeting the academic needs of different kinds of gifted learners has been discussed. No instructional strategy, program type, or administrative arrangement is known that is exclusively useful for these students, but there are approaches that have proven helpful in supporting the growth of high-potential and high-performing gifted learners—particularly when they are used with students' readiness, interests, and learning preferences in mind and when they are vehicles to help students explore high-quality curriculum. With a high-quality curriculum in place, strategies must be aligned with learning goals, selected on the basis of best fit with those goals, and modified according to learner traits, namely, variance in readiness, interest, and learning profile. Certain program types and administrative arrangements are means of facilitating effective differentiation but will not necessarily meet the needs of advanced learners unless they are modified to do so.

QUESTIONS FOR THOUGHT AND REFLECTION

1. Read the profiles for Adam, Bettina, Catie, and Diego again. What additional characteristics do these learners manifest that might require instructional, administrative, or programmatic attention?
2. How can a teacher decide which instructional strategies to use with advanced learners? What factors should he or she consider?
3. Discuss the advantages and disadvantages of acceleration and enrichment strategies and program types for (a) Adam, Bettina, Catie, and Diego and (b) high-performing and high-potential students in your class(es).
4. Describe your classroom and school grouping practices. What grouping arrangements are most common in your classroom or school? When do you typically use groups? On what basis do you or does the school make grouping decisions?
5. Use The Equalizer (Figure 10–2) to think about ways you can modify a task for a high-performing or high-potential student in your classroom.

RESOURCES

Websites

Accelerated Schools Project
www.acceleratedschools.net

National Research Center on the Gifted and Talented: Training Module on Curriculum Compacting
www.gifted.uconn.edu/siegle/Curriculum Compacting/INDEX.HTM

WebQuest Portal
http://webquest.org

Web Inquiry Projects: Using Web Resources to Promote Classroom Inquiry
http://edweb.sdsu.edu/wip

BOOKS

Cohen, E. G. (1994). *Designing groupwork: Strategies for the heterogeneous classroom* (2nd ed.). New York: Teachers College Press.

Cole, R. W. (1995). *Educating everybody's children: Diverse teaching strategies for diverse learners*. Alexandria, VA: Association for Supervision and Curriculum Development.

Houk, F. A. (2005). *Supporting English language learners: A guide for teachers and administrators*. Portsmouth, NH: Heinemann.

Marzano, R. J., Pickering, D. J., & Pollock, J. E. (2001). *Instructional strategies that work*. Alexandria, VA: Association for Supervision and Curriculum Development.

Nottage, C., & Morse, V. (2000). *Independent investigation method: A 7-step method for student success in the research process*. Kingston, NH: Active Learning Systems.

Tomlinson, C. A. (1999). *The differentiated classroom: Responding to the needs of all learners*. Alexandria, VA: Association for Supervision and Curriculum Development.

Tomlinson, C. A. (2003). *Fulfilling the promise of the differentiated classroom*. Alexandria, VA: Association for Supervision and Curriculum Development.

Winebrenner, S. (1992). *Teaching gifted kids in the regular classroom*. Minneapolis: Free Spirit.

Winebrenner, S. (1996). *Teaching kids with learning difficulties in the regular classroom*. Minneapolis,: Free Spirit.

REFERENCES

Archambault, F. X., Westberg, K. L., Brown, S. W., Hallmark, B. W., Emmons, C. L., & Zhang, W. (1993). *Regular classroom practices with gifted students: Results of a national survey of classroom teachers* (Research Monograph 93102). Storrs: National Research Center on the Gifted and Talented, University of Connecticut.

Berliner, D. C., & Biddle, B. J. (1995). *The manufactured crisis: Myths, fraud, and the attack on America's public schools*. Cambridge, MA: Perseus.

Cohen, E., Lotan, R., Scarloss, B., & Arellano, A. (1999). Complex instruction: Equity in cooperative learning classrooms. *Theory Into Practice, 28*(2), 80–86.

Colangelo, N., Assouline, S. G., & Gross, M. U. M.(Eds.). (2004). *A nation deceived: How schools hold back America's brightest students*. Philadelphia: Templeton Foundation.

Davis, G. A., & Rimm, S. B. (2004). *Education of the gifted and talented*. Boston: Allyn & Bacon.

Gamoran, A. (1992). The variable effects of high school tracking. *American Sociological Review, 57,* 812–828.

Gentry, M. (1999). *Promoting student achievement and exemplary classroom practices through cluster grouping: A research-based alternative to heterogeneous elementary classrooms* (Research Monograph 99138). Storrs: National Research Center on the Gifted and Talented, University of Connecticut.

Gentry, M., & Owen, S. V. (1999). An investigation of total school flexible cluster grouping on identification, achievement, and classroom practices. *Gifted Child Quarterly, 43,* 224–243.

Goldberg, M. (2001). A concern with disadvantaged students. *Phi Delta Kappan, 82,* 632–634.

Gordon, W. J. J. (1961). *Synectics*. New York: Harper & Row.

Great Books Foundation. (1987). *An introduction to shared inquiry*. Chicago: Author.

Gross, M. (2004). *Exceptionally gifted children* (2nd ed.). London: Routledge Falmer.

Kaplan, S. N. (1974). *Providing programs for the gifted and talented: A handbook*. Ventura, CA: Office of the Ventura County Superintendent of Schools.

Kulik, J. A. (1992). *An analysis of the research on the research on ability grouping: Historical and contemporary perspectives*. Storrs: National Research Center on the Gifted and Talented, University of Connecticut.

Kulik, J. A., & Kulik, C-L. C. (1984). Effects of acceleration on students. *Review of Educational Research, 54,* 409–425.

Kulik, J. A., & Kulik, C-L. C. (1992). Meta-analytic findings on grouping programs. *Gifted Child Quarterly, 36,* 73–77.

Landrum, M. S. (2001). An evaluation of the Catalyst Program: Consultation and collaboration in gifted education. *Gifted Child Quarterly, 45,* 139–151.

Levin, H. (1987). Accelerating schools for disadvantaged students. *Education Leadership, 44*(6), 19–21.

Maker, C. J. (1982). *Curriculum development for the gifted*. Rockville, MD: Aspen Systems Corporation.

Molebash, P., Dodge, B., Bell, R., Mason, C., & Irving, K. (n.d.). *Promoting student inquiry: Webquests to web inquiry projects (WIPS)*. Retrieved from June 8, 2007, *http://edweb.sdsu.edu/wip/WIP_Intro.htm*

Moon, T. R., Callahan, C. M., Tomlinson, C. A., & Miller, E. M. (2002). *Middle school teachers' reported practices and student perceptions* (Research Monograph 02164). Storrs: National Research Center on the Gifted and Talented, University of Connecticut.

Moon, T. R., Tomlinson, C. A., & Callahan, C. M. (1995). *Academic diversity in the middle school: Results of a national survey of middle school administrators and teachers* (Research Monograph 95124). Storrs: National Research Center on the Gifted and Talented, University of Connecticut.

Oakes, J. (1986). Tracking, inequality, and the rhetoric of reform: Why schools don't change. *Journal of Education, 168,* 60–80.

Oakes, J. (2005). *Keeping track: How schools structure inequality* (2nd ed.). New Haven, CT: Yale University Press.

Osborn, A. (1948). *Your creative power*. New York: Charles Scribner.

Passow, A. H. (1982). *Differentiated curricula for the gifted/talented*. Ventura, CA: Office of the Ventura County Superintendent of Schools.

Purcell, J. H., & Leppien, J. H. (1998). Building bridges between general practitioners and educators of the gifted: A study of collaboration. *Gifted Child Quarterly, 42,* 172–181.

Reis, S. M., & Purcell, J. H. (1993). An analysis of content elimination and strategies used by elementary classroom teachers in the curriculum compacting process. *Journal for the Education of the Gifted, 16,* 147–170.

Reis, S. M., & Westberg, K. L. (1994). The impact of staff development on teachers' ability to modify curriculum for gifted and talented students. *Gifted Child Quarterly, 38,* 127–135.

Reis, S. M., Westberg, K. L., Kulikowich, J., Caillard, F., Hebert, T., Plucker, J., et al. (1993). *Why not let high ability students start school in January? The curriculum compacting study* (Research Monograph 93106). Storrs: National Research Center on the Gifted and Talented, University of Connecticut.

Renzulli, J. S. (1977). *The Enrichment Triad Model: A guide for developing defensible programs for the gifted and talented.* Mansfield Center, CT: Creative Learning Press.

Renzulli, J. S., & Reis, S. M. (1997). *The Schoolwide Enrichment Model: A how-to guide for educational excellence* (2nd ed.). Mansfield Center, CT: Creative Learning Press.

Rogers, K. B. (1991). *The relationship of grouping practices to the education of the gifted and talented learner.* Storrs: The National Research Center on the Gifted and Talented, University of Connecticut.

Rogers, K. B. (1993). Grouping the gifted and talented: Questions and answers. *Roeper Review, 16,* 8–12.

Rogers, K. B. (2002). *Re-forming gifted education: How parents and teachers can match the program to the child.* Scottsdale, AZ: Great Potential.

Rogers, K. B. (2004). The academic affects of acceleration. In N. Colangelo, S. G. Assouline, & M. U. M. Gross (Eds.), *A nation deceived: How schools hold back America's brightest students* (pp. 47–57). Philadelphia: Templeton Foundation.

Schiever, S. W., & Maker, C. J. (1997). Enrichment and acceleration: An overview and new directions. In N. Colangelo & G. A. Davis (Eds.), *Handbook of gifted education* (2nd ed., pp. 113–125). Boston: Allyn & Bacon.

Schumm, J. S., Moody, S. W., & Vaughn, S. (2000). Grouping for reading instruction: Does one size fit all? *Journal of Learning Disabilities, 33,* 477–488.

Shore, B. M., Cornell, D. G., Robinson, A., & Ward, V. S. (1991). *Recommended practices in gifted education.* New York: Teachers College Press.

Sisk, D. A. (2005). Teaching the gifted through simulation. In F. A. Karnes & S. M. Bean (Eds.), *Methods and materials for teaching the gifted* (2nd ed., pp. 543–574). Waco, TX: Prufrock.

Slavin, R. E. (1991). Synthesis of research on cooperative learning. *Educational Leadership, 48,* 71–82.

Southern, W. T., & Jones, E. D. (1991). *The academic acceleration of gifted children.* New York: Teachers College Press.

Southern, W. T., & Jones, E. D. (2004). Types of acceleration: Dimensions and issues. In N. Colangelo, S. G. Assouline, & M. U. M. Gross (Eds.), *A nation deceived: How schools hold back America's brightest students* (pp. 5–12). Philadelphia: Templeton Foundation.

Stanley, J. C. (1976). The case for extreme educational acceleration of intellectually brilliant students. *Gifted Child Quarterly, 20,* 65–75.

Stevenson, C. (1992). *Teaching ten- to fourteen-year-olds.* New York: Longman.

Tannebaum, A. J. (1986). The enrichment matrix model. In J. S. Renzulli (Ed.), *Systems and models for developing programs for the gifted and talented* (pp. 126–152). Mansfield Center, CT: Creative Learning Press.

Tomlinson, C. A. (1997). Good teaching for one and all: Does gifted education have an instructional identity? *Journal for the Education of the Gifted, 20,* 155–174.

Tomlinson, C. A. (1999). *The differentiated classroom: Responding to the needs of all learners.* Alexandria, VA: Association for Curriculum and Supervision Development.

Tomlinson, C. A. (2001). *How to differentiate instruction in the mixed-ability classroom* (2nd ed.). Alexandria, VA: Association for Curriculum and Supervision Development.

Tomlinson, C. A. (2004). Differentiation for gifted and talented students. In S. Reis (Series Ed.), *Essential readings in gifted education.* Thousand Oaks, CA: Corwin.

Tomlinson, C. A. (2005). Quality curriculum and instruction for high ability students. *Theory Into Practice, 44,* 160–166.

Tomlinson, C. A., Brighton, C., Hertberg, H., Callahan, C. M., Moon, T. R., Brimijoin, K., (2003). Differentiating instruction in response to student readiness, interest, and learning profile in academically diverse classrooms: A review of literature. *Journal for the Education of the Gifted, 27,* 119–145.

VanTassel-Baska, J. (1985). Appropriate curriculum for the gifted. In J. Feldhusen (Ed.), *Toward excellence in gifted education* (pp. 175–189). Denver: Love.

Ward, V. S. (1961). *Educating the gifted: An axiomatic approach.* Columbus: Charles E. Merrill.

Westberg, K. L., & Archambault, F. X. (1997). A multi-site case study of successful classroom practices for high ability students. *Gifted Child Quarterly, 41,* 42–51.

CHAPTER 11

TEACHING MODELS FOR GIFTED LEARNERS

Joan Franklin Smutny, Director
The Center for Gifted, National-Louis University

INTRODUCTION

The models described in this chapter offer a rich resource for meeting the academic, creative, and emotional needs of advanced learners. They span a time period of over four decades and have contributed significantly to the field of gifted education. Countless teachers and researchers have used the philosophies, ideas, and strategies from these models to guide generations of gifted students.

The aim of this chapter is to help readers appreciate what these models have brought to advanced learners. Providing a detailed portrait of each model is impossible given the limited space of this chapter. Hence, descriptions are confined to those aspects that specifically address the needs of gifted learners and to those strengths or features that are most appropriate for classrooms today. Descriptions of each model focus on (a) the basic concept of the model, (b) the structure, and (c) its benefits to gifted learners. The models are grouped under general domains merely as a way of highlighting their contribution to gifted education. The domains and models to be considered under each include the following:

1. Foundations
   a. J. P. Guilford: Structure of the Intellect
   b. Jerome Bruner: Basic Structure of the Discipline
2. Taxonomies
   a. Benjamin Bloom: Cognitive Taxonomy
   b. David Krathwohl: Affective Taxonomy
3. Procedures for Applying Thinking Strategies
   a. Hilda Taba: Teaching Strategies Program
   b. Lawrence Kohlberg: Discussion of Moral Dilemmas
   c. Frank E. Williams: Cognitive Affective Interaction
   d. Sidney Parnes: Creative Problem-Solving Model
4. Comprehensive Approaches
   a. Joseph Renzulli: The Enrichment Triad Model
   b. John Feldhusen: Purdue Three-Stage Enrichment Model
   c. John Feldhusen: Purdue Secondary Model
5. Multiple Abilities
   a. June Maker and Shirley W. Schiever: DISCOVER Model
   b. Calvin Taylor: Multiple Talents Model
6. Independent Learning
   a. Donald J. Treffinger: Self-Directed Learning Model
   b. George Betts: Autonomous Learner Model

FOUNDATIONS

The pioneering work of J. P. Guilford and Jerome Bruner prepared the foundation for a new conceptual understanding of intelligence and learning in American schools. Guilford (1967) contributed to the field a much broader and multidimensional concept of intelligence than the accepted definition of the intellect as a fixed, unitary trait. Through his theory and practical understanding about the process of learning, Bruner (1960) created the possibility for students to actively engage in a subject rather than receive it passively. Their combined influence opened the door to a wide range of teaching ideas and approaches that continue to have a profound impact on gifted education today.

J. P. Guilford: Structure of the Intellect

Concept. Guilford's (1967) fundamental concept is that intelligence is multifaceted or multidimensional. Before Guilford, educators believed that even if the intellect has different aspects or elements, it nevertheless remains *one general level of intelligence.* In contrast, Guilford presents a morphological model in which the facets or dimensions of intelligence, though related, are separate and distinct; there is no general intelligence factor operating through all these abilities.

Structure. The structure of Guilford's model is a simple one. Guilford (1967) conceptualizes human intelligence in terms of three overarching dimensions: (a) content, (b) operations (processes), and (c) products. Each human ability includes, in some fashion, these three dimensions and manifests itself through the subcategories within each dimension. With such a variety of combinations, up to 120, the model provides the means to identify and respond to exceptional ability across a broad spectrum of domains.

Benefit to Gifted Students. Guilford's expanded view of intelligence was his greatest gift to the gifted. The theory affected all levels of program planning from identification to philosophy, curriculum design, and teaching strategies (Maker & Nielson, 1995). Table 11–1 demonstrates how gifted children from a variety of backgrounds and learning orientations can benefit from a model that embraces less recognized kinds of intelligence. Including the figural, symbolic, and behavioral in the content dimension, for example, provides more opportunities for these students to show their ability than if they had to confine themselves to the semantic aspect (Meeker & Meeker, 1986).

Meeker (1969), a colleague of Guilford, significantly extended the usefulness of the model by translating it into more accessible, practical forms. She designed testing materials, workbooks to use with children, and computer programs and also developed materials for training teachers (Meeker & Meeker, 1986).

Jerome Bruner: Basic Structure of the Discipline

Concept. Jerome Bruner (1960) challenged conventional notions about learning that existed in his time and

TABLE 11–1 Guilford's Structure of the Intellect Model

Operations	Content	Product
Cognition (perceive/understand)	Figural (concrete/sensory)	Units (single item)
Memory (remember/store)	Semantic (meaning of information)	Classes (categories)
Convergent production (generate answers that "converge" on a solution)	Symbolic (representations/signs)	Relations (connections)
Divergent production (generate ideas that "diverge" from conventional)	Behavioral (nonverbal information/ body language)	Systems (complex structures)
Evaluation (assess/measure/decide)		Transformations (changes within that make something new)
		Implications (predictions from data analysis)

Examples:

Divergent production of semantic systems. A child studies the story of Cinderella and writes a fractured fairytale version of the story.

Cognition of figural relations. A child accurately "reads" the body language of a small crowd on the street and takes steps to avoid them.

Memory of behavioral classes. A child identifies the barn swallow because of the flight patterns in the air.

revolutionized curriculum theory and practice. In his view, the outcome of a student's learning should be to understand the fundamental structure of a discipline with its concepts, relations, practices, and elements. This understanding should emerge from the discovery process of an active, inquiring mind. Primarily a content model, the Basic Structure of the Discipline constitutes a major shift from passive reception to lively engagement. It involves selecting, constructing, and decision making that evolve from conceptual models that the students already have and that bring meaning to new knowledge. In Bruner's model, a child, instead of learning the *results* of scientific studies, would instead *do science* by conducting an inquiry, performing an experiment, and evaluating data, thereby gaining an understanding of its underlying structure.

Structure. Bruner's Basic Structure of the Discipline is a *total approach to content.* Implementing all the themes examined by Bruner is a vast and detailed process. Instead, what follows are key areas of emphasis (for a fuller treatment of this subject, see Maker & Schiever, 2005):

- **Structure of knowledge**—To learn, students need to participate in the processes, practices, and fundamental concepts of a discipline. Activities should lead to abstract ideas and an increasingly more complex understanding. Economy is also emphasized. Students should not waste time on tasks that are not related to core concepts. Examples:
  1. The content of each lesson relates to some fundamental concept and process within a discipline (e.g., a science lesson involves learners in testing and hypothesizing).
  2. Students practice and strengthen advanced skills essential to a discipline (e.g., they edit and rewrite as part of the craft of creative writing).
  3. Students work in environments that maximize the possibility of discovery and advancement beyond current level of understanding.
- **Readiness for learning**—To learn, children need to be motivated and feel an interest and passion in the mysteries before them. Examples:
  1. There is an appropriate match between level of content and child.
  2. Activities stimulate interest and relate to core concepts to be discovered.
  3. Resources are rich and varied and come from the real world (e.g., books, nature materials, art, and science supplies, *not* school texts or worksheets).
- **Intuitive and analytic thinking**—To learn in a meaningful way, children need to experience discovery. Examples:
  1. Students acquire enough understanding of a particular subject to analyze and explore (e.g., to discover a new pattern in the migration of the whooping crane depends on some fundamental knowledge about the natural history of this particular species).
  2. Teachers sequence activities in such a way as to nurture inductive thinking, deductive thinking, analysis, and intuitive leaps.
  3. Students practice making hypotheses and gathering evidence with teachers supporting posing questions, encouraging risks, and making suggestions.

Benefit to Gifted Students. Bruner's focus on the structure of the discipline has had a profound impact on gifted education programs (Maker & Schiever, 2005). The model offers abstract and complex content (concepts, ideas, and themes), with sequences and processes that stimulate and nurture discovery with depth, challenge, and flexibility. Students approach content in a participatory way as scientists, historians, and mathematicians. Depending on the topic and learning goals, a lesson may involve logic, analysis, inquiry, synthesis, and so forth. In keeping with his vision of the active learner, Bruner particularly focused on the process of discovery, such as guided inquiry and exploration in an open-ended context. Also beneficial to gifted students is the value he placed on intuitive leaps rather than step-by-step analysis in discovering new ideas. Gifted children frequently draw on this quality to arrive at their most startling and insightful solutions.

TAXONOMIES

Benjamin S. Bloom: Cognitive Taxonomy; David R. Krathwohl: Affective Taxonomy

Although not specifically designed for advanced learners, Bloom's (1956) cognitive taxonomy and Krathwohl's (Krathwohl, Bloom, & Masia, 1964) affective taxonomy have had a profound influence on gifted education. Whether in the regular classroom or in a resource room or summer program, teachers have particularly used the cognitive taxonomy to create learning goals at higher levels of complexity in order to design more challenging units of study and to select resources and materials appropriate for advanced thinkers. Although less well known, the affective taxonomy has taken its place in current efforts to understand and address the affective needs of the gifted (Nugent, 2005).

In recent years, Robert Marzano (2000) addressed some of the shortcomings of Bloom's taxonomy by designing a more comprehensive alternative that he calls a New Taxonomy of Educational Objectives. Integrating a wider range of factors that affect student learning, Marzano's New Taxonomy embraces three systems: (a) the *Self-System*, which deals with the realm of beliefs, attitudes, and emotions as they relate to knowledge; (b) the *Metacognitive System*, which focuses on how the mind sets goals, applies knowledge, and manages and monitors its own progress; and (c) the *Cognitive System,* which includes processes such as knowledge retrieval, comprehension, and analysis. This new taxonomy reflects a contemporary trend toward integrating the cognitive and affective processes.

Concept. Both the cognitive and the affective taxonomies present a hierarchical order of thinking and feeling/valuing. The higher levels depend on those beneath them. Students cannot analyze the role of metaphor in a story without first knowing what metaphor is, understanding it in a variety of contexts, and applying it themselves. Nor can they assess, prioritize, and relate different values to a complex moral question without first deciding what they feel has worth and why.

Structure. Although the two taxonomies are often seen as occupying separate domains of human behavior, they intersect in many ways (see Table 11–2). The process of valuing, for example, is inextricably linked to a child's motivation to engage in comprehending and analyzing a phenomenon. Scholars and educators are increasingly recognizing the importance of the affective domain in nurturing gifted learners (Nugent, 2005).

The following are examples of the taxonomies combined:

Comprehension/valuing. Fifth-grade gifted students explore the cultural and religious stereotypes and misunderstandings between peoples of the Middle East and the West. They consider the value of knowledge and understanding between the two and provide a rationale for increasing opportunities for intercultural exchange.
Characterizing/synthesis. Seventh-grade gifted students conduct a research project on different cultural attitudes about animals and their treatment. While synthesizing this information, they formulate a coherent position on the value of animals and what they consider the proper relationship between people and animals.
Analysis/receiving. A fourth-grade cluster group analyzes the actions and motives of several characters in a novel. They reread a number of passages, attending to symbols, signs, hints, and metaphoric language that might provide clues to the questions they have.
Responding/application. Third-grade gifted students learn about the science of testing freshwater for contaminants and other problems. They eagerly seek out, with parental help, local freshwater sources and bring a sample to school, where they will conduct their own tests.

TABLE 11–2 Taxonomies

Bloom's Cognitive Taxonomy	Krathwohl's Affective Taxonomy
Knowledge Remembering information Behaviors: describe, name, tell, show	**Receiving** Attending, focusing awareness, being open Behaviors: sense, listen, see, feel
Comprehension Translating, interpreting, extrapolating Behaviors: rephrase, explain, show, infer	**Responding** Active engagement, willing participation Behaviors: feel inspired or interested, actively participate
Application Implementing a principle or theory in a new situation. Behaviors: inquire, test, solve, demonstrate	**Valuing** Deciding what has worth based on adherence to value Behaviors: sensing worth, exploring different views, assessing, clarifying
Analysis Breaking down a thing into its essential parts in order to understand the underlying structure and relations between parts Behaviors: examine, compare, distinguish, reason	**Organizing** Prioritizing and ordering different values, synthesizing values into a coherent system Behaviors: comparing values, questioning, applying logic, creating rationales
Synthesis Weaving together different elements and parts to create a new structure Behaviors: combine, interrelate, create, conclude	**Characterizing** Evolving an overarching set of values that inform how individuals approach situations Behaviors: formulating a principle or general conclusion, showing an integrated set of values
Evaluation Assessing value of something within the context of a specific goal or purpose Behaviors: Analyze evidence, measure against criteria, judge, check	

Benefit to Gifted Students. The usefulness of the taxonomies to teachers can be readily seen in almost any district in the United States. Certainly Bloom's taxonomy is the more popular. In combining them, however, teachers can help their advanced students reach learning goals in both the cognitive and the affective domains. Close parallels have been noted between, for example, receiving and knowledge, analysis/synthesis and conceptualization, and evaluation and organization/characterization (Maker & Schiever, 2005). It's important to note that these combinations do not have to occur on the same level. There are times when an analytical process benefits most from a mind in a "receiving" mode where new impressions and thoughts can appear.

The taxonomies, particularly Bloom's, continue to guide educators in addressing the needs of gifted students, as can be seen in differentiated instruction (Gregory & Chapman, 2002). The taxonomies enable teachers to evaluate the level of content, process, and student products as well as resources and materials.

Supporting Research. A study by Roberts, Ingram, and Harris (1992) assessed the effect of a school's special programming on the higher-level cognitive processing skills of gifted and nongifted third, fourth, and fifth graders. The school adapted the Renzulli Triad Model (Renzulli, 1977) to stimulate and develop higher-level thinking skills. Activities drew on Bloom's taxonomy and Guilford's Structure of the Intellect. In the study, researchers used the Ross Test of Higher Cognitive Processes (Ross & Ross, 1976) to measure the effects of the intervention on thinking ability among students of various ability levels. The results showed significant growth in all populations. Gifted students who received special programming showed a marked increase in higher levels of thought processes than those in a comparison school who did not.

PROCEDURES FOR APPLYING THINKING STRATEGIES

The models in this section evolved during a time when the *transmission* approach to education (Miller & Seller, 1985), where teachers literally "transmit" knowledge to students, was being challenged. In contrast, these models propose a *transaction* philosophy, where learning happens in the process of a variety of interactions between students and the teacher, students and each other, and students and the content at hand. All four explore specific strategies for teaching students to think.

Hilda Taba: Teaching Strategies Program

Concept. Hilda Taba's model concerns itself largely with the development of inductive thinking and rests on several related ideas (Joyce & Weil, 1986). First, thinking is something that can and should be taught. Although Taba adhered to Piaget's theory of cognitive development, she nevertheless understood that, given the proper environmental conditions and support by the teacher, students' thinking could evolve (Maker & Schiever, 2005). Second, this kind of learning involves an active exchange between student and the data before him or her. Third, growth in thinking ability results from a precise sequence, arranged to build on and extend from the previous steps.

Influenced by the theories of Piaget, Taba designed a model that enables students at specific levels of cognitive development to master particular kinds of thinking skills. Her research led to the conclusion that children can best develop inductive thinking skills by making their own inquiries with the help of guiding questions from the teacher. She challenged the notion that students require a prescribed amount of knowledge in order to extend their thinking. Taba's philosophy stressed the vital role of sequential questioning techniques, such as open ended, embracing different perspectives and levels of thinking, to guide inductive thought processes.

Structure. The model includes four basic strategies:

- **Concept development**—Students organize information, identify categories, and develop concepts while interacting with it. Taba used a sequence of what she called "eliciting questions" (1967, p. 92) to stimulate certain kinds of thinking about the data (Joyce & Weil, 1986, p. 43).
- **Interpretation of data**—Students identify and explore relationships and make generalizations and inferences in response to eliciting questions by the teacher.
- **Application of generalizations**—Students apply previously learned generalizations and facts to new situations.
- **Resolution of conflict**—Students resolve conflicts that arise between the known and the new.

The success of Taba's model lies in the carefully sequenced questions and activities that lead students through each level of discovery, from exploring unfamiliar data and forming concepts to explaining and interpreting data to applying and extending the principles learned. In the process, students become increasingly more experienced and confident in the art of inductive thinking.

A sixth-grade math teacher has made extensive use of this kind of approach:

> A clear directive to me about the need for inductive thinking came from an offhand remark made by my professor. . . . He pointed out that, for 12 or even 16 years of mathematics instruction, students are judged by their ability to apprehend mathematics that has already been formulated by others. Then, when they

begin work on their Ph.D., they are expected to discover something new—and they sometimes have no idea how to proceed. When I heard this, I thought to myself, why not give students the opportunity to formulate mathematical principles while they are young? Over many years, I have developed activities that do just that. I present a situation of some mathematical interest; let the students explore it, and encourage them, through leading questions, to formulate the fundamental mathematical principles that govern it. (Freeman, 2003, p. 73)

In this math teacher's class, inductive thinking can result in new insights only if the children have sufficient time to mull over the different possibilities and test their hypotheses. To facilitate this, the teacher must allow students to confront real problems, manipulate and/or construct objects, and collaborate with each other when appropriate. This takes more time than just memorizing math formulas and practicing them.

Benefit to Gifted Students. Taba's inductive thinking model emphasizes higher-level thinking and complex content, which in turn stimulates more sophisticated and original student responses. Her social studies curriculum (1967) illustrates her inductive teaching approach. The model offers practical guidance on teaching strategies and techniques that educators can learn gradually and then expand and adapt to their own classrooms.

Supporting Research. A study on an alternative method for assessing critical thinking skills among gifted middle school students (Udall & High, 1989) showed that Taba's strategies provide a highly effective vehicle for teaching gifted learners not only how to engage specific kinds of data and problems but also how to decide which strategies to use. Two teachers in separate middle schools participated in the study, which involved videotaping and interviews of both teachers and selected students to yield in-depth information on how well the latter could identify their teachers' intentions and articulate their own processes. A high level of congruence between the instructional goals of teachers and perceptions and achievements of students demonstrated that Taba's strategies resulted in significant learning among gifted learners.

Lawrence Kohlberg: Discussion of Moral Dilemmas

Concept. Influenced by Piaget's "stage theory" of cognitive development, Lawrence Kolberg designed methods for stimulating growth in moral thinking (DeVries & Kohlberg, 1987; Kohlberg, 1976). The stages unfold in three general levels. Within those, Kohlberg posits two stages each. To illustrate these stages clearly, imagine that two sisters find some money on a city sidewalk. One sister quickly picks it up even though both saw it at the same time. The mother insists that the sister who picked it up share it with the other sister.

Preconventional Level. Goodness relates to punishment and rewards:

1. **Obedience and punishment orientation.** "I'll share with my sister the money we found on the sidewalk." or "My Mom won't give me any cake after supper if I don't share with my sister."
2. **Instrumental relativist orientation.** "I'm sharing the money because then we'll each get half of the amount for finding it."

Conventional Level. Goodness means doing right in the social order:

1. **Interpersonal concordance or "good boy–nice girl" orientation.** "I'll share with my sister because then my parents will approve of me."
2. **"Law and order" orientation.** "I'll share the money with my sister because it's right to divide something that two people find at the same time."

Postconventional, Autonomous, or Principled Level. Goodness is understood in terms of principles that transcend any one group of people:

1. **Social contract legalistic orientation.** "I'm sharing the money with my sister because we've decided that even though I *touched* it first, we both *saw* it at the same time, and seeing is finding."
2. **Universal ethical principle orientation.** "I'm sharing the money with my sister because sharing is a quality I value, particularly with a family member or friend."

Understanding this development enables teachers to design what Kohlberg termed "moral dilemmas," where students can grapple with challenging issues and gradually reach new perspectives and insights that they didn't have before.

Structure. Centered on the discussion of moral dilemmas (Kohlberg & Mayer, 1972), Kohlberg's teaching model actively engages learners in complex questions and a careful consideration of the issues they raise. In the process, students become aware of their own and others' values and experience the "dilemma" of two or three convincing rationales for different courses of action.

Kohlberg structures his model in such a way that students explore a particular moral dilemma by carefully considering alternative, seemingly appropriate actions. The process can involve role-playing, imaginative games, and questioning and debating, as children weigh the values of conflicting positions and formulate a position of their own. An example of the six-step sequence is demonstrated in Table 11–3.

Benefit to Gifted Students. Kohlberg's model applies to the unique learning needs of the gifted even though it wasn't designed for them specifically. Gifted students attain higher levels of moral reasoning sooner than their peers (Karnes & Brown, 1981) and express a readiness, often an eagerness, to explore complex problems around issues of justice, human rights, animal rights, conservation, and so forth. The model's emphasis on reaching progressively higher levels of thinking and reasoning and developing sensitivity to universal principles is appropriate for gifted learners. At the same time, while the model provides for more complexity in content, it also lacks a clear structure for moving discussion to higher levels of thinking. To make this model truly practical, teachers of the gifted need to determine how a child will actually reach more advanced levels of moral thinking and reasoning.

Frank E. Williams: Cognitive Affective Interaction Model

Concept. Frank Williams's (1972) model operates on the assumption that students learn best when they actively produce something and when thinking and feeling are equally encouraged. The Cognitive Affective Interaction Model develops the thinking processes of fluency, flexibility, originality, and elaboration in combination with the feeling processes of curiosity, risk taking, complexity, and imagination. The framework applies to curriculum planning, instruction, and teacher training. It offers a means for integrating a subject with any teaching strategy to produce student behavior that is creative.

Like earlier morphological models before it (e.g., Guilford, 1967), the elements of Williams's approach cohere as a whole and are not hierarchical. In fact, Williams was concerned that developmental stage theory could impose inappropriate limits by postponing a creative challenge for younger students, for example, on the grounds that their higher-level thinking abilities are insufficiently developed for the task (Maker & Schiever, 2005). Both practical and simple, the Cognitive Affective Interaction Model allows teachers to apply strategies within all subject areas, and Williams (1972, 1982) provides plenty of practical guidance and tools for doing so.

Structure. Although originally intended to enrich the education of all students, Williams's model became a popular option for gifted learners. The model includes three dimensions: (a) the curriculum, (b) teaching strategies, and (c) student behaviors. These domains interact with each other. Thus, with 18 teaching strategies, six subject areas, and eight student behaviors, a total of 864 classroom activities are possible (see Table 11–4).

TABLE 11–3 Kohlberg's Moral Dilemmas

Steps	Example: The Case of the Burrowing Owl
1. A dilemma, loosely based on Carl Hiaasen's book *Hoot* (2002), is presented to students.	A small community receives news that a new restaurant will be built on a lot that has a colony of burrowing owls. The community is divided between those who see it as a source of jobs for the local people and those who want to prevent devastation of the owl population.
2. Students clarify the facts of the situation and identify the issues involved.	Students list pertinent facts on both sides of the issue (explore community needs on the one hand and natural history of burrowing owls on the other; examine impact that different actions might have).
3. Students identify a tentative position on the action the central character should take and state one or two reasons for that position.	Students weigh the different points of view as well as mitigating circumstances and choose a position based on the facts known and their own values.
4. Class is divided into small groups.	Students share their position and rationale with each other. Questions they consider include the following: What facts most influenced your decision? What values? They also do further research into the issues (e.g., learn more about the burrowing owl and about similar conflicts; also research small communities in need of business).
5. Class engages in a full-class discussion of the dilemma.	Following small-group work, students come together to argue their cases in a full-class session. They debate the issues, sharing new and different facts and insights.
6. Students reevaluate their original positions individually.	After discussing and sharing information and insights, students reevaluate their position. Did their original position take into account the most pertinent facts on both sides?

TABLE 11–4 Williams's Cognitive Affective Interaction Model

Teaching Strategies	Content	Student Behaviors
1. Paradoxes	Language arts	Fluent thinking
2. Attributes	Social studies	Flexible thinking
3. Analogies	Mathematics	Original thinking
4. Discrepancies	Science	Elaborative thinking
5. Provocative questions	Music	Curiosity (willingness)
6. Examples of change	Art	Risk taking (courage)
7. Examples of habit		Complexity (challenge)
8. Organized random search		Imagination (intuition)
9. Skills of search		
10. Tolerance of ambiguity		
11. Intuitive expression		
12. Adjustment to development		
13. Study creative people and process		
14. Evaluate situations		
15. Creative reading		
16. Creative listening		
17. Creative writing		
18. Visualization		

Here is an example of how a teacher might use the Williams approach:

Student behavior. Fluent and original thinking, imagination
Content. Language arts and art
Teaching strategies. Attributes, intuitive expression, creative writing, visualization

The teacher presents a series of paintings, prints, or photographs as catalysts for ideas. The students explore and then select several as sources for developing a short story. On the basis of the images before them, they list and develop a series of plots and characters that emerge from their imagined world. Working in pairs, they share their ideas, evaluate their potential as story material, and select one on which to expand.

Benefit to Gifted Students. The model provides gifted students with activities that draw both on advanced thinking and on characteristics common to high-ability learners, such as risk taking, curiosity, and tolerance toward ambiguity. It enhances open-ended discovery and freedom of choice and emphasizes a more individualized approach to learning. Williams's model is also unique in developing thinking and feeling processes simultaneously (Maker & Schiever, 2005).

Sidney Parnes: Creative Problem-Solving Model

Concept. Sidney Parnes's (1967, 1981) model operates on the assumption that creative thinking is a learned, cultivated behavior, not a fixed characteristic (Maker & Schiever, 2005). Each step of the process includes a divergent thinking phase by generating many ideas, facts, definitions of the problem, potential solutions, and so forth, and a convergent thinking phase by selecting the most promising ideas for further inquiry. Creative behavior involves a combination of knowledge, imagination, and evaluation that act in response to a practical need for a solution. The model enables students to approach a range of problems through a far more creative process and to develop tools for harnessing their creative powers overall.

Structure. Based on the five-step model pioneered by Alex Osborn (1963), Parnes updated it in 1981, emphasizing both divergent and convergent thinking. Treffinger and his associates created another version (e.g., Treffinger & Firestien, 1989) and then an additional model (Isaksen, Puccio, & Treffinger, 1993) that responded to specific criticisms about the process being too linear and failing to address the artistic dimension.

Briefly, the steps in Parnes's (1981) Creative Problem Solving Model (CPS) involved the following activities:

- **Fact finding.** List all known facts about the problem (who, what, when, where, why and how).
- **Problem finding.** Consider different ways of defining the problem.
- **Idea finding.** Generate ideas through divergent thinking and brainstorming.
- **Solution finding.** Establish criteria for evaluating ideas and identify most important elements for a viable solution.
- **Acceptance finding.** Apply/adapt solution to individuals/organizations involved in addressing the issue/problem.

Example of Creative Problem Solving. Several gifted students in a cluster group do a project on the sharp declines in migratory bird populations in the United States.

Fact finding. They ask themselves, What do birds need? Each student chooses a specific focus to research (e.g., food sources, habitat needs, migratory flight patterns, and so on). When they pool their research, they record on index cards the most important data that account for the decline in bird populations.

Problem finding. The teacher has the students examine all the index cards and asks, What is the cause of each problem the birds are facing? What is the main problem the birds are having if you put all this information together? After some discussion, the students decide that people are the problem. They decimate the habitat, build large cities in the middle of migratory routes, and so forth. The teacher asks, What is the root cause of the problem(s) people create for birds? Ignorance of birds and the environment? Overpopulation? Corporate greed? Students choose a position.

Idea finding. All the identified problems have to do with the underlying challenge that birds face from having to share the environment with humans. The students focus on bird habitat needs and human habitat needs in order to think about the different conditions and circumstances under which birds and humans could coexist on the planet without harm to either.

Solution finding. A main interest that surfaces is the problem of millions of migratory birds colliding with buildings in the major cities of North America. Students explore various solutions: city design, architectural design, restoration of habitat, glass treatments, and so forth. One student finds several bird rescue groups online who are working on reducing bird collisions.

Acceptance finding. Students create charts, designs, drawings, and reports on their proposed solutions. Members of local bird groups agree to meet with the students and also to display their findings in the local ecology center.

Benefit to Gifted Students. Although not originally intended for gifted students, the model offers a simply structured method for approaching problems in a creative way through inquiry method, higher-level thinking, open-endedness, and freedom of choice. Extremely versatile in the situations and subjects where it can be used, the model enables high-ability learners to engage in divergent, complex thinking and to expand the number of approaches for tackling problems. The practice of deferring judgment is particularly helpful to gifted students who can be impatient with themselves and with a process that doesn't yield quick results. As long as teachers take a flexible approach to the five steps, gifted students can gain long-term benefits from having this model become second nature. The five steps were meant to act as a general guide rather than a formula (Parnes, 1981), and gifted learners should be free to change the sequence or skip steps.

Supporting Research. Schack (1993) investigated the CPS model with 276 gifted, honors, and average learners in six middle schools and found that the process benefited all students. In the study, six classroom teachers developed a CPS curriculum, and six others did not. Schack assessed the growth of students' problem-solving skills through their approach to a real-world problem and focused on such processes as problem finding, fluency of ideas, managing the process according to criteria, flexibility, and originality. Results clearly indicated that *all* the students in the classrooms with a CPS curriculum grew in significant ways compared to those that lacked the CPS curriculum. Although gifted learners advanced to higher levels than their less able peers, there were no marked differences in cognitive growth due to ability level.

COMPREHENSIVE APPROACHES

The three models that follow distinguish themselves in two ways: (a) they are specifically designed for gifted students and therefore evolve from the unique abilities, traits, and learning styles of this population, and (b) they are comprehensive in nature. Hence, in both models teachers can find, for example, systems that respond to the need for accelerated instruction *and* for enrichment opportunities; in addition, they address the social-emotional challenges common among exceptional learners, such as isolation, perfectionism, boredom, underachievement, and pressure to get high grades.

Joseph Renzulli: The Enrichment Triad Model

Concept. Joseph Renzulli's (1977; Renzulli & Reis, 1986) Enrichment Triad Model has been one of the most popular in the schools and stands today as perhaps the most comprehensive and detailed system on what to do for gifted students in an educational setting. It rests on a much broader concept of giftedness (Renzulli & Reis, 1986) that is based, in large part, on the distinguishing characteristics of highly productive and eminent people. Renzulli theorizes that gifted students manifest three clusters of traits: (a) above-average ability, (b) task commitment, and (c) creativity. He makes a strong case for focusing attention more on gifted *behaviors* than on gifted *people* (Renzulli & Reis, 1986).

Although the fundamental concepts never changed, this model underwent a few incarnations, including the Secondary Triad Model (Reis & Renzulli, 1986), which orients itself more toward the needs and characteristics of high school students, and the Revolving Door Model (Renzulli, Reis, & Smith, 1981), which eventually became the Schoolwide Enrichment Model (SEM; Renzulli & Reis, 1985). In keeping with his more expansive approach to identifying high ability, Renzulli designed within the Enrichment Triad/Revolving Door Program a "Talent Pool" (Renzulli & Reis, 1986, p. 226) that includes the top 15% to 20% of a school's population (rather than 3% to 5%) and that involves *all* students in some form of enrichment.

Renzulli's model offers individualized pacing, a variety of choices; freedom from pressure and grading, and alternatives in content, learning styles, and teaching strategies. The kind of learning emphasized by the model reconnects learners to the world and nurtures the development of passion and interest in making new discoveries. Although students in an enrichment program clearly have to master basic competencies in order to proceed, they pursue subjects and topics far beyond those competencies and engage in activities that center around individual interests and learning styles (e.g., architectural drawing, planning and implementing community action, the legal rights of animals in the United States, constructing Tibetan masks, musical composition in the blues tradition, and so forth).

Structure. The Enrichment Triad Model addresses a broad spectrum of learning needs in the classroom by designing three tiers or levels of enrichment: Types I and II enrichment (for most of the school population) and Type III (for gifted and highly motivated learners). To implement the Enrichment Triad approach, Renzulli employs his Revolving Door Identification Model (Renzulli et al., 1981), which essentially allows students from the "talent pool" pursuing enrichment at the type I or II level to tackle a Type III project whenever they feel motivated and ready. The model is structured as follows:

- **Assessment of students' strengths.** Teachers explore the full spectrum of learners' strengths, abilities, interests, and learning styles. Cultural background, special areas of expertise, and life experiences among others are also considered.
- **Curriculum compacting.** Regular curriculum is modified (condensed) so that gifted students can spend more time on advanced enrichment activities.
- **Type I—general exploratory activities.** Students are introduced to a wide range of topics or areas of study not usually included in the regular curriculum. Type I demands an abundance of resources and access to a variety of fields for students to explore.
- **Type II—group training activities.** Students develop cognitive and affective skills (e.g., research, reference, and communication skills). For gifted students, this kind of enrichment provides the crucial tools and process skills (e.g., how to script a play, use science equipment, and so forth) that enable them to advance to Type III activities. Renzulli and Reis (1991) especially focused on process development:

  1. **Thinking.** Creative thinking, problem solving, critical thinking, decision making, affective processes—sensing, appreciating, valuing
  2. **Procedural skills.** Listening, observing, note taking, outlining, interviewing and surveying, classifying, analyzing and organizing data, drawing conclusions, and so forth.
  3. **Using reference and resource materials.** Reader's guides, directories, abstracts, and information retrieval systems
  4. **Communication skills.** Written, oral, and visual skills that maximize impact of students' work on audiences

- **Type III—individual and small-group investigations of real problems**—Most applicable to gifted students, Type III enrichment involves using the processes and skills of firsthand inquirers to pursue a question, a puzzle, or an interest in a variety of fields. Gifted students become researchers, investigators, inventors, artists, and so forth. In the Bruner sense, they take on the role of professionals and pursue knowledge in order to experiment, discover, invent, write, and research. Hence, they don't write a report *about* information they amassed. Rather, they use data as a source, which, in combination with other sources (e.g., fieldwork, interviews, experiments, and so forth), they employ to formulate a problem or project or design a plan with the teacher acting as mentor. An important part of this enrichment type is also locating venues for students to share their findings through performances, art installations, and so forth.

Examples of Type III Enrichment.

1. Gifted bilingual students produce a multimedia representation (text, art, video, theater, or photography) of the immigration experience as a result of readings, Internet/library research, and interviews of family and relatives. They create maps of the routes traveled, analyze the information for general themes expressed, and stage a theatrical event featuring the stories they gathered.
2. A couple of gifted students create a plan on what to do about invasive plant species in their area. They collect information on the Internet and local environmental newsletters and magazines, visit ecology centers, and participate in projects rooting out harmful species. They consult with ecologists about the feasibility of their plan.

Benefit to Gifted Students. This model stimulates transformation in both the content and the process dimensions of the regular curriculum. Benefits to gifted learners include emphasis on discovery, hands-on orientation, higher-level thinking, complexity, open-ended inquiry, flexibility, and accommodating with regard to different learning styles and cultural backgrounds. The model is designed with gifted students in mind but includes all learners in the scope and variety of the enrichment offered. As such, the model relates to the regular curriculum in helpful ways and allows teachers to use it for everyone in the classroom.

Supporting Research. A great deal of research has been conducted on the SEM. The model has shown itself to be adaptable to hundreds of school districts in the United States (Burns, 1998). Students who have participated in self-selected independent studies in SEM programs initiated their own creative products both inside and outside school more often than students who did not receive these services (Starko, 1986).

In a multicase study of secondary students (Delcourt, 1988), positive changes were observed in the skills needed for implementing projects, in personal characteristics (e.g., perseverance, patience, and so forth), and in career planning. Other researchers have also documented marked improvements among secondary students in terms of helping them discover and define new directions for their lives and clarify long-term interests (Delcourt, 1993; Taylor, 1992).

Because of its nontraditional and open-ended approach to identification and enrichment, SEM has also helped gifted students with special problems, such as those with learning disabilities (Baum, 1988; Olenchak, 1991). As an intervention for gifted/learning-disabled learners, SEM notably improved attitudes about learning at both the elementary and the high school level and increased self-esteem among those who completed Type III projects (Olenchak, 1991). The model has also helped reverse the plight of underachieving gifted students by drawing on their learning styles and strengths; compacting the curriculum, and supporting their progress through advanced, Type III enrichment projects (Emerick, 1988). A school district in London (Warwick, 2001), for example, used Renzulli's model to create a video project for underachieving gifted students that advanced their abilities and skills and connected them to areas of special interest.

John Feldhusen: Purdue Three-Stage Enrichment Model

Concept. Responding to the broad spectrum of abilities and needs among gifted elementary children, the Purdue Three-Stage Enrichment Model (Feldhusen & Kolloff, 1986) presents a combination of accelerated instruction, talent development, independent learning, and self-actualization. Although essentially an enrichment model, this approach nevertheless supports in-depth assessment and use of individualized education plans to teach basic subjects at an appropriate level and pace. It embraces the needs of the whole gifted child, encompassing higher-level and creative thinking as well as the development of self-directed learning.

Structure. The Purdue Model is often implemented as a pullout/resource room program but has also worked in self-contained classes, in cluster groups of gifted learners, as well as in enrichment classes on weekends and summers (Feldhusen & Kolloff, 1986). It centers around three levels of skill development. Creativity plays a key role, although the model also develops other kinds of thinking, such as convergent problem solving, research skills, and independent learning.

These are the three stages of the model:

Stage 1. This foundational stage provides instruction and experience in basic *divergent and convergent thinking abilities.* Applying to different content areas, activities balance verbal and nonverbal processes and emphasize fluency, flexibility, originality, and elaboration. Resources have included, for example, the creativity workbooks by Stanish (1977) and Harnadek (1976). The goal at this stage is to enhance thinking skills (classifying, comparing, logic, analysis, synthesis, evaluation, and so forth).

Stage 2. This stage encourages the *development of creative problem-solving abilities.* The model provides more complex and practical strategies and systems. Creative thinking techniques include brainstorming, the CPS model, Future Problem Solving (based on CPS), Odyssey of the Mind, and other applications. At this stage, strategies of inquiry are both teacher led and student initiated.

Stage 3. At this stage, the model focuses on the *development of independent study skills.* Projects involve gifted students in defining a problem, researching published works and other sources, interpreting findings, and developing creative ways of communicating results. Student initiated with guidance from the teacher, stage 3 projects could involve writing stories, producing plays, investigating a problem or situation, and creating a means to synthesize and communicate the findings.

Benefits to Gifted Students. The Purdue Three-Stage Model has proven its effectiveness as a system for supporting the advancement and independence of gifted learners in thinking ability, educational challenge, and interest development. Gregory (1982) applied the model in designing art courses for students in the Purdue Super Saturday Program (Feldhusen & Sokol, 1982) and providing practical guidance to art teachers. Flack and Feldhusen (1983) similarly found the model adaptable to teaching future studies in an enrichment program for gifted youth.

The model also performed as the foundation for PACE in eight elementary schools in grades 3 through 6 (Feldhusen & Kolloff, 1986). Tests assessing differences between the program and control groups on creative thinking demonstrated the model's effectiveness in developing both verbal and figural originality in participants.

Perhaps most important, the model provides a structure for gifted learners to begin building their own futures. On its basis, Feldhusen and Wood (1997) formulated an approach to talent development that actively engages able learners (in grades 3 to 12) in planning their own programming for the coming year. They examine their interests and achievements and identify goals of their own. This kind of model instills confidence in gifted students and the capacity for long-term self-directed and personal development.

John Feldhusen: Purdue Secondary Model

Concept. Designed around the unique needs of gifted secondary students, this model (Feldhusen & Robinson-Wyman, 1986) is an eclectic one, embracing both acceleration and enrichment. As shown in Table 11–5, Feldhusen sees giftedness in terms of general intellectual ability, positive self-concept, achievement motivation, and talent. This model followed his earlier Purdue Three-Stage Enrichment Model (Feldhusen & Kolloff, 1986), which focused on the development of creativity as well as other areas, such as research skills, convergent thinking, and independent learning (Davis & Rimm, 1994). In the secondary model, Feldhusen places particular emphasis on individuality since gifted students at this level diverge more with respect to their needs and interests.

Structure. The structure is informed both by the needs of gifted adolescents and by an eclectic, integrative approach to educating advanced learners. This approach rejects the notion of there being any disparity between acceleration and enrichment. Characterized by faster pace, higher level, and greater depth and complexity, the model offers a comprehensive structure for designing and developing appropriate programming at the secondary level. It features 11 components that span enrichment and acceleration options, with each

TABLE 11–5 Feldhusen's Purdue Secondary Model

General Intellectual Ability	Positive Self-Concept	Achievement Motivation	Talent
Mastery of basic skills and concepts	Development of self-awareness and self-acceptance	Stimulation to pursue higher-level goals and aspirations	Learning experiences involving creative thinking
Learning activities at a high level and rapid pace	Development of independence, self-direction, and discipline in learning	Exposure to fields of study, art, professions, and occupations	Stimulation of spatial abilities, imagery, and imagination
Development of convergent abilities	Experience in relating intellectually, artistically, and affectively with other gifted and talented students		
A significant amount of information about diverse topics			
Access and stimulation to reading			

component offering guidance on an appropriate provision for secondary gifted students. They include:

1. **Counseling services.** Fundamental to the model's success, counseling ensures accurate and fair identification, education and career counseling as well as support for personal growth.
2. **Seminars.** Seminars provide in-depth study, topics of interest to secondary students, instruction in advanced research skills, information on careers, and support for personal growth.
3. **Advanced placement courses.** This option should be and is often provided for high school students in all subject areas.
4. **Honors classes.** These include advanced course work, usually in English, social studies, science, mathematics, and foreign languages.
5. **Math/science acceleration.** Acceleration in mathematics is highly important and effective (Stanley, Keating, & Fox, 1974). Feldhusen's model recommends beginning algebra in seventh grade, providing accelerated math instruction thereafter, and opening science courses to earlier admission.
6. **Foreign languages.** Gifted students need opportunities to study languages at an advanced level, including such languages as Russian, Chinese, Latin, or Greek.
7. **Arts.** Gifted students need more opportunities to explore artistic expression. This would include visual arts as well as drama, music, and dance.
8. **Cultural experiences.** These include concerts, plays, exhibits, field trips, tours abroad, and museum programs.
9. **Career education.** At the secondary level, gifted students need opportunities to explore their own long-term interests, potential career paths, and future educational needs.
10. **Vocational programs.** To include high-ability students not interested in college, programs need to offer information and content in home economics, agriculture, business, and industrial arts.
11. **Extraschool instruction.** Learning *outside* of school could include weekend workshops, summer courses, study through correspondence or the Internet, and college classes (Feldhusen & Robinson-Wyman, 1986).

Benefit to Gifted Students. The primary benefits of this model for gifted students are, first of all, the fact that it addresses the needs of secondary students and, second, the eclectic, comprehensive nature of the model. Most models don't focus exclusively on gifted secondary students. However, as Feldhusen proves, gifted secondary students have unique needs that require special handling (Feldhusen & Robinson-Wyman, 1986). This model addresses the whole spectrum, from sensitive social-emotional needs to career education to the students' readiness for in-depth projects beyond the scope of their regular classes.

The second significant benefit of the model is the combination of acceleration and enrichment. Gifted learners need both advanced, accelerated content and the enrichment of in-depth, multidimensional learning experiences that allow flexibility and the free exploration of ideas and concepts across the disciplines. In addition, Feldhusen's inclusion of the arts as well as vocational programs recognizes that not all exceptionally able students belong in an academic context and expresses a commitment to giftedness across a much broader spectrum of domains.

MULTIPLE ABILITIES

The following models address a broader range of gifts and talents than most models. For gifted learners from non-mainstream populations (e.g., multicultural, bilingual, creatively gifted, urban poor, or learning disabled), these approaches significantly expand the number of avenues for expressing and developing ability.

June Maker: DISCOVER Model

Concept. June Maker (1996), like Renzulli (1977) and other scholars, sees intelligence in far broader and multidimensional terms than the conventional notion of a predetermined general intelligence or "*g*." The DISCOVER model (Maker, Nielson, & Rogers, 1994; Maker & Schiever, 2005), which includes both assessment and curriculum, is a response to the serious lack of resources provided for gifted children from multicultural and economically disadvantaged communities. The assessment and curriculum dimensions of the model are fully integrated.

Influenced in particular by Gardner (1985, 1992), the DISCOVER approach to assessment focuses on the behaviors and processes of students as they explore materials, consider possibilities, and solve problems. The information this yields in a variety of intelligence domains then shapes the development of a curriculum where learners draw on their strengths (knowledge, skills, and abilities) to build new concepts, address weaknesses, and make discoveries.

Structure.

Assessment. In the context of assessment, DISCOVER is an acronym that means Discovering Individual Strengths and Capabilities through Observation while allowing for Varied Ethnic Responses. Three assessment procedures were designed: one for preschool, one for high school, and a three-level process for elementary and middle school (Nielson, 2003). Students work on a series of five activities in different "intelligence" domains while a trained team carefully observes and rates the students whose eligibility will be subsequently discussed by the whole team.

Teaching. In the context of teaching, DISCOVER means Developing Individual Strengths and Creativity through Varied Opportunities for real-world problem solving. The DISCOVER Curriculum Model provides structure for units, yearlong activities, and special projects. The process begins with problem finding, where teachers explore and decide on broad themes or big ideas to study across disciplines. They then brainstorm problems within different intelligences and combinations of intelligences and arrange them on a continuum from highly structured (less creative) to completely unstructured (highly creative). These are the different problem types:

- **Type I**—Problem clearly structured with correct method identified and one correct solution
- **Type II**—Problem clearly structured with choice in method and a correct solution
- **Type III**—Problem clearly structured with choice from a variety of methods and a range of solutions possible
- **Type IV**—Problem partially structured with some parameters with choice of methods to solve it and evaluation of multiple solutions to choose best
- **Type V**—Problem conceived and structured by solver with choice of methods and evaluation of variety of solutions to select best (Maker et al., 1994)

Benefit to Gifted Students. Maker's and Schiever's model provides both alternative assessment and comprehensive programming for high-ability students from multicultural and low-socioeconomic communities. The focus on multiple intelligences, higher-level thinking, problem solving, and creativity are highly responsive to the unique characteristics and needs of these learners.

The classroom environment is student centered, flexible, and accepting and fosters risk taking and independent learning. The DISCOVER Curriculum Model provides complex content structured around abstract themes. At the same time, students undertake projects and problems that interest them and relate to their lives in some way. They use methods commonly employed by professionals in different fields and apply their discoveries to the creation of products that they can display, perform, or show to real audiences.

Supporting Research. A study by Maker, Rogers, Nielson, and Bauerle (1996) used pre- and post-assessments to measure the impact of the DISCOVER approach both on problem-solving behaviors of children (male and female, Spanish speaking, and English speaking) and on the identification of gifted learners. The study involved two classrooms with children of similar ages and ethnic, linguistic, and economic backgrounds. The assessments included interviews of teachers on their identification processes and beliefs/attitudes about giftedness. Classroom observations took place with multiple observers who recorded details on classroom setup, the use of multiple intelligences, the problem types employed, integration of cultural and linguistic features, and the content/process/product modifications.

The most dramatic changes in problem-solving behaviors took place in the domains of spatial reasoning and storytelling. High-level application of the DISCOVER approach undoubtedly stimulates significant growth, particularly in areas less emphasized in school, such as spatial abilities, that are not related to logical thinking (artistic, creative aspects) as well as artistry and imagination in storytelling.

Another finding of this study was that in a classroom with an enriched environment and a high level of DISCOVER features in the curriculum and daily teaching practices, more children show their abilities and make notable progress as a result of the focus on multiple intelligences, problem types, and integration of cultural and linguistic content, processes, and materials.

Although limited in scope (two classrooms), this study provides clear evidence that the DISCOVER approach can successfully develop the abilities of gifted learners who need real alternatives to mainstream programming for gifted students.

Calvin Taylor: Multiple Talents Model

Concept. Calvin Taylor's (1978, 1986) model operates on the assumption that most learners have special strengths in more than one area and that schools should develop this fuller spectrum of student abilities. Taylor's project was intended to create a change of focus from a predominantly academic paradigm to one of multiple abilities where the potential of more students could be engaged and developed.

Taylor drew on the research of J. P. Guilford (1967), particularly his identification of 120 abilities of the human intellect, to develop his model. Taylor grouped a number of these abilities into six areas: (a) academic, (b) communication, (c) creative, (d) planning, (e) decision making, and (f) forecasting. He presented these abilities as "Talent Totem Poles" (Taylor, 1986, p. 316), where students can occupy different positions depending on their strengths. The Multiple Talents Model emphasizes activities that relate to the world of work and to fields of study that most students can learn about only outside of school.

Structure. Taylor lists a variety of talent areas in his model (Stevenson, 1971):

- **Academic**—Academic talent is the one most rewarded by the schools and is most often seen in the ability to quickly grasp concepts and information, to engage easily in higher-level thinking (e.g., analysis and synthesis), and to express understanding in a variety of ways (math problems, science experiments, and written reports).
- **Creative**—Creative talent is seen in terms of *fluency* (producing many different ideas about a topic or problem), *flexibility* (creating many various, divergent ideas, solutions, and viewpoints), and *originality* (generating unique ideas and solutions and making unique connections and novel insights).
- **Decision making**—This talent is an ability to evaluate data carefully and includes experimental evaluation, logical evaluation, and judgment. In *experimental evaluation,* a person considers solutions from different viewpoints and explores conditions that might limit or enhance the solution. In *logical evaluation,* the potential solutions are examined in light of an established set of criteria, goals for a successful solution, the process to be engaged, and the end result. *Judgment* is the final step of actually reaching a reasoned, well-thought-out conclusion.
- **Planning**—According to Taylor, the ability to plan well involves three domains: elaboration, sensitivity to problems, and organization. *Elaboration* focuses on what needs to be done—the purpose, process, and end product. *Sensitivity to problems* involves understanding the influence of outside or personal factors on how things are done. *Organization* has to do with the logistics of accomplishment; such as locating materials and human resources and arranging for times, locations, and funds.
- **Forecasting**—This ability enables students to evaluate cause-and-effect sequences and decide what is likely to happen. It involves conceptual foresight, a firm and detailed grasp on all aspects of a situation, and social awareness (a sense of how people will respond).
- **Communication**—The ability to communicate is critical to any endeavor. It involves *expressional fluency* (effectively expressing thoughts and needs as well as understanding them when expressed by others), *associational fluency* (understanding relationships between ideas and thoughts of ones self and of others), and *word fluency* (ability to use words masterfully to convey precise meanings, to inspire, to clarify, and so forth) (Maker & Nielson, 1995).

Included in this approach are Taylor's guidelines for developing productive thinking skills, such as divergent, convergent, and evaluative thinking. Although he doesn't specify how to draw on these skills and in what contexts, the implication (Maker & Nielson, 1995) is that they can and should be developed in a number of talent areas.

Further research has produced models that translate Taylor's ideas. Schlichter's (1986) Talents Unlimited (Schlichter & Palmer, 1993) is a staff development model that trains teachers to recognize and nurture potential in the six talent areas. It focuses on the skills involved in the multiple talent areas, methods for using these areas to enhance learning, a teacher training program for nurturing multiple thinking abilities, and a system for student assessment (Schlichter, 1986).

Benefit to Gifted Students. Taylor's model offers to the gifted population a broader range of talents and abilities to explore as well as a greater variety of real-world fields and subjects to investigate. It gives students practice in addressing subjects in more complex, multilayered, and unconventional ways.

The Taylor model has the advantage of a broader, more inclusive concept of giftedness, meaning that teachers can integrate the talents into their curriculum for a larger portion of their students. The model also coincides with current approaches to differentiation, providing modifications in content, process, and product areas (Maker & Nielson, 1995).

INDEPENDENT LEARNING

The following models are intended to develop independent learning skills in gifted students. An often-neglected need, the process of becoming more self-managing and confident in implementing independent projects is a critical one for many advanced learners.

Donald Treffinger: Self-Directed Learning Model

Concept. The fundamental concept behind Treffinger's (1978, 1986) model is that gifted students need to develop the skills to become self-directed and independent learners. The impact of teacher-directed instruction is such that gifted students lack the practice of initiating projects and managing their time and processes.

The model builds on the strengths and interests of gifted students to develop skills sequentially, enabling them to assume more control over their own learning. It focuses on four basic areas: (a) identifying goals and objectives, (b) assessing behavior, (c) identifying and implementing instructional procedures, and (d) assessing performance. As they acquire skill, students gradually become engaged in all four areas. This structure provides the support system that gifted students need to direct a study or special project of their own and evaluate their progress.

Structure. Treffinger (1978, 1986) created a four-step plan for leading gifted students toward a higher degree of independent, self-initiated learning:

1. **Command style.** The teacher directs all aspects of learning for the students.
2. **Task style.** This is the first step toward self-directed learning where the teacher provides options from which the students make choices.
3. **Peer-partner style.** Students take a more active role in decisions about their learning activities, goals, and evaluation.
4. **Self-directed style.** In this final step, students are prepared to make informed choices, plan and implement activities, and evaluate their own progress. The teacher supports the students as needed.

Benefit to Gifted Students. The model enables gifted students to advance from a teacher-directed setting to one where they gain more independence as learners. The model provides a wide range of choices in content, process, and products and builds on the characteristics and strengths of gifted students to develop the practical skills required for self-directed learning. For high-ability students, Treffinger's model responds to an overlooked need for the kind of organizational and self-management skills that best support independent learning.

Supporting Research. A study by Zimmerman and Martinez-Pons (1990) sheds light on the relation between students' perceptions of academic efficacy and their use of self-regulated learning strategies. Through a structured interview process, the authors assessed 14 kinds of strategies (e.g., self-evaluating, goal setting, planning, organizing, seeking information, and so forth) in the area of mathematical problem solving and verbal comprehension. Forty-five students in fifth, eighth, and eleventh grades in a school for the gifted and the same number from regular schools were assessed in their verbal and mathematical efficacy and provided details on their use of self-regulated learning strategies. The students came from middle-class homes and included a range of ethnicities.

The gifted population showed notably higher efficacy in verbal and mathematical areas as well as in strategy use than students from regular classrooms. They demonstrated greater ability to apply self-regulating strategies than did students in the regular schools, though this is in part due to the fact that they attended a school with a highly accelerated academic program. Clearly, the development of skills that increase independent learning has to become an essential element in the education of the gifted.

George Betts: Autonomous Learner Model

Concept. Betts's (1985, 1986) Autonomous Learner Model also addresses the need of gifted and talented students to assume more responsibility for developing their own potential. This includes understanding their gifts and social-emotional needs; developing thinking, decision-making, and problem-solving skills; and becoming more creative and independent learners. As the cognitive, emotional, and social needs of the gifted are met, they naturally become more able to initiate, implement, and evaluate their own learning.

Betts's model is a comprehensive approach: a resource room plan at the elementary level and an elective course at the junior and senior high school levels. Implemented in a number of school districts in the United States and Canada, the model has five major dimensions: (a) orientation, (b) individual development, (c) enrichment activities, (d) seminars, and (e) in-depth study.

Structure. The five dimensions of the Autonomous Learner Model address the needs of gifted learners in the intellectual, creative, emotional, and social realms. Summaries of these dimensions follow:

1. **Orientation.** This dimension exposes students, teachers, administrators, and parents to the fundamental concepts and elements of the model. Activities strengthen group dynamics and self-understanding.
2. **Individual development.** This dimension develops skills, concepts, and attitudes that enhance lifelong independent learning. It focuses on learning skills, personal understanding, interpersonal skills, and career involvement.
3. **Enrichment activities.** This dimension emphasizes student-generated content. Gifted learners study topics and subjects that interest them and design a project (e.g., a performance, charity effort, intervention, research plan, and so forth).
4. **Seminars.** This dimension provides opportunities not only to research a topic but also to share it according to criteria selected by the group. Students practice presenting information on a topic to an audience, stimulating and leading discussion of the topic, and concluding discussion and activities in appropriate ways.
5. **In-depth study.** The fifth dimension involves students in investigating an idea or topic in long-term study. At this level, gifted students plan what they will learn; what they will explore, develop, and design; what resources they will need; what the end product will be; how it will be applied and presented; and how they will evaluate the process.

Benefit to Gifted Students. This model empowers gifted students to effectively direct and manage their own learning. It addresses growth and development across a full spectrum of needs: organizational, cognitive, creative, emotional, social, and so forth. It nurtures in gifted students the ability to design, plan, and implement a project idea; to evaluate their own work; and to formulate an alternative plan if necessary. The model is open ended, innovative, practical, and multidimensional.

SUMMARY AND CONCLUSIONS

Certainly, any decision as to the suitability of a model must begin with the gifted students themselves—their special abilities, learning needs, cultures, interests, and state of development. Today, teachers are facing an increasingly diverse student body in both general and gifted populations. Teaching models that have evolved over the past four decades provide a wide range of responses to this diversity.

Because of J. P. Guilford's Structure of the Intellect and Jerome Bruner's Basic Structure of the Discipline, conventional understandings about intelligence and learning have given way to more expansive ideas. Guilford introduced the idea of intelligence as multidimensional rather than a fixed, unitary quantity. Bruner demonstrated that real learning had less to do with committing facts to memory and more to do with discovering and building conceptual understanding. The cognitive and affective taxonomies by Benjamin Bloom and David Krathwohl further advanced this newly found freedom in education by providing tools that facilitate identifying and stimulating cognitive processes.

A number of models offer useful procedures for applying thinking strategies to specific kinds of content. Hilda Taba's Teaching Strategies Program emphasizes inductive thinking and uses precisely sequenced questioning techniques to elicit specific responses. Lawrence Kohlberg's Moral Dilemmas Model designs complex scenarios to advance moral thinking. Students analyze circumstances, weigh different values and viewpoints, and choose and defend their positions. In Frank Williams's Cognitive Affective Interaction Model, teachers can design dozens of activities within six subject areas by combining specific content with teaching strategies and his eight "thinking and feeling" processes. Sidney Parnes's Creative Problem-Solving Model guides and shapes creative thinking to inspire entirely novel approaches to problems.

Some models take a comprehensive approach to educating gifted students. Both Joseph Renzulli's and John Feldhusen's models evolved from a particular understanding of advanced learners. Renzulli's model is structured to address their special strengths, specifically, above-average ability, task commitment, and creativity. The Enrichment Triad Model provides three levels of enrichment, a comprehensive approach that matches enrichment learning to the ability, knowledge, and skill level of each student. John Feldhusen's Purdue Three-Stage Enrichment Model is a comprehensive approach to the educational needs of highly able learners in the elementary years. It aims to lay a solid foundation for advanced thinking that will enable students to become increasingly more self-directed in mastering research skills, engaging in the creative process, and pursuing talents and interests that they most care about. John Feldhusen's Purdue Secondary Model focuses on the unique needs of gifted secondary learners who distinguish themselves by high intellectual ability, positive self-concept, and motivation to achieve. His comprehensive model features 11 components that span enrichment and acceleration options, from counseling services to advanced courses, seminars, special instruction in the arts, vocational training, and extracurricular experiences.

Some models specifically concern themselves with expanding the definition of giftedness and providing opportunity for high-ability learners who are currently underserved in the schools. June Maker's DISCOVER model is one of these. The DISCOVER model proposes viable alternatives in both identifying and serving gifted learners from nonmainstream populations. Maker draws on multiple intelligences to design activities that can then be observed and assessed. The teaching model includes curriculum units, yearlong activities, and special projects that engage students in explorative and problem-solving processes across the disciplines. Calvin Taylor's Multiple Talents Model, inspired by Guilford's Structure of the Intellect, groups the wide and varied abilities of the human mind within six areas: academic, communication, creative, planning, decision making, and forecasting. The model emphasizes productive thinking skills, such as convergent, divergent, and evaluative processes.

Teaching models for the gifted don't focus exclusively on academic and/or creative development. Donald Treffinger and George Betts address the need for gifted students to develop independent learning skills in order to master the art and skill of planning, designing, and implementing a research project, experiment, community outreach program, or arts production and then assess their own growth and progress. Treffinger's Self-Directed Learning Model develops these skills in the form of a gradual, four-step sequence, beginning with the conventional, teacher-directed style and ending with a self-managing process. In Betts's Autonomous Learner Model, gifted students also attain more independence, but they acquire these skills through different dimensions (e.g., enrichment activities, seminars, and in-depth study) rather than through a sequence of steps.

QUESTIONS FOR THOUGHT AND REFLECTION

1. Why are teaching models necessary to prepare appropriate learning experiences for gifted students?
2. In what ways does an expanded view of human intelligence as proposed by some of these models accommodate gifted children from nonmainstream populations (e.g., multicultural, bilingual, urban, rural, low income, and so forth)?
3. What connections exist between the concepts underlying these models and current ideas behind the use of multiple intelligences, differentiation, and acceleration?
4. What models help teachers provide both acceleration *and* enrichment in their classrooms, and what are the benefits of this combination?
5. When selecting a teaching model or models for gifted students, what are the most important factors that should guide such a decision?
6. In a school where gifted students represent a diverse cultural and socioeconomic population, what model(s) would be most responsive to their needs and most versatile in the classroom? Why?
7. What model(s) could be combined to better accommodate the abilities and needs of gifted learners? Provide a rationale for the choice.

RESOURCES

Websites

Hoagies' Gifted Education Page

www.hoagiesgifted.org

This site is one of the most comprehensive resources with approximately 900 pages on many topics related to gifted children and gifted education. Resources on the website come from teachers, parents, psychologists, and even gifted students. It also includes an extensive collection from the ERIC Clearinghouse for Disabilities and Gifted Education.

Multiple Intelligences (MI)

www.newhorizons.org/bibmishelf.html

New Horizons for Learning is a network of educators interested in identifying, communicating, and implementing the most effective teaching and learning strategies for all ages and abilities. It uses the Theory of Multiple Intelligences as a framework for its website and offers a quarterly online journal that seeks to gather and disseminate the best from educational research and experience.

National Foundation for Gifted and Creative Children

www.nfgcc.org

Designed primarily for parents, this website provides a wide range of information and current research on gifted children. It focuses on contemporary concerns, most recently on the current debate about attention-deficit/hyperactivity disorder and giftedness.

National Research Center on the Gifted and Talented

www.gifted.uconn.edu/nrcgt.html

A cooperative of researchers, practitioners, policymakers, and others, this website pools knowledge and expertise on a broader conception of giftedness and on creating appropriate learning opportunities for all of America's students. It consistently offers high-quality research based both on sound theory and practice and on the most current experiences and studies performed in the field.

Odyssey of the Mind

www.odysseyofthemind.com

An international educational program that offers creative problem solving for students from kindergarten through college. They apply their creativity to solve problems, which involve evaluating ideas and making decisions, gaining greater self-confidence, and increasing self-esteem.

BOOKS

Betts, G., & Kercher, K. (1999). *Autonomous learning model: Optimizing ability.* Greeley, CO: ALPS.

Bloom, B. S. (Ed.). (1985). *Developing talent in young people.* New York: Ballantine.

Delisle, R. (1997). *How to use problem-based learning in the classroom.* Alexandria, VA: Association for Supervision and Curriculum Development.

Eberle, B., & Hall, R. E. (1986). *Affective education guidebook: Classroom activities in the realm of feelings.* Buffalo, NY: D.O.K.

Eberle, B., & Stanish, B. (1996). *CPS for kids.* Waco, TX: Prufrock.

Feldhusen, J. H. (1993). *Individualized teaching of gifted children in regular classrooms.* West Lafayette, IN: Star Teaching.

Genshaft, J., Bireley, M., & Hollinger, C. L. (Eds.). (1995). *Serving gifted and talented students: A resource for school personnel.* Austin, TX: PRO-ED.

Guilford, J. P. (1977). *Way beyond the IQ.* Buffalo, NY: Creative Education Foundation.

Karnes, F. A., & Bean, S. M. (Eds.). (2005). *Methods and materials for teaching the gifted* (2nd ed.). Waco, TX: Prufrock.

Maker, C. J., & Nielson, A. (1995). *Teaching models in education of the gifted* (2nd ed.). Austin, TX: PRO-ED.

Maker, C. J., & Schiever, S. W. (2005). *Teaching models in education of the gifted* (3rd ed.). Austin, TX: PRO-ED.

Parke, B. N. (2003). *Discovering programs for talent development.* Thousand Oaks, CA: Corwin.

Renzulli, J. S. (Ed.). (1986). *Systems and models for developing programs for the gifted and talented.* Mansfield Center, CT: Creative Learning Press.

Renzulli, J. S., Leppien, J., & Hayes, T. (2000). *The multiple menu model: A practical guide for developing differentiated curriculum*. Mansfield, CT: Creative Learning Press.

Ross, E. W. (1998). *Pathways to thinking: Strategies for developing independent learners K–8*. Norwood, MA: Christopher-Gordon.

Ruggiero, V. R. (1997). *The art of thinking: A guide to critical and creative thought* (5th ed.). New York: Longman.

Smutny, J. F., & von Fremd, S. E. (2004). *Differentiating for the young child: Teaching strategies across the content areas (K–3)*. Thousand Oaks, CA: Corwin.

Smutny, J. F., Walker, S. Y., & Meckstroth, E. A. (1997). *Teaching young gifted children in the regular classroom: Identifying, nurturing, challenging ages 4–9*. Minneapolis: Free Spirit.

Tomlinson, C. A. (1999). *The differentiated classroom: Responding to the needs of all learners*. Alexandria, VA: Association for Supervision and Curriculum Development.

Tomlinson, C. A., Kaplan, S. N., Renzulli, J. S., Purcell, J., Leppien, J., & Burns, D. (2001). *The parallel curriculum: A design to develop high potential and challenge high-ability learners*. Thousand Oaks, CA: Corwin.

Udall, A., & Daniels, J. (1991). *Creating the thoughtful classroom: Strategies to promote student thinking*. Tucson, AZ: Zephyr.

Wiggins, G., & McTighe, J. (2005). *Understanding by design* (2nd ed.). Alexandria, VA: Association for Supervision and Curriculum Development.

Winebrenner, S. W. (1992). *Teaching gifted kids in the regular classroom: Strategies and techniques every teacher can use to meet the academic needs of the gifted and talented*. Minneapolis: Free Spirit.

JOURNAL ARTICLES

Dixon, F. A. (2002). Designing critical thinking activities that stimulate synthesis and evaluation among verbally gifted adolescents. *Journal of Secondary Gifted Education, 13, 73–84.*

Plucker, J. A. (2001). Looking back, looking around, looking forward: The impact of intelligence theories on gifted education. *Roeper Review, 23*, 124–125.

Rash, P. K., & Miller, A. D. (2000). A survey of practices of teachers of the gifted. *Roeper Review, 22*, 192–194.

Reid, C., & Romanoff, B. (1997). Using multiple intelligence theory to identify gifted children. *Educational Leadership, 55*, 71–74.

Renzulli, J. S., & Reis, S. M. (2002, Fall). What is schoolwide enrichment? How gifted programs relate to total school improvement. *Gifted Child Today, 25*, 18–25, 64.

Stein, S. J., Ginns, I. S., & McRobbie, C. J. (2003). Grappling with teaching design and technology: A beginning teacher's experiences. *Research in Science and Technological Education, 21*, 141–157.

Sternberg, R. J., & Grigorenko, E. L. (2002). The theory of successful intelligence as a basis for gifted education. *Gifted Child Quarterly, 46*, 265–277.

Treffinger, D. J., Borgers, S. B., Render, G. F., & Hoffman, R. M. (1976). Encouraging affective development: A compendium of techniques and resources. *Gifted Child Quarterly, 20*, 47–65.

REFERENCES

Baum, S. (1988). An enrichment program for the gifted learning disabled student. *Gifted Child Quarterly, 32*, 226–230.

Betts, G. T. (1985). *Autonomous learner model: For the gifted and talented*. Greeley, CO: ALPS.

Betts, G. T. (1986). The autonomous learner model for the gifted and talented. In J. S. Renzulli (Ed.), *Systems and models for developing programs for the gifted and talented* (pp. 29–56). Mansfield Center, CT: Creative Learning Press.

Bloom, B. S. (Ed.). (1956). *Taxonomy of educational objectives: The classification of educational goals*. New York: Longman.

Bruner, J. S. (1960). *The process of education*. Cambridge, MA: Harvard University Press.

Burns, D.E. (1998). *SEM network directry*. Storrs, CT: University of Connecticut, Neag Center for Gifted Education and Talent Development.

Davis, G. A., & Rimm, S. B. (1994). *Education of the gifted and talented* (3rd ed.). Boston: Allyn & Bacon.

Delcourt, M. A. B. (1988). *Characteristics related to high levels of creative/productive behavior in secondary school students: A multi-case study*. Unpublished doctoral dissertation, University of Connecticut, Storrs.

DelCourt, M.A.B. (1993). Creative productivity among secondary school students. Combining energy, interest, and imagination. *Gifted Child Quarterly, 37*, 23–31.

DeVries, R., & Kohlberg, L. (1987). *Constructivist early education: Overview and comparison with other programs*. Washington, DC: National Association for the Education of Young Children.

Emerick, L. (1988). *Academic underachievement among the gifted: Student's perceptions of factors relating to the reversal of the academic underachievement pattern*. Unpublished doctoral dissertation, The University of Connecticut, Storrs.

Feldhusen, J. F., & Kolloff, P. B. (1986). The Purdue Three-Stage Enrichment Model for gifted education at the elementary level. In J. S. Renzulli (Ed.), *Systems and models for developing programs for the gifted and talented* (pp. 126–152). Mansfield Center, CT: Creative Learning Press.

Feldhusen, J. F., & Robinson-Wyman, A. (1986). The Purdue Secondary Model for gifted education. In J. S. Renzulli (Ed.), *Systems and models for developing programs for the gifted and talented* (pp. 153–179). Mansfield Center, CT: Creative Learning Press.

Feldhusen, J. F., & Sokol, L. (1982). Extra-school programming to meet the needs of gifted youth. *Gifted Child Quarterly*, 26, 51–56.

Feldhusen, J. F., & Wood, B. K. (1997, November/December). Developing growth plans for gifted students. *Gifted Child Today,* 20, 24–28.

Flack, J. D., & Feldhusen, J. F. (1983, March/April). Future studies in the curriculum framework of the Purdue three-stage model. *Gifted Child Today*, 27, 1–9.

Freeman, C. (2003). Designing math curriculum to encourage inductive thinking by elementary and middle school students: Basic principles to follow. In J. F. Smutny (Ed.), *Designing and developing programs for gifted students* (pp. 69–85). Thousand Oaks, CA: Corwin.

Gardner, H. (1985). *Frames of mind*. New York: Basic Books.

Gardner, H. (1992). Assessment in context: The alternative to standardized testing. In B. R. Gifford & M. C. O'Connor (Eds.), *Changing assessments: Alternative views of aptitude, achievement, and instruction* (pp. 77–120). Boston: Kluwer.

Gregory, A. (1982, January/February). Super Saturday: A description of Purdue University's special programs for gifted children with special emphasis on the studio arts. *Gifted Child Today,* 21, 13–16.

Gregory, G. H., & Chapman, C. (2002). *Differentiated instructional strategies: One size doesn't fit all.* Thousand Oaks, CA: Corwin.

Guilford, J. P. (1967). *The nature of human intelligence.* New York: McGraw-Hill.

Harnadek, A. (1976). *Critical thinking*. Pacific Grove, CA: Midwest Publications.

Hiassen, C. (2002). *Hoot*. New York: Knopf.

Isaksen, S. G., Puccio, G. J., & Treffinger, D. J. (1993). An ecological approach to creativity research: Profiling for creative problem solving. *Journal of Creative Behavior, 27*(3), 149–170.

Joyce, B., & Weil, M. (1986). *Models of teaching* (3rd ed.). Englewood Cliffs, NJ: Prentice Hall.

Karnes, F. A., & Brown, K. E. (1981). Moral development and the gifted: An initial investigation. *Roeper Review, 3,* 8–10.

Kohlberg, L. (1976). Moral states and moralization: The cognitive developmental approach. In T. Lickona (Ed.), *Moral development and behavior* (pp. 31–53). New York: Holt, Rinehart and Winston.

Kohlberg, L., & Mayer, R. (1972). Development as the aim of education *Harvard Educational Review, 42,* 449–496.

Krathwohl, D. R., Bloom, B. S., & Masia, B. B. (1964). *Taxonomy of educational objectives: The classification of educational goals: Vol. 2. Affective domain*. New York: David McKay.

Maker, C. J. (1996). Identification of gifted minority students: A national problem, needed changes, and a promising solution. *Gifted Child Quarterly, 40,* 41–50.

Maker C. J., & Nielson, A. (1995). *Teaching models in education of the gifted* (2nd ed.). Austin TX: PRO-ED.

Maker, C. J., Nielson, A., & Rogers, J. A. (1994). Multiple intelligences: Giftedness, diversity, and problem solving. *Teaching Exceptional Children, 27,* 4–19.

Maker, C. J., Rogers, J. A., Nielson, A. B., & Bauerle, P. R. (1996). Multiple intelligences, problem solving, and diversity in the general classroom. *Journal for the Education of the Gifted, 19,* 437–460.

Maker, C. J., & Schiever, S. W. (2005). *Teaching models in education of the gifted* (3rd ed.). Austin, TX: PRO-ED.

Marzano, R. J. (2000). *Designing a new taxonomy of educational objectives*. Thousand Oaks, CA: Corwin.

Meeker, M. N. (1969). *The structure of intellect: Its interpretation and uses.* Columbus: Merrill.

Meeker, M. N., & Meeker, R. (1986). The SOI system for gifted education. In J. S. Renzulli (Ed.), *Systems and models for developing programs for the gifted and talented* (pp. 194–215). Mansfield Center, CT: Creative Learning Press.

Miller, J. P., & Seller, W. (1985). *Curriculum perspectives and practice*. New York: Longman.

Nielson, A. B. (2003). The DISCOVER assessment and curriculum models. In J. F. Smutny (Ed.), *Underserved gifted populations: Responding to their needs and abilities* (pp. 205–237). Cresskill, NH: Hampton.

Nugent, S. A. (2005). Affective education: Addressing the social and emotional needs of gifted students in the classroom. In F. A. Karnes & S. M. Bean (Eds.), *Methods and materials for teaching the gifted* (2nd ed., pp. 409–438). Waco, TX: Prufrock.

Olenchak, F. R. (1991). Assessing program effects for gifted/learning disabled students. In R. Swassing & A. Robinson (Eds.), *NAGC 1991 Research Briefs.* Washington, DC: National Association for Gifted Children.

Osborn, A. F. (1963). *Applied imagination: Principles, procedures and creative problem solving* (3rd rev. ed.). New York: Scribner.

Parnes, S. J. (1967). *Creative potential and the education experience* (Occasional Paper No. 2). Buffalo, NY: Creative Education Foundation.

Parnes, S. J. (1981). *The magic of your mind.* Buffalo, NY: Creative Education Foundation.

Reis, S. M., & Renzulli, J. S. (1986). The Secondary Triad Model. In J. S. Renzulli (Ed.), *Systems and models for developing programs for the gifted and talented* (pp. 267–305). Mansfield Center, CT: Creative Learning Press.

Renzulli, J. S. (1977). *The Enrichment Triad Model: A guide for developing defensible programs for the gifted and talented.* Mansfield Center, CT: Creative Learning Press.

Renzulli, J. S., & Reis, S. M. (1985). *The Schoolwide Enrichment Model: A comprehensive plan for educational excellence.* Mansfield Center, CT: Creative Learning Press.

Renzulli, J. S., & Reis, S. M. (1986). The Enrichment Triad/Revolving Door Model: A schoolwide plan for the development of creative productivity. In J. S. Renzulli (Ed.), *Systems and models for developing programs for the gifted and talented* (pp. 216–266). Mansfield Center, CT: Creative Learning Press.

Renzulli, J. S., & Reis, S. M. (1991). The Schoolwide Enrichment Model: A comprehensive plan for the development of creative productivity. In N. Colangelo & G. A. Davis (Eds.), *Handbook of gifted education* (pp. 111–141). Boston: Allyn & Bacon.

Renzulli, J. S., Reis, S. M., & Smith, L. H. (1981). *The Revolving Door Identification Model.* Mansfield Center, CT: Creative Learning Press.

Roberts, C., Ingram, C., & Harris, C. (1992). The effect of special versus regular classroom programming on higher cognitive processes of intermediate elementary aged gifted an average ability students. *Journal for the Education of the Gifted, 15,* 332–343.

Ross J. D., & Ross, C. M. (1976). *Ross Test of Higher Cognitive processes.* Novato, CA: Academic Therapy Publications.

Schack, G. D. (1993). Effects of a creative problem-solving curriculum on students of varying ability levels. *Gifted Child Quarterly, 37,* 32–38.

Schlichter, C. L. (1986). Talents Unlimited: Applying the multiple talent approach in mainstream and gifted programs. In J. S. Renzulli (Ed.), *Systems and models for developing programs for the gifted and talented* (pp. 352–390). Mansfield Center, CT: Creative Learning Press.

Schlichter, C. L., & Palmer, W. R. (1993). *Thinking smart. A primer of the Talents Unlimited Model.* Mansfield Center, CT: Creative Learning Press.

Stanish, B. (1977). *Sunflowering.* Carthage, IL: Good Apple.

Stanley, J. C., Keating, D., & Fox, L. (Eds.). (1974). *Mathematical talent: Discovery, description, and development.* Baltimore: Johns Hopkins University Press.

Starko, A. J. (1986). *The effects of the Revolving Door Identification Model on creative productivity and self-efficacy.* Unpublished doctoral dissertation, The University of Connecticut, Storrs.

Stevenson, G. (1971). *Igniting creative potential.* Salt Lake City, UT: Project Implode.

Taba, H. (1967). *Teacher's handbook for elementary social studies.* Palo Alto, CA: Addison-Wesley.

Taylor, C. W. (1978). How many types of giftedness can your program tolerate? *Journal of Creative Behavior, 12*(1), 39–51.

Taylor, C. W. (1986). Cultivating simultaneous student growth in both multiple creative talents and knowledge. In J. S. Renzulli (Ed.), *Systems and models for developing programs for the gifted and talented* (pp. 306–351). Mansfield Center, CT: Creative Learning Press.

Taylor, L, A. (1992). *The effects of the secondary enrichment triad model and a career counseling component on the career development of vocational-technical school students.* Unpublished doctoral dissertation, University of Connecticut, Storrs.

Treffinger, D. J. (1978). Guidelines for encouraging independence and self-direction among gifted students. *Journal of Creative Behavior, 12*(1), 14–20.

Treffinger, D. J. (1986). Fostering effective, independent learning through individualized programming. In J. S. Renzulli (Ed.), *Systems and models for developing programs for the gifted and talented* (pp. 429–459). Mansfield Center, CT: Creative Learning Press.

Treffinger, D. J., & Firestien, R. L. (1989, November/December). Update: Guidelines for effective facilitation of creative problem solving. *Gifted Child Today, 12,* 35–39.

Udall, A. J., & High, M. H. (1989). What are they thinking when we're teaching critical thinking? *Gifted Child Quarterly, 33,* 156–160.

Warwick, I. (2001). Providing for under-achieving students using *Renzulli's* Type III Enrichment Activities: Gifted and talented video projects at Holland Park Comprehensive School. Gifted Education International, 16(1), 29-42.

Williams, F. E. (1972). *A total creativity program for individualizing and humanizing the learning process: Identifying and measuring creative potential* (Vol. 1). Englewood Cliffs, NJ: Educational Technology.

Williams, F. E. (1982). *Classroom ideas for encouraging thinking and feeling* (Vol. 2). Buffalo, NY: D.O.K.

Zimmerman, B. J., & Martinez-Pons, M. (1990). Student differences in self-regulated learning: Relating grade, sex, and giftedness to self-efficacy and strategy use. *Journal of Educational Psychology, 82,* 51–59.

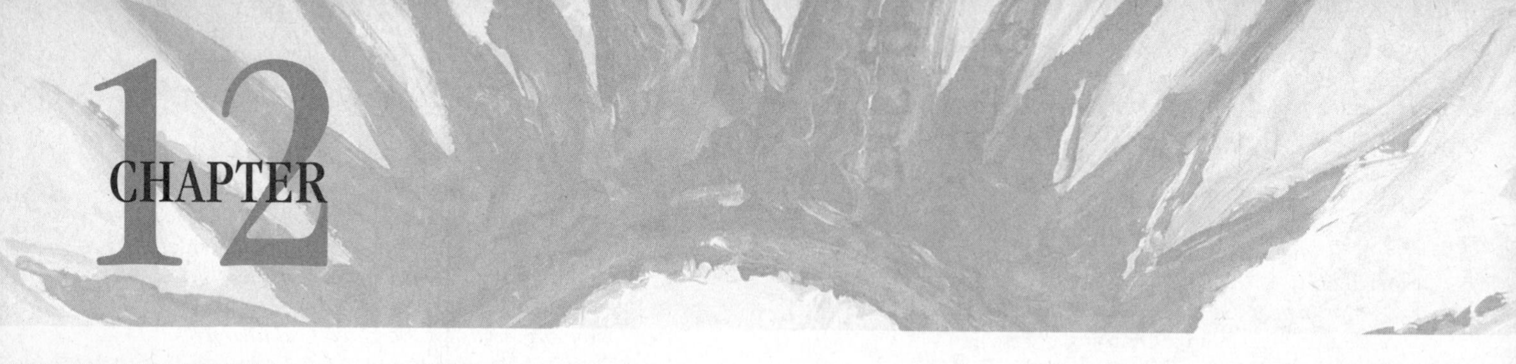

SPECIALIZED PROGRAMS SERVING THE GIFTED

Paula Olszewski-Kubilius, Ph.D.
NORTHWESTERN UNIVERSITY

Seon-Young Lee, Ph.D.
NORTHWESTERN UNIVERSITY

INTRODUCTION

There is a history in the United States of specialized services for children classified as special education students. In most states, however, this category does not include gifted children. Nevertheless, many specialized services for gifted children already exist and are growing in number and variety. These may be sponsored by schools, cultural institutions, state governments, and institutions of higher education. Why are these specialized programs increasing? What need do they fill? What is their role in talent development? What research evidence is there about their efficacy? Who has access to such programs, and who does not? These are some of the issues that are explored in this chapter.

WHY SPECIALIZED PROGRAMS?

The main reason for specialized programs is the needs of gifted children, including the following:

1. Advanced curriculum and a faster instructional pace of instruction that is matched to students' learning abilities (Goldstein & Wagner, 1993; Olszewski-Kubilius 1989, 1997, 1998b; Olszewski-Kubilius & Limburg-Weber, 2002; Renzulli, 1987a, 1987b; VanTassel-Baska, 1988)
2. Access to and sustained interaction with true intellectual peers in order to support and encourage high levels of achievement and to affirm oneself as a gifted individual (Olszewski-Kubilius & Limburg-Weber, 2002; Olszewski-Kubilius, Grant, & Seibert, 1994)
3. Challenging classes that require students to stretch themselves intellectually and that will motivate and assist them in developing effective study and work habits while taking personal responsibility for their learning and fostering an increased desire for intellectual challenges (Olszewski-Kubilius & Grant, 1996)
4. Access to teachers with subject-matter expertise who can help students acquire the tools of the field and understand the major concepts and structure of the discipline (VanTassel-Baska, 1988)

Another reason for specialized programs outside of school is the nature of the talent development process that may require additional, intensive instruction beyond what schools can or are willing to provide (Bloom, 1985; Goldstein & Wagner, 1993; Olszewski-Kubilius, 1997, 2003). Supplementary and specialized educational services such as out-of-school programs (e.g., Saturday or summer programs) can fill in the missing pieces of a school program for a gifted child (Feldhusen, 1991, 1997). It is well known and widely accepted that developing musical or athletic talent to a high level requires lessons, special teachers, and long hours of devoted study over a period of years. In these areas, school programs typically provide only initial exposure to the talent field and an arena for identification of talent by coaches or teachers. Parents can supplement their children's learning and development through outside programs. So it is for academic talent as well. Even in the best schools, the amount of instruction in an area for a gifted child may not be sufficient to develop the talent or to satisfy the child's hunger for learning (Thompson, 2001).

Specialized programs for gifted children are also needed because schools simply fail to provide for these children, especially for special subgroups of gifted learners such as underrepresented minorities (Alamprese, Erlanger, & Brigham, 1989; Ford, 1996; VanTassel-Baska, Patton, & Prillaman, 1990) and the profoundly gifted (Gross, 2000). Reasons include insufficient funds or other resources, shortage of qualified teachers, too few students to establish classes in some settings, and the lack of commitment to gifted learners. For all gifted students, but particularly for special groups of students, being with intellectually stimulating and emotionally supportive peers through special educational programs such as Saturday or summer programs can be a way to ameliorate the effects of poverty or isolation, augment social networks, and obtain increased social support. Parental demand for special opportunities has often fueled the development of specialized programs.

SUMMER AND WEEKEND PROGRAMS

Instructional Models and Program Types

Summer and Saturday programs vary on many dimensions, such as content, duration, intensity, sponsorship, and overall purpose. There are many different programs and instructional models. Program attributes are important because they determine the type of student for whom the experience is most appropriate. Summer programs that offer intensive accelerated courses are a better match for very gifted students with good study skills, an ability to learn independently, and a desire or need to accelerate (Bartkovich & Mezynski, 1981; Benbow & Stanley, 1983; Lynch, 1992; Olszewski-Kubilius, Kulieke, Willis, & Krasney, 1989). These programs typically use techniques such as telescoping or curriculum compacting to reduce the amount of time students spend on a course by as much as 50%. Programs that offer students an opportunity to study a single subject in great depth are more suited to students with intense, focused interests (VanTassel-Baska, 1988) and identified specific talent areas.

Enrichment programs give students the chance to sample one or more areas of study and are especially appropriate for younger children who are still discovering their interests and talents. Programs offering mentorships, internships, or shadowing of an adult professional on the job are particularly suitable for older students who are trying to explore career interests. Residential summer programs on college campuses can also help older gifted students test their independent living skills and expose them to college life. Summer programs offering study abroad opportunities are a good match for students desiring increased facility with another language and broadened cultural perspectives (Limburg-Weber, 1999/2000; Olszewski-Kubilius & Limburg-Weber, 2002).

Research on the Effects of Summer and Weekend Programs

While there are many summer and weekend programs around the country, the research evidence about them is sparse other than for one particular type of program—accelerated summer residential programs held on college campuses involving middle or high school–aged students. The majority of these programs have been sponsored by talent search institutions.

Summer Programs. Empirically documented effects for students who participate in summer programs include the following:

1. Experiencing greater academic challenge while in the program (Enersen, 1993; Mills, Ablard, & Lynch, 1992)
2. Taking a more rigorous course of study with more advanced courses (Barnett & Durden, 1993)
3. Higher educational aspirations (Olszewski-Kubilius & Grant, 1996)
4. Greater participation in math-related extracurricular activities (Olszewski-Kubilius & Grant, 1996)
5. Increased use of accelerative options (Barnett & Durden, 1993; Olszewski-Kubilius & Grant, 1996)
6. Greater likelihood of getting a National Merit Letter of Commendation (Olszewski-Kubilius & Grant, 1996)
7. More likely to pursue professional degrees and careers in math (Olszewski-Kubilius & Grant, 1996)
8. Selection of more academically selective institutions of higher education (Swiatek & Benbow, 1991) subsequent to the program

In addition, achievement in such programs is high and similar to older students who typically take these courses (Bartkovich & Mezynski, 1981; Lynch, 1992; Olszewski-Kubilius et al., 1989).

There is a paucity of research on the effects of non–academically oriented summer programs, such as programs in the arts. However, at least one study found effects 10 years later for adolescents who took college-level classes in art, music, dance, theater, or creative writing at a university in the summer. Effects included persistence in the arts field, confirmation of the student's identity as an artist, and peer support (Confessore, 1991).

Most of the research on summer programs has dealt with students' academic performance and long-term achievement, while relatively few have examined the impact on social and emotional areas. Enersen's (1993) study is one exception. She investigated the effects of an intensive, residential summer program on student self-perceptions, attitudes, and feelings. While this study involved only 12 students, ages 13 to 18, identified as having high academic abilities, interview data showed that the students built and received reinforcement for a positive self-image through interactions with intellectual peers during the program. The student participants expressed that they felt they were similar to other students in personality and received greater acceptance by fellow campers.

Another body of research that touches on the social-emotional arena is that on self-concept. Much of this research is guided by the "big fish, small pond" concept, which includes the belief that individuals' self-concepts are formed on the basis of comparisons to others and are affected by the social dimensions of situations. For gifted students, this means that their self-concepts, particularly their academic self-concepts, can decline when they are placed in classes with other gifted students. This effect has been found for special schools (Marsh & Hau, 2003) and for in-school gifted programs (Rogers, 1991), although the latter effect was deemed small and temporary in nature. The evidence regarding summer programs is equivocal in large part because of differences in samples and the self-concept instruments used. Previous studies have found positive increases from preprogram to post–summer program for self-concept (Kolloff & Moore, 1989) and self-esteem (VanTassel-Baska & Kulieke; 1987), declines in academic self-concept, an initial decline and then an increase in social acceptance, and positive changes for physical and athletic competence over the course of summer programs (Olszewski, Kulieke, & Willis, 1987). However, the effect sizes for these changes were not reported but were probably small, consistent with research on in-school gifted programs (Rogers, 1991).

In summary, although the research results are mixed, it appears that negative effects of placement in special summer or weekend programs on self-esteem, self-concept, and self-perceptions, because of a higher-level comparison group, do occur but do not permanently or significantly affect students.

Effects of Fast-Paced Summer Programs. The one instructional model that has been extensively studied is fast-paced summer classes. These programs emerged subsequent to the creation of the regional talent searches for seventh and eighth graders that began over 25 years ago. Fast-paced summer courses are typically open to middle school–aged students scoring at levels on the ACT or SAT comparable to college-bound seniors. They include an array of honors-level high school courses that students complete in a reduced time frame (150 hours of in-school instruction is reduced to 75 hours of instruction during the summer).

Research has shown that the SAT scores used as cutoffs for entrance into these types of programs are valid and select students who will succeed academically (Olszewski-Kubilius, 1998a; Olszewski-Kubilius et al., 1989). Research has also shown that student achievement is high. Students with SAT math scores over 600 can complete as much as two courses in precalculus mathematics within only 50 hours of instruction (Bartkovich & Mezynski, 1981) and perform higher on standardized tests than students who spend an entire year in similar mathematics classes (Stanley, 1976). Similarly high levels of achievement have been found for fast-paced science classes (Lynch, 1992). Better performance in such classes, especially in mathematics, is associated with well-developed, independent study skills (Olszewski-Kubilius et al., 2002) that can compensate for somewhat lower initial SAT entry scores. Students who take fast-paced summer classes perform well in subsequent classes in school (Lynch, 1992).

Research has shown that participation in fast-paced, accelerative summer programs can significantly influence many aspects of students' academic careers, occupational choices, and aspirations. Documented effects include taking advanced placement (AP) calculus earlier in high school, taking more college courses while still in high school, pursuing a more rigorous course of study in mathematics, and entering more academically competitive colleges than students with similar scores who do not participate in a summer program (Barnett & Durden, 1993). Females who participate in fast-paced classes seem to particularly benefit, especially those who take mathematics in the summer (Olszewski-Kubilius & Grant, 1996). The female students subsequently accelerated themselves more in mathematics, earned more honors in math, took more AP classes of any type in high school and more math classes in college, participated more in math clubs, more often majored in math or science in college, and had higher-educational aspirations. A summer program designed specifically for mathematically talented females helped them remain competitive with mathematically talented boys in math through high school (Brody & Fox, 1980; Fox, Brody, & Tobin, 1985). Additional long-term effects of summer programs for girls included a greater commitment to consistent, full-time work in the future, and higher-educational aspirations (Fox et al., 1985). See Olszewski-Kubilius (1998b) for a summary of research on fast-paced summer programs.

As of yet, questions that remain unanswered are why summer programs impact students in these ways and how such programs affect talent development. While isolated effects of summer programs have been documented, the process underlying them has not been elucidated. One possibility is that when students succeed in challenging accelerated course work, such as fast-paced summer classes, confidence in their abilities is bolstered, enabling them to select other challenging educational opportunities. Success in such programs increases self-efficacy, raises expectations, and increases motivation to achieve.

Additional Issues. One of the issues about summer programs, particularly those that offer typical high school classes, is how these are viewed and articulated with students' home school experiences. The evidence regarding this is equivocal. Many gifted students enroll in such classes for their personal and private enrichment and do not care how their schools respond to their summer course work. But some students are using summer courses, particularly fast-paced ones, to speed up their progress through their school curriculum, possibly to graduate early or to supplement meager offerings in their high school. Many of these students want recognition and credit for their summer course work. The percentage of students who get credit for fast-paced classes varies across studies with reports of 80% for subsets of students who specifically ask for credit (Lynch, 1990) and 50% for those students who achieve proficiency in the subject as measured by performance on standardized tests and thus qualified for credit (Olszewski-Kubilius, 1989). It is easier for summer students to get appropriate placement subsequently in their local schools than credit for summer course work (Lynch, 1990; Olszewski-Kubilius, 1989). Additionally, credit rates vary by subject area and are higher for cumulatively organized subjects such as algebra or Latin and lower for verbal classes such as writing or literature (Olszewski-Kubilius, 1989).

The awarding of credit by schools for summer courses is facilitated by accreditation of the program by an outside educational agency (Lee & Olszewski-Kubilius, 2005; Olszewski-Kubilius, Laubscher, Wohl, & Grant, 1996). Lee and Olszewski-Kubilius (2005) reported that after a summer program at a major midwestern university had been accredited by the North Central Association of Colleges and Schools and thus was able to award credit to middle and high school students who successfully completed high school courses, the percentage of summer students whose schools honored the credit increased significantly from 28% preaccreditation to 64% 8 years postaccreditation. How summer program experiences relate to in-school curricula and programming is important for students' talent development but at the present is largely left up to parents to manage.

Weekend Programs. Relatively little research exists on the effects of weekend programs, in part because they have short and intermittent formats (e.g., 1 to 10 Saturdays with sessions of 2 to 3 hours each), making their effects difficult to detect. In addition, most of these programs serve younger elementary school children who are often unable to articulate effects or read and complete surveys.

One study on a weekend program (Olszewski-Kubilius & Lee, 2004b) found that a Saturday enrichment program involving children in grades pre-K through 6 might have impacted students indirectly through raising parental expectations regarding their children's achievement in school. While most parents increased their expectations, the majority did not contact their children's school regarding their school curricula. Among those who did, however, almost 50% reported that their children subsequently received more challenging work. Parents also perceived that their children gained scholastic skills, were more motivated to learn, were more interested in the subject areas they studied, and gained academic competence as a result of participation in the Saturday program.

DISTANCE EDUCATION

Distance education is now widespread, especially at the college level. It is being utilized for transmitting instruction across geographic boundaries and extending educational opportunities nationally and internationally (Timpson & Jones, 1989). Distance education transcends the constraints of time and space through media such as computer- or Internet-based programs, which enable educators and learners to "interact" but not necessarily in face-to-face situations ("Accessing Distance Learning," 1995; Hofmeister, 1994; Washington, 1997). Distance education programs may never replace existing classrooms and schools but can be used to compensate for educational deficits and lack of advanced course work in schools (Adams & Cross, 1999/2000; Ravaglia & Sommer, 2000; Washington, 1997; Wilson, Litle, Coleman, & Gallagher, 1997/1998) or as part of a homeschooling program (Ravaglia & Sommer, 2000; Washington, 1997).

Distance education was historically designed primarily for students who were not succeeding in a traditional school setting or were unable to attend a regular school (Olszewski-Kubilius & Limburg-Weber, 2002; Timpson & Jones, 1989). As a result, studies on the effectiveness of distance education have been limited to these groups of students (Adams & Cross, 1999/2000; Belcastro, 2001; Lewis, 1989; McBride & Lewis, 1993; Ravaglia & Sommer, 2000; Threlkeld, 1991) and have not focused on gifted students enrolled in such programs. While distance education programs are proliferating, there are only a few that are specifically designed for gifted students.

Need for Distance Education Programs for Gifted Students

Despite the scarcity of research on distance education for the gifted, gifted educators appear interested in distance education as a means to increase their ability to serve gifted learners, especially those with limited access to advanced courses (Adams & Cross, 1999/2000; Olszewski-Kubilius & Limburg-Weber, 2002). Distance education programs may be a good option for a variety of types of gifted students, including students who attend rural schools where advanced courses and gifted programs are limited, students who cannot obtain early access to advanced courses, students who want to take additional advanced courses but cannot fit them into their school schedules, gifted students who are not thriving in a typical school setting (Goodrich, 1994; Lewis, 1989; Lewis & Talbert, 1990; McBride, 1991b; McBride & Lewis, 1993; Ravaglia & Sommer, 2000; Savage & Werner, 1994; Wilson et al., 1997/1998), or homebound or home-schooled learners (Ravaglia & Sommer, 2000). One of the significant advantages of distance education for schools is the ability to provide appropriate courses for gifted students without having to remove them from their peers or regular school environment, thus avoiding transportation costs and problems associated with placing younger students in classes with older students (Ravaglia & Sommer, 2000).

In a sample of middle and high school (grades 6 through 12) gifted students, most of whom (83%) were enrolled in public schools, students' interests in specific subjects, a desire to enrich or add to their home school curriculum, a desire to accelerate or move faster through the curriculum, and the unavailability of the courses in their home schools were the major reasons for enrolling in the distance education program (Olszewski-Kubilius & Lee, 2004a). Less salient (less than 10% of students) were reasons such as a desire to accumulate another AP credit for college or to take a course offered in their schools but unavailable to their age-group. Parents who enrolled their fourth through sixth graders in enrichment classes in a distance education program did so primarily because they desired academic challenge for their children and because of their children's interest in the subject matter. Other less significant reasons for this age-group were the lack of courses in their school and a desire by parents that their children spend more time on academic pursuits (Dershewitz, Lee, & Johnson, 2006).

It is difficult to gauge how many gifted students are participating in distance education programs. A national study of four talent search centers that offer distance education programs found that 34,644 students in grades 3 through 12 had participated in distance education courses since their inception in the 1990s and that 7,468 participated in 2003–2004 (Lee, Matthews, & Olszewski-Kubilius, in press). For the year 2003–2004, males (53.9%) surpassed females (45.9%) in their participation in these courses. More than half (54.2%) of the students were seventh through ninth graders, 43.1% were third through sixth graders, and 2.8% were tenth through twelfth graders.

Many other gifted students may be participating in distance education programs through state-supported virtual high schools. A recent book aimed at helping high school students find an online high school lists 113 programs (Kiernan, 2005). While the overwhelming majority of these are not geared specifically toward gifted learners, individual programs may have courses appealing to or appropriate for them.

Distance Education Program Features and Models

Contrary to most people's beliefs that distance education is passive, distance education programs are actually based on the premise that students are active participants and collaborators (McLoughlin, 1999) who construct their own knowledge (Hull, Bull, Montgomery, May, & Overton, 2000). Hull et al. (2000) contend that distance education, such as online courses, entails authentic problem solving, which assumes that learners are able to transform given information into knowledge. It is comparable to a student-centered learning approach, in which learners are central to the learning process and take responsibility for their learning. Teachers assist learners as an "educational resource" and encourage students to engage in learning activities as active participants (Wilson et al., 1997/1998). Thus, students enrolling in distance education must be independent problem solvers and take initiative and responsibility for their academic activities ("Accessing Distance Learning," 1995; University of Plymouth, 2006; Wilson et al., 1997/1998). Indeed, research has shown that students are more likely to challenge their teachers in a setting where geographic distance and lack of face-to-face contact lessens their concern about actively questioning their teachers (McBride, 1991a).

Distance education is often thought of as a lonely or a solitary type of experience, but this is not necessarily the case with current technologies. By posting discussions or participating in real-time class discussions online, students can actively engage with others. Although researchers (Glennan & Melmed, 1996) allege that limited access to and use of computers and other educational technologies are still problems for many students, they also suggest that technologies make distance education programs active and engaging learning experiences for students.

With the development of various forms of communication technologies, especially Internet and broadband technologies, not only has distance education spread in the past few years ("Accessing Distance Learning," 1995), but there are now multiple venues and delivery modes available. Most courses are currently provided online or with some kind of computer teleconferencing. The technologies enable students to have a variety of learning experiences beyond classes, including virtual field trips to cultural institutions and historical sites that allow students to have broader cultural exposure to the arts. Technologies can also afford students the opportunity to communicate and collaborate with a more diverse group of students, thereby cultivating an understanding of multicultural perspectives via interactions across classrooms, countries, and continents (Cifuentes, Murphy, & Davis, 1998).

Some university-based gifted centers have distance education programs designed specifically for gifted students of precollege age. The Center for Talented Youth program at Johns Hopkins University offers computer-based multimedia courses in mathematics and computer science for elementary through beginning college level, writing classes for students beginning in fifth grade, and some AP courses. Students interact with their instructors using e-mail or telephone or by means of an interactive, Internet-based whiteboard. Students can earn high school credit for high school–level classes.

Duke University's Talent Identification Program (Duke TIP) offers distance education courses through their E-Studies program to gifted students in grades 8 through 12. Courses are Web based, and students interact with their instructors and peers through online discussions, virtual lectures, and real-time collaborations. Currently, eight courses are offered, including Anatomy and Physiology, History of the Ancient World, JAVA for Video Games, Mathematical Problem Solving, Academic Writing, Social Psychology, and Short Fiction Workshops I and II. Duke TIP does not grant credit for successfully completion of E-Studies courses, but students may seek this on their own from their local schools.

The Center for Talent Development at Northwestern University has offered a distance education program, LearningLinks, for gifted students in grades 4 through 12 for more than 20 years. Classes include 22 enrichment classes (e.g., The Wonders of Ancient Egypt, Classic American Novels, Writing Workshops, Latin, and Topics in Math) for younger students, 30 or more high school honors-level classes (e.g., Creative Writing, Literary Analysis, Economics, U.S. History, Biology, and Chemistry), and 19 different AP classes. Students receive "textboxes" (boxes filled with needed course materials) that include introductory course materials, textbooks, course syllabi, and more. Courses are Web based, and students participate with others in online discussions and communicate with teachers via e-mail. Some college-level classes are also available, and students earn credit for high school–level classes.

The Education Program for Gifted Youth at Stanford University offers multimedia, computer-based distance education courses in mathematics (kindergarten through advanced undergraduate classes), English (fourth grade through AP), physics (secondary through advanced undergraduate level), and computer science (secondary level). Writing classes are offered from fourth grade through the AP level. Students receive Stanford University credit for successfully completing undergraduate-level courses.

The Renzulli Learning System is an online program for students in grades 2 through 10 through the University of Connecticut Research and Development Corporation Company. The program is based on the Enrichment Triad Model (Renzulli, 1977; Renzulli & Reis, 1997) with the goal of matching students with enriching and challenging educational experiences commensurate with their interests and learning styles. Based on students' individual talent development profiles, various educational activities and options are offered in 14 enrichment categories, including virtual/real field trips, creativity training, critical thinking, independent studies, books (fiction and nonfiction), and research skills. All these activities are selected to encourage students' interests and enhance their hands-on investigative skills.

Research About the Effects of Distance Education Programs

Empirical research about the effectiveness of distance education programs is sparse, specifically regarding gifted students. Not all gifted students are good candidates for a distance education course. Wilson et al. (1997/1998) suggest that there are four characteristics that contribute to success in a distance education course: (a) ability to work independently, (b) desire to take the course, (c) motivation to persist, and (d) prerequisite background knowledge. Completion rates nationally for distance education courses are about 50%, but at least one distance education program for gifted learners reports significantly higher rates, around 66% to 80% (lower for AP classes, higher for enrichment classes), and grades of A or B for over 95% of students (L. Dershewitz, personal communication, January 25, 2006; Olszewski-Kubilius & Lee, 2004a). Olszewski-Kubilius and Lee (2004a) found that students who took AP classes via a distance education program specifically designed for gifted students reported that the classes prepared them well for their AP examinations (64% of students completed the AP exam, and 63% earned a 4 or 5 on the exam).

Despite limited data on how successful gifted students actually are in distance education courses, researchers have documented evidence about the positive effects of distance education programs on gifted and talented students academically and socially, primarily through self-reports of students on questionnaires and surveys after the program. Effects found include the following:

1. Greater independence on the part of students regarding their learning and the development of close relationships with peers for rural gifted students who took advanced high school mathematics courses in a telelearning program (Lewis, 1989)
2. Enhanced independent study and thinking skills, new means of communication, academic challenge and growth, and a more realistic assessment of how one's abilities compared to others among high school–aged students from multiple schools who participated in a distance education program through a state-supported residential school (Wilson et al., 1997/1998)
3. Increases in students' collaboration skills and higher-order thinking skills, such as logical explanation, critical inquiry, interpretation, and reflection as a result of participation in a program that augmented teaching with audiographic conference technology for secondary students (McLoughlin, 1999)
4. Increases in students' problem-solving abilities, logical thinking skills, and collaborative learning skills, motivation, task commitment, leadership ability, and responsibility for learning in a program that connected elementary and secondary gifted students from multiple schools (Ewing, Dowling, & Coutts, 1997)
5. Higher interest in the subject studied, increased confidence in one's academic abilities, and improved study and organizational skills for fourth through sixth graders who took enrichment classes via a distance education program (Dershewitz, Lee, & Johnson, 2006)

Regarding gifted students' preferences for certain features of their distance education classes, Olszewski-Kubilius and Lee (2004a) found that among gifted students who took either honors or AP courses through a distance education program, the lack of interactions with teachers was a source of dissatisfaction for some students and that most students wanted to use computer technologies that enabled them to have easy communication with teachers, other students, and course information but still desired to have traditional textbooks and written course materials as part of the learning tools. Thus, students need to know and understand their learning styles and preferences in order to find those distance education classes appropriate for them.

There continues to be concerns about distance education on the part of both educators and students. Concerns include the inability to use students' body language as an indication of student engagement and understanding (Gallagher, 2001), technological problems (Lewis & Talbert, 1990), and insufficient contact with and therefore support from other students and the teacher (University of Plymouth, 2006). In addition, distance education programs suffer from some of the same articulation issues as summer and other out-of-school programs. Olszewski-Kubilius and Lee (2004a) found that 20% of students who took a distance education course and wanted credit did not get it from their high schools, but only 6% of those who asked for placement in the next course in sequence were denied. However, almost half the students could not skip ahead to the next course because none was available.

TALENT SEARCH PROGRAMS

Talent search programs have been in existence for over 25 years and have successfully assisted hundreds of thousands of students by identifying their abilities, nurturing their talents through educational programs, and connecting schools and families to appropriate resources, services, and programs (VanTassel-Baska, 1998). As documented in numerous articles (e.g., Assouline & Lupkowski-Shoplik, 1997; Benbow, 1992b; Brody, 1998; Jarosewich & Stocking, 2003; Lee et al., in press; Olszewski-Kubilius, 1998c; VanTassel-Baska, 1998), talent search testing was initiated in the early 1970s by Dr. Julian Stanley at Johns Hopkins University as part of the Study of Mathematically Precocious Youth. Its primary goal at that time was to identify mathematically talented pre–high school students using SAT math scores. Talent search testing has expanded to include other above-grade-level tests that assess both mathematical and verbal areas in elementary and middle school children.

The idea of talent searches came from the belief that gifted children need to be assessed with tests commensurate with their abilities, developmental rates, and preexisting knowledge and skills, not with those designed for their chronological age or grade. Several major university–based gifted institutes, such as the Center for Talent Development at Northwestern University, Duke University's Talent Identification Program, the Center for Talented Youth at Johns Hopkins University, and the Rocky Mountain Talent Search at the University of Denver, conduct talent search testing annually in order to provide students with more accurate information about their academic abilities.

Talent search programs include the following major components: the diagnosis and evaluation of the area and level of students' abilities via above-level tests such as the ACT, SAT, or EXPLORE; educational placement for individual students based on test scores; access to further talent developing opportunities, such as weekend programs, summer programs, and distance education programs; and guidance and expert advice via newsletters, magazines, and conferences (Olszewski-Kubilius, 1998a).

Talent search programs have become a major force within gifted education and are the key provider of out-of-school, specialized programming. Lee et al., (in press) collated data from the various talent search programs to produce a comprehensive, national picture of how many children are being served by these programs annually. Based on data from 2004, almost a quarter of a million students in grades 3 through 9 participated in above-level testing programs offered by talent search programs. Of these, 33,900 subsequently participated in a talent search–sponsored educational program in 2004. Almost half the program participants were in summer programs, 10,300 in Saturday and weekend programs, 7,500 in distance education courses, and 460 in leadership programs through the talent search institutions. Males (55%) participate at slightly higher rates than females (45%), and minority students are underrepresented, more so in the educational programs than in the talent search testing. Yet only a small proportion of the students (around 14%) identified annually through testing participate in a talent search–related educational program. Many are limited by the tuition costs involved in these programs.

Research on the Effects of Talent Search and Talent Search Educational Programs

There is a rather substantial body of research about talent search testing and talent search participants—literally hundreds of published research studies. These studies document the following:

1. The validity of using the ACT and SAT with middle school students based on students' performances on these tests, which is similar to the average college-bound senior (Bartkovich & Mezynski, 1981; Benbow, 1992a; Olszewski-Kubilius, 1998b)
2. The predictive validity of talent search scores for later school achievement and career success, which has been found to be substantial (Barnett & Durden, 1993; Benbow, 1992a, 1992b; Benbow & Arjmand, 1990; Lubinski, Webb, Morelock, & Benbow, 2001; Webb, Lubinski & Benbow, 2002; Wilder, Casserly, & Burton, 1988)
3. The predictive validity of talent search scores within the gifted population discriminating different patterns of achievement into adulthood for students scoring at the top versus bottom quartile of the top 1% (Benbow, 1992a; Wai, Lubinski, & Benbow, 2005)

Research has documented that talent search participation gives students better knowledge about the nature of their academic abilities (Ablard, Mills, & Hoffhines, 1996; Assouline & Lupkowski-Shoplik, 1997; Brody, 1998; Jarosewich & Stocking, 2003; VanTassel-Baska, 1989) and thus can raise their educational and career aspirations (Benbow & Arjmand, 1990; Brody, 1998; Wilder et al., 1988; VanTassel-Baska, 1989). Participation in talent search testing has an impact that is magnified by also participating in talent search–sponsored educational programs. A higher degree of academic acceleration and a greater level of participation in academic opportunities were found for students who participated in both talent search testing and subsequent educational programs (Barnett & Durden, 1993). However, Barnett and Durden also found that students who participated only in talent search testing were as academically successful as the former. A sizable percentage of these "talent search testing only" students accelerated in specific subject areas, especially in math and computers; performed well (usually A to B+) on college-level math or computer courses taken in high school (Kolitch & Brody, 1992); graduated from high school almost 1 year earlier than their age-equivalent peers; and earned high grade-point averages (3.4 on average) in college.

The testing in talent searches has spawned educational program models such as the fast-paced summer classes described earlier in this chapter. The academic performance of students in these talent search educational programs and their effects on students are strong, substantial, and positive (Ablard et al., 1996; Assouline & Lupkowski-Shoplik, 1997; Barnett & Durden, 1993; Benbow, 1992b; Benbow & Arjmand, 1990; Brody, 1998; Jarosewich & Stocking, 2003; Kolitch & Brody, 1992; Olszewski-Kubilius & Grant, 1996; VanTassel-Baska, 1989; Wilder et al., 1988). Students in fast-paced, 3-week accelerated summer classes perform as well as or better than high school students who typically take the courses for a full academic year at school. Middle school students who took high school science classes in a 3-week summer program scored at or above the 70th percentile on standardized tests in biology, chemistry, and physics compared to norms for high school juniors or seniors who had a full year of instruction (Lynch, 1992). Students with higher scores can accelerate at a faster pace. For example, mathematically talented seventh graders who scored about 600 or above on SAT math were able to successfully complete two high school precalculus math courses in less than 50 hours of instruction (Bartkovich & Mezynski, 1981) and achieved at high levels in a special program in which 4 years of high school math were compressed into 2½ years (Benbow, Perkins, & Stanley, 1983).

Summer programs and other programs offered by talent search centers enable gifted students to significantly augment their school programs and accelerate their progress through the school curriculum. Many students chose talent search–related programs because their schools lack classes or because they are seeking contact with intellectual peers. Research shows that learning material in a fast-paced context does not result in lower levels of mastery (Lynch, 1990) although that is a common misperception of schools. While talent search testing has opened many opportunities for many gifted students; one of the major criticisms of the program is that it is still viewed as a primarily out-of-school program with little impact on in-school curricula, services, and eligibility for in-school gifted programs (Olszewski-Kubilius & Lee, 2005).

SPECIALIZED SCHOOLS

Types and Variety of Special Schools

There are varied types of specialized schools for children who are gifted academically or in the arts. These schools are operated by school districts, universities, state governments, and private entities. Most focus on a particular talent area, such as performing arts, music, or a few related disciplines such as mathematics, science, and technology, or a specialized population, such as gifted children with learning disabilities. Most exist in physical space and real time but some are virtual (e.g., the A. Linwood Holton Governor's School for the Gifted in southwestern Virginia). Many exist at the level of elementary and secondary education, but some operate across levels such as combined high school/college programs. Two major categories of specialized schools include state-supported residential high schools (Kolloff, 2003) and university-based early college entrance programs (Brody, Muratori, & Stanley, 2004).

Currently there are 13 residential schools for gifted students chartered by state legislatures. For most of these, students enter after their sophomore year of high school; a few take students after the completion of ninth grade, such as the Illinois Mathematics and Science Academy. Students are typically admitted on the basis of scores on college entrance exams, such as the ACT and SAT, and since state dollars are involved, selection is handled so that the school population reflects that of the state in terms of race, ethnicity, and geography. These schools have advanced offerings beyond what is available in even the best high schools in the state. They also typically have faculty with exceptionally high levels of content area expertise. In addition, these schools have a select population of students who are more homogeneous with respect to ability levels and interests.

Many more special schools for academically gifted students exist around the United States (e.g., over 90 schools are currently listed as members of the National Consortium for Specialized Secondary Schools of Mathematics, Science and Technology) as well as schools for students gifted in the performing arts, and these are typically 4-year specialized secondary high schools. These schools may or may not use the word *gifted* in their title, although they may be selective in their admissions and may call themselves magnet schools or conservatories. Such schools may also have an array of advanced offerings, teachers with advanced training and performance experience in the case of performing arts schools, and a more homogeneous school population in terms of abilities and interests compared to a typical secondary school (for a fuller description, see Sayler, 2006).

Research on the Effects of Special Schools

Specialized schools measure their success in varied ways. Indicators can include the numbers of students who pursue advanced study or careers in the areas that the schools specialize in as well as the number of awards and honors, contests, and competitions won by students. For example, the Illinois Mathematics and Science Academy (a state-supported school for grades 10 to 12) tracks the number of students who work with scientists to complete research projects, win competitions and awards, pursue mathematics and science majors and careers, gain admission to prestigious colleges and universities, and get merit-based scholarships for higher education (Illinois Mathematics and Science Academy, 2005). Internally, these schools may promote certain values; thus, track indicators, such as the number of students who do volunteer work or changes in attitudes and beliefs toward science, are assessed by surveys (K. Hallowell, personal communication, January 12, 2006). State-supported schools often have their mission to contribute scholars and professionals to the state in key areas or to provide professional development or leadership in the areas of curriculum to schools within their states. Unfortunately, most of the data about success on these and other indicators are contained in reports to state boards and not in journals or other professional outlets. State-supported schools are held accountable by state legislators, but other specialized schools need to demonstrate success on indicators valued by parents to attract students.

Brody et al. (2004) listed 17 early college entrance programs in the United States: 10 residential and seven commuter-only programs. Most of the residential, early college entrance programs enable students to enter college 1 to 2 years earlier. Many residential programs house early entrance students together in separate dorms, at least for the first year. The commuter-only, early college entrance programs generally take students earlier, some as early as at the end of eighth grade. These programs take many different forms, but all allow students early access to college courses. Some have a particular curricular focus, such as leadership and the humanities or science and technology. Some admit students automatically into the honors college of the school. Early college entrance programs provide students with a bridging experience during the first year or summer before their college studies begin, thus helping prepare students for college-level work and the college environment. Students finish high school during the first 2 to 3 years of the program and do college studies during the last 1 or 2 years of enrollment in the school (e.g., combining 4 years of high school and the first 2 years of college into 4 years). A few grant high school diplomas, and a few more arrange for the diploma to be granted by the students' home high school (for a complete listing and further description, see Brody et al., 2004). Some early entrance programs offer extracurricular programs and some do not, but many have special supports for young students, including special counselors, closer supervision, and special social activities, to foster camaraderie and support.

Both special secondary schools and early entrance programs are accelerative programs. Many special secondary schools offer advanced courses, including AP classes and college-level classes. Often the decision about whether a special secondary school versus an early college entrance program is more appropriate for a child comes down to access (proximity to home), match to the child's talent domain or interests, the child's maturity for handling living away from home and mingling with older students, and desire for acceleration. One advantage of some special schools is that they have rich curricular offerings that allow students to stay in high school for 4 years.

Specialized schools and early college entrance programs can offer a more advanced curriculum to students as well as some specialized opportunities that typical secondary schools cannot. These include working in research laboratories or other research experiences, receiving training in how to audition, and acquiring the professional tools, values, and attitudes important to success in the field (Subotnik & Jarvin, 2005).

Research about early college entrance programs suggests that effects are positive and substantial for students (Gross & van Vliet, 2005). Early entrants earn higher grade-point averages than regular freshman (Eisenberg & George, 1979; Janos & Robinson, 1985; Janos, Sanfilippo, & Robinson, 1986; Muratori, Colangelo, & Assouline, 2003; Noble, Robinson, & Gunderson, 1993), typically within the B+ to A− range (Stanley & McGill, 1986; Swiatek & Benbow, 1991), and equal to those of a group of National Merit Scholars at the same university (Janos & Robinson, 1985; Janos et al., 1986). Compared to typical college students, they are more likely to do the following:

1. Complete college (Pressey, 1967) and on time (Brody, Assouline, & Stanley, 1990; Stanley & McGill, 1986)
2. Earn general and departmental honors (Stanley & McGill, 1986; Brody et al., 1990)
3. Make the dean's list (Eisenberg & George, 1979)
4. Have plans to enter graduate school (Noble et al., 1993)
5. Complete concurrent master's degrees (Brody et al., 1990)

The majority of these results are based on students who entered (1 to 2 years early) a private, selective, academically prestigious university that did not have a special early entrance program. A few are based on a large state institution that admitted students immediately after the seventh or eighth grade into a yearlong transition school. Thus, the demands of these experiences, because of either the academic reputation of the institution or the age of the student, were great, yet the students were very successful. In addition, early entrance students fare well later in their educational careers, earn Ph.D. degrees and work in prestigious positions, are admitted as transfer students to highly selective universities (often with scholarships), and are accepted to prominent graduate programs (Sayler & Lupkowski, 1992; Sethna, Wickstrom, Boothe, & Stanley, 2001; Stanley, 1985).

While the results of these studies are very positive, it must be remembered that students who do poorly generally leave the program and are not included in research studies. There are not much data in the published research about dropout rates, and what does exist suggest that dropout rates may be high, 30% to 45%, in the initial years of a program (Callahan, Cornell, & Lloyd, 1992; Sayler, 1993) but decline rapidly to around 5% to 10% once programs have selection procedures refined (Noble et al., 1993). Regarding low achievement, again, few published statistics are available. Janos et al. (1986) reported that about 12% of students who entered college after the seventh or eighth grade were earning grade-point averages 1.5 standard deviations below other similarly aged early entrants and that underachieving students tended to be immature or did not balance their academic and social lives. Few of these students dropped out, but they tended to alternate between good and very poor regarding their grades and achievement. Sayler (1993) reported that 28% of students admitted to an early entrance program after the tenth grade had academic difficulties, but this was in the early years of the program, and this percentage was reduced quickly by half and then to zero. Thus, most students admitted to early college entrance programs are academically successful.

Regarding social emotional adjustment, the picture for early college entrants is positive. Relatively few have adjustment problems (Sayler, 1993). Most find friends, initially among other early college entrants who provide an important support group in the first few years (Noble & Drummond, 1992), especially for the younger students (Janos & Robinson, 1985; Janos et al., 1986), but eventually among typically aged college students. The only study that found a high percentage (50%) of early entrance with mental health and adjustment problems was in the early years of the program before selection procedures were refined (Cornell, Callahan, & Lloyd, 1991). Similarly, Muratori (2003) suggested that social and emotional factors, including motivation, perseverance, and homesickness, should be considered prior to admitting students to college early because these factors may lead to underachievement and failure to complete college for some young entrants. Few students express strong regrets, and any of these regrets tended to be about missing social events in high school or decreased eligibility for college scholarships (Noble & Drummond, 1992; Noble et al., 1993).

Students who fared best in early college entrance programs seem to be the following:

1. Those who have taken and succeeded in college-level classes, such as AP classes, prior to full-time college studies (Brody et al., 1990)
2. Those who were independent, unconventional, and less conforming (Janos & Robinson, 1985)
3. Those who were more focused, motivated, and persevering (Muratori, 2003)
4. Those who had more harmonious family relationships (Cornell et al., 1991)
5. Those who had well-developed study and organizational skills (Schumacker, Sayler, & Bembry, 1995)

These are not very different from predictors of success in college for typically aged college freshman.

Why Choose Special Schools?

The decision to attend a special school is dependent on many factors, including but not limited to the student's desire and maturity to cope with living away from home, the lack of other alternatives within the student's local community, the degree to which a student has specific, well-identified and developed areas of talent and interest, the student's motivation to excel and ability to work independently, family support, and the student's need for and availability of a supportive peer group.

GENERAL ISSUES WITH SPECIAL PROGRAMS

Regardless of who sponsors special programs or their content, there are some general issues that result from their existence.

Relationship to In-School Programs

A frequent concern of educators is the articulation between in-school and out-of-school programs. When students accelerate themselves in a content area through a special program, there can be both immediate and long-term consequences. Immediate consequences include how to respond to the course just completed and in what kind of course the student should now be placed. Long-term consequences include how to accommodate a high school junior who has completed all the mathematics courses that the high school has to offer. Schools may actively discourage students from participating in special programs because of these articulation issues, or they may indirectly discourage them by not responding appropriately after the special program. Providers of specialized services and local schools need to view themselves as partners in the education of a gifted child, each contributing resources and important experiences. Programs that involve collaboration, such as early college entrance programs that work with students' local high schools to secure a high school diploma, are examples of the kind of cooperation that can occur for the benefit of gifted children.

Access to Special Programs

Special programs are most often sponsored by institutions of higher education, and most charge tuition. As a result, many are simply out of reach for academically gifted children who are economically disadvantaged. Minority children are less likely to be identified as gifted and less likely to be placed in special programs within their schools (Alamprese et al., 1989; VanTassel-Baska et al, 1990). They are also underrepresented in talent search testing and other out-of-school educational programs. But gifted minority students, especially those who are economically disadvantaged, are in dire need of the services provided by special programs. The costs of residential summer programs are often too high for even moderate-income families. And commuter programs may be too distant, especially in more rural areas. Thus, though special summer and Saturday programs are increasingly seen as vital to talent development, access to them is too often limited to the more economically advantaged gifted students and those in resource-rich geographic locations.

Distance education programs are becoming increasingly available in our technologically oriented society, particularly Web-based courses, but these also typically involve tuition, which makes them inaccessible to many of the same students (Adams & Cross, 1999/2000).

The Future of Special Programs

Specialized programs and their services offered have become vital to the talent development of academically gifted students. It is difficult to predict whether there will be increased demand for them from parents, legislators, and educators. Gifted education is very vulnerable to political and budgetary issues. Some aspects of specialized programs, such as the educational models they embody, including fast-paced instruction or problem-based learning, can easily be incorporated into the local school curriculum, while other aspects, such as the environments of like-minded peers, are more difficult to replicate.

The increases in the variety of different types of supplemental programs, the number of institutions that offer them, and the number of students who participate have had some negative consequences for students. Rather than deal with the myriad of programs and make decisions about student credit and placement on the basis of evaluations of their quality, schools sometimes opt for general blanket policies that do not allow credit for any out-of-school courses or programs. However, with a growing number of states instituting legislation to support dual enrollment and the increasing number of programs seeking accreditation, the precedent is set to accept credits from outside institutions. Special programs for gifted students have the potential to link schools and universities and other institutions in significant, important ways. The most important component, however, is educators' knowledge about specialized programs and their openness to having students participate in them and be rewarded for such achievements by their schools.

SUMMARY AND CONCLUSIONS

Different types of supplementary and special educational services exist for gifted students in the United States, and the number of students served in these programs is growing. The underlying assumptions for special programs and schools for the gifted have to do with the needs of gifted students, including advanced, challenging, and stimulating academic experiences and social and emotional support for high achievement and healthy psychological development. Program types include summer and Saturday programs, distance education programs, talent search programs, specialized schools, and early college entrance programs. A substantial amount of research attests to the positive influence of participation in special programs for gifted students, affecting their motivation, persistence, and achievement and altering their choices of courses and educational and career paths.

Despite the growing quantity of institutions providing special educational programs for gifted learners and a greater interest among gifted students in such programs for their own academic enrichment or acceleration, issues regarding the articulation between in-school and out-of-school programs and the inaccessibility of programs due to tuition costs still remain as major limitations. Cooperative work between local schools and outside institutions offering specialized services for gifted students, especially regarding issues of credit and academic placement, is needed to optimize the benefits of the special services for students and to ensure the fullest development of their abilities.

QUESTIONS FOR THOUGHT AND REFLECTION

1. Compare, through discussion or by preparing a chart, the characteristics of early college entrance programs, distance learning programs, summer and weekend programs, and specialized schools. Your comparison should include but not be limited to access to and opportunities for sustained interactions with intellectual peers, diversity of environment, level of academic challenge, appropriateness for highly gifted students, required level of maturity, special skills needed for success, and articulation with regular schooling.
2. Prepare a profile of a gifted student who would benefit most from or be best matched to each of the following: specialized school in mathematics and science, performing arts school, distance learning program, and summer program.
3. Based on your reading, identify five areas of needed research regarding specialized programs and services for gifted children.
4. Develop a list of recommendations for either educators or parents regarding use of specialized services for gifted students, including distance learning programs, summer or weekend programs, special schools, and early college entrance programs.

RESOURCES

Distance Education Programs for Gifted Students

Center for Talent Development
www.ctd.northwestern.edu

Education Program for Gifted Youth
www.epgy.stanford.edu

Center for Talented Youth at Johns Hopkins University
www.jhu.edu/gifted/cde

Duke University's Talent Identification Program, E-Studies Program
www.tip.duke.edu/e-studies/index.html

Directories of Summer Programs

Summer Opportunities for Gifted Kids (National Association for Gifted Children)
www.nagc.org/index.aspx?id=1103

Peterson's Guide to Summer Programs
www.petersons.com/summerop/ssector.html

Educational Opportunity Guide (Duke TIP)
www.duketipeog.com

Special Schools

National Consortium of Specialized Secondary Schools of Mathematics, Science and Technology (NCSSSMST)
www.ncsssmst.org

BOOKS AND ARTICLES

Brody, L., Muratori, M. C., & Stanley, J. C. (2004). Early entrance to college: Academic, social, and emotional considerations. In N. Colangelo, S. Assouline, & M. Gross (Eds.), *A nation deceived: How schools hold back America's brightest students* (Vol. 2). Iowa City: University of Iowa.

Kiernan, V. (2005). *Finding an online high school.* Alexandra, VA: Mattily.

Olszewski-Kubilius, P., & Limburg-Weber, L. (2004). *Designs for excellence: A guide to educational program options for academically talented middle and secondary students.* Evanston, IL: Center for Talent Development, Northwestern University.

REFERENCES

Ablard, K. E., Mills, C. J., & Hoffhines, V. L. (1996). *The developmental study of talented youth (DSTY): The participants* (Technical Report No. 13). Baltimore: Institute for the Academic Advancement of Youth, Johns Hopkins University.

Accessing distance learning. (1995, November/December). *Imagine, 3,* 1–4.

Adams, C. M., & Cross, T. L. (1999/2000). Distance learning opportunities for academically gifted students. *Journal of Secondary Gifted Education, 11,* 88–96.

Alamprese, J. A., Erlanger, W. J., & Brigham, N. (1989). *No gift wasted: Effective strategies for educating highly able, disadvantaged students in mathematics and science* (Vols. 1–2). Washington, DC: COSMOS.

Assouline, S., & Lupkowski-Shoplik, A. (1997). Talent searches: A model for the discovery and development of academic talent. In N. Colangelo & G. A. Davis (Eds.), *Handbook of gifted education* (2nd ed., pp. 170–179). Boston: Allyn & Bacon.

Barnett, L. B., & Durden, W. G. (1993). Education patterns of academically talented youth. *Gifted Child Quarterly, 37,* 161–168.

Bartkovich, K. G., & Mezynski, K. (1981). Fast-paced precalculus mathematics for talented junior-high students: Two recent SMPY programs. *Gifted Child Quarterly, 25,* 73–80.

Belcastro, F. P. (2001). Electronic technology and its use with rural gifted students. *Roeper Review, 25,* 14–16.

Benbow, C. P. (1992a). Academic achievement in mathematics and science of students between ages 13 and 23: Are there differences among students in the top one percent of mathematical ability? *Journal of Educational Psychology, 84,* 51–61.

Benbow, C. P. (1992b). Mathematical talent: Its nature and consequences. In N. Colangelo, S. G. Assouline, & D. L. Ambroson (Eds.), *Talent development: Proceedings from the 1991 Henry B. and Jocelyn Wallace National Research Symposium on Talent Development* (pp. 95–123). Unionville, NY: Trillium.

Benbow, C. P., & Arjmand, O. (1990). Predictors of high academic achievement in mathematics and science by mathematically talented students: A longitudinal study. *Journal of Educational Psychology, 82,* 430–441.

Benbow, C. P., Perkins, S., & Stanley, J. C. (1983). Mathematics taught at a fast pace: A longitudinal evaluation of SMPY's first class. In C. P. Benbow & J. C. Stanley (Eds.), *Academic precocity: Aspects of its development* (pp. 51–78). Baltimore: Johns Hopkins University Press.

Benbow, C. P., & Stanley, J. C. (Eds.). (1983). *Academic precocity: Aspects of its development.* Baltimore: Johns Hopkins University Press.

Bloom, B. S. (Ed.). (1985). *Developing talent in young people.* New York: Ballantine.

Brody, L. E. (1998). The talent searches: A catalyst for change in higher education. *Journal of Secondary Gifted Education, 9,* 124–133.

Brody, L. E., Assouline, S. G., & Stanley, J. C. (1990). Five years of early entrants: Predicting successful achievement in college. *Gifted Child Quarterly, 34,* 138–142.

Brody, L., & Fox, L. H. (1980). An accelerative intervention program for mathematically gifted girls. In L. H. Fox, L. Brody, & D. Tobin (Eds.), *Women and the mathematical mystique: Proceedings of the eighth annual Hyman Blumberg Symposium on Research in Early Childhood Education* (pp. 164–178). Baltimore: Johns Hopkins University Press.

Brody, L. E., Muratori, M. C., & Stanley, J. C. (2004). Early entrance to college: Academic, social, and emotional considerations. In N. Colangelo, S. Assouline, & M. U. M. Gross (Eds.), *A nation deceived: How schools hold back America's brightest students* (Vol. 2). Iowa City: The Connie Belin and Jacqueline N. Blank International Center for Gifted Education and Talent Development, University of Iowa.

Callahan, C. M., Cornell, D. G., & Lloyd, B. H. (1992). The academic development and personal adjustment of high ability young women in an early college entrance program. In N. Colangelo, S. G. Assouline, & D. L. Ambroson (Eds.), *Talent development: Proceedings from the 1991 Henry B. and Jocelyn Wallace National Research Symposium on Talent Development* (pp. 248–260). Unionville, NY: Trillium.

Cifuentes, L., Murphy, K., & Davis, T. (1998). Cultural connections: Promoting self-esteem, achievement, and multicultural understanding through distance learning. In N. J. Maushak (Ed.), *Proceedings of selected research and development presentations at the national convention of the Association for Educational Communications and Technology,* St. Louis, MO. (ERIC Document Reproduction Service No. ED423831)

Confessore, G. J. (1991). What became of the kids who participated in the 1981 Johnson Early College Summer Arts Program? *Journal for the Education of the Gifted, 15,* 64–82.

Cornell, D. G., Callahan, C. M., & Lloyd, B. H. (1991). Socioemotional adjustment of adolescent girls enrolled in a residential acceleration program. *Gifted Child Quarterly, 35,* 58–66.

Dershewitz, L., Lee, S.-Y., & Johnson, P. (2006, February). *Parents' perceptions of the effects of distance education on gifted children.* Paper presented at the annual convention of Illinois Association for Gifted Children, Chicago, IL.

Eisenberg, A., & George, W. (1979). Early entrance to college: The Johns Hopkins Experience Study of Mathematically Precocious Youth. *College and University,* pp. 109–118.

Enersen, D. L. (1993). Summer residential programs: Academics and beyond. *Gifted Child Quarterly, 37,* 169–176.

Ewing, J., Dowling, J., & Coutts, N. (1997). *STARS: Report on superhighway teams across rural school projects.* Dundee, Scotland: Northern College. (ERIC Document Reproduction Service No. ED421319)

Feldhusen, J. F. (1991). Saturday and summer programs. In N. Colangelo & G. A. Davis (Eds.), *Handbook of gifted education* (1st ed., pp. 197–208). Boston: Allyn & Bacon.

Feldhusen, J. F. (1997). Secondary services, opportunities, and activities for talented youth. In N. Colangelo & G. A. Davis (Eds.), *Handbook of gifted education* (2nd ed., pp. 189–197). Boston: Allyn & Bacon.

Ford, D. Y. (1996). *Reversing underachievement among gifted black students.* New York: Teachers College Press.

Fox, L. H., Brody, L., & Tobin, D. (1985). The impact of early intervention programs upon course-taking and attitudes in high school. In S. F. Chipman, L. R. Brush, & D. M. Wilson (Eds.), *Women and mathematics: Balancing the equation* (pp. 249–274). Hillsdale, NJ: Lawrence Erlbaum Associates.

Gallagher, J. J. (2001). Personnel preparation and secondary education programs for gifted students. *Journal of Secondary Gifted Education, 12,* 133–138.

Glennan, T. K., & Melmed, A. (1996). *Fostering the use of educational technology: Elements of a national strategy.* Retrieved February 3, 2003, from *http://www.rand.org/pubs/monograph_reports/MR682/contents.html*

Goldstein, D., & Wagner, H. (1993). After school programs, competitions, school olympics, and summer programs. In K. A. Heller, F. J. Mönks, & H. Passow (Eds.), *International handbook of research and development of giftedness and talent* (pp. 593–604). New York: Pergamon.

Goodrich, B. E. (1994). Creating a "virtual" magnet school. *T.H.E. Journal,* pp. 73–75.

Gross, M. U. M. (2000). Issues in the cognitive development of exceptionally and profoundly gifted individuals. In K. A. Heller, F. J. Mönks, R. J. Sternberg, & R. F. Subotnik (Eds.), *International handbook of giftedness and talent* (2nd ed., pp. 179–192). New York: Elsevier.

Gross, M. U. M., & van Vliet, H. E. (2005). Radical acceleration and early entry to college: A review of the research. *Gifted Child Quarterly, 49,* 154–171.

Hofmeister, A. (1994). Technological tools for rural special education. *Exceptional Children, 50,* 326–331.

Hull, D. F., Bull, K. S., Montgomery, D., May, J. R., & Overton, R. (2000). Designing an online, introductory gifted education. In *Capitalizing on leadership in rural special education: Making a difference for children and families.* Conference Proceedings, Alexandria, VA. (ERIC Document Reproduction Service No. ED439873)

Illinois Mathematics and Science Academy. (2005). *A pioneering educational community* (Fiscal Year 2005 Performance Report). Aurora: Office of Research and Evaluation, Illinois Mathematics and Science Academy.

Janos, P. M., & Robinson, N. M. (1985). The performance of students in a program of rapid acceleration at the university level. *Gifted Child Quarterly, 19,* 175–180.

Janos, P. M., Sanfilippo, S. M., & Robinson, N. M. (1986). "Underachievement" among markedly accelerated college students. *Journal of Youth and Adolescence, 15,* 303–311.

Jarosewich, T., & Stocking, V. B. (2003). Talent Search: Student and parent perceptions of out-of-level testing. *Journal of Secondary Gifted Education, 14,* 137–150.

Kiernan, V. (2005). *Finding an online high school: Your guide to more than 4,500 high school courses offered over the Internet.* Alexandria, VA: Mattily.

Kolitch, E. R., & Brody, L. E. (1992). Mathematics acceleration of highly talented students: An evaluation. *Gifted Child Quarterly, 36,* 78–86.

Kolloff, P. B. (2003). State-supported residential high schools In N. Colangelo & G. A. Davis (Eds.), *Handbook of gifted education* (3rd ed., pp. 238–246). Boston: Allyn & Bacon.

Kolloff, P. B., & Moore, A. D. (1989). Effects of summer programs on the self-concepts of gifted children. *Journal for the Education of the Gifted, 12,* 268–276.

Lee, S.-Y., Matthews, M. S., & Olszewski-Kubilius, P. (in press). A national picture of talent search and talent search educational programs. *Gifted Child Quarterly.*

Lee, S.-Y., & Olszewski-Kubilius, P. (2005). Investigation of high school credit and placement for summer coursework taken outside of local schools. *Gifted Child Quarterly, 49,* 37–50.

Lewis, G. (1989). Telelearning: Making maximum use of the medium. *Roeper Review, 11,* 195–198.

Lewis, G., & Talbert, M. (1990). Telelearning: Reaching out to the gifted in rural schools. *Educating Able Learners, 15,* 2–3, 10.

Limburg-Weber, L. (1999/2000). Send them packing: Study abroad as an option for gifted students. *Journal of Secondary Gifted Education, 11,* 43–51.

Lubinski, D., Webb, R. M., Morelock, M. J., & Benbow, C. P. (2001). Top 1 in 20,000: A 10-year follow-up of the profoundly gifted. *Journal of Applied Psychology, 85,* 718–729.

Lynch, S. J. (1990). Credit and placement issues for the academically talented following summer studies in science and mathematics. *Gifted Child Quarterly, 34,* 27–30.

Lynch, S. J. (1992). Fast-paced high school science for the academically talented: A six-year perspective. *Gifted Child Quarterly, 36,* 147–154.

Marsh, H. W., & Hau, K.-T. (2003). Big-fish-little-pond effect on academic self-concept: A cross-cultural (26-country) test of the negative effects of academically selective schools. *American Psychologist, 58,* 364–376.

McBride, R. (1991a). Courses offered despite cutbacks. *American School Board Journal, 178,* A26.

McBride, R. (1991b). Strategies for implementing teletraining systems in education K–12. In *ITCA teleconferencing yearbook.* McLean, VA: International Teleconferencing Association.

McBride, R. O., & Lewis, G. (1993). Sharing the resources: Electronic outreach programs. *Journal for the Education of the Gifted, 16,* 372–386.

McLoughlin, C. (1999). Providing enrichment and acceleration in the electronic classroom: A case study of audiographic conferencing. *Journal of Special Education Technology, 14,* 54–69.

Mills, C. J., Ablard, K. E., & Lynch, S. J. (1992). Academically talented students' preparation for advanced-level coursework after individually-paced precalculus class. *Journal for the Education of the Gifted, 16,* 3–17.

Muratori, M. C. (2003). *A multiple case study examining the adjustment of ten early entrants.* Unpublished doctoral dissertation, University of Iowa, Iowa City.

Muratori, M., Colangelo, N., & Assouline, S. (2003). Early-entrance students: Impressions of their first semester of college. *Gifted Child Quarterly, 47,* 219–237.

Noble, K. D., & Drummond, J. E. (1992). But what about the prom? Students' perceptions of early college entrance. *Gifted Child Quarterly, 36,* 106–111.

Noble, K. D., Robinson, N. M., & Gunderson, A. (1993). All rivers lead to the sea: A follow-up study of gifted young adults. *Roeper Review, 15,* 124–130.

Olszewski, P., Kulieke, M. J., & Willis, G. B. (1987). Changes in the self-perceptions of gifted students who participate in rigorous academic programs. *Journal for the Education of the Gifted, 10,* 287–303.

Olszewski-Kubilius, P. (1989). Development of academic talent: The role of academic programs. In J. VanTassel-Baska & P. Olszewski-Kubilius (Eds.), *Patterns of influence on gifted learners: The home, the self, and the school* (pp. 214–230). New York: Teachers College Press.

Olszewski-Kubilius, P. (1997). Special summer and Saturday programs for gifted students. In N. Colangelo & G. A. Davis (Eds.), *Handbook of gifted education* (2nd ed., pp. 180–188). Boston: Allyn & Bacon.

Olszewski-Kubilius, P. (1998a). Early entrance to college: Students' stories. *Journal of Secondary Education, 10,* 226–247.

Olszewski-Kubilius, P. (1998b). Research evidence regarding the validity and effects of talent search educational programs. *Journal of Secondary Gifted Education, 9,* 134–138.

Olszewski-Kubilius, P. (1998c). Talent search: Purposes, rationale, and role in gifted education. *Journal of Secondary Gifted Education, 9,* 106–114.

Olszewski-Kubilius, P. (2003). Special summer and Saturday programs for gifted students. In N. Colangelo & G. A. Davis (Eds.), *Handbook of gifted education* (3rd ed., pp. 219–228). Boston: Allyn & Bacon.

Olszewski-Kubilius P., & Grant, B. (1996). Academically talented women and mathematics: The role of special programs and support from others in acceleration, achievement and aspiration. In K. D. Noble & R. F. Subotnik (Eds.), *Remarkable women: Perspectives on female talent development* (pp. 281–294). Cresskill, NJ: Hampton.

Olszewski-Kubilius, P., Grant, B., & Seibert, C. (1994). Social support systems and the disadvantaged gifted: A framework for developing programs and services. *Roeper Review, 17,* 20–25.

Olszewski-Kubilius, P., Kulieke, M. J., Willis, G. B., & Krasney, N. (1989). An analysis of the validity of SAT entrance scores for accelerated classes. *Journal for the Education of the Gifted, 13,* 37–54.

Olszewski-Kubilius, P., Laubscher, L., Wohl, V., & Grant, B. (1996). Issues and factors involved in credit and placement for accelerated summer coursework. *Journal of Secondary Gifted Education, 13,* 5–15.

Olszewski-Kubilius, P., & Lee, S.-Y. (2004a). Gifted adolescents' talent development through distance learning. *Journal for the Education of the Gifted, 28,* 7–35.

Olszewski-Kubilius, P., & Lee, S.-Y. (2004b). Parent perceptions of the effects of the Saturday Enrichment Program on gifted students' talent development. *Roeper Review, 26,* 156–165.

Olszewski-Kubilius, P., & Lee, S.-Y. (2005). How schools use talent search scores for gifted adolescents. *Roeper Review, 27,* 233–240.

Olszewski-Kubilius, P., & Limburg-Weber, L. (2002). *Designs for excellence: A guide to educational program options for academically talented middle and secondary school students.* Evanston, IL: Center for Talent Development, Northwestern University.

Pressey, S. (1967). "Fordling" accelerates ten years after. *Journal of Counseling Psychology, 14,* 73–80.

Ravaglia, R., & Sommer, R. (2000, January). Expanding the curriculum with distance learning. *Principal, 79,* 10–13.

Renzulli, J. S. (1977). *The enrichment triad model: A guide for developing defensible programs for the gifted and talented.* Mansfield Center, CT: Creative Learning Press.

Renzulli, J. S. (1987a). The difference is what makes differentiation. *Journal for the Education of the Gifted 10,* 265–266.

Renzulli, J. S. (1987b). The positive side of pull-out programs. *Journal for the Education of the Gifted, 10,* 245–254.

Renzulli, J. S., & Reis, S. M. (1997). *The schoolwide enrichment model: A how to guide for educational excellence* (2nd ed.). Mansfield Center, CT: Creative Learning Press.

Rogers, K. B. (1991). *The relationship of grouping practices to the education of the gifted and talented learner.* Storrs: National Research Center on the Gifted and Talented, University of Connecticut.

Savage, L., & Werner, J. (1994). Potpourri of resources to tap gifted education in rural areas. In D. Montgomery (Ed.), *Rural partnerships: Working together* (pp. 127–132). Austin, TX: American Council on Rural Education. (ERIC Document Reproduction Service No. ED369601)

Sayler, M. F. (1993, November). *Profiles of successful male and female early entrants.* Paper presented at the annual conference of the National Association for Gifted Children, Atlanta, GA.

Sayler, M. F. (2006). Special schools for the gifted and talented. In F. A. Dixon & S. M. Moon (Eds.), *The handbook of secondary gifted education* (pp. 547–559). Waco, TX: Prufrock.

Sayler, M. F., & Lupkowski, A. E. (1992, March/April). Early entrance to college: Weighing the options. *Gifted Child Today, 15,* 24–29.

Schumacker, R. E., Sayler, M., & Bembry, K. L. (1995). Identifying at-risk gifted students in an early college entrance program. *Roeper Review, 18,* 126–129.

Sethna, B. N., Wickstrom, C. D., Boothe, D., & Stanley, J. C. (2001). The Advanced Academy of Georgia: Four years as a residential early-college-entrance program. *Journal of Secondary Gifted Education, 13,* 11–21.

Stanley, J. C. (1976). Special fast-mathematics classes taught by college professors to fourth- through twelfth-grades. In D. P. Keating (Ed.), *Intellectual talent, research and development: Proceedings of the sixth annual Hyman Blumberg Symposium on Research in Early Childhood Education* (pp. 132–159). Baltimore: Johns Hopkins University Press.

Stanley, J. C. (1985, Fall). How did six highly accelerated gifted students fare in graduate school? *Gifted Child Quarterly, 29,* 180.

Stanley, J. C., & McGill, A. M. (1986). More about "young entrants to college: How did they fare?" *Gifted Child Quarterly, 30,* 70–73.

Subotnik, R. F., & Jarvin, L. (2005). Beyond expertise: Conceptions of giftedness as great performance. In R. J. Sternberg & J. E. Davidson (Eds.), *Conceptions of giftedness* (2nd ed., pp. 343–357). New York: Cambridge University Press.

Swiatek, M. A., & Benbow, C. P. (1991). Ten-year longitudinal follow-up of ability-matched accelerated and unaccelerated gifted students. *Journal of Educational Psychology, 83,* 528–538.

Thompson, M. (2001). *Developing verbal talent.* Retrieved May 12, 2006, from *http://www.ctd.northwestern.edu/resources/talentdevelopment/verbaltalent.html*

Threlkeld, R. (1991). Increasing educational options through distance learning. *Gifted Education Communicator, 21*(1), 12–14.

Timpson, W. M., & Jones, C. S. (1989, September/October). Increasing education choices for the gifted: Distance learning via technology. *Gifted Child Today, 12,* 10–11.

University of Plymouth. (2006, March 31). *Distance education: Why distance learning?* Retrieved May 29, 2006, from *http://www2.plymouth.ac.uk/distancelearning*

VanTassel-Baska, J. (1988). *Comprehensive curriculum for gifted learners.* Boston: Allyn & Bacon.

VanTassel-Baska, J. (1989). Profiles of precocity: A three-year study of talented adolescents. In J. VanTassel-Baska & P. Olszewski-Kubilius (Eds.), *Patterns of influence on gifted learners: The home, the self, and the school* (pp. 29–39). New York: Teachers College Press.

VanTassel-Baska, J. (1998). Key issues and problems in secondary programming. In J. VanTassel-Baska (Ed.), *Excellence in educating gifted and talented learners* (3rd ed., pp. 241–259). Denver: Love.

VanTassel-Baska, J., & Kulieke, M. J. (1987). The role of community-based scientific resources in developing scientific talent: A case study. *Gifted Child Quarterly, 31,* 111–115.

VanTassel-Baska, J., Patton, J., & Prillaman, D. (1990). The nature and extent of programs for the disadvantaged gifted in the United States and Territories. *Gifted Child Quarterly, 34,* 94–96.

Wai, J., Lubinski, D., & Benbow, C. P. (2005). Creativity and occupational accomplishments among intellectually precocious youths: An age 13 to age 33 longitudinal study. *Journal of Educational Psychology, 97,* 484–492.

Washington, M. F. (1997, November/December). Real hope for the gifted. *Gifted Child Today, 20,* 20–22.

Webb, R. M., Lubinski, D., & Benbow, C. P. (2002). Mathematically facile adolescents with math-science aspirations: New perspectives on their educational and vocational development. *Journal of Educational Psychology, 94,* 785–794.

Wilder, G. Z., Casserly, P. L., & Burton, N. W. (1988). *Young SAT-takers: Two surveys* (College Board Report No. 88-1). New York: College Entrance Examination Board.

Wilson, V., Litle, J., Coleman, M. R., & Gallagher, J. (1997/1998). Distance learning: One school's experience on the information highway. *Journal of Secondary Gifted Education, 9,* 89–100.

CHAPTER 13

CURRICULUM DEVELOPMENT IN GIFTED EDUCATION: A CHALLENGE TO PROVIDE OPTIMAL LEARNING EXPERIENCES

Joyce VanTassel-Baska, Ph.D.
The College of William and Mary

Susannah Wood, Ph.D.
University of Iowa

INTRODUCTION

Curriculum development for gifted learners has been a serious subject in the field since the 1970s, when several approaches emerged in servicing the gifted learner that became translated into formalized curricula. Other models that evolved in the 1980s and beyond focused exclusively on approaches for the direct design of curriculum. While models are useful for curriculum development, they need to be augmented by a clear sense of development and design processes that will produce viable curricular products. This chapter explores existing models for curriculum development and the research base supporting them as well as the processes needed to develop effective curriculum.

RECENT AND SEMINAL RESEARCH ON CURRICULUM MODELS

The following models represent both accelerative and enrichment approaches to working with the gifted (VanTassel-Baska, 2003b). Some of the curriculum models cited ascribe solely to an enriched view of curriculum development for the gifted and use a broader conception of giftedness, taking into account principles of creativity, motivation, and independence as crucial elements in the development of high ability (Maker & Nielson, 1996a, 1996b; Renzulli, 1986; VanTassel-Baska, 2003b).

The models discussed in this chapter meet five primary criteria for use in gifted curriculum development:

1. They provide a system for developing and designing appropriate curriculum for the target population,
2. They can be easily applied to all major content areas of school-based learning,
3. They are applicable to different age and grade levels, and
4. They differentiate according to principles of gifted education.

The first two models cited are not, strictly speaking, only curriculum models. They are overall programs of talent development. Yet data have been collected on the effects of student learning in the curriculum model aspect of each.

The Stanley Model of Talent Identification and Development

The overall purpose of the Stanley model is to educate for individual development over the life span. Major tenets of the model include the following: (a) the use of a secure and difficult testing instrument that taps into high-level verbal and mathematical reasoning to identify students; (b) a diagnostic testing-prescriptive instructional approach in teaching gifted students through special classes, allowing for appropriate level of challenge in instruction; (c) the use of subject-matter acceleration and fast-paced classes in core academic areas as well as advocacy for various other forms of acceleration; and (d) curriculum flexibility in all schooling.

From 1972 through 1979, the Study of Mathematically Precocious Youth (SMPY) pioneered the concept of searching for youth who reason exceptionally well mathematically (i.e., a talent search). In 1980, others at Johns Hopkins University extended the talent search to verbally gifted youth. The SMPY provided educational facilitation to these students by utilizing acceleration or curricular flexibility and by developing fast-paced academic programs at centers, other universities, and organizations, including residential and commuter academic programs in several disciplines. Almost 250,000 gifted students in seventh and eighth grade are eligible to participate every year in these talent searches by taking the College Board's SAT or the ACT.

The research work of SMPY has been strong over the past 27 years. Findings of multiple studies have consistently focused on the benefits of acceleration for continued advanced work in an area by precocious students (Stanley, Keating, & Fox, 1974), a clear rationale for the use of acceleration in intellectual development (Keating, 1976), and the long-term positive repeated impacts of accelerative opportunities (Benbow & Arjmand, 1990).

Longitudinal data, collected over the past 20 years on 300 highly gifted students, have demonstrated the viability of the Stanley model in respect to the benefits of accelerative study, early identification of a strong talent area, and the need for assistance in educational decision making (Lubinski & Benbow, 1994). A 50-year follow-up study (1972–2022) is ongoing with 6,000 students in the sample. A recent review of longitudinal studies on acceleration continues to demonstrate the positive results of accelerative practices and the lack of negative consequences, such as knowledge gaps or loss of interest (Swiatek, 2000). A major national report, *A Nation Deceived*, has also documented the evidence of the use of various forms of acceleration that can be applied in curriculum for the gifted (Colangelo, Assouline, & Gross, 2004).

The Schoolwide Enrichment Model

The Schoolwide Enrichment Model (SEM) evolved after 15 years of research and field-testing by both educators and researchers (Renzulli, 1988). It is the combination of the previously developed Enrichment Triad Model (Renzulli, 1977) with a more flexible approach to identifying high-potential students, the Revolving Door Identification Model (Renzulli, Reis, & Smith, 1981).

In the SEM, a talent pool of 15% to 20% of above-average ability/high-potential students is identified through a variety of measures, including achievement tests, teacher nominations, assessment of potential for creativity and task commitment, as well as alternative pathways of entrance (e.g., self-nomination and parent nomination). High achievement test scores and IQ scores automatically include a student in the talent pool, enabling those students who are underachieving academically in school to be considered. Once students are identified for the talent pool, they are eligible for several kinds of services, including interest and learning style assessments, curriculum compacting, and various enrichment experiences.

Type I Enrichment consists of general exploratory experiences designed to expose students to new and exciting topics, ideas, and fields of knowledge not ordinarily covered in the regular curriculum. Type II Enrichment promotes the development of thinking, feeling, research, communication, and methodological processes. In Type III Enrichment, the most advanced level of the model, the learner assumes the role of a firsthand inquirer: thinking, feeling, and acting like a practicing professional, with involvement pursued at a level as advanced or professional as possible, given the student's level of development and age.

There have been a wide range of studies conducted on the effects of SEM, including evaluation (Olenchak & Renzulli, 1989), longitudinal studies (Delcourt, 1993, 1994; Hébert, 1993), research focused on compacting (Reis & Purcell, 1993; Reis, Westberg, Kulikowich, & Purcell, 1998), student behaviors such as creative production (Baum, Renzulli, & Hébert, 1995; Burns, 1988; Schack, Starko, & Burns, 1991), and underserved gifted populations (Baum, 1988). These studies have documented mostly positive results of the SEM model on student motivation and sustained interest in learning.

The Betts Autonomous Learner Model

The autonomous learner model for the gifted and talented was developed to meet the diverse cognitive, emotional, and social needs of gifted and talented students in grades K–12 (Betts & Knapp, 1980). As the needs of gifted and talented students are met, gifted students will develop into autonomous learners who are responsible for the development, implementation, and evaluation of their own learning. The model is divided into five major dimensions: (a) orientation, (b) individual development, (c) enrichment activities, (d) seminars, and (e) in-depth study. To date, no research evidence of effectiveness has been shown with regard to this model's student learning impact or longitudinal effectiveness with gifted learners. However, several curriculum units and curriculum guides have been produced as a result of the dissemination of its ideas (Betts, 1986).

Gardner's Multiple Intelligences

Multiple intelligences as a curriculum approach were built on a multidimensional concept of intelligence (Gardner, 1983). Seven areas of intelligence were defined in the original published work in 1983, with an eighth intelligence added by Gardner in 1995. They are (a) verbal/linguistic, (b) logical/mathematical, (c) visual/spatial, (d) musical/rhythmic, (e) bodily/kinesthetic, (f) interpersonal, (g) intrapersonal, and (h) naturalistic.

The multiple intelligences approach has been used in the formation of new schools, in identifying individual differences, for curriculum planning and development, and as a way to assess instructional strategies. A plethora of curriculum materials has been produced and marketed on the basis of multiple intelligences. This approach holds widespread appeal for many educators because it can be adapted for any learner, subject domain, or grade level. While the model has been readily adapted to curricula, it remains primarily a conception of intelligence applied broadly to school settings as a way to promote talent development for all learners.

Evidence of research based on multiple intelligences translated into practice has been documented (Latham, 1997; Smith, Odhiambo, & El Khateeb, 2000; Strahan, Summey, & Banks, 1996). Most of the research, however, lacks control groups; therefore, generalizations about the model are difficult to infer (Latham, 1997). Longitudinal evidence of effectiveness with gifted students over at least 3 years has not been documented, although some research has been conducted on incorporating multiple intelligences with other curriculum approaches (Maker, Nielson, & Rogers, 1994).

The Purdue Three-Stage Enrichment Model for Elementary Gifted Learners (PACE) and the Purdue Secondary Model for Gifted and Talented Youth

The concept of a three-stage model, initiated by Feldhusen and his graduate students, was first introduced as a course design for university students in 1973. It evolved into the Three-Stage Model by 1979. It is primarily an ordered enrichment model that moves students from stage I (development of divergent and convergent thinking skills) to stage II (creative problem solving) and to stage III (application of research and independent study skills) (Feldhusen & Kolloff, 1986).

The Purdue Secondary Model is a comprehensive structure for programming services at the secondary level. It has 11 components supporting enrichment and acceleration options, including (a) counseling services, (b) seminars, (c) advanced placement courses, (d) honors classes, (e) math/science acceleration, (f) foreign languages, (g) arts, (h) cultural experiences, (i) career education, (j) vocational programs, and (k) extraschool instruction (Feldhusen & Robinson-Wyman, 1986).

Research has documented student learning gains in the enhancement of creative thinking and self-concept using the Three-Stage Enrichment Model for Elementary Gifted Students (Kolloff & Feldhusen, 1984), and one study was conducted documenting limited long-term effects of the elementary program, PACE (Moon & Feldhusen, 1994; Moon, Feldhusen, & Dillon, 1994).

The Parallel Curriculum Model

The Parallel Curriculum Model is a model for curriculum planning based on the composite work of Tomlinson, Kaplan, Renzulli, Purcell, Leppien, and Burns (2002).

The heuristic model employs four dimensions, or parallels, that can be used singly or in combination. The parallels include the following:

1. **The core curriculum.** Acts as the basis for all other curricula, and it should be combined with any or all of the three other parallels. It establishes the basis of understanding within relevant subjects and grade levels. National, state, and/or local school district's standards should be reflected in this dimension.
2. **The curriculum of connections.** Supports students in discovering the interconnectedness among and between disciplines of knowledge and has students exploring connections for both intra- and interdisciplinary studies.
3. **The curriculum of practice.** Extends students' understandings and skills in a discipline through application and promotes student expertise as a practitioner of a given discipline.
4. **The curriculum of identity.** Serves to help students think about themselves within the context of a particular discipline and is used as a catalyst for self-definition and self-understanding.

To date, no research-based evidence of effectiveness has been shown with regard to this model's use with gifted or nongifted learners. However, several curriculum units and curriculum guides have been produced as a result of a wide dissemination effort by the National Association for Gifted Children. In addition, the creation of curriculum units is currently underway by practitioners at various levels, guided by the authors of the model.

The Schlichter Models for Talents Unlimited Inc. and Talents Unlimited to the Secondary Power

Talents Unlimited was based on Guilford's (1967) research on the nature of intelligence. Taylor, Ghiselin, Wolfer, Loy, & Bourne (1964), also influenced by Guilford, authored the Multiple Talent Theory, which precipitated the development of a model to be employed in helping teachers identify and nurture students' multiple talents. Talents Unlimited features four major components:

- A description of specific skill abilities, or talents, in addition to academic ability that includes productive thinking, communication, forecasting, decision making, and planning
- Model instructional materials
- An in-service training program for teachers
- An evaluation system for assessing students' thinking skills development (Schlichter, 1986).

Partially because of the strong emphasis on teacher training, the model has been used most effectively as a classroom-based approach with all learners. Research has documented the model's effectiveness in developing students' creative and critical thinking (Schlichter & Palmer, 1993), with young children in an English setting (Rodd, 1999), and in the enhancement of academic skill development on standardized achievement tests (McLean & Chisson, 1980).

Sternberg's Triarchic Componential Model

Sternberg's (1981) Triarchic Componential Model is based on an information-processing theory of intelligence. The interaction and feedback between the individual and his or her environment within any given context allows cognitive development to occur. In the model, the following three components represent the mental processes used in thinking: (a) the executive process component used in planning, decision making, and monitoring performance; (b) the performance component processes used in executing the executive problem-solving strategies within domains; and (c) the knowledge-acquisition component used in acquiring, retaining, and transferring new information.

Initial studies have shown the effectiveness of the triarchic model with students learning psychology in a summer program (Sternberg & Clinkenbeard, 1995), while more recent work conducted in studies using psychology as the curriculum base show growth patterns when assessment protocols are linked to measuring ability profiles (Sternberg, Ferrari, Clinkenbeard, & Grigorenko, 1996). Other studies include the validation of the *Sternberg Triarchic Abilities Test* and the use of triarchic instructional processes in elementary and middle school classrooms (Sternberg, Torff, & Grigorenko, 1998a, 1998b), which suggest slightly stronger effects for triarchic instruction over traditional and critical-thinking approaches.

VanTassel-Baska's Integrated Curriculum Model

The VanTassel-Baska (1986) Integrated Curriculum Model (ICM) was specifically developed for high-ability learners, based on existing research about "what works" with gifted students in classrooms and the literature on individual differences. It has three dimensions: (a) an advanced content focus in core areas; (b) high-level process and product work in critical thinking, problem solving, and research; and (c) intra- and interdisciplinary concept development and understanding. VanTassel-Baska has used the ICM as a basis to develop specific curriculum frameworks and underlying units in language arts, mathematics, and social studies content areas that are aligned with state standards yet differentiated for high-ability students.

Quasi-experimental and experimental research has been conducted to support the effectiveness of these curriculum units with gifted populations within a variety of educational settings. Findings indicate the following:

- Significant growth and educationally important gains in literary analysis and interpretation, persuasive writing, and linguistic competency in language arts have been demonstrated for experimental gifted classes using the developed curriculum units in comparison to gifted groups not using them (VanTassel-Baska, Johnson, Hughes, & Boyce, 1996; VanTassel-Baska, Zuo, Avery, & Little, 2002).
- Use of the problem-based science units embedded in an exemplary science curriculum significantly enhances the capacity for experimental students in integrating higher-order process skills in science regardless of the grouping approach employed over comparison students with moderate effect sizes (VanTassel-Baska, Bass, Ries, Poland, & Avery, 1998).
- Positive change occurs in teacher attitude, student motivational response, and school and district change as a result of using the ICM curriculum in both science and language arts over at least 3 years (VanTassel-Baska, Avery, Little, & Hughes, 2000).
- The language arts units are successful with low-income students, can be used in all grouping paradigms, and learning increases with multiple units employed (Feng & VanTassel-Baska, 2004; VanTassel-Baska et al., 2002).
- Use of the social studies units significantly impacts critical thinking and content mastery for experimental students over comparison groups (Little, Feng, VanTassel-Baska, Rogers, & Avery, 2002).
- The language arts units show significant and important gains for all groups of learners in Title I schools, including gifted learners, promising learners, and typical learners, on measures of critical thinking and reading achievement (VanTassel-Baska & Bracken, 2006).
- Teacher growth in differentiated classroom behaviors is significantly and importantly enhanced across 2 years of unit implementation and teacher training (VanTassel-Baska & Bracken, 2006).

Conclusions

A strong body of research evidence exists supporting the use of advanced curricula in core areas of learning at an accelerated rate for high-ability learners. Moreover, recent meta-analytic studies and reports continue to confirm the superior learning effects of acceleration over enrichment in tandem with grouping the gifted (Colangelo et al., 2004; Kulik & Kulik, 1992).

Some evidence also exists that more enrichment-oriented models are effective. For example, units developed on the ICM model appear to be effective with all learners, given certain teaching modifications. Therefore, content-based accelerative approaches and well-designed curriculum found to be effective with gifted learners should be employed routinely in school-based programs for the gifted, ensuring that curriculum models are applied faithfully and thoroughly to realize their potential impacts over time.

DIFFERENTIATING CURRICULUM FOR GIFTED LEARNERS BASED ON CHARACTERISTICS AND NEEDS

When reflecting the concept of giftedness through the curriculum, curriculum planners must analyze the characteristics and needs of gifted children and organize curricula that are responsive to them. Figure 13–1 illustrates the relationship between conceptions of giftedness and curriculum planning. School disctricts' conceptions of giftedness and the interaction of those conceptions with group and individual student characteristics and needs feed into curriculum planning, while appropriately tailored curriculum, instruction, and assessment systems foster gifted student creativity and productivity. Once a program is in place, educators must be continously mindful of each gifted student's identification data and adapt the curriculum to guarantee that student profiles are utilized in the classroom.

Curriculum for gifted learners is based on several critical assumptions that should be persistently applied in practice to ensure that gifted students receive appropriate services (VanTassel-Baska, 2003a, 2005).

1. All children can learn, but in different ways at different times in different contexts.

    This fundamental principle of the standards-based reform movement has been both applauded and supported by gifted educators. In the effort to improve the education of all students, however, the implementation of a common set of standards must also value individual differences and accommodate them through flexible means.

2. Gifted children differ from each other in learning rates and in what curriculum areas they find easy.

    Although this assumption has been demonstrated repeatedly by research, the power of the difference in individual learning rate is minimized and obscured by age-grade notions of curriculum readiness. Gifted students can learn new material at least twice as fast as typical learners, and their learning rates can increase radically if the curriculum is reorganized in "larger chunks." Gifted learners vary as much from one another as they do from the nongifted population in both rate of learning and areas in which they may be ready for advanced learning.

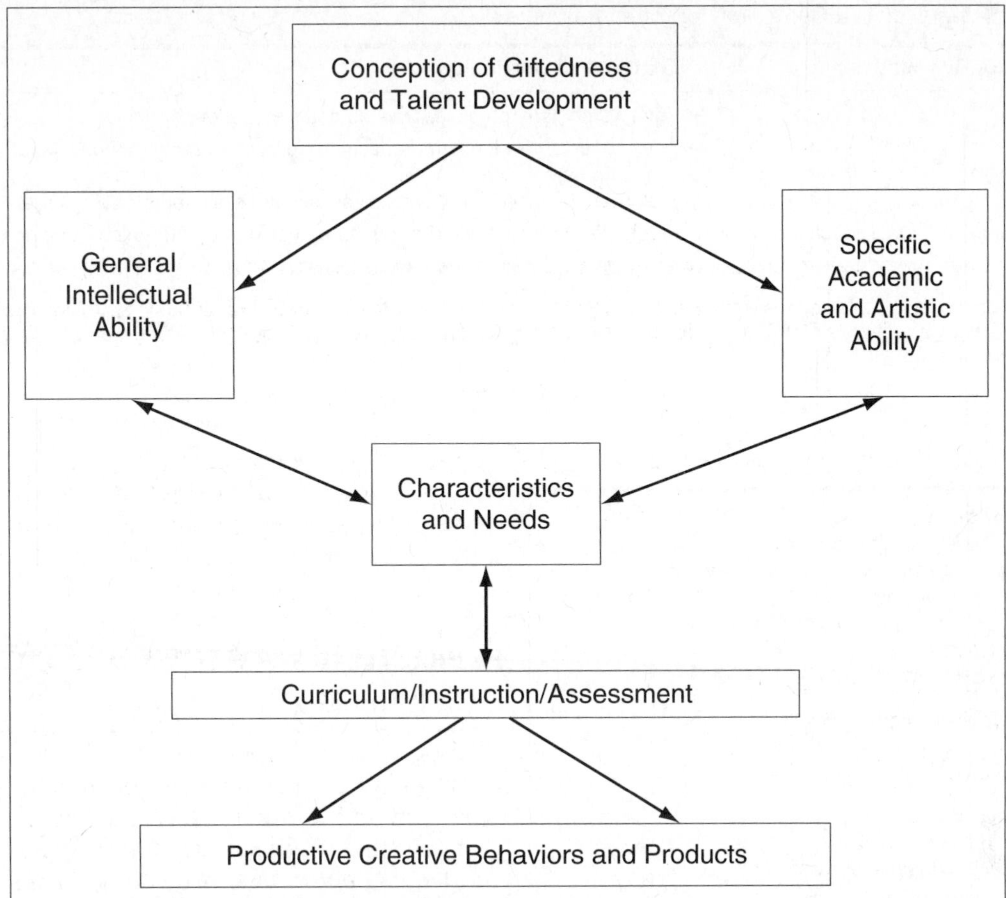

FIGURE 13–1 The Embedded Context for Designing Differentiated Curriculum
Source: From *Curriculum Planning and Instructional Design for Gifted Learners* (p. 90), by J. VanTassel-Baska, 2003, Denver, CO: Love. Copyright © 2003 Love Publishing Company. Reprinted with permission.

3. Gifted students vary considerably among themselves in intrinsic motivation for cognitive learning.

   Individual differences in motivation for learning, which may be related to cognitive capacity, tend to manifest in critical ways as students attempt schoolwork.

4. Not every student (or gifted student) will attain a useful mastery of concepts and skills beyond a certain level of complexity and abstraction.

   Many students, including some gifted learners, cannot handle advanced mathematics and science, both very abstract subject matters. Other gifted students encounter difficulty in interpreting complex passages of written text. At some point they may encounter the maximal degree of abstraction they are capable of handling in a given subject area. Thus, curriculum levels must be carefully matched to the capacity of the learners.

5. Learning should provide "a basic diet but also favorite foods."

   One of the assumptions regarding curriculum for the gifted is that "specialization" is fundamental to strong growth in essential areas. However, opportunities such as self-selected subjects, special project work, mentorships, and so on provide broader opportunities and are also important to learning.

6. Intra- and interindividual variability is the rule in development.

   The unique cognitive abilities of each child, which interact with subtle and complex classroom dynamics, determine the nature and degree of his or her understanding at any point in time. Neither gifted students nor any other group of learners can or should be seen as a monolithic group for purposes of learning. As Demetriou and Valanides (1998) observe, "Classrooms are developmental mixers in which each student's developmental dynamics constrain and are constrained by the developmental dynamics of every other student and of the classroom as a whole" (p. 195). A thoughtful examination of, deep appreciation for, and careful incorporation of individual and group characteristics and needs of the gifted must be the beginning point for all meaningful curricula for this population of learners. Existing curricula found to be effective with the gifted have evolved primarily from this understanding (Maker et al., 1994; VanTassel-Baska, 2003a).

TABLE 13–1 Integration in a Curriculum for Gifted Learners

Dimensions of Connectivity	Features of Curriculum
Organization	Employs content, process, product, and concept opportunities
Models	Uses concept development, reasoning skills, and research models that transcend curriculum areas studied
Assessments	Performance-based and portfolio assessment are integrated into regular use
Reform elements and gifted education	Emphasis is on meaning making through student-centered challenging activities

Source: From "Domain-Specific Giftedness: Applications in School and Life," by J. VanTassel-Baska, 2005, in R. J. Sternberg & J. E. Davidson (Eds.), *Conceptions of Giftedness* (p. 371). New York: Cambridge University. Copyright © 2005 Cambridge University Press. Reprinted with permission.

TABLE 13–2 Differentiation Features Checklist

1. **Acceleration**
   a. Fewer tasks assigned to master standards
   b. Standards-based skills assessed earlier or prior to teaching
   c. Standards clustered by higher-order thinking skills
2. **Complexity**
   a. Used multiple higher-level skills
   b. Added more variables to study
   c. Required multiple resources
3. **Depth**
   a. Studied a concept in multiple applications
   b. Conducted original research
   c. Developed a product
4. **Challenge**
   a. Employed advanced resources
   b. Used sophisticated content stimuli
   c. Made cross-disciplinary applications
   d. Made reasoning explicit
5. **Creativity**
   a. Designed/constructed a model based on principles or criteria
   b. Provided alternatives for tasks, products and assessments
   c. Emphasized oral and written communication to a real world audience

Source: From *Curriculum Planning and Instructional Design for Gifted Learners*, (p. 43), by J. VanTassel-Baska, 2003, Denver, CO: Love. Copyright © 2003 Love Publishing Company. Reprinted with permission.

Table 13–1 illustrates the integration in a curriculum of gifted learners.

Any curriculum to be used with gifted learners should incorporate the following five elements: acceleration, complexity, depth, challenge, and creativity. While any individual standard may contain only one of these elements, what is important is that the total curriculum in a particular area addresses all five. The checklist illustrated in Table 13–2 is designed to provide educators with a means to quickly ascertain the degree to which each curriculum standard is appropriate for use with the gifted. Using this checklist, educators can assess how much modification of a standard may be necessary. The list can also facilitate translation of the standards into archetypal activities.

PRACTICAL STRATEGIES FOR DEVELOPING CURRICULUM

Program developers need to be sensitive to several major issues in planning curriculum for gifted learners. Clearly, curriculum models and their underlying philosophy are important, but other issues also affect the planning effort. One issue is the definition being used for curriculum. *Curriculum* is defined as a set of organized experiences appropriate for gifted learners that are written down and adopted for use in a school district (VanTassel-Baska & Stambaugh, 2006b, p. 37). The articulation and codification of the goals, objectives, and activities of a gifted program is represented in this term. At the point that curriculum development work is undertaken, it is wise to examine the current curriculum and make appropriate modifications in the core content areas before developing a new curriculum.

Program developers will need to decide on the *appropriate goals* to address in developing a curriculum for gifted learners, and outcomes then can be developed from the overall goals of the program. Model goals for gifted learners follow (VanTassel-Baska & Stambaugh, 2006b).

Gifted Program Goals

1. **To provide for the mastery of the basic skills of reading and mathematics at a pace and depth appropriate to the capacities of able learners.** Students will participate in a diagnostic-prescriptive model of reading and mathematics instruction that would allow for individual rates of mastery, regardless of age or grade. *(Content Acceleration Goal)*
2. **To promote critical thinking and reasoning abilities.** Students will be instructed in the areas

of inference, deductive and inductive reasoning, analogies, and evaluation of arguments. These reasoning tools will be applied to all areas of the curriculum. *(Critical Thinking Goal)*
3. **To provide an environment that encourages divergent thinking.** Students will be encouraged in the development of originality, fluency, flexibility, and elaboration in their thought processes. *(Creative Thinking Goal)*
4. **To develop high-level oral and written skills.** Students will become confident in expressing ideas through class discussions, panel discussions, debates, and oral reports; students will learn expository and creative writing skills and technical report writing. *(Communication Goal)*
5. **To develop research skills and methods.** Students will be able to understand the scientific method and its application to all areas of inquiry. *(Research Goal)* (VanTassel-Baska & Stambaugh, 2006b, p. 37).

As they progress through school, gifted students need to be exposed to increasingly complex and difficult material. Articulation of skills and concepts in core curriculum areas is but part of the task; skills such as critical thinking, creative thinking, problem solving, and research all need to be structured hierarchically so that higher-level skills are taught through a progressive developmental system. Product requirements also need to be articulated across content and grade-level dimensions (Karnes & Stephens, 2000).

Needs Assessment

One of the most practical aspects of the curriculum development process is a thorough needs assessment. VanTassel-Baska and Stambaugh (2006b) propose the use of a needs assessment model that links student needs to program components and links developmental concerns to the nature and extent of staff development. Other perspectives on needs assessment more precisely focus on decision making in the area of curriculum.

Needs assessment must also occur at the local level, involving students, parents, and administrators in order to determine what currently exists or needs to in the curriculum for gifted students. This task can be accomplished by asking multiple stakeholders to comment formally on this aspect of the district's educational plan. To begin, it may be helpful to start with a list of questions that can guide the needs assessment process. These might include the following:

1. Based on the characteristics of gifted children in this district, what are the educational needs for which we are responsible?
2. What are the gaps in our current program that must be addressed in order to respond to the needs of gifted students?
3. What technical assistance will be needed in order to develop and implement new directions in curriculum?

In summary, a needs assessment strategy must recognize (a) general needs of gifted learners derived from research-based models, (b) specific curriculum needs of gifted students, (c) discrepancies between what existing curriculum for the gifted currently provides and what it should provide, and (d) specific curriculum resources needed to codify and guide curriculum efforts (VanTassel-Baska & Stambaugh, 2006b). All of these elements are useful in ascertaining what appropriate curriculum for the gifted might be.

Curriculum Development Teams

As one examines the possibility of developing meaningful curriculum for the gifted, it becomes apparent that if the curriculum is content based or interdisciplinary in nature, curriculum developers must be well acquainted with the content areas to be examined and have the ability to construct an organizational schema that focuses on the most important skills, concepts, and "cutting-edge" ideas in that field.

Because an individual teacher may or may not have these insights, it is useful to develop a team approach to curriculum development. Such a team approach allows the strength of each individual member to emerge. Good teachers know intuitively what is workable for the gifted in the classroom and can translate ideas at an appropriate level for gifted learners. Content experts, who may be university professors or practicing professionals, know their particular field of inquiry and are engaged in active research within it; thus, they can supply key ideas and concepts that can provide the curricular structure. The combined effort of teachers and scholars in this type of curriculum effort is most productive. The extent of the undertaking, number of members, member role, and representation are all critical aspects to forming curriculum teams (VanTassel-Baska & Stambaugh, 2006b).

The makeup of district curriculum teams should be determined by the scope of the curriculum effort. First, if the task is to be a comprehensive one, such as restructuring a K–12 curriculum for the gifted, then there will be a need for multiple teams that are guided by a central steering committee. Second, clear boundaries need to be drawn between data-gathering tasks, planning, and writing tasks when considering the constituents of the committees. Curriculum writers and data gatherers should be a subset of the committee or, if needed, a separate task force that works with the committee. Third, the number of people on a curriculum development committee is also an essential consideration. Ideal sizes for curriculum planning committees range from 6 to 12 people, depending on the size of the district and the scope of the effort. One to four individuals work best in conducting a data-gathering and writing task force.

Finally, representation on the committee is a critical variable. The individual in a school district who is responsible for curriculum leadership for the gifted program has several responsibilities, including chairing the committee, communicating the work of the committee with clarity, and moving the agenda along a predetermined schedule to ensure that the committee work will be implemented (VanTassel-Baska & Stambaugh, 2006b). Involving building-level administrators who can represent their counterparts on curriculum committees is integral to the process. In addition, teacher involvement is also important but should be reserved for teachers who have knowledge and experience in working with gifted learners in a variety of classroom settings.

Representation by content disciplines rather than grade level only may be an important consideration for teacher selection (VanTassel-Baska & Stambaugh, 2006b). First, the education of the gifted, as it is translated through school curriculum, needs to be at an advanced level and have a clear emphasis on maximum rather than minimum competency issues; thus, electing primary teachers based on their understanding of reading or mathematics rather than their teaching style is preferable. Second, gifted students' capabilities obscure the boundaries of traditional grade-level designations (VanTassel-Baska & Stambaugh, 2006b). Thus, the development of curriculum can be simplified by structuring committees by content area.

The traditional consultant mode approach model may be preferable if the focus of the curriculum work is on planning rather than writing and the style of teamwork is discussion and deliberation. In this approach, an educator within the school district leads the curriculum team, and outside consultants participate at particular stages of the process. If school political issues tend to dominate curriculum deliberations, the consultant can provide a more objective assessment of any curriculum issue or problem. Moreover, he or she has an in-depth knowledge of the key areas being considered. For example, in considering an appropriate sequence of mathematics courses for gifted students at the secondary level, a consultant in mathematics can share major approaches to organizing such courses, where exemplary programs based on those approaches may be operating, and the advantages and disadvantages of any given sequence.

The Curriculum Development Approach: Data Gathering, Adapting, and Writing

School district practitioners should never assume that appropriate curriculum for the gifted must be developed completely from scratch. Too much time, energy, and resources have already been used by school districts on an individual basis to create their own unique curriculum for the gifted or to allow individual teachers the freedom for creative license with the gifted curriculum. While some new development may need to be completed as the process goes on, creating new units of study, for example, is clearly not a first step.

Data Gathering. Gathering existing curriculum that may be appropriate for gifted learners is the first step. Procedurally, this involves the following:

1. Contact appropriate commercial publishers and other sources for materials related to the curriculum under study. Obtain materials that are appropriate for high-ability learners. Review and critique these materials for possible inclusion in the program.
2. Contact state consultants for the gifted who should be able to provide lists of curriculum guides developed in their state for the gifted through special projects or collaboration with local efforts.
3. Review curriculum materials from research-based projects, such as those of The College of William & Mary and others, cited as promising or exemplary by the U.S. Department of Education.
4. Contact at least five coordinators of established gifted programs across the country and gather ideas on effective curricula employed in those programs.
5. Determine what may be usable from all these sources for your program and the degree to which the materials obtained may need to be adapted or supplemented.

Adapting Existing Curriculum. Another task that a curriculum development team must consider is modifying the core curriculum to make it more appropriate for gifted learners. After completing the data-gathering process, it will become clear that most published curricula designed solely for gifted learners are not sufficient in breadth or depth to carry a program for a school year. There is no way to avoid the difficult task of reorganizing and restructuring state standards in order to make them more appropriate for able learners.

The following list developed by VanTassel-Baska (2003a) suggests potential strategies to employ for more effective and efficient implementation of standards with gifted students:

1. Recognize that many of the standards focus on higher-level thought processes and that task demands for gifted learners may be developed directly from them.
   For example, historical analysis skills are stressed from primary grades through high school in the social studies standards. These standards do not have to be changed to make them more appropriate for gifted learners; rather, they should be translated into appropriate teaching–learning task demands.

2. Read and interpret individual standards carefully to discern their scope and intent.
   One of the major problems with many of the standards is their lack of easy translation into appropriate task demands. This is true within and across subject areas; particularly in language arts and social studies, the standards are written at a general level that requires interpretation before task demands can be developed.
3. Use the essence of the standards as a rubric for assessing student learning.
   It is easier to determine key aspects students must master if the interpretation of the standards is specific. Rubrics can be developed to verify how well students have mastered the demands of the standards, and, on the basis of student scores, teachers can elect to reteach the specific element of the standard, meet with individual students to discuss, or provide additional applications for students to work through to increase their mastery.
4. Organize standards according to higher-order skills and then teach across subject areas.
   Most state standards include a strand on reasoning within math and science, a strand on communication within language arts and math, a strand on research in language arts (which also is captured as the scientific process in the science standards), and a set of standards related to technology, that may be embedded or stand-alone (VanTassel-Baska, 2003c). These areas of the standards have relevance for all subject areas and could be used to organize direct teaching across subject areas.
5. Accelerate student work in the standards after carefully pretesting within strands and across levels.
   To determine if the standards delineated for particular grade levels within subject areas may be too low level for gifted students in that grade, teachers can pretest students using standards across grade levels. For example, in mathematics, each strand could be pretested with gifted students to ensure appropriate-level work. Standards across multiple grade levels may be collapsed to create a more meaningful instructional module for gifted students, such as in the area of research, if pretesting indicates that acceleration is in order.
6. Design student project choices that address multiple standards within and across subject areas.
   One way to teach effectively to multiple standards is to design student project work around the attainment of several standards. Often this process results in addressing standards across disciplines. At the secondary level, interdisciplinary teams of teachers could plan out such options in advance to focus the project work for the year in a more streamlined way.

This standards modification approach is particularly useful as an alternative to total curriculum change for several reasons. First, the approach starts with the standards, which are familiar and required for all teachers to address. Second, the standards approach also keeps the curriculum focus on the core content dimensions around which schools are organized yet moves beyond basal text materials and forces schools to alter curriculum scope and sequence in the face of individual learner needs. Moreover, the approach allows us to infuse the teaching of such process skills as critical thinking, creative thinking, and research into individual fields of inquiry rather than teach them in isolation. In this way, these skills can adapt to the idiosyncratic nature of individual disciplines rather than be viewed as applicable in all respects to every discipline. Finally, this approach allows for project development that is meaningful in the context of a student's total program of studies.

Through the use of such a standards-based modification model, coupled with appropriate delivery methods, curriculum for gifted learners can maximize its opportunity for being integrated at a policy level in a given school district. Furthermore, differentiation of curriculum in all the basic areas is achieved, thus eliminating fragmentation, gaps, and a general lack of curriculum coordination.

Curriculum Writing: Unit Development. Table 13–3 illustrates the salient aspects of unit development from a content, process/product, and concept perspective. Decisions regarding the topics of the units to be developed should flow out of the earlier phases of data gathering and adaptation. As school districts begin to consider the infusion of process/product curriculum and concept curriculum, frequently the need for teaching units emerges. As new topics are added to the core content areas, the need for new units may surface as well. Thus, careful planning for unit development needs to be undertaken.

CURRICULUM IMPLEMENTATION AND MANAGEMENT

Whether one is adopting a prepackaged curriculum, adapting a currently existing curriculum, or creating new units of instruction, pilot testing is critical. There is often a "leap of faith" that occurs with the development of a curriculum piece. It is assumed that teachers can use it effectively in the dynamic context of the classroom. Frequently, the gulf between intended curriculum and delivered curriculum is great. The piloting stage thus allows individual teachers as well as outside process observers to monitor the use of a new curriculum in a systematic way. Tracking curriculum efficacy at this stage of development also allows the opportunity for important feedback to curriculum writers who may

TABLE 13–3 Sample Outline for Curriculum Units

Unit Elements	Question It Answers
1. General instructions on the use of the unit including grade levels, prerequisite skills, type of learner	Who is the unit for?
2. Unit rationale and goals	What is the purpose of the unit?
3. Unit objectives	What will students learn from the unit?
4. Specific learner activities (including sample questions for discussion, sample exercises, and study sheets)	What will students do? What questions will teachers/ students ask?
5. Dominant teaching strategies	How will teachers carry out instruction?
6. Key materials and other resources	What tools will teachers need to implement this unit in the classroom?
7. Appropriate tests and other evaluative tools such as inventories, checklists, etc.	How will teachers assess student learning?
8. Student self-study material	What aspects of this unit can students explore on their own?
9. Student and teacher references	What books, films, etc. increase understanding about this topic?
10. Relationship of the unit to other aspects of the curriculum	How does this unit fit into the larger curriculum schemata?

Source: From *Comprehensive Curriculum for Gifted Learners* (p. 59), by J. VanTassel-Baska & T. Stambaugh, 2006, Boston: Allyn & Bacon. Copyright © 2006 Pearson Education, Inc. Adapted with permission.

alter and revise learning segments on the basis of teacher or observer responses.

Field-testing, disseminating, and institutionalizing curriculum within the political context of schools is a major phase in the curriculum process (VanTassel-Baska, 2003c). Change agents, including developers of curriculum for the gifted, can encounter many problems along the road of implementation. An effective strategy of curriculum change must therefore proceed on a double agenda, working simultaneously to change ideas about curricula and to change human dynamics. Taba (1962) delineated key issues in the implementation process:

1. Curriculum change requires a systematic sequence of work that deals with all aspects of the curriculum, ranging from goals to means.
2. A strategy for curriculum change involves creating conditions for productive work.
3. Effecting curriculum change involves a large amount of training.
4. Change always involves human and emotional factors.
5. Since curriculum development is extremely complex, it requires many kinds of competencies in different combinations at various points of work.
6. Managing curriculum change requires skilled leadership.

Curriculum implementation should be viewed as the most complex stage of curriculum development, for it involves the translation of ideas from written form into classroom action, the transforming of individuals' thoughts and behaviors to new paradigms, and the accomplishment of this evolution in a reasonable period of time (VanTassel-Baska, 2003c).

Successful implementation of curriculum takes a cooperative and total effort by all staff to ensure a smooth and successful transition. Because one of the first issues of curriculum implementation that confronts educational personnel is deciding on the scope of the implementation effort (VanTassel-Baska, 2003c), it may be useful to limit the unit of analysis utilized in the first stage of implementation by grade levels, content disciplines, or schools.

A second issue in curriculum implementation involves a thorough understanding of the change process on the part of the administrator responsible for instituting it (VanTassel-Baska, 2003c). This understanding, at a very fundamental level, involves an awareness of and appreciation for the school climate into which the curriculum innovation will be placed as well as having a clear idea about how key personnel will respond to the demands placed on them in implementing new curriculum.

A third issue revolves around the selection of staff for the first stage of implementation (VanTassel-Baska, 2003c). Even though the total staff may

1. What is working in this lesson?

2. What is not?

3. What would I change before teaching it again?

FIGURE 13–2 Sample Teacher Log

eventually become involved with several aspects of the gifted curriculum, the number of staff involved with implementation should be limited initially. Willingness and enthusiasm for the new direction, a capacity to adapt curriculum appropriately in the classroom, and an interest in training fellow teachers in the use of the new curriculum all should be considered in criteria for considering staff selection. It is also important to select schools on the basis of the interest and follow-through involvement that may be anticipated at the principal level.

It is rare that curriculum implementation can occur without some problems (VanTassel-Baska, 2003c). One common problem is the lack of supplementary materials to carry out the implementation tasks at the most effective level. In order to maximize the potential for obtaining such materials, several steps should be taken prior to this stage of the process, including the following: establishing lists of the types of materials needed by teachers and students in the course of using the curriculum, setting criteria for selection of such materials, and careful budgeting to ensure purchasing power.

An additional consideration at the implementation stage is a work plan that charts progress (VanTassel-Baska, 2003c). This work plan should detail the implementation schedule according to pivotal points in the process, such as when teachers have demonstrated a full understanding of what the purposes are of the new curriculum and the specifics of how to implement it in the context of the classroom. The work plan should also be revised as the process goes along, with notes recorded on problems or issues encountered along the way. Figure 13–2 illustrates a sample work log that teachers can use.

In addition, it is important to consider the monitoring that needs to occur to ensure that classroom implementation is indeed taking place. Are new materials being used? Are teachers applying appropriate strategies in teaching the new curriculum? Do students respond to what is being implemented? All these questions are important checks on the actual degree of implementation that may be occurring in a given school. It is the responsibility of the administrator of a school and the coordinator of the gifted program to monitor the implementation process according to a predetermined agreement (i.e., with teachers regarding what behaviors and content pedagogy are being looked for in the classroom).

An additional consideration at the implementation stage is to have a process in place that will allow adjustments and adaptations in the curriculum to occur immediately rather than waiting for the next formal phase (VanTassel-Baska, 2003c). If something is not working, then make the necessary changes and document accordingly. Consequently, fine-tuning of the curriculum can occur during implementation rather than being seen as an outcome of evaluation.

A final consideration is that of professional development. Professional development work at this stage of the curriculum development process is another issue vital to the success of the effort (VanTassel-Baska & Stambaugh, 2006b). Professional development tasks critical to the implementation of curriculum include sensitizing and training personnel to use a new curriculum, laying out expectations regarding its implementation, and disseminating the work of the curriculum teams.

Professional development on new curriculum should occur in stages (VanTassel-Baska, & Stambaugh, 2006b). To begin, a 2-day period of time should be set aside for an orientation session. During this session, the implementation plan is presented, and the curriculum teams who piloted the materials are introduced. Outside consultants, if they were utilized in the earlier stages, may serve as presenters or discussants for such an orientation session. Follow-up sessions at 3-month intervals should focus on strengths and weaknesses in the curriculum as it is being used. Classroom observations should also be conducted, including the videotaping of teachers implementing the curriculum for consideration in the curriculum critique. Hence, classroom dynamics become the focus for judging curriculum efficacy by the following criteria:

1. Consonant with curriculum design features (i.e., goals, outcomes, activities/tasks, instructional strategies and management approaches, assessment, and evaluation and revision)
2. Consonant with exemplary features of the content being studied and its related pedagogy
3. Consonant with principles of differentiation for gifted learners (i.e., acceleration, depth, complexity, creativity, and challenge)
4. Consonant with the use of cognitive science principles (i.e., use of concept mapping, metacognitive strategies, teaching for conceptual learning)

CURRICULUM ASSESSMENT AND EVALUATION

Curriculum developers must be concerned with the assessment of learning and effectiveness of the curriculum as much as they are with the planning and execution of it (VanTassel-Baska & Stambaugh, 2006a). The real test of a gifted program is how it answers the guiding question, "What have students learned as a direct result of being in a gifted program over 1 or more years?" Documentation and student data used to answer this question must be collected annually and provided by the program coordinator and by each teacher who has responsibility for instructing these learners so that teachers can make adjustments in their curriculum design to improve student performance the next year.

However, evidence of program success is needed over time in order for gifted education to become an institutionalized part of a school system (VanTassel-Baska & Stambaugh, 2006a). Long-term evaluation of curriculum, including strategies for data collection and analysis, requires a careful evaluation plan that ensures that systematic data are available at key stages of the program. A thorough evaluation of the curriculum should occur every 3 years and include several steps. VanTassel-Baska and Stambaugh (2006a, p.357) suggest the following:

1. **A review of existing curriculum documents, including texts, units of study, and other supplementary materials that frame the substance of content delivery.** These documents should be reviewed according to criteria for general curriculum, criteria for the relevant subject area, and criteria for appropriateness for gifted learners. In respect to gifted learners, the materials used should be advanced, require students to exhibit higher-order processes in order to interact with the materials, and be organized at a conceptual level. Opportunities for open-ended work should abound.
2. **An analysis of classroom instructional practices that reveal patterns of use of higher-order instructional strategies, such as critical thinking, problem solving, creative thinking, and research.** Classroom observation data should be collected annually to use for staff development planning purposes. However, over time, such data should be employed to judge whether instructional practices match desired ones with respect to working effectively with gifted learners.
3. **A trend analysis of gifted student outcome data using standardized on- and off-level tests, performance-based assessments, and portfolios.** These data, examined over a 3-year period, would provide important insights into the efficacy of the curriculum and the program as it has been implemented. Lack of growth among individual cohorts of students over time would signal a need for curriculum change. Lack of student data would signal the need for a clear evaluation design that is activated annually by the coordinator.

The nature of questions to be asked in an evaluation of a curriculum for the gifted over time matters, as do the data sources used to render judgments (Feng & VanTassel-Baska, 2004). The following questions developed by VanTassel-Baska and Stambaugh (2006a, p. 356) may be useful in considering the design of such an evaluation:

1. **What are the patterns of growth in students in the areas in which the gifted program focuses?** A strong gifted program must show evidence of student growth in those areas in which it has chosen to put resources. Thus, if the program has decided to emphasize product development, then the processes underlying the products and the products themselves should demonstrate incremental growth over time.
2. **What are the predominant instructional strategies used by teachers of the gifted to deliver a differentiated curriculum?** Teachers should be employing higher-level strategies in the curriculum areas for which they have responsibility. Evidence of more differentiated strategy use should be documented in these classrooms in comparison to regular education classrooms. Over 60% of the instructional time of gifted learners should be used in the pursuit of higher-level, advanced activities.
3. **What evidence exists that the curriculum is appropriately tailored to the needs of gifted learners?** A curriculum base for the gifted must be effectively differentiated with respect to level, processes emphasized, and products expected. The curriculum should be described in ways that suggest it extends beyond the regular school

curriculum to meet the needs of gifted learners. The curriculum should be well defined in written form so that reviewers can make relevant judgments.

4. **What is the relationship of the gifted curriculum to the standard one?** The curriculum for the gifted should be designed in relationship to state and local standards. Thus, it should reflect desirable learning in the areas identified as important in those standards. However, there is an obligation for the curriculum to go beyond the standards with respect to advanced learning with focus on higher-order skills and processes and an emphasis on creative work.
5. **What are stakeholder perceptions about the efficacy of the curriculum?** How educators, parents, and students themselves view the curriculum is a critical part of curriculum evaluation. Results should suggest commonality across groups with respect to curriculum efficacy, with teachers of the gifted and students often reflecting the most positive reactions to it.
6. **What evidence exists that gifted learners are academically successful when they leave the school district and beyond?** The long-term impact of a gifted curriculum should be seen by the time students graduate from a district. It should be reflected in higher grade-point averages, in higher test scores on relevant off-level assessments like Advanced Placement and International Baccalaureate examinations, and in being accepted to prestigious universities.

Utility of Results

Once the central evaluation questions have been addressed and results obtained through the approaches outlined, then the question arises about how to interpret and use the data to the best advantage (VanTassel-Baska & Stambaugh, 2006a). All evaluation data should be seen as a basis for program improvement (Avery, VanTassel-Baska, & O'Neill, 1997). The first group that should have access to such data and use it for active planning is the gifted program staff, including the teachers and administrators, who should develop an action plan using available data. The action plan should identify specific goals and outcomes along with strategies and assessment procedures on the basis of a thorough analysis of the evaluation. Because gifted program curriculum is most deficient with respect to student outcome data, action plans should focus on methods to improve the processes of assessing student learning as a part of the program.

In addition to action planning by staff, the utility of a curriculum evaluation should be sought by the program administrator by deciding which audiences would benefit from hearing the results and discussing the implications. Such audiences should include, at a minimum, the school board (VanTassel-Baska & Stambaugh, 2006a). Because program improvement usually carries fiscal implications, the board may need to know that more human resources are needed in order to collect assessment data on the program to make good program decisions or that defective curriculum may need to be replaced, adding to the cost of program materials and professional development. Other audiences would include stakeholders such as parents, administrators, and teachers who care about gifted student learning.

SUMMARY AND CONCLUSIONS

This chapter has described what we know as a field about appropriate curriculum for the gifted, the basic considerations for differentiating such a curriculum, and the processes that program developers must accomplish in order to make curriculum work. In educational contexts that may devalue such efforts, in favor of a one-size fits all orientation, it is important to emphasize the mantra that gifted students have a right to learn something new every day. Their needs for advanced learning opportunities cannot be ignored in the rush to impose education for all. The use of sound curriculum design and development practices is one way to institutionalize a differentiated curriculum philosophy in schools. It is a route we must take to ensure optimal learning for our best students.

Designing and developing curriculum for the gifted requires careful attention to three phases of the work: curriculum planning and writing, curriculum implementation and management, and curriculum assessment and evaluation. Only when all three phases are carefully and systematically addressed will strong curriculum emerge, worthy of use with our best learners.

Revision work at each stage of the process is also a key consideration; thus, tools to help with that work are critical to success. The use of classroom observation, teacher log notes, student pre–post results, and careful review by outside experts of the curriculum products enhances the chance for quality curriculum. The involvement of a team approach also ensures that more than one pair of eyes is engaged with the development work at critical periods.

Attention to the learner and his or her defining characteristics and needs continues to have primacy in the thinking of curriculum developers at all stages of the process, nowhere more so than in the revision process where learning outcomes of students can be analyzed for deeper understanding of the flaws in the design process and recycled into a new version of the work.

Curriculum effectiveness, based on evidence of student learning, should be the goal of all curricula designed for gifted learners. The mechanism to pilot and then revise and implement those revisions is crucial for schools to employ to ensure that the best learners are optimally matched to the best curriculum. Only then can we say that gifted education truly has relevance in classrooms.

QUESTIONS FOR THOUGHT AND REFLECTION

1. What are the stages of curriculum development, and why are they each important to the overall result?
2. What models of curriculum may be viable for use with gifted learners? What is the evidence base supporting each of your choices?
3. What is differentiation for gifted learners? How can it be designed into curriculum units of study?
4. Research strongly suggests that the level of the curriculum must be above the tested level of the learner at each stage of development in order to ensure challenge. How can this be accomplished in each subject area?
5. Assessing gifted learning in advanced curriculum requires different assessment tools. What approaches can be successfully applied to make judgments about advanced learning? How do these findings become relevant to curriculum revision?

RESOURCES

Website

The College of William and Mary, Center for Gifted Education

http://cfge.wm.edu

BOOKS

VanTassel-Baska, J. (2003). *Curriculum planning and instructional design for gifted learners.* Denver: Love.

VanTassel-Baska, J., & Little, C. (2003). *Content-based curriculum for high ability learners.* Waco, TX: Prufrock.

VanTassel-Baska, J., & Stambaugh, T. (Eds.). (2006). *Comprehensive curriculum for gifted learners.* Boston: Allyn & Bacon.

WILLIAM & MARY RESEARCH-BASED CURRICULUM DESIGNED FOR GIFTED LEARNERS

Language Arts

The College of William & Mary Center for Gifted Education. (1997). *Change through choices.* Williamsburg, VA: Author.

The College of William & Mary Center for Gifted Education. (1998). *Language arts unit: Autobiographies.* Dubuque, IA: Kendall/Hunt.

The College of William & Mary Center for Gifted Education. (1998). *Language arts unit: Journeys and destinations.* Dubuque, IA: Kendall/Hunt.

The College of William & Mary Center for Gifted Education. (1998). *Language arts unit: Persuasion.* Dubuque, IA: Kendall/Hunt.

The College of William & Mary Center for Gifted Education. (1998). *Language arts unit: The 1940s: A decade of change.* Dubuque, IA: Kendall/Hunt.

The College of William & Mary Center for Gifted Education. (1998). *Language arts unit: Threads of change in 19th century American literature.* Dubuque, IA: Kendall/Hunt.

The College of William & Mary Center for Gifted Education. (2000). *Language arts unit: Literary reflections.* Dubuque, IA: Kendall/Hunt.

The College of William & Mary Center for Gifted Education. (2001). *Language arts unit: Beyond words.* Dubuque, IA: Kendall/Hunt.

The College of William & Mary Center for Gifted Education. (2003). *Language arts unit: Patterns of change.* Dubuque, IA: Kendall/Hunt.

The College of William & Mary Center for Gifted Education. (2003). *Language arts unit: Utopia.* Dubuque, IA: Kendall/Hunt.

Navigators

The *Navigators* are a series of novel study guides developed as a resource for teachers and students. These guides encourage advanced readers to develop their skills at analyzing and interpreting literature through structured questions and activated that highlight themes and concepts, literary elements, and real-world connections contained within the books. Students are also able to develop their own vocabulary and writing skills by exploring and emulating the language and style used by different authors. In addition, several research activities are included in each *Navigator.*

Baska, A. (2004). *Navigator: Twelfth night.* Williamsburg, VA: The College of William & Mary Center for Gifted Education.

Baytops, J. (2003–2004). *Navigator: Bud, not buddy.* Williamsburg, VA: The College of William & Mary Center for Gifted Education.

Baytops, J. (2003–2004). *Navigator: Talk about a family.* Williamsburg, VA: The College of William & Mary Center for Gifted Education.

Beeler, R. (2003–2004). *Navigator: An angel for Solomon Singer.* Williamsburg, VA: The College of William & Mary Center for Gifted Education.

Beeler, R. (2003–2004). *Navigator: The garden of Abdul Gasazi.* Williamsburg, VA: The College of William & Mary Center for Gifted Education.

Benson, D. (2002). *Navigator: The dark is rising.* Williamsburg, VA: The College of William & Mary Center for Gifted Education.

Benson, D., & McGowan, S. (2004). *Navigator: The day they came to arrest the book.* Williamsburg, VA: The College of William & Mary Center for Gifted Education.

Brigham-Lampert, R. (2004). *Navigator: Hamlet.* Williamsburg, VA: The College of William & Mary Center for Gifted Education.

Brigham-Lampert, R. (2004). *Navigator: Henry IV, part 1.* Williamsburg, VA: The College of William & Mary Center for Gifted Education.

Brown, E. (2002). *Navigator: Number the stars.* Williamsburg, VA: The College of William & Mary Center for Gifted Education.

Carey, M. (2002). *Navigator: The Egypt game.* Williamsburg, VA: The College of William & Mary Center for Gifted Education.

Carey, M. (2003–2004). *Navigator: Charlie and the chocolate factory.* Williamsburg, VA: The College of William & Mary Center for Gifted Education.

French, H. (2003–2004). *Navigator: The door in the wall.* Williamsburg, VA: The College of William & Mary Center for Gifted Education.

Ginsburgh, P. (2004). *Navigator: Call of the wild.* Williamsburg, VA: The College of William & Mary Center for Gifted Education.

Henshon, S. (2002). *Navigator: Sarah, plain and tall.* Williamsburg, VA: The College of William & Mary Center for Gifted Education.

Little, C. (2002). *Navigator: Everything on a waffle.* Williamsburg, VA: The College of William & Mary Center for Gifted Education.

Little, C. (2003). *Navigator: Charlotte's web.* Williamsburg, VA: The College of William & Mary Center for Gifted Education.

Little, C. (2003). *Navigator: Summer of my German soldier.* Williamsburg, VA: The College of William & Mary Center for Gifted Education.

Massey, H. (2002). *Navigator: Tuck everlasting.* Williamsburg, VA: The College of William & Mary Center for Gifted Education.

Pleiss, M. (2005). *Navigator: A year down yonder.* Williamsburg, VA: The College of William & Mary Center for Gifted Education.

Pleiss, M. (2005). *Navigator: The great Gilly Hopkins.* Williamsburg, VA: The College of William & Mary Center for Gifted Education.

Struck, J. (2003). *Navigator: Snow treasure.* Williamsburg, VA: The College of William & Mary Center for Gifted Education.

VanTassel-Baska, J. (2002). *Navigator: Walk two moons.* Williamsburg, VA: The College of William & Mary Center for Gifted Education.

Worley, B. (2003). *Navigator: Sarah Bishop.* Williamsburg, VA: The College of William & Mary Center for Gifted Education.

Science

These curriculum units contain simulation of real-world problems that face today's society. The units are geared toward different grade-level clusters yet can be adapted for use at all levels K–8. The goals of each unit are to allow students to analyze several real-world problems, understand the concept of systems, and design and conduct scientific experiments. These units also allow students to explore various scientific topics and identify meaningful scientific problems for investigation. Through these units, students experience the work of real science in applying data-handling skills, analyzing information, evaluation results, and learning to communicate their understanding to others. A guide to using the curriculum is also available.

The College of William & Mary Center for Gifted Education. (1997). *Guide to teaching a problem-based science curriculum.* Dubuque, IA: Kendall/Hunt.

The College of William & Mary Center for Gifted Education. (1997). *Science unit: Acid, acid everywhere.* Dubuque, IA: Kendall/Hunt.

The College of William & Mary Center for Gifted Education. (1997). *Science unit: The Chesapeake Bay.* Dubuque, IA: Kendall/Hunt.

The College of William & Mary Center for Gifted Education. (1997). *Science unit: Dust Bowl.* Dubuque, IA: Kendall/Hunt.

The College of William & Mary Center for Gifted Education. (1997). *Science unit: Electricity city.* Dubuque, IA: Kendall/Hunt.

The College of William & Mary Center for Gifted Education. (1997). *Science unit: Hot rods.* Dubuque, IA: Kendall/Hunt.

The College of William & Mary Center for Gifted Education.(1997). *Science unit: No quick fix.* Dubuque, IA: Kendall/Hunt.

The College of William & Mary Center for Gifted Education. (1999). *Science unit: What a find!* Dubuque, IA: Kendall/Hunt.

Clarion Science Units for Primary Grades

The Clarion Science Units for Primary Grades have been designed to introduce young students to science concepts, science processes, and overarching concepts. A hands-on, constructivist approach is used to allow children to build their knowledge base and their skills as they explore science topics through play and planned investigations. Students are engaged in creative and critical thinking, problem finding and solving, process skill development, and communication opportunities. Each unit is designed to strengthen essential concepts, including quantity, direction/position, comparison, colors, letter identification, numbers/counting, size, self- and social awareness, texture/material, shape, and time/sequence. The units also focus on overarching concepts of systems, patterns, change, and cause and effect.

The College of William & Mary Center for Gifted Education: Project Clarion. (2004–2005). *Changes in earth and sky* (K). Williamsburg, VA: Author.

The College of William & Mary Center for Gifted Education: Project Clarion. (2004–2005). *Commotion in motion: Investigation in force and motion.* (grade 1). Williamsburg, VA: Author.

The College of William & Mary Center for Gifted Education: Project Clarion. (2004–2005). *Going full circle* (K). Williamsburg, VA: Author.

The College of William & Mary Center for Gifted Education: Project Clarion. (2004–2005). *Investigating simple machines* (grade 3). Williamsburg, VA: Author.

The College of William & Mary Center for Gifted Education: Project Clarion. (2004–2005). *Lots and lots of stripes and spots* (pre-K). Williamsburg, VA: Author.

The College of William & Mary Center for Gifted Education: Project Clarion. (2004–2005). *Natural and man-made environmental changes* (grade 1). Williamsburg, VA: Author.

The College of William & Mary Center for Gifted Education: Project Clarion. (2004–2005). *Return of the wolves* (grade 3). Williamsburg, VA: Author.

The College of William & Mary Center for Gifted Education: Project Clarion. (2004–2005). *Save it! Everything comes from something* (grade 3). Williamsburg, VA: Author.

The College of William & Mary Center for Gifted Education: Project Clarion. (2004–2005). *Tinkering with toys* (K). Williamsburg, VA: Author.

Fithian, E. (2004–2005). *What's the matter?* (grade 2). Williamsburg, VA: The College of William & Mary Center for Gifted Education.

Holub, C. (2004–2005). *Budding botanists* (grade 2). Williamsburg, VA: The College of William & Mary Center for Gifted Education.

Social Studies

The social studies units utilize a heavy emphasis on primary source analysis, critical thinking, and concept development to help students develop understanding of high-level social studies content in key areas. Thus, the units reflect the focus of national and state-level standards on historical thinking and research and on the integrating of major concepts across disciplines. The unit series covers a wide range of topics while maintaining consistent models for understanding issues, documents, and artifacts. Interdisciplinary connections are explored through in-class activities and student projects. The units also emphasize the development of student skills in the areas of discussion, writing, and research.

The College of William & Mary Center for Gifted Education. (2002). *Social studies unit: The 1920s in America: A decade of tensions.* Dubuque, IA: Kendall/Hunt.

The College of William & Mary Center for Gifted Education. (2003). *Social studies unit: A house divided? The Civil War, its causes and effects.* Dubuque, IA: Kendall/Hunt.

The College of William & Mary Center for Gifted Education. (2003). *Social studies unit: Ancient Egypt: Gift of the Nile.* Dubuque, IA: Kendall/Hunt.

The College of William & Mary Center for Gifted Education. (2003). *Social studies unit: Building a new system: Colonial America 1607–1763.* Dubuque, IA: Kendall/Hunt.

The College of William & Mary Center for Gifted Education. (2003). *Social studies unit: The 1930s in America: Facing Depression.* Dubuque, IA: Kendall/Hunt.

The College of William & Mary Center for Gifted Education. (2003). *Social studies unit: The road to the White House: Electing the American president.* Dubuque, IA: Kendall/Hunt.

The College of William & Mary Center for Gifted Education. (2003). *Social studies unit: The world turned upside down: The American Revolution.* Dubuque, IA: Kendall/Hunt.

The College of William & Mary Center for Gifted Education. (2004). *Social studies unit: Ancient China: The Middle Kingdom.* Dubuque, IA: Kendall/Hunt.

The College of William & Mary Center for Gifted Education. (2005). *Social studies unit: The Renaissance and Reformation in Europe.* Dubuque, IA: Kendall/Hunt.

The College of William & Mary Center for Gifted Education. (2006). *Social studies unit: Defining Nations: Cultural identity and political tension.* Dubuque, IA: Kendall/Hunt.

The College of William & Mary Center for Gifted Education. (2006). *Social studies unit: Primary sources and historical analysis.* Dubuque, IA: Kendall/Hunt.

Mathematics

The mathematics units emphasize the development of student skills in the areas of mathematical computation and spatial reasoning.

Johnson, D. (2005). *Math unit: Numbers and numerals: On what are they based?* Williamsburg, VA: The College of William & Mary Center for Gifted Education.

Johnson, D. (2005). *Math unit: Spatial reasoning.* Williamsburg, VA: The College of William & Mary Center for Gifted Education.

OTHER CURRICULUM

Mathematics

Hands-On Equations
www.borenson.com
This program for advanced elementary students provides a sound foundation for algebraic skills using manipulatives to illustrate abstract concepts

Mathematics the Human Endeavor
www.whfreeman.com
This textbook teaches advanced mathematical concepts in an applied way. Landmark mathematical problems such as the billiard problem and the birthday problem are included.

Social Studies

Contemporary Perspectives Series
www.gale.com/greenhaven
This series includes pro and con articles on a variety of contemporary and historical issues for students to examine multiple perspectives and defend a perspective through debate or essay.

Law Related Education Programs
www.abanet.org/publiced (see Educators link)
This supplementary program provides curriculum and contest options such as Mock Trial or other simulated debate and trial opportunities on varied social studies topics

Science

A GEMS (Great Explorations in Math and Science)
www.lhsgems.org/gems.html
This science series is rated as an Exemplary or Promising Program by the U.S. Department of Education, 2001. Each unit includes an integrated approach to learning content through scientific processes such as inquiry, experimentation, and reporting results.

Modeling Instruction in High School Physics
http://modeling.la.asu.edu/modeling-HS.html
This research-based high school physics program is on the Exemplary or Promising Science Program list as rated by the U.S. Department of Education, 2001.

Language Arts

The Magic Lens and The Word Within A Word
(vols. 1 & 2) by Michael Clay Thompson; Trillium Press
Both of these series provide students with the linguistic competencies to study vocabulary by examining word etymology, word roots, prefixes, suffixes, and grammar.

Junior Great Books
www.greatbooks.org
Junior Great Books applies Socratic questioning methods to enhance students' critical reading skills. This research-based program is one of the only national reform reading programs that reports growth in critical thinking.

REFERENCES

Avery, L. D., VanTassel-Baska, J., & O'Neill, B. (1997). Making evaluation work: One school district's experience. *Gifted Child Quarterly,* 41, 124–132.

Baum, S. (1988). An enrichment program for gifted learning disabled students. *Gifted Child Quarterly, 32,* 226–230.

Baum, S., Renzulli, J., & Hébert. T. P. (1995). Reversing under-achievement: Creative productivity as a systematic intervention. *Gifted Child Quarterly, 39,* 224–235.

Benbow, C. P., & Arjmand, O. (1990). Predictors of high academic achievement in mathematics and science by mathematically talented students: A longitudinal study. *Journal of Educational Psychology, 82,* 430–431.

Betts, G. T. (1986). The Autonomous Learner Model for the gifted and talented. In J. S. Renzulli (Ed.), *Systems and models for developing programs for the gifted and talented* (pp. 27–56). Mansfield Center, CT: Creative Learning Press.

Betts, G. T., & Knapp, J. (1980). Autonomous learning and the gifted: A secondary model. In A. Arnold (Ed.), *Secondary programs for the gifted* (pp. 29–36). Ventura, CA: Ventura Superintendent of Schools Office.

Burns, D. (1988). The effects of group training activities on students' creative productivity. In J. S. Renzulli (Ed.), *Technical report of research studies related to the Revolving Door Identification Model* (2nd ed., pp. 147–174). Storrs: Research Report Series, School of Education, University of Connecticut.

Colangelo, N., Assouline, S. G., & Gross, M. (2004). *A nation deceived: How schools hold back America's brightest students.* Iowa City: University of Iowa.

Delcourt, M. A. B. (1993). Creative productivity among secondary school students: Combining energy, interest, and imagination. *Gifted Child Quarterly, 37,* 23–31.

Delcourt, M. A. B. (1994). Characteristics of high-level creative productivity: A longitudinal study of students identified by Renzulli's three misconceptions of greatness. In R. Subotnik & K. D. Arnold (Eds.), *Beyond Terman: Contemporary longitudinal studies of giftedness and talent* (pp. 375–400). Norwood, NJ: Ablex.

Demitriou, A., & Valanides, N. (1998). A three-level theory of the developing mind: Basic principles and implications for instruction and assessment. In R. Sternberg & W. Williams (Eds.), *Intelligence, instruction and assessment* (pp. 149–199). Mahwah, NJ: Lawrence Erlbaum Associates.

Feldhusen, J. F., & Kolloff, M. B. (1986). The Purdue Three-Stage Model for gifted education. In J. S. Renzulli (Ed.), *Systems and models for developing programs for the gifted and talented* (pp. 126–152). Mansfield Center, CT: Creative Learning Press.

Feldhusen, J. F., & Robinson-Wyman, A. (1986). The Purdue Secondary Model for gifted education. In J. S. Renzulli (Ed.), *Models for developing programs for the gifted and talented* (pp. 153–179). Mansfield Center, CT: Creative Learning Press.

Feng, A., & VanTassel-Baska, J. (2004). Collecting student impact data in gifted programs: Problems and processes. In J. VanTassel-Baska & A. Feng (Eds.), *Designing and utilizing evaluation for gifted program improvement* (pp. 133–154). Waco, TX: Prufrock.

Gardner, H. (1983). *Frames of mind: The theory of multiple intelligences.* New York: Basic Books.

Guilford, J. P. (1967). *The nature of human intelligence.* New York: McGraw-Hill.

Hébert, T. P. (1993). Reflections at graduation: The long-term impact of elementary school experiences in creative productivity. *Roeper Review, 16,* 22–28.

Karnes, F. A., & Stephens, K. R. (2000). *The ultimate guide for student product development and evaluation.* Waco, TX: Prufrock.

Keating, D. P. (Ed.). (1976). *Intellectual talent: Research and development.* Baltimore: Johns Hopkins University Press.

Kolloff, P. B., & Feldhusen, J. F. (1984). The effects of enrichment on self-concept and creative thinking. *Gifted Child Quarterly, 28,* 53–57.

Kulik, J., & Kulik, C. L. (1992). Meta analytic findings on grouping programs. *Gifted Child Quarterly, 36,* 73–77.

Latham, A. S. (1997). Quantifying MI's gains. *Educational Leadership, 55*(1), 84–85.

Little, C. A., Feng, A. X., VanTassel-Baska, J., Rogers, K. B., & Avery, L. D. (2002). *Final report on social studies curriculum effectiveness study.* Williamsburg, VA: College of Willam & Mary Center for Gifted Education.

Lubinski, D., & Benbow, C. P. (1994). The study of mathematically precocious youth: The first three decades of a planned 50-year study of intellectual talent. In R. Subotnik & K. D. Arnold (Eds.), *Beyond Terman: Contemporary longitudinal studies of giftedness and talent* (pp. 375–400). Norwood, NJ: Ablex.

Maker, C. J., & Nielson, A.G. (1996a). *Curriculum development and teaching strategies for gifted learners* (2nd ed.) Austin, TX: PRO-ED.

Maker, C. J., & Nielson, A. B. (1996b). *Teaching models in education of the gifted* (2nd ed.). Austin, TX: PRO-ED.

Maker, C. J., Nielson, A. B., & Rogers, J. A. (1994). Multiple intelligences: Giftedness, diversity, and problem solving. *Teaching Exceptional Children, 27,* 4–19.

McLean, J. E., & Chisson, B. S. (1980). *Talents Unlimited program: Summary of research findings for 1979–80.* Mobile, AL: Mobile County Public Schools.

Moon, S. M., & Feldhusen, J. F. (1994). The program for academic and creative enrichment (PACE): A follow-up study 10 years later. In R. Subotnik & K. D. Arnold (Eds.), *Beyond Terman: Contemporary longitudinal studies of giftedness and talent* (pp. 375–400). Norwood, NJ: Ablex.

Moon, S. M., Feldhusen, J. F., & Dillon, D. R. (1994). Long-term effects of an enrichment program based on the Purdue Three-Stage Model. *Gifted Child Quarterly, 38,* 38–48.

Olenchak, F. R., & Renzulli, J. S. (1989). The effectiveness of the Schoolwide Enrichment Model on selected aspects of elementary school change. *Gifted Child Quarterly, 33,* 36–46.

Reis, S. M., & Purcell, J. H. (1993). An analysis of content elimination and strategies used by elementary classroom teachers in the curriculum compacting process. *Journal for the Education of the Gifted, 16,* 147–170.

Reis, S. M., Westberg, K. L., Kulikowich, J. M., & Purcell, J. H. (1998). Curriculum compacting and achievement test scores: What does the research say? *Gifted Child Quarterly, 42,* 123–129.

Renzulli, J. S. (1977). *The Enrichment Triad Model: A guide for developing defensible programs for the gifted and talented.* Mansfield Center, CT: Creative Learning Press.

Renzulli, J. S. (1986). *Systems and models for developing programs for the gifted and talented.* Mansfield Center, CT: Creative Learning Press.

Renzulli, J. S. (Ed.). (1988). *Technical report of research studies related to the Revolving Door Identification Model.* Storrs: Bureau of Educational Research, University of Connecticut.

Renzulli, J. S., Reis, S. M., & Smith, L. (1981). The Revolving-Door Model: A new way of identifying the gifted. *Phi Delta Kappan, 62,* 648–649.

Rodd, J. (1999). Encouraging young children's critical and creative thinking skills: An approach in one English elementary school. *Childhood Education, 75,* 350–354.

Schack, G. D., Starko, A. J., & Burns, D. E. (1991). Self-efficacy and creative productivity: Three studies of above average ability children. *Journal of Research in Education, 1,* 44–52.

Schlichter, C. (1986). Talents Unlimited: Applying the multiple talent approach in mainstream and gifted programs. In J. S. Renzulli (Ed.), *Systems and models for developing programs for the gifted and talented.* Mansfield Center, CT: Creative Learning Press.

Schlichter, C. L., & Palmer, W. R. (Eds.). (1993). *Thinking smart: A premiere of the Talents Unlimited model.* Mansfield Center, CT: Creative Learning Press.

Smith, W., Odhiambo, E., & El Khateeb, H. (2000, November). *The typologies of successful and unsuccessful students in the core subjects of language arts, mathematics, science, and social studies using the theory of multiple intelligences in a high school environment in Tennessee.* Paper presented at the annual meeting of the Mid-South Educational Research Association, Bowling Green, KY.

Stanley, J. C., Keating, D., & Fox, L. (1974). *Mathematical talent.* Baltimore: Johns Hopkins University Press.

Sternberg, R. (1981). A componential theory of intellectual giftedness. *Gifted Child Quarterly, 25,* 86–93.

Sternberg, R., & Clinkenbeard, P. R. (1995). A triarchic model applied to identifying, teaching, and assessing gifted children. *Roeper Review, 17,* 255–260.

Sternberg, R. J., Ferrari, M., Clinkenbeard, P., & Grigorenko, E. L. (1996). Identification, instruction, and assessment of gifted children: A construct validation of a triarchic model. *Gifted Child Quarterly, 40,* 129–137.

Sternberg, R. J., Torff, B., & Grigorenko, E. L. (1998a). Teaching for successful intelligence raises school achievement. *Phi Delta Kappan, 79,* 667–699.

Sternberg, R. J., Torff, B., & Grigorenko, E. L. (1998b). Teaching triarchically improves school achievement. *Journal of Educational Psychology, 90,* 374–384.

Strahan, D., Summey, H., & Banks, N. (1996). Teaching to diversity through multiple intelligences: Student and teacher responses to instructional improvement. *Research in Middle Level Education Quarterly, 19,* 43–65.

Swiatek, M. A. (2000). A decade of longitudinal research on academic acceleration through the study of mathematically precocious youth. *Roeper Review, 24,* 141–144.

Taba, H. (1962). *Curriculum development, theory, and practice.* New York: Harcourt, Brace, & World.

Taylor, C. W., Ghiselin, B., Wolfer, J., Loy, L., & Bourne, L. E., Jr. (1964). *Development of a theory of education from psychology and other basic research findings* (Final Report, USOE Cooperative Research Project, No. 621). Salt Lake City: University of Utah.

Tomlinson, C. A., Kaplan, S. N., Renzulli, J. S., Purcell, J., Leppien, J., & Burns, D. (2002). *The parallel curriculum: A design to develop high potential and challenge high-ability learners.* Washington, DC: National Association for Gifted Children.

VanTassel-Baska, J. (1986). Effective curriculum and instruction models for talented students. *Gifted Child Quarterly, 30,* 164–169.

VanTassel-Baska, J. (2003a). The nature and curriculum needs of gifted learners. In *Curriculum Planning and instructional design for gifted learners* (pp. 83–106). Denver: Love.

VanTassel-Baska, J. (2003b). Research on curriculum models in gifted education. In *Curriculum Planning and instructional design for gifted learners* (pp. 13–34). Denver: Love.

VanTassel-Baska, J. (2003c). Standards of learning and gifted education. In *Curriculum Planning and instructional design for gifted learners* (pp. 205–222). Denver: Love.

VanTassel-Baska, J. (2005). Domain-specific giftedness: Applications in school and life. In R. J. Sternberg & J. E. Davidson (Eds.), *Conceptions of giftedness* (pp. 358–376). New York: Cambridge University Press.

VanTassel-Baska, J., Avery, L. D., Little, C. A., & Hughes, C. E. (2000). An evaluation of the implementation: The impact of the William and Mary units on schools. *Journal for the Education of the Gifted, 23,* 244–272.

VanTassel-Baska, J., Bass, G. M., Ries, R. R., Poland, D. L., & Avery, L. D. (1998). A national study of science curriculum effectiveness with high ability students. *Gifted Child Quarterly, 42,* 200–211.

VanTassel-Baska, J., & Bracken, B. (2006). *Evaluation report to the United States Department of Education Javits Program.* Williamsburg, VA: College of William and Mary Center for Gifted Education.

VanTassel-Baska, J., Johnson, D. T., Hughes, C. E., & Boyce, L. N. (1996). A study of the language arts curriculum effectiveness with gifted learners. *Journal for the Education of the Gifted, 19,* 461–480.

VanTassel-Baska, J., & Stambaugh, T. (2006a). Assessment of gifted student learning. In *Comprehensive curriculum for gifted learners* (pp. 346–360). Boston: Allyn & Bacon.

VanTassel-Baska, J., & Stambaugh, T. (2006b). Curriculum development process. In *Comprehensive curriculum for gifted learners* (pp. 31–45). Boston: Allyn & Bacon.

VanTassel-Baska, J., Zuo, L., Avery, L. D., & Little, C. A. (2002). A curriculum study of gifted student learning in the language arts. *Gifted Child Quarterly, 46,* 30–44.

CHAPTER 14

ASSESSING AND IMPROVING SERVICES PROVIDED TO GIFTED STUDENTS: A PLAN FOR PROGRAM EVALUATION

Carolyn M. Callahan, Ph.D.
University of Virginia

INTRODUCTION

How well is the gifted program serving the students in your school? Are students achieving the goals and objectives of particular lessons and units? Are they moving toward attainment of the goals of the program? Why or why not? Answers to these and many other questions about the quality of gifted programs are necessary to ensure that high-quality educational programs are offered to gifted students. While schools evaluate our students and provide them with grades and feedback, they seldom scrutinize the services offered to the students with the same careful lens. As with any educational enterprise, constant examination of practice is necessary to ensure that goals are accomplished, and strategies should be revised accordingly to improve all aspects of educational programs, including the curriculum and instruction.

Certainly everyone involved in developing and delivering instruction and services to gifted and talented students should be making decisions on the basis of a body of theory and research. Using such knowledge, sound decisions are made, and quality programs can be implemented at the local level. However, once these programs are established, systematic information should be gathered about their effectiveness. If such evaluations do not occur, valuable educational time is wasted, resources are squandered, and a false sense of confidence prevails. Reliable and valid feedback identifies how programs can be improved, provides an assessment of student achievement that can be attributed to program efforts, and allows the overall impact of the program to be effectively communicated to the public.

WHY CAN'T WE JUST RELY ON "BEST PRACTICE" GUIDES AND GOOD PLANNING?

Best practices and standards such as those endorsed by the National Association for Gifted Children (NAGC; Landrum, Callahan, & Shaklee, 2001) can serve as guides in planning and revising programs. Appropriate implementation in the right context with specific groups of students should lead to expected outcomes. However, as with many things, there is often a large gap between intentions and practice. What translates into best practice in one school setting or classroom may not translate into best practice in another. The ways in which individual administrators and teachers translate best practice guidelines into program administration, curriculum, or classroom instruction may be flawed in minor or fundamental ways. As a result, inadequate services and inferior learning opportunities may persist.

The time has passed when the good intentions of educators will suffice. It is critical that programs are evaluated on the basis of the degree to which they are driven by sound theory and research and their implementation represents best practice. Further, it is imperative to confirm, through thorough and sound evaluations, that similar outcomes would not have been achieved without the specialized educational services provided by the gifted program. Sustainability of a quality gifted program requires the continued examination and evaluation of services to gifted students.

MODELS OF PROGRAM EVALUATION

General Models

Many models for evaluating educational programs representing differing philosophical approaches have been used to evaluate gifted programs. Fitzpatrick, Sanders, and Worthen (2004) classify these into five categories: objectives oriented, management oriented, consumer oriented, expertise oriented, and participant oriented.

Objectives Oriented. When evaluators focus on specifying goals and objectives and judging the degree to which those have been achieved, their methodology is referred to as objectives-oriented evaluation. The first model in this category was developed by Tyler (1942). A similar model, the Discrepancy Evaluation Model (Provus, 1971), focuses on identifying all the components of a program, the program resources (inputs), program activities (processes), and the objectives or expected outcomes (outputs) and provides a guide to the evaluator in assessing the ways the relationships between these components work toward achieving program goals, the degree to which goals and objectives are achieved, and the contributions or limitations of certain components in contributing to program success. The outcomes-oriented model was directly countered by Scriven's (1972) proposal of goal-free evaluation. Scriven advocated for not assuming that goals were a given or necessarily appropriate. When this approach is used, the goals and their worthiness should be examined as part of the evaluation process, and evaluation should focus on *actual* outcomes, not just intended outcomes.

Management Oriented. Evaluations designed to assist decision makers in the collection of data directly related to issues of program operation, such as Stufflebeam's (2001) CIPP model (context, input, process, and product), are called management evaluation models. Stufflebeam outlined four categories of focus for examining components of educational programs. In using this model, the evaluator will focus on (a) the situation in which a program exists and evaluate the program relative to the potential for productivity that the environment provides, (b) the resources available to the program and whether they are adequate for the program design and are being used effectively and efficiently, (c) the activities of the program to judge whether they are being implemented as planned and that they are likely to produce desired goals, and (d) the outcomes of the program to ascertain whether the goals of the program have been achieved.

Consumer Oriented. Consumer-oriented evaluation approaches are used primarily in evaluating education materials. These models are generally applied to educational products in relation to particular educational contexts. An evaluator may, for example, be asked to evaluate the effectiveness of The materials that constitute a whole program of studies, such as The William & Mary curriculum model products, or a particular book, medium, or website, such as Web Quest. In these evaluations, the evaluators are attending primarily to categories of information of interest to the potential users of materials. For example, in evaluation of a new instrument to be used in assessing giftedness, the evaluator would consider the cost, the ease of administration of the instrument, the likelihood that qualified staff would be available to administer the instrument, the readability and appropriateness of reading level for the target student group, and so on.

Expertise Oriented. In expertise-oriented models, the focus is on using professional expertise to judge the institution, program, product, or curriculum. The model of evaluation that falls within this category and that most educators are familiar with is the accreditation or certification model. In this model, aspects of a program are evaluated against a set of standards established by an accrediting agency (e.g., public school accreditations that are carried out by state departments of education). Eisner (1975, 1991) notes that this model is reliant on connoisseurship and criticism (the art of appreciation and "the art of disclosing the qualities of events objects" [p. 197]).

Participant Oriented. Stake (1967) provided the impetus for participant-oriented evaluation, which begins by focusing on the values and needs of the individuals and groups served by the program. This form of evaluation has evolved into responsive evaluation and case study approaches, such as the methods outlined by Lincoln and Guba (1985) and Stake (1995). These models have been widely used in evaluations focusing on in-depth understanding of how a program is functioning with regard to the values and interests of all the stakeholders[1] involved and have a basis in qualitative methodology.

Patton (1997, 2002) has advocated utilization-focused evaluation, which focuses on using stakeholders to identify the ways in which evaluation data will be utilized. This model is similar to responsive evaluation (Stake, 1980), which seeks to provide differing data to meet the needs of differing stakeholder groups.

As Fitzpatrick et al. (2004) indicate, no research exists that clearly identifies the relative merits of one model over the other in the realm of evaluating either general education programs or gifted programs, leaving the choice among alternatives a matter of the evaluator's preference and the purpose of the evaluation.

Gifted Education Program Evaluation Models

In gifted education, three models have evolved on the basis of an amalgamation of the principles and approaches of the standard models in the general field of program evaluation.

Key Features Model. The first to emerge in the literature was the Key Features Model (Renzulli, 1975). In this model, prime interest groups are identified and then surveyed and interviewed to determine the major concerns or questions they deem important to examine. The organization of these issues and questions about the key features of program quality, identified by Renzulli in earlier research, serve as a basis for proceeding to gather data.

Modified Discrepancy Evaluation Model. Callahan and Caldwell (1995) developed the Discrepancy Evaluation Model, which was updated on the basis of the current emphasis on stakeholder input and concerns that emerged from the responsive evaluation models. Still focusing on evaluating the adequacy of the resources expended by the program and the activities carried out in pursuit of achieving student outcomes appropriate for gifted students, the evaluator begins with a description of the gifted program and then identifies and confirms the major operations and desired outcomes of the program identified by stakeholders. Outcomes are identified for every component (e.g., students who are identified using current best practice in gifted identification, a curriculum that is matched to the needs of identified students, and staff development that has changed teacher behavior in specified ways), including student outcomes (e.g., increase in the number of students who enroll in Advanced Placement [AP] courses and earn scores greater than 3 on the AP exam). Evaluation questions are then developed to examine the degree to which the various components contribute effective and efficient program implementation and assessment of outcomes.

William & Mary Model. Finally, an eclectic model, the William & Mary Model, has been outlined by VanTassel–Baska and Feng (2004) and is based on the responsive evaluation model of Stufflebeam (2001) and the utilization model of Patton (1997, 2002). The steps in this model include determining evaluation purposes and questions, creating an evaluation design, creating or tailoring instruments, implementing the evaluation design through data collection, analyzing and cross-validating data, and answering evaluation questions.

Basic Principles and Issues in Evaluating Services Provided to Gifted Students

All these models are similar in basic principles, and all evaluations of gifted services must grapple with a particular set of unique issues. The principles are best summarized in the Program Evaluation Standards developed by the Joint Committee on Standards for Educational Evaluation (1994). This set of principles is organized around the *utility* of the information that is collected and reported, the *feasibility* of collecting the data needed, the *propriety* of the design (ethical and moral standards), and the *accuracy* of information. These standards are designed to ensure that the time and effort devoted to collecting data is effectively and efficiently expended in documenting program outcomes and in improving program functioning. Table 14–1 presents these standards and sample interpretations of the standards relative to the evaluation of gifted programs.

GETTING STARTED

The goal of program evaluation should be to maximize the effectiveness and efficiency of the program offered to gifted students through the systematic collection and interpretation of data. A good education plan to achieve that goal begins with a plan to do what is manageable. It is self-defeating to try to do more than resources or time will support. Further, to ensure that data will be utilized and that recommendations from the evaluation

[1] Stakeholders are all those individuals who are either affected by the gifted program directly (e.g., gifted students, their parents, and teachers of the gifted), may be affected indirectly (e.g., other students in the school, regular classroom teachers, and building level administrators), or may have a vested interest in the success of the program (e.g., school board members and superintendents).

TABLE 14–1 Program Evaluation Standards Summarized with Illustrative Interpretations

Standard	Illustrative Interpretation in Evaluation of Services for Gifted Students
Utility	
Stakeholders (persons involved in or affected by the evaluation) are identified, and their needs and interests are considered.	Concerns that parents of gifted students might have are addressed in the evaluation questions (e.g., Does leaving the classroom to go to a resource room have negative effects on my child's social relationship?).
The persons carrying out the evaluation are trustworthy and competent.	The evaluators know both good procedures for carrying out an evaluation and good practice in delivering curriculum and services to gifted students.
Data should address important and relevant evaluation questions that are of interest to stakeholders and decision makers.	Issues of equity in identification processes are addressed in order to ensure that all members of the community view the process as fair and unbiased. Evidence is collected that documents achievement of program goals.
The bases for making judgments are clear, and the reporting process provides information that is easily understood and interpreted.	The evaluation identifies whether goals have been achieved and *why* or *why not*.
Data are presented in a timely fashion that includes interim feedback if necessary. There should be clear direction for and encouragement for follow-through by stakeholders.	If the evaluation data suggest there are needed changes to ensure that staff have the instructional skills to appropriately differentiate, those data are presented in time to affect the budget and scheduling of the next year's staff development program.
Feasibility	
Evaluation procedures should collect information necessary to answer questions but be practical and minimize disruptions.	It is not necessary to do classroom observations in all schools and all classrooms. But in order to know whether instruction is really differentiated for the level of the students in the program, classes must be observed, so choose representative classrooms and schools for visitations.
The positions of interest groups who hold different points of view should be considered.	If there have been parents or teachers who have questioned given aspects of the program (such as children leaving the classroom to go to resource rooms), their views should be considered in defining what data to collect and to ensure that those voices are heard in the data collection process.
Evaluations should be cost effective.	
Propriety	
The evaluation should provide data that assist the school in effectively serving target populations.	Evaluation data should focus on making services more effective for gifted students, not on whether services should exist.
Before the evaluation process begins, all parties involved in carrying out the evaluation should be clear on who is doing what, when, and where.	Be sure that if teachers are expected to rate student performance or administer tests or assessments, they are given adequate notice and opportunity to review procedures and are involved in the scheduling of the assessments.
Protect the rights and welfare of all involved (e.g., students, teachers, parents, and administrators).	Individual students and their parents and teachers should not be identified as informant in any reports unless they have given specific permission for that to occur. Every respondent in an interview should have the option of not answering a question or not participating. Respondents should never be pushed to answer questions that make them uncomfortable.
Treat all involved in the evaluation with dignity.	Teachers should be given advance notice of any classroom visits and be given the opportunity to discuss the classes observed to comment on any aspect of instruction or interaction.
The evaluation should be fair and complete with appropriate attention to strengths that can be built on and problem areas that can be remediated.	Be sure that those things taken for granted as positive aspects of the program are highlighted. If an aspect of the program is criticized, then there should be specific recommendations for making them more effective and efficient.

(*continued*)

TABLE 14–1 *(continued)*

Standard	Illustrative Interpretation in Evaluation of Services for Gifted Students
All limitations should be explicitly stated, and all evaluation results should be accessible to those who are affected by the evaluation.	Teachers who directly deliver services to gifted students and other classroom teachers and/or staff who have instructional responsibility should be provided with both executive summaries and full reports.
Deal with all conflicts of interest fairly. Use money wisely and be prepared to account for all expenditures.	
Accuracy	
Describe and document the program.	Specify exactly how identification takes place and how services are delivered to those identified. Identify the expected outcomes of instruction in terms of student learning.
Examine the context of the program.	A gifted program exists within a system and a school that has a philosophy and values, and they may affect the program functioning. For example, how does the school deal with other special needs students? Is the gifted program in concert with that philosophy?
Describe the evaluation process and purpose and procedures.	If the purpose is to judge the degree to which a specific model is implemented, not only should the model be described with statements of expected outcomes, but the ways to assess the implementation and outcomes should be explicitly stated as well.
Select information sources to be sure they yield accurate data and reveal all information sources.	
Be sure that valid data are collected. That is, be sure that data are relevant to the evaluation questions.	If you wish to know whether student outcomes are achieved, it is imperative to find student measures and not rely on reports of student change.
Be sure that information is reliable.	Be sure to ask survey questions that clearly will result in reliable responses. For example, ask, "How many times last month did you allow students independence in choice of what they studied?" Then give options of never, once, two to five times, or more than five times. Do not use never, sometimes, often, almost always, and always since different respondents interpret these terms differently.
Review all information to be sure that it does not contain errors of reporting or analysis. Both quantitative and qualitative data should be appropriately and systematically analyzed.	Check quotations and data tables to be sure that you are reflecting the true picture of the data. For example, to say, "100% of the parents agree that communication is adequate," when only 2 of 50 parents answered the question, is not fully revealing of the response.
Conclusions should be explicitly stated.	Avoid statements open to interpretation, such as, "Administrators at some levels are supportive of the gifted program, while administrators at other levels are not." Specify the level of support.
Guard against distortion that comes from personal feelings and biases.	If you are not a supporter of acceleration as a program service, guard against interpreting data to support your position. It is helpful to have a peer who has an alternative point of view look at the interpretation of your data to ensure that your biases have not affected your conclusions.

will be considered, the evaluation process should supply data in a timely manner that allows sufficient opportunity for decision makers to process, reflect on, and integrate recommendations into their overall planning. Finally, evaluation plans should provide for cost-efficient data collection plans. Useful data document the degree to which goals are achieved, assess the degree to which the program is using its resources wisely, and highlight areas where program improvement is needed. The goal of program evaluation should be to maximize the effectiveness and efficiency of the program offered to gifted students through the systematic collection and interpretation of data, and all planning should reflect that goal.

Research on the most effective gifted programs evaluations identifies several critical planning steps in the evaluation process (Tomlinson, Bland, Moon, & Callahan, 1994). The first of these is the identification and involvement of an evaluation planning team. This team is a critically useful resource in specifying the long-term goals of the program and in identifying the areas of concern to be evaluated. The team can also provide guidance in decision making relative to identifying the potential audiences for the evaluation, clarifying the purposes of the evaluation, selecting sources of information, identifying strategies for data collection, and finding ways to effectively communicate results and recommendations and for their implementation. The composition of an evaluation planning team should reflect those who have a stake in the quality of services delivered to gifted students (e.g., the parents of students, school board members, teachers [specialists in gifted and generalists], building-level administrators, and central office–level administrators; Reineke, 1991). Individuals who know the political landscape of the school district and are influential with their peer group are valuable assets in ensuring that stakeholders will attempt to implement those recommendations that flow from the evaluation.

If a gifted advisory board exists that is representative of the school community, representatives should be appointed to the evaluation planning team. But the evaluation planning team should *not* be the gifted advisory board. The evaluation planning team needs a broader base of representation than is typically found on a gifted advisory board, and it is very important to bring in new and different perspectives for this activity. While those who have been acting in an advisory role know the program and while their perspective should be included, sometimes they can be blind to the shortcomings of the program. In addition, they may be unable to see the more positive aspects of the program and may take the functioning aspects of the program for granted.

Beginning the Discussion with the Evaluation Advisory Team

The first step involved in planning an evaluation is to be sure that everyone agrees on what the program really is,[2] the resources needed to make the program work, the activities carried out as part of delivering services to gifted students, and the expected outcomes of all the these activities. This process and discussion is most fruitful if the evaluation team begins with a complete and careful description of the gifted program. All components or major facets of the program should be considered: definition of giftedness, identification, curriculum development, instructional delivery, teacher selection, teacher training, staff development, program management and administration, communication, and so on. The description of the program will allow for the comparison of the program philosophy, activities, and processes against best practice and will guide decisions about what outcomes can and should be measured. All the key players in the delivery of the services should agree on the veracity and completeness of the program description before the evaluation proceeds.

Initial discussions with the evaluation planning team should be aimed at identifying key stakeholders, outlining key areas of concern, and generating possible evaluation questions to be addressed. To guide the discussion, the team might be asked to consider questions such as the following:

- Which groups have a vested interest in this program and its outcomes? How will their interests and concerns be tapped?
- What areas or components of the program are most critical to its success?
- What outcomes are expected for the gifted program?
- What components of the program are significant for student learning and success? Which may be in need of revision?
- What decisions need to be made about changes to improve services to gifted students? What changes are teachers, administrators, and others willing to make?
- Does the description of the program identify areas where there may be weaknesses or missing elements for the quality programming for gifted students?

In addition, the team may be asked to examine the NAGC standards and prioritize those areas on which the evaluation might focus.

The next job of the evaluation team is to specify evaluation questions. This stage of generating all the possible evaluation questions is identified as the divergent phase of planning an evaluation (Cronbach, 1982). Reflecting on the discussions around the previous questions, the leader of the team can provide examples that may be useful as models for the group in generating a wide range of evaluation questions. Examples include the following:

- Does the curriculum offered to gifted students meet the criteria for quality-differentiated curriculum outlined by the NAGC?
- Do students produce products that are more creative and that represent deep and sophisticated understanding of the methodologies of the practicing professional in the discipline?
- Is staff development training providing counselors with appropriate skills in noting the social and emotional needs of gifted students?

Supplementing the input of the advisory group by holding focus group meetings with key stakeholders may produce different—but significant—additional questions for consideration. Key questions to pose to focus group participants might include the following:

- We are interested in the areas that you would deem relevant to evaluation of the gifted program. These might relate to the scheduling of services, curriculum,

[2] It is critical to determine where discrepancies exist between program documents and actual program implementation in order to determine what should be evaluated. Often, program documents do not reflect the actual program, and the stakeholders and advisory team need to determine which program will be evaluated.

instruction, expected outcomes of the program, facilities, and so on. Would you help us by telling us what is of most concern to you?
- If you were evaluating this program, what questions would you ask?
- (Follow-up) What kinds of data would you collect to help answer (insert question here)?

Once focus group responses have been collected, the evaluation team should weigh these questions using guidelines from Fitzpatrick et al. (2004) and others to determine the usefulness of the input, potential biases in the questions, and the degree to which the new questions will enrich the decision-making process:

- Why is this group concerned about this particular aspect of the gifted program? Is their concern one that would affect the effectiveness of the program?
- Is this a concern shared by other groups?
- Why would this group value these particular outcomes?
- Did the group suggest other approaches they think would be useful for achieving the outcomes?
- How would this group or others use the answers to particular questions they have raised?

Finally, it is useful to reflect on the key features of programs for the gifted presented in Table 14–2 (Renzulli, 1975) to determine the degree to which the program is providing high-quality implementation of the specified areas. The table provides sample evaluation questions relating to each of the key features.

Once the team has generated ideas for evaluation questions, it is likely that there will be far more areas that could be evaluated than there is the time, energy, or money to address. So the next step (convergent) is to work with the evaluation team to prioritize and narrow down the possibilities. Consider whether the data collected will do the following:

- Be useful in effective decision-making
- Lead to changes that will have a significant impact on improving the education of the gifted students
- Help in documenting the outcomes of the program and aid in understanding why the goals and objectives of the program are or are not being achieved
- Help determine the degree to which our students are achieving goals that could not otherwise be achieved
- Be of use to other program developers
- Be of importance to a key stakeholder group

Effective evaluations are based on limited but very *specific* and *focused* evaluation questions (Tomlinson, Bland, & Moon, 1993; Tomlinson et al., 1994). Evaluation questions should be clear with all terms sufficiently defined, and everyone should agree on their meaning. For example, if the committee agrees that one goal is the development of creativity, then the definition of that construct in behavioral terms and observable performance is critical in guiding the next stages of the evaluation design. Or if the evaluation question focuses on the determination of the degree to which the curriculum reflects current best practice and research, the committee will need to determine how best practice will be defined and evaluated.

Further, evaluations focused on both formative and summative questions are most useful in helping leaders make decisions about appropriate changes in program services (Hunsaker & Callahan, 1993; Tomlinson et al., 1993, 1994). Formative evaluation questions are those that focus on process and are used to make decisions that will improve the program and increase the likelihood that the desired outcomes will be achieved. For example, consider this evaluation question: Are compacting forms appropriately completed? Suppose that a program has adopted the Enrichment Triad Model (Renzulli, 1977) or the Schoolwide Enrichment Model (Renzulli & Reis, 1985), both of which have the core expectation that students' traditional curriculum will be compacted to allow time for in-depth investigations. If teachers do not carry out this core aspect of the model, it is unlikely that the goals of the program will be achieved.

Summative evaluation questions focus on outcomes. For example, asking whether students demonstrate more advanced, in-depth learning of major concepts, principles, and generalizations of the disciplines is asking a summative evaluation question. In the finalization of the evaluation questions, the evaluation team can also be useful in helping to gather input from stakeholder groups to ensure that their major concerns have been reflected in the evaluation questions.

How Else Can an Evaluation Task ForceHelp You?

The evaluation team is also useful in delineating the plan for carrying out the evaluation and in ensuring that key decision makers are included in the process. If networks that will support the evaluation process are identified and cultivated both inside and outside the school district, the chances that the evaluation efforts will be fruitful are increased substantially.

DESIGNING DATA COLLECTION

An evaluation planning team is also helpful in brainstorming the kinds and sources of data that can provide useful information in answering selected evaluation questions. Of course, it is critical to (a) choose or create data collection strategies and instruments that will give you valid and reliable answers to the evaluation questions posed, (b) collect data from multiple sources using a variety of strategies to add veracity and completeness to the findings, and (c) gather information that will be credible and useful in decision making. Collecting data that no one will pay attention to is not only wasteful but also frustrating.

As mentioned previously, the best guide to data collection is the specification of clear, unambiguous evaluation questions (Joint Committee on Standards for Educational Evaluation, 1994). These questions should address program goals, including those that direct the data collection with regard to the identification process, curriculum development efforts, staff development, instruction, communication, program management, and so on. The questions should be carefully examined to

TABLE 14–2 Key Features of Programs for Gifted Students (Renzulli, 1975) and Potential Questions

Feature	Potential Questions
Philosophy and Objectives	
Existence and adequacy of document	Does the current document reflect state-of-the-art thinking about gifted students and their needs? Do the stakeholders know about, understand, and agree with the stated philosophy and objectives?
Application of the document	Do the philosophy statement and the objectives guide decisions about identification and instructional decision?
Student Identification and Placement	
Validity of conception and adequacy of procedures	Do the instruments used in the identification process yield valid and reliable indicators of the underlying construct of giftedness that is defined in the philosophy statement? Do the persons involved in the identification process have skills in interpreting test score and other identification information?
Appropriateness of relationship between capacity and curriculum	Are students placed in services and provided instruction that matches the needs identified in the screening and placement process?
The Curriculum	
Relevance of conception	Does the curriculum truly reflect differentiation of content, process, and product that will meet the needs of gifted students? Does the curricular and instructional plan lead to the expected outcomes?
Comprehensiveness	Are there curricular and instructional modifications in place to meet the needs of all identified students across all areas of identification?
Articulation	Do the offerings across grade levels build on earlier outcomes and goals and objectives?
Adequacy of instructional facilities	Do teachers have adequate space to carry out the planned instruction?
The Teacher	
Selection	Are teachers who are selected to provide services to gifted students certified to teach those students?
Training	Is there a carefully articulated staff development plan based on a systematic needs assessment of teacher knowledge as well as strengths and weaknesses in implementation?
Program Organization and Operation	
General staff orientation	Do administrators, regular classroom teachers, counselors, media specialists, and other support staff have an adequate understanding of the program to provide necessary support?
Administrative responsibility and support	Do those who have the charge of guiding any and all aspects of the program have adequate background and knowledge to carry out leadership and advocacy roles?
Functional adequacy of the organization	Does the school division have an adequate plan for incorporating this program into its planning and day-to-day operation?
Financial operation	Are there adequate funds provided to support the services proposed?
Provision for evaluation	Does the school district have a plan for systematic formative and summative evaluation? Does the school division have a plan for data warehousing that will provide appropriate outcome data on the program?

ensure that the data they generate will have a positive impact on the services for gifted students and, subsequently, on the students themselves. Finally, the questions should be comprehensive, covering (a) all the important components of the program, (b) both cognitive and affective outcomes for students, and (c) long-term and short-term outcomes. Table 14–3 provides a sample of evaluation questions addressing those critical areas involved in delivering services and instruction to gifted students.

Identifying Data Sources and Types of Data to Collect

There are two key guiding principles that must be kept in mind in choosing the data collection strategies for answering the selected evaluation questions:

1. Are data being gathered from the most direct and best sources?
2. Are data being collected that will have credibility with key decision makers?

TABLE 14–3 Sample Evaluation Questions

Area of Evaluation Concern	Sample Evaluation Questions
Definition and philosophy	1. Does the school district have a clearly agreed-on definition of giftedness? 2. Does the definition of giftedness adopted by the school district reflect current theory and research in gifted education? 3. Does the school district communicate the definition of giftedness to primary stakeholders? 4. Is the definition of giftedness broad enough to reflect the variety of talents valued by the community? 5. Does the philosophy of the school district with regard to services for gifted provide options for a continuum of services across grades K–12?
Student identification	1. Does the identification process reflect the definition of giftedness adopted by the school district? 2. Are the instruments used in the identification process valid for identifying the types of giftedness reflected in the definition of giftedness adopted by the school division? 3. Are the instruments used in the identification process free of racial, gender, and other biases that would discriminate against the identification of subpopulations of students? 4. Is the nomination process ongoing, and does it allow for identification at any time? 5. Is the process for identifying gifted students understood by key stakeholders and those responsible for input? 6. Does the identification process yield data useful for appropriate placement of students and for guiding curricular differentiation for the students identified?
Curriculum development	1. Is there a well-defined curriculum scope and sequence that is likely to lead to the stated goals of services offered to gifted students? 2. Is the curriculum structured to address needs of students defined and identified by the school division? 3. Does the curriculum reflect differentiated content, process, and products that are differentiated from those of the regular curriculum and representative of the most current theory and research in gifted education? 4. Does the curriculum provide for modification based on a preassessment of the current level of student performance? 5. Does the curriculum provide appropriate levels of challenge for all identified gifted learners? 6. Does the curriculum provide the opportunity for the development of both cognitive and affective outcomes (including habits of mind) that are differentiated appropriately for gifted students?
Instruction	1. Do students produce real-life solutions to real problems using the methodology of professionals in the discipline? 2. Do students develop more complex and in-depth understandings of key concepts from the disciplines? 3. Do students develop greater mastery of the critical thinking skills of analytical reasoning, discriminating fact from opinion, inference, and prioritizing than they would have gained from the regular instructional program? 4. Do students develop independence and confidence in planning for self-directed projects? 5. Does instruction provide for modification according to student interests, readiness, and learning style? 6. Do instructional modifications include both acceleration and enrichment as appropriate? 7. Do students demonstrate increased interest in the disciplines studied?

(*continued*)

TABLE 14–3 *(continued)*

Guidance and counseling	1. Do the counselors working with gifted students have knowledge of and training to work with gifted students? 2. Is the career and college guidance program differentiated for gifted students? 3. Are gifted underachievers provided services as gifted students? 4. Is there adequate support for gifted underachievers?
Program administration and management	1. Is communication between and among stakeholders adequate for informed decision making? 2. Do students and teachers have access to state-of-the-art technology to support the curriculum and instructional program? 3. Is there clear coordination between the general education program and services for gifted students? 4. Are teaching staff fully informed of the goals and objectives of the program—cognitive and affective? 5. Is strategic planning an ongoing and effective component of program administration?
Staff development	1. Is there a clearly articulated staff development plan based on teacher, support staff, and administrator needs assessment? 2. Is staff allotted sufficient time to prepare and practice (with coaching support) the implementation of skills presented during staff development workshops? 3. Do teachers develop and demonstrate greater competency and use of compacting skills? 4. Do teachers implement preassessment strategies prior to the teaching of a unit? 5. Are teachers able to articulate the variety of ways in which particular characteristics of giftedness will be manifested in diverse populations?
Program design	1. Do gifted learners have access to a continuum of program services based on learner needs? 2. Is program design reflective of the school district's philosophy of gifted education? 3. Are options provided for early entrance to kindergarten, grade skipping, ability grouping, and dual enrollment, and are all students provided access to these services based on careful assessment of need? 4. Are program options integrated with the school program? 5. Is flexible grouping used and appropriate both in the regular classroom and in special classes for gifted students?

Adequately addressing the first question requires a match between the sources of the information and question. In many instances, evaluations of gifted programs have relied too heavily on surveys from parents, teachers, and students to address all evaluation questions. While such surveys may provide data about perceptions, beliefs, and attitudes, they are insufficient in answering evaluation questions regarding the quality of the curriculum, the outcomes of instruction, or the demonstrated changes in teacher or student behavior. For example, what is the most direct way to find out what students have learned? Of course, the best strategy is to measure students with a test, observation, or other assessment strategy that measures student behavior and performance. This is not to deny other input into assessing student learning. Others' perceptions of student learning may also be of interest because the perceptions of stakeholders (i.e., parents and teachers) are important as well. In addition, some sources may add to the understanding of student change. For example, through interviews, teachers may be able to supply data on student growth.

In program evaluation, information is gathered from multiple sources using a process called triangulation (collecting data using multiple instruments from a variety of sources). For example, if the goal is to increase knowledge, understanding, and the ability to apply advanced content knowledge, AP test scores, student and teacher interviews, and grades of students in their first year in college may be examined. The concordance of results from these multiple inputs strengthens confidence in conclusions. The challenge to the evaluation planning team is to identify those evaluation questions for which perceptions and attitudes are sufficient data for decision making and then to generate ideas for collecting data that will go beyond opinion to answer other evaluation questions. Table 14–4 lists the types and potential sources of data that might be collected that can be useful starting points for the panel in determining the types of data that should be collected.

It is unreasonable to expect an evaluation team to be experts in measurement. Consultation with experts is usually required in selecting those published instruments to be used in the evaluation process. The Buros *Mental Measurements Yearbook* (Spies & Plake, 2005)[3] or other sources of information on test score

[3] The latest *Mental Measurements Yearbook* is referenced here. A new edition is published each year; however, not all tests are reviewed each year, so in searching for instruments, it is useful to consult volumes from the past several years and to consult the online resource available in most college libraries.

TABLE 14–4 Suggested Types and Sources of Data Used in the Evaluation of Gifted Programs

Potential Types of Data	Potential Sources of Data
Measures of cognitive outcomes • Student objective, standardized • Objective, teacher constructed • Essay, standardized • Essay, teacher constructed • Performance assessments • Student products • Portfolios	Students
Measures of affective outcomes • Checklist • Rating scales	Teachers, outside observers
Observation	Classrooms and their teachers (general educators and/or specialists)
Interviews	Administrators, parents, teachers, students, counselors
Surveys/questionnaires	Administrators, parents, teachers, students
Exert ratings of documents/document reviews (e.g., curriculum or identification protocols)	Outside consultants
Existing data such as books checked out of library, attendance records, awards received, AP enrollments, and exam scores	School records

reliability and validity can be helpful once the evaluation team identifies the range of credible data needed to assist in decision making and identifies the types of instruments they would deem useful in collecting data.

Choosing or Constructing the Specific Instruments to Collect the Data

Ensuring that data are reliable and valid is the core of quality evaluation. First, instruments must be free of the influence of random error. The score that a student earns one day on an instrument should be about the same as the score he or she earns on a subsequent day (test–retest reliability), scores that are assigned by one rater should be similar to scores assigned by a second scorer (interrater reliability), and scores a student earns on one form of a test should be similar to scores earned on another form of the same test (equivalent forms or parallel forms reliability). Reliability of test scores is important because changes from one administration of the test (pretest) to a second (posttest) should be due to changes in students and not to variability in test scores attributable to other sources. For example, if Sally earns 10 more points on the *Cornell Critical Thinking Test,* it should be because she has become a better critical thinker, not because she guessed better, because a more lenient scorer rated her responses, or because the second form of the test was easier. Evaluations of the reliability of test scores are expressed in terms of correlations ranging from 0.0 (no reliability) to 1.0 (perfect reliability). In general, reliability of test scores of 0.65 or greater is desirable for measuring changes in groups.

But even more important than the reliability of test scores is the validity of the scores. The test scores should be reflective of the characteristic being measured. For example, if the expected outcome is a change in critical thinking abilities, the test scores should reflect changes in critical thinking, not reading ability. Data on the reliability and validity of test scores derived from a particular published test can be found in the test's technical manual, the various editions of the Buros *Mental Measurements Yearbook,* and published reviews of the test.

Student Outcome Data. Cognitive outcomes are one dimension of instruction that might be assessed in an evaluation. When considering cognitive outcomes, it is important to take into account the dimensions of content, process, and product in specifying the type of outcome expected. However, it is also critical to assess goals reflecting the affective outcomes of the program. For example, a program may have goals that include positive attitudes toward learning, acceptance of challenge, increase in student independence, and development of a positive self-concept or self-efficacy. If changes in these attributes or behaviors are goals of the program, then assessment on these dimensions is warranted.

The Buros *Mental Measurements Yearbook* (Spies & Plake, 2005), *Tests in Print* (Murphy, Plake, Impara, & Spies, 2002), and the Internet are valuable resources for identifying potential instruments for measuring the outcomes of instruction. For example, CriticalThinking.Net (*www.criticalthinking.net/CTTestList1199.html*) provides an annotated list of critical thinking measures compiled by Robert Ennis, a leading expert in the measurement of critical thinking. Other useful websites for locating assessment instruments are listed in the resource section at the end of this chapter.

Nonstandardized Instruments to Measure Student Outcomes. Because of the lack of reliable and valid instruments to measure the outcomes of classroom instruction, program evaluators may use performance assessments, product rating scales or rubrics, checklists, or other nonstandardized, evaluator- or teacher-constructed instruments for assessing changes in student learning. These assessments should also be constructed or selected on the basis of the satisfactory reliability and validity of scores obtained from these tools. Some examples include the rubric developed by Schack (1994) for rating student research products and the *Student Product Assessment Form* developed by Reis (Reis & Renzulli, 1991). Many performance assessments addressing differentiated state standards across disciplines have been developed by the National Research Center on the Gifted and Talented.[4] These tools are constructed to reflect interdisciplinary achievements across the domains of social studies, language arts, science, and mathematics from elementary through middle school grades. Wiggins (1996) has pointed out that the construction of any rubric for scoring student products should stress high-level, professional performance as the ultimate goal of student production. This principle is important in program evaluation to ensure that the ceiling on these instruments is set at a level that will provide for measurement of growth over time and for full evaluation of the highest level of productivity of gifted students.

Issues in the Use of Standardized Assessments for Evaluating the Outcomes of Services Provided to Gifted Students

The Dearth of Published Instruments. When selecting or constructing instruments to use in the evaluation of gifted services, several challenges face the evaluator. The first of these is the limited number of instruments that are specifically designed to measure the types of outcomes that typically are specified as goals for these services (e.g., critical or creative thinking, production of authentic products, and more abstract, complex, and in-depth thinking in a discipline). The testing industry is able to operate profitably only if it produces instruments that will be widely used. The small market for the types of instruments measuring outcomes commonly associated with gifted programs and services has restricted the development of new instruments beyond a few. Those instruments (e.g., *Ross Test of Critical Thinking, Cornell Critical Thinking Test,* and *Torrance Tests of Creative Thinking)* have specific limitations that are discussed in the Buros *Mental Measurements Yearbook,* in Callahan and Caldwell (1995), and in the websites listed at the end of this chapter.

The Issues Surrounding the Use of Scores from Standardized Achievement Tests. Often, program evaluations in education rely on the use of standardized tests scores, either norm referenced (e.g., *Iowa Test of Basic Skills)* or criterion referenced (e.g., state-level, standards based assessments), to judge the success of programs. These scores have limited validity in assessing the outcomes of gifted services because they measure the outcomes of the standard curriculum rather than the more advanced and differentiated outcomes of the curriculum provided through gifted services. A second limitation is the low ceiling of these instruments. A group of students who are gifted will often score at the top of the scale on the grade-level forms of the test (ceiling effect), so there is no room to demonstrate growth. If posttest scores alone are used, there is no way to judge whether the students would have achieved the given scores without any program at all. If students are placed in a program that relies primarily on acceleration through the regular curriculum, scores may be valid if out-of-level assessments are used (using the form that measures achievement in grade levels above the levels where the student is currently enrolled and matching the curricula the students have studied).

The Issue of Comparing Growth to Standards or to Comparing Change to Other Gifted Students in a Control or Comparison Group. In developing evaluation designs, one may specify expectations (e.g., at least 75% of gifted students will enroll in and earn a minimum of a 4 on at least 3 AP exams), or one may look to see if the level of performance compares favorably to those who do not have gifted services available. Unfortunately, the field has not been researched sufficiently to allow for specificity on the level one might expect gifted students of a given grade or level of exceptionality to achieve. Therefore, setting standards against which to compare the achievement of a given group of students may be quite arbitrary. As an alternative, examination of the past performance of students may be used as a baseline and considered in setting goals that reflect the community expectations of the outcomes for such services.

An alternative is to establish a control or comparison group or to compare student performance to that of other students of similar ability who did not participate in given services. More detailed options for approaching this issue are outlined in Callahan and Caldwell (1995), Fitzpatrick et al. (2004), and VanTassel-Baska and Feng (2004).

---

[4] Information about these performance assessments can be obtained from the National Research Center on the Gifted and Talented, 179 Ruffner Hall, PO Box 400265. Charlottesville, VA 22904-4265.

Other Measures Used in Evaluations

Instruments and observation protocols used to gather data for making decisions about program effectiveness must be scrutinized to ensure that they (a) are appropriate, (b) will provide data that are reliable and valid, and (c) will be regarded by decision makers as providing valued evidence. These instruments include classroom observation protocols used to assess whether teachers are implementing the program model as designed, surveys designed to collect perceptions and levels of satisfaction with program elements, interview protocols, and checklists or rating scales to assess whether relevant program documents and identification procedures represent state-of-the-art practice in gifted education.

SPECIFYING THE DATA COLLECTION STRATEGIES

The evaluation team will again be useful in specifically identifying key students to interview, representative schools to visit, classrooms to observe, and other sources of information in order to gain the broadest perspective on instructional practice and program outcomes. As plans are made as to *whom* to interview and *where* to observe, the team can help ensure that a broad and representative sample of "informants" has been included in the evaluation process. The evaluation planning team can also assist by reviewing surveys, observation protocols, and interviews to eliminate jargon and clarify wording. All instruments should be field-tested prior to administration.

As the data collection process is designed, some key questions should be asked:

- Are there plans for collecting a variety of data on each question?
- Will data be collected from multiple data sources to ensure that the perspectives of various stakeholders have been addressed?
- Will varied data collection procedures/modes be used in order to ensure that the complex nature of the program has been documented?
- Has the use of data and its impact on the operation of the program been considered?
- Has consideration been given to the use of existing data as a source of information to address the evaluation questions (e.g., documents such as handbooks, agendas, and minutes of meetings from gifted and talented staff meetings and parent advisory committee meetings; newsletters, report cards, and other communications with parents/families; and teacher and/or student journals)?

Once all the data collection strategies and sources of data are determined, a careful plan for who will collect which data at what point in time is critical to ensure that responsibilities are clear and appropriate. Further, at this point in time, discussions should be held and procedures put in place to ensure confidentiality and anonymity of data as appropriate.

Finally, the evaluation planning team is critical in helping to decide how the results and recommendations can be communicated most effectively and in planning specific strategies for implementing those recommendations that result from the evaluation. Use of the political expertise of the group and their experiences in bringing about the changes that address the outcomes of the evaluation is essential. This requires careful thought about how and when evaluation results are best shared. It may be that some findings are shared long before the final report is ready because decisions must be made for budgetary reasons. It may be that some information is shared with certain stakeholders and not with others, using "need to know" criteria in making that decision. The best efforts to develop important evaluation questions, choose sound instruments, carefully collect and interpret data, and develop significant recommendations are all for naught if none pays attention to the results.

One other function, not mentioned thus far, that may be undertaken by the evaluation team is the decision of whether the evaluation will be best accomplished by using local staff and resources or whether the evaluation will have the most effect and be most informative if undertaken by an external evaluator or team of evaluators.

SHOULD WE HAVE SOMEONE ELSE DO THIS EVALUATION?

The question often arises about whether the evaluation of an educational program should be implemented by internal staff or whether an outside expert or expert team should be hired. Of course, the key to effective evaluation is buy-in by the key stakeholders to the process and the product produced by the evaluation. Even though the evaluation team carries out every step that was described previously with the greatest of competency and care, there may remain doubts because the evaluation is internal and thus deemed biased. In that case, engaging an evaluator from outside is warranted. Sometimes a school district does not have staff with the expertise or time to carry out an evaluation. In those cases, an outside evaluator or evaluation team is selected. If the decision is made to employ an outside evaluator, the criteria for choosing an evaluator should include the following:

- Knowledge about both evaluation and gifted programming
- Understanding of both quantitative and qualitative evaluation strategies
- Sufficient political sophistication to understand the implications of evaluation

Even if an outside individual or agency is hired to conduct the evaluation, the evaluation team should play a critical role in the planning process, particularly in (a) selecting the evaluator, (b) identifying stakeholders, (c) developing the evaluation questions, (d) determining how the results will be used and communicated, and (e) conveying recommendations.

SUMMARY AND CONCLUSIONS

The evaluation process that has been described is characterized by intense involvement of key stakeholders in a set of procedures that are based on careful examination of all components of the gifted program. An evaluation team may decide to focus on only certain aspects of a program at any given time, but an overall plan is necessary to ensure that the best use is made of resources to implement the best program possible. The plan must include the following:

- The identification of key questions
- The identification of key sources of information
- The use of reliable and valid instruments in data collection
- A careful balance between qualitative and quantitative information
- The provision of both formative and summative evaluation data
- The careful analysis and triangulation of data
- The identification of and communication with key decision makers using data they find credible

Because of the complexity of the process described here and the threat that evaluation poses, administrators and teachers are often reluctant to engage in this course of action. Hence, evaluation is too often a neglected aspect of program administration. As a result, gifted services may suffer in two serious ways. In one scenario, gifted services are sometimes eliminated or severely curtailed because the success of the program has not been appropriately documented. In the other, gifted children are not provided an adequate curriculum or adequate services because the models or the resources for delivering the model are not of the highest quality possible. A comprehensive evaluation based on the support of an evaluation planning team is a positive first step in protecting a gifted program from the whims of uniformed decision makers and our gifted students from inadequate services.

It is important that gifted program administrators come to view the evaluation process as one that will provide good information for improving practice; as ammunition for arguing for the implementation of the most effective models of curriculum, instruction, and service in the school district; as support for existing structures that are effective; as guidance in maximizing the effects of limited resource allocations; and as information that informs the community of the program and its value. To do so requires an investment of time and energy beyond the normal delivery of services, but the potential for creating excellence in programming far outweighs the cost.

QUESTIONS FOR THOUGHT AND REFLECTION

1. Consider a gifted program with which you are familiar. Who are all the potential stakeholders?
2. What are the major components of the program? (identification? curriculum development? instruction of students? mentorships? teacher selection and training? communication? other?)
3. What are three crucial questions you would suggest to an evaluator who was designing an evaluation of the program? What evidence would you want to see to provide you with an answer to your question? What would be good tools for collecting this evidence? Who should provide the evidence?

RESOURCES

Websites

CriticalThinking.net
www.criticalthinking.net/CTTestList1199.html
An annotated list of critical thinking tests categorized by general, specific skill, and subject areas.

Creativity Assessments
www.creativelearning.com/Assess/index.htm
Descriptions and brief reviews of more than 70 instruments for assessing creativity prepared by Donald J. Treffinger and colleagues, leading experts in the measurement of creativity.

Measures for the Study of Creativity in Scientific Problem-Solving
www.ets.org/Media/Research/pdf/GREB-78-01SR.pdf
A set of "tests of scientific thinking" developed for use as criterion measures of creativity. Scores on the tests describe both quality and quantity of ideas produced in formulating hypotheses, evaluating proposals, solving methodological problems, and devising methods for measuring constructs.

Evaluation Center at the University of Western Michigan
www.wmich.edu/evalctr/checklists/plans_operations.pdf
www.wmich.edu/evalctr/checklists/makingevalmeaningful.pdf
www.wmich.edu/evalctr/checklists/evaldesign.pdf
These three documents produced by the Evaluation Center at the University of Western Michigan provide checklists against which to compare the quality of an evaluation design.

BOOKS

Callahan, C. M. (Ed.). (2004). *Program evaluation in gifted education*. Thousand Oaks, CA: Corwin.

Callahan, C. M., & Caldwell, M. S. (1995). *A practitioner's guide to evaluating programs for the gifted*. Washington, DC: National Association for Gifted Children.

Fitzpatrick, J. L., Sanders, J. R., & Worthen, B. R. (2004). *Program evaluation: Alternative approaches and practical guidelines* (3rd ed.). Boston: Allyn & Bacon.

JOURNAL ARTICLES

Avery, L. D., & VanTassel-Baska, J. (1997). Making evaluation work: One school district's experience. *Gifted Child Quarterly, 41,* 124–132.

Callahan, C. M. (1986). Asking the right questions: The central issues in evaluating programs for the gifted and talented. *Gifted Child Quarterly, 30,* 38–42.

Callahan, C. M. (1995). Using evaluation to improve programs for the gifted. *The School Administrator, 52* (4), 22–24.

Carter, K. (1992). A model for evaluation programs for the gifted under non-experimental conditions. *Journal for the Education of the Gifted, 16,* 190–200.

Tomlinson, C. A., & Callahan, C. M. (1994). Planning effective evaluations of programs for the gifted. *Roeper Review, 17,* 46–51.

REFERENCES

Callahan, C. M., & Caldwell, M. S. (1995). *A practitioner's guide to evaluating programs for the gifted*. Washington, DC: National Association for Gifted Children.

Cronbach, L. J. (1982). *Designing evaluations of educational and social programs*. San Francisco: Jossey-Bass.

Eisner, E. W. (1975, April). *The perceptive eye: Toward the reformation of educational evaluation*. Paper presented at the annual meeting of the American Educational Research Association, Minneapolis, MN.

Eisner, E. W. (1991). Taking a second look: Educational connoisseurship revisited. In M. W. McLaughlin & D. C. Phillips (Eds.), *Evaluation and education at quarter century: Ninetieth yearbook of the National Society for the Study of Education, Part II* (pp. 169–187). Chicago: University of Chicago Press.

Fitzpatrick, J. L., Sanders, J. R., & Worthen, B. R. (2004). *Program evaluation: Alternative approaches and practical guidelines* (3rd ed.). Boston: Allyn & Bacon.

Hunsaker, S. L., & Callahan, C. M. (1993). Evaluation of gifted programs: Current practices. *Journal for the Education of the Gifted, 16,* 190–200.

Joint Committee on Standards for Educational Evaluation. (1994). *The program evaluation standards* (2nd ed.). Thousand Oaks, CA: Sage.

Landrum, M. S., Callahan, C. M., & Shaklee, B. D. (2001). *Aiming for excellence: Gifted program standards*. Waco, TX: Prufrock.

Lincoln, Y. S., & Guba, E. G. (1985). *Naturalistic inquiry*. Thousand Oaks, CA: Sage.

Murphy, L. L., Plake, B. S., Impara, J. C., & Spies, R. A. (2002). *Tests in print VI*. Lincoln: Buros Institute of Mental Measurements, University of Nebraska.

Patton, M. Q. (1997). *Utilization-focused evaluation: The new century text* (3rd ed.). Thousand Oaks, CA: Sage.

Patton, M. Q. (2002). *Qualitative research and evaluation methods*. (3rd ed.). Thousand Oaks, CA: Sage.

Provus, M. M. (1971). *Discrepancy evaluation for educational program improvement and assessment*. Berkeley, CA: McCutchan.

Reineke, R. A. (1991). Stakeholder involvement in evaluation: Suggestions for practice. *Evaluation Practice, 12,* 39–44.

Reis, S. M., & Renzulli, J. S. (1991). The assessment of creative products in programs for gifted and talented students. *Gifted Child Quarterly, 35,* 128–134.

Renzulli, J. S. (1975). *A guidebook for evaluating programs for the gifted and talented*. Ventura, CA: Office of the Ventura County Superintendent of Schools.

Renzulli, J. S. (1977). *The Enrichment Triad Model: A guide for developing defensible programs for the gifted and talented*. Mansfield Center, CT: Creative Learning Press.

Renzulli, J. S., & Reis, S. M. (1985). *The Schoolwide Enrichment Model: A comprehensive plan for educational excellence*. Mansfield Center, CT: Creative Learning Press.

Schack, G. D. (1994). Authentic assessment procedures for secondary students' original research. *Journal of Secondary Gifted Education, 6,* 38–43.

Scriven, M. (1972). Pros and cons about goal-free Evaluation. *Evaluation Comment, 3,* 1–7.

Spies, R. A., & Plake, B. S. (Eds.). (2005). *The sixteenth mental measurements yearbook*. Lincoln: Buros Institute of Mental Measurements, University of Nebraska.

Stake, R. (1995). *The art of case study research*. Thousand Oaks, CA: Sage.

Stake, R. E. (1967). The countenance of educational evaluation. *Teachers College Record, 68,* 523–540.

Stake, R. E. (1980). Program evaluation, particularly, responsive education. In W. B. Dockrell & D. Hamilton (Eds.), *Rethinking educational research* (pp. 72–87). London: Hodder & Stoughton.

Stufflebeam, D. L. (2001). *Evaluation models*. San Francisco: Jossey-Bass.

Tomlinson, C. A., Bland, L., & Moon, T. R. (1993). Evaluation utilization: A review of the literature with implications for gifted education. *Journal for the Education of the Gifted, 16,* 171–189.

Tomlinson, C. A., Bland, L., Moon, T. R., & Callahan, C. M. (1994). Case studies of evaluation utilization in gifted education. *Evaluation Practice, 15,* 153–158.

Tyler, R. W. (1942). General statement on evaluation. *Journal of Educational Research, 35,* 492–501.

VanTassel-Baska, J., & Feng, A. X. (2004). *Designing and utilizing evaluation for gifted program improvement*. Waco, TX: Prufrock.

Wiggins, G. P. (1996) Anchoring assessment with exemplars: Why students and teachers need models. *Gifted Child Quarterly, 40,* 66–69.

CHAPTER 15

TEACHERS OF THE GIFTED AND TALENTED

Julia L. Roberts, Ed. D.
Western Kentucky University

INTRODUCTION

When a preservice teacher inquired about what modifications the classroom teacher made for gifted children, the answer was "I don't make any." While not true of all teachers, this candid comment represents a response that characterizes many teachers. Students are the losers in classes where few, if any, strategies are employed to see that all students make continuous progress, including those who are gifted and talented. Each year, young people at all levels of their education need to make an achievement gain of at least a year. When this is not the case, they miss opportunities to develop their potential.

If a sixth grader completes class work easily and makes straight As or 100s, what does he or she not learn that others already have by that time? Responses to this question are numerous. The student doesn't learn the following:

1. To work hard on challenging tasks
2. That effort is a key component in learning at high levels
3. To persist in order to accomplish a goal
4. Study skills

This list of what a student doesn't learn includes many factors that are necessary for success in high school as well as in postsecondary opportunities. Students who find that everything comes easily in classrooms do not learn lessons that are essential for being successful in their careers. The loss is tremendous to the child and to society.

Teachers may shortchange students who are ready for advanced learning opportunities. This occurs because teachers don't know how to differentiate to challenge them and do not make necessary accommodations because they feel "these kids will make it on their own," a widely believed myth about gifted children. Preparing teachers to challenge all students, including those who are gifted and talented, is very important. After all, students who don't *earn* their accomplishments (grades, scores, and recognition), don't *own* them.

Understanding the needs of gifted and talented learners is essential for all educators if individuals of high ability are to thrive in school and in life. The fact that gifted children and adolescents have social-emotional and cognitive needs is missed by many teachers because such students may not look "needy." Their needs aren't obvious, as they result from their strengths rather than deficiencies. Many teachers do not recognize the intensity of gifted students' needs, which are as great as those of other exceptional children. In fact, the gifted differ from students with average abilities as much as exceptional students with identified deficiencies do.

Who should be prepared to teach gifted and talented students? All teachers with gifted and talented students in their classrooms for any portion of the school day must be prepared to address the needs of these students. Counselors, administrators, gifted resource teachers, and teachers of special subjects (art, music, and so on) work with gifted students at some point.

Other questions that appear to cloud decision making are issues concerned with fairness. Is it fair to do something different for students who are advanced in a particular area? An example of one view of fairness is evidenced in a middle school where educators have decided to eliminate honors classes so that all students can have the same opportunities. It is apparent from this example that these educators equate fairness with sameness. What is the future of our society if all students receive the same instruction, on the same time schedule, and with the same expectations? If the same opportunities are offered to all young potential athletes, they will never have the opportunity to develop their potentials. For example, there would be no Tiger Woods or Annika Sorenstam in golf. Their talents and abilities were developed to world-class standards because instruction was matched to their readiness to move on to the next level of knowledge and skill. World-class scholars are needed too, and such status is reached only when fairness is seen as matching instruction to readiness to learn at higher levels. Providing opportunities for continuous progress for all students, including the gifted and talented, is the key to developing their potentials in all content areas. Fairness must involve removing the learning ceiling and is an important consideration in classrooms and schools if all students are to be ensured opportunities to learn at the highest levels for which they are capable.

This chapter examines the key role teachers have in student achievement, the preservice and in-service preparation of teachers, and special factors related to teaching gifted students. Effective teachers must develop the strengths of all students, including those who are gifted and talented. Without the opportunity to make continuous progress, gifted students will often fail to develop to their potential.

TEACHERS OF THE GIFTED AND TALENTED

Undoubtedly, all students need teachers who are well qualified. Being well qualified includes having knowledge of the content being taught and knowledge and understanding of the students. It also includes having attitudes and dispositions that encourage the development of potentials in students and an understanding of the fact that gifted students are exceptional as the result of strengths rather than deficiencies:

> Gifted students appear to be more profoundly impacted by their teachers' attitudes and actions than are other students. Although their teachers must possess the same characteristics and competencies of all good teachers, the most successful teachers of the gifted develop areas of specific expertise not required in general education. (Croft, 2003, p. 558)

The Essentials for Teachers

What are the essentials necessary for teachers and other educators to effectively teach the gifted and talented? What do they need to know and be able to do to teach gifted students so that they make at least 1 year of achievement gain annually and develop to their maximum potential? "To provide appropriate learning experiences for gifted and talented students, key personnel need to possess knowledge and understanding of:

- The nature of individual differences, especially as applied to exceptional abilities
- The origin and nature of various manifestations of giftedness
- The cognitive, social, emotional, and environmental factors that enhance or inhibit the development of giftedness in all populations
- A variety of methods for identifying and assessing students with extraordinary potential
- The historical and theoretical foundations of the field of gifted education, current trends and issues, and potential future directions of the field
- A research-based rationale for differentiated programs and services for gifted students
- Theoretical models, program prototypes, and educational principles that offer appropriate foundations for the development of differentiated curriculum for gifted students
- The unique potentials of gifted students from underserved populations, including but not limited to gifted females, students who have disabilities, or students who are racially or ethnically diverse, economically disadvantaged, or underachieving
- Curriculum and instruction that is appropriate for meeting the needs of gifted learners
- State mandates that guide district program design, identification procedures, delivery of services, and evaluation guidelines
- Program evaluation as a systematic study of the value and impact of services provided
- Current educational issues, policies, and practices including their relationships to the field of gifted education" (Leppien & Westberg, 2006, pp. 162–163).

Gifted young people in a summer program in 2004 voiced their opinions about teachers in an open-ended questionnaire (Roberts, 2004). When asked for the characteristics they valued most in their teachers, the five characteristics most frequently given were being knowledgeable, having a sense of humor, being creative, understanding, and having an enthusiasm for teaching. These middle and high school students were asked what teachers do to encourage students to learn at high levels. Sample responses were the following:

- They personally "zoom in" on you and your work and help you learn at a different level.
- They expect a high level of performance from you.
- They give me stimulating questions to answer and something new to learn.
- If the teacher is excited and passionate about his or her subject, it makes it much easier for me to put a lot of effort into whatever I'm doing. Recommending extracurricular learning opportunities also encourages me.

When asked what teachers do that discourages them from learning at high levels, sample responses were the following:

- Busywork (excessive amounts of work that requires little thought but takes a lot of time).
- Regular questions in assignments that we already know about. They should give us work that makes us think a lot.
- Worksheets. They don't help at all; they just keep you busy (Roberts, 2004).

Teachers as Talent Developers

Bloom (1985) conducted a study of talent development among individuals who had attained eminence in their field by the age of 40. He determined "the study has provided strong evidence that no matter what the initial characteristics (or gifts) of the individuals, unless there is a long and intensive process of encouragement, nurturance, education, and training, the individuals will not attain extreme levels of capability in these particular fields" (p. 3). In this study of talent development, Bloom and other researchers found that a different type of teacher was needed at various stages of the individual's development. Initially, the student needs a teacher who will teach the basics in ways that make the student enjoy learning. The next teacher needs to be one who will have the expertise to develop skills and knowledge to a high level. The final teacher must be one who can take them to the level of expert. Without the appropriate opportunities, talent will not be developed:

> No matter how precocious one is at age ten or eleven, if the individual doesn't stay with the talent development process over many years, he or she will soon be outdistanced by others who do continue. A long-term commitment to the talent field and an increasing passion for talent development are essential if the individual is to attain the highest levels of capability in the field. (p. 538)

Teachers must have the knowledge, skills, and dispositions to develop the potentials of their students, including developing talents that are exceptional. Quality teaching focuses on developing all learners, including those who are more advanced or have the potential to advance at a rapid pace and to learn content that is more complex than what their age-mates are ready to learn.

Teacher Impact on Student Achievement

In the 21st century, student achievement is often equated to high test scores. Certainly, test scores have become important as a measure of success in school; however, the tests that are typically being administered often have low ceilings and do not measure the achievement levels of the most advanced students. Above-level testing is an important component in the assessment of students who are gifted and talented. For example, Jack and Sirona are two seventh graders who took the ACT as participants in one of the national talent searches. The ACT is a test designed for college-bound juniors and seniors. Jack scored a 32 on the language portion and a 14 on the mathematics section of the ACT. Sirona obtained scores of 27 and 29 on these two sections of the test, respectively. These scores provide a great deal of information to any teachers who are planning appropriately challenging learning opportunities that will ensure continuous progress in these students' areas of strength. Grade-level assessments, because of their low ceilings, cannot provide the same information as above-level tests.

The teacher is the most important factor in the achievement of students. Using the Tennessee Value-Added Assessment System database to examine the magnitude of teacher effects on student achievement, Wright, Horn, and Sanders (1997) found that "the teacher effect is highly significant in every analysis and has a larger effect size than any other factor" (p. 61). The researchers conclude, "Differences in teacher effectiveness were found to be the dominant factor affecting student academic gain" (p. 66). In other words, the teacher is the key influence on what a student learns in the classroom. Furthermore, Sanders (1998) states that the highest-ability students are less likely to make 1-year achievement gains than other students.

Highly qualified teachers are prepared in the subject matter they are teaching. "The strongest, consistently negative predictors of student achievement . . . are the proportions of new teachers who are uncertified . . . and the proportions of teachers who hold less than a minor in the field they teach" (Darling-Hammond, 2000, p. 27). The effects of teachers who are well prepared can be greater on student achievement than such influences of student background as language, minority status, and poverty (p. 38). Mastery of content is basic to being effective in teaching subject matter to students. The teacher who has a background in the content being taught can use that knowledge to plan in ways to facilitate learning, while a teacher with a limited knowledge of the content is hampered in planning and teaching.

The Role of Assessment in Learning

Assessment is an important aspect of teaching for all effective teachers. The emphasis on assessment has broadened to include preassessment as both formative assessment and summative assessment. Atkin, Black, and Coffey (2001) use three questions to frame the teaching–learning process:

1. Where are you trying to go?
2. Where are you now?
3. How can you get there? (p. 26)

"A landmark review by Black and Williams (1998) found that focused efforts to improve formative assessment provided learning gains greater than one-half standard deviation, which would be equivalent to raising the score of an average student from the 50th percentile to the 85th percentile" (Darling-Hammond, 2000, p. 277). Assessment focuses on what the student learns and how the student learns, key features to understand if the teacher is to have a significant impact on student learning.

TEACHER PREPARATION AND PROFESSIONAL DEVELOPMENT

Preservice Teacher Education Programs

How can preservice teacher education programs prepare future teachers to address the needs of all children, including those with exceptionalities who need more time and less complexity as well as those who need more complexity and less time to learn a new concept? What strategies must teachers utilize if they are to ensure that all students, including the gifted and talented, make continuous progress and that all children make at least a year's achievement gain annually? What are the attitudes or dispositions that preservice teachers need to possess if they are to understand diversity in its broad context and employ strategies that respect differences in learning preferences, in readiness and preparation to learn specific content and skills, and in ethnic and racial backgrounds?

Darling-Hammond and Bransford (2005) present a conceptual framework for teaching and learning that highlights key factors that come together in the "preparation of teachers for a changing world" (p. 11). This framework (see Figure 15–1) describes the major elements in a professional education curriculum. In order to teach students so that they become lifelong learners, teachers need knowledge of (a) learners and their development in social contexts, (b) subject matter and curriculum goals, and (c) teaching. Knowledge of teaching includes knowledge of subject matter, diverse learners, assessment, and classroom management.

In 2002, the National Council for Accreditation of Teacher Education (NCATE) changed its focus and established six standards that must be met in order to be accredited as a teacher preparation program. Standard 4 addresses diversity, including "the knowledge, skills, and dispositions necessary to help all students learn" (p. 29). In the 21st century, the focus of NCATE standards has shifted to outputs, assessing what teacher candidates should know and be able to do rather than inputs, such as the courses they must take and experiences they must have during their preservice program. "NCATE expects institutions to assess teacher candidate dispositions based on observable behavior in the classroom. NCATE does not recommend that attitudes be evaluated" (Wise, 2006). The standards describe what teachers need to understand and be able to do in order to facilitate learning for all students, and "all" includes students who are gifted and talented. Student learning is the desired end product of initial preparation programming:

> What effective teachers know and are able to do has a tremendous impact on the learning opportunities available to young people. Teachers who have the knowledge and repertoire of skills to teach their content at high levels challenge all students to work hard learning what they don't already know. They nurture and develop the talents of young people in their classes. (Roberts, 2006, p. 572)

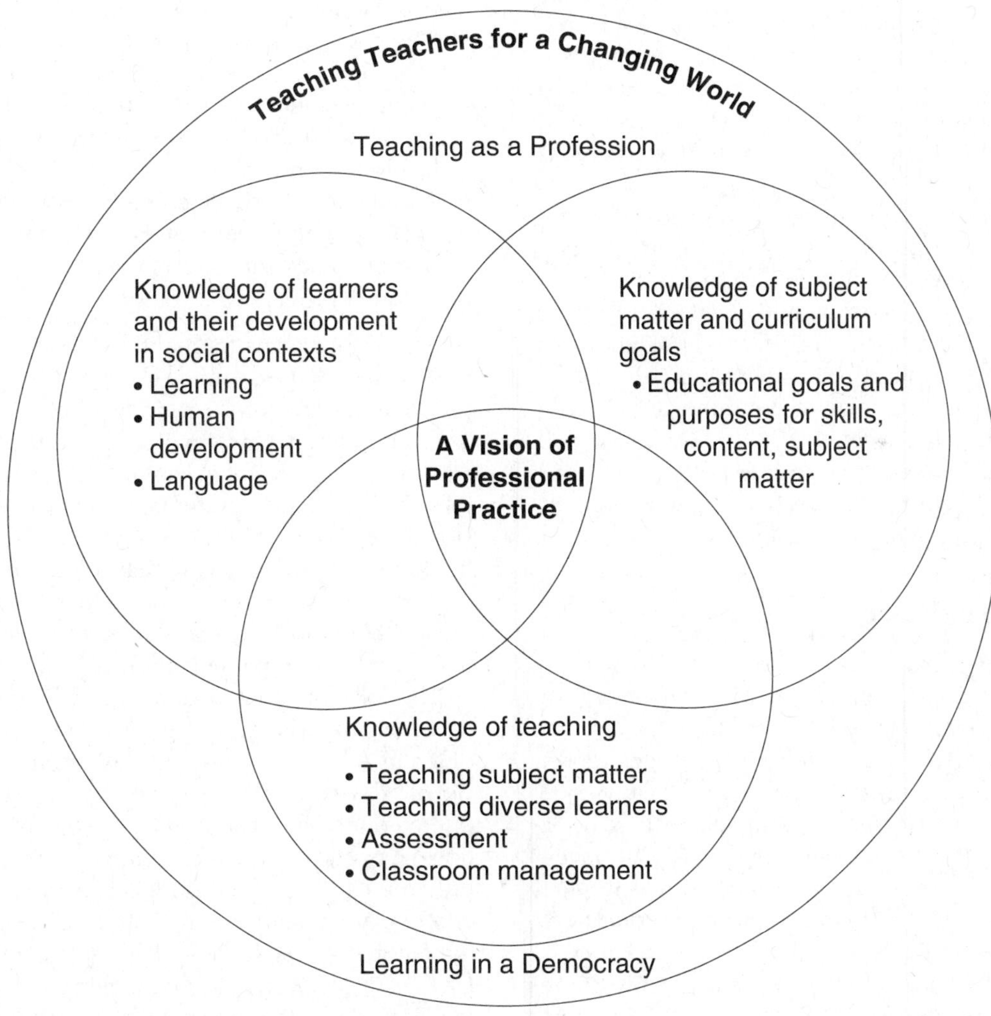

FIGURE 15–1 A Framework for Understanding Teaching and Learning
Source: From *Preparing Teachers for a Changing World, ed. By L. Darling-Hammond and J. Bransford, 2005, San Francisco: Wiley & Sons.*

At the preservice level in teacher education, there is little preparation to work with students who are gifted and talented, yet teachers in regular classrooms provide most of the instruction for such students. The 2004–2005 *State of the States* report (National Association for Gifted Children [NAGC], 2005) reveals that "LEAs [local education agencies] relied upon the *regular classroom* as one of the top two delivery methods for gifted services. However, survey responses from the *State of the State* questionnaire indicate Washington is the only state to require regular classroom teachers to have coursework in gifted and talented education despite the fact that these teachers are most often relied upon to meet the diverse educational needs of our most able students" (p. vi).

If teachers in the regular classroom provide the majority of the instruction for students who are gifted and talented, what modifications do they make to address the wide range of learner needs in their classrooms? On the basis of observations, anecdotal accounts, and research, it is highly likely that few adaptations are made in classrooms across the country to accommodate the needs of students who are ready to learn more complex content at a more rapid pace than others in their class. One study reveals that teachers reported doing little differentiation to meet the needs of high-ability learners. Ten years later, teachers in a follow-up study reported making few, if any, modifications for high-ability students (Westberg & Daoust, 2003).

Accreditation to address the diverse needs of learners could provide appropriate preparation for teaching gifted students; however, current information indicates that this preparation is not routinely a part of preservice teacher education programs. The fact that teachers do not have this background has implications for professional development. Any plan to educate teachers concerning their students' cognitive and social-emotional needs, as well as strategies to promote continuous progress, must include professional development as well as teacher preparation programs.

Professional Development

"The overarching goal of professional development in gifted education is to prepare school personnel for making appropriate decisions about the education of gifted students" (Dettmer, Landrum, & Miller, 2006, p. 625). How well this goal is met differs greatly from state to state, district to district, and school to school. States and districts make numerous professional development requirements, yet few states or districts require linking professional development to gifted education. The *State of the States* (NAGC, 2005) reports that only three states (Oklahoma, Pennsylvania, and South Carolina) require annual professional development in gifted education for regular classroom teachers. A survey of professional development practices in gifted education found that districts spend 4% of their professional development budget on gifted education, including teaching practices (Westberg et al., 1998). Educators, including principals, counselors, and special area teachers, may or may not have had any course work or professional development in gifted education.

Professional development makes a difference in student achievement. Wenglinsky (2000) studied indicators of teacher quality that relate to student performance, and the results were reported in *How Teaching Matters: Bringing the Classroom Back into Discussion of Teacher Quality,* a report of the Milken Foundation. The results highlight the importance of professional development opportunities that emphasize strategies that have been the hallmark of gifted education:

- When teachers participated in professional development focused on working with diverse learners, students in mathematics outperformed their peers by more than a full grade level.
- When teachers participated in professional development emphasizing higher-order thinking skills, students in mathematics outperformed their peers by 40% of a grade level.
- When teachers participated in professional development focusing on hands-on learning activities, their students outperformed their peers by 70% of a grade level in math and 40% of a grade level in science.
- When teachers participated in professional development on laboratory skills, their students outperformed their peers by 40% of a grade level in science (p. 9).

Professional development increases in its effectiveness if it is focused and ongoing. The focus can be on professional goals for the individual, team, or school. The ongoing nature involves follow-up discussions, support, and/or feedback. When the follow-up is built into the evaluation system, the subject of the professional development is seen as important and likely to be implemented. Knowing that the principal, gifted coordinator, or other school or district leader will expect the teacher to implement the strategies will enhance the likelihood that implementation will be tried.

The following is an example of effective professional development. The school goal is to increase the use of differentiation strategies in all classrooms. Various professional development opportunities are planned and offered during the school year. The planners have the National Association for Gifted children's program standards in hand to facilitate developing a configuration map for differentiation that is in line with these standards. A configuration map establishes what implementation will look like if it is successful. The configuration map serves as a guide through the implementation process. Having a "coach" who is accessible further enhances the chances that implementation will be successful. The coach can be an educator in various capacities who is on-site and has the knowledge and skills to help others in the building implement, in this example, differentiation strategies. Certainly, implementation is most likely to occur if it is seen as important to the school leaders and if on-site help is provided to assist in implementation when questions arise and problems occur. Thus, if differentiation is to be successfully implemented, teachers need to know what it will look like when implemented and have help and encouragement throughout the process.

Effective professional development is well planned, and it comes in many formats. It isn't limited to 3-hour-, 1-day, or any-length-of-time workshops. Professional development can be a book study involving educators who choose to learn together and support each other through the implementation process. It may involve placing a short article in mailboxes or sending it via e-mail with the awareness that the article will be the subject of discussion at the next faculty meeting. It may involve a team of teachers visiting a school with a successful model that is under consideration for adoption at other sites. Sending an individual teacher or a team of educators to a conference with the charge to learn and then to come back to lead a discussion at a faculty meeting is another form that professional development can take. Educators who view professional development in the broadest perspective have the greatest opportunity to have it make a difference in practices and attitudes.

Professional development needs to be differentiated. It needs to address the fact that "teachers themselves differ in readiness, interest, and learning profile" and that "staff development that models for teachers the beliefs, and practices that differentiation commends for their students provides powerful images of what the practice looks like and how it benefits individual human beings" (Tomlinson, 2005, p. 3).

Graduate Preparation in Gifted Education

States vary in requiring or not requiring gifted endorsement or certification as well as in the number of graduate hours, professional development hours, or continuing education units to earn the endorsement. The *State of the States* (NAGC, 2005) reported responses from 23 states that require certification or endorsement in gifted education for professionals in gifted and talented programs and from 21 states that do not have such a requirement. The number of graduate credits to obtain endorsement ranged from 6 to 24.

In April 2006, the Council for Exceptional Children (CEC)–NAGC Initial Knowledge and Skill Standards for Gifted and Talented Education became the official standards for initial preparation in gifted education. These 10 standards serve to guide the development of programs to prepare gifted educators. They will become the official standards to be used by institutions seeking accreditation by NCATE. The standards were developed by the two organizations with a focus on children who are gifted and talented, and they are the first set of joint standards in gifted education (see Appendix A for the CEC–NAGC Initial Knowledge and Skill Standards for Gifted and Talented Education). Key features of the standards are shown in Table 15–1.

The new standards for graduate programs in gifted education will be used not only by universities in the preparation of teachers but also by schools and districts as guides in professional development. For example, districts can determine if the presentations of consultants follow the CEC–NAGC standards in order to ensure that the district is aligned with recommended standards for instructional planning, assessment, and teaching strategies.

The Need to Describe What Successful Teachers Do

Do gifted education courses make a difference? Hansen and Feldhusen (1994) concluded that teachers who had completed three to five graduate courses in gifted education were more effective teachers than those who had not had such training. The study showed that teachers trained in gifted education "demonstrated greater teaching skills and developed more positive class climates than did teachers who had no training in gifted education" (p. 115).

An important question addresses the specific behaviors and strategies of successful teachers of the gifted. Croft (2003) states, "Isolating the characteristics and competencies unique to effective teachers of the gifted is a challenge. Many of the attributes delineated in research in gifted education correspond to characteristics necessary for any teaching success" (p. 560).

Graffam (2006) conducted a case study of two exemplary teachers of gifted learners in which he described practices used by these teachers. Central findings included the following:

1. Teaching gifted learners requires the teacher to frame individualized and whole-group learning simultaneously.
2. The path a person takes to become a teacher of gifted learners is significant. Personal background, preservice training, and professional reflection all help prepare the teacher for her task.
3. Some elements of the "canon" of gifted education, often seen as individual concepts, are fused into the practice of excellent teachers of gifted learners.
4. The relationships a teacher of gifted learners develops with students are the keys to opening doors (and setting fires) to higher challenge, motivation, and personal investment on the parts of the students.

More research on the behaviors and practices of exemplary teachers of the gifted is needed. Such research will inform the field of education as we move to describe what works for teachers of children and young people who are gifted and talented.

TABLE 15–1 Joint Initial Teacher Standards

Standard	Description
Foundations	Local, state/provincial, federal laws; Definition and identification; Historical foundations Philosophies, theories, models; Social, cultural, economic factors; Issues and trends
Development and characteristics of learners	Cognitive, effective characteristics; Effects of culture and environment; Role of families and communities; Developmental milestones; Learner similarities and differences
Individual learning differences	Influences of diversity on talents; Individuals with talents and disabilities; Differences in learning patterns; Variations in beliefs, traditions, values; Perspectives of diverse groups
Instructional strategies	Identify resources; Describe strategies; Apply content pedagogical knowledge; Interest-based research; Preassess learning/adjust instruction; Pacing; Multicultural curricula; Information and assistive technologies
Learning environments and social interactions	Analyze stereotypes; Social and emotional development; Affective learning experiences; Develop lifelong learning; Individual and group learning; Appreciate linguistic/cultural differences; Social interaction and coping skills
Language and communication	Communication; Effects of diversity on communication; Exceptional communication needs; Communicate with families; Advanced communication tools
Instructional planning	Theories/research models of curriculum; Distinguish general from differentiated curricula; Articulate cognitive, affective, aesthetic, social curricula; Align curricular standards; Design learning plans; Develop scope and sequence; Select resources, strategies, products; Advanced curricular content; Integrate academic and career guidance
Assessment	Critique identification processes; Uses, limitations, interpretation of assessments; Equitable approaches for identification; Technically adequate assessment; Develop differentiated curriculum-based assessments
Professional and ethical practice	Reflection; Identify organizations/publications; Comply with laws, ethics, standards; Improve practice
Collaboration	Culturally responsive collaboration; Respond to concerns of families; Collaborate to deliver services; Advocacy; Communicate with families, communities, school personnel

Source: From *The Handbook of Secondary Gifted Education*, ed. by F. Dixon and S. Moon, 2006, Waco, TX: Prufrock. Copyright © 2006 by Prufrock Press. Adapted with permission.

WHAT DO PARENTS, PRINCIPALS, AND EDUCATORS WANT IN TEACHERS?

The importance of teachers understanding the needs (often created by strengths) of gifted children cannot be underestimated. A parent, a principal, and a teacher provide their perspectives about this important topic.

Perspective of a Parent

Jake's last year of middle school! These 2 years have zoomed by with learning and challenge and growth and an excited son who didn't make excuses not to go to school. I remember his first science test in seventh grade: "Mom, it wasn't really like a test at all! She just walked around while we were doing this way cool experiment asking us questions and stuff! It was so cool! You know, Mom, I think middle school is going to be different." And so it was. His middle school years were mostly filled with hands-on and minds-on learning. They were filled with teachers who didn't always give the same assignments to every child in the class and teachers who encouraged him to take high school algebra while still in middle school. His mind stretched. His perspective widened. And he even learned how to study! No longer could he just sit in class, take little to no notes, and ace everything. He had to work. What a life lesson! He even made a couple of Bs! I guess that's a strange thing for a parent to be excited about, but for the first time, Jake was working hard at some tasks that really made him think. A B in a class like that means so much more than those As he brought home without having to think.

Now I wonder what his freshman year will bring. As a former high school teacher, I am so afraid that it will be filled with teachers who care more about content than kids, who have not been trained on how to differentiate the curriculum, and who think that taking an Advanced Placement class meets gifted kids needs.

What do I wish for in his teachers?

- *That they understand the characteristics and needs of gifted children and that they care enough about them as people to change how or what they teach. I don't want them to believe all those myths out there. Jake will not learn all he needs to learn on his own; he will not learn best by tutoring other kids; he is not elitist. He just learns differently from the norm (just as other exceptional kids learn differently from the norm).*
- *That they have had training on how to meet gifted kids' needs, how to differentiate the curriculum, and how to increase the pace or deepen the levels. I want them to read, attend conferences, and continue learning throughout their careers.*
- *That they find out what he already knows, then not "reteach" those concepts. Even in honors or AP classes, Jake will already know some material and not know other material. I'd want to know that every unit in every class was preassessed and that the results were used to guide his learning. Then I'd know that he was having continuous progress.*
- *That they group ability within his classroom giving different assignments to different groups. Then I'd love for them to group in other ways, too, such as interest or learning style. This way he learns how to work with a wide variety of people in a variety of ways.*
- *That they'd be open to new ways to learn. For example, don't force Jake to do 30 repetitions of a math problem that he can learn in three. Give options in homework.*
- *That they offer classes that are for gifted children. By this I don't mean AP; those are designed for any college-bound student. How about a class focusing on leadership development since gifted children will be leaders in their academic fields? A class on creativity or a special topics course pertinent to their area of giftedness would help meet needs.*
- *That they offer a wide variety of services to meet his needs, not just his academic needs but his social-emotional ones as well. I want to see monthly sessions wherein the counselor meets with small groups of young people who are gifted and talented. They could talk about peer pressure, the best college match for them, what it means to be a gifted teen, and the ethical responsibility that comes with having extraordinary abilities.*

The potential is tremendous—as is Jake's. What I want for him is what any parent wants for her child: continuous progress.

Tracy Inman, Parent

Perspective of a Principal

Teachers need special skills and abilities in order to recognize exceptional potential and demonstrated talent in children and to be able to facilitate the personal, social, and academic development of gifted and talented children. Teachers working with gifted children need to show great enthusiasm and love for learning, display an interest in a wide variety of subjects, and possess flexibility and open-mindedness. Gifted children typically have a wide range of interests, and teachers cannot be knowledgeable about all areas a child might have a driving need to know, but teachers must show an interest and help the child find information, including experts in the field (online or in person) who can mentor the particular interest. Gifted children often think "outside the box," and their teachers need to be open-minded and flexible to support the ideas being presented even though the teacher may not understand the origin of the idea or see the relationship to the topic being discussed. Often at a later time, the connection will be made, and the "Aha!" moment will occur.

Teachers of gifted children should have high intelligence and have demonstrated achievement both in and out of the classroom. They should be successful teachers who appreciate giftedness and easily build relationships with children and take an interest in their students beyond the time they are in their classroom. Being knowledgeable of the affective needs of gifted students will help them support the social-emotional concerns of their students.

Teachers of gifted children should be confident in their ability to motivate children to think at high levels, and they should enjoy the challenge of stimulating discussions and creative production. They should have good questioning skills and realize that asking good questions is more important than answering questions.

Dr. Mary Evans, Elementary Principal

Perspective of a Teacher

As a veteran teacher of 18 years, I truly thought I knew everything about teaching the gifted, as over the years I've had numerous classes with rosters full of students from various academic levels, including students identified as gifted. Nevertheless, in the past few years, I've been fortunate enough to teach some classes with only gifted/talented-identified students. Of course, these classes were more challenging, as I was constantly attempting to locate various teaching materials that would enhance the students' academic growth. I cannot begin to inform you of how much knowledge I've gained from these unique students of the accelerated level.

It is a known fact that gifted students sometimes pose a challenge to the ordinary teacher. Students may seem arrogant and bored with simple classroom tasks. This could be portrayed to the teacher as students who are somewhat rebellious with a poor work ethic and attitude. Many of these students could be chatty or constantly conversational. This scenario, of course, could possibly present a behavior problem in the classroom. Finally, teachers of the gifted student could view the student as being simply different and standoffish and therefore will not allow him or her to flourish in their classrooms because of their unusual characteristics. Some instructors may even shy away from these students as the student often presents the "I know more than you do" persona.

Due to the fact that I am a veteran teacher with special, gifted classes during my day's schedule, I am constantly approached by teachers who need assistance or simply want to complain about "my" children. Usually, their statements begin with eye rolls and a sigh, "Your gifted students . . ." and sometimes end with "will not stop talking . . . drive me crazy as they are always indifferent to my activities . . . will not complete their homework because they are lazy and irresponsible." My response to the teachers varies depending on the situation. I do not admit to knowing everything about the gifted, but when I am approached, I do add my insight because I have them for one period a day—they are now "my" students. Therefore, in a polite way, I often explain that "the students are talkative because their minds work nonstop and must be kept busy with useful activities" and "they need challenge, and if they are required to complete the same problems as the other nongifted students in your classroom, they may need some accelerated assignments to keep them interested and involved."

Over the years, I will not admit to knowing everything about the field of education. However, I will disclose to having grown immensely as a teacher in part because of having gifted students in my classroom. I've learned that such students have unique personalities and a wealth of knowledge, both of which, if allowed to flourish, can add a great deal of knowledge and insight into a classroom. I cannot begin to tell you how much I anticipate my second- and fifth-period gifted classes everyday. The students enrolled are special children with unique personalities and individualities that enhance my role as a teacher. As stated earlier, they do keep me on my toes because I am constantly searching for interesting activities and opportunities that such students need to grow and flourish. A veteran teacher must know how to take the uniqueness of the gifted and address their special characteristics and knowledge rather than retreat from the gifted. When both the teacher and the gifted student work together in the classroom, they will both learn immensely from the educational opportunities presented.

Vangie Altman, Middle School Teacher with National Board Certification

SUMMARY AND CONCLUSIONS

Teachers are very important to all students, and their attitudes and strategies make opportunities for students who are gifted and talented or shut off opportunities by creating a learning ceiling that is too low. Effective teachers create a classroom culture that promotes achievement, and they have a repertoire of strategies that promote continuous progress.

Teacher preparation at the preservice, in-service, and graduate levels as well as professional development can provide educational experiences to prepare educators to accommodate the wide range of learner needs. The NCATE standards as well as the CEC-NAGC Initial Knowledge and Skill Standards for Gifted and Talented Education can be vehicles to facilitate the integration of gifted education into teacher preparation programs at various levels. After all, all students deserve teachers who have the dispositions, knowledge, and skills to facilitate their optimal learning and implement strategies that allow all students to make continuous progress.

The shift to focusing on outputs rather than inputs has changed the accreditation of educators. Student learning is the goal. A parallel change has occurred in state accreditation standards. Both NCATE's and the new CEC-NAGC joint standards are in line with this change.

Teachers make the difference in a child's opportunity to learn. Observable behaviors are the key to identifying what effective teachers do that facilitate learning. Teachers of the gifted need the knowledge, skills, and dispositions to facilitate high-level learning. Even the dispositions need to be assessed by observable behaviors. It is what teachers do that determines what a gifted child learns. What a teacher does reflects his or her beliefs. Therefore, it is very important for educators to understand the cognitive and the social-emotional needs of all learners, including those who learn at a faster pace and a more complex level. Teachers indeed make the difference for a child.

QUESTIONS FOR THOUGHT AND REFLECTION

1. What preparation for teaching gifted children are educators in your state required to have? Counselors? Administrators? Teachers in specialized programs for the gifted and talented?

2. What differences will the shift in national accreditation standards from inputs to outputs (student learning) make on the preparation of teachers and their accountability for student learning?
3. What strategies have your teachers used (at any point in your education) that have encouraged you to learn at high levels?
4. Describe the differences you see in the knowledge, skills, and dispositions needed by teachers of the gifted and general classroom teachers.

RESOURCES

Websites

The Davidson Institute's State Policy Database

www.GT-Cybersource.org/policy

Details pertinent statistical information and state legislation and policy regarding gifted and talented education.

National Association for Gifted Children's Gifted Program Standards

www.nagc.org/index.aspx?id=546

Pre-K through grade 12 program standards designed to assist school districts in examining the quality of their programming for gifted learners.

BOOKS

Dixon, F. A., & Moon, S. M. (Eds.). (2006). *The handbook of secondary education.* Waco, TX: Prufrock.

Purcell, J. H., & Eckert, R. D. (Eds.). (2006). *Designing services and programs for high-ability learners.* Thousand Oaks, CA: Corwin.

REFERENCES

Atkin, J. M., Black, P., & Coffey, J. (2001). *Classroom assessment and the National Science Education Standards.* Washington, DC: National Academy Press.

Black, P., & William, D. (1998). Assessment and classroom learning. *Assessment and Education: Principles, Policy and Practice, 5* (1), 7–75.

Bloom, B. S. (1985). (Ed.). *Developing talent in young people.* New York: Ballantine.

Croft, L. J. (2003). Teachers of the gifted: Gifted teachers. In N. Colangelo & G. A. Davis (Eds.), *Handbook of gifted education* (pp. 558–571). Boston: Allyn & Bacon.

Darling-Hammond, L. (2000). Teacher quality and student achievement: A review of state policy evidence. *Education Policy Analysis Archives, 8,* 1–49. Retrieved August 1, 2006, from *http://epaa.asu.edu/epaa/v8n1*

Darling-Hammond, L., & Bransford, J. (Eds.). (2005). *Preparing teachers for a changing world: What teachers should learn and be able to do.* San Francisco: Wiley.

Dettmer, P. A., Landrum, M. S., & Miller, T. N. (2006). Professional development for the education of secondary gifted students. In F. A. Dixon & S. M. Moon (Eds.), *The handbook of secondary gifted education* (pp. 611–648). Waco, TX: Prufrock.

Graffam, B. (2006). A case study of teachers of gifted learners: Moving from prescribed practice to described practitioners. *Gifted Child Quarterly, 50,* 119–131.

Hansen, J. B., & Feldhusen, J. F. (1994). Comparison of trained and untrained teachers of gifted students. *Gifted Child Quarterly, 38,* 115–123.

Leppien, J. H., & Westberg, K. L. (2006). Roles, responsibilities, and professional qualifications of key personnel for gifted education services. In J. H. Purcell & R. D. Eckert (Eds.), *Designing services and programs for high-ability learners: A guidebook for gifted education* (pp. 161–182). Thousand Oaks, CA: Corwin.

National Association for Gifted Children. (2005). *2004–2005 State of the states: A report by the National Association for Gifted Children and the Council of State Directors of Programs for the Gifted.* Washington, DC: Author.

National Council for Accreditation of Teacher Education. (2002). *Professional standards for the accreditation of schools, colleges, and departments of education.* Washington, DC: Author.

Roberts, J. L. (2004). *Middle and high school gifted students' perceptions of teachers.* Unpublished manuscript.

Roberts, J. L. (2006). Teachers of secondary gifted students: What makes them effective. In F. A. Dixon & S. M. Moon (Eds.), *The handbook of secondary gifted education* (pp. 567–580). Waco, TX: Prufrock.

Sanders, W. L. (1998, December). Value-added assessment. *School Administrator, 55,* 24–27.

Tomlinson, C. A. (2005, Fall). Traveling the road to differentiation in staff development. *Journal of Staff Development (JSD), 26.* Retrieved August 1, 2006, from *http://www.nsdc.org/library/publications/jsd/tomlinson264.cfm*>

Wenglinsky, H. (2000). *How teaching matters: Bringing the classroom back into discussion of teacher quality* (Policy Information Center Report). Princeton, NJ: Educational Testing Service. (ERIC Document Reproduction Service No. ED447128)

Westberg, K. L., Burns, D. E., Gubbins, E. J., Reis, S. M., Park, S., & Maxfield, L. R. (1998, Spring). Professional development practices in gifted education: Results of a national survey. *The National Research Center on the Gifted and Talented Newsletter,* pp. 3–4.

Westberg, K. L., & Daoust, M. E. (2003, Fall). The results of the replication of the classroom practices survey replication in two states. *The National Research Center on the Gifted and Talented Newsletter,* pp. 3–8.

Wise, A. (June, 2006). *A statement from NCATE on professional dispositions.* Retrieved August 15, 2006, from *http://www.ncate.org/public/0616_messageAWise.asp?ch=150*

Wright, S. P., Horn, S. P., & Sanders, W. L. (1997). Teacher and classroom contexts effects on student achievement: Implications for teacher evaluation. *Journal of Personnel Evaluation in Education, 11,* 57–67.

APPENDIX A

CEC–NAGC Initial Knowledge and Skill Standards for Gifted and Talented Education

Standard 1: Foundations

Educators of the gifted understand the field as an evolving and changing discipline based on philosophies, evidence-based principles and theories, relevant laws and policies, diverse and historical points of view, and human issues. These perspectives continue to influence the field of gifted education and the education and treatment of individuals with gifts and talents both in school and society. They recognize how foundational influences affect professional practice, including assessment, instructional planning, delivery, and program evaluation. They further understand how issues of human diversity impact families, cultures, and schools, and how these complex human issues can interact in the delivery of gifted and talented education services.

K1	Historical foundations of gifted and talented education including points of view and contributions of individuals from diverse backgrounds.
K2	Key philosophies, theories, models, and research supporting gifted and talented education.
K3	Local, state/provincial, and federal laws and policies related to gifted and talented education.
K4	Issues in conceptions, definitions, and identification of gifts and talents, including those of individuals from diverse backgrounds.
K5	Impact of the dominant culture's role in shaping schools and the differences in values, languages, and customs between school and home.
K6	Societal, cultural, and economic factors, including anti-intellectualism and equity vs. excellence, enhancing or inhibiting the development of gifts and talents.
K7	Key issues and trends, including diversity and inclusion, connecting general, special, and gifted and talented education.

Standard 2: Development and Characteristics of Learners

Educators of the gifted know and demonstrate respect for their students as unique human beings. They understand variations in characteristics and development between and among individuals with and without exceptional learning needs and capacities. Educators of the gifted can express how different characteristics interact with the domains of human development and use this knowledge to describe the varying abilities and behaviors of individuals with gifts and talents. Educators of the gifted also understand how families and communities contribute to the development of individuals with gifts and talents.

K1	Cognitive and affective characteristics of individuals with gifts and talents, including those from diverse backgrounds, in intellectual, academic, creative, leadership, and artistic domains.
K2	Characteristics and effects of culture and environment on the development of individuals with gifts and talents.
K3	Role of families and communities in supporting the development of individuals with gifts and talents.
K4	Advanced developmental milestones of individuals with gifts and talents from early childhood through adolescence.
K5	Similarities and differences within the group of individuals with gifts and talents as compared to the general population.

Standard 3: Individual Learning Differences

Educators of the gifted understand the effects that gifts and talents can have on an individual's learning in school and throughout life. Moreover, educators of the gifted are active and resourceful in seeking to understand how language, culture, and family background interact with an individual's predispositions to impact academic and social behavior, attitudes, values, and interests. The understanding of these learning differences and their interactions provides the foundation upon which educators of the gifted plan instruction to provide meaningful and challenging learning.

K1	Influences of diversity factors on individuals with exceptional learning needs.
K2	Academic and affective characteristics and learning needs of individuals with gifts, talents, and disabilities.
K3	Idiosyncratic learning patterns of individuals with gifts and talents, including those from diverse backgrounds.
K4	Influences of different beliefs, traditions, and values across and within diverse groups on relationships among individuals with gifts and talents, their families, schools, and communities.
S1	Integrate perspectives of diverse groups into planning instruction for individuals with gifts and talents.

Standard 4: Instructional Strategies

Educators of the gifted possess a repertoire of evidence-based curriculum and instructional strategies to differentiate for individuals with gifts and talents. They select, adapt, and use these strategies to promote challenging learning opportunities in general and special curricula and to modify learning environments to enhance self-awareness and self-efficacy for individuals with gifts and talents. They enhance the learning of critical and creative thinking, problem solving, and performance skills in specific domains. Moreover, educators of the gifted emphasize the development, practice, and transfer of advanced knowledge and skills across environments throughout the lifespan leading to creative, productive careers in society for individuals with gifts and talents.

K1	School and community resources, including content specialists, which support differentiation.
K2	Curricular, instructional, and management strategies effective for individuals with exceptional learning needs.
S1	Apply pedagogical content knowledge to instructing learners with gifts and talents.
S2	Apply higher-level thinking and metacognitive models to content areas to meet the needs of individuals with gifts and talents.
S3	Provide opportunities for individuals with gifts and talents to explore, develop, or research their areas of interest or talent.
S4	Preassess the learning needs of individuals with gifts and talents in various domains and adjust instruction based on continual assessment.
S5	Pace delivery of curriculum and instruction consistent with needs of individuals with gifts and talents.
S6	Engage individuals with gifts and talents from all backgrounds in challenging, multicultural curricula.
S7	Use information and/or assistive technologies to meet the needs of individuals with exceptional learning needs.

Standard 5: Learning Environments and Social Interactions

Educators of the gifted actively create learning environments for individuals with gifts and talents that foster cultural understanding, safety and emotional well being, positive social interactions, and active engagement. In addition, educators of the gifted foster environments in which diversity is valued and individuals are taught to live harmoniously and productively in a culturally diverse world. Educators of the gifted shape environments to encourage independence, motivation, and self-advocacy of individuals with gifts and talents.

K1	Ways in which groups are stereotyped and experience historical and current discrimination and implications for gifted and talented education.
K2	Influence of social and emotional development on interpersonal relationships and learning of individuals with gifts and talents.
S1	Design learning opportunities for individuals with gifts and talents that promote self-awareness, positive peer relationships, intercultural experiences, and leadership.
S2	Create learning environments for individuals with gifted and talents that promote self-awareness, self-efficacy, leadership, and lifelong learning.
S3	Create safe learning environments for individuals with gifts and talents that encourage active participation in individual and group activities to enhance independence, interdependence, and positive peer relationships.
S4	Create learning environments and intercultural experiences that allow individuals with gifts and talents to appreciate their own and others' language and cultural heritage.
S5	Develop social interaction and coping skills in individuals with gifts and talents to address personal and social issues, including discrimination and stereotyping.

Standard 6: Language and Communication

Educators of the gifted understand the role of language and communication in talent development and the ways in which exceptional conditions can hinder or facilitate such development. They use relevant strategies to teach oral and written communication skills to individuals with gifts and talents. Educators of the gifted are familiar with assistive technologies to support and enhance communication of individuals with exceptional needs. They match their communication methods to an individual's language proficiency and cultural and linguistic differences. Educators of the gifted use communication strategies and resources to facilitate understanding of subject matter for individuals with gifts and talents who are English learners.

K1	Forms and methods of communication essential to the education of individuals with gifts and talents, including those from diverse backgrounds.
K2	Impact of diversity on communication.
K3	Implications of culture, behavior, and language on the development of individuals with gifts and talents.
S1	Access resources and develop strategies to enhance communication skills for individuals with gifts and talents including those with advanced communication and/or English language learners.

S2 Use advanced oral and written communication tools, including assistive technologies, to enhance the learning experiences of individuals with exceptional learning needs.

Standard 7: Instructional Planning

Curriculum and instructional planning is at the center of gifted and talented education. Educators of the gifted develop long-range plans anchored in both general and special curricula. They systematically translate shorter-range goals and objectives that take into consideration an individual's abilities and needs, the learning environment, and cultural and linguistic factors. Understanding of these factors, as well as the implications of being gifted and talented, guides the educator's selection, adaptation, and creation of materials, and use of differentiated instructional strategies. Learning plans are modified based on ongoing assessment of the individual's progress. Moreover, educators of the gifted facilitate these actions in a collaborative context that includes individuals with gifts and talents, families, professional colleagues, and personnel from other agencies as appropriate. Educators of the gifted are comfortable using technologies to support instructional planning and individualized instruction.

K1 Theories and research models that form the basis of curriculum development and instructional practice for individuals with gifts and talents.

K2 Features that distinguish differentiated curriculum from general curricula for individuals with exceptional learning needs.

K3 Curriculum emphases for individuals with gifts and talents within cognitive, affective, aesthetic, social, and linguistic domains.

S1 Align differentiated instructional plans with local, state/provincial, and national curricular standards.

S2 Design differentiated learning plans for individuals with gifts and talents, including individuals from diverse backgrounds.

S3 Develop scope and sequence plans for individuals with gifts and talents.

S4 Select curriculum resources, strategies, and product options that respond to cultural, linguistic, and intellectual differences among individuals with gifts and talents.

S5 Select and adapt a variety of differentiated curricula that incorporate advanced, conceptually challenging, in-depth, distinctive, and complex content.

S6 Integrate academic and career guidance experiences into the learning plan for individuals with gifts and talents.

Standard 8: Assessment

Assessment is integral to the decision-making and teaching of educators of the gifted as multiple types of assessment information are required for both identification and learning progress decisions. Educators of the gifted use the results of such assessments to adjust instruction and to enhance ongoing learning progress. Educators of the gifted understand the process of identification, legal policies, and ethical principles of measurement and assessment related to referral, eligibility, program planning, instruction, and placement for individuals with gifts and talents, including those from culturally and linguistically diverse backgrounds. They understand measurement theory and practices for addressing the interpretation of assessment results. In addition, educators of the gifted understand the appropriate use and limitations of various types of assessments. To ensure the use of nonbiased and equitable identification and learning progress models, educators of the gifted employ alternative assessments such as performance-based assessment, portfolios, and computer simulations.

K1 Processes and procedures for the identification of individuals with gifts and talents.

K2 Uses, limitations, and interpretation of multiple assessments in different domains for identifying individuals with exceptional learning needs, including those from diverse backgrounds.

K3 Uses and limitations of assessments documenting academic growth of individuals with gifts and talents.

S1 Use non-biased and equitable approaches for identifying individuals with gifts and talents, including those from diverse backgrounds.

S2 Use technically adequate qualitative and quantitative assessments for identifying and placing individuals with gifts and talents.

S3 Develop differentiated curriculum-based assessments for use in instructional planning and delivery for individuals with gifts and talents.

S4 Use alternative assessments and technologies to evaluate learning of individuals with gifts and talents.

Standard 9: Professional and Ethical Practice

Educators of the gifted are guided by the profession's ethical and professional practice standards. They practice in multiple roles and complex situations across wide age and developmental ranges. Their practice requires ongoing attention to professional and ethical considerations. They engage in professional activities that promote growth in individuals with gifts and talents and update themselves on evidence-based best practices. Educators of the gifted view themselves as lifelong learners and regularly reflect on and adjust their practice. They are aware of how attitudes, behaviors, and ways of communicating can influence their practice. Educators of the gifted understand that culture and language interact with gifts and talents and are sensitive to the many aspects of the diversity of individuals with gifts and talents and their families.

K1	Personal and cultural frames of reference that affect one's teaching of individuals with gifts and talents, including biases about individuals from diverse backgrounds.
K2	Organizations and publications relevant to the field of gifted and talented education.
S1	Assess personal skills and limitations in teaching individuals with exceptional learning needs.
S2	Maintain confidential communication about individuals with gifts and talents.
S3	Encourage and model respect for the full range of diversity among individuals with gifts and talents.
S4	Conduct activities in gifted and talented education in compliance with laws, policies, and standards of ethical practice.
S5	Improve practice through continuous research-supported professional development in gifted education and related fields.
S6	Participate in the activities of professional organizations related to gifted and talented education.
S7	Reflect on personal practice to improve teaching and guide professional growth in gifted and talented education.

Standard 10: Collaboration

Educators of the gifted effectively collaborate with families, other educators, and related service providers. This collaboration enhances comprehensive articulated program options across educational levels and engagement of individuals with gifts and talents in meaningful learning activities and interactions. Moreover, educators of the gifted embrace their special role as advocate for individuals with gifts and talents. They promote and advocate for the learning and well being of individuals with gifts and talents across settings and diverse learning experiences.

K1	Culturally responsive behaviors that promote effective communication and collaboration with individuals with gifts and talents, their families, school personnel, and community members.
S1	Respond to concerns of families of individuals with gifts and talents.
S2	Collaborate with stakeholders outside the school setting who serve individuals with exceptional learning needs and their families.
S3	Advocate for the benefit of individuals with gifts and talents and their families.
S4	Collaborate with individuals with gifts and talents, their families, general, and special educators, and other school staff to articulate a comprehensive preschool through secondary educational program.
S5	Collaborate with families, community members, and professionals in assessment of individuals with gifts and talents.
S6	Communicate and consult with school personnel about the characteristics and needs of individuals with gifts and talents, including individuals from diverse backgrounds.

CHAPTER 16

PARENTING GIFTED CHILDREN

Sylvia Rimm, Ph.D.
FAMILY ACHIEVEMENT CLINIC

INTRODUCTION

Gifted children benefit when educators and parents ally in raising and teaching them. While parental involvement in gifted education may include primarily seeking information about their own children (Rash, 1998; Silverman, 1992; Tolan, 1990), as parents become more informed about giftedness, they may become full, instructional partners in their children's education (Radaszewski-Byrne, 2001). Since this text is directed primarily toward educators, this chapter focuses on information that teachers can share with parents about appropriate parenting of gifted children. Parents of gifted children are frequently interested in their children's progress, thus giving educators many opportunities to share their own knowledge about parenting. Teachers will need to be careful not to take on counseling responsibilities because they aren't trained or certified in that role. Nevertheless, teachers can provide information without becoming invasive or personal. By suggesting books, videos, or CDs or providing general principles about parenting gifted children, teachers can support and inform parents. Gifted programs can sponsor general e-mails or newsletters with information that parents can then apply as they see appropriate. Open house, classroom meetings, or individual conferences provide additional opportunities to share information with parents. Counselors who are knowledgeable about parenting can also provide parenting classes and presentations. Such presentations can include general principles of good parenting as well as information that is specific to the needs of gifted children.

Parents often trust educators of the gifted as their main source of information about giftedness. Respect between parents and educators is reciprocal; that is, parents are more likely to respect and support educators who are supportive and understanding of their parenting responsibilities. Gifted children are more likely to achieve and adjust well if parents understand principles of parenting gifted children.

Some key issues that educators will surely want to address and convey to parents are the following:

1. How to recognize the varieties of giftedness
2. The importance of assessment
3. Guidelines for encouraging learning without pressure
4. Ideas for fostering creativity and thinking skills
5. Strategies for supplementing school learning
6. Tips for setting appropriately high expectations
7. Information regarding how to help children cope with social and emotional issues
8. An understanding of the impact of giftedness on family dynamics
9. Methods for guiding children toward a balanced future career and relationship life

RECOGNIZING CHILDREN'S GIFTED ABILITIES

It is frequently assumed that all parents think their children are gifted. However, a survey of 1,039 parents contradicts this assumption (Gogul, McCumsey, & Hewett, 1985). Seventy percent of parents in the survey sample accurately identified their child as gifted by the age of 3. Most parents are good identifiers of their children's giftedness. Firstborn children tend to be recognized by parents more frequently than later born (Silverman, 1992). Although when one child is gifted, other children in the family are frequently gifted as well. Figure 16–1 lists some of the earliest signs by which parents may be able to recognize a young child's giftedness (Silverman, 1992).

Gifted children aren't all alike. Different kinds of giftedness may manifest in a variety of surprising ways. Although some children are gifted in multifaceted directions, others may be precocious in a single area. While some kinds of giftedness are readily apparent to parents, teachers may wish to heighten parents' sensitivity to less obvious forms of giftedness. Verbal giftedness is often easily identified by both parents and teachers, but there are some surprises even in this area.

Early reading is characteristic of verbal giftedness (Smutny, 2001; Stamm, 2003), although some gifted children do not learn to read until kindergarten or first grade. While some early readers learn letters and phonic sounds early, others seem to skip the typical learning-to-read sequence and proceed directly to reading full sentences, as illustrated in the following example.

Charles's mother discovered his verbal giftedness on a visit to the bank. Unlike most verbally gifted children, Charles was not an early talker. When he began talking at age 2, he spoke in full sentences, had an extensive vocabulary, and learned the alphabet quickly. He was sitting in his stroller while his mom waited in line to make her bank deposit and suddenly exclaimed, "Mommy, look! That sign says, 'Interest rates haven't been this low since shag carpets were in style.'" Needless to say, his mother was stunned when she discovered that her $2\frac{1}{2}$-year-old son could read virtually everything.

Miller (1990) lists characteristics that can alert parents to mathematical talent: (a) an intense curiosity about numeric information; (b) an unusual quickness in learning, understanding, and applying mathematical ideas; (c) an advanced ability to think and work abstractly and the ability to see mathematical patterns and relationships; (d) a tendency to think and work with mathematical problems in flexible, creative ways rather than in a stereotypic fashion; and (e) an extraordinary ability to transfer learning to new, untaught mathematical situations.

Children with spatial giftedness think in images and three dimensions and may show their gift in remarkable creations with Legos or blocks. Early school environments are often unfriendly places for visual-spatial talent, making it difficult to identify early in school (Silverman, 2003). Early grade curriculum is geared toward learning basic skills such as reading, math facts, and spelling and writing—none of which are spatial. Building projects that might reveal spatial giftedness are relegated to play and are more difficult to measure as skills. Higher mathematics involves spatial ability but is typically postponed until children have learned fundamental computational skills.

Artistic talent may be uncovered by children's sophisticated or detailed drawings, and musical talent may be recognized when a young child is musically aware, moves to music more rhythmically than most, or picks out tunes on an available piano (Haroutounian, 2001). Solo violinist Pamela Frank recalls that when she was 3 or 4, she attended serious music concerts with her parents and would get chills and tears in her eyes as she viscerally felt the beauty of the music. Symphonic flutist Martha Aarons remembers falling in love with Puccini's opera *Tosca* when she was in second grade (Rimm & Rimm-Kaufman, 2001). This musical sensitivity is quite different than the typical music addiction to iPods that might be observed among many adolescents. iPod absorption might also alert a parent to musical awareness if accompanied by more serious involvement with music.

Renzulli, Sytsma, and Schader (2003) suggest that children may identify themselves as likely to contribute their

Some of the earliest signs of giftedness include the following:

- unusual alertness in infancy
- less need for sleep in infancy
- long attention span
- high activity level
- smiling or recognizing caretakers early
- intense reactions to noise, pain, frustration
- advanced progression through the developmental milestones
- extraordinary memory
- enjoyment and speed of learning
- early and extensive language development
- fascination with books
- curiosity
- excellent sense of humor
- abstract reasoning and problem-solving skills
- vivid imagination (e.g., imaginary companions)
- sensitivity and compassion

FIGURE 16–1 Early Signs of Giftedness

Source: From *"How Parents can Support Gifted Children,"* by L. K. Silverman, 1992, ERIC Document Reproduction Service No. ED352776. Reston, VA: Clearinghouse on Handicapped and Gifted Children. Reprinted with Permission. Also available at *www.gifteddevelopment.com.*

giftedness toward social service and making the world a better place by showing a strong sense of right and wrong, sensitivity to the feelings of others, a heightened awareness of the needs of others, and observations about "fairness." Such heightened social awareness could be categorized as potential positive leadership talent.

Solow (2001) reminds us that parents' conceptions of giftedness are likely to affect what they identify as giftedness and, in turn, what they choose to cultivate in their children. Thus, a highly verbal parent may both encourage a child's verbal ability and also be more likely to identify a child's verbal giftedness, while a more artistic parent might recognize and encourage a child's advanced art abilities.

ARRANGING ASSESSMENT FOR GIFTED CHILDREN

Parents who recognize early signs of intellectual giftedness should be advised to have their children tested, even during the preschool years (Davis & Rimm, 2004; Rimm, 2006b; Silverman, 1992), although test scores can be somewhat unreliable for preschool children and may be influenced by shyness, fears of a teacher, or by no experience with test taking. Following are some reasons for early testing:

1. Children who are intellectually gifted may benefit from early entrance to kindergarten, special curriculum planning within kindergarten, or a uniquely enriched preschool environment.
2. Test scores give quantitative data, which parents may choose to share with the school when communicating about their child's special needs. These quantitative data are usually normative, permitting parents to compare their child's intellectual development to that of a sample of children of similar age.
3. Weak areas may be discovered that may be masked by the child's intellectual giftedness. It is not unusual to find verbally gifted children who score poorly in tests of spatial abilities or small motor skills. Preschool testing permits parents to assist children in improving weak skills during a time that brain growth is very rapid.
4. Test scores give parents confidence in their personal observations, or they can correct them appropriately. Some children are very verbal but do not have abstract thinking skills yet and may appear to be gifted. Thus, such tests can prevent parents from placing too much pressure on their children.
5. Early test scores provide baseline information for monitoring children's intellectual growth and progress over time (Rimm, 2006b).

Intellectual assessments for school-age children may be conducted under the auspices of the school district and can include IQ and academic testing by the school psychologist. However, school services are variable for gifted children. Parents who recognize their children's giftedness might be required to arrange for assessments by a private psychologist. Finding a school or private psychologist who does appropriate testing and also knows about gifted children can be difficult in some communities. A nearby university center, the state association for gifted children, or the state department of education is a likely resource for identifying a qualified tester. In addition to the reasons given for testing preschool children, there are several others for testing school-age children:

1. Teachers may not have identified the extent of a child's intellectual giftedness.
2. Gifted children may also have learning disabilities that are easily masked by accomplishing, at least, average work. Teachers may thus assume they only have average abilities.
3. Spatial giftedness is unlikely to be identified in the early grades because the curriculum does not give children the opportunity to display such talent (Silverman, 2003).
4. By identifying strengths and weaknesses in a gifted child, one can often prevent the child from falling into an underachievement pattern.
5. Test scores assist parents in advocating for appropriate educational programs for their gifted children.
6. Psychologists who test gifted children and are aware of their needs can often support parents in advocacy.

PROVIDING HOME ENRICHMENT

Learning at home typically sets the stage for children's love of learning. Thus, the enrichment parents provide contributes to the high IQ scores, interests, and motivation that gifted children show. Just as there is great value in providing these learning opportunities for children, there are also pitfalls that parents can avoid.

Encouraging Learning Without Pressure

Parent attention and interest in reading, playing with numbers, experimenting with science, and learning about nature are naturally inviting to children. Most gifted children have been read to regularly and talked with a lot. Even the typically negatively described workbooks are used by parents to teach their children skills, although many parents will not use them for fear they will be accused of pushing their children. Technology has entered the scene with video game-like learning tools that entice children toward reading and math in fun and intrinsically interesting involvement (see the resources section at the end of this chapter).

Home learning should be fun, but it can become a pressure. If parents expect young children to spend too much time on skills, if they continuously show off the child's advanced abilities to others, or if parents overreact to children's mistakes, it can feel like pressure to children. Even extreme praise, using words like *brilliant, extraordinary,* and *smartest,* can cause children to experience learning as pressure (Rimm, 1995b, 1996). Understanding that cognitive development proceeds unevenly will prevent parents from becoming impatient (Roedell, 1990). A gifted 3- or 4-year-old may know only letters and a few sight words and 6 months later may be reading full sentences. Furthermore, young children who are reading *Harry Potter* may not know addition facts or have the courage or social skills to invite a friend over. Sophisticated adult vocabulary may be paired alternately with babyish tears of protest when big brother knocks down a block tower or childish silliness among same-age friends. The unevenness of cognitive abilities coupled with unpredictable social and emotional development can stun even the most alert parents and teachers.

Fostering Creativity and Thinking Skills

The curiosity and adult-sounding reasoning can be stifled when parents emphasize learning as only a memory or reciting skill. Helping a child respond to the question "Why are some states large and others small?" may be more effective than getting him or her to recite the names of all 50 states. From preschool through young adulthood, parental encouragement of thinking will help children define giftedness as more than committing facts to memory (Shade & Garrett, 2001). Cook, Wittig, and Treffinger (2004) propose a three-part goal for parents who are interested in developing children in a healthy way; the parts include becoming (a) a healthy, effective person; (b) an independent learner; and (c) a creatively productive person. Parents should keep these goals in mind as they organize learning opportunities for their children. It is suggested that parents encourage their children to generate many ideas, defer judgment, and view options from different perspectives. Children can also have gradually increasing difficulty in levels of material so that they can learn to persevere. Collaboration, team building, and healthy competition should be included in their learning experiences. It is also important to apply these creative thinking skills to a real-world interest or talent area. In summary, parents should balance academic challenge, physical challenge, social activity, and relaxation. That balance is often precarious for gifted children who frequently experience intense imbalance in their personal development.

Torrance (1969) suggests the following ways that parents can foster creativity:

1. Encourage curiosity, exploration, experimentation, fantasy, questioning, testing, and the development of creative talents. For example, experiment by measuring how much surface area is covered when different amounts and different liquids are spilled.
2. Provide opportunities for creative expression, creative problem solving, and constructive response to change and stress. For example, have children correctly solve a math problem in at least three different ways or make up new rules to a board or card game.
3. Prepare children for new experiences and help develop creative ways of coping with them. For example, arrange for children to go to a new summer camp where they don't know anyone. Help them role-play how to meet people and make friends.
4. Find ways of changing destructive behavior into constructive, productive behavior rather than relying on punitive methods of control. For example, reward children who have difficulty concentrating by permitting them to work on the computer on days when they stay on task.
5. Find creative ways of resolving conflicts between an individual's needs and the needs of the other family members. For example, have regular family meetings to solve scheduling and responsibility issues.
6. Make sure that every member of the family receives individual attention and respect and is given opportunities to make significant, creative contributions to the welfare of the family as a whole. For example, chart regular family fun time.
7. Use what the school provides imaginatively, and supplement the school's efforts. For example, If children are learning about Egypt in school, enrich that study by visiting museums.
8. Give the family purpose, commitment, and courage. For example, plan ways the family can contribute to others, such as by sending supplies to hurricane or earthquake victims, participating in a walk for hunger, or writing letters to soldiers in service.

The Homeschooling Alternative

A significant number of parents of gifted children choose to homeschool their children (Ensign, 2005; Rivero, 2002). Parents who decide to take on this project will need to recognize that it will involve a huge time commitment on their part. As with all decisions, there are always tradeoffs. Homeschooling can often be most effective with profoundly gifted children whose academic skills are many years ahead of their developmental and social skills (Davidson & Davidson, 2004; Julicher, 2000). Variations in academic ability, such as extraordinary math ability with only above-average reading skills, might not fit with what schools are willing to provide for gifted students and may be better supported by partial homeschooling.

Although today's homeschoolers often bring children together for social and sports activities, grouping children with intellectual peers is frequently missed by homeschooled children—a gap that can't easily be filled. Parents' decision to partially homeschool children may help alleviate such problems.

SOCIAL AND EMOTIONAL ISSUES

Gifted children are much more than learning machines. Most parents are very concerned with raising gifted children, with attention to their social and emotional adjustment as well. Furthermore, children who feel lonely or are rejected by peers are often so distracted by their emotional pain that even their intellectual learning suffers (Freedman & Jensen, 1999; Tolan, 1990).

Setting High Expectations

Setting appropriately high expectations for gifted children makes a positive difference in their motivation (DeVries, 2005; Rimm & Rimm-Kaufman, 2001; Rimm, Rimm-Kaufman, & Rimm, 1999). There is the risk that what parents may feel as appropriate children may internalize as too high expectations. Continuous success causes children to expect further success, and perfectionism (Rimm, 1996, 2002; Rimm et al., 1999) can frustrate and inhibit children's motivation. Here's an example: Jessica, a highly gifted kindergartner, sat at her computer busily writing a story. A glimpse of the monitor showed interesting conversation between characters, extraordinary vocabulary, correctly placed quotation and punctuation marks, and a plot that resembled what a talented middle school student might write. Every adult observer who passed and read her story described it as "perfect."

One can hardly blame adults for their exuberant praise for such unusually precocious talent, but the risk of pressure for perfectionism is great. That pressure potentially brings with it difficulty in accepting criticism, internalizing corrections as inadequacies, and terrible fears of failure. Perhaps this "little writer" will be a published author some day, but even excellent writers have to cope with editorial changes and writer's block.

Praise words often convey expectations so that overpraise or too highly competitive praise can actually contribute to feelings of pressure (Rimm, 1995b, 1996). Praising process rather than ability is recommended and serves to motivate the child. Commenting on children being good learners, hard workers, good thinkers, and persevering encourages children to make strong efforts and become more thoughtful.

Teaching Healthy Competition

The many successes that gifted children feel may accustom them to continuous success. Success is exhilarating and motivating to children, but gifted children also need to experience failure to develop the resilience that will ensure accomplishment in a highly competitive society (Karnes & Riley, 2005; Rimm, 2006c; Rimm et al., 1999). In order for parents to teach children to function in a competitive society, they will have to not only facilitate participation in intellectual, artistic, musical, creative, and physical interests but also applaud victories, be supportive during defeats, and, most important, not support alibis, excuses, or "pity parties" when children lose in competition. Feeling too sorry for children who lose in contests justifies their feeling too sorry for themselves. Instead of learning from losses, they may sulk, get angry, or avoid competition in the future. The habit of avoiding competition puts them at risk of never working to their potential.

Facilitating Social Adjustment

The social adjustment of gifted children has not been found to be any worse than that of average children, but some children in all ability groups have difficulty with social adjustment (Gross, 2002; Neihart, Reis, Robinson, & Moon, 2002; Robinson & Noble, 1992). Characteristic social-skill deficits that tend to cause gifted children problems are bragging, being too competitive, talking too much and listening too little, inability to collaborate, argumentativeness, bossiness, poor anger management, and being disrespectful of children who are not as capable. Profoundly gifted children seem to have more problems with social adjustment than those in the more typically gifted range (Gross, 2002; Rimm, 2006a). They also seem to report feeling different more frequently. That is not surprising in light of the fact that their thinking is often very different than that of their chronological peers. Part of the reason for social deficits for these gifted children who do have problems may come from the attention given at home to their strengths, which are their intellectual abilities. From early childhood on, that differential attention could cause children to believe that social skills are not as important as intellectual skills. Parents can easily help children to value social skills and friendship by placing emphasis on both intellectual and social abilities. However, placing too much emphasis on social skills can cause worse problems than not enough emphasis if children believe that popularity should be their priority. Socializing could easily distract them from learning, especially from middle school forward (Colangelo, 2006; Rimm, 1994, 2005).

Parents or counselors can work with children on these skills since there are many books and CDs directed specifically at improving such skills (see the resource list at the end of this chapter). Awareness of deficits in these areas may be all that is needed to teach these skills to children. Sometimes, however, the gifted parents may not be socially skilled either ("the apple doesn't fall far from the tree"). Counselors who specialize in gifted children will understand and be able to teach them, and teachers of the gifted can include these social skills in their programming (Rimm, 1990, 2003; Rimm & Priest, 1990; Verdick & Lisovskis, 2003).

Feeling Different

Many gifted children describe themselves as feeling different. In the *Jane* studies of the childhoods of successful women (Rimm & Rimm-Kaufman, 2001; Rimm et al. 1999), the women who struggled with feelings of difference or loneliness coped best by joining interest groups of like-minded youth. Sports, drama, debate, music, math teams, art groups, religious groups, and scouts often provided the outlets and friends that reassured them during those difficult times in their development. Maslow (1954) described self-actualized people as typically surrounding themselves with small groups of friends who shared similar interests rather than many friends.

Coping with the Emotional Component of Twice-Exceptional Abilities

The emotional component of feeling highly intelligent and yet feeling "stupid" in some ways is often one with which parents need to help twice-exceptional children cope. Helping children understand they can have extreme differences in their abilities is difficult enough, but encouraging them to value their strengths while struggling with areas of disability is a much more difficult task. The contrast is often so great that they would prefer to completely neglect their areas of disability to avoid the stress. Yet overcoming or adjusting to a disability may be a powerful learning experience and may be key to developing resilience. Successful attorney Martha Lindner credited her early struggles with dyslexia for her later success in law school. In eighth grade, she realized that because reading was slow and difficult for her, she would have to study material three times as long as average students in order to feel intelligent. In law school, other students more accustomed to quickly skimming material struggled with inordinate time demands required for understanding complex law, while repetition and slow, cautious interpretation were already a habit to Martha (Rimm & Rimm-Kaufman, 2001). Parents should be cautious not to foster an avoidance posture with respect to disabilities. In communicating with schools, it is important to be sure that needs are met in both areas of giftedness and disabilities. This may be difficult to communicate since disabilities can overshadow giftedness and vice versa and schools may, indeed, neglect the responsibility to provide for both exceptionalities (Trail, 2006).

FAMILY INTERACTIONS

There is considerable evidence that families make a difference in a child's life. Research on over 5,400 middle school children found that the children's perceptions of their family relationships affected almost everything (Rimm, 2005). If they perceived that family relationships were above average rather than average or below average, they were less likely to worry about being smart; about having enough self-confidence; about being pretty, popular, or overweight; or about peer pressure to try alcohol and drugs. These findings should be translated to busy parents who often assume that tweens and teens would rather not be with their parents. Actually, these early adolescent years are ideal for knitting close family relationships. During this difficult developmental time, game playing, joking and laughing, work projects, reading and learning together, attending concerts and theater, travel, camping and hiking, and even watching television as a family provide the security needed by children who are gradually becoming adults. These activities provide the bonding that permits children to talk about their feelings and worries in supportive environments and also prevent children from dwelling on their anxieties. Just as adults take vacations to escape temporarily from their own pressures, family activities are effective for providing tweens and teens with temporary relaxation from their pressured peer environments.

United Parenting

Parents rarely have identical values or lifestyles, but if parents are willing to compromise on their expectations for effort and success and if they are respectful of each other, children are more likely to achieve in school and life (Rimm, 1995b, 1996; Rimm et al., 1999). Parents united in respect for teachers will also help children achieve to a level commensurate with their abilities. These compromises among adults are rarely easy because each parent and teacher usually believes he or she has the correct approach for guiding their children. If one parent sides with a child against another parent or teacher, it gives the child adult power. Thus, if a parent or teacher thinks the child isn't working hard and scolds or punishes the child and the other parent takes the child's side against the parent who expects the child to work harder, the child is inadvertently taught the "easy way out." If such a pattern occurs repeatedly, the child gets in the habit of "getting by" or avoiding challenge.

In effect, the parent who makes excuses for the child is sabotaging the other parent or teacher in their efforts to teach the child to deal with challenge. As a result, the "rescuing" parent disempowers the "expecting" adult. Unfortunately, such conflict between adult expectations denies the child the opportunity to struggle with even reasonable challenges and in turn prevents him or her from building confidence. If the adults in a child's life can manage to compromise and support the child with reasonable challenges, the child will move forward, achieve, and build confidence. Children build confidence only when they undertake and succeed in a task that feels difficult. Accomplishing easy tasks does not build confidence because children realize that anyone can do them. The compromises between adults can be difficult, but they are an effective way to encourage achievement and avoid patterns of underachievement (Rimm, 1995b, 1996).

Single Parenting and Parenting After Divorce

Approximately half of marriages end in divorce, so there are sure to be some gifted kids whose parents are divorced. Furthermore, some single adults intentionally give birth to or adopt children, and, unfortunately, some parents are left to raise their children alone following the death of a spouse. Parenting as a single parent or blending families to include stepparents can be extremely challenging. By reason of a gifted child's adult-sounding vocabulary, reasoning, and sensitivity, there is more risk of adultizing a child under these unique circumstances. It becomes very natural to confide in a gifted child about adult matters because the child seems wise beyond his or her age and may be capable of providing sensitivity beyond that which other adults show. The loneliness after the death of a spouse or the feelings of rejection after divorce can cause a parent to feel like the child is his or her only reason for living and can tempt an adult to treat a child as a partner and confidant. Such adultlike relationships can convey both power and pressure to a child. Children may, indeed, enjoy the confidential relationships because of the feelings of specialness they convey, but typically such relationships fail later. The parent who takes the role of equal partner loses forever the respect garnered from the parent role. While parents should be friendly to children, this is different than treating the child like an adult friend, which suggests equality. If children become accustomed to equal power, they may refuse to accept limits. When parents tell them no, they debate or ignore the parental limit because they believe their opinion is as valuable as their parent's despite their lack of experience.

It is important that boys brought up in single-parent families led by mothers have opportunities to communicate with men (Hébert, 2001). Communication with women is also important, but boys have difficulty developing confidence without being comfortable with both kinds of communication. Differences in communication style between men and women and girls and boys have been documented by considerable research (Gilligan, 1982; Pollack, 1998; Tannen, 1990). During adolescence, when children are building their sense of sexual identity, a boy who does not feel comfortable communicating with other boys and men may lose confidence in his sense of masculinity. He may be taunted as being "gay." Although such bullying is inappropriate for any children, it is especially damaging to a boy's fragile self-confidence, whether or not he is actually homosexual. Particularly at early adolescence, peers can be very nonaccepting of boys with characteristics they view as feminine. Therefore, when boys see effective men in their lives as role models, whether these men are heterosexual or homosexual, they are more likely to feel good about their sense of self (Farrell, 2001). This is less of a problem for girls brought up with single dads because there are so many women teachers in school who serve as role models. Following are some suggested guidelines for single parenting after divorce:

- Both parents should assure the children of their love and explain that the divorce was not caused by any of the children. Parents should also assure the children that they can continue to love both parents and don't have to take sides.
- Even if one parent believes the divorce to be the fault of the other parent, they shouldn't blame the divorce on that parent when speaking to the children.
- Parents should not confide in children about intimate details of the divorce. Older children, particularly, will often wish to take the role of confidant. Children may want the status of adults, but in the long run, treating them like an adult too soon will cause them to feel insecure. They often turn on the confiding parent and become more rebellious than typical during adolescence.
- Parents shouldn't say negative things about the other parents or encourage their children to say bad things about the other parent.
- Parents should emphasize positive achieving aspects of the other parent so that he or she can be a constructive role model. Children will see that person as a role model even if he or she is described negatively. The more emphasis placed on the negative characteristics of the other parent, the more likely that children will feel helpless to do anything about their own, similar negative characteristics.
- Children who live with and visit parents in separate homes should have two places where they can learn about work and play. Parents should avoid the image of one "work parent" and one "play parent" and try to make the two home lives as consistent as possible.
- When parents are angry at their children's behavior, they shouldn't tell the children that they're like the other parent. This will not help the children with any problem but will probably cause the children to believe they have no other choice but to be like that parent (Rimm, 2002, p. 5).

Sibling Issues

Siblings (or even the lack thereof) always affect children in any family. Whether a sibling is a role model for a younger sibling or develops in competition with other siblings or whether an only child becomes accustomed to being the center of adult attention, sibling issues are all involved. Sibling effects happen for all children, whether or not all or any are gifted children. Following are some parenting concerns that are specific to sibling issues with gifted children.

One Child In, One Child Out. A difficult issue is when parents have one child in a gifted program and another child who is not eligible for the program. Either parents tend to want to persuade the school to allow the ineligible child to be in the program, or they may consider taking the eligible child out of the gifted program. Both decisions come because they are fearful that the ineligible child will suffer. Parents should always be sure to do what is best for each child. In some cases, the ineligible child may have missed by only a point or two on an identification matrix, and it may be reasonable to advocate for the child being included since the difference is so small. On the other hand, if the child is far from eligible, the experience in the gifted program could be inappropriate and frustrating. It would make more sense to assure the child that everyone has different abilities, and the regular classroom would be more appropriate to develop his or her best learning. Parents can reassure the child that most people would like to be smarter, prettier, or a better athlete than others, but doing the best one can with what one has is truly most satisfying. After all, we do not move through life with IQ scores engraved on our foreheads, and many people are successful who have never been in gifted programs. Once the discussion of the decision is over, both children become accustomed to their assigned place, and if both have an interesting and challenging education, they are likely to adjust well. As Tomlinson (2005) indicates, differentiating at home helps one understand differentiating in school, and both help children to feel safe being themselves.

Achievers and Underachievers. Another frequent sibling issue is a family where all children are gifted but some are achievers and others underachievers. Younger children may feel great pressure to achieve as well as their older siblings, and rather than work at that task, their fears of inadequacy cause them to avoid challenge. Avoiding challenge becomes a habit, thus causing them to underachieve. While more often it is the younger child who underachieves, sometimes the reverse takes place. The older child is an achieving child at first, the center of attention, and a powerful "king" or "queen" of the family. When a second child displaces the older child as the center of attention, the older child feels "dethroned," or rejected, and his or her positive, achieving personality changes to become negative, aggressive, or depressed as well as underachieving (Rimm, 1995b, 1996, 2006c).

The sibling competition seems keenest between two children of the same sex or a brother following a perfect sister. It is good to assure children that it is normal to feel competition but that to act negatively on those feelings may do harm to themselves and others.

Only Children. While many only children are successful and learn to share attention with cousins, friends, and classmates, sometimes only children feel overshadowed by their classmates. Acting out, behaviors like those seen in attention-deficit/hyperactivity disorder, or underachieving can be the symptoms that suggest they are struggling with attention. If parents of only children are conscientious about not giving these children too much adult power or if they have early opportunities in preschool or day care where they learn to share attention, this may not be an issue at all (Rimm, 1995b, 1996).

Including the Valuable Extended Family

Grandparents, aunts, uncles, and cousins can provide plenty of opportunities for enrichment and sharing attention for gifted children.

Grandparents. Grandparents may be in a position to contribute time, especially if they do not work outside the home. They may be able to host museum trips or hikes or may patiently assist with science experiments. Some grandparents may also be able to provide resources that younger parents may not be able to afford. Parents who are respectful to their own parents model respect to their children. Children observe these family interrelationships continuously and learn how to treat others by what they see. Grandparent disrespect is less problematic when families do not live near each other, but proximity offers wonderful opportunities for enrichment and relationship building if families are sensitive to each other's needs (Webb, Gore, Karnes, & McDaniel, 2004).

Aunts, Uncles, and Cousins. While aunts and uncles may be busy with their own children, they can provide excellent relationships for their nieces and nephews. They make great role models and wonderful confidants and can provide special visits at their homes. They can broaden the interests of gifted children by introducing them to new experiences. If a child has no parent, either by choice of a single parent or by divorce or death, an aunt or uncle can fill a special need. In much the same way as grandparents provide enrichment, time, and resources, aunts and uncles can contribute to the raising of gifted children.

One great risk is an aunt or uncle who plays out his or her own sibling rivalry by sabotaging the sibling parent. They can be "too understanding" and negate parental guidelines or suggest that the parent expects too much or is an "ogre." A second pitfall is when an aunt or uncle acts in a jealous way, negating a child's talents because his or her own children are not as successful.

Cousins can develop very close relationships with each other and provide opportunities for sharing attention and enrichment, or cousin relationships can take on the competitive nuances of siblings or of the parents' earlier sibling competition. Again, it is important to understand that competitive feelings are normal and that cousins can cope with such feelings with regard to gifted programs, grades, and accomplishments in arts, music, or sports. The respect for and the valuing of talents and a sensitivity to problems are important components of teaching children to live in the world with others.

ENSURING A BRIGHT FUTURE

Parents should be aware of the challenges gifted children deal with in decision making about the future so that their high school preparation is suitable for college entrance and eventually into a satisfying career. Although research on middle school children has found that students in gifted programs are significantly more optimistic about their futures and less fearful about them than students not identified as gifted, there remain some special issues (Rimm, 2006a). Kerr (1990) brings together four subcategories of concern for parents, based on research by others, to consider when helping their child plan for the future. These categories include multipotentiality, early emergers, minority students, and gifted girls.

Multipotentiality

Frederickson and Rothney (1972) describe gifted children who have many talent areas and could do equally well in all as having multipotentiality. Such children continue to win awards and prizes in areas like music, mathematics, science, and creative writing. However, they delay decision making regarding a career or college major focus until college or beyond because of the variety of their interests and their unwillingness to drop a favorite talent area.

In high school these children may fill their schedules beyond capacity, skipping lunch or taking gym during the summer so that they can fit in the many electives and honors classes they wish to take. In college they may have multiple majors because it feels impossible to decide between them. Parental and counselor guidance at every level is helpful for guiding these children in deciding which courses will lead to careers they can truly engage in and which areas they might continue as hobbies and recreation with lesser involvement and intensity.

Early Emergers

Marshall (1981) refers to gifted students who decide their path of interest early on as early emergers. They are enthusiastic, engaged, and clear in their choices, and parents often struggle finding educational experiences for them to pursue their passions. There is the risk that they will lose interest because they cannot find sufficient opportunities to develop their talent, but early emergers usually continue their engagement through life. Occasionally, some change their direction in high school, college, or even adulthood. The challenge for parents is to provide their child with opportunities to explore these intense interests while not setting specific expectations that prevent children from having the courage to change career direction if they choose to do so.

Minority Students and Gifted Girls

The lower expectations placed on gifted minority students and girls, despite their talents, is a continuing problem. For example, despite her perfect grade-point average, interest in science, and excellent SAT scores, Ana Casa's high school counselor was blinded to her potential and recommended she become a secretary. Today, Dr. Ana Casa is a cardiothoracic surgeon. Had she not been Hispanic and a girl, the recommendation would have probably been different (Rimm et al., 1999). Parents, counselors, and teachers who have stereotypical ideas of what minority students or girls can accomplish may not direct these students to the high-powered classes or the most challenging colleges and universities.

Minority and female students need to be prepared for higher expectations, the struggles they will meet trying to prove themselves, and, for girls, the added issues of balancing a high-level, challenging career with child rearing.

Career Guidance That Provides Challenge

Gifted children require guidance as they select from the many available colleges and universities. In some schools, peers will pressure students toward applying only to the most prestigious and expensive colleges, while in other high schools, students may have less challenging aspirations regarding college. Berger (1996) recommends that parents encourage children to begin exploring possible colleges by seventh and eighth grades. By eleventh and twelfth grades, if high schools do not have active college counselors, parents may need to further assist their children with the practical processes of required test preparation, completing applications, and scholarship searches. Figure 16–2 provides a matrix for college decision making so that parents and children can weigh each of the variables involved in making this important decision (Rimm, 1995a, p. 4).

For many gifted children, their first 4 years of college education are only the beginning, and it is helpful for students and parents to view potential long-range plans. Obviously, such long-range plans need to be only exploratory for most students since it is not unusual for students to change career directions while attending college. A priority for gifted students is to recognize that a career that may have seemed appealing to them in

How Do You Choose a College?

Now that you've been accepted to colleges, you'll need to make a choice. Hopefully, you have several to choose from. Here's a step-by-step program for making this exciting choice that will affect the direction of your adult life:

1. Brainstorm for all the possible criteria to use in evaluating your college. Here are some possible criteria: cost, size of college, major, distance from home, proximity to large city, etc. You'll find many more.
2. List your criteria in order of importance to you. You may have some that are tied for importance, and you may drop some from your original list because you decide they're not important enough to you.
3. Assign numerical weights to each criterion depending on their importance. Use numbers between 1 and 3 to avoid making your evaluation too complex. Higher numbers represent greatest importance to you.
4. Make a matrix for yourself listing colleges to which you've been accepted at the left and the criteria and their weight numbers across the top.
5. Rate each college using numbers between 1 and 3 for each criterion.
6. Working down, multiply each college rating by the weight for each criterion. Working across for each college will cause bias.
7. Add up the scores across to determine what colleges score highest.
8. Use the matrix and the total scores for guidance as you discuss your college choice with your parents.
9. Be willing to add other criteria suggested by your parents and change weights if necessary. Redo the matrix and the totals if you and your parents have decided to add or change criteria.
10. Don't feel bound by the numbers. The matrix is meant to help you focus your thinking for discussion, not to provide an absolute choice.

Sample Matrix for Choosing a College

	Wt Cost 3*	Wt Size 1	Wt Major 2	Wt Distance 1	Total Scores**
University of Michigan	(3) 9	(1) 1	(3) 6	(3) 3	19
Carleton College	(2) 6	(3) 3	(1) 2	(2) 2	13
Kenyon College	(2) 6	(3) 3	(2) 4	(2) 2	15
Brown University	(3) 9	(2) 2	(3) 6	(2) 2	19

FIGURE 16–2 Choosing a College

**Cost factor should include actual costs, scholarships available, and so on. High numbers indicate most reasonable costs; low numbers, most expensive.*

***Although this score indicates rank by your criteria, further discussion with your parents may encourage you to weight criteria differently or add other criteria, which could total scores. Parentheses indicate college rating for criteria; number outside parentheses equals college rating times criteria weight.*

Source: From *"Sample Matrix for Choosing a College,"* by S. Rimm, 1995, *Sylvia Rimm On Raising Kids Newsletter, 5, p. 4.* Copyright © 1995 Sylvia Rimm. Reprinted with permission.

childhood could be one they might outgrow if not sufficiently challenging and creative. Mentorships could help students find direction. For example, shadowing a pediatrician and a pediatric medical researcher could help a student differentiate between these two professions.

ADVOCACY ALL THE WAY

Gifted programs would not exist if it weren't for the efforts of advocates at every level. Thus, parents do need to be pleasant, "pushy parents" (DeVries, 1999) for their own children, for their school or district, and at the state and national level. Because schools, states, and Congress are not likely to pay attention to any one person, it is best for parents to join with others. Parents and educators together can forge ahead toward the achievement of appropriately challenging learning experiences for gifted children.

Supporting Children at School

Parents should communicate as allies with teachers and principals and assume that they, too, would like children to achieve in school. A battling attitude will alienate those whose help parents require and may cause their gifted children to believe their education needs to be a constant fight. Children who enjoy arguing with teachers reluctantly admit that at first their curriculum was too easy, so there was reason to argue, but now the arguing has become a habit, which they enjoy. They further add that such arguments with teachers bring peer admiration, especially when they can "out-argue" their teachers. DeVries (1999) recommends establishing rapport with the school by volunteering to help students directly and by contributing to advisory committees that support gifted children. Parents who join with others in advocating for gifted children in their school district have more impact. Using the media, including local radio, television, and the press, can provide the positive public relations necessary for making a difference (Karnes & Lewis, 1997).

The State Needs to Hear from Parents

Parents can have enormous power by advocating for legislation that requires gifted education for every qualified child. Forming a knowledgeable group at the state level will enable communication to legislators. The California Association for the Gifted (2003) has assembled an excellent advocacy handbook that provides both information on advocacy and diplomatic strategies. Being systematic in planning will channel parents' energies in the right direction (Mitchell, 1981). Once state legislation is in place, the local district has directives to follow responsibly. Because there is no federal legislation that protects the rights of gifted children, it is important that parents understand the legal obligations of their respective state (Karnes & Marquardt, 1997). The knowledge of these rights can lead to more effective advocacy and mediation. In the most extreme cases, parents may even have to resort to litigation to obtain an appropriate education for their child.

SUMMARY AND CONCLUSIONS

Gifted children benefit when educators and parents ally in raising and teaching them. This chapter focuses on information that teachers can share with parents about appropriate parenting of gifted children.

Most parents are good identifiers of their children's giftedness. Parents who recognize early signs of intellectual giftedness should be advised to have their children tested, even during the preschool years (Davis & Rimm, 2004; Rimm, 2006b; Silverman, 1992).

The enrichment parents provide contributes to the high IQ scores, interests, and motivation that gifted children show. Just as there are great values in providing these learning opportunities for children, there are also pitfalls that parents can avoid. Home learning should be fun, but it can become a pressure.

Cook et al. (2004) propose a three-part goal for parents who are interested in developing children in a healthy way.

Most parents are very concerned with raising gifted children, with attention to their social and emotional adjustment as well. Setting appropriately high expectations for gifted children makes a positive difference in their motivation. Praise words often convey expectations so that overpraise or too highly competitive praise can actually contribute to feelings of pressure (Rimm, 1995b, 1996). Success is exhilarating and motivating to children, but gifted children also need to experience failure to develop the resilience that will ensure accomplishment in a highly competitive society (Karnes & Riley, 2005; Rimm, 2006c; Rimm et al., 1999).

The social adjustment of gifted children has not been found to be any worse than that of average children, but profoundly gifted children seem to have more problems with social adjustment than those in the more typically gifted range (Gross, 2002; Rimm, 2006a).

Characteristic social skill deficits that tend to cause gifted children problems are bragging, being too competitive, talking too much and listening too little, inability to collaborate, argumentativeness, bossiness, poor anger management, and being disrespectful of children who are not as capable. Teachers of the gifted can include these social skills in their programming.

Many gifted children describe themselves as feeling different. In the *Jane* studies of the childhoods of successful women (Rimm & Rimm-Kaufman, 2001; Rimm et al. 1999), the women who struggled with feelings of difference or loneliness coped best by joining interest groups of like-minded youth.

There is considerable evidence that families make a difference in a child's life. Research on over 5,400 middle school children found that the children's positive perceptions of their family relationships affected almost everything (Rimm, 2005).

Parents rarely have identical values or life styles, but if parents are willing to compromise on their expectations for effort and success and if they are respectful of each other, children are more likely to achieve in school and life. Parents united in respect for teachers will also help children achieve to a level commensurate with their abilities. Parenting as a single parent or blending families to include stepparents can be extremely challenging.

Siblings (or even the lack thereof) always affect children in any family. Grandparents, aunts, uncles, and cousins can provide plenty of opportunities for enrichment and sharing attention for gifted children.

Parents should be aware of the challenges gifted children deal with in decision making about the future so that their high school preparation is suitable for college entrance and eventually into a satisfying career. A priority for gifted students is to recognize that a career that may have seemed appealing to them in childhood could be one they might outgrow if not sufficiently challenging and creative.

Gifted programs would not exist if it weren't for the efforts of advocates at every level. Using the media, including local radio, television, and the press, can provide the positive public relations necessary for making a difference

(Karnes & Lewis, 1997). Parents can have enormous power by advocating for legislation that requires gifted education for every qualified child. Because there is no federal legislation that protects the rights of gifted children, it is important that parents understand the legal obligations of their respective state (Karnes & Marquardt, 1997).

QUESTIONS FOR THOUGHT AND REFLECTION

1. If a parent came to you, as an educator, to indicate that she believed her child was gifted and needed different programming, what kinds of questions could you ask to assist you in responding sensitively to the parent?
2. What kinds of suggestions could you make to parents who indicate they'd like to be partners with you in their gifted child's education?
3. If only the mother of an underachieving boy asked for help with his underachievement and she indicated that the boy's father didn't seem concerned, what suggestions could you make about involving the father in motivating the son?
4. What could you do to encourage parents to support legislation for gifted programming in your state?

RESOURCES

Websites

ERIC Digests (former ERIC Clearinghouse System)
www.ericdigests.org
Provides access to educational articles produced by the former ERIC Clearinghouse system.

Hoagies Gifted Education Page
www.hoagiesgifted.org
Offers resources, articles, books, and links for parents; educators, counselors, administrators, and other professionals; and for kids and teens.

Sylvia Rimm's Websites
www.sylviarimm.com
Offers articles about giftedness, underachievement, perfectionism, parenting, attention-deficit/hyperactivity disorder, creativity, and other relevant topics. It also includes Dr. Rimm's books and assessment instruments.

See Jane Win
www.seejanewin.com
Offers articles and books especially related to encouraging gifted girls toward success.

BOOKS

Adderholdt, M., & Goldberg, J. (1999). *Perfectionism: What's bad about being too good.* Minneapolis: Free Spirit.

Benson, P. L., Galbraith, J., & Espeland, P. (1998). *What kids need to succeed: Proven, practical ways to raise good kids.* Minneapolis: Free Spirit.

Beyer, R., & Winchester, K. (2001). *Speaking of divorce: How to talk with your kids and help them cope.* Minneapolis: Free Spirit.

California Association for the Gifted. (2003). *Advocacy in action: An advocacy handbook related to gifted and talented students* (2nd ed.). Sacramento: Author.

Drew, N. (2000). *Peaceful parents, peaceful kids: Practical ways to create a calm and happy home.* Minneapolis: Free Spirit.

Fox, A., Kirschner, R., & Verdick, E. (2005). *Too stressed to think?* Minneapolis: Free Spirit.

Frankel, F. (1996). *Good friends are hard to find: Help your child find, make, and keep friends.* Minneapolis: Free Spirit.

Galbraith, J. (1999). *The gifted kids' survival guide: For ages 10 and under.* Minneapolis: Free Spirit.

Galbraith, J. (2000). *You know your child is gifted when . . .* Minneapolis: Free Spirit.

Galbraith, J., & Delisle, J. (1996). *The gifted kids' survival guide: A teen handbook.* Minneapolis: Free Spirit.

Greenspon, T. S. (2001). *Freeing our families from perfectionism.* Minneapolis: Free Spirit

Piirto, J. (2004). *Understanding creativity.* Scottsdale, AZ: Great Potential.

Rimm, S. (1990). *Gifted kids have feelings too—and other not-so-fictitious stories for and about teenagers.* Watertown, WI: Apple.

Rimm, S. (1994). *Rimm's parenting for achievement: Six-hour training course, including gifted module.* Watertown, WI: Apple.

Rogers, K. B. (2002). *Re-forming gifted education: How parents and teachers can match the program to the child.* Scottsdale, AZ: Great Potential.

Strip, C. A. (2000). *Helping gifted children soar: A practical guide for parents and teachers.* Scottsdale, AZ: Great Potential.

Walker, S. Y. (2002). *The survival guide for parents of gifted kids: How to understand, live with, and stick up for your gifted child.* Minneapolis: Free Spirit.

ORGANIZATIONS

National Association for Gifted Children
www.nagc.org
Dedicated specifically to providing resources to families and educators to develop the potential of gifted children. The organization provides a wide variety of resources through its conferences, websites, and publications.

Supporting Emotional Needs of the Gifted
www.sengifted.org
A national organization to foster environments that particularly target the social and emotional needs of gifted adults and children.

Council for Exceptional Children
www.cec.sped.org
Provides resources to families and educators for all educational exceptionalities, including gifted children.

Mensa International
www.mensa.org
An international organization that provides lectures, discussions, journals, special-interest groups, and local, regional, national, and international gatherings related to projects dealing with intelligence.

The Davidson Institute for Talent Development
www.ditd.org
Recognizes, nurtures, and supports profoundly intelligent young people and provides opportunities for them to develop their talents to make a positive difference.

NEWSLETTERS AND MAGAZINES

Parenting for High Potential
www.nagc.org/index.aspx?id=1180
A quarterly magazine published by the National Association for Gifted Children designed for parents who want to make a difference in their children's lives, who want to develop their children's gifts and talents, and who want to help them develop their potential to the fullest.

Twice-Exceptional Newsletter
www.2enewsletter.com
A newsletter that strives to provide understanding of twice-exceptional children. It features articles, profiles of experts, organizations, and resources for and about twice-exceptional children and columns that offer insight into living and working with twice-exceptional children.

EDUCATIONAL MATERIALS BY SYLVIA RIMM

Student Stepping Stones Q-Cards
Practical commonsense ideas on study habits for students.

Parent Pointers Q-Cards (Available in English and Spanish)
Tips for parenting in easy-to-use form.

ELECTRONIC MEDIA BY SYLVIA RIMM

The Pressures Gifted Children Feel and Why They Underachieve [DVD]
Illustrates how praise can lead to pressures that underlie underachievement.

The Psychological Importance of Classroom Challenge for Gifted Children's Achievement [DVD]
Illustrates why curriculum needs to be appropriately challenging to prevent boredom and underachievement.

A United Front for Gifted Children's Achievement [DVD]
Demonstrates how parents and other adults can compromise on differences to lead children to respect of other adults and thus achievement.

How to Respond Counterintuitively to Dependent and Dominant Gifted Underachievers [DVD]
Details how parents and teachers can respond more appropriately to gifted underachievers.

How to Parent so Children Will Learn [CD]
Provides basic strategies for guiding children from birth to young adulthood.

OTHER ELECTRONIC MEDIA

My Turn, Your Turn [CD]
By Cathy Bollinger
Provides songs for building social skills.

REFERENCES

Berger, S. (1996). *How can I help my gifted child plan for college?* [Brochure]. Washington, DC: U.S. Department of Education. Retrieved May 9, 2006, from *http://www.kidsource.com/kidsource/content2/Help_My_gifted_child.html*

California Association for the Gifted. (2003). *Advocacy in action: An advocacy handbook related to gifted and talented students* (2nd ed.). Sacramento: Author.

Colangelo, N. (2006, Spring). Counseling gifted and talented students. *Gifted Education Communicator, 37,* 42–45.

Cook, N. A., Wittig, C. V., & Treffinger, D. J. (2004, March). The path from potential to productivity: The parent's role in the levels of service approach to talent development. *Parenting for High Potential,* pp. 22–27.

Davidson, J., & Davidson, B. (2004). *Genius denied: How to stop wasting our brightest young minds.* New York: Simon & Schuster.

Davis, G. A., & Rimm, S. B. (2004). *Education of the gifted and talented* (5th ed.). Boston: Allyn & Bacon.

DeVries, A. R. (1999, Summer). "Pushy parents" . . . bad rap or necessary role? *Gifted Education Communicator,* 30. Retrieved May 9, 2006, from *http://www.giftedbooks.com/aart_devries.html*

DeVries, A. R. (2005). *Appropriate expectations for the gifted child.* Retrieved May 9, 2006, from *http://www.giftedbooks.com/aart_devries2.html*

Ensign, J. (2005). *Homeschooling gifted students: An introductory guide for parents.* Arlington, VA: The ERIC Clearinghouse on Disabilities and Gifted Education. (ERIC Digest No. 543) Retrieved May 9, 2006, from *http://www.kidsource.com/kidsource/content4/homeschool.gifted.html*

Farrell, W. (2001). *Father and child reunion: How to bring the dads we need to the children we love.* New York: Putnam.

Frederickson, R. H., & Rothney, J. (1972). *Recognizing and assisting multipotential youth.* Columbus: Merrill.

Freedman, J., & Jensen, A. (1999). *Joy and loss: The emotional lives of gifted children*. Retrieved May 9, 2006, from *http://www.kidsource.com/ kidsource/ content4/joy.loss.eq.gifted.html*

Gilligan, C. (1982). *In a different voice: Psychological theory and women's development.* Cambridge, MA: Harvard University Press.

Gogul, E. M., McCumsey, J., & Hewett, G. (1985, November/December). What parents are saying. *Gifted Child Today, 41,* 7–9.

Gross, M. M. (2002). Social and emotional issues for exceptionally intellectually gifted students. In M. Neihart, S. Reis, N. Robinson, & S. Moon (Eds.), *Social and emotional development of gifted children: What do we know?* (pp. 19–30). Waco, TX: Prufrock.

Haroutounian, J. (2001, September). Nurturing musical potential one step at a time. *Parenting for High Potential,* pp. 6–7, 26–27.

Hébert, T. (2001, June). Man to man, heart to heart. *Parenting for High Potential,* pp. 18–22.

Julicher, K. H. (2000, Fall). Removing the barriers. *Gifted Education Communicator, 31,* 10–11.

Karnes, F. A., & Lewis, J. D. (1997). *Public relations: A necessary tool for advocacy in gifted education.* Arlington, VA: ERIC Clearinghouse on Disabilities and Gifted Education. (ERIC Digest No. E542)

Karnes, F. A., & Marquardt, R. (1997). *Know your legal rights in gifted education.* Reston, VA: Council for Exceptional Children. (ERIC Document Reproduction Service No. ED415590)

Karnes, F. A., & Riley, T. L. (2005). *Competitions for talented kids.* Waco, TX: Prufrock.

Kerr, B. (1990). *Career planning for gifted and talented youth.* Reston, VA: Council for Exceptional Children. (ERIC Document Reproduction Service No. ED321497)

Marshall, B. C. (1981). Career decision-making patterns of gifted and talented adolescents. *Journal of Career Education, 7,* 305–310.

Maslow, A. H. (1954). *Motivation and personality.* New York: Harper.

Miller, R. C. (1990). *Discovering mathematical talent.* Reston, VA: Council for Exceptional Children. (ERIC Document Reproduction Service No. ED321487)

Mitchell, P. B. (1981). Effective advocacy: Understanding the process and avoiding the pitfalls. In P. B. Mitchell (Ed.), *An advocate's guide to building support for gifted and talented education* (pp. 5–23). Washington, DC: National Association of State Boards of Education.

Neihart, M., Reis, S. M., Robinson, N. M., & Moon, S. (2002). *The social and emotional development of gifted children: What do we know?* Waco, TX: Prufrock.

Pollack, W. (1998). *Real boys: Rescuing our sons from the myths of boyhood.* New York: Random House.

Radaszewski-Byrne, M. (2001, Spring). Parents as instructional partners in the education of gifted children: A parent's perspective. *Gifted Child Today, 24,* 32–43.

Rash, P. K. (1998, September/October). Meeting parents' needs. *Gifted Child Today, 21,* 14–17.

Renzulli, J. S., Sytsma, R. E., & Schader, R. M. (2003, December). Developing giftedness for a better world. *Parenting for High Potential,* pp. 18–22.

Rimm, S. B. (1990). *Gifted kids have feelings too: And other not-so-fictitious stories for and about teenagers.* Watertown, WI: Apple.

Rimm, S. B. (1994). Why do bright children underachieve? The pressures they feel. *Sylvia Rimm On Raising Kids Newsletter, 4*(3), 1–3.

Rimm, S. B. (1995a). Sample matrix for choosing a college. *Sylvia Rimm On Raising Kids Newsletter, 5*(4), 4.

Rimm, S. B. (1995b). *Why bright kids get poor grades: And what you can do about it.* New York: Crown.

Rimm, S. B. (1996). *How to parent so children will learn.* New York: Three Rivers.

Rimm, S. B. (2002). What's wrong with perfect? *Sylvia Rimm On Raising Kids Newsletter, 12*(4), 5.

Rimm, S. B. (2003). *See Jane win® for girls: A smart girl's guide to success.* Minneapolis: Free Spirit.

Rimm, S. B. (2005). *Growing up too fast: The Rimm Report on the secret world of America's middle schoolers.* Emmaus, PA: Rodale.

Rimm, S. B. (2006a, March). Growing up too fast—and gifted. *Parenting for High Potential,* pp. 6–11.

Rimm, S. B. (2006b). *Keys to parenting the gifted child* (3rd ed.). Scottsdale, AZ: Great Potential.

Rimm, S. B. (2006c). Teaching healthy competition. *Sylvia Rimm On Raising Kids Newsletter, 16*(3), 1–4.

Rimm, S. B., & Priest, C. E. (1990). *Exploring feelings: Discussion book for gifted kids have feelings too.* Watertown, WI: Apple.

Rimm, S. B., & Rimm-Kaufman, S. (2001). *How Jane won: 55 successful women share how they grew from ordinary girls to extraordinary women.* New York: Crown.

Rimm, S. B., Rimm-Kaufman, S., & Rimm, I. (1999). *See Jane win®: The Rimm Report on how 1,000 girls became successful women.* New York: Crown.

Rivero, L. (2002). *Creative home schooling for gifted children: A resource guide.* Scottsdale, AZ: Great Potential.

Robinson, N. M., & Noble, K. D. (1992). Social-emotional development and adjustments of gifted children. In M. Wang, M. Reynolds, & H. Walberg (Eds.), *Handbook of special education: Research and practice* (Vol. 4, pp. 57–76). Oxford: Pergamon.

Roedell, W. C. (1990). *Nurturing giftedness in young children.* Reston, VA: Council for Exceptional Children. (ERIC Document Reproduction Service No. ED321492)

Shade, R. A., & Garrett, P. (2001, March). Teach your child to think and make parenting fun again. *Parenting for High Potential,* pp. 15, 28.

Silverman, L. K. (1992). *How parents can support gifted children.* Reston, VA: Clearinghouse on Handicapped and Gifted Children. (ERIC Document Reproduction Service No. ED352776)

Silverman, L. K. (2003, Spring). The power of images: Visual-spatial learners. *Gifted Education Communicator, 34,* 14–40.

Smutny, J. F. (2001). *Stand up for your gifted child: How to make the most of kids' strengths at school and at home.* Minneapolis: Free Spirit.

Solow, R. (2001, Spring). Parents' conceptions of giftedness. *Gifted Child Today, 24,* 14–22.

Stamm, M. (2003, Spring). Looking at long-term effects of early reading and numeracy ability: A glance at the phenomenon of giftedness. *Gifted and Talented International, 18*, 7–16.

Tannen, D. (1990). *You just don't understand: Women and men in conversation.* New York: Morrow.

Tolan, S. S. (1990). *Helping your highly gifted child.* Reston, VA: Council for Exceptional Children. (ERIC Document Reproduction Service No. ED321482)

Tomlinson, C. A. (2005, September). Differentiation at home as a way of understanding differentiation at school. *Parenting for High Potential*, pp. 5–9.

Torrance, E. P. (1969). *Creativity.* San Rafael, CA: Dimensions.

Trail, B. (2006, March). Parenting twice-exceptional children through frustration to success. *Parenting for High Potential*, pp. 26–30.

Verdick, E., & Lisovskis, M. (2003). *How to take the grrrr out of anger.* Minneapolis: Free Spirit.

Webb, J. T., Gore, J. L., Karnes, F. A., & McDaniel, S. A. (2004). *Grandparents' guide to gifted children.* Scottsdale, AZ: Great Potential.

NAME INDEX

SUBJECT INDEX